Applying International Humanitarian Law in Judicial and Quasi-Judicial Bodies

Derek Jinks · Jackson N. Maogoto
Solon Solomon
Editors

Applying International Humanitarian Law in Judicial and Quasi-Judicial Bodies

International and Domestic Aspects

ASSER PRESS

Springer

Editors
Derek Jinks
School of Law
University of Texas
Austin, TX
USA

Solon Solomon
Dickson Poon School of Law
King's College London
London
UK

Jackson N. Maogoto
School of Law
University of Manchester
Manchester, Lancashire
UK

ISBN 978-94-6265-007-7 ISBN 978-94-6265-008-4 (eBook)
DOI 10.1007/978-94-6265-008-4

Library of Congress Control Number: 2014936006

Published by T.M.C. ASSER PRESS, The Hague, The Netherlands www.asserpress.nl

Produced and distributed for T.M.C. ASSER PRESS by Springer-Verlag Berlin Heidelberg

Printed on acid-free paper

Springer is part of Springer Science+Business Media (www.springer.com)

Contents

Chapter 1
Introducing International Humanitarian Law to Judicial and Quasi-Judicial Bodies

Derek Jinks, Jackson Nyamuya Maogoto and Solon Solomon

Contents

1.1 International Humanitarian Law and the Judiciary

Traditionally, domestic courts have been inclined to deal with international humanitarian law (IHL) issues at arm's length. However, progressively, particularly after World War II, issues of refugee status or war crimes prosecutions granted the opportunity to these courts to apply IHL. International courts and

D. Jinks (✉)
School of Law, University of Texas, Austin, TX, USA
e-mail: djinks@law.utexas.edu

J. N. Maogoto
School of Law, University of Manchester, Manchester, UK
e-mail: Jackson.Maogoto@manchester.ac.uk

S. Solomon
Dickson Poon School of Law, King's College London, London, UK
e-mail: solon.solomon@kcl.ac.uk

D. Jinks et al. (eds.), *Applying International Humanitarian Law in Judicial and Quasi-Judicial Bodies*, DOI: 10.1007/978-94-6265-008-4_1,

tribunals have also addressed IHL, yet as demonstrated in a number of chapters in this volume, not always adequately.[1]

The national security dilemmas that the war on terror introduced left in some cases international courts unable or unwilling to engage in the dialogue that has to be developed between IHL and these national security parameters.[2] In this sense, it is mostly domestic courts which have tried to apply IHL in the realms of these national security challenges.[3] IHL issues such as civilian casualties or whether the warriors' combatant status enables the former to claim protection under the human rights provisions, have been adjudicated by domestic courts[4] and in certain cases the domestic courts' utterance has caused international courts like the European Court of Human Rights to also postulate a position.[5] Accordingly, IHL application has come to be perceived not just as a technical legalistic exercise, but also as part of the more general legal response to some of the harsh realities of modern warfare. It will be accordingly viewed in the realms of this volume. Thus, some of the chapters, like those penned by Roberta Arnold or Makane Mbengue and Brian McGarry, assess also the judicial response to crimes such as genocide or crimes against humanity, which do not necessarily have to occur in the realms of an armed conflict and thus do not always generate IHL violations, yet are deeply interrelated with war crimes.[6]

---

[1] See for example in this volume the chapters penned by Stephens and McLaughlin, Tabak, Hartridge.

[2] Roach 2009. See for example the assertion of the European Court of Human Rights in the Kelly case involving the lethal shooting by SAS forces of nine men in Northern Ireland, that it "considers that in the circumstances of this case it would be inappropriate and contrary to its subsidiary role under the Convention to attempt to establish the facts of this case by embarking on a fact-finding exercise of its own by summoning witnesses. Such an exercise would duplicate the proceedings before the civil courts which are better placed and equipped as fact finding tribunals." Kelly v. United Kingdom, App. No. 30094/96, Judgment of 4 May, 2001, para 101. See also the case of the ICJ's Advisory Opinion on the issue of Israel's security fence, where the Court refused to acknowledge the security language argumentation raised for the justification of the project. On this see Legal Consequences of the Construction of a Wall in the Occupied Palestinian Territory, ICJ Re 2004, 136 paras 116, 121; Shany 2005, pp. 236–237; Solomon 2009, p. 106.

[3] Joseph 2013, p. 129. See for example the stance of the Canadian Supreme Court that "the challenge for democracies in the battle against terrorism is not whether to respond, but rather how to do so. It is because Canadians value the importance of human life and liberty, and the protection of society through respect for the rule of law. Indeed, a democracy cannot exist without the rule of law… Consequently, the challenge for a democratic state's answer to terrorism calls for a balancing of what is required for an effective response to terrorism in a way that appropriately recognizes the fundamental values of the rule of law". (Application under s. 83.28 of the Criminal Code (Re), 2004 SCC 42, [2004] 2 S.C.R. 248 at paras 5 and 7). For a similar position of the Israeli Supreme Court see HCJ 2056/04 Beit Sourik Vill. Council v. Israel [2004] 43 I.L.M. 1099.

[4] For these issues see the analysis in the next paras.

[5] On this see infra Chap. 9, Hartridge.

[6] It can be argued that according to the jurisprudence of the ICTY, genocide constitutes a more severe level of behavior in the same scale that includes also war crimes and crimes against

1.2 The Judicial Factual Expansion of IHL

1.2.1 The Classification of an Armed Conflict

Modern warfare raises important, often difficult questions about conflict classification and applicable legal frameworks. These challenges typically concern whether a conflict should be deemed as international or non-international and which legal regime applies in virtue of this classification. It is this issue that Noëlle Quénivet develops in her chapter. Focusing on non-international conflicts, she examines the impact of the international criminal tribunals' jurisprudence on the classification of non-international conflicts as either falling under Common Article 3 or under the Additional Protocol II.

Quénivet sketches the difference between the two treaty regimes as far as application of IHL is concerned, with Common Article 3 permitting such application in cases of dissident groups fighting each other, whereas the Additional Protocol II requires the conflict to be between a government and internal belligerent forces. Proceeding to explain that the Additional Protocol II cannot be considered either lex posterior or lex generalis to Common Article 3, Quénivet illustrates this through reference to state practice, demonstrating that there exists a bifurcation as regards legal regulation for non-international armed conflicts.

Consequently and based on these premises, Quénivet explores the applicability test of these two different treaties in the jurisprudence of various international criminal courts and tribunals. She notes that the International Criminal Tribunal for the former Yugoslavia (ICTY) has endorsed a single definition to this applicability test, in contrast to the ICTR which has held that the Additional Protocol II develops and supplements Common Article 3. On the contrary, the Special Court for Sierra Leone has appeared more reluctant to apply the Additional Protocol II test.

For Quénivet, the central challenge for the International Criminal Court (ICC) is whether it will stress the actual distinction of the applicability of the Common Article 3 and Additional Protocol II legal regimes or follow along the lines of the ICTY, which left this distinction blurred.

The maturation of transnational terror as exemplified in the 9/11 attacks on the U.S. and the unprecedented barrage of suicide attacks against Israel at the beginning of the new century, has prompted calls to characterize these manifestations of non-state violence[7] as 'armed attacks' able to trigger the right of self-defense under the UN Charter.[8] Immediately after 9/11, UN Security Council Resolution 1373

(Footnote 6 continued)
humanity and that the differentiation is being made for reasons of gradation in the punishment of these behaviors. On this see Shany 2013, p. 22.

[7] For the fact that terrorists are considered as non-state actors see Maogoto Nyamuya 2005, p. 52.

[8] Solomon 2010, pp. 505–506; Melzer 2008, p. 52.

acknowledged that the U.S. right to self-defense was enlivened. With regard to Israel, the International Court of Justice's (ICJ) stance that this right did not apply was criticized by members of the Court and international commentators alike.[9] Yet, both regarding the armed conflict of the U.S. with Al Qaeda as well as that of Israel with the Palestinians, no accord clearly addresses whether confronting the dangers of terrorism leads to an international or non-international armed conflict.[10] This was augmented by the fact that in some cases like that of the U.S. and Al Qaeda, the UN Security Council Resolution itself was silent over whether the U.S. right to self-defense was toward Al Qaeda or toward Afghanistan as the harboring state.[11]

In that sense, the task of the conflict's characterization moved to domestic courts which were called to adjudicate on U.S. or Israeli policies associated with the conflict. Thus, in the Hamdan case, the U.S. Supreme Court was called to decide whether the conflict with Al Qaeda should be deemed as non-international, justifying Hamdan's detention or international and accordingly Hamdan should be given a prisoner of war status.[12]

In its ruling, the Court held that the conflict with Al Qaeda was non-international within the meaning of Common Article 3 of the Geneva Conventions. Yet, as put by Lesley Wexler in her chapter, the Court did not specify whether its stance referred only to Afghanistan or expanded to include also other countries where the U.S. is waging its war on terror, such as Yemen. Thus, the Hamdan ruling leaves issues open regarding the standards any IHL application must meet in U.S. operations, such as drone strikes. It is these issues that Wexler examines in this volume.

Similarly, in Israel, as suicide attacks occurred almost on a daily basis, the State described the situation as that of an 'armed conflict short of war'.[13] In 2002, a one ton bomb released from an Israel Air Force (IAF) jet killed a major Hamas member, Shahade, injuring at the same time many civilians, including women and children.[14] The outcry that the particular targeted killing brought, led to a petition before the Israeli Supreme Court. In 2006, in its Targeted Killings case, the Court

---

[9] For the opinions of the Court's Judges holding otherwise than the Court's majority on the issue see Separate Opinion of Judge Higgins, at paras 33–34; Separate Opinion of Judge Kooijmans, at paras 35–36; Declaration of Judge Buergenthal, at paras 5–6. For some of the scholars acknowledging the right to self-defense in cases of transnational terrorist attacks with no state requirement, see Dinstein 2001, p. 214; Franck 2001; Brown 2003; Stahn 2003; Kretzmer 2005; Solomon 2010.

[10] De Cock 2010, p. 110; Ohlin 2013. For publicists arguing for the international character of such conflicts see Ben-Naftali and Michaeli 2003; Jinks 2003; Dinstein 2009. For publicists arguing for the non-international character of such conflicts see Bellal et al. 2011; Kretzmer 2005; Ben-Naftali and Shany 2006, p. 124.

[11] Maogoto Nyamuya 2003, pp. 436–437.

[12] For the fact that the Israeli Supreme Court has denied any prisoner of war status to terrorists on account of their violating the laws of war see HCJ 2967/00, Arad v. The Knesset, 54 PD (2) 188, 191.

[13] Kretzmer 2005, p. 207.

[14] Ibid at p. 172, n. 6.

held that an international conflict existed between Israel and the Palestinians.[15] For a Court that has opted to remain mum on other IHL issues such as the legality of the settlements,[16] the uttering of a clear view on an IHL issue with major legal implications for the State should be applauded.

Such conclusion should not be deemed self-evident. In both the cases of the U.S. and Israeli Supreme Courts, it is human rights protections that have compelled domestic judicial bodies to take this position. In turn, this judicial readiness to articulate a clear stance on IHL issues has instigated a dialogue which extends also to the executive branch. As Wexler demonstrates, it is the Al-Aulaqi lawsuits that instigated the U.S. administration to articulate clearer rules with regard to circumstances that would permit the targeting of U.S. citizens.

On similar lines, Stephens and McLaughlin examine the impact of the flotilla incident on the laws of naval warfare. Noting that the existing ICJ jurisprudence so far, particularly in the Nicaragua and Oil Platforms cases, opted either to deal with selected jus in bello aspects of maritime IHL or did not adequately address them, Stephens and McLaughlin note in contrast the direct manner in which various quasi-judicial bodies tackled maritime IHL issues, such as that of the blockade, in light of the Gaza flotilla incident. Moreover, these reports also provided input on other cardinal IHL issues that refer to naval warfare, such as the characterization of the conflict or the interrelation of IHL and International Human Rights Law (IHRL). While Stephens and McLaughlin convincingly argue that the treatment of these issues has not always been satisfactory, the fact that these quasi-judicial bodies dared to touch cardinal contested issues of IHL in their naval context, is laudable.

Despite these difficulties concerning conflict classification and applicable legal frameworks, the international community has not crafted a new treaty to resolve the matter. In her contribution to this volume, Ashley Deeks argues that new rules are emerging that purport to govern transnational armed conflicts with non-state actors—and that these rules stem from non-international sources. Domestic courts of a number of states—through the interpretation, extension, and prudential modification of IHL—are developing a "domestic humanitarian law" to fill the gaps and resolve the ambiguities perceived in prevailing IHL. Deeks maintains that this "domestic humanitarian law" is important because it provides specific, legally binding rules governing a broad range of issues in transnational armed conflicts with non-state actors. Deeks also suggests that "domestic humanitarian law" will have a significant impact on the development of conventional and customary IHL.

---

[15] HCJ 769/02, Public Committee Against Torture in Israel v. Israel, Judgment of 13 December 2006, para 21 at http://elyon1.court.gov.il/Files_ENG/02/690/007/a34/02007690.a34.pdf.

[16] Barak Erez 2009, p. 122; Shany 2005, p. 244.

1.2.2 Direct Participation in Hostilities

Modern warfare has broadened the parameters and challenges for IHL. The fact that terrorist groups like Hamas, Hezbollah, or Al Qaeda have developed into significant political actors, raises the question of whether mere membership to these organizations is enough in order for an individual to be considered a legitimate target. In other words, when could the "direct participation in hostilities" requirement as embedded in the Additional Protocol I to the Geneva Conventions be deemed to have been satisfied?

A clear and uniform definition of direct participation in hostilities does not exist.[17] On one hand, the traditional view of the "direct participation" requirement is embedded in the view of Professor Cassese, that to hold that killing civilians suspected of terrorism, while they are not engaged in military action, is internationally lawful would involve a blatant departure from the fundamental principles of international humanitarian law.[18] Certain states, such as the United Kingdom, seem to abide by this stance.[19]

On the other hand, the need for this direct participation to be broadened in order to cover also preparatory stages of an attack was also diagnosed.[20] Yet, where this broadening of the notion should stop is an issue that remains unresolved among publicists. It has been noted that direct participation should not include support for or affiliation to the adversary.[21] According to the third report of the Inter-American Commission on Human Rights

> Civilians whose activities merely support the adverse party's war or military effort or otherwise only indirectly participate in hostilities cannot on these grounds alone be considered combatants. This is because indirect participation, such as selling goods to one or more of the armed parties, expressing sympathy for the cause of one of the parties or, even more clearly, failing to act to prevent an incursion by one of the armed parties, does not involve acts of violence which pose an immediate threat of actual harm to the adverse party.[22]

On the other hand, it was equally argued that the issue of the civilians' direct participation in hostilities should be interpreted liberally, in asserting such

---

[17] Henckaerts and Doswald-Beck 2005, p. 23. For the fact that the ICRC Interpretive Guidance on the Notion of Direct Participation in Hostilities under International Humanitarian Law does not shed much light on certain aspects of direct participation see Goodman and Jinks 2010.

[18] Antonio Cassese, Expert Opinion on Whether Israel's Targeted Killings of Palestinian Terrorists Is Consonant with International Humanitarian Law (http://www.stoptorture.org.il/files/cassese.pdf.

[19] Dapo Akande, The UK's Use of Drones in Afghanistan and its Definition of "Civilians", EJIL!Talk, January 31, 2013 available at http://www.ejiltalk.org/the-uks-use-of-drones-in-afghanistan-and-its-definition-of-civilians/.

[20] Pilloud et al. 1987, p. 516; Watkin 2004, p. 17.

[21] Duffy 2005, p. 230.

[22] Inter-American Commission on Human Rights, Third Report on Human Rights in Colombia, paras 53, 56 (1999).

participation in disputed cases. Thus, ultimately, civilians would stay distant from the conflict.[23]

It is in this normative background that domestic courts have been called to formulate a stance. Thus, in Hamdan, the U.S. Supreme Court held that the position of Hamdan as Bin Laden's driver was enough to render him the combatant status. In the Targeted Killings case, the Israeli Supreme Court expanded the notion of direct participation to include also stages before the actual resort to force.[24] This position while frequently criticized by publicists as lowering the burden for demonstrating that a civilian can be an object of an attack,[25] represents at the same time efforts by domestic courts to balance IHL's normative standards with practical considerations of the exigencies that characterize many times the nature of terrorist organizations and participation in them.

The implications of this judicial stance are mapped in this volume. Wexler, in her chapter, takes the Hamdan "direct participation" ruling one step forward and examines how this can apply to the role of CIA agents in drone strikes. Institutionally, Buchan examines how quasi-judicial bodies such as the Israeli Turkel Commission integrated the Israeli Supreme Court's direct participation standards in their own findings. He holds a critical stance toward the Commission's conclusion that the Mavi Marmara passengers and crew should be deemed as combatants, since according to Buchan their resolution to break the Israeli blockade should not be considered an act of direct support to Hamas' conflict with Israel.

On her part, in her chapter, Kimberley Trapp examines whether this 'direct participation' doctrine can be widened to include also acts of moral support for Al Qaeda and the Taliban in Afghanistan. Trapp examines the Gul case, where the Court of Appeal of England and Wales convicted Gul for conspiracy with terrorist groups because he uploaded in YouTube a video depicting Taliban forces killing members of the Coalition forces in Afghanistan. Trapp critically questions whether such a conviction should take place under Article 19 of the Terrorist Bombing Convention. As Trapp clarifies also elsewhere, this does not mean that insurgents should not be prosecuted at all; her criticism relates only to such prosecution taking place on account of terrorism.[26]

Terrorism-based prosecution opens in turn also other issues. For example, it raises the question of how IHL compliance can be better ensured. It has been noted that designating the Taliban fighting Coalition forces in Afghanistan as terrorists, although they do comply with the laws of war, constitutes a disincentive for them to continue abiding by the IHL legal framework.[27] The same concern is found in

[23] Schmitt 2004.

[24] HCJ 769/02, Public Committee against Torture v. Israel, para 37.

[25] Eichensehr 2007.

[26] Trapp K (2012) R v. Mohammed Gul: Are you a Terrorist If you Support the Syrian Insurgency? EJIL!Talk at http://www.ejiltalk.org/r-v-mohammed-gul-are-you-a-terrorist-if-you-support-the-syrian-insurgency/#_edn3.

[27] Coco 2013.

Yuval Shany's reservations to Marco Sassoli's suggestion that the principle of equality in warfare should be reconsidered in the era of asymmetric warfare.[28]

In essence, both these debates are about the extent to which IHL should adapt to a changing warfare environment. This is, of course, a long-standing problem for IHL. International humanitarian law aims to establish a realistic set of constraints on war fighting. The difficulty is that accommodation of shifting strategic, operational and tactical concerns might undermine protection of humanitarian values. And protection of these values without regard to shifting realities of the battlefield risks rendering IHL irrelevant. Striking the right balance is as important as it is difficult.

Furthermore, the Gul case opens a new window to the relationship between domestic and international courts in IHL issues, since the Court of Appeal endorsed the definition of terrorism that the Appeals Chamber of the Special Court for Lebanon had coined about a year before the Gul judgment.[29] The fact that a domestic court opts to be guided in the ruling of a cardinal issue to the case, as to what constitutes terrorism, by the dicta of an international tribunal, shows the readiness with which domestic courts have sought to absorb jus in bello-jus ad bellum debates formulated in the international arena. In IHL matters, the nexus between international and domestic law becomes more intense on a jurisprudential level. The fact that this does apply on a normative level, is something that the current volume will examine through Patricia Hobb's chapter on the Extraordinary Chambers in the Courts of Cambodia.

Interestingly, the Gul case invites us to think about the vertical intrusion of IHLR in IHL to the extent that IHLR can apply also to combatants concerned. The two extremes taken by the two litigant parties hinge on whether in non-international armed conflicts armed forces are or are not subject to combatant immunity,[30] or otherwise stated, whether or not they are under the protective umbrella of IHL. In reflection, it can be argued that even if this is not the case, in some instances, it is actually IHRL that extends to offer protective status.

Traditionally, combatants have been perceived as lawful targets. Yet, in all cases and under all circumstances? Recent developments in international theory have restructured the identity of combatant. Thus, in life-threatening situations and operations, such as targeted killings decisions, it is not incontestable that the right to life of soldiers cannot be taken into consideration.[31] Domestic jurisprudence seems to be following this line of thought. Thus, in the case of Smith, the UK Supreme Court held that the soldiers' human rights applied while on duty. Accordingly, the State was found accountable for not providing the soldiers with the necessary equipment and conditions for the better protection of their lives.

---

[28] Shany 2011; Sassoli 2011.

[29] Ibid.

[30] R v. Mohammed Gul, EWCA Crim. 280 (22 February 2012).

[31] Blum 2010; Solomon 2007.

These domestic decisions raise the question of combatants' judicial protection to another, higher level. If man is considered as a union of body and soul, till now IHL has focused on the corporal aspect. From the mid-nineteenth century and the Solferino battle, all debates on instituting laws of war focused on enemy combatants. The Hague Regulations, enacted at the beginning of the twentieth century, place accordingly an emphasis on how hostilities are to be conducted. After World War II, Geneva Convention IV reached to embrace the plight of civilians by offering a concrete legal framework. The latest developments in international theory and jurisprudence seem to put again the stress on combatants, this time fellow combatants. This closes a circle in IHL's evolution.

These developments also relate to the behavioral context of IHL. International humanitarian law regulates human behavior under extremely adverse circumstances. As a consequence, advances in our understanding of human psychology – particularly in the context of highly adversarial encounters – will be important in debates about IHL reform. Along these lines, Eliav Lieblich's chapter opens the volume's second part by addressing the intersection between IHL and psychology.

1.3 The Thematic and Institutional Expansion of IHL

1.3.1 Expanding Thematically

1.3.1.1 IHL and Psychology

In his chapter, Lieblich examines the role the psychological impact of warfare on the civilian population and how this psychological factor can be legally evaluated. Lieblich stresses that mental harm needs a thorough doctrinal examination as part of the wider civilian harm, particularly in light of modern asymmetric conflicts or conflicts waged in the proximity of a civilian population. This doctrinal examination is utterly tied to the inclusion of mental harm as a parameter to be taken into account in the proportionality equation. In his careful assessment of the doctrine, Lieblich examines IHL's development, state practice, and more importantly, the stance of judicial and quasi-judicial bodies.

On a judicial level, Lieblich posits the readiness by the Peshawar High Court in Pakistan in its judgment to declare the unlawfulness of U.S. drone strikes, also due to the harm caused to the cattle, beyond any economic aspects and on account of 'the worst kind of cruelty to the animals' as is characteristically mentioned. As far as quasi-judicial bodies are concerned, Lieblich notes that in the case of Israel and Gaza both the Goldstone Report as well as the Palmer Report have referred to the psychological trauma suffered by civilians. In 2013, the UN Human Rights Council Report on Syria referred to acts meant to cause terror among civilians. Lieblich notes that this treatment of mental harm on a quasi-judicial level, albeit signaling a development in the inclusion of feelings and thoughts as parameters in IHL, refers to the causing of intentional and not incidental mental harm.

Lieblich notes a number of reasons why mental harm is not more widely included in IHL judicial and quasi-judicial application, most significantly due to problems of its definition and discernment. However, Lieblich suggests that this 'intangibility' of mental harm, can be solved both on an interdisciplinary basis, through resort to notions of psychiatry such as the Post-Traumatic Stress Disorder (PTSD), as well as through other branches of law, like tort law and most importantly, through the jurisprudence of the international criminal courts and tribunals. Citing the Krstic, Tolimir, Kajelijeli, and Kayishema cases, his chapter deals with the fact that both the ICTY as well as the ICTR have recognized that mental harm can be inflicted and be criminally punishable as a crime, in cases where it is lasting and impacts on a permanent basis to a person's ability to have a normal and constructive life.

1.3.1.2 IHL and Human Rights Law

The civil war in former Yugoslavia, the Rwanda genocide led to the establishment of international criminal tribunals, assigned to investigate the criminal facets of combat behavior.[32] In parallel, also the International Court of Justice (ICJ) was called to adjudicate the question of whether war conduct in the framework of the Yugoslavian civil war could amount to genocide.[33]

With the establishment of these tribunals, the international community signaled that a page should be turned in the legal evaluation of war atrocities. This perception proved not to be temporal. With the establishment of the International Criminal Court in 1998, international criminal accountability for the Geneva Convention IV grave breaches was entrenched and even sometimes allegedly expanded from the existent customary law.[34] The perception that international criminal law could interact with IHL on a norm-formation basis emerging from the blending of the two fields, is directly linked to the fact that IHL had already been perceived as able to interact with IHRL not on a distinct, parallel basis, but through the forging of a lex specialis relationship.[35]

---

[32] On this see Maogoto Nyamuya 2004, p. 8 (noting that international criminal tribunals…have become the international community's primary response to humanitarian crises.).

[33] Application of the Convention on the Prevention and Punishment of the Crime of Genocide (Bosnia and Herzegovina v. Serbia and Montenegro) ICJ Rep. 2007.

[34] This is the case with the ICC Settlement Provision, where the addition of the word 'indirectly' in the ICC Statute regarding population transfers in an occupied territory, led to arguments that the provision did not reflect customary law in this particular point. On this see Zemach 2003.

[35] Lubell 2005; Schabas 2007; Verdirame 2008; Legality of the Threat or Use of Nuclear Weapons, Advisory Opinion [1996] ICJ Rep. 226; Legal Consequences of the Construction of a Wall in the Occupied Palestinian Territory (2004) 43 I.L.M. 1009; Armed Activities on the Territory of Congo (Democratic Republic of Congo v. Uganda), Judgment, ICJ Rep. 2005, p. 168, para 180; Report of the Secretary-General's Panel of Experts on Accountability in Sri Lanka (March 31, 2011), para 184. For the fact that initially the two fields—IHL and IHRL—were seen as two distinct fields, the one applying in wartime the other in times of peace, see Kretzmer 2005, p. 185.

The question is how far horizontally, meaning vis-a-vis other courts and tribunals, and vertically, regarding its entrenchment, this IHL-IHRL nexus has expanded. This question is explored in this volume through the comparison of two different regional Human Rights Systems, the Inter-American and the European one.

Shana Tabak provides in her chapter an exhaustive summary of the interpretation and application of IHL in the Inter-American System. As Tabak notes, the Inter-American Commission of Human Rights and the Inter-American Court of Human Rights have often encountered human rights allegations in conflict situations. For example, many cases have arisen out of the conflicts involving governments or non-state armed groups in El Salvador, Colombia, Guatemala, Mexico, Peru, and the United States. Although the Commission and Court have jurisdiction over only human rights instruments, the application and interpretation of these instruments in time of armed conflict has required the interpretation of IHL. As such, both the Commission and Court have developed a rich jurisprudence on IHL as well as the relationship between IHL and human rights law.

Both the Commission and the Court have concluded that human rights law and IHL are complementary and that both bodies of law apply in time of armed conflict. Even so, Tabak maintains, the Commission and Court have refused to apply IHL directly as a general matter—having resort to IHL principally as an aid in the interpretation of human rights law. Tabak argues that the limited jurisdiction *ratione materiae* of the Inter-American System accounts for this approach—and that various institutional and procedural constraints within the System have reinforced the approach.

Similarly, Sam Hartridge argues in his chapter, that although the European Court of Human Rights has rendered rulings on IHL issues, it still has not clarified how exactly IHL interacts with IHRL. In Hartridge's words "while there is no express rejection of the *lex specialis* doctrine, neither is there any express application of it." Bringing the example of the notion of "effective control" in the law of occupation, and the fact that this has been raised in cases involving the extraterritorial application of human rights conventions, Hartridge argues that the Court should consider the notion's different role in IHL and IHRL, respectively, and elaborate more on the nexus between the two fields of international law. In that aspect, Hartridge brings to the forefront the jurisprudential challenges that arise out of a mere application of IHRL to situations of armed conflict, which involve different factual and normative backgrounds and which the Hassan case was called to address.[36]

Turning to non-international armed conflicts (NIACs), Hartridge points out that the Court consistently overlooks IHL. Citing a number of ECHR cases, he shows how the Court, despite the arguments advanced by various parties, has not systematically considered IHL in the application of the European Convention.

---

[36] Marko Milanovic, Hassan v. United Kingdom, IHL and IHRL and Other News in (Extra-) Territoriality and Shared Responsibility, December 18, 2013 available at http://www.ejiltalk.org/hassan-v-united-kingdom-ihl-and-ihrl-and-other-news-in-extra-territoriality-and-shared-responsibility/

Particularly in cases relating to the conflict in Chechnya which Hartridge cites, the Court avoided altogether any reference to IHL, although the facts demanded an elucidation of the question whether the armed conflict threshold had been met. In the closing sections of his chapter, Hartridge demonstrates how this reluctance of the Court to apply IHRL viewed through the prism of IHL extends also to substantive rights such as the right to life and freedom from arbitrary detention.

1.3.1.3 IHL and Domestic Law

In her chapter, Patricia Hobbs examines how IHL is applied in the Extraordinary Chambers in the Courts of Cambodia (ECCC). In the case of Cambodia, there is a tendency to associate certain acts of the Khmer Rouge regime with grave breaches of IHL. This necessitates an international armed conflict background. In part, this is provided by the Vietnam Cambodian military intervention. Yet, as Hobbs points out, the Vietnamese intervention cannot adequately provide the necessary international armed conflict background in all cases, even regarding crimes that had to do more with internal social Cambodian issues, such as the efforts of the Khmer Rouge regime to ideologically cleanse the country. Thus, while IHL can help toward the prosecution of the crimes committed in Cambodia, it ultimately meets limits. It is in this aspect that domestic law interacts with IHL, rendering possible the connection with the criminal jurisdiction. Hobbs lauds this normative involvement of domestic law. She explains that such an involvement can bolster the legitimacy of such tribunals and can create also an effective criminal judicial model.

At the same time, it is interesting to note how also in the case of Cambodia, the domestic law environment, reminiscent of Law No. 10 that in the aftermath of World War II rendered possible Nazi prosecutions in domestic courts, though under an international legal regime that the Allied Powers had drafted,[37] works in order not to impede the role of international criminal and the indictment of IHL breaches, but actually to promote it, even if resort to novice approaches has to be undertaken. Thus, for example, in the Duch case that Hobbs analyzes, although planning and superior responsibility did not form part of the Cambodian Penal Code, the ECCC was not led to the conclusion that no prosecution should take place, but reinterpreted in essence the Criminal Code, inserting the element of foreseeability or relied on customary international law. Questions whether the particular judgment respected the principle of legality can be raised.[38] Moreover, this function of domestic law, totally disregarded when it cannot provide corroborative authority for rules the Tribunal has already adopted, can ultimately undermine the Tribunal's hybrid character.[39] The ECCC provides no hierarchy between international and domestic law and as such it becomes on one hand more

---

[37] Maogoto Nyamuya 2009.

[38] Kielsgard 2012.

[39] Ibid at p. 136.

doctrinally anarchic, but on the other hand also more practically flexible to substantially apply IHL by rendering punishments on IHL grave breaches.[40]

Moreover, in her chapter Hobbs expands on how the acts under prosecution, especially for crimes related to the destruction of cultural property, can be disengaged from the requirement of any armed conflict and be punished as crimes against humanity. This highlights the interrelation between war crimes and crimes against humanity and depicts what the present volume aspires to stress, namely that IHL in so much as it is a technical field governed by the Hague Regulations and the Geneva Conventions, it is also a substantial field spreading its arms to embrace notions strictly belonging to other related legal fields, such as jus ad bellum, human rights, and international criminal law.

The ECCC had to apply IHL taking into consideration international criminal law principles. Hobbs aptly demonstrates how this was the case with the principle of legality in reference to the doctrine of Joint Criminal Enterprise or the principle of *ne bis in idem* in the Ieng Sari case, which involved the question of whether amnesties granted were valid.

The ECCC push new legal ground since as Hobbs notes, "they represent a new judicial model, attempting to bring standards of international criminal justice closer to home." In a sense, they inaugurate a new era in the expansion of the institutional application of IHL, which is discussed in the third part of this volume.

1.3.2 Expanding Institutionally

1.3.2.1 IHL and Domestic Courts

In 2013, writing in the Leiden Journal of International Law, Yael Ronen observed that domestic jurisprudence on the laws of armed conflict is not plentiful.[41] Yet, the last few years have seen domestic jurisprudence more willing to deal with international law issues to the extent that whereas traditional emphasis has been on how international law configures domestic law, more recently international legal theory has started seriously to explore also how domestic law actually shapes international law.[42] The current volume aspires to examine this question by focusing on how domestic judicial bodies have dealt with IHL issues.

---

[40] Along the same lines see also the ECCC's assertion on claims of Duch that his due process rights had been violated due to his prolonged detention that "...the prolonged detention under the jurisdiction of the Military Court, in comparison with the crimes against humanity alleged against the accused, cannot be considered a sufficiently grave violation of the rights of the accused. On this see Office of the Co-Investigating Judges (OCIJ) Detention Order at http://www.eccc.gov.kh/english/cabinet/indictment/1/Order_of_Provisional_Detention-DUCH-EN.pdf, para 21. For criticism of this stance see Ryngaert 2008, p. 730.

[41] Ronen 2013.

[42] See on this the relevant symposium published in 2013 in volume 26 of the Leiden Journal of International Law.

The chapters contained herein palpably demonstrate the shift in IHL application in the realms of domestic judicial bodies. From cases dealing primarily with issues of refugee law, due to the internalization of conflict on one hand and various countries' participation to the war on terror and the readiness of states to exercise their universal jurisdiction competence on the other, in the last decade domestic courts have come to pronounce also on IHL issues arising from armed conflicts, pertaining *inter alia* to treatment of war prisoners or to war crimes.[43] This is not confined to the Supreme Courts of various states, but finds voice also in courts of lower instance. However, even this judicial intervention meets certain limits.[44]

In 2013, a civil case was opened before the German Bonn Regional Court by relatives of victims of the Kunduz airstrike in Afghanistan.[45] This was on the basis of a NATO lethal airstrike ordered by a German officer, which caused the death of scores of civilians.[46] Despite the nature of the incident involving as it did matters of state personnel engaged in a traditional non-justiciable activity, once proceedings were opened, the judges did not throw out the case but asked to see video footage of the incident in order to form their opinion.[47]

Evidently, this is a window into how lower instance courts appear increasingly willing to adjudicate on IHL issues and consequently award compensation to the victims. This far from being a one-off instance is reinforced by the Varvarin bombing incident, an incident similar to that of Kunduz, that arose in the context of the civil war in former Yugoslavia. The German Court of Appeal held that the rules of IHL can be invoked in order for the individual to present claims under national law.[48] On the contrary, the German Federal Constitutional Court held that Germany did not have to compensate victims since it was NATO and not German forces that conducted the bombing as well as the fact that any relevant proceedings could be instigated by other states and not by individuals. The Varvarin decision demonstrates also the limits of domestic judicial bodies in engaging with issues of IHL application utterly tied to actions of their respective governments.[49]

The current volume contains analyses of IHL treatment both in continental as well as common law jurisdictions, which are historically and geographically diverse. Close to Germany, yet having its distinct judicial treatment of the issue, Roberta Arnold through her chapter focusing on Switzerland, maps the legislative

---

[43] Ronen 2013, pp. 600–601.

[44] O' Keefe 2013, p. 547. For these limits as experienced in the application of universal jurisdiction in the Belgium judicial context see Langer 2011, pp. 26–31.

[45] Carla Christina Bleiker, German Court to Rule on Kunduz Airstrike, Deutsche Welle, March 20, 2013 at http://www.dw.de/german-court-to-rule-on-kunduz-airstrike/a-16680014.

[46] Ibid.

[47] German Court Demands Video Footage of Kunduz Airstrike, Deutsche Welle, Apr. 17, 2013 at http://www.dw.de/german-court-demands-video-footage-of-kunduz-airstrike/a-16750847.

[48] Schwager 2005, p. 433.

[49] O'Keefe 2013. For the fact that these limits in the treatment of international law issues are inherent to international law itself see Solomon 2013.

background that ultimately enables Swiss courts to become involved with cases pertaining to IHL.

If in the case of Germany the limits of IHL domestic application have been demonstrated, in Switzerland, cases like that of Jagath Dias or even that of the criminal complaint against then US President George W. Bush depict exactly the dynamics embedded in the augmenting interaction of domestic jurisdictions with IHL. Dias, deputy Sri Lankan ambassador to Switzerland, and a previous senior army officer, had played an important role in the government's armed conflict with the Tamil Tigers. In 2011, a report of the European Centre for Constitutional and Human Rights accused him of war crimes being undertaken between 2008 and 2009.[50] In particular, he was accused that the army division he was heading completely devastated the city of Kilinochchi, a Tamil Tigers stronghold, causing a bloodbath and subsequently kept bombarding the civilians who were trying to flee.[51]

Eventually, two associations in Switzerland filed a criminal complaint with the Federal Attorney General, calling for Dias' arrest on account of war crimes.[52] Shortly after, Dias was stripped of his diplomatic immunity and recalled back to Sri Lanka.[53] In response, the Federal Attorney General confirmed that the existing suspicions against Dias were enough in order for a criminal investigation to be opened, yet investigation would not proceed further since Dias was no longer in Switzerland.[54] Nevertheless, the file remained open, meaning that Dias would be investigated the moment he stepped back on Swiss soil.[55] It is of note that in August 2013, the United States refused to grant Dias entry to attend a training program as member of the Sri Lankan armed forces.[56]

---

[50] European Centre for Constitutional and Human Rights, ECHHR Dossier, Major General Jagath Dias, Allegations of War Crimes Committed by the 57 Division of Major General Dias in Northern Sri Lanka between April 2008 and May 2009 at http://www.trial-ch.org/fileadmin/user_upload/documents/affaires/SriLanka/Dias_dossier_en.pdf.

[51] Ibid, pp. 11, 13, 17.

[52] Criminal Complaint filed against Deputy Ambassador of Sri Lanka for War Crimes, August 3, 2011 at http://www.trial-ch.org/srilanka-en/press_files/41476ca5f20ba3e8df168e8eb01fe3ef-5.html.

[53] TRIAL-Swiss Association against Impunity,Jagath Dias at http://www.trial-ch.org/en/activities/litigation/trials-cases-in-switzerland/jagath-dias-sri-lanka-2011.html, July 30, 2013; Sri Lanka Recalls Diplomat Accused of War Crimes, Swiss Broadcasting Corporation, Sept, 13, 2011 at http://www.swissinfo.ch/eng/news_digest/Sri_Lanka_recalls_diplomat_accused_of_war_crimes.html?cid=31128290.

[54] Ordonance of Non Entry, Swiss Federal Prosecutor's Office, Sept. 16, 2011, p. 4 at http://www.trial-ch.org/fileadmin/user_upload/documents/affaires/SriLanka/DiasMPCDecision16.09.2011.pdf.

[55] Ibid.

[56] US, Switzerland Reject Jagath Dias as Probable War Criminal; Gov't Appoints Dias to Head Weliweriya Military Probe, Colombo Telegraph, August 22, 2013 at https://www.colombotelegraph.com/index.php/us-switzerland-reject-jagath-dias-as-probable-war-criminal-govt-appoints-dias-to-head-weliweriya-military-probe/.

An interesting case, which shows the potential that IHL has in domestic fora when linked with international criminal accountability, is the Bush case. On account of the US tactics in the realms of the war on terror and in particular treatment of prisoners in Guantanamo Bay, Swiss associations prepared a criminal complaint against the U.S. president, due to be filed on account of the latter's visit to Geneva.[57] The complaint related indirectly also to the Bush administration claim that Taliban and Al Qaeda detainees did not merit the protection of the Geneva Conventions since they did not qualify as combatants.[58] This touched the very heart of the question of the Afghanistan conflict's categorization, an issue pronounced upon by the U.S. Supreme Court in the Hamdan case. Quite interestingly, in Switzerland, the criminal complaint was based on the provisions of the Convention against Torture, which negates any immunity for heads of states. Ultimately, the complaint was not filed because George W. Bush cancelled his Geneva trip.[59] Yet, the impact such initiatives of IHL application in domestic fora implant, remains palpable.

Swiss courts have also been involved in issues arising out of IHL violations in the case of Khaled Nezzar, where the Swiss Federal Court rejected any claims of state immunity, despite the Switzerland's Office of Foreign Affairs opinion to the opposite.[60] Nezzar was suspected of war crimes perpetrated during the Algerian civil war and the Court was of the opinion that he could be tried in Switzerland. This was a seismic moment since the Court's stance demonstrated that domestic courts can utter a different word from the executive branch even in matters touching issues of foreign policy and bilateral relations.[61]

In addressing Mr. Nezzar's claim that Swiss courts lacked any competence to judge him since he was not present in Switzerland at the time of the trial, the Federal Court noted that while indeed Swiss law required the presence of the defendant, the seriousness of the accusations compelled the Court to adopt a broad interpretation regarding the necessary link between Switzerland and the defendant. Thus, the Federal Court held that the presence of the accused at the moment of the prosecutor's interrogation was enough in order for Swiss jurisdiction to be asserted, despite the fact that the accused was not in Switzerland at the time of proceedings.[62] As such, through this particular stance, the Court affirmed that war

---

[57] Preliminary "Indictment for Torture": George W. Bush Brought Pursuant to the Convention Against Torture, Centre for Constitutional Rights at http://ccrjustice.org/files/FINAL%207%20Feb%20BUSH%20INDICTMENT.pdf.

[58] Memorandum for Chairman of the Joint Chiefs of Staff, Status of Taliban and Al Qaida, Jan. 19, 2002 at http://www.defense.gov/news/Jun2004/d20040622doc1.pdf.

[59] George W. Bush Cancels Visit to Jewish Charity Gala Over Fears he Could be Arrested on Torture Charges, Daily Mail, Feb. 6 2011 at http://www.dailymail.co.uk/news/article-1354211/George-W-Bush-cancels-Switzerland-visit-fears-arrest-torture-charges.html.

[60] Katzenstein 2012, p. 699.

[61] Wuerth 2012, pp. 822–823.

[62] Federal Criminal Tribunal, A vs. Ministere Public de la Confederation, Decision, July 25, 2012 available at http://www.trial-ch.org/fileadmin/user_upload/documents/affaires/algeria/BB.2011.140.pdf para 3.1.

crimes accusations can impact on domestic jurisprudence not only as far as substantial law is concerned, but also on procedural aspects like the defendant's in abstentia trial.

On account of the augmenting role that the Swiss judicial bodies play when questions of IHL arise, Roberta Arnold maps in her chapter the legal landscape that through the revision of the Criminal and Military Criminal Codes has offered a new impetus to the application of IHL in Swiss courts. Moreover, Arnold analyzes the landmark cases of G. as well as that of Niyonteze that ushered the Swiss judicial world into an era of more thorough involvement with issues of IHL application.

Two other jurisdictions that have seen application of IHL extending further beyond traditional cases of refugee law and asylum cases are Australia and Canada. In her chapter, Emily Crawford covers IHL application in Australian courts. She analyzes the transition from the less than successful prosecution of World War II war criminals living in Australia toward the end of the previous century to the more recent attempts to prosecute Australian soldiers for alleged war crimes. Similar to the case of Switzerland, Crawford analyzes how the Australian judicial system faced issues of foreign heads of state immunity when criminal charges were filed in the Melbourne Magistrates' Court against the President of Sri Lanka for his role in the commission of alleged war crimes throughout the Sri Lankan civil war.

Indeed, the whole question of whether immunity of state officials should be preserved even in cases of war crimes has been in the heart of a debate-dialogue between international and domestic courts. Thus, in the Arrest Warrant case, the ICJ held that a court of a foreign state can try an official of another State for acts committed during the period in office in a private capacity.[63] On the other hand, domestic courts have been more ready to convict state officials for crimes they have perpetrated while in office.[64] The debate is captured in soft law international instruments, such as the reports of the International Law Commission on immunity of State officials from foreign criminal jurisdiction. Thus, in the relevant report of 2011, the immunity versus impunity nexus is evident in the stance of the Special Rapporteur that no immunity exceptions should be allowed even in cases of crimes allegations and the criticism voiced by members of the Commission who have referred to the domestic jurisprudence that has developed for the prosecution of war crimes in domestic courts notwithstanding any immunity claims.[65]

---

[63] Arrest Warrant of 11 April 2000 (Democratic Republic of Congo v. Belgium), Judgment, ICJ Rep. 2002 para 61.

[64] On this see Joanne Foakes, Immunity for International Crimes? Developments in the Law on Prosecuting Heads of States in Foreign Courts, November 2011, Chatham House Briefing Paper at http://www.chathamhouse.org/sites/default/files/public/Research/International%20Law/bp1111_foakes.pdf.

[65] United Nations, Report of the International Law Commission, Sixty-third session (26 April-3 June and 4 July-12 August 2011), General Assembly, Official Records, Sixty-sixth session, Supp. No.10 (A/66/10), paras 113–114, 121–124, 131.

As such, it is interesting that in the case of Australia immunity rhetoric did ultimately prevail. Ultimately, as Crawford palpably describes in her chapter, less than a day after the indictment was filed, the Attorney General quashed the charges.

Some important cases stemming from Australia's augmenting role in the regional and international arena form part of the analytic pivot in Crawford's chapter. For example, in the Balibo-Five case, an Australian war crimes investigation was opened in 2009 regarding the death of five journalists in Timor Leste during the Indonesian invasion in 1975. A Coroner's investigation found that the five journalists—two Australians, two Britons and one New Zealander—were caught alive and it was the Captain of the Indonesian Special Forces that ordered their execution. Crawford demonstrates the hurdles IHL application in domestic fora faces, noting that almost five years since the investigation opened, it is yet to yield any results and it is uncertain how proceedings will move forward.

Australia's participation in the war on terror has also led to some relevant cases reaching Australian courts. The Habib case is significant. Mamhoud Habib, an Australian citizen, claimed that following his arrest in 2001 in Afghanistan, he had been subject to torture and that Australian officials were complicit in the acts of torture, because they provided intelligence that was employed during his interrogation and in all cases knew about the torture he was subject to.

The Full Court of the Federal Court appeared willing to hear the case, brushing aside the Australian government's resort to the act of state doctrine.[66] Ultimately, and amidst reports that Australian officials seemed indeed to have been involved in Habib's torture, the latter reached an out of court settlement with the Australian government.

Similar to the Dias and Bush cases in Switzerland, the Habib case unveils the limits of judicial bodies in the application of IHL, but at the same time also the war crimes accountability drive that escorts such IHL application initiatives. Thus, although the Habib case was settled out of court, it still led to the appointment of an independent body, the Inspector General of Intelligence and Security, to examine the conduct of Australian officials in the affair.[67]

The application of IHL in the Australian domestic jurisdiction holds a particular importance due, *inter alia*, to the fact that it has initiated charges against Australian soldiers serving in Afghanistan and having been accused for allegedly unlawfully targeting civilians. Yet, charges against these soldiers were not brought on grounds of any war crimes commission, but for manslaughter, based on the Australian criminal code. In her chapter, Crawford raises her voice in tandem with the stance of also other prominent members of the Australian international law community, such as Professor Tim McCormack, against these charges, echoing concerns that members of the Australian armed forces were asked to rely on

---

[66] For the distinction between the act of state doctrine and the principle of non-justiciability see Alderton 2011, pp. 11–13.

[67] Roach 2013, p. 929.

standards higher than those imposed by IHL. Moreover, such charges that have been pressed also in other countries like Israel[68] raise the issue also of whether combatants can be accused for negligence in the realms of blurred combat conditions. This takes us back to Finogenov as discussed above, placing Crawford's chapter in a direct dialectic with Lieblich's chapter. The issue of how the thoughts and emotions of warfare's protagonists impact on their criminal accountability is one that the international law community will ultimately have to address, on account of the fact that in modern warfare combatants are many times hiding in the civilian population.[69]

Aside these cases, Crawford refers also to cases regarding refugee protection and extradition, which albeit referring to a more traditional field of IHL application in Australian jurisprudence, still, they offer important insights into the way international law is applied once the Australian domestic courts want to ensure the entrenchment of IHL. As Crawford notes, in the SRYYY case, the Full Court of the Federal Court held that the Administrative Appeals Tribunal had correctly applied law, when it interpreted the crimes against humanity, and war crimes in tandem with the ICC Rome Statute, which was not though in force the time the relevant crimes constituting the object of the SRYYY case took place. It is interesting—and Crawford notes it—that the Federal Court in essence accepted thus the dynamic character of international legal rules, which can be seen also in other facets of IHL, such as the law of occupation.[70]

The tension between IHL application through traditional venues and the challenges modern warfare connotes is expansive. Turning to Canada, in his chapter James Yap analyzes the traditional extradition and immigration cases that involve application of IHL in Canadian Courts and how these are associated with individuals residing in Canada and being suspected of having committed war crimes as well as grave breaches of IHL in their countries of origin. This nexus is particularly evident, since Canada has adopted a policy of preventing suspected war criminals from immigrating to Canada and deporting such individuals who already reside in Canadian soil.[71] Similar to Australia, also in Canada there were fears that the country had become a safe haven for Nazi-era war criminals. This is one of the principal reasons that extraterritorial jurisdiction for war crimes and crimes against humanity was introduced.

Under this lens, Yap proceeds to examine the Munyaneza and Mungwarere cases, involving Rwandan nationals tried *inter alia* on war crimes, crimes against humanity and genocide charges. As Yap notes, while the Mungwarere judgment brings forth the dialogue between domestic courts and international criminal

---

[68] Harriet Sherwood, Israeli Soldier Charged with Manslaughter during Gaza Offensive, The Guardian, July 6, 2010 at http://www.theguardian.com/world/2010/jul/06/israeli-soldier-charged-gaza-manslaughter.

[69] Brooks 2004, p. 710, n. 124.

[70] Solomon 2012.

[71] Weiss 2012, p. 588.

tribunals, a dialogue discerned also in other Canadian judgments that Yap analyzes, the Munyaneza decision raises some issues of IHL application, which the chapter critically addresses. More interestingly, Yap brings forth the fact that Munyaneza was found guilty of war crimes even though it was not clear that customary international law at the time recognized acts committed in non-international armed conflicts as war crimes.

This issue is linked with legal dilemmas in the application of IHL we encountered also in the chapter on the ECCC as well as in other jurisdictions, albeit tackled in a different manner. As such, in the Mpambara case, another case similar to that of Munyaneza involving a Rwandan national before Dutch courts, the latter lacked universal jurisdiction for genocide and crimes against humanity.[72] Yet, the Dutch juridical authorities did not attempt to expand their jurisdiction *ratione materiae*. Rather, charges were brought only for war crimes and torture. Ultimately, these war charges failed before the Hague District Court owing to the lack of nexus with an armed conflict.[73]

Yap stays doctrinally on the nexus between the administrative immigration and deportation proceedings and the criminal charges the Canadian juridical world opts to settle once IHL breaches are at play. He notes that the administrative leeway has been deplored by scholars. Yap concedes it is imperfect. At the same time though he stresses that practical reasons render it preferable in cases where charges cannot be established beyond any reasonable doubt or logistical concerns pose as an obstacle to the opening of domestic proceedings.

Highlighting issues of possible corporate liability for war crimes, Yap proceeds to examine also the civil claims against Canadian corporations for allegedly committing war crimes overseas. In that sense, domestic Canadian jurisdiction is enlivened to IHL application on account of armed conflicts in which Canada does not form a belligerent party. Yap extends a critical tone on the Canadian courts' decisions on the issue. He notes that Canadian courts should find themselves competent both in the Yassin as well as the Anvil Mining case, the former involving a Canadian corporation undertaking in projects in the West Bank, the latter a corporation in the Democratic Republic of Congo.

The question of whether domestic courts could constitute the natural forum for the legal pronouncement of internationally contested issues without getting prone to criticism of excessive politicization is indeed sensitive. At the same time, it may account also for the reluctance of domestic courts to deal with highly contested and politicized issues such as these that are many times brought up in the realms of IHL.[74] For example, regarding the question of Israel's occupation of the West Bank and on account of potential liability of French companies for participating in

---

[72] Ferdinandusse 2009.

[73] Ibid.

[74] Milena Sterio, French Companies May Build in the West Bank-An Assessment of the Versailles Court of Appeals Case, May 8, 2013 at http://opiniojuris.org/2013/05/08/guest-post-french-companies-may-build-in-the-west-bank-an-assessment-of-the-versailles-court-of-appeals-case/.

the construction of a light railway system there, the French Versailles Court of Appeals held that violations of Article 49 of the Geneva Convention IV could not be put forth against individuals and thus rejected similar adjudication pleas.[75] A jurisprudential gap is thus created, with domestic courts sliding back. One of the purposes of this volume is to discern how this gap is filled by quasi-judicial bodies.

This gap, this time not procedural but substantial, yet equally caused by the Canadian courts' reluctance to take a stance on IHL issues, is discerned also in the judgments of Canadian courts regarding matters stemming from the war on terror. For example, Canadian courts ruled that the transfer by Canadian forces of non-Canadian detainees to Afghan authorities despite a known and substantial risk of torture does not violate these peoples' rights under the Canadian Charter. Critically poised toward the particular judgment, Yap compares the Canadian stance with that of UK courts, which have adjudicated similar cases.

India is a country where IHL application issues have traditionally found their way in Indian courts. At the same time, India is also a country impacted by terrorism, as demonstrated in various incidents such as the failed attempt to take over the Indian Parliament in 2001 or the Mumbai attacks in 2009. In his chapter, Chintan Chandrachud maps the application of IHL in Indian courts. Notably, he proceeds to examine cases of misapplication or non-application, rendering his critical voice on opportunities Indian courts missed to actually make IHL more tangible to the Indian juridical consciousness.

Chandrachud analyzes the cases of IHL application in Indian courts under four themes: occupation and annexation of territory, prisoners of war, terrorism, and the meaning of aggression.

On the theme of occupation, interesting regarding also cases of contemporary occupations, is the Indian Supreme Court's decision in the Monterio case. Dealing with Goa's annexation by India, the country's Supreme Court made a distinction between "premature annexation" and "true annexation." The former refers to cases where hostilities are continuing, the latter applies once the territory is conquered and subjugated. This stands in contrast with modern international law dicta, according to which, invasion and annexation of a territory is unlawful.[76]

In his chapter, Chandrachud additionally notes the tension between the Court's ruling and the *de lege lata* existent legal mapping. Interestingly, he adds an important parameter to the discussion of how IHL is to be applied. As he notes "although the Court's analysis that the annexation led to a transfer of title may seem flawed when examined exclusively through the funnel of IHL, it finds greater justification when viewed in the context of the broader political and legal issues of de-colonisation, self-determination and acceptance by the international community of states, all of which were precipitated by the annexation of Goa". In that sense, Chandrachud puts on the table the issue of whether IHL application should take

[75] Cour d'Appel de Versailles, AFP v. Societe Alstom Transport SA, http://www.volokh.com/wp-content/uploads/2013/04/French-Ct-decision.pdf.

[76] Crawford 2007, p. 137; Grant 2000, p. 274.

into account new realities on the ground that have been created or the general will of the international community to accept a new factual reality. It has been pointed out by Robert Jennings that the ban on acquisition of territory by force has not prevented eventual title by consolidation and recognition by other states.[77]

This is revolutionary for IHL and in a sense iconoclastic. But, it has to be mentioned that similar lines of thought have been found in international jurisprudence in the last few years. Thus, in the Demopoulos case, the European Court of Human Rights noted in the context of northern Cyprus' Turkish occupation that

> .....Some 35 years after the applicants, or their predecessors in title, left their property, it would risk being arbitrary and injudicious for it [the Court] to attempt to impose an obligation on the Respondent State [Turkey] to effect restitution in all cases....It cannot be within this Court's task in interpreting and applying the provisions of the Convention to impose an unconditional obligation on a Government to embark on the forcible eviction and rehousing of potentially large numbers of men, women and children even with the aim of vindicating the rights of victims of violations of the Convention.[78]

Whether this trend in associating doctrinal IHL with the political and social reality is to be continued, remains to be seen. Yet, as Steven Ratner notes "the trend is hardly over," pointing *inter alia* to the cases of Morocco and Western Sahara and Israel and the West Bank, where relevant groups "look forward to a day when so called facts on the ground displace legal norms".[79] It may seem as a legal Armageddon, but in the end it may prove that it isn't.

In their chapter, Michael Lewis and Peter Margulies provide a survey of over two centuries of US jurisprudence on the interpretation of IHL. Lewis and Margulies make clear that US tribunals and courts have engaged IHL since the nation's founding. This engagement, they maintain, has been driven and limited by an enduring commitment to US membership in the community of nations. The central claim of the chapter is that this conception of the scope, content, and function of IHL has greatly influenced US judicial interpretation of IHL. They also point out a variety of ways in which the conception has influenced the development of IHL more generally.

Although the policy and practice of the political branches of the US government has generally reflected this "membership conception" of IHL, the executive branch has, at times, taken wartime measures inconsistent with this approach. Lewis and Margulies provide a detailed and provocative account of how US courts have responded to these departures—and, in turn, the effect that this response has had on the development of IHL domestically and internationally. In the course of elaborating their argument, Lewis and Margulies provide detailed accounts of US jurisprudence from the US Civil War, World War II, and the contemporary conflict with Al Qaeda.

---

[77] Jennings 1963, p. 67.

[78] Demopoulos et al. v. Turkey, 2010 Eur. Ct. H. R. For a discussion of why such line of thought regarding the Israeli occupation of the West Bank, as put forward by the Levi Commission Report, was not endorsed see Solomon 2012.

[79] Ratner 2006, p. 812.

1.3.2.2 IHL and Quasi-Judicial Bodies

Another theme that the present volume deals with is the question of how IHL is applied in the realms of quasi-judicial bodies. Although the establishment of such quasi-judicial bodies is a known practice,[80] during the last few years, their function has acquired an additional epistemological and institutional impetus through the readiness of international actors to entrust to these quasi-judicial bodies the treatment of disputed international law issues, particularly as far as IHL is concerned.[81]

As such, it is utterly indispensable to examine also the application of IHL in these quasi-judicial bodies if a spherical picture is to be provided.[82] This is true in particular because these quasi-judicial bodies, domestic or international, have tried to postulate an authoritative stance on highly controversial issues, this stance sometimes negating the general international legal and political consensus.[83] As Russell Buchan underlines in his contribution to this volume, citing Jose Alvarez, "it is apparent that quasi-judicial and judicial dispute settlers' contribution to the law is considerable." At the same time, it is important not to forget that these quasi-judicial bodies are largely based on state consent. When this consent is lacking, as Buchan argues was the case with the Panel of Experts on Accountability in Sri Lanka, the very foundations of the quasi-judicial body become shaky.

The present volume does not aspire to examine the application of IHL in all relevant quasi-judicial bodies. On the contrary, it aspires to focus on international and domestic commissions instituted on account of two international events that have sparked lengthy international law discussions either due to their unanimous factual acceptance or due to their factually contested character; the Darfur genocide, and the Gaza flotilla incident.

Makane Mbengue and Brian McGarry examine IHL application in the realms of the International Commission of Inquiry on Darfur. In their chapter, they argue that exactly the fact that the Commission itself acknowledged it was not a judicial body gave it on one hand certain freedom of action, as for example, the obligation to apply standard criminal law thresholds concerning evidentiary burdens, but on the other hand, turned out to be also a setback in the sense that the Commission, albeit did not preclude that certain individuals might have committed atrocities with genocidal intent, referred this possibility to the analysis of the ICC. Mbengue and

---

[80] Thus for example, in the course of the twentieth century fact-finding missions have been established by various international organizations such as the League of Nations and the African Commission on Human and People's Rights. On this see Robertson 2010, pp. 19–21; Mutangi 2006. For the establishment of fact-finding missions on a domestic level by Latin American states to investigate the atrocities committed by the various dictatorial regimes see Galvan 2013, p. 14.

[81] For a list of such quasi-judicial bodies established since the beginning of the twenty first century, see infra Chap. 17 Buchan, n. 107.

[82] Robertson 2010, p. 15.

[83] See for example the Levi Committee Report, arguing that Israeli settlements are legal under international law. For a critical stance on the Committee's conclusions see Solomon 2012.

McGarry rightfully question whether despite the fact that the Commission had a mandate to identify perpetrators of genocide, resort from its part to the ICC judicial scheme, demonstrates a weakness of quasi-judicial bodies to deliver their task.

At the same time, Mbengue and McGarry note correctly the normative gap that has been created due to the fragmentation of judicial bodies and which quasi-judicial bodies such as the International Commission on Darfur have been called to fill. In particular, the authors bring the tension between the ICJ's judgment in the Bosnia and Herzegovina v. Serbia and Montenegro case and the stance of the ICTY regarding the question of genocide. The Darfur Commission was endowed with such a task which went beyond its capacities. The result was that the report of the Commission was replete with systemic errors which Mbengue and McGarry pinpoint.

Thus for example in his contribution to the current volume, Buchan explicitly deals with how the various quasi-judicial bodies—international and domestic—that were established to investigate the Gaza flotilla incident and the tension between Turkey and Israel in its aftermath, applied IHL. Buchan concludes that such IHL application was inadequate by all the relevant bodies, albeit for different reasons. For example, Buchan critically notes that both the Turkish as well as the UN Human Rights Council Report did not utter a stance whether the conflict between Hamas and Israel was international or non-international, an issue utterly linked to the question of whether the law of blockade could apply. Similarly, Buchan holds that the UN Palmer Report and the Israeli Turkel Report erroneously held that the conflict was international. As a result, Buchan argues that the law of blockade, meant according to the San Remo Manual to apply only in international armed conflicts, could not apply in the case of Gaza and that the examples that the Palmer and the Turkel Reports provided in an attempt to demonstrate the blockade's application also in non-international conflicts, are unconvincing.

It is in this regard that Buchan delicately yet robustly diagnoses the potential hidden behind the dicta of quasi-judicial bodies and views in the Palmer Report's doctrinal expansion of the law of blockade, an attempt to alleviate the tension between the *de lege lata* and *de lege ferenda* law pillars.[84]

1.4 Conclusion

In this volume, we attempt to provide the reader with an outlook of the status of international humanitarian law in international and domestic courts and tribunals. Accordingly, some of the volume's chapters map the legal landscape, rendering

---

[84] For another example of the tension between these pillars on account of the Gaza flotilla incident see Solon Solomon and Jackson Nyamuya Maogoto, Jurisdictional Aspects of the Article 12(2) Rome Statute Vessel Provision: Some Thoughts on the Provision's Dogma and Implementation in light of the Comoros Referral, Opinio Juris, July 21, 2013 available at http://opiniojuris.org/2013/07/21/jurisdictional-aspects-of-the-article-122-rome-statute-vessel-provision-some-thoughts-on-the-provisions-dogma-and-implementation-in-light-of-the-comoros-referral/.

the necessary information even to someone not extensively acquainted with the field of IHL. At the same time, the volume also aspires to embrace the debate that the challenges behind any IHL application beget.

Asymmetric warfare, the militarization of counter-terrorist measures, the introduction of lawfare have obliged courts and tribunals to reshape their traditional interpretations of the laws of war if they want to render decisions that are not only doctrinally correct, but are also perceived as just and relevant to the exigencies of our times. In that sense, the present volume is equally addressed to the legal scholar or judge that has already been exposed to the problematic around IHL application and wishes to look for novel ideas in order to advance the relevant debate in the field.

Last, but not least, we wish not to exclude the general public from the IHL debate. Ethical and legal dilemmas arise directly from issues like targeted killings and the war on terror. Our aspiration is that this volume will serve as a useful manual also for non-legal experts, in order for the latter to examine the response international law has to offer to contemporary IHL problems.

The fact that international and domestic judicial bodies have started uttering such a response—even sometimes with deficiencies—is particularly encouraging. Moreover, the growing interaction of quasi-judicial bodies with major IHL issues has to be applauded in principle. The impact though of these quasi-judicial bodies on international and domestic jurisprudence has to be further measured, depending on whether the quasi-judicial bodies will be able to postulate their conclusions on an epistemological basis. In a sense, maybe we are before a judicial revolution in the application of IHL. This volume tries not necessarily to herald it, but at least to discern it.

References

Alderton M (2011) The act of state doctrine: questions of validity and abstention from Underhill to Habib. Melbourne J Int Law 12:1

Barak Erez D (2009) Broadening the scope of judicial review in Israel: between activism and restraint. Indian J Const Law 3:118

Bellal A, Giacca G, Casey-Maslen S (2011) International Law and armed non-state actors in Afghanistan. Int Rev Red Cross 93(47):51

Ben-Naftali O, Michaeli K (2003) 'We must not make a Scarecrow of the Law': a legal analysis of the Israeli policy of targeted killings. Cornell Int Law J 36:233

Ben-Naftali O, Shany Y (2006) International Law between war and peace. Ramot Publications, Tel Aviv University, Tel Aviv

Blum G (2010) The dispensable lives of soldiers. J Legal Anal 2:115

Brooks R (2004) War everywhere: rights, National Security Law and the Law of Armed Conflict in the age of terror. Univ Pa Law Rev 153:675

Brown D (2003) Use of force against terrorism after September 11th: state responsibility, self-defence and other responses. Cardozo J Int Comp Law 11:1

Coco A (2013) The mark of Cain: national prosecution of international crimes: legislation and cases: the crime of terrorism in times of armed conflict as interpreted by the Court of Appeal of England and Wales in R v. Mohammed Gul J Int Crim Justice 11:425

Crawford J (2007) The creation of states in International Law. Oxford University Press, Oxford
De Cock C (2010) Counter-insurgency operations in Afghanistan. What about the 'Jus Ad Bellum' and the 'Jus in Bello': is the Law still accurate? Yearb Int Humanit Law 13:97
Dinstein Y (2001) War, aggression and self-defence, 3rd edn. Cambridge University Press, Cambridge
Dinstein Y (2009) Concluding remarks on terrorism and Afghanistan. Israel Yearb Hum Rights 39:325
Duffy H (2005) The 'War on Terror' and the framework of International Law. Cambridge University Press, Cambridge
Eichensehr K (2007) On target? The Israeli supreme court and the expansion of targeted killings. Yale Law J 116:1873
Ferdinandusse W (2009) The prosecution of grave breaches in national courts. J Int Crim Justice 7:723
Franck T (2001) Editorial comments: terrorism and the right of self-defence. AJIL 94:839
Galvan J (2013) Latin American dictators of the 20th century: the lives and regimes of 15 rulers. McFarland and Company Inc., Jefferson
Goodman R, Jinks D (2010) The ICRC interpretive guidance on the notion of direct participation in hostilities under international humanitarian law. NYU J Int Law Polit 42:637
Grant T (2000) East Timor, the UN system and enforcing non-recognition in International Law. Vanderbilt J Trans Law 33:273
Henckaerts J, Doswald Beck L (2005) Customary international humanitarian law, vol I. Rules. Cambridge University Press, Cambridge
Jennings R (1963) The acquisition of territory in International Law. Manchester University Press, Oxford
Jinks D (2003) September 11 and the Law of War. Yale J Int Law 28:1
Jinks D (2004) Protective parity and the Laws of War. Notre Dame Law Rev 79:1493–1494
Joseph R (2013) The war prerogative: history, reform and constitutional design. Oxford University Press, Oxford
Katzenstein S (2012) International adjudication and custom breaking by domestic courts. Duke Law J 62:671
Kielsgard M (2012) The legality principle in sentencing at the ECCC: making up law as it goes along? Asian J Int Law 2:119
Kretzmer D (2005) Targeted killing of suspected terrorists: extra-judicial executions or legitimate means of defence? EJIL 16:171
Langer M (2011) The diplomacy of universal jurisdiction: the political branches and the transnational prosecution of international crimes. AJIL 105:1
Lubell N (2005) Challenges in applying human rights law to armed conflict. In Rev Red Cross 87:737
Maogoto Nyamuya J (2003) War on the enemy: self-defence and state-sponsored terrorism. Melbourne J Int Law 4:406
Maogoto Nyamuya J (2004) War crimes and real politik: international justice from World War I to the 21st century. Lynne Rienner Publishers Inc, Boulder
Maogoto Nyamuya J (2005) Battling terrorism: legal perspectives on the use of force and the war on terror. Ashgate, Aldershot
Maogoto Nyamuya J (2009) The work of national military tribunals under Control Council Law 10. In: Doria J, Gasser H, Bassiouni C (eds) The legal regime of the International Criminal Court: essays in memory of Igor Blischenko. Brill Publishing, Leiden
Melzer N (2008) Targeted killing in international law. Oxford University Press, Oxford
Mutangi S (2006) Fact-finding missions or omissions: a critical analysis of the African Commission on Human and Peoples' Rights and lessons to be learned from the Inter-American Commission on Human Rights. East Afr J Peace Human Rights 1
O'Keefe R (2013) Domestic courts as agents of development of the international law of jurisdiction. Leiden J Int Law 26:541
Ohlin JD (2013) The duty to capture. Minnesota Law Rev 97(1268):1276–1277

Pilloud C, Sandoz Y, Swinarski C, Zimmermann B (1987) Commentary on the additional protocols of 8 June 1977 to the Geneva Conventions of 12 August 1949. Martinus Nijhoff Publishers, Dordrecht
Ratner S (2006) Land feuds and their solutions: finding international law beyond the tribunal chamber. AJIL 100:808
Roach K (2009) Judicial review of the state's anti-terrorism activities: the post 9/11 experience and normative justifications. Indian J Const Law 3:138
Roach K (2013) Substitute justice? Challenges to American counterterrorism activities in non-American Courts. Miss Law J 82:907
Robertson G (2010) Human rights fact-finding: some legal and ethical dilemmas. UCL Human Rights Rev 3:15
Ronen Y (2013) Silent Enim Leges inter Arma-but beware the background noise: domestic courts as agents of development of the law on the conduct of hostilities. Leiden J Int Law 26:599
Ryngaert C (2008) The doctrine of abuse of process: a comment on the Cambodia tribunal's decisions in the case against Duch (2007). Leiden J Int Law 21:719
Sassoli M (2011) Introducing a sliding-scale of obligations to address the fundamental inequality between armed groups and states? Int Rev Red Cross 93:426
Schabas W (2007) Lex specialis? Belt and suspenders? The parallel operation of human rights law and the law of armed conflict and the conundrum of Jus Ad Bellum. Isr Law Rev 40:592
Schmitt M (2004) Direct participation in hostilities and 21st century armed conflict. In: Fischer H et al (eds) Crisis management and humanitarian protection: Festschrift fur Dieter Fleck. Berliner Wissenschafts-Verlag, Berlin, pp 505–509
Schwager E (2005) The right to compensation for victims of an armed conflict. Chin J Int Law 4:417
Shany Y (2005) Capacities and inadequacies: a look at the two separation barrier cases. Isr Law Rev 38:230
Shany Y (2011) A rebuttal to Marco Sassoli. Int Rev Red Cross 93:432
Shany Y (2013) Seeking domestic help: the role of domestic criminal law in legitimizing the work of international criminal tribunals. J Int Crim Justice 11:5
Slovic P, Zionts D, Woods A, Goodman R, Jinks D (2013) Psychic numbing and mass atrocity. In: Eldar S (ed.) The behavioral foundations of public policy. Princeton University Press, Princeton
Solomon S (2007) Targeted killings and the soldiers' right to life. ILSA J Int Law 14:99
Solomon S (2009) The justiciability of international disputes: the advisory opinion on Israel's security fence as a case study. Wolf Legal Publishers, Oisterwijk
Solomon S (2010) The Great Oxymoron: Jus in Bello violations as legitimate non-forcible measures of self-defense: the post-disengagement Israeli measures towards Gaza as a case study, vol 9, p 501
Solomon S (2012) The dynamic law of occupation: inaugurating international thematic constitutionalism. Harvard Int Law J Online 54:59
Solomon S (2013) The quest for self-determination: defining international law's inherent interstate limits. Santa Clara J Int Law 11:397
Stahn C (2003) Terrorist acts as "Armed Attack": the right to self-defense, Article 51 (1/2) of the UN charter, and international terrorism. Fletcher Forum World Aff 27:35
Verdirame G (2008) Human rights in wartime: a framework for analysis. Eur Human Rights Law Rev 6:689
Watkin K (2004) Controlling the use of force: a role for human rights norms in contemporary armed conflict. AJIL 98:1
Weiss N (2012) Somebody else's problem: how the United States and Canada violate international law and fail to ensure the prosecution of war criminals. Case W Res J Int Law 45:579
Wuerth I (2012) International Law in domestic courts and the jurisdictional immunities of the state case. Melbourne J Int Law 13:819
Zemach A (2003) Fairness and moral judgments in international criminal law: the settlement provision in the Rome Statute. Colum J Trans Law 41:895

Part I
The Judicial Factual Expansion of International Humanitarian Law

Chapter 2
Applicability Test of Additional Protocol II and Common Article 3 for Crimes in Internal Armed Conflict

Noëlle Quénivet

Contents

Noëlle Quénivet is Associate Professor and Head of the International Law and Human Rights Unit, Department of Law, University of the West of England, United Kingdom.

N. Quénivet (✉)
Department of Law, University of the West of England, Bristol, UK
e-mail: noelle.quenivet@uwe.ac.uk

D. Jinks et al. (eds.), *Applying International Humanitarian Law in Judicial and Quasi-Judicial Bodies*, DOI: 10.1007/978-94-6265-008-4_2,

2.1 Introduction

International humanitarian law (IHL) is based on the premise that armed conflicts can be categorised as either international under Common Article 2 of the Geneva Conventions[1] or Article 1(4) of Additional Protocol I or non-international under Common Article 3 of the Geneva Conventions and/or Article 1 of Additional Protocol II. Depending on their qualifications, different rules apply.[2] What is more two different mechanisms of enforcement were applicable until the mid-1990s. While in international armed conflicts state responsibility and individual liability could be used to ensure the proper application of IHL, in times of non-international armed conflicts only state responsibility could be attached to violations of IHL, a system that failed inasmuch as there was no legal forum to address such issues and, thus, violations were left unpunished. Hence, the distinction was of utmost significance.

The statutes and jurisprudence of various international criminal tribunals altered this position inasmuch as they proclaimed that acts in contravention of IHL committed during non-international armed conflicts could also be viewed as criminal acts and prosecuted as such. Undoubtedly the criminalisation of IHL provisions emerged as the most suitable solution to deal with serious breaches of the laws of armed conflict. Further, 'the law of internal armed conflict has drawn on international criminal law to fill out its substance content.'[3]

However, although the use of international criminal law to ensure that individuals are protected in times of armed conflict is to be welcome some questions are left unanswered, notably relating to the qualification of a non-international armed conflict. As aforementioned, treaty law knows of two types of non-international armed conflicts. This could appear as a purely legalistic distinction if it did not entail a distinction in the content and scope of the protection offered to certain persons and in the prohibition of certain types of acts. The problem increased as those norms were criminalised[4] through jurisprudence[5] and Statutes of international

---

[1] Article 2 common to the Four Geneva Conventions; Geneva Convention for the Amelioration of the Condition of the Wounded and Sick in armed forces in the field, 12 August 1949, 75 UNTS 31; Geneva Convention for the amelioration of the condition of the wounded, sick and shipwrecked members of the armed forces at sea, 12 August 1949, 75 UNTS 85; Geneva Convention relative to the treatment of prisoners of war, 12 August 1949, 75 UNTS 135; Geneva Convention relative to the protection of civilian persons in time of war, 12 August 1949, 75 UNTS 287 (GCs).

[2] Akande 2012, p. 34.

[3] Sivakumaran 2011, p. 220.

[4] This chapter does not aim to discuss the criminalisation of violations of international humanitarian law occurring in non-international armed conflicts. It takes the stance that this criminalisation is now entrenched in international criminal law and that the current problem lies in the definition of an armed conflict.

[5] ICTY Tadic 1995, Prosecutor v. Tadic, Case No IT-94-1-AR72, Decision on Defence Motion for Interlocutory Appeal on Jurisdiction, 2 October 1995, paras 127 and 130 [hereafter ICTY

criminal tribunals.[6] It became hence of utmost relevance to qualify properly the non-international armed conflict as one falling within the purview of Common Article 3 or Additional Protocol II. While it is widely accepted that violations of Common Article 3 entail criminal liability because of their customary nature, this seems to be less true for all violations contained in Additional Protocol II. To add to the already complicated array of types of armed conflicts, international tribunals have adopted definitions of armed conflicts that do not fall squarely in any of the above-mentioned provisions or their customary equivalent. In addition, the Statute of the International Criminal Court, that is deemed to represent the current status of the law, offers definitions of armed conflict that appear *prima facie* to be different from those expounded in treaty law and in the jurisprudence.

The chapter does not aim to focus on the applicability threshold of international humanitarian law, rather it examines whether international legal rules, including treaty, customary international law and jurisprudence, provide for one, two or potentially three types of non-international armed conflicts. In particular, it investigates whether the definitions used by the international criminal tribunals and courts to trigger the application of war crimes[7] provisions coincide with the definitions expounded in treaty and customary law.

2.2 Applicability Tests in Treaty Law: Additional Protocol II and Common Article 3

Treaty law recognises two types of non-international armed conflicts: a distinction deeply entrenched in the 1949 Conventions and the 1977 Additional Protocols. The Geneva Conventions offer a first definition while the Additional Protocol II to the same conventions imparts a second one.

(Footnote 5 continued)
Tadic 1995]. In the same decision the Court explained that for an offence to fall within the purview of criminal prosecution by the ICTY it must fulfil four requirements, namely 'the violation must constitute an infringement of a rule of international humanitarian law', 'the rule must be customary in nature or, if it belongs to treaty law, the required conditions must be met', 'the violation must be "serious"' and 'the violation of the rule must entail, under customary or conventional law, the individual criminal responsibility of the person breaching the rule'. Paragraph 94.

[6] Statute of the International Criminal Tribunal for Rwanda. '[T]he ICTR Statute can be regarded as an important document in introducing the concept of war crimes in an internal armed conflict, a development that has subsequently been consolidated in the ICC Statute.' Van den Herik 2005, p. 273.

[7] 'The term war crime alludes to the violation of a recognised obligation of the rules of armed conflict which must be respected by conflicting parties.' Bassiouni 1999, p. 101.

2.2.1 Common Article 3

Common Article 3 provides a set of international humanitarian rules applicable in 'case of armed conflict not of an international character occurring in the territory of one of the High Contracting Parties'. Unfortunately for lawyers, it is remarkably silent on the circumstances when it is applicable since it does not impart a definition. The only pieces of information it contains relate to territorial issues, i.e. Common Article 3 only applies in the territory of a state party, and the contra-distinction made with conflicts covered by the rules enshrined in the Geneva Conventions, i.e. Common Article 3 conflicts covers conflict that are not of international nature. This vague formulation leaves room for interpretation since neither 'armed conflict' nor 'non-international character' are defined. Neither objective nor subjective criteria are included in the first sentence of Common Article 3 as the article was a political compromise.[8] This lack of definition is welcomed by Pictet in his Commentary on the Geneva Conventions,[9] and according to some authors was the aim of the drafters of the said treaties.[10]

Indeed, a proposal to clarify the material field of application of Common Article 3 put forward at the XXIst International Conference of the Red Cross and Red Crescent Society in Istanbul in September 1969 was rejected.[11] Meaning must be sought outside the treaty itself and notably by perusing the *travaux préparatoires* and the Commentary to the convention. The crucial question for states is to determine Common Article 3's threshold of applicability, as during the drafting of the provision, many delegations expressed their fear that any sort of internal trouble would trigger it. As Jinks explains, 'the coherence of the "armed conflict" concept turns on the viability of the distinction between internal disturbances or insurrections and internal armed conflicts.'[12]

Yet, the ICRC pushed for recognising situations with a low threshold of violence.[13] Different criteria were enumerated during the discussions and may be of some help in determining the threshold of applicability, although they should be regarded as neither an exhaustive, nor a legally binding list. In fact the actual boundary is determined on a case-by-case basis.

In this regard, Pictet imparts a number of possible criteria to gauge whether Common Article 3 is applicable. First, hostilities have to be conducted by

---

[8] Tahzib-Lie and Swaak-Goldman 2004, p. 243. See also Pejic 2007, p. 85. For a detailed drafting history of Common Article 3 see Moir 1998, p. 337.

[9] Pictet 1960, p. 49. Abi-Saab also argues that '[t]his vague formulation, which was considered at the time as one of the major defects of Article 3, is now considered, however, as one of its main advantages, in the sense that it does not formally exclude a broad interpretation.' Abi-Saab 1991, p. 216.

[10] Jinks 2003, p. 2.

[11] See Verri 1972, p. 99.

[12] Jinks 2003, p. 2.

[13] Kretzmer 2009, p. 40.

organised armed groups and exhibit such intensity that the government cannot rely simply on ordinary policing methods. Second, the hostilities carried out by the insurgents must have a collective character. Third, the insurgents must show some degree of organisation (a responsible command and a capacity to meet the minimal humanitarian requirements).[14] These criteria are reminiscent, if only distantly, of those inscribed in Article 1 of Protocol II.[15]

Common Article 3 applies in the case of a classic civil war when the state's armed forces are confronted with armed opposition groups within the state's territory. Moreover, this provision is applicable when two dissident groups fight against each other within the territory of one state which may, or may not, be a party to the armed conflict.

2.2.2 *Additional Protocol II*

Owing due to the aforementioned deficiencies in the international legal machinery states agreed to enhance the regime of Common Article 3. Additional Protocol II is 'the first and only international agreement exclusively regulating the conduct of the parties in a non-international conflict.'[16] Sadly, in comparison to Common Article 3 Additional Protocol II adopts a more restrictive approach to internal conflicts and 'even formally excludes some situations, that, with a broad interpretation, could be included in the scope of application of Article 3'.[17] According to Article 1, Additional Protocol II is only applicable when a conflict between an incumbent government and internal belligerent forces arises, not when the state is shaken by conflicts among different dissident groups, in which case only Common Article 3 is pertinent.[18] The conservative shift to more demanding criteria was a compromise to allow some states to obtain a treaty that contains more specific rules pertaining to non-international armed conflicts and other states to deny its applicability due to the high threshold.

Additional Protocol II is to be applied automatically when the stringent requirements of Article 1 are met. This provision stipulates that dissident forces must be 'under responsible command' and 'exercise such control over a part of its territory as to enable them to carry out sustained and concerted military operations and to implement this Protocol.' This happened despite the fact that 'the ICRC

[14] These were in fact some of the criteria proposed during the drafting negotiations to the 1949 Geneva Conventions. See Elder 1979, pp. 52–53.

[15] Protocol Additional to the Geneva Conventions of 12 August 1949, and relating to the protection of victims of non-international armed conflicts, 8 June 1977, UN Doc A/32/144, Appendix II (1977) 16 International Legal Materials 1442. See also International Institute of Humanitarian Law and International Committee of the Red Cross 2003, pp. 5–7.

[16] Green 2002, p. 61.

[17] Abi-Saab 1991, p. 216. See also Vité 2009, p. 79.

[18] Sandoz et al. 1987, para 4461.

persistently tried to avoid writing into Article 1 phraseology relating to the degree of organization necessary for armed forces or other armed groups; the duration of the conflict; the amount of territory to be controlled by a nongovernmental party; and other factors that would reduce the scope of the Protocol by establishing conditions that had to be fulfilled before the instrument came into force.'[19] '[T]he three criteria that were finally adopted on the side of the insurgents ... restrict the applicability of the Protocol to conflicts of a certain degree of intensity'.[20]

The very high threshold set by Additional Protocol II[21] means that in reality the protocol applies 'to situations at or near the level of a full-scale civil war'[22] or belligerency, a highly improbable case when one examines contemporary armed conflicts where territorial control is not anymore one of the priorities of armed opposition groups. In addition, the problem remains as to the exact time when a situation develops into an armed conflict within the terms of Additional Protocol II.

Further at first sight Article 1 Additional Protocol II lowers the bar of the applicability of the treaty since it excludes 'internal disturbances and tensions, such as riots, isolated and sporadic acts of violence and other acts of a similar nature'. However, practice shows that Common Article 3 is not applied either under these circumstances.[23]

2.2.3 Relationship Between These Two Instruments

As illustrated above, Common Article 3 and Additional Protocol II apply a different applicability standard. The relationship between the two conventional instruments is, thus, of great importance when considering which one prevails. Pursuant to the general rules of international law and notably the *lex posterior*[24] and *lex specialis*,[25] Additional Protocol II should contain the universal rules applicable to conflicts of non-international nature.

---

[19] Forsythe 1978, p. 284.

[20] Sandoz et al. 1987, para 4453.

[21] See discussion in Spieker 2001, pp. 142–143.

[22] See United Nations Secretary-General 1998, Minimum Humanitarian Standards: Analytical Report of the Secretary-General Submitted pursuant to Commission on Human Rights Resolution 1997/21, UN Doc E/CN.4/1998/87, 12 January 1998, para 74 and Ambos 2001, p. 338.

[23] See below the case-law of ICTY and ICTR. See also Vité 2009, p. 76 and Tahzib-Lie and Swaak-Goldman 2004, p. 249.

[24] The full sentence is 'lex posterior derogat legi priori' and means that the newer norm is preferred over the elder one.

[25] The full sentence is 'lex specialis derogat legi generali' and means that 'whenever two or more norms deal with the same subject matter, priority should be given to the norm that is more specific.' United Nations General Assembly (International Law Commission) 2006, Fragmentation of International Law: Difficulties Arising from the Diversification and Expansion of International Law, UN Doc A/CN.4/L.702, 18 July 2006, para. 14.2(5) [hereafter UNGA (ILC) 2006].

2.2.3.1 Lex Posterior

According to Article 30(2) of the 1969 Vienna Convention on the Law of Treaties (VCLT) '[w]hen a treaty specifies that it is subject to or that it is not to be considered as incompatible with, an earlier or later treaty, the provisions of that other treaty prevail.'[26] In the case at hand the Additional Protocol II is not considered as incompatible with the Geneva Conventions. First, as its name says, the aim of an Additional Protocol is to develop the law in an area which the drafters of the initial conventions think to be underdeveloped.[27] Second, Additional Protocol II clearly indicates that it *develops* and *supplements* common Article 3. That Additional Protocol II and Common Article 3 should have the same scope of application was the original intention of the ICRC.[28] Hence, at first sight Additional Protocol II should 'override' the provisions contained in the Geneva Conventions.

To some degree, this simultaneous validity has been conserved, for if Additional Protocol II is applicable then Common Article 3 is also since the latter's threshold is lower than the one expounded in Article 1 AP II. Without a doubt Additional Protocol II has a much narrower field of application. Yet, in the same sentence, Article 1(1) AP II also underlines the autonomy of Common Article 3 in relation to Additional Protocol II as it expounds that its intention is not to modify the existing conditions or application of common Article 3. The first words of Article 1(1) AP II are welcome since sponsors to Article 1(2) AP II intended to impose thereby a restrictive interpretation of the scope of application of Common Article 3.[29] As a result of this autonomy, treaty law identifies two distinctive kinds of conflicts.[30]

Additionally, one must bear in mind that in pursuance of Article 30(4) VCLT '[w]hen the parties to the later treaty do not include all the parties to the earlier one:

(a) as between states Parties to both treaties the same rule applies as in paragraph 3;
(b) as between a state party to both treaties and a state party to only one of the treaties, the treaty to which both states are parties governs their mutual rights and obligations.'[31]

---

[26] Vienna Convention on the Law of Treaties 1969, 1155 UNTS 331, 23 May 1969.

[27] Turns argues that 'Protocol II can be regarded as "new" law in the sense that it represents the first—and, to date, the only—major attempt to apply the laws of war in a comprehensive manner to non-international armed conflicts.' Turns 1995, p. 817.

[28] UNGA (ILC) 2006, para 14.2(5). Abi-Saab 1991, p. 215.

[29] Abi-Saab 1986, pp. 145–148.

[30] 'It should be noted that this fairly restrictive definition applies only to Protocol II. The definition does not apply to Article 3 common to the four Geneva Conventions.' Sassoli and Bouvier 1999, p. 90.

[31] The application of this rule may appear awkward when referring to conflicts that do not cross the borders of a state and, hence, only involve a party to the Convention. However, the Geneva Conventions and Additional Protocol II are international treaties regulated by the 1969 Vienna Convention on the Law of Treaty as far as it provisions reflect the state of customary international law.

In the case where states are parties to both treaties and unless otherwise provided for in a treaty, the earlier instrument applies only to the extent its provisions are compatible with the later treaty (in conformity with the latin maxim *lex posterior derogat legi priori*).[32] Since Additional Protocol II, as explained earlier, regulates the scope of application of both instruments, both treaties are simultaneously applicable and, therefore, two thresholds of applicability of norms relating to non-international armed conflict exist. In the instance where a state has only ratified the Geneva Conventions, Additional Protocol II is not applicable and only one type of non-international armed conflict is possible.

2.2.3.2 Lex Specialis

In the case where two treaties cover the same subject, the rule of the *lex specialis* may be used for interpretation purposes, the rationale being that the 'special law, being more concrete, often takes better account of the particular features of the context in which it is to be applied than any applicable general law'.[33] Undoubtedly the rules spelled out in Common Article 3 are universally applicable and are of general nature. First, as per the *travaux préparatoires* Common Article 3 reiterates basic norms that were entrenched in domestic legislation relating basically to the protection of the human rights and physical integrity of persons not taking part in the hostilities, or who have laid down their arms, or who are *hors de combat*. The Commentary asserts that Common Article 3 include 'rules which were already recognised as essential in all civilized countries and embodied in the national legislation of the states in question, long before the convention was signed'.[34]

Second, 'the entire philosophy of the provisions of common Article 3, whether explicitly reaffirmed or not, is included in [AP II]',[35] thereby giving the impression that Additional Protocol II is the *lex specialis* of Common Article 3. Indeed, the International Court of Justice plainly explained in the *Nicaragua* case that the norms encapsulated in Common Article 3 represent universal values, a 'minimum yardstick',[36] more, they reflect 'elementary considerations of humanity'.[37] This cannot be said of Additional Protocol II which goes beyond these fundamental

---

[32] Vienna Convention on the Law of Treaties 1969, 1155 UNTS 331, 23 May 1969, Article 30(3).

[33] UNGA (ILC) 2006, para 14.2(7). For a discussion on the concept of lex specialis, see McCarthy 2008, p. 101.

[34] Pictet 1960, p. 36.

[35] Explanations of Vote on Protocol II 1978, Belgium, VII Official records of the diplomatic conference on the reaffirmation and development of international humanitarian law applicable in armed conflicts, Geneva, 1974–1977, Federal Political Department, Bern, 1978, Annex, p. 76.

[36] ICJ Nicaragua 1986, para 218.

[37] It is remarkable that the Italian proposal concerning Common Article 3 during the 1949 negotiations stipulated that the rules contained therein 'constitute the basis of universal humanitarian law'. See Final Record of the Diplomatic Conference of Geneva of 1949, 1951, p. 113.

principles since it clarifies certain rules. For example Article 4 AP II which contains the fundamental guarantees draws heavily upon the prohibition expounded in Common Article 3,[38] a position also supported by Van den Herik who explains that 'Article 4 may only come into play to the extent that it directly supplements common Article 3'.[39] Abi–Saab goes as far as to declare that 'these additions are not new in themselves, but appear more as a detailed interpretation of existing rules, particularly as concerns fundamental guarantees, and they do not go much beyond what had been provided in very general terms by common Article 3'.[40] Additional Protocol II offers greater protection to civilians and civilian objects[41] as well as detained persons.[42]

At first glance Additional Protocol II is the *lex specialis* of Common Article 3. Yet, it must be underlined that the *lex specialis* presumption does not apply when 'the application of the special law might frustrate the purpose of the law'[43] or 'where the parties have intended otherwise'.[44] As aforementioned the drafters of Additional Protocol II clearly endowed the general norm, i.e. Common Article 3, with autonomous application and, hence, the *lex specialis* cannot be applied in this context.

As a conclusion, treaty law as envisaged in the Geneva Conventions and the Additional Protocol II knows of two types of non-international armed conflicts, granting individuals different kinds of protection from the ghastly effects of armed conflicts.

2.3 Applicability Tests in Customary Law

In keeping with the *Nicaragua* jurisprudence, international customary law continues to exist besides norms regulated in treaty law.[45] This means that along the treaty provisions on the qualification of an armed conflict, customary law provisions must be pinpointed all the more as authors contend that '[c]ustomary law has accelerated the development of the law of armed conflict, particularly in relation to

---

[38] The United Nations Secretary-General explained that Common Article 3 is more 'fully elaborated in Article 4 of the 1977 Additional Protocol II'. United Nations Secretary General 1995, Report Pursuant to Para 5 of Security Council Resolution 955 (1994), UN Doc S/1995/134, 13 February 1995, para 11.

[39] Van den Herik 2005, p. 205.

[40] Abi-Saab 1991, p. 219.

[41] See generally Part IV of AP II.

[42] Articles 5 and 6 AP II.

[43] UNGA (ILC) 2006, para 14.2(10).

[44] UNGA (ILC) 2006, para 14.5(27).

[45] International Court of Justice 1986, Military and Paramilitary Activities in and against Nicaragua (Nicaragua v. USA), Judgment, [1986] ICJ Rep 14, 27 June 1986, para 179 [hereafter ICJ Nicaragua 1986].

crimes committed in internal conflicts'.[46] Nevertheless, one must bear in mind that '[i]t is unlikely that there is any body of customary international law applicable to internal armed conflict which does not find its root in … treaty provisions'[47] to the extent that any discussion on customary law must be based on the aforementioned treaties.

2.3.1 Study on Customary International Humanitarian Law

Unfortunately the Study on Customary International Humanitarian Law does not offer a readily available answer to the types of armed conflicts that are known to customary law. Indeed the Study, despite its breadth and detailed approach to its aim, namely that of clarifying customary norms of international humanitarian law, does not discuss the issue of the characterisation of the conflict. The Study simply refers to international and non-international armed conflicts and all norms are accordingly described. As Meron states '[i]t does not adopt the three-tiered approach of the Geneva Conventions and Additional Protocols'.[48]

Remarkably, on the face of it, the International Committee of the Red Cross did not consider it worth a discussion. However, as intrigued as the author of this chapter, McLauren and Schwendimann speculate about the reason for this lack that shakes the edifice of the Study inasmuch as its bases appear to be rather weak. Since no definition of a non-international armed conflict is provided, it is easy to argue that a particular event or series of events are not to be considered as a non-international armed conflict and, thus, the rules pertaining to such conflicts as ascertained in the Study are not binding upon states via their customary nature.[49]

Obviously tortured by the issue, McLauren and Schwendimann asked Henckaerts, legal advisor of the International Committee of the Red Cross and one of the masterminds of the Study, to clarify the reasons that led to this major legal flaw. He replied that no customary definition was included because doing so 'would require a study in and of itself. [Short of that] all we could have done was to repeat the various provisions in treaty law (Geneva Conventions, Articles 2 and 3; Additional Protocol II, Article 1(1); Statute of the International Criminal Court (ICC)) and possibly some dicta from case-law of the ICTY'.[50]

In brief, the issue of the customary nature of the definition of armed conflict is very complicated and hence would have merited an investigation of its own. In an

---

[46] Greppi 1999, pp. 531–553. See also Schindler 2003, p. 178.

[47] United Nations Commission of Experts Appointed to Investigate Violation of International Humanitarian Law in the Former Yugoslavia, Letter Dated 24 May 1994 from the Secretary General to the President of the Security Council, UN Doc S/1994/674, 27 May 1994, para 52.

[48] Meron 2000, p. 261.

[49] McLauren and Schwendimann 2005, p. 1227.

[50] Cited in McLauren and Schwendimann 2005, p. 1227.

article published in 2011, Pejic however states that the Study did not distinguish between the two categories because 'it was found that states did not make such a distinction in practice'.[51] No references support her statement. Regrettably for us there is no readily available answer to the question of whether international customary law provides for a single definition of non-international armed conflict.

2.3.2 Establishing Customary International Humanitarian Law

Consequently, one needs to resort to the traditional method of establishing customary law. In pursuance of Article 38 of the Statute of the International Court of Justice, a customary norm is formed of two elements, state practice[52] and *opinio juris sive necessitates*,[53] 'the latter of which is dominant in the formation of humanitarian and human rights law'.[54]

State practice must be constant and uniform[55] as well as of some duration.[56] To establish actual practice one should hold to acts but also to *inter alia* treaties, diplomatic correspondence, and unilateral declarations.[57] Practice, although scarce, reveals that states, having ratified Additional Protocol II, indeed consider that two sets of norms are applicable in times of non-international armed conflicts, depending on whether the threshold of Additional Protocol II is reached.

States have on several occasions distinguished between Additional Protocol II and Common Article 3 conflicts. For example, during the conflict in Chechnya the Constitutional Court of Russia clearly asserted that the rules pertaining to Additional Protocol II were applicable. It could have left it to acknowledging the applicability of Common Article 3 inasmuch as its provisions reflect basic principles applicable in all types of armed conflicts and, moreover the Russian Federation had not incorporated the Additional Protocol II rules into the domestic

---

[51] Pejic 2011, p. 191.

[52] As Henckaerts notes '[a]lthough decisions of international courts are subsidiary sources of international law, they do not constitute state practice'. Henckaerts 2005, p. 5.

[53] International Court of Justice Statute 1945, 26 June 1945, Article 38.

[54] Meron 1998, p. 9.

[55] International Court of Justice 1950, Asylum Case (Columbia v. Peru), [1950] ICJ Rep 266, 27 November 1950, p. 277. However, in the Nicaragua case, the International Court of Justice explained that the practice does not need to be absolutely rigorous with regard to the conformity principle. ICJ Nicaragua 1986, para 186.

[56] International Court of Justice 1969, North Sea Continental Shelf Cases (Federal Republic of Germany/Denmark and Federal Republic of Germany/Netherlands), [1969] ICJ Rep 3, 20 February 1969, paras 73–74. However, since this decision, the International Court of Justice has not emphasised the time element anymore.

[57] International Court of Justice 1970, Barcelona Traction, Light and Power Company, Limited (Belgium v. Spain), Second Phase, [1970] ICJ Rep 3, 5 February 1970.

legal system. Yet, it preferred to state that Additional Protocol II (though it regrettably did not prop up its standpoint by any legal reasoning) was applicable.[58] Likewise the Federal Government of Germany informed the Russian Federation that it classified the conflict as one covered by Additional Protocol II.[59] Other examples of states examining whether Additional Protocol II is applicable include Switzerland. The Directorate for Public International Law of Switzerland qualified the conflict in El Salvador in 1986 as one falling within the purview of Additional Protocol II after careful examination of the factual situation and legal implications.[60]

Furthermore, United Nations bodies refer to both sets of norms. For example, when creating the International Criminal Tribunal for Rwanda the Security Council mentioned Additional Protocol II.[61] Yet, recently, a growing number of resolutions do not distinguish between these two times of conflicts, let alone between international and non-international armed conflicts.[62]

As for the laws expounded in military manuals, some military manuals like the one for the Canadian forces[63] or the British Forces[64] distinguish between Common Article 3 and Additional Protocol II non-international armed conflicts.

On the factual side, states have also distinguished between two sets of non-international armed conflicts. For example, the applicability of Common Article 3 hinges on facts and not on the willingness of the state to admit the facts.[65] Yet, in practice, many states are unwilling to acknowledge the applicability of Common Article 3, owing to a concern that they would thereby be admitting their reduced

58 See Gaeta 1996, pp. 563–570.

59 German Bundestag, Document 13/718, 13th legislative period, 9 March 1995, reproduced in parts in Sassoli and Bouvier 1999, p. 1404.

60 Note of the Directorate for Public International Law of the Federal Department of Foreign Affairs, 20 January 1986, cited in Annuaire Suisse de Droit International 1987, pp. 185–187.

61 United Nations Security Council 1994, Resolution 955 (1994), UN Doc S/RES/955 (1994), 8 November 1994.

62 United Nations Security Council 2013, Resolution 2106 (2013), UN Doc S/RES/2106 (2013), 24 June 2013, pream para 13; United Nations Security Council 2012, Resolution 2068 (2012), UN Doc S/RES/2068 (2012), 19 September 2012, pream para 3.

63 Canada National Defence 2001, Joint doctrine manual: law of armed conflict at the operational and tactical levels, Office of the Judge Advocate General, B-GJ-005-104/FP-021, 13 August 2001, Chap. 17.

64 United Kingdom Ministry of Defence 2005, para 3.5 explains that if 'the dissident or anti-government armed forces exercise sufficient territorial control as to enable them to carry out sustained and concerted military operations and implement Additional protocol II, that Protocol applies in addition to Common Article 3.' See also para 3.9.

65 ICTR Akayesu 1998, Prosecutor v. Akayesu, Case No ICTR-96-4-T, 2 September 1998, para 603 [hereafter ICTR Akayesu 1998]. See also the Explanations of Vote on Protocol II 1978, Brazil, VII VII Official records of the diplomatic conference on the reaffirmation and development of international humanitarian law applicable in armed conflicts, Geneva, 1974–1977, Federal Political Department, Bern, 1978, Annex, p. 76.

control of their territory[66] and particularly to a fear that they would thereby be according some status to the non-state fighters. Nevertheless 'whilst states may not be willing to admit to the application of Common Article 3 as a matter of law, its provisions are frequently applied in fact.'[67] They do not, on the other hand, apply *de facto* Additional Protocol II rules. Practice hence shows that states distinguish between Additional Protocol II and Common Article 3 conflicts.

To pinpoint *opinio juris* it must be demonstrated that states generally recognise that a legal and not only a moral, political obligation is involved in their attitude. They must also believe that this practice is obligatory and settled.[68] The aforementioned example of the Constitutional Court of Russia[69] also demonstrates that certain states believe they must decide upon the applicability of Common Article 3 or Additional Protocol II and cannot simply brand the conflict 'non-international'; they must determine the exact characterisation of the armed conflict. The stance of the Colombian government to apply Additional Protocol II in its conflict with FARC also illustrates the point.[70] In other words, in conflicts where Additional Protocol II was obviously applicable, states did recognise its application and did not shun away from characterising the conflict as such and apply the higher standards enshrined in Additional Protocol II.

One must nonetheless consider that according to the authors of the Study of Customary International Humanitarian Law that a customary rule exists 'when that rule is a desirable one for international peace and security or for the protection of the human person, provided that there is no important contrary *opinio juris*'.[71] Although this interpretation of customary international law may be interesting for lawyers who think in terms of how the law ought to be and those who trust that 'contemporary exigencies of humankind require[] the conscious, deliberate use of law as an instrument of policy',[72] it does not satisfy the criteria of classical international law, even those relating human rights and humanitarian norms. On the other hand, it is clear that '[i]n situations where practice is ambiguous ... *opinio juris* plays an important role in determining whether or not that practice counts towards the formation of custom'.[73] As a result, there are two sets of rules regulating non-international armed conflicts, both based or linked to treaty rules.

---

66 When American President Clinton visited Russia in May 1995, he was informed that the Russian army was only conducting a 'police action against terrorists'. Tskhovrebov 1995, footnote 55.

67 United Kingdom Ministry of Defence 2005, para 3.6.1.

68 International Court of Justice 1969, North Sea Continental Shelf Cases (Federal Republic of Germany/Denmark and Federal Republic of Germany/Netherlands), [1969] ICJ Rep 3, 20 February 1969.

69 Acts may both constitute the objective element and be evidence of subjective element in the same time. Henckaerts also recognises that 'it prove[s] very difficult and largely theoretical to strictly separate elements of practice and legal conviction.' Henckaerts 2005, p. 8.

70 Szesnat and Bird 2012, p. 240.

71 Henckaerts and Doswald-Beck 2005, p. xlii.

72 Lasswell and McDougal 1992, p. xxii.

73 Henckaerts 2005, p. 8.

Further, as far as the minimum threshold of applicability of international humanitarian law in times of non-international armed conflicts is concerned, 'state practice since 1949 indicates that banditry, criminal activity, riots, or sporadic outbreaks of violence and acts of terrorism do not amount to an armed conflict'.[74] Although Common Article 3 does not specifically refer to a minimum threshold of applicability and although Common Article 3 is autonomous in relation to Additional Protocol II the minimum threshold expounded in Additional Protocol II is also applicable to Common Article 3. In some instances, states have admitted *expressis verbis* the applicability of Common Article 3 but that seems to be only the case when the conflict drags on beyond several weeks and months.[75]

2.4 Jurisprudence of International Criminal Tribunals

Although the jurisprudence of international criminal courts only count as subsidiary source of international law, it is nevertheless important because it might point at existing persuasive evidence of customary law.[76] Further, 'because of the precedential value of their decisions, international courts can also contribute to the emergence of a rule of customary international lay by influencing the subsequent practice of states and international organizations'.[77] Hence, examining the jurisprudence of the *ad hoc* but also permanent international criminal tribunals, one must investigate whether they simply restate the law, adduce customary evidence of a certain rule or go beyond that rule thus pushing towards the creation of new norms.

As Abi–Saab explains

> '[f]rom the time when common Article 3 was first discussed in the 1949 Diplomatic Conference, until today, we see the shift of the pendulum between those who wanted to extend the definition contained in this Article as widely as possible to cover all situations, and those who wanted to confine it within very restrictive limits'.[78]

The main question in this regard is whether the jurisprudence of international criminal tribunals has not set the pendulum on the side of those who wished for a broad application of Common Article 3.

---

74 United Kingdom Ministry of Defence 2005, para 3.5.1.

75 Bond 1974, p. 60. For example, the French government in 1956, after several years of asserting that the conflict in Algeria was a suppression of an uprising, admitted the applicability of Common Article 3 and 'recognise[d] a separate legal status for Algerian detainees in order to mitigate the impact of French law.' Forsythe 1978, p. 277.

76 Henckaerts 2005, p. 5.

77 Henckaerts 2005, p. 5.

78 R. Abi-Saab 1991, p. 213.

2.4.1 *The International Criminal Tribunal for the Former Yugoslavia*

Despite the fact that the Statute of the International Criminal Tribunal for the former Yugoslavia (ICTY) does not expressly refer to non-international armed conflicts, the ICTY has on the basis of Article 3 of its Statute[79] established jurisdiction over crimes committed in such conflicts.[80] In this regard, it appears that the ICTY knows of only one threshold of non-international armed conflict. Indeed, whilst the well-known *Tadic Jurisdiction* decision refers to Common Article 3 crimes the ICTY has on numerous occasions applied crimes deriving from Additional Protocol II[81] and yet failed to discuss the threshold of applicability of Additional Protocol II. Technically, in pursuance of treaty law, the ICTY should have verified that the conflict fell within the remit of Additional Protocol II.

Relying on the ICRC Commentary to the Geneva Conventions[82] the *Tadic Jurisdiction* decision created the following test for the existence of an armed conflict, irrespective of its international or non-international characterisation: '[A]n armed conflict exists whenever there is a resort to armed force between states or protracted armed violence between governmental authorities and organized armed groups or between such groups within a state'.[83] Under this test 'well settled in the jurisprudence of the Tribunal',[84] the twin requirements are the intensity of the conflict and the organisation of the parties.[85] The ICTY however, noted in *Boskoski* that the temporal element of the adjective 'protracted' had 'not received much explicit attention in the jurisprudence of the Tribunal'.[86]

---

79 Updated Statute of the International Criminal Tribunal for the Former Yugoslavia.

80 ICTY Tadic 1995, para 93.

81 See e.g. ICTY Nikolic 1995, Prosecutor v. Nikolic, Case No IT-95-2-R61, Review of Indictment Pursuant to Rule 61, Trial Chamber, 20 October 1995 [hereafter ICTY Nikolic 1995]. See discussion in Sivakumaran 2011, pp. 230–231.

82 See especially discussion in ICTY Milosevic 2004, Prosecutor v. Milosevic, Case No IT-02-54-T, Decision on Motion for Judgement of Acquittal, Trial Chamber, 16 June 2004, para 19 [hereafter ICTY Milosevic 2004].

83 ICTY Tadic 1995, para. 70.

84 ICTY Oric 2006, Prosecutor v. Oric, Case No IT-03-68-T, Judgment, Trial Chamber, 30 June 2006, para 254.

85 ICTY Limaj 2005, Prosecutor v. Limaj et al. Case No IT-03-66-T, Judgment, Trial Chamber, 30 November 2005, para 84 [hereafter ICTY Limaj 2005]. See also the review of the case-law in ICTY Haradinaj 2008, Prosecutor v. Haradinaj et al., Case No IT-04-84-T, Judgment, Trial Chamber, 3 April 2008, paras 39–60 [hereafter ICTY Haradinaj 2008].

86 ICTY Boskoski and Tarculovski 2008, Prosecutor v. Boskoski and Tarculovski, Case No IT-04-82-T, Judgment, Trial Chamber, 10 July 2008, para 186 [hereafter]. As Akande explains, '[w]hile the word "protracted" suggests that the criterion relates exclusively to the time over which armed conflict takes place, it has come to be accepted that the key requirement here is the intensity of the force.' Akande 2012, p. 52. For an earlier discussion on the adjective 'protracted' and its use by the ICTY, see Tahzib-Lie and Swaak-Goldman 2004, p. 248.

As the ICTY Trial Chamber in *Limaj* noted,[87] this position is consistent with other persuasive commentaries on the matter, as for example a comment of the International Committee of the Red Cross on the ICC Elements of Crimes which noted:

> 'The ascertainment whether there is a non-international armed conflict does not depend on the subjective judgment of the parties to the conflict; it must be determined on the basis of objective criteria; the term 'armed conflict' presupposes the existence of hostilities between armed forces *organised to a greater or lesser extent*; there must be the opposition of armed forces and *a certain intensity* of the fighting'.[88]

A range of indicative factors has been used to ascertain the intensity of the conflict and the organisation of the parties.[89] Nonetheless, the ICTY has always stressed that none of these factors is preponderant in deciding upon the existence of an armed conflict;[90] 'These are not minimum factors that must be present but rather indicators of organization'.[91]

Interestingly, the ICTY highlights that under the *Tadic* test which governs the applicability of Article 3 of its Statute[92] it only needs to prove that there was an armed conflict in contradistinction to acts that do not fall within the purview of international humanitarian law.[93] The Trial Chamber held in *Limaj*:

> 'The two determinative elements of an armed conflict, intensity of the conflict and level of organisation of the parties, are used "*solely for the purpose*, as a minimum, of distinguishing an armed conflict from banditry, unorganized and short-lived insurrections, or terrorist activities, which are not subject to international humanitarian law".'[94]

In *Haradinaj* the Court restated that the 'test serves to distinguish non-international armed conflict from banditry, riots, isolated acts of terrorism, or similar situations'.[95]

---

[87] ICTY Limaj 2005, para 89.

[88] International Committee of the Red Cross, Working Paper, 29 June 1999 (submitted by the ICRC as a reference document to assist the Preparatory Commission in its work to establish the elements of crimes for the ICC) (italics in original).

[89] With regard to intensity of the conflict, see ICTY Haradinaj 2008, para 49 and ICTY Boskoski and Tarculovski 2008, para 177; and organisation of the parties see ICTY Haradinaj 2008, para 60 and ICTY Boskoski and Tarculovski 2008, paras 199–203.

[90] With regard to intensity of the conflict, see ICTY Haradinaj 2008, para 49 and organisation of the parties at para 60.

[91] Akande 2012, p. 52.

[92] Article 3 ICTY is viewed as 'a general, residual clause covering all serious violations of international humanitarian law not falling under Articles 2, 4 and 5 of the Statute, as well as violations of Common Article 3 of the Geneva Conventions, which specifically applies to cases of armed conflict not of an international character.' ICTY Milosevic 2004, para 15. See also Boelaert-Suominen 2000a, p. 75.

[93] See discussion in Bartels 2009, p. 38.

[94] ICTY Limaj 2005, para 89. Similar statements were made in ICTY Delalic et al. 1998, Prosecutor v. Delalic et al., Case No IT-96-21-T, Judgment, Trial Chamber, 16 November 1998, para 184; ICTY Kordic and Cerkez 2004, Prosecutor v. Kordic and Cerkez, Case No IT-95-14/2-A, Appeals Chamber, 17 December 2004, para 341; ICTY Milosevic 2004, para 26.

[95] ICTY Haradinaj 2008, para 38.

In *Prosecutor v. Limaj* et al. the defence challenged the Court's approach, arguing that the Trial Chamber should apply the stricter test of Article 1 of Additional Protocol II.[96] Sadly, the Trial Chamber's arguments are not convincing as it simply reiterates the position that it needs to prove that a minimum threshold has been attained and that 'the nature of the armed conflict is irrelevant to the application of Article 3 of the Statute'[97] and later confirms on the basis of previous case-law[98] that 'violations of Common Article 3 fall within the scope of Article 3 of the Statute'.[99] Nevertheless, it should be noted that the ICTY in *Limaj* only dealt with Common Article 3 and not Additional Protocol II crimes and thus there was no compelling reasons to warrant an examination of the threshold of applicability of Additional Protocol II. In fact in most cases in which the ICTY discussed the applicability test it was confronted with charges deriving directly from Common Article 3 and not from Additional Protocol II (i.e. collective punishment, acts of terrorism, pillage or threat to commit the forgoing act).

Unfortunately and surprisingly, the ICTY did not discuss this matter in cases where it directly applied Additional Protocol II crimes. For example, in cases where the Court had to deal with charges stemming from Article 4 AP II it found a legal trick to sidestep a discussion on the applicability of Additional Protocol II and declared that 'the only charge not coming under common Article 3 of the Geneva Conventions concerns the prohibition on plunder of private property but that is specifically mentioned in Article 3(e) of the Statute'.[100] In *Hadzihasanovic* the Court took the view that Article 3 of the ICTY Statute was broad enough to confer jurisdiction over other crimes.[101] As a result, it pointed out that wanton destruction as well as pillage could be prosecuted pursuant to Article 3(b) and 3(e), respectively, of the ICTY Statute even though they were not mentioned in Common Article 3 though prohibited under Additional Protocol II and, most significantly, under customary international law.[102]

---

[96] ICTY Limaj 2005, para 88.

[97] ICTY Limaj 2005, para 92.

[98] See ICTY Delalic et al. 2001, Prosecutor v. Delalic et al., Case IT-96-21-A, Appeals Judgment, Appeals Chember, 20 February 2001, para 136 and ICTY Kunarac et al. 2002, Prosecutor v. Kunarac, Kovac and Vukovic, Case IT-96-23 & IT-96-23/1-A, Appeals Judgment, Appeals Chamber, 12 June 2002, para 68 [hereafter ICTY Kunarac et al. 2002].

[99] ICTY Limaj 2005, para 176. As the ICTY noted 'Article 3 of the Statute is a general and residual clause covering serious violations of international humanitarian law not falling under Articles 2, 4 or 5 of the Statute'. ICTY Kunarac et al. 2002, para 68.

[100] ICTY Nikolic 1995, para 31.

[101] ICTY Hahdzihasanovic and Kubura 2005, Prosecutor v. Hadzihasanovic and Kubura, Case No IT-01-47-AR3.3, Decision on Joint Defence Interlocutory Appeal of Trial Chamber Decision on Rule 98bis Motions for Acquittal, Appeals Chamber, 11 March 2005, para 14 [hereafter ICTY Hahdzihasanovic and Kubura 2005].

[102] ICTY Hahdzihasanovic and Kubura 2005, paras 29 and 37.

In *Milosevic* the Trial Chamber boldly stated that 'the Tadic test is consistent with Additional Protocol II to the Four Geneva Conventions';[103] nonetheless it hinted that the threshold of applicability of Additional Protocol II was higher inasmuch as it denied 'such control of territory [as] a requirement for the existence of an armed conflict'.[104] Later, in *Boskoski*, the ICTY distinguished between the threshold of applicability of Additional Protocol II and Common Article 3, stressing that it is mainly one relating to the degree of organisation of the armed groups and explained that

> 'Additional Protocol II requires a higher standard than Common Article 3 for establishment of an armed conflict. It follows that the degree of organisation required to engage in "protracted violence" is lower than the degree of organisation required to carry out "sustained and concerted military operations"'.[105]

The ICTY is no doubt aware that the threshold of applicability of Additional Protocol II is higher.

In conclusion, the ICTY appears to favour a single definition in regard to the applicability test of a non-international armed conflict, this being dictated by its Statute. That being said, the test set out in *Tadic* appears to be lower than the one expounded in the ICRC Commentary.

As a result, Boelaert-Suominen explains that 'the threshold suggested by the ICRC Commentary has failed to crystallise into customary international law'. In particular, there is no requirement in the ICTY judgments that the non-state entities should somehow exert control over part of a territory, or that such armed forces have a responsible command[106] or be willing to respect the laws and customs of warfare.[107] Undoubtedly the ICTY jurisprudence has lowered the threshold of applicability of Common Article 3.

2.4.2 The International Criminal Tribunal for Rwanda

The greatest innovation in terms of international criminal law relating to non-international armed conflicts was the inclusion in Article 4 of the Statute of the International Criminal Tribunal for Rwanda (ICTR) of crimes derived from Common Article 3 GCs and Article 4 of Additional Protocol II. Therefore the Statute of the ICTR 'fully deserves the epithet "historic"'.[108] In particular three sets of crimes derive from Additional Protocol II only and are not found in

[103] ICTY Milosevic 2004, para 21.
[104] ICTY Milosevic 2004, para 36.
[105] ICTY Boskoski and Tarculovski 2008, para 197.
[106] Boelaert-Suominen 2000b, pp. 633–634.
[107] Tahzib-Lie and Swaak-Goldman 2004, pp. 250–251.
[108] Turns 1995, p. 822.

Common Article 3.[109] As the specified crimes are not all crimes deriving from Common Article 3 the applicability and threshold of the two distinctive treaties would, so it seems, be of utmost importance.

As far as the threshold issue is concerned, the ICTR has applied an 'evaluation test' to determine whether a non-international, in contradistinction to an international, armed conflict exists[110] and whether an armed conflict, in contradistinction to internal disturbances, exists.[111] Under this test the Court must, similar to the *Tadic* case, appraise the 'intensity and organisation of the parties to the conflict'.[112] Alike the ICTY the ICTR uses this test to rule out 'mere acts of banditry, internal disturbances and tensions, and unorganized and short-lived insurrections'[113] from the application of the Statute.[114]

With regard to the relation between the Additional Protocol II and the Common Article 3 GCs thresholds the Court adopts the view that Additional Protocol II develops and supplements the rules under Common Article 3 GCs.[115] The Trial Chamber in *Akayesu* noted the different thresholds between Additional Protocol II and Common Article 3 and considered separately which convention applied.[116] The Court clearly specified that 'if an offence [...] is charged under both Common Article 3 and Additional Protocol II, it will not suffice to apply Common Article 3 and take for granted that Article 4 of the Statute, hence Additional Protocol II, is therefore automatically applicable'.[117] It held that both standards applied to the conflict in question.

A different approach to the *Akayesu* 'bifurcation thesis' was adopted by the Trial Chamber in *Kayishema and Ruzindana*, for by declaring that '[a]n armed conflict which takes place in the territory of a High Contracting Party between its armed forces and dissident armed forces or other organised armed groups, in accordance with Protocol II, should be considered as a non-international armed conflict'[118]

[109] This is the case for collective punishment, acts of terrorism, pillage and threats to commit any of the forgoing acts. Article 4(b)(d)(h) and (g) AP II respectively.

[110] ICTR Musema 2000, Prosecutor v. Musema, Case No ICTR-96-13-T, Judgment, Trial Chamber, 27 January 2000, para 247 [hereafter ICTR Musema 2000].

[111] ICTR Akayesu 1998, para 601; ICTR Musema 2000, para 248.

[112] ICTR Akayesu 1998, para 620; ICTR Musema 2000, para 250; ICTR Rutaganda 1999, Prosecutor v. Rutaganda, Case No ICTR-96-3-T, Judgment, Trial Chamber, 6 December 1999, para 93 [hereafter ICTR Rutaganda 1999]; ICTR Baglishema 2001, Prosecutor v. Baglishema, Case No ICTR-95-1A-T, Judgment, Trial Chamber, 7 June 2001, para 101 [hereafter ICTR Baglishema 2001].

[113] ICTR Rutaganda 1999, para 92.

[114] ICTR Akayesu 1998, para 620.

[115] ICTR Kayishema and Ruzindana 1999, Prosecutor v. Kayishema and Ruzindana, Case No ICTR-95-1-T, Judgment, Trial Chamber, 21 May 1999, para 170 [herafter ICTR Kayishema and Ruzindana 1999]; ICTR Musema 2000, para 252.

[116] ICTR Akayesu 1998, para 607. As Cullen notes, 'the ICTR Trial Chamber found it necessary to establish the applicability of common Article 3 and Additional Protocol II individually'. Cullen 2010, p. 133.

[117] ICTR Akayesu 1998, paras 607 and 618. See also ICTR Musema 2000, para 252.

[118] ICTR Kayishema and Ruzindana 1999, para 170.

the ICTR seems to list most of, albeit not all, the elements of the *Tadic* definition of an armed conflict whilst referring to Additional Protocol II in the same breath. This odd phrasing in fact means that the Court deems Common Article 3 and Additional Protocol II to have to be satisfied 'conjunctively'. Indeed, in *Rutaganda* the Trial Chamber stated that '[c]onsequently, the Prosecutor must prove that at the time of the events alleged in the Indictment there existed an internal armed conflict in the territory of Rwanda, which, at the very least, satisfied the material requirements of Additional Protocol II, as these requirements subsume those of Common Article 3.'[119] This finding was confirmed in *Baglishema* stating that if the higher threshold of applicability of Additional Protocol II was met, the material requirements of applicability *ipso facto* meet those of Common Article 3.[120] This undoubtedly supports the aforementioned simultaneous application of both standards when the more restrictive requirements set out in Additional Protocol II are fulfilled. Yet, this does not seem to cover situations that fall short of the threshold of Additional Protocol II but might be covered by Common Article 3 GCs.

It appears on the face of it that the ICTR is applying only one applicability standard, that is the Additional Protocol II standard, but this is due to the fact that the conflict in Rwanda was an Additional Protocol II conflict and there was thus no need to assess situations that fall solely within the remit of applicability of Common Article 3. Further, Article 4 of the ICTR specifically refers to 'Violations of Article 3 Common to the Geneva Conventions and of Additional Protocol II' which led the Court to believe correctly that both thresholds had to be met.[121] In this regard, the ICTR has identified four requirements that must be satisfied: (i) an armed conflict between the armed forces of a High Contracting Party and dissident armed forces or other organised armed groups; (ii) dissident forces were under responsible command; (iii) dissident forces were able to exercise control over a part of territory to carry out sustained and concerted military operations and (iv) dissident forces were able to implement Additional Protocol II.[122]

The first requirement is fulfilled by the presence of state armed forces 'understood in the broadest sense, so as to cover all armed forces as described within national legislation'[123] and armed opposition groups. As for the second requirement, i.e. that of responsible command, it is closely knitted with (i) how 'organised' the armed group is, (ii) the ability to carry out sustained and concerted military operations and (iii) the ability to ensure the implementation of international humanitarian law.

Indeed, the ICTR explained in *Musema* that dissident armed forces or other armed groups need not be hierarchically organized as a formal military

---

119 ICTR Rutaganda 1999, para 435.

120 ICTR Baglishema 2001, para 100. See also ICTR Rutaganda 1999, para 94.

121 ICTR Musema 2000, para 245.

122 ICTR Akayesu 1998, paras 619, 623; ICTR Rutaganda 1999, para 95; ICTR Baglishema 2001, para 100; ICTR Kayishema and Ruzindana 1999, para 171.

123 ICTR Akayesu 1998, para 625; ICTR Musema 2000, para 256.

structure,[124] but that there must be a level of organisation that is capable of 'on the one hand, planning and carrying out sustained and concerted military operations—operations that are kept up continuously and that are done in agreement according to a plan, and on the other, of imposing discipline in the name of the de facto authorities'.[125]

Yet, the Court does not leave it at that as it also stresses that

> '[t]he armed forces must be able to dominate a sufficient part of the territory so as to maintain sustained and concerted military operations and to apply Additional Protocol II. In essence, the operations must be continuous and planned. The territory in their control is usually that which has eluded the control of the government forces'.[126]

As mentioned by Vité, the distinctive criterion between an Additional Protocol II and a Common Article 3 armed conflict is that of the armed opposition group's control of territory.[127] This criterion (which assists in ascertaining the armed group's ability to carry out sustained and concerted military operations) for the applicability of Additional Protocol II, in contrast to Common Article 3, is strongly reaffirmed in the jurisprudence of the ICTR.

2.4.3 *The Special Court for Sierra Leone*

In a similar manner to the ICTR, the war crimes provision in the Statute of the Special Court for Sierra Leone (SCSL),[128] derive from Common Article 3 GCs and Article 4 of Additional Protocol II. As mentioned above collective punishment, acts of terrorism, pillage and threats to commit the foregoing acts derive specifically from Article 4 of Additional Protocol II. The first three offences have been charged in all cases before the SCSL. In contrast, the ICTR and ICTY have been more reluctant to charge crimes deriving directly and solely from Additional Protocol II. Therefore, the cases before the SCSL could potentially add clarifications to the questionable applicability standard.

Regrettably, the SCSL adds more doubtful jurisprudence. The SCSL Appeals Chamber in *Fofana* has followed the broader test stating in regard to Article 3 of the SCSL Statute: 'In respect of Article 3, therefore, the court need only be satisfied that an armed conflict existed and that the alleged violations were related to the armed conflict'.[129]

---

[124] ICTR Musema 2000, para 257.

[125] ICTR Musema 2000, para 257. See also ICTR Akayesu 1998, para 626.

[126] ICTR Akayesu 1998, para 626; ICTR Musema 2000, para 258.

[127] Vité 2009, p. 79.

[128] Statute of the Special Court for Sierra Leone.

[129] SCSL Fofana 2004, Prosecutor v. Fofana, Case No SCSL-04-14-PT-101, Decision on Preliminary Motion on Lack of Jurisdiction Materiae: Nature of the Armed Conflict, Appeals Chamber, 25 May 2004, para 25 [hereafter SCSL Fofana 2004].

The SCSL does not fall short to give an explanation for such an interpretation stating

> '[i]t has been observed that "even though the rules applicable in internal armed conflict still lag behind the law that applies in international conflict, the establishment and work of the ad hoc Tribunals has significantly contributed to diminishing the relevance of the distinction between the two types of conflict". The distinction is no longer of great relevance in relation to the crimes articulated in Article 3 of the Statute as these crimes are prohibited in all conflicts.'[130]

The ICTY principle that there are minimum standards once a situation can be described as an armed conflict has without a doubt been readily adopted by the SCSL.[131] In this regard, the SCSL reiterates the *Tadic* definition of an armed conflict and uses the same criteria, that of the intensity of the conflict and the organisation of the parties.[132] Such criteria are essential to distinguish an armed conflict from other acts that do not fall within the purview of international humanitarian law.[133]

Yet, such a statement appears to be ground-breaking. Indeed the conflict in Sierra Leone took place only two years after the conflict in Rwanda and yet whilst the ICTR assesses the applicability of Additional Protocol II the SCSL does not appear to feel obliged to do so. It is all the more surprising as both Article 3 of the ICTR Statute and Article 3 of the SCSL Statute refer to violations of Common Article 3 *and* Additional Protocol II. The SCSL also analyses the ICTR position, acknowledging that the ICTR understands its jurisdiction in relation to non-international armed conflict to be ascertained when the requirements set out in Additional Protocol II are satisfied.[134] Yet, after reviewing the ICTY and ICTR jurisprudence, the SCSL Appeals Chamber explains that the crimes spelled out in Article 3 of its Statute are of customary nature and as the distinction between international and non-international armed conflict 'is no longer of great relevance in relation to the crimes articulated in Article 3 of the Statute'[135] the Court only needs to be satisfied that an armed conflict existed.[136] As a result, the SCSL considers that as the distinction between international and non-international armed conflicts is irrelevant with regard to the crimes listed in Article 3 of the Statute, the

---

[130] SCSL Fofana 2004, para 25; See also SCSL Brima et al. 2007, Prosecutor v. Brima et al. Case No SCSL-04-16-T, Judgment, Trial Chamber, 20 June 2007, para 243 [hereafter SCSL Brima et al. 2007]; SCSL Taylor 2012, Prosecutor v. Taylor, Case No SCSL-03-01-T, Judgment, Trial Chamber, 18 May 2012, para 563 [hereafter SCSL Taylor 2012].

[131] SCSL Fofana 2004, para 23; SCSL Fofana and Kondewa 2007, Prosecutor v. Fofana and Kondewa, Case No SCSL-04-14-T, Trial Chamber, 2 August 2007, para 123 [hereafter SCSL Fofana and Kondewa 2007]; SCSL Brima et al. 2007, paras 243–244.

[132] SCSL Fofana and Kondewa 2007, para 124; SCSL Brima et al. 2007, paras 243–244; SCSL Taylor 2012, paras 563–564.

[133] SCSL Fofana and Kondewa 2007, para 124; SCSL Taylor 2012, para 564.

[134] SCSL Fofana 2004, para 20.

[135] SCSL Fofana 2004, para 25.

[136] See also SCSL Brima et al. 2007, paras 251.

distinction between the two types of non-international armed conflict is also irrelevant.

Nonetheless, the SCSL has at times examined whether the conflict fell within the purview of Additional Protocol II. In the *Fofana* case, the Court spelled out the classical criteria for the application of Additional Protocol II, stressing that an Additional Protocol II conflict automatically satisfies the criteria for the applicability of Common Article 3.[137] Yet, in the Court's application of the law there are no references to Additional Protocol II.[138] In the *Sesay* et al. Case, the Trial Chamber felt the need to investigate the applicability of Additional Protocol II as three counts charged by the Prosecution—collective punishment, acts of terrorism and pillage—were solely found in Additional Protocol II.[139] Although it spelled out the three criteria of responsible command, control over territory (combined with the ability to carry out sustained and concerted military operations) and implementation of Additional Protocol II[140] it only focused on the first two criteria and ignored the last one.[141] Moreover, the succinctness of the application of the criteria and the conclusion that anyway 'an armed conflict satisfying this higher threshold would necessarily constitute an armed conflict under Common Article 3'[142] conveys the impression that the Trial Chamber applied the Additional Protocol II test with extreme reluctance.

In conclusion, although the provision of the SCSL Statute in relation to crimes perpetrated in non-international armed conflict is similar to that of the ICTR, the SCSL has adopted the ICTY approach, namely that it only needs to be satisfied that there is an armed conflict.

2.4.4 The International Criminal Court

Last but not least, the Rome Statute of the International Criminal Court and the jurisprudence of its Chambers need to be scrutinised in order to resolve the question of whether there are two or only one type of non-international armed conflict. Two articles of the Statute relate to such conflicts. Article 8(2)(c) enumerates war crimes for serious violations of Common Article 3 that are committed against 'persons taking no active part in hostilities…'. It applies to armed conflicts not of an international character and thus does not apply to situations of internal disturbances and tensions, such as riots, isolated and sporadic acts of violence or

---

[137] SCSL Fofana and Kondewa 2007, paras 126–127.

[138] SCSL Fofana and Kondewa 2007, paras 695–700.

[139] SCSL Sesay et al. 2009, Prosecutor v. Sesay et al., Case No SCSL-04-15-T, Judgment, Trial Chamber, 2 March 2009, para 966 [hereafter SCSL Sesay et al. 2009].

[140] SCSL Sesay et al. 2009, para 966.

[141] SCSL Sesay et al. 2009, paras 978–981.

[142] SCSL Sesay et al. 2009, para 981.

other acts of a similar nature.[143] Article 8(2)(e) of the Rome Statute, which enumerates war crimes for other serious violations of the laws and customs applicable in non-international armed conflicts (similar to Article 4 of the SCSL Statute) adduces an additional requirement (stipulated in Article 8(2)(f) such that it only 'applies to armed conflicts that take place in the territory of a state when there is protracted armed conflict between governmental authorities and organized armed groups or between such groups'.[144]

Inevitably the question is whether these two provisions reflect Common Article 3 and Additional Protocol II, respectively, or any other standard adopted by the previous international criminal tribunals. Certainly both Articles 8(2)(c) and 8(2)(e) could cover situations falling within the purview of Common Article 3, for the ICTY has consistently stressed the distinction between an armed conflict and other situations such as internal disturbances and tensions. Common Article 3 is now viewed as encapsulating the lowest threshold of a non-international armed conflict.

Still, there are doubts as to whether Article 8(2)(f)—which clarifies the condition of applicability for Article 8(2)(e)—reflects the standards of Additional Protocol II. The language used is reminiscent of, albeit not identical to, the *Tadic* threshold as it defines a non-international armed conflict by reference to 'protracted armed conflict' and 'organised armed groups'.[145] The reference to a 'protracted' armed conflict is certainly a lower standard than the expression 'sustained and concerted military operations' enshrined in Article 1(1) of Additional Protocol II.[146] Moreover, unlike Additional Protocol II, the Rome Statute also formally captures situations where governmental authorities are not directly involved in the armed conflict, but where the conflict is merely between organized armed groups and which, in the past, were only covered by Common Article 3. As a matter of fact, during the drafting of the article delegates rejected a proposal to introduce the Additional Protocol II threshold and agreed on the one propounded in the *Tadic* case, thereby indicating 'that the latter test was considered to be distinct from, and a lower threshold than, the test under Additional Protocol II'.[147] The drafters of the Rome Statute considered that this broader definition of the scope of application of the law relating to non-international armed conflicts now constitutes customary law.[148]

The question is whether this creates another threshold. In other words, can Article 8(2)(e) be considered as a hybrid threshold between Additional Protocol II and Common Article 3? This is particularly significant as the drafters only stipulated conditions for the applicability of Article 8(2)(e) by referring in Article 8(2)(f)

143 Article 8(2)(d) Rome Statute.

144 Article 8(2)(f) Rome Statute; emphasis added.

145 ICTY Limaj 2005, para 87.

146 Zimmermann 1999, p. 285.

147 ICTY Boskoski and Tarculovski 2008, para 197.

148 'The incorporation of [the Tadic threshold] into the Rome Statute of the International Criminal Court has been cited as indicative of its customary status.' Cullen 2010, pp. 121–122.

to an amended version of the *Tadic* test.[149] Furthermore, Article 8(2)(c) expressly refers to Common Article 3[150] whilst Article 8(2)(c) relates to the *Tadic* test mentioned in Article 8(2)(f), thereby conveying the impression that the *Tadic* test is different from the one encapsulated in Common Article 3.

Many jurists argue that Article 8(2)(f) has the same threshold as Common Article 3.[151] Likewise, Akande does not think that the intention was to create different thresholds of application, noting that 'Article 8(2)(f) is better interpreted as simply stating the intensity test with the protracted nature of the conflict being a factor to be assessed determining intensity'.[152]

In *Bemba* the Pre-Trial Chamber noted that a non-international armed conflict occurs when it reaches a 'level of intensity, exceeding that of internal disturbances and tensions, such as riots, isolated and sporadic acts of violence or other acts of a similar nature, and which takes place within the confines of a state territory. The hostilities may break out (i) between government authorities and organized dissident armed groups or (ii) between such groups'.[153] This formulation tends to reflect the *Tadic* test, i.e. that of a minimum threshold to distinguish an armed conflict from other situations and the idea of two *organised* groups whose clashes reach a certain level of *intensity*. However, the Pre-Trial Chamber goes further, affirming that the group must be under responsible command so as to be able to impose discipline and carry out military operations,[154] criteria that are reminiscent of those stipulated in Additional Protocol II.

Some legal experts also contend that a temporal element is introduced by way of the word 'protracted', thereby creating a separate category of non-international armed conflict.[155] The ICC jurisprudence seems to confirm this viewpoint, for, when dealing with Article 8(2)(f) the ICC links the concept of 'protracted' to the ability of the armed groups to plan and carry out military operations rather than solely the intensity and the organisation of the armed groups as in the *Tadic* test.[156] In *Bemba* although the Pre-Trial Chamber specifically raises the issue of the temporal element it deems it unnecessary to address the argument in detail (i.e. spell out relevant factors), for the period during which the alleged crimes were committed was regarded as 'protracted'.[157] The position of the ICC is best summarised in the *Lubanga* judgment in which the Trial Chamber stated:

---

149 See discussion in Vité 2009, p. 81.

150 See discussion in Boelaert-Suominen 2000a, p. 87.

151 Pejic 2011, pp. 192–193; Meron 2000, p. 260; Cullen 2007, p. 445.

152 Akande 2012, p. 56.

153 ICC Bemba 2009, Prosecutor v. Bemba, Case No ICC-01/05-01/08, Decision Pursuant to Article 61(7)(a) and (b) of the Rome Statute on the Charges of the Prosecutor against Jean-Pierre Bemba Gombo, Pre-Trial Chamber, 15 June 2009, para 231 [hereafter ICC Bemba 2009].

154 ICC Bemba 2009, para 234. See also ICC Lubanga 2007, Prosecutor v. Lubanga, Case No ICC-01/04-01/06-803, Decision on the Confirmation of Charges, Pre-Trial Chamber I, 29 January 2007, para 23 [hereafter ICC Lubanga 2007].

155 Provost 2002, pp. 268 f.

156 ICC Lubanga 2007, para 234.

157 ICC Bemba 2009, para 235.

> '[i]t is argued a non-international armed conflict is established when states have not resorted to armed force and i) the violence is sustained and has reached a certain degree of intensity, and ii) armed groups with some degree of organisation, including the capability of imposing discipline and the ability to plan and carry out sustained military operations, are involved. Additionally, Article 8(2)(f) of the Statute stipulates that the conflict must be "protracted" for these purposes'.[158]

This *Lubanga* test is narrower than the one applied under the customary interpretation of Common Article 3 as it requires the fighting to take place over a certain period of time and yet, to a certain extent, broader than the one expounded in Additional Protocol II as it does not require the armed group to be in control of a section of the territory.[159] Whilst Vité concludes, this is a new test 'half way between the categories referred to in common Article 3 and in Additional Protocol II' it is argued that the interpretation imparted by the ICC is in fact closer to the original intention of the drafters of Common Article 3 than the interpretation by the ICTY. After all, the Commentary to Common Article 3 explains that '[s] peaking generally, it must be recognized that the conflicts referred to in Article 3 are armed conflicts, with "armed forces" on either side engaged in "hostilities"—conflicts, in short, which are in many respects similar to an international war, but take place within the confines of a single country'.[160] Common Article 3 was not meant to cover situations in which organised groups were engaged in acts that just reached a minimum level of intensity.

2.5 Conclusion

International humanitarian law identifies two types of non-international armed conflict: first those covered by Common Article 3 and, second those falling within the purview of Article 1 AP II. There can be no doubt that the jurisprudence of the international criminal tribunals—the International Criminal Tribunal for the Former Yugoslavia, the International Criminal Tribunal for Rwanda, the Special Court for Sierra Leone and the International Criminal Court—has led to changes in relation to the distinction between the different types of non-international armed conflicts. The inconsistencies in the case law, however, mean that the tribunals have not had the significant impact on treaty law that might have been expected.

For example, the ICTR appears to be the only tribunal that closely follows this distinction and makes a conscious effort to verify that a situation falls within one and/or the other type of non-international armed conflict.

In contrast the ICTY has chosen to apply only one threshold of applicability. In *Tadic* it focused its attention on the distinction between armed conflicts and other

[158] ICC Lubanga 2012, Prosecutor v. Lubanga, Case No ICC-01/04-01/06, Judgment, Trial Chamber I, 14 March 2012, para 506.

[159] See discussion in Vité 2009, p. 82.

[160] Pictet 1960, p. 37.

situations. This minimum threshold that allows a distinction between armed conflicts and other situations as well as the factors adopted by the ICTY to ascertain whether a conflict is taking place—intensity of conflict and organisation of the armed groups—are now widely accepted by the ICTR, the SCSL and the ICC. As Bartels explains '[d]espite the lack of a formal treaty-given definition, it seems reasonably clear nowadays what is to be considered an IAC or an NIAC, and thus what constitutes the distinction between the two types'.[161] Although the ICTY argues that it has based its case-law on the commentary there are however doubts that this threshold is similar to the one originally intended by the drafters of Common Article 3.[162] Common Article 3 has been extended[163] and distorted, inasmuch as it now applies as a minimum threshold (see jurisprudence of the ICTY, ICTR and SCSL) rather than to internal situations that are similar to international armed conflicts, yet occurring on the territory of a single state.

To further complicate matters, it appears that the drafters of the ICC Statute have in Article 8(2)(f) introduced a third type of armed conflict, a hybrid version of Common Article 3 and Additional Protocol II.[164] A closer and thorough examination nevertheless reveals that the threshold set in Article 8(2)(f) and the interpretation thereof are likely to be similar to the original intention of the drafters of Common Article 3. The question is whether the interpretation of the ICC will override the one by the ICTY in the *Tadic* case now so ingrained in customary international law. Will the ICC test slowly, but assuredly, find its way in customary international law? Time will tell.

References

Abi-Saab R (1991) Humanitarian law and internal conflicts: the evolution of legal concern. In: Delissen AJM, Tanja GT (eds) Humanitarian law of armed conflict. Challenges ahead. Essays in honour of Frits Kalshoven. Martinus Nijhoff, Dordrecht, pp 209–223

Abi-Saab R (1986) Droit humanitaire et conflits internes. Origines et évolution de la réglementation internationale. Institut Henry Dunant/Pedone, Genève/Paris

Akande D (2012) Classification of armed conflicts: relevant legal concepts. In: Wilmhurst E (ed) International law and the classification of conflicts. Oxford University Press, Oxford, pp 32–79

Ambos K (2001) Zur Bestrafung von Verbrechen im internationalen, nicht-internationalen und internen Konflikt. In: Hasse J et al (ed) Humanitäres Völkerrecht. Politische, rechtliche und strafgerichtliche Dimensionen. Nomos Verlag, Baden-Baden, pp 325–353

Ash RW (2007) Square pegs and round holes: Al-Qaeda detainees and common Article 3. Indiana Int Comp Law Rev 17:269

Bartels R (2009) Timelines, borderlines and conflicts. The historical evolution of the legal divide between international and non-international armed conflicts. Int Rev Red Cross 873:35

Bassiouni MC (1999) International criminal law. Transnational Publishers, Ardsley

161 Bartels 2009, p. 40.

162 Ash 2007, p. 275.

163 Bartels 2009, p. 36.

164 Vité 2009, p. 82.

Boelaert-Suominen S (2000a) Grave breaches, universal jurisdiction and internal armed conflict: is customary law moving towards a uniform enforcement mechanism for all armed conflicts? J Conflict Secur Law 5:63

Boelaert-Suominen S (2000b) The Yugoslav tribunal and the common core of humanitarian law applicable to all armed conflicts. Leiden J Int Law 13:619

Bond JE (1974) The rules of riot: internal conflict and the law of war. Princeton University Press, Princeton

Cullen A (2007) The definition of non-international armed conflict in the Rome Statute of the International Criminal Court: an analysis of the threshold of application contained in Article 8(2)(f). J Conflict Secur Law 12:419

Cullen A (2010) The concept of non-international armed conflict in international humanitarian law. Cambridge University Press, Cambridge

Elder DA (1979) The historical background of common Article 3 of the Geneva Convention of 1949. Case W Reserve J Int Law 11:37

Forsythe DP (1978) Legal management of internal war: the 1977 protocol on non-international armed conflicts. Am J Int Law 72:272

Gaeta P (1996) The armed conflict in Chechnya before the Russian Constitutional Court. Eur J Int Law 7:563

Green LC (2002) The contemporary law of armed conflict. Manchester University Press and Juris Publishing, Manchester

Greppi E (1999) The evolution of individual criminal responsibility under international law. Int Rev Red Cross 835:531

Henckaerts J-M (2005) Study on customary international humanitarian law: a contribution to the understanding and respect for the rule of law in armed conflict. Int Rev Red Cross 857:175

Henckaerts J-M, Doswald-Beck L (eds) (2005) Customary international humanitarian law, vol 1. Cambridge University Press, Cambridge

Jinks D (2003) The temporal scope of application of international humanitarian law in contemporary conflicts. HPCR Policy Brief, January 2003

Kretzmer D (2009) Rethinking the application of international humanitarian law in non-international armed conflicts. Isr Law Rev 42:8

Lasswell HD, McDougal MS (1992) Jurisprudence for a free society. New Haven Press, New Haven

McCarthy C (2008) Legal conclusion or interpretative process? Lex specialis and the applicability of international human rights standards. In: Arnold R, Quénivet N (eds) International humanitarian law and human rights law: towards a new merger in international law. Martinus Nijhoff, The Hague, pp 109–126

McLauren N, Schwendimann F (2005) An exercise in the development of international law: the new ICRC study on customary international humanitarian law. German Law J 6:1217

Meron T (1998) Is international law moving towards criminalization. Eur J Int Law 9:18

Meron T (2000) The humanization of humanitarian law. Am J Int Law 94:239

Moir L (1998) The historical development of the application of humanitarian law in non-international armed conflict to 1949. Int Comp Law Q 47:337

Pejic J (2007) Conflict classification and the law applicable to detention and the use of force. In: Wilmhurst E (ed) International law and the classification of conflicts. Oxford University Press, Oxford, pp 80–115

Pejic J (2011) The protective scope of common Article 3: more than meets the eye. Int Rev Red Cross 881:189

Pictet J (1960) Commentary on the Geneva Conventions. International Committee of the Red Cross, Geneva

Provost R (2002) International human rights and humanitarian law. Cambridge University Press, Cambridge

Sandoz Y et al (eds) (1987) Commentary on the additional protocols to the Geneva Conventions. Martinus Nijhoff/International committee of the Red Cross, Geneva

Sassoli M, Bouvier AA (1999) How does law protect in war? Cases, documents and teaching materials on contemporary practice in international humanitarian law. International Committee of the Red Cross, Geneva

Schindler D (2003) International humanitarian law: its remarkable development and its persistent violation. J Hist Int Law 5:165

Sivakumaran S (2011) Re-envisaging the international law of internal armed conflict. Eur J Int Law 22:219

Spieker H (2001) Twenty-five years after the adoption of Additional Protocol II: breakthrough or failure of humanitarian legal protection? Yearb Int Humanit Law 4:129

Szesnat F, Bird AR (2012) Colombia. In: Wilmhurst E (ed) International law and the classification of conflicts. Oxford University Press, Oxford, pp 203–241

Tahzib-Lie B, Swaak-Goldman O (2004) Determining the threshold for the application of international humanitarian law. In: Lijnzaad L, van Sambeek J, Tahzib-Lie B (eds) Making the voice of humanity heard. Essays on humanitarian assistance and international humanitarian law in honour of HRH Princess Margriet of the Netherlands. Martinus Nijhof, The Hague, pp 239–253

Tskhovrebov Z (1995) An unfolding case of genocide: Chechnya, world order and the 'right to be left alone'. Nordic J Int Law 64:501

Turns D (1995) War crimes without war?—The applicability of international humanitarian law to atrocities in non-international armed conflicts. Afr J Int Compa Law 7:804

United Kingdom Ministry of Defence (2005) The manual of the law of armed conflict. Oxford University Press, Oxford

Van den Herik L (2005) The contribution of the Rwanda tribunal to the development of international law. Martinus Nijhoff, Leiden

Verri P (1972) Considérations sur l'application dans les conflits modernes des Articles 3 et 4 des Conventions de Genève de 1949. Revue de droit militaire et de droit de la guerre 11:93

Vité S (2009) Typology of armed conflicts in international humanitarian law: legal concepts and actual situations. Int Rev Red Cross 873:69

Zimmermann A (1999) Preliminary remarks on paras 2(c)-(f) and 3. In: Triffterer O (ed) Commentary on the Rome Statute of the International Criminal Court. Nomos Verlag, Baden-Baden, pp 475–501

Jurisprudence

ICC Bemba 2009, Prosecutor v Bemba, Case No ICC-01/05-01/08, Decision pursuant to Article 61(7)(a) and (b) of the Rome Statute on the Charges of the Prosecutor against Jean-Pierre Bemba Gombo, Pre-Trial Chamber, 15 June 2009

ICC Lubanga 2007, Prosecutor v Lubanga, Case No ICC-01/04-01/06-803, Decision on the confirmation of charges, Pre-Trial Chamber I, 29 January 2007

ICC Lubanga 2012, Prosecutor v Lubanga, Case No ICC-01/04-01/06, Judgment, Trial Chamber I, 14 March 2012

ICTR Akayesu 1998, Prosecutor v Akayesu, Case No ICTR-96-4-T, Judgment, Trial Chamber, 2 September 1998

ICTR Baglishema 2001, Prosecutor v Baglishema, Case No ICTR-95-1A-T, Judgment, Trial Chamber, 7 June 2001

ICTR Kayishema and Ruzindana 1999, Prosecutor v Kayishema and Ruzindana, Case No ICTR-95-1-T, Judgment, Trial Chamber, 21 May 1999

ICTR Musema 2000, Prosecutor v Musema, Case No ICTR-96-13-T, Judgment, Trial Chamber, 27 January 2000

ICTR Rutaganda 1999, Prosecutor v Rutaganda, Case No ICTR-96-3-T, Judgment, Trial Chamber, 6 December 1999

ICTY Boskoski and Tarculovski 2008, Prosecutor v Boskoski and Tarculovski, Case No IT-04-82-T, Judgment, Trial Chamber, 10 July 2008

ICTY Delalic 2001, Prosecutor v Delalic et al., Case IT-96-21-A, Appeals Judgment, Appeals Chamber, 20 February 2001

ICTY Delalic et al. 1998, Prosecutor v Delalic et al., Case No IT-96-21-T, Judgment, Trial Chamber, 16 November 1998

ICTY Hahdzihasanovic and Kubura 2005, Prosecutor v Hadzihasanovic and Kubura, Case No IT-01-47-AR3.3, Decision on Joint Defence Interlocutory Appeal of Trial Chamber Decision on Rule 98bis Motions for Acquittal, Appeals Chamber, 11 March 2005

ICTY Haradinaj 2008, Prosecutor v Haradinaj et al., Case No IT-04-84-T, Judgment, Trial Chamber, 3 April 2008

ICTY Kordic and Cerkez 2004, Prosecutor v Kordic and Cerkez, Case No IT-95-14/2-A, Appeals Judgment, Appeals Chamber, 17 December 2004

ICTY Kunarac et al. 2002, Prosecutor v Kunarac, Kovac and Vukovic, Case IT-96-23 & IT-96-23/1-A, Appeals Judgment, Appeals Chamber, 12 June 2002

ICTY Limaj 2005, Prosecutor v Limaj et al., Case No IT-03-66-T, Judgment, Trial Chamber, 30 November 2005

ICTY Milosevic 2004, Prosecutor v Milosevic, Case No IT-02-54-T, Decision on Motion for Judgment of Acquittal, Trial Chamber, 16 June 2004

ICTY Nikolic 1995, Prosecutor v Nikolic, Case No IT-95-2-R61, Review of Indictment Pursuant to Rule 61, Trial Chamber, 20 October 1995

ICTY Oric 2006, Prosecutor v Oric, Case No IT-03-68-T, Trial Chamber, Judgment, 30 June 2006

ICTY Tadic 1995, Prosecutor v Tadic, Case No IT-94-1-AR72, Decision on Defence Motion for Interlocutory Appeal on Jurisdiction, 2 October 1995

International Court of Justice 1950, Asylum case (Columbia v Peru), [1950] ICJ Rep 266, 27 November 1950

International Court of Justice 1969, North Sea continental shelf cases (Federal Republic of Germany/Denmark and Federal Republic of Germany/Netherlands), [1969] ICJ Rep 3, 20 February 1969

International Court of Justice 1970, Barcelona Traction, Light and Power Company, Limited (Belgium v Spain), Second Phase, [1970] ICJ Rep 3, 5 February 1970

International Court of Justice 1986, Military and paramilitary activities in and against Nicaragua (Nicaragua v USA), Judgment, [1986] ICJ Rep 14, 27 June 1986

SCSL Brima et al. 2007, Prosecutor v Brima et al., Case No SCSL-04-16-T, Judgment, Trial Chamber, 20 June 2007

SCSL Fofana 2004, Prosecutor v Fofana, Case No SCSL-04-14-PT-101, Decision on Preliminary Motion on Lack of Jurisdiction Materiae: Nature of the Armed Conflict, Appeals Chamber, 25 May 2004

SCSL Fofana and Kondewa 2007, Prosecutor v Fofana and Kondewa, Case No SCSL-04-14-T, Judgment, Trial Chamber, 2 August 2007

SCSL Sesay, Prosecutor v Sesay, Kallon and Gbao, Case No SCSL-04-15-T, Judgment, Trial Chamber, 2 March 2009

SCSL Taylor 2012, Prosecutor v Taylor, Case No SCSL-03-01-T, Judgment, Trial Chamber, 18 May 2012

Chapter 3
The Role of the U.S. Judicial Branch During the Long War: Drone Courts, Damage Suits, and Freedom of Information Act (FOIA) Requests

Lesley Wexler

Contents

Lesley Wexler is Professor of Law and Thomas A. Mengler Faculty Scholar, University of Illinois College of Law. 504 E. Pennsylvania, Champaign, IL 61820 USA. Thanks to Gary Solis, Dan Shalmon, Rachel Levinson, Ariel Waldman, and Rob Knowles for helpful comments. Many thanks also to J. R. Hand and Elizabeth Deshaies for excellent research assistance.

L. Wexler (✉)
College of Law, University of Illinois, Pennsylvania, IL 61820, USA
e-mail: lmwexler@illinois.edu

D. Jinks et al. (eds.), *Applying International Humanitarian Law in Judicial and Quasi-Judicial Bodies*, DOI: 10.1007/978-94-6265-008-4_3,

3.1 Introduction

The current U.S. practice of using drones to engage in overseas killings raises difficult legal questions with incredibly high stakes. The fate of potential targets and collateral damage hangs in the balance along with grave concerns about national and foreign security. Over the past decade, expansive deference to the executive branch has allowed a substantial increase in the number and rate of drone strikes. The use of drones for targeted killing is becoming a regular tool of the U.S. government and perhaps will become so for other governments as well. What role, if any, do courts have to play in regulating this practice?

Critics of the status quo would like greater transparency and accountability with regard to targeted killings. In addition to constitutional concerns, some worry the executive branch is violating International Humanitarian Law (IHL). They want the executive branch to reveal its legal understandings of IHL and its application to drone strikes. They also seek greater information regarding review processes for targeted killings as to both prospective listings and retrospective assessments of compliance. These skeptics contend that the lack of judicial oversight and the opacity of the government's legal position risk the deaths of innocent foreign civilians, violate democratic accountability norms, erode the compliance reputation of the United States with allies, and help recruit a new generation of anti-American insurgents. Even if the current approach is lawful, many worry about future administrations or other governments that may adopt drone strikes without sufficient IHL protections. As this chapter describes, some of these critics have proposed the use of courts to foster either transparency or accountability or both.

In contrast, many, including those within the executive and judicial branches themselves, believe that the judicial role regarding drone strikes and targeted killings should be a minimal one.[1] They suggest that an active court reviewing names of those to be targeted, providing damages to victims of unlawful strikes, or demanding agencies declassify information on drone strikes would compromise an effective strategy in the war on terror.[2] They fear judicial intervention would pose great danger to U.S. soldiers, foreign civilians, and in worst-case scenarios, to U.S. citizens at home without enhancing IHL compliance. In particular, government actors have argued that greater transparency may compromise intelligence efforts and provide targets with additional opportunities to act strategically.[3] It could sour

[1] See e.g. Memorandum in Opposition to Plaintiff's Motion for Preliminary Injunction, *al-Aulaqi v. Obama*, 727 F. Supp. 2d (D.D.C. 2010) (No. 10-cv-101469), 2010 WL 3863135, p. 22.

[2] Ibid at 29.

[3] C Muñoz (Feb. 13, 2013) No court for drone oversight, says GOP. http://thehill.com/blogs/defcon-hill/policy-and-strategy/282687-no-court-for-drones-says-gop.

relations with states currently willing to provide covert permission for strikes. Meanwhile, these court opponents suggest that sufficient internal and congressional oversight can prevent unlawful activity.[4] They also push back on the opacity charge by noting the information provided through a series of high-level administration speeches and unacknowledged leaks.[5]

The U.S. judiciary itself is often reluctant to aggressively intervene in national security matters and other legal issues arising out of armed conflicts. Federal courts frequently employ a variety of procedural postures and substantive doctrines to avoid deciding live IHL controversies.[6] But the judicial branch sometimes surprises, as when the Supreme Court spoke to detention policy and its relationship to IHL in the trio of war on terror cases *Hamdi*,[7] *Hamdan*,[8] and *Boumediene*.[9] U.S. courts considering a more aggressive role might look to other countries, like Israel, whose courts have issued numerous rulings applying IHL to national security issues.[10]

This chapter suggests the U.S. judiciary may play an important role in the debate over the executive branch's decisions regarding IHL even if it declines to speak to the substance of such cases. First, advocates may use courts as a visible platform in which to make their arguments and spur conversations about alternative, nonjudicially mandated transparency and accountability measures. Perhaps they can leverage underlying constitutional concerns about the treatment of citizens to stimulate interest in the larger IHL issues. Second, litigants may use courts to publicize and pursue Freedom of Information Act (FOIA) requests and thus enhance transparency. Even if courts decline to grant FOIA requests, the lawsuits can generate media attention about what remains undisclosed. Third, and most robustly, Congress may pass legislation that would facilitate either prospective review of kill lists through a so-called drone court or remove procedural barriers to retrospective damage suits for those unlawfully killed by a drone strike. Even the threat of such a judicial role may influence executive branch behavior.

Section 3.1 identifies the underlying reasons for the expanding use of drones in targeted killings. It explains why the U.S. government frequently engages in a kill

---

[4] Associated Press (Feb. 11, 2013) Former Pentagon chief says lawmakers should have oversight of drone strikes against al-Qaida, Fox News, http://www.foxnews.com/us/2013/02/11/former-pentagon-chief-says-lawmakers-should-have-oversight-drone-strikes/.

[5] See *generally* K Anderson and B Wittes, 2013, Speaking the Law http://www.lawfareblog.com/speaking-the-law-the-obama-administrations-addresses-on-national-security-law/. Accessed 14 Aug 2013.

[6] See e.g. *El-Shifa Pharmaceuticals v. United States*, 607 F.3d 836, 849 (D.C. Cir. 2010)(en banc); *al-Aulaqi v. Obama*, 727 F. Supp. 2d 1, 33, 46 (D.D.C. 2010) (employing the political question and standing doctrines to avoid reaching a decision on the merits).

[7] *Hamdi v. Rumsfeld*, 542 U.S. 507 (2004).

[8] *Hamdan v. Rumsfeld*, 548 U.S. 557 (2006).

[9] *Boumediene v. Bush*, 553 U.S. 723 (2008).

[10] In fact, as discussed in Sect. 3.1, Israel's high court has ruled on targeted killings and issued guidelines informed by IHL to govern future behavior. *The Public Committee Against Torture in Israel v. Government of Israel* (Targeted Killings Case). HCJ 769/02 (2006).

rather than capture strategy in countries such as Pakistan, Somalia, and Yemen. It further addresses why the government might often prefer drone strikes to more traditional boots on the ground operations. After establishing the reasons for drone strikes, this section identifies the targets and unintended victims of drone strikes. In so doing, it distinguishes between traditional personality strikes of high level operatives and the newer approach of signature strikes in which the targeted individual's identity is unknown.

Section 3.2 then identifies the relevant IHL that might govern targeted killings and the use of drone strikes in various locations.[11] The first questions raised are whether IHL applies at all and if so, which body of IHL should govern? To the extent that IHL norms of proportionality and discrimination do apply, how are they implicated in this context? Lastly, is the executive branch's use of the Central Intelligence Agency (CIA) to conduct drone strikes protected under IHL? Should CIA operatives be viewed as combatants entitled to engage in the use of force? Or rather should one view CIA employees as civilians taking direct part in hostilities?

Given these various questions, Sect. 3.3 identifies the potential judicial roles in promoting accountability and transparency regarding drone strikes. This section opens with a brief description of the Israeli targeted killing case as a possible model for a court's substantive intervention. It then surveys existing U.S. lawsuits. One set of suits, *al-Aulaqi v. Obama* & *al-Aulaqi v. Panetta*, challenges the application of IHL to targeted killings outside of Afghanistan, but argues as a second-best that courts ought to find the executive branch's application of IHL norms to be unlawful. Another set of suits seeks judicial involvement in FOIA requests regarding the drone program.

Section 3.3 then moves to a discussion of the recommendations for a more robust role for the judicial branch in seeking accountability and transparency. One recent proposal suggests the creation of drone courts modeled after the Foreign Intelligence Surveillance (FIS) court for surveillance of domestic citizens.[12] Such a court might review individual listings and/or specific strikes. A second proposal urges the legislature to establish a judicial cause of action allowing nominal damages for those unlawfully killed.[13]

While this chapter remains skeptical that courts will ever reach the merits on IHL questions, Sect. 3.4 suggests creative use of the judiciary has helped insert IHL into the public debate over targeted killings and encouraged greater accountability. This chapter concludes by discussing the executive branch's behavior in the shadow of the judicial and legislative branches. First, even as the

---

[11] This section identifies, but does not attempt to answer, these questions. For high quality legal approaches to these questions, see Alston 2011; Anderson 2009; Blum and Heymann 2010; Chesney 2010; Daskal 2013.

[12] S Shane (Feb. 8, 2013) A court to vet kill lists. N.Y. Times p. A1.

[13] R Brooks 2010, The Constitutional and Counterterrorism Implications of Targeted Killing, Testimony Before the Senate Judiciary Subcommittee on the Constitution, Civil Rights, and Human Rights, pp. 18–19. Available at http://www.judiciary.senate.gov/pdf/04-23-13BrooksTestimony.pdf.

Obama administration failed to acknowledge drone strikes explicitly, a number of government officials gave speeches providing some sense of the justifications for and the limitations upon targeted killings. Second, members of the Obama administration began leaking documents providing extensive details on legal questions surrounding targeted killings including some relating to the application and interpretation of IHL norms. Lastly, the Obama administration's efforts to institutionalize its targeted killing practices may enhance compliance with IHL norms and create more significant internal oversight and review. This final section closes the chapter by noting additional reform measures to bolster these protections in the absence of a stronger judicial role.

3.2 Background

After September 11, 2001, the United States became enmeshed in a war on terror against al-Qaeda. The Bush and the subsequent Obama administrations sought out members of this group not only in Afghanistan, but across the globe. President Bush carried out a limited number of drone attacks to engage in targeted killings of members of al-Qaeda in Afghanistan, Yemen, and Pakistan. President Obama dramatically escalated the drone program by multiplying the quantity of strikes, expanding the geographic locations, emphasizing the use of signature strikes, and increasing the number of targetable groups. The following section explains why the United States has used drones to pursue targeted killings and who it has allegedly killed with these drones.

3.2.1 Why?

The United States and its allies face many threatening groups and individuals. When that threat is serious enough, the government must consider the appropriate course of action. If the government wants to neutralize the threat, it must then make a second strategic decision about how. The traditional choice has been framed as "kill or capture." As a legal matter, if the threat arises during an armed conflict and the individual has been classified as either a combatant or a civilian directly participating in hostilities, IHL allows both options.[14]

In the war on terror, both the Bush administration and the Obama administration have engaged in a mixed strategy, favoring kills in some situations and captures in others. Each strategy presents a different, largely context-dependent

---

[14] A combatant may be targeted up until the individual surrenders. If, however, the individual surrenders, the United States must then either detain or release the individual. For civilians directly participating in hostilities (CDPH), see Sect. 3.2.

mix of risk and reward. If the government believes a threatening individual possesses important intelligence, capture can be particularly valuable.[15]

Additionally, if the government lacks confidence in its assessment of an individual's threat, detention provides a reversible decision that allows more room for good faith mistakes. Yet capture also raises a host of thorny political and legal questions.[16] To list just a few: Where will detainees be kept and what are the relevant standards for their detention? Does the government intend for such detention to be indefinite? Is the individual eligible for judicial proceedings? When must such proceedings occur in civilian courts and when may they occur via military commissions? If one wants to elicit information, how can the government make sure such operations comply with international and domestic law standards?

In the war on terror, forging a domestic or international consensus on these questions has proven quite difficult. The United States has been harshly criticized for its creation of and behavior at detention sites such as Guantanamo, Bagram, and floating facilities in international waters. While the United States has never acknowledged the difficulties of detention as a reason for the increase in targeted killings, many suspect it motivates the current emphasis on killing.

Of course, the choice to kill rather than capture presents its own mix of risk and reward. Killing threats absolutely neutralizes an individual; he can never return to the battlefield or provide useful information to opponents.[17] Killing threats also allows a quicker conclusion of operations. U.S. forces need not be concerned with how they will transport the threat to a detention facility or how to protect the facility from attack. Yet killing may present more significant concerns about correctly identifying individuals and the risk of collateral damage to civilians and property. It also eliminates the possibility of extracting information.

Once the government decides to kill, it must then choose between drone or manned air strikes, or boots on the ground. CIA director and former Deputy National Security Advisor for Homeland Security and Counterterrorism John Brennan has outlined a variety of reasons the Obama administration may prefer drones to boots on the ground. He noted that the presence of U.S. soldiers abroad is expensive, an irritant to the local population, and may "inspire the next generation of terrorists."[18] The presence of soldiers creates escalation opportunities, posing an additional risk to civilians as well as to our troops. In contrast, drones strikes do not require the physical presence of our troops. Some also argue that drones even enhance law compliance as they are better suited to engage in pattern of life analysis and drone operators sitting in an office in the United States do not suffer the same sort of

[15] For example, the United States engaged in a snatch and grab of al-Qaeda in the Arabian Peninsula (AQAP); al Shabab liason Ahmed Abdulkadir Warsame whose subsequent interrogation produced a treasure trove of information on the structure and operational capabilities of both al Shabab and AQAP.

[16] Chesney and Goldsmith 2008, p. 180.

[17] For example, by using a drone strike to kill al-Aulaqi, the United States guaranteed he could no longer direct any of al-Qaeda's or AQAP's activities.

[18] Brennan 2012a, para 44.

physical or emotional stressors as pilots in planes or on the ground.[19] For good or for bad, the American public may be more willing to allow forceful engagement when the direct risk to troops is eliminated[20] and the financial cost is lower. That said, many worry without direct engagement, troops might develop a "Playstation mentality to killing"[21] lowering IHL compliance. Relatedly, some suggest the multi-day hovering physical presence of drones and accompanying stress and uncertainty can increase militancy of the local population. At least for now, the Obama administration appears to increasingly prefer to kill threats located outside of traditional battlefields, though it certainly engages in captures as well.

3.2.2 Who?

Against whom is the United States using drone strikes? Who are its intended targets? Who are its unintended victims? This subsection identifies three categories of persons that have allegedly been struck by U.S. drones. First, in personality strikes, the United States relies on intelligence data to target particular high-value individuals. Second, in signature strikes, the United States relies on intelligence data to target groups of individuals possessing characteristics associated with terrorist activity, but whose distinct identities are unknown. Third, the United States sometimes kills civilians who are not the target of the strike. This might happen as an unintended side effect of either personality or signature strikes. This subsection provides more details on each of these groups because they raise different legal concerns.

3.2.2.1 High Value Targets: Personality Strikes

A personality strike is one in which the government targets a specific individual based on intelligence data linked to that particular person. Several drone strikes in the last 10 years have been personality strikes.[22] The most notable of these have focused on high value targets; the personality strike that killed Anwar Al-Aulaqi (alleged high-level AQAP operative) is a prime example. The United States reasons that if it decapitates members essential to military organizations, the groups' ability to engage in terror or war-fighting will erode. In addition, losing top leadership in such a visible way should depress the morale of the rank and file members. Obama official John Brennan has publicly defended this strategy as

---

[19] Blank 2012, p. 716.

[20] O'Connell 2011, p. 136.

[21] P. Alston 2010, Study on targeted killings. Special Rapporteur on Extrajudicial, Summary or Arbitrary Executions, U.N. Doc. A/HRC/14/24/Add.6, para 84 (herafter "Alston Report 2010").

[22] New America Foundation, 2013, The year of the drone: leaders killed. counterterrorism.newamerica.net/about/militants.

slowing al-Qaeda's recruitment drive and degrading its capacity "to plan and execute large scale, potentially catastrophic attacks against our homeland … ."[23]

Regardless of the policy wisdom of personality strikes, high value targeting seems to play a shrinking role in overall targeting strategy.[24] While the Bush administration seemed to favor leadership strikes, under Obama, leaders comprise less than 15 % of its drone deaths.[25] Instead, Obama's strikes seemingly aim at the more rank and file of organizations like al-Qaeda, the Taliban, and the Haqqani network. Some of the strikes rely on individualized data to strike specific and known militants, but as explained below, many kills are not personality strikes at all.

3.2.2.2 Generalized Terrorist Targets: Signature Strikes

In addition to personality strikes, the Obama administration has also authorized so-called "signature strikes" or strikes based on targeting "groups of men who bear certain signatures, or definite characteristics associated with terrorist activity, but whose identities aren't known."[26] Status-based targeting is not unique to drone strikes—militaries have often relied on status markers such as uniforms rather than individualized intelligence to lawfully target combatants. Not much is known about the current practice as Obama administration officials have never officially acknowledged signature strikes nor identified legally adequate signatures,[27] although anonymous officials have claimed that "the criteria for signature strikes is 'tighter' today than when Obama entered office."[28] Nor has the practice yet received much serious scholarly criticism, though the revelation of more information will probably pave the way for more sustained academic attention.[29] At the very least, publicly available evidence indicates the vast majority of CIA strikes are signature, rather than personality, strikes.[30]

3.2.2.3 Civilians

Lastly, drone strikes, whether personality or signature, raise the possibility of unintended civilian casualties. Such deaths might occur in a variety of ways. The government might use a drone strike, but hit the wrong target. Or it might strike

[23] Brennan 2012a, para 11.

[24] Bergen and Tiedemann 2011, p. 12.

[25] New America Foundation 2013.

[26] Klaidman 2012, p. 41.

[27] Stanford Law School & New York U Law School, Living under drones: death, injury and trauma to civilians from US drone practices in Pakistan, 2012, p. 13.

[28] M Zenko (July 17, 2012), para 13, Targeted killings and signature strikes. blogs.cfr.org/zenko/2012/07/16/targeted-killings-and-signature-strikes.

[29] Heller 2013, noting dearth of legal literature on these questions.

[30] D Cloud (May 5, 2010) CIA drones have broader list of targets. LA Times, para 12.

the correct target, but the targeted individual might be misclassified based on inadequate intelligence or inappropriate legal standards of permissible targets. A government might also accept some civilian deaths as collateral damage necessary to successfully strike the intended target. Most controversially, the government might intentionally strike civilians. Some sources suggest that the U.S. practice of "double tapping" or striking a target site multiple times in quick succession is designed to kill first responders to the scene such as emergency workers and those recovering dead bodies.[31]

3.2.2.4 Significance

The United States has caused a significant number of deaths across these three categories. While the government has refused to disclose casualty estimates,[32] several well-known and widely cited drone strike data aggregators provide some sense of the toll.[33] While the aggregators reach different conclusions, the three big ones agree that more than 2,000 individuals have been killed and the number may reach over 4,000.[34] In addition, clinics at Stanford and NYU released a study assessing these data aggregators, compiling their own estimates and providing first person narratives of specific drone strikes.[35] Some, but not all, of the aggregators suggest a high percentage of civilian deaths, though they all agree the number and rate of civilian deaths has declined in the last year.[36]

Given that the known fact that the United States has caused the deaths of some combination of high-level operatives, low-level militants, and civilians,[37] a next

---

[31] G Greenwald (Aug. 20, 2012) US drone strikes target rescuers in Pakistan-and the West stays silent. The Guardian. http://www.guardian.co.uk/commentisfree/2012/aug/20/us-drones-strikes-target-rescuers-pakistan.

[32] Columbia Law School Human Rights Clinic 2012, Counting drone deaths, p. 9.

[33] These sources are the Foundation for the Defense of Democracy's *The Long War Journal*, New America Foundation's *Year of the Drone*, and The Bureau of Investigative Journalism's (TBIJ) *Covert Drone War*.

[34] For instance, the New American Foundation estimates that from 2004 to 2013, the U. S. drone strikes in Pakistan and Yemen killed 2439–3982 individuals in Pakistan and Yemen. New American Foundation 2013. The Long War Journal suggests that from 2006 to 2013, U.S. drone strikes in Pakistan and Yemen killed 3065 individuals. Roggio, B and Mayer, A (2013) Charting the data for US airstrikes in Pakistan, 2004–2013. http://www.longwarjournal.org/pakistan-strikes.php. (hereafter "Roggio and Mayer 2013") The Bureau of Investigative Journalism suggests from 2004 to 2013 U.S. drone strikes killed 2773–3866 individuals. Bureau of Investigative Journalism, The (2013) Casualty estimates. http://www.thebureauinvestigates.com/category/projects/drones. Accessed 5 May 2013.

[35] Stanford Law School & New York U Law School, Living under drones: death, injury and trauma to civilians from US drone practices in Pakistan, 2012, p. 13.

[36] The Long War Journal suggests that from 2006 to 2013, U.S. drone strikes in Pakistan and Yemen killed 3065 individuals. Roggio and Mayer 2013, supra n. 34.

[37] Columbia Law School Human Rights Clinic, p. 9.

logical inquiry is whether such deaths occurred in a lawful manner. The following section sets out the relevant legal questions that some have called upon courts to either answer or to reveal information necessary for others to answer.

3.3 The Application of IHL Norms to Drones

In some ways, drone strikes are no different than any other means used to kill those believed to present a threat to the United States. One could lodge many of the same complaints against boots on the ground operations or conventional bomb and missile strikes. Yet the drone program may be special in starkly raising a variety of legal issues regarding targeted killings. U.N. Special Rapporteur Ben Emmerson has noted the fundamental disputes regarding both the relevant legal framework for targeted killings as well as appropriate application and refinements within those legal frameworks, lamenting the lack of a "critical mass of concurrent opinion."[38] In this section, I identify the host of difficult legal questions raised by such strikes and for which advocates are calling for greater executive transparency and accountability.

3.3.1 Which, If Any, Bodies of IHL Apply to Drone Strikes?

First, states wishing to use force must address the threshold question of IHL's applicability. IHL governs at least two distinct sets of conflicts: international and non-international armed conflicts. The set of facts on the ground necessary to trigger the application of IHL for these two types of conflicts differs. Relatedly, the relevant substantive rules that apply to these two conflicts also differs. For instance, international armed conflicts are governed by the substantive rules contained in the entirety of the 1949 Geneva Conventions, whereas non-international armed conflict receive the lesser protections under Common Article 3 as well as the possible application of Additional Protocol II.[39] Whether and when terrorists may trigger the application of either of these bodies of law presents subsequent complications. And of course, the possibility always remains that no armed conflict exists at all. In such situations, a state may decide instead to apply some combination of the criminal law and human rights framework or it may believe that terrorist activity has triggered its independent and free standing right to self-defense justifying the use of force. Even under the self-defense justification, however, states are still governed by basic IHL principles of proportionality and discrimination discussed below.

---

[38] B. Emmerson 2013, Lawfare Podcast Episode 31: Interview with Ben Wittes. Lawfare, 3:45, http://www.lawfare.blog.com/2013/05/lawfare-podcast-episode-31-special-edition-ben-emmerson-discusses-his-investigation/. Accessed 3 Jun 2013 (hereafter Emmerson 2013a).

[39] The United States has not ratified Additional Protocol II.

The United States must determine the appropriate body of law for each location where it deploys drones to engage in targeted killing. To do so, it must assess the relevant facts on the ground and determine whether an armed conflict exists. While the Bush administration originally maintained that no IHL applied to its struggle with al-Qaeda in Afghanistan,[40] the U.S. Supreme Court definitively rejected this view in *Hamdan*, holding that the United States is engaged in a non-international armed conflict with al-Qaeda in Afghanistan.[41] In contrast, the courts have not explicitly spoken as to whether such reasoning also applies to the use of force in places like Pakistan, Yemen, Somalia, and Libya. For each of these locations and as well as for future sites, the government must decide whether the United States is using drone strikes to: (a) pursue its own non-internationalized armed conflict against al-Qaeda and their affiliates wherever located; (b) join a state ally in its fight against an insurgent group in its own pre-existing non-international armed conflict; (c) create a distinct non-international armed conflict separate from the Congressionally authorized one governing al-Qaeda and its affiliates; (d) create a new international armed conflict; (e) exercise its free standing right to self-defense; or (f) engage in law enforcement activities distinct from any armed conflict.

3.3.2 How Do Targeting Principles Apply to Drone Strikes?

If a body of IHL applies to drone strikes, then the next set of questions implicate its targeting principles. For all armed conflicts, IHL makes clear that the only legitimate object of the state in using force is to weaken the military forces of the enemy. Thus, under IHL, states may not lawfully target civilians.[42] In international armed conflicts, civilians can, however, lose their immunity from targeting if they directly participate in hostilities, but only for such time as they participate.[43] For non-international armed conflicts, some states adopt a broad understanding of direct participation, and others might use the ICRC Interpretive guidance that individuals who assume a "continuous combat function" (CCF) in an organized armed group may be targeted at any time.[44] The range of activities that constitute direct participation is hotly contested. United States military commission manuals have tried to

---

40 *Hamdan* 548 U.S. at 628 ("The conflict with al Qaeda is not, according to the Government, a conflict to which the full protections afforded detainees under the 1949 Geneva Conventions apply because Article 2 of those Conventions…renders the full protections applicable only to 'all cases of declared war or of any other armed conflict which may arise between two or more of the High Contracting Parties.'").

41 Id at 631–632 ("Common Article 3, then, is applicable here and, as indicated above", requires that Hamdan be tried by a "regularly constituted court affording all the judicial guarantees…").

42 Additional Protocol I Article 51(2); HPCR Commentary C18.

43 See Targeted Killings Case 2006, supra n. 10.

44 International Committee of the Red Cross (2009) Interpretive guidance on the notion of direct participation in hostilities under International Humanitarian Law. pt. I, Article VII.

sidestep this debate,[45] but the exact domestic understanding of direct participation is still open.[46] Some evidence suggests that the United States may believe mere membership in an organized armed group is sufficient to be targeted.[47]

These questions can come up in personality strikes in which you have a significant amount of detail about an individual or in signature strikes in which you may only know about an individual's participation in a particular activity. For the war on terror context, it has been suggested that legally adequate signatures would include planning attacks, transporting weapons, handling explosives, presence at al-Qaeda compounds, or identification at a training camp.[48] More controversial are alleged Bush and Obama administration signatures such as "military age males in a strike zone";[49] those who consort with known militants;[50] and armed men travelling in trucks in terrorist controlled areas.[51]

In addition to the deaths of combatants and civilians directly participating in hostilities, IHL does sometimes permit the indirect deaths of civilians, also known as collateral damage.[52] Such deaths must be "proportionate" to the military advantage sought.[53] In other words, if the use of force is militarily necessary, then any anticipated military advantage must be "considered in light of the expected harm to civilians" and cannot be found to be excessive. In doing the proportionality analysis, questions come up both regarding the correct balancing and also

---

[45] Manual for Military Commissions, 2010, IV-13(15)(c)(comment) http://www.mc.mil/Portals/0/2010_Manual_for_Military_Commissions.pdf (.. , an accused may be convicted in a military commission for these offenses if the commission finds that the accused employed a means…or method…prohibited by the law of war; intentionally attacked a "protected person" or "protected property" under the law of war; or engaged in conduct traditionally triable by military commission (e.g., spying; murder committed while the accused did not meet the requirements of privileged belligerency) even if such conduct does not violate the international law of war.).

[46] Former Legal Advisor to the State Department, Harold Koh voiced concern that the government's efforts to criminalize direct participation in hostilities under the Military Commissions Act "would acknowledge that CIA drone operators were criminals." The relevant language was changed to avoid this problem. C Savage (May 28, 2010) U.N. official to ask U.S. to end C.I.A. drone strikes, N.Y. Times, http://www.nytimes.com/2010/05/28/world/asia/28drones.html?_r=0.

[47] H Koh 2010, The Obama Administration and international law. American Society of International Law, Washington D.C. http://www.state.gov/s/l/releases/remarks/139119.htm. Accessed 24 May 2013 (arguing that individuals who are *part of an armed group* are "belligerents and, therefore, lawful targets under international law.").

[48] Heller 2013, p. 94.

[49] Zenko, supra n. 28, para 3.

[50] Heller 2013, p. 12, citing D Filkins (Sept. 19, 2011) The Journalist and the Spies. The New Yorker. http://www.newyorker.com/reporting/2011/09/19/110919fa_fact_filkins.

[51] Heller 2013, p. 13, citing B Roggio (Apr. 2012) US Predators strike again in southern Yemen. http://www.longwarjournal.org/archives/2012/04/us_predators_strike_35.php.

[52] Additional Protocol I Articles 51(5)(b) & 57; International Committee of the Red Cross (2005) Customary international humanitarian law. Rule 14 Proportionality in Attack. http://www.icrc.org/customary-ihl/eng/docs/v1_rul_rule14.

[53] Ibid.

how to count particular individuals in the balance.[54] For instance, states may differ on how to treat civilians who have directly participated in hostilities but are not doing so at the moment or have acted as voluntary or involuntary shields for militants.

In order to satisfy both discrimination and proportionality requirements, IHL also requires that Parties must undertake precautions to protect civilians.[55] These include taking "constant care [to]...spare the civilian population [and] civilians."[56] Under Additional Protocol I, which the United States has largely accepted as customary international law, states must do everything feasible to ensure that targets are military objectives. Once a military objective has been chosen, states must also "take all feasible precautions in the choice of means and methods of attack" to minimize[e] incidental loss of civilian life..."[57] In order to satisfy these requirements, forces must seek out and act upon relevant information.

Are drone strikes capable of satisfying proportionality and discrimination principles? Even if they are inherently capable of doing so in the abstract, one may also question the actual practice of drone strikes. Compliance with IHL is assessed both by the state's interpretation of the legal framework and its application of that framework to specific facts on the ground. Are U.S. decision makers applying the correct legal tests to determine if proportionality and discrimination are satisfied? Similarly, are U.S. decision makers applying those legal tests to the facts in a reasonable manner? When mistakes are made, what standard governs their categorization? How, if at all, does the Obama administration assess IHL compliance after the fact?

3.3.3 Who May Engage in Drone Strikes?

Another set of questions relate to the personnel conducting the drone strikes. IHL provides the privilege of belligerency to those who wear uniforms, distinctive signs recognizable at a distance, carry arms openly, and participate in an organization that follows the laws and customs of war.[58] Such individuals may be targeted in an international armed conflict, and if captured, these combatants receive prisoner of war status and may not be tried simply for participating in armed conflict. In contrast, as explained above, civilians are immune from attack unless

---

[54] McNeal 2013, p. 77.

[55] International Committee of the Red Cross (2005) Customary international humanitarian law. Rule 15 Precautions in attack. http://www.icrc.org/customary-ihl/eng/docs/v1_cha_chapter5_rule15#Fn_64_20.

[56] Additional Protocol I, Article 57(2).

[57] The feasibility requirement has been interpreted to mean "those measures that are practicable or practically possible, taking into account all circumstances ruling at the time." International Committee of the Red Cross 2005, Rule 15, para 9.

[58] Additional Protocol I, Articles 51(5)(b), 57.

they directly participate in hostilities.[59] In addition, captured civilians who take a direct part may be tried under domestic law for their unlawful activities.[60]

The involvement of the CIA in drone strikes raises a host of legal questions. Though the administration has not directly confirmed the exact nature of the CIA's role in any individual strike, it seems that CIA agents have supplied targeting data as well as armed and piloted drones in places like Afghanistan and Pakistan.[61] Are these particular strikes part of an armed conflict and if so, should the CIA participants be viewed as civilians directly participating in hostilities? Should lawfulness turn on whether CIA operatives wear uniforms? Is a drone itself an openly carried arm or would agents have to do something else to meet the "carry arms openly" requirement? If they are individuals with continuous combatant functions, are CIA operatives unlawfully employing human shields by returning to their civilian dwellings after piloting and killings?[62] When, if it all, can they be targeted by opposing forces? Can they be prosecuted under the domestic laws where such strikes occur?

For those who believe the IHL framework applies, commentators are divided as to whether CIA operatives act as civilians directly participating in hostilities or as lawful combatants with the respective burdens and privileges under the Geneva Conventions. Under the first view, the CIA is a civilian organization which has not been incorporated into the armed forces[63] and operatives are unlikely to have received any IHL training.[64] Accordingly, CIA operatives with the requisite involvement in the drone program are civilians who may be targeted for such time

59 Additional Protocol I, Article 51(3).

60 Schmitt 2004.

61 G Solis (Mar. 1, 2010) CIA Drone Attacks Produce America's Own Unlawful Combatants, Wash. Post. http://www.washingtonpost.com/wpdyn/content/article/2010/03/1/AR2010031103653.html; Alston 2011, pp. 284–285.

62 A Mukharji (Mar. 28, 2013) Drone operators: soldiers or civilians? International law does not allow combatants to kill in the morning and enjoy dinner with their children later in the evening. The Atlantic, paras 6–8.

63 Vogel 2010–2011, p. 134 ("Even under a liberal reading of Article 4 from GC III, the CIA would not meet the requirements of lawful belligerency as a militia or volunteer corps because, while they do report to a responsible chain of command (albeit not always a military chain of command), as a group they do not wear uniforms or otherwise distinguish themselves, nor do they carry their arms openly"); Barnidge 2012, p. 445 (relying on Protocol I Article 43(3)).

64 Sterio 2012, p. 208 (noting that "CIA operatives are not trained in the use of force and do not face court-martial or other disciplinary action."); McChrystal Apologizes as Airstrike Kills Dozens in Afghanistan (Feb. 22, 2010) http://www.cnn.com/2010/WORLD/asiapcf/02/22/afghanistan.civilian.strike/index.html. (noting the transparency of military policy and constraints placed on operations by the military chain of command, as compared to the secrecy of the CIA program); M O'Connell, 2010, Rise of Drones II: Unmanned Systems and the Future of Warfare: Hearing before the U.S. House Subcommittee on National Security and Foreign Affairs, 111th Cong. 2 p. 6 (written testimony of Mary Ellen O'Connell, Professor, University of Notre Dame Law School). http://oversight.house.gov/images/stories/subcommittees/NS-Subcommittee/4.2810-DronesII/OConnellStatement.pdf. (noting that the CIA is not trained in the law of war and implying that the constraints of IHL are not considered by CIA when conducting strikes).

as they directly participate in hostilities.[65] Their physical assets, such as the buildings where they engage in targeting or their weapon supplies, may also be lawfully targeted.[66] Many who hold this view do not believe the CIA's actions violate IHL per se as nothing in IHL either "prohibits or privileges" civilian participation.[67] That said, they believe CIA operatives may be subject to prosecution under the domestic law of the country where the targeted killing takes place.[68]

Under the opposing view, CIA operatives should be viewed as lawful combatants.[69] These commentators suggest that while the CIA may not have as detailed a chain of command as the military, President Obama serves as the operatives' commander. While CIA operatives do not currently wear insignia, such uniform requirements could easily be met. Moreover, under a functional view of IHL, the lack of uniform is irrelevant since those involved with drone operation in the United States do not need to distinguish themselves from the civilian population abroad.[70] And although the CIA's role in drone strikes is unconfirmed, the widespread knowledge as to their involvement might suffice as evidence of carrying their arms openly. Under such a view, IHL authorizes their activities and CIA operatives would be both targetable and afforded POW protections.

---

[65] Solis supra n. 61 (concluding "CIA agents are...like the fighters they target, unlawful combatants...[T]hey are fighters without uniforms or insignia, directly participating in hostilities, employing armed force contrary to the laws and customs of war. Even if they are sitting in Langley, the CIA pilots are civilians violating the requirement of distinction, a core concept of armed conflict, as they directly participate in hostilities...[and as such, are] legitimate targets whenever and wherever they may be found..."); Barnidge 2012, p. 445 (relying on Protocol I Article 51(3), Protocol II Article 13(3), ICRC Customary International Humanitarian Law Rule 6); Alston Report 2010, supra n. 21, para 71 (because they are "directly participating in hostilities" by conducting targeted killings, intelligence personnel may themselves be targeted and killed).

[66] Barnidge 2012, p. 445 (concluding the extensive nature of the CIA drone program means that the CIA's physical assets do indeed make an 'effective contribution to military action'...and, as such, could lawfully be targeted.").

[67] Barnidge 2012, p. 445; Alston Report 2010, supra n. 21, para 71; Sterio 2012, p. 212.

[68] Alston Report 2010, supra n. 21 (adding they could also be prosecuted for violations of applicable US law); Vogel 2010–2011 p. 445. *But see* Radsan and Murphy (2011–2012), p. 445 (arguing that other nations' domestic laws are irrelevant to US drone operators: "as long as the President and his agents do not fall into the jurisdictional grasp of a nation in which drone strikes occur, that nation's laws lack force for U.S. operators.").

[69] See generally Radsan and Murphy (2011–2012), p. 458 (citing N Melzer 2008, at p. 317, who observes that the "notion of 'armed forces'" as used in the Additional Protocols "remains functionally wide enough to include police forces, intelligence agents, and border guards assuming combat function for the States, without formally qualifying as members of its armed forces under domestic law.").

[70] More problematically, they also do not distinguish themselves from the purely civilian population domestically either.

3.4 Using Courts to Seek Transparency and Accountability

Although U.S. administrations have used drones since the early 2000s, they did not receive extensive congressional, judicial, or public scrutiny until Obama accelerated the rate of drone strikes in the late 2000s.[71] One might attribute this relative inattention to some combination of: the perceived national security benefits of such killings, a zero risk to those operating drone aircraft, the lack of information surrounding the program, and disinterest in the imposition of harm upon foreigners far away. Yet many now decry the lack of transparency and accountability as problematic from both a domestic and international perspective.[72] The absence of official information decreases the legitimacy of the Obama administration's counterterrorism strategy with domestic constituencies, allies needed for cooperation, and the foreign populations of whom the U.S. wishes to win their hearts and minds. The dearth of detailed information also prevents any meaningful outside assessment of IHL compliance. Courts, congress, and the public at large simply lack the legal and factual information to have any meaningful sense of whether norms of proportionality and discrimination are being satisfied or even whether the executive branch has sufficient accountability mechanisms for those purposes.

Over time, various groups have called on the Obama administration to provide more transparency and more accountability. This should be attributed to a number of factors such as the distance in time away from 9/11, the significant expansion of the drone program and its rising death toll, and probably most importantly, the intentional and unintentional killings of American citizens. In seeking answers about the government's IHL compliance, civil rights groups, human rights groups, and journalists have invoked courts in a number of ways.[73]

The federal judiciary usually steers clear of resolving IHL questions. While the Supreme Court has spoken to the existence of an armed conflict in Afghanistan and how to conduct the status determination of those being detained, U.S. courts have shied away from substantive rulings in targeting cases. For instance, in a conventional strike case *El-Shifa*, the Second Circuit declined to reach the merits on political question grounds.[74] It concluded that targeting decisions must be resolved by the political branches. This raises the questions of whether courts will choose to speak to IHL issues and why advocates choose courts as a venue for their arguments.

The current wave of lawsuits comes in the two forms detailed below. Some actors seek a substantive ruling from the courts as to whether a conflict exists and

---

[71] V Hanson 2013, Game of drones. Hoover Institution J. http://www.hoover.org/publications/defining-ideas/article/143451. Accessed 24 May 2013.

[72] Alston 2011, p. 283.

[73] D Ingram (May 23, 2013) Lawsuits seek more than U.S. acknowledgment of drone killings. Chicago Tribune. http://articles.chicagotribune.com/2013-05-23/news/sns-rt-us-usa-justice-drone-lawsuitsbre94m1b5-20130523_1_drone-attacks-drone-program-drone-killings.

[74] *El-Shifa Pharmaceuticals*, 607 F.3d at 849.

IHL has been properly applied.[75] These suits seek remedies such as damages and injunctions.[76] Others simply seek access to information that the government will not release in the absence of judicial intervention.[77] This section begins with a brief description of the Israeli Targeted Killings case as a possible model for an active judiciary willing to wrestle with the application and interpretation of IHL.

Then, this section moves to introduce the most notable of these U.S. lawsuits and where they currently stand. In assessing the cases described below, I posit at least four reasons why individuals might employ the courts. First, and most aggressively, they may hope that a court disgusted with the lack of transparency and accountability will decide to substantively intervene as the Supreme Court did in the trio of *Hamdi*, *Hamdan*, and *Boumediene*.[78] Like with *Hamdi* and *Hamdan*,[79] advocates may hope that tying their concerns to constitutional questions regarding citizens will make the court more likely to intervene. Second, they may believe that the lawsuit will produce useful government information that can create the opportunity for public accountability. Third, they may use lawsuits as a platform from which to seek attention and publicity. Lawsuit filings and rulings create opportunities for media coverage that may be difficult to generate in the absence of high profile events. Last, and relatedly, the lawsuits provide a narrative from which advocates can frame their approach to the application and interpretation of IHL. This forum constitutes a venue in which advocates can elucidate their arguments and creates a story that runs contrary to the executive branch's national security narrative.

3.4.1 Israel as Substantive Example

Like the United States, Israel developed a legal framework for the use of targeted killings against terrorists.[80] Also like the United States, Israel had to determine whether and how to apply the body of IHL in this framework. By way of background, in 2000, disgruntled Palestinians had killed over 900 Israelis and wounded thousands during the second intifada.[81] Israel described the situation as "closer to war than peace," and the government adopted rules of engagement that allowed use of force beyond self-defense permitted in human rights and law enforcement

[75] See e.g. *Al-Aulaqi v. Panetta* (D.D.C.) No. 1:12 CV 01192 FMC.

[76] See e.g. Complaint for Declaratory and Injunctive Relief, *Al-Aulaqi v. Obama*, 727 F. Supp. 2d 1 (D.D.C. 2010)(No. 1:10-cv-01469), 2010 WL 3478666, p 11; Complaint, *Al-Aulaqi v. Panetta* (D.D.C.) No. 1:12 CV 01192 RMC, p. 16.

[77] See e.g. *Al-Aulaqi v. Obama*, 727 F. Supp. 2d at 1.

[78] *Boumediene* 553 U.S. at 723 (2008); *Hamdan*, 548 U.S at 631; *Hamdi*, 542 U.S at 533.

[79] *Hamdan*, 548 U.S. at 575; *Hamdi*, 542 U.S. at 511.

[80] See Targeted Killings Case 2006, supra n. 10.

[81] Ibid, para 16.

models.[82] These rules authorized the Israeli Defense Force to employ a 'policy of targeted frustration' against terrorists. This policy authorized security forces to "kill members of terrorist organizations involved in the planning, launching, or execution of terrorist attacks against Israel."[83] By 2002, the Israeli Defense Force's Judge Advocate General clarified the policy by disclosing targeting criteria. These criteria required: (1) well-supported information showing the terrorist will plan or carry out a terror attack in the near future; (2) a prior appeal to the Palestinian Authority calling for the terrorist's arrest; and (3) a failed attempt by IDF troops to arrest the suspect.[84]

After significant use and criticism of this policy,[85] the Public Committee against Torture challenged the legality of Israel's targeted killing policy.[86] The Israeli Supreme Court began its opinion in this case by determining the status of events leading to the policy of targeted killings. The Court concluded that Israel was engaged in an international armed conflict[87] and thus resolved to apply IHL as the relevant body of law.[88] The court next assessed the status of targeted individuals. Adopting a test that requires "combatants" to be commanded by a person responsible for his subordinates, to have a fixed distinctive emblem recognizable at a distance, to carry arms openly, and conduct operations in accordance with the laws and customs of war,[89] the court found that the targeted individuals failed this test.[90] As the court rejected the creation of a new category of "unlawful combatants," for these purposes,[91] it instead accepted IHL's traditional binary approach[92] and thus concluded that if the targeted individuals were not combatants, they were necessarily civilians.[93]

---

[82] D Reisner (Nov. 15, 2000) Press Briefing. IDF Legal Division (http://mfa.gov.il/MFA/Press Room/2000/Pages/Press%20Briefing%20by%20Colonel%20Daniel%20Reisner-%20Head%20 of.aspx).

[83] Targeted Killings Case 2006, supra n. 10, para 2.

[84] G Alon and A Harel (Feb. 4, 2002) IDF Lawyers Set 'Conditions' for Assassination Policy, Haaretz. http://www.haaretz.com/print-edition/news/idf-lawyers-set-conditions-for-assassination-policy-1.53911 (English Edition).

[85] Targeted Killings Case 2006, supra n. 10, para 4. See e.g. Ben-Naftali and Michaeli 2009, p. 256.

[86] Targeted Killings Case 2006, supra n. 10, para 3.

[87] Ibid, paras 16–21 (discussing the significant casualties, the military capabilities of the terrorists, and dismissing the need for state actors on both sides of the conflict).

[88] Ibid, paras 19–20.

[89] Ibid, para 24 (Relying on the definition of combatant from the Hague Regulations and the Geneva Conventions).

[90] Ibid, para 24 (Relying on the definition of combatant from § 3.1 of the Hague Regulations, Article 13 of the First and Second Geneva Conventions, and Article 4 of the Third Geneva Conventions).

[91] Ibid, paras 25–28.

[92] Ibid, paras 26–30.

[93] Ibid, para 26.

The Court next considered whether Israel may target civilians for direct participation in hostilities. It concluded that Additional Protocol I to the Geneva Convention reflects binding customary international law[94] and therefore civilians taking a direct part in hostilities are not protected from attack at such time as they participate. The Court defined hostilities as "acts which by nature and objective are intended to cause damage to the army" or civilians.[95] Noting the lack of consensus in international law regarding "direct participation," the court advocated a case-by-case determination with an expansive understanding of "direct,"[96] and provided signposts for the analysis: a civilian who carries arms, transports combatants (or ammunition) to or from the place where the hostilities are taking place, operates or services weapons which combatants use, or plans operations, regardless of distance from the battlefield, is directly participating; but a civilian providing support (food, shelter, logistic support, medicine, propaganda) is not.[97] Likewise, the Court found no international consensus regarding the length of time direct participation lasts once triggered, and created a case-by-case analysis that protects the sporadic or one-time participant while allowing the systematic but noncontinuous participant to be targeted, even while not actively participating.[98]

The Court concluded by limiting the state's ability to engage in targeting killings with four guiding principles. Israel may only engage in targeted killings if (a) it possesses well-based information; (b) no less harmful means may be employed without great risk to soldiers; (c) it performs an after the fact independent, thorough investigation regarding the precision of the identification of the target and the circumstances of the attack; and (d) collateral damage is anticipated to be proportionate. If these guidelines are satisfied, a civilian directly participating in hostilities forfeits his immunity from attack and if captured, may not claim prisoner of war status.[99]

While commentators have criticized the case on numerous grounds,[100] it possesses the virtue of providing a clear statement of the applicable rules, its reasoning, and the supporting legal analysis upon which it relies. Some in the United

[94] Ibid, para 30.

[95] Ibid, para 33.

[96] Ibid, para 34.

[97] Ibid, para 34.

[98] Ibid, para 40 (attempting to find a balance between international law's protection of civilians and creating a "revolving door" of immunity for hostiles at all times except when actually firing a weapon).

[99] Ibid, para 31.

[100] Schondorf 2007, pp. 303–306 (rejecting the classification of the conflict as international); Bradley 2009, pp. 403–405 (rejecting the need for a binary classification system and urging consideration of the unlawful combatant category); Eichensehr 2007, pp. 1878–1879 (noting that the expansive definition of direct participation may lead to unnecessary targeted killings and increased collateral damage); Blum and Heymann 2010, p. 159 (expressing concerns about the merger of the Human Rights Law/Law enforcement model with IHL).

States may have even seen the case as evidence that courts may and should actively intervene in the practice of targeted killing.[101]

3.4.2 *Current Judicial Activity*

3.4.2.1 Al-Aulaqi v Obama

In early 2010, the Obama administration placed its first American citizen, Anwar al-Aulaqi,[102] on a list of terrorists approved for targeted killing.[103] Some believed al-Aulaqi played a key operational role in terrorist activities against the United States.[104] Others viewed him as a very powerful propagandist, but rejected his classification as a civilian directly participating in hostilities.[105] At the time of his listing, the government was reluctant to disclose information demonstrating al-Aulaqi's exact roles, citing concerns about intelligence gathering.[106]

Although all targeted killings during the war on terror raise some IHL questions, the listing of an American citizen raised an additional set of questions about the interaction of citizenship, constitutional law, and IHL. Questions that few had raised previously were now being asked more vigorously with special attention to whether citizenship ought to change the answers. These questions included: How and under what authority did the government target individuals outside of Afghanistan? What legal standards guide the decision to list? What evidentiary standards does the government use to determine if the legal standards are satisfied? Who reviews the determinations and how frequently? Does the listed individual have an opportunity to challenge his placement? Does the executive possess sole discretion on these decisions or is it subject to Congressional or judicial oversight?

Al-Aulaqi's father contacted the American Civil Liberties Union (ACLU) and the Center for Constitutional Rights (CCR) to file suit on his son's behalf.

---

[101] F Mohamed (Feb. 6, 2013) The targeted killing memo- What the United States could learn from Israel. Huffington Post. http://www.huffingtonpost.com/feisal-g-mohamed/the-targeted-killing-memo_b_2634078.html. (lauding the case's creation of mandatory after action review).

[102] Anwar al-Aulaqi is also known as Anwar al-Alwaki. Commentators differ on the translation of al-Aulaqi's name. For consistency's sake, this article will employ the same spelling that the al-Aulaqi family used in filing the litigation.

[103] See *Al-Aulaqi v. Obama*, 727 F. Supp. 2d at 11.

[104] C Savage (Oct. 9, 2011) Secret U.S. memo made legal case to kill a citizen. N.Y. Times. http://www.nytimes.com/2011/10/09/world/middleeast/secret-us-memo-made-legal-case-to-kill-a-citizen.html?pagewanted=all (hereafter "Savage 2011").

[105] Foreman 2013, p. 938.

[106] See ACLU (2010) ACLU Seeks Information On Predator Drones Program, http://www.aclu.org/national-security/aclu-seeks-information-predator-drone-program. Accessed 9 Aug 2013.

Although the suit largely focused on the constitutional questions,[107] it did ask for a court to speak on IHL controversies. For instance, the ACLU and CCR's complaint alleged that the U.S. was not at war with Yemen or within its boundaries, and thus IHL did not govern targeted killings in those locations.[108] A supporting memo further outlined the legal analysis for why the ACLU believed no non-international armed conflict existed with al-Qaeda outside of Afghanistan.[109] The complaint also sought an injunction to force the government to "disclose standards under which it determines whether U.S. citizens can be targeted for death" which may include the application of IHL.[110]

The government's response brief and supporting memoranda spoke to IHL issues in fairly conclusory ways. The government relied on the President's Commander in Chief powers to target individuals and articulated dual authority under both the armed conflict outlined in the Congressional Authorization to Use Military Force (AUMF) and also the inherent right to self-defense.[111] The government noted its determinations that al-Aulaqi played an operational role in Al Qaida in the Arabian Peninsula (AQAP) and that AQAP was covered by the AUMF, thus triggering the application of IHL, though it provided little detail justifying its conclusions.[112]

The government strongly resisted judicial oversight of executive and congressional answers to IHL questions. For instance, it posited that courts had no authority and no competence in the targeted killing context to determine "whether and in what circumstances the U.S. armed conflict with al Qaeda might extend beyond the borders of Iraq and Afghanistan."[113] The government also rejected the need for disclosure of its listing processes, but did not rely heavily on its assertion of the state secrets privilege.[114]

Unsurprisingly, the ACLU and CCR defended the judiciary's authority and competence to use IHL to resolve statutory construction issues and determine the legality of targeted killings. They noted that courts already used IHL to assess the existence and nature of an armed conflict in the detention setting and other courts

---

[107] J Ku (Aug. 31, 2010) ACLU sues Obama Administration over targeted killings of U.S. citizens. http://opiniojuris.org/2010/08/31/aclu-sues-obama-administration-over-targeted-killings-of-us-citizens.

[108] Complaint for Declaratory and Injunctive Relief, *al-Aulaqi v. Obama*, 727 F. Supp. 2d (D.D.C. 2010)(No. 10-cv-01469), 2010 WL 347866, paras 3–4.

[109] Memorandum in Support of Plaintiff's Motion, *al-Aulaqi v. Obama*, 727 F. Supp. 2d 1 (D.D.C. 2010) (No. 10-cv-101469), 2010 WL 3555385 (hereafter Memorandum in Support of Plaintiff's Motion, *al-Aulaqi*).

[110] Ibid, p. 2.

[111] Memorandum in Opposition to Plaintiff's Motion, *al-Aulaqi v. Obama*, 727 F. Supp. 2d (D.D.C. 2010)(No. 10-cv-101469), 2010 WL 3863135, pp. 4–5.

[112] Ibid, p. 8.

[113] Ibid, p. 22.

[114] Ibid, pp. 1, 43.

have spoken to similar questions in a variety of settings.[115] The ACLU and CCR also used their responses as an opportunity to speak to the facts on the ground and explain why AQAP ought not be viewed as part of an armed conflict either in Yemen or as an affiliate, associated force, or co-belligerent with al-Qaeda.[116]

In dismissing the case, the district court largely accepted the government's position on the non-justiciability of IHL questions. For instance, it decried any role in resolving questions like whether AQAP is covered by the AUMF for targeting purposes.[117] The court relied on *El-Shifa*'s reasoning to emphasize that courts are in no position to elucidate standards for presidential evaluations of military intelligence.[118] Nor was it sympathetic to the possibility of an injunction enforced by an after-the-fact contempt ruling or the provision of damages, as it did not wish to second guess presidential decision-making in this area.

Although this specific case has drawn to a close, first with the ACLU and the CCR abandoning their opportunity for an appeal, and second with al-Aulaqi's death, these IHL questions remain important ones. The al-Aulaqi court suggests significant judicial hostility to before the fact assessments and after the fact review of targeted killings. It voiced significant skepticism of judicial assessment of IHL application to domestic authorizations. From a merits perspective, this ruling was a major loss. Yet, as explained below, the lawsuit itself may have served other goals.

3.4.2.2 Al-Aulaqi v Panetta

After the government used a drone strike in Yemen to kill Anwar al-Aulaqi, the ACLU and CCR filed a second lawsuit alleging that the U.S. government unlawfully killed three U.S. citizens, Anwar Al-Aualqi, his minor son Abdulrahaman al-Aulaqi, and alleged AQAP propagandist Samir Khan.[119] Like the first suit, the complaint asserts that IHL governs some targeted killings, like those in Afghanistan and Iraq, but remains inapplicable to those in Yemen, Somalia, Pakistan, Sudan, and the Philippines.[120]

In contrast, the complaint also maintains that if the United States was engaged in an armed conflict in Yemen, it violated several major IHL prohibitions. First, the ACLU alleges al-Aulaqi was not directly participating in hostilities and thus not a legitimate target.[121] Second, the ACLU alleges that the government's failure to meet the requirements of distinction and proportionality resulted in Samir Khan

---

[115] Memorandum in Support of Plaintiff's Motion, *al-Aulaqi*, p. 37.

[116] Ibid.

[117] *Al-Aulaqi v. Obama*, 727 F. Supp. 2d at 9.

[118] Ibid at 45.

[119] Complaint, *al-Aulaqi v. Panetta*, paras 1–6.

[120] Ibid, paras 1, 4.

[121] Ibid, para 4.

and Abdulrahaman al-Aulaqi's deaths.[122] The complaint laments the "incomplete and inconsistent explanations of the legal standards that govern the placement of U.S. citizens on the kill lists."[123] The plaintiffs sought monetary damages for constitutional violations under the Fourth and Fifth Amendment.[124]

The government's motion to dismiss reiterated its stance on non-justiciability. It suggested courts are ill suited to make any determinations relating to issues surrounding the executive's entitlement to strike enemy forces abroad.[125] Relying again on *El-Shifa*, the government argued the court was not able to "assess the merits of the President's (alleged) decision to launch an attack on a foreign target."[126] Moreover, the government argued that injecting courts into the decision-making process would disrupt military discipline.[127] Subordinates might question whether orders from superiors would be second guessed by courts. As to the issue of compensation, the government argued that implied civil damages against federal officials is inappropriate in the wartime context for actions taken on the battlefield as it would risk "fettering commanders in their operations."[128]

In April 2014 the district court concluded the case was justiciable, but concluded neither Samir Khan's nor Abdulraham al-Aulaqi's Fourth or Fifth Amendment claims should survive summary judgment. It further determined that no remedy existed for any potential deprivation of Anwar al-Aulaqi's due process rights emphasizing "[i]n this delicate area of warmaking, national security, and foreign relations, the judiciary has an exceedingly limited role."

3.4.2.3 FOIA Lawsuits

In addition to suits seeking court rulings on substantive IHL issues, several groups have asked courts to grant FOIA requests regarding information on drone strikes. At least three different high-profile lawsuits currently seek some combination of: Office of Legal Counsel (OLC) opinions and memos regarding the legal status of targeted killing of people suspected of ties to terrorist groups,[129] OLC opinions and memos analyzing the legality of targeting a United States citizen,[130] records

---

[122] Ibid, para 5.

[123] Ibid, paras 41, 42.

[124] Id at Prayer for Relief.

[125] See *Al-Aulaqi*, p. 6.

[126] Ibid, p. 10.

[127] Motion to Dismiss, *al-Aulaqi v. Panetta*, pp. 25–26.

[128] Ibid, p. 24.

[129] J King, 2011, DOJ must explain missile attacks on U.S. citizens abroad. http://www.nacdl.org/NewsReleases.aspx?id=22748. Accessed 24 May 2013.

[130] First Amendment Coalition (2012) FAC sues US for memo on "lethal targeting" of al Qaeda figure (& US citizen) al-Awlaki, killed in 2010 drone strike. http://firstamendmentcoalition.org/2012/02/fac-sues-us-for-memo-on-lethal-targeting-of-al-qaeda-figure-us-citizen-al-awlaki-killed-in-2010-drone-strike/.

on specific targets like al-Aulaqi,[131] and records on "the selection of human targets; civilian casualties; post-strike assessments; limits to the use of drones; the agency of government or branch of the military involved",[132] and records on the supervision, oversight, discipline, or training of drone operators and those involved in targeting decisions, and more."[133]

The various agencies have generally not produced the requested documents and many have issued a so-called "Glomar response" which neither confirms nor denies the existence of such documents.[134] In some instances, this Glomar response has led to subsequent litigation in the federal courts. In an ACLU case, Judge Collyer of the D.C. District court granted summary judgment for the CIA concluding that even the mere acknowledgement of such records could "reveal information on the CIA's internal structure and its capabilities and potential interests and involvement in/ operation of the drone program" and could lead to the unauthorized disclosure of intelligence sources and/or methods.[135] Judge Collyer concluded that the CIA had not publically acknowledged any role or interest in a drone strike program nor the existence of any CIA records.[136] In March 2013, however, the D.C. Court of Appeals rejected the CIA's neither confirm nor deny response because top government officials, like Obama, had subsequently acknowledged drone strikes.[137] With this appellate decision, the Court did not guarantee the release of requested documents, but the CIA must provide some disclosure regarding the documents it possesses. This may come in the form of merely acknowledging the existence of documents or listing and describing said documents.

A second notable set of FOIA requests asked for access to State department embassy cables.[138] WikiLeaks, an online group which publicizes classified information, initially released these cables, some of which included communications regarding drone use.[139] The government initially failed to respond to the ACLU's FOIA request, prompting a lawsuit. The State Department then released redacted portions of 11 of the 23 requested cables.[140] The ACLU continued to press for the

---

[131] Judicial Watch (June 7, 2012) Judicial Watch sues Obama State Department, FBI and CIA for records regarding Anwar al-Awlaki, American citizen killed by CIA-led drone attack in September 2011. http://www.judicialwatch.org/press-room/press-releases/judicial-watch-sues-obama-state-department-fbi-and-cia-for-records-regarding-anwar-al-awlaki-american-citizen-killed-by-cia-led-drone-attack-in-september-2011/.

[132] *ACLU v. Dep't of Justice*, 808 F. Supp. 2d 280 (D.D.C. 2011).

[133] Ibid, p. 298.

[134] See e.g., *ACLU v. CIA*, 710 F.3d 422 (D.D.C. 2013); *Moore v. CIA*, 666 F.3d 1330, (D.C. Cir. 2011).

[135] *ACLU v. CIA*, 710 F.3d at 289, 93.

[136] *ACLU v. Dep't of Justice*, 808 F. Supp. 2d at 296–297.

[137] *ACLU v. CIA*, 710 F.3d at 429–430.

[138] See generally ACLU (2012) *ACLU v. Department of State*. http://www.aclu.org/national-security/aclu-v-department-state. Accessed 23 July 2012.

[139] Ibid.

[140] Ibid; *ACLU v. Dep't of State*, 878 F. Supp. 2d 215, 219 (D.D.C. 2012).

full cables, but a district court refused concluding that official disclosure "reasonably could be expected to result in damage to the national security."[141]

In addition to the ongoing lawsuits, several FOIA requests may lead to future litigation. One particularly notable request regards a drone strike in the al-Majalah region of Yemen. During the December 2009 strike on an al-Qaeda camp, cruise missiles delivering cluster bombs are alleged to have killed 14 members of al-Qaeda as well as 41 civilians including 20 children.[142] Although Yemen initially took credit for the attack, many believe the United States itself engaged in the strike.[143] The ACLU and CCR seek to learn the legal and factual basis for the strike as well as measures taken to limit collateral damage, and any efforts to provide compensation.[144] Thus far, none of the eight relevant agencies have responded.

3.5 Movement Toward Oversight and Accountability

These various lawsuits are part of a larger movement pressing for greater transparency and accountability. These lawsuits, particularly the ones regarding al-Aulaqi, provided a platform for media attention to the issue.[145] Many, including the editorial pages of major newspapers,[146] the ACLU, scholars,[147] politicians, high ranking UN Special Rapporteurs,[148] and even former officials of the Obama administration[149] have called for the declassification of targeted killing related memos and an ensuing public debate over their contents. Other noteworthy events regarding drone strike accountability and transparency include the U.N. Special

141 *ACLU v. Dep't of State*, 878 F. Supp. 2d at 222.

142 Center for Constitutional Rights (2012) Al-Majalah Freedom of Information Act Request, http://ccrjustice.org/files/FOIA%20request.pdf.

143 Ibid.

144 Ibid.

145 See e.g. D Romero and V Warren (Sept. 9, 2010) Sentencing terrorisms suspects to death-without trial. Wash. Post. http://www.washingtonpost.com/wp-dyn/content/article/2010/09/02/AR2010090204463.html.

146 See e.g. Editorial Board (Mar. 5, 2012) It's time to release the drone memos. Wash. Post. http://articles.washingtonpost.com/2012-03-05/opinions/35446598_1_drone-strikes-al-awlaki-drone-policy; Editorial Desk (7 March 2012) Death by drone rules. LA Times. http://articles.latimes.com/2012/mar/07/opinion/la-ed-holder-20120307.

147 J Goldsmith (Oct. 3, 2011) Release the al-Aulaqi OLC opinion, or its reasoning. Lawfare. http://www.lawfareblog.com/2011/10/release-the-al-aulaqi-olc-opinion-or-its-reasoning/.

148 J Burns (Jan. 25, 2013) U.N. panel to investigate rise in drone strikes. NY Times. http://www.nytimes.com/2013/01/25/world/europe/un-panel-to-investigate-rise-in-drone-strikes.html.

149 J Bellinger (Oct. 2, 2011) Obama's drone danger. Wash. Post. http://www.washingtonpost.com/opinions/will-drone-strikes-become-obamas-guantanamo/2011/09/30/gIQA0ReIGL_story.html.

Rapporteur's condemnation of U.S. targeted killings,[150] the letter from several members of Congress asking for more information on signature strikes,[151] Senator Rand Paul's filibuster of John Brennan's appointment as CIA director,[152] and recent Congressional hearings on drone strikes.[153] As mentioned earlier, another motivating factor for calls to action might be the public availability of drone strike aggregators.[154]

As part and parcel of this growing demand for transparency and accountability, several high profile members of Congress have now called for more significant oversight of the executive branch.[155] Even former administration officials such as Harold Koh (former head State Department attorney), Anne-Marie Slaughter (former director of policy planning at State Department)[156] and Jeh Johnson (former general counsel of the Defense Department)[157] have echoed these suggestions. This section details the two most prominent suggestions for an enhanced role for the judiciary branch: the creation of a drone court and judicially enforcement right to damages for unlawful killings.

---

[150] B Emmerson 2012, Press Release Concerning the Launch of an Inquiry into the Civilian Impact, and Human Rights Implications of the Use of Drones and other Forms of Targeted Killings for the Purpose of Counter-Terrorism. http://www.foreignpolicy.com/files/fp_uploaded_documents/130124_SRCTBenEmeersonQCStatement.pdf. Accessed 20 May 2013. (hereafter Emmerson 2012).

[151] J Herb (June 13, 2012) Lawmakers want legal justification for drone strikes, The Hill, http://thehill.com/blogs/defcon-hill/operations/232523-lawmakers-want-legal-justification-for-drone-strikes.

[152] E O'Keefe and A Blake (Mar. 6, 2013) Rand Paul launches talking filibuster against John Brennan, Wash. Post. http://www.washingtonpost.com/blogs/post-politics/wp/2013/03/06/rand-paul-begins-talking-filibuster-against-john-brennan/.

[153] K Holman 2013, Congress Begins to Weigh In On Drone Strikes Policy, PBS Newshour, http://www.pbs.org/newshour/rundown/2013/04/congress-begins-to-weigh-in-on-drone-strikes-policy.html. Accessed 9 Aug 2013.

[154] Of course, these studies only raise questions about legality, rather than answer them. For instance, we do not know how the U.S. valued the military targets so we do not know if they considered strikes to be proportionate. Similarly, we do not know when civilian deaths were unintentional collateral damage and when they were the result of mistaken intelligence or misapplication of legal standards for legitimate targets.

[155] J Rogin (Mar. 20, 2013) Corker calls for more congressional oversight of drone strikes. Foreign Policy. http://thecable.foreignpolicy.com/posts/2013/03/20/corker_calls_for_more_congressional_oversight_of_drone_strikes.

[156] K DeYoung (Apr. 6, 2013) Drone use remains cloaked despite Obama's promise for transparency. Wash. Post. http://articles.washingtonpost.com/2013-04-06/world/38325214_1_drone-program-u-s-citizen-anwar-strikes (hereafter DeYoung 2013).

[157] J Johnson (2013) A drone court: some pros and cons. Keynote Address at the Center on National Security at Fordham Law School, New York, New York (noting that the lack of transparency puts the government in a "lose-a lose-lose proposition: it fails to officially confirm many of its counterterrorism successes, and fails to officially confirm, deny or clarify unsubstantiated reports of civilian casualties.").

3.5.1 Drone Court

Public officials, political analysts, and others have floated the idea of a drone court.[158] Some evidence suggests the Obama administration itself has considered such proposals.[159] Such a court might be similar to the FIS court created for wiretapping or to specialized courts proposed to execute torture warrants. By way of background, the FIS court is comprised of 11 judges[160] who individually review evidence presented by the government in a high security courtroom.[161] The individuals to be surveilled do not have an opportunity to challenge the warrant and it is not an adversarial process.[162] The judges make the final determination on whether to grant surveillance warrants.[163]

Advocates are currently debating the contours of a possible drone court. Such a court might only review the placement of citizens on a kill list[164] or instead the placement of all individuals outside traditional battlefields. The review process might include considerations such as the individual's status under IHL. A drone court might also consider questions about specific strike operations such as whether the government is acting sufficiently to minimize civilian casualties.[165]

Whether such a court would increase either transparency or accountability is also an open question. While advocates believe the judicial oversight will enhance the decision making process and improve compliance with IHL and domestic law, skeptics worry it only creates the appearance of accountability[166] while providing

---

[158] G Miller (Feb. 8, 2013) Proposal to Give Judges a Role in Drone Strikes Faces Obstacles. Para. 1, Wash. Post. http://articles.washingtonpost.com/2013-02-08/world/36988536_1_drone-program-special-court-judicial-review (hereafter Miller 2013); J Oliphant (Mar. 4, 2013) Vetting the kill list. National Journal. www.nationaljournal.com/magazine/vetting-the-kill-list-20130404 (hereafter "Oliphant 2013"); Shane 2013, A1.

[159] Miller 2013, supra n. 158, para 10.

[160] Foreign Intelligence Surveillance Act, 50 U.S.C. §1803(a)(1).

[161] D Wilber (Mar. 2, 2009) Surveillance Court Quietly Moving. Washington Post. http://articles.washingtonpost.com/2009-03-02/news/36900081_1_chief-judge-secretive-court-federal-courthouse.

[162] Seamon and Gardner 2005.

[163] Federal Judicial Center, History of the Federal Judiciary. http://www.fjc.gov/history/home.nsf/page/courts_special_fisc.html. Accessed 24 Jul 2013.

[164] E Robinson (Feb. 8, 2013) The burden of drones: judge, jury, executioner. Wash. Post, p. A17.

[165] S Vladeck (Mar. 6, 2013) Why I don't mind the Rand Paul filibuster. Lawfare. http://www.lawfareblog.com/2013/03/why-i-dont-mind-the-rand-paul-filibuster/ (hereafter Vladeck 2013b).

[166] Some suggest the President as the Commander in Chief ought to remain the primary responsibility rather than being able to hang blame for failures or mistakes on the courts. G McNeal (Mar. 31, 2013) How a drone court might work, National Public Radio, Weekend Edition http://www.npr.org/2013/03/31/175829140/how-a-drone-court-might-work (hereafter McNeal 2013a).

a rubber stamp of its approval.[167] Other opponents worry instead that searching and protracted judicial review will disrupt effective military operations and often eliminate the narrow window for successful targeted killings.[168]

Such courts may not be particularly likely for a variety of reasons.[169] Congress created the FIS court in the wake of Watergate and other domestic surveillance scandals. Two presidents and the majority of the public supported the FISA legislation. In contrast, it is not clear the public wants judicial oversight as a majority of the current public supports drone strikes and particularly so when conducted against foreign citizens.[170] Even if legislative will existed, the constitutional issues raised by drone courts may be insurmountable.[171] That said, the threat of their creation may still exert a disciplining effect on the Obama administration.

3.5.2 Damage Suits

Law professor Stephen Vladeck has instead suggested legislation to establish a judicial damages regime for unlawful targeted killings.[172] Such legislation would create an express cause of an action for nominal damages arising out of unlawful targeted killings and reform the barriers identified in the al-Aulaqi suits such as the state secrets privilege and sovereign and official immunity doctrines. Unlike a drone court's focus on prospective listing, damage suits use a retrospective view. Vladeck believes that by avoiding prospective rubber stamping, damage suits will not facilitate an increase in targeted killings.[173] Vladeck contends that judges are better suited to such a back end role given their experience in activities like reviewing combatant status for detention and determining after the fact legitimacy in police officer excessive force suits. Although these suits would likely be resolved "under extraordinary secrecy" and thus provide only very limited public transparency, they may enhance accountability beyond the status quo or beyond a drone court. Yet such accountability would be fairly deferential as Vladeck notes

---

[167] S Vladeck (Feb. 10, 2013) Why a 'drone court' won't work but (nominal) damages might. Lawfare. http://www.lawfareblog.com/2013/02/why-a-drone-court-wont-work/ (hereafter Vladeck 2013a). The FISA court has been criticized for its exceedingly low rate of rejections for electronic surveillance and physical searches. Some worry that the courts lack sufficient competence to engage in before-the-fact review and that may lead to excessive deference to experts. McNeal 2013a, supra n. 166, para 4.

[168] Oliphant 2013, supra n. 158; McNeal 2013a, supra n. 166.

[169] Shane 2013, p. A1.

[170] Brown, A and Newport, F (2013) In the U.S., 65 % support drone attacks on terrorists abroad. http://www.gallup.com/poll/161474/support-drone-attacks-terrorists-abroad.aspx?version . Accessed 24 May 2013.

[171] Vladeck 2013a, supra n. 167, para 5.

[172] Vladeck 2013a, supra n. 167, para 2.

[173] Vladeck 2013a, supra n. 167, para 14.

such suits might integrate the executive branch's internal procedures and accord some respect to executive branch after-action reviews.

3.5.3 Other Options

Of course, reforms need not occur through the judicial branch. Scholars and advocates have proposed a variety of other suggested reforms to occur within the executive branch. On the accountability front, Neal Katyal has proposed the executive branch host its own "national security court."[174] On the transparency front, Gregory McNeal has identified several reforms including: a more substantial defense of the existing process it uses to identify targets and evaluate strikes; performance reporting to provide a sense of whether it believes collateral damage has occurred; and publication of targeting criteria.[175] Notably, even administration supporters suggest that more reforms are necessary to legitimize targeted killings conducted via drone strikes.[176]

3.5.4 Quasi-Judicial Activity

In addition to domestic actors using domestic courts, international actors are also promoting accountability and transparency through quasi-judicial activity. In particular, UN Special Rapporteurs have been very active on the issue of drone strikes. As early as 2005, the UN Special Rapporteur Philip Alston began making inquiries about drone strikes.[177] The United States responded that "international human rights law did not apply to the incident; that the laws that did apply could not be addressed by the Special Rapporteur or, implicitly, by the Human Rights Council; and that each State could determine for itself whether any particular

[174] Katyal, N (Feb. 21, 2013) Who will mind the drones. NY Times. http://www.nytimes.com/2013/02/21/opinion/an-executive-branch-drone-court.html. Unlike the drone court proposal, both sides would be staffed by expert lawyers who would switch sides every few years. Rather than use a single article III judge, a panel of the president's highest national security advisers would render decisions. The Congressional intelligence committee would later have the opportunity to review these decisions. Also unlike the regular judicial process Katyal suggests the president should retain the opportunity to overrule this court, but any action taken in contravention of the panel decisions would have to be explained to Congress after the fact. Katyal suggests that this proposal overcomes the limitations on using regular Article III judges unaccustomed to this work and prevents the president from blame shifting to the court.

[175] McNeal 2013a, supra n. 166.

[176] Johnson 2013b, para XX. Jeh Johnson has encouraged the President to "institutionalize his own process, internal to the Executive Branch, to ensure the quality of the decision-making."

[177] P Alston 2007, Report of the Special Rapporteur on Extrajudicial, Summary or Arbitrary Executions, U.N. Doc. A/HRC/4/20/Add.1.

incident could be addressed by the Council."[178] By 2007, Alston submitted this series of letters and a response to the Human Rights Council alleging that U.S. strikes in Pakistan caused civilian casualties.[179] The response requested the United States clarify which body of law it believes governs the targeted killings. The United States gave a little ground by stating that it was in an armed conflict with al-Qaeda governed by IHL, but reiterated that the activities fell outside the Special Rapporteur's mandates.

The Special Rapporteur continued to press for clarification on targeting policies and their real justifications. In 2010, the Special Rapporteur issued a study on targeted killings.[180] This study outlined the basic legal framework that governs target killings. While it acknowledged that IHL can govern drone strikes, it concluded that the right of self-defense had not been triggered in Pakistan because unlike Iraq and Afghanistan, the conflict was not of sufficient intensity.[181] It also concluded that if Article 51 right to self-defense had been triggered, IHL still applies to that use of force.[182] The report expresses skepticism about the ICRC's category of continuous combatant function and suggests targeting of civilians should be purely activity based and when the relevant activity ceases, so too does the ability to target.

Furthermore, like the U.S. lawyers pursuing judicial action, the drafters of the report implore the U.S. to disclose its criteria for civilians directly participating in hostilities. It also provides guidelines to States in implementing a lawful targeted killing program. The report suggests that states must ensure agents have reliable intelligence when making targeting decisions, guidelines on proportionality, processes for aborting faulty attacks, and investigative measures in place to identify unlawful killings.[183] In 2012, Special Rapporteur Christof Heyns lamented the lack of transparency, reiterated these requests, and called for disaggregated tracking of drone related casualties.[184]

UN Special Rapporteur on Counterterrorism and Human Rights Ben Emmerson has recently begun an investigation to "look at the evidence that drone strikes and other forms of remote targeted killings have caused disproportionate civilian casualties…and to make recommendations concerning the duty of States to conduct thorough independent and impartial investigations into such allegations with a view toward securing accountability and reparation."[185] Those conducting the

---

178 Ibid, para 3.

179 P Alston 2007, Statement from the Special Rapporteur on Extrajudicial, Summary, or Arbitrary Executions: UN Expert on Extrajudicial Killings Tells United States War on Terror Could Undermine Human Rights Accountability. Addendum 1. http://www.ohchr.org/EN/NewsEvents/Pages/DisplayNews.aspx?NewsID=1655&LangID=E. Accessed 24 Jul 2013.

180 Alston Report 2010, supra n. 21.

181 Ibid, paras 52–53.

182 Ibid, paras 42–44.

183 Ibid, para 93.

184 Heyns, C (2012) Report of the Special Rapporteur on Extrajudicial, Summary or Arbitrary Executions Addendum 3. UN Doc. A/HRC/20/22.Add.3 para 81.

185 Emmerson 2012, supra n. 150.

study will use 25 case studies to determine whether allegations of unlawful killings trigger international law obligations. This inquiry opened with an evidence gathering phase. During this time, the UN consulted with lawyers, journalists, NGOs, states and made country visits to Pakistan, Yemen, and the Sahel. It has led to statements about sovereignty violations in Pakistan, though no assessment of particular IHL violations.[186] The UN then solicited views and responses from the relevant states. Then, the UN will draft a final report to include conclusions and recommendations to be submitted to the UN general assembly. In addition to the case studies concerning the civilian casualties, the Special Rapporteur is engaged in a number of high level conversations to help forge a consensus on the appropriate legal framework to apply to targeted killings.[187]

While the activities of U.N. Special Rapporteurs may exercise a disciplining effect on the President, they get little direct commentary from the Executive branch. Emmerson himself has acknowledged that the U.S. is skeptical about engagement with the process and believes "nothing good can come out of it."[188] Some have suggested that the U.N.'s real target is the CIA, not the US or targeted killings more generally.[189]

3.6 Executive Response

Rather than capitulate, create, or allow a role for the courts to review the executive branch's approach to targeted killings, the Obama administration has instead used a multitiered strategy of speeches, leaks of legal analysis, and revelations regarding enhanced executive and congressional oversight to demonstrate its commitment to IHL. Early in Obama's first term, the President took only minimal efforts to assure public audiences that he was acting lawfully. As plaintiffs' advocates, the media, and members of Congress intensified their call for greater transparency,[190] administration officials provided significantly more legal detail through public speeches and unofficial leaks and finally formally acknowledging the drone program.[191]

---

186 B Emmerson 2013b, Statement of the Special Rapporteur Following Meetings in Pakistan. http:www.ohchr.org/EN/NewsEvents/Pages/DisplayNews.aspx?NewsID=13146&LangID=E.

187 Emmerson 2012, supra n. 150.

188 Emmerson 2013a, supra n. 38, 13:30.

189 J Goldsmith (Feb. 9, 2013) The Meaning of the U.N. Special Rapporteur's Endorsement of Brennan for CIA Director. Lawfare. http://www.lawfareblog.com/2013/02/the-meaning-of-the-u-n-special-rapporteurs-endorsement-of-brennan-for-cia-director.

190 Vladeck 2013b, supra n. 165, para 4.

191 J Gerstein (Feb. 2013) Official memo justifying drone strikes leaks. Politico. http://www.politico.com/blogs/under-the-radar/2013/02/official-memo-justifying-drone-strikes-leaks-156106.html; Miller, G (Jul. 25, 2012) Brennan speech is first Obama acknowledgment of use of armed drones. Wash. Post. http://articles.washingtonpost.com/2012-04-30/world/35452340_1_drone-strikes-drone-program-brennan-speech.

In addition to disseminating this increased information, the Obama administration has taken some actions to enhance both internal and Congressional oversight. This section discusses what is known about the Congressional role in drone strokes, the use of the National Counter Terrorism Center to institutionalize targeted killing practices, and the possible transfer of strike authority away from the CIA. This section concludes by discussing the role of President Obama's 2013 discussions of drone policy and Presidential Policy guidance in the transparency ecosystem.

3.6.1 Speeches

The Obama administration has largely controlled the information flow about the drone program by pursuing a strategy of framework speeches and leaks while asking courts to stay on the sidelines. Under the early Obama administration (2008–2009), the President was fairly quiet on targeted killings and did not acknowledge the U.S. role in drone strikes,[192] while he simultaneously made rhetorical appeals to transparency and accountability in the war on terror.[193] Some of his early public addresses directly acknowledged the need for accountability in the IHL context.[194] Yet he provided no detail as to how the U.S. was upholding that role in regard to targeted killings. In contrast, by 2010, the Obama administration deployed high level executive branch officials to lay out a basic legal framework for targeted killings. While this set of speeches provided substantially more guidance to the administration's approach, this framework maintained the administration's opacity as to the drone strikes themselves. Legal Adviser to the Department of State Harold Koh started sketching out the administration's approach in a March 2010 speech to the American Society of International Law.[195] He foregrounded the details with a clear statement of the importance of IHL compliance and IHL's application to "lethal operations conducted with the use of

---

[192] B Obama 2009, Remarks on national security, para 10, The National Archives, Washington D.C.

[193] For example, in May 2009, Obama promised "whenever possible, my administration will make all information available to the American people so that they can make informed judgments and hold us accountable… Whenever we cannot release certain information to the public for valid national security reasons, I will insist that there is oversight of my actions—by Congress or by the courts." He pledged reforms to the classification system and to the invocation of the state secrets privilege. B Obama 2009, Address to the nation on the way forward in Afghanistan and Pakistan, para 55, United States Military Academy at West Point.

[194] For instance, at his December 2009 Nobel Prize Lecture, Obama referenced the importance of the Geneva Conventions and the need for the U.S. to be a standard bearer in upholding them. B Obama, A just and lasting peace. The 2009 Nobel Peace Prize Lecture, para 30, Oslo, Norway.

[195] Koh 2010, para III, B, 1, b. He emphasized that IHL principles "are implemented rigorously throughout the planning and execution of lethal operations to ensure that such operations are conducted in accordance with all applicable law."

unmanned aerial vehicles." He distinguished the targeting of leaders of enemy forces as legitimate because "individuals who are part of such an armed group are belligerents and, therefore, lawful targets under international law." This first speech also emphasized the importance of distinction and proportionality in keeping collateral damage to a minimum. It embraced the application of IHL principles, but studiously avoided any discussion of how the administration applies those rules in specific cases.

After interested groups filed both damages suits and FOIA requests to gather more information and challenge the government's assertion of compliance, Obama officials began to flesh out the legal framework a bit more. Koh began with the May 2011 Opinio Juris blogpost applying the framework to the Osama bin Laden raid.[196] In September 2011, then Deputy National Security Advisor for Homeland Security and Counterterrorism John Brennan provided a more in-depth view on the specific IHL question regarding the legitimacy of force outside of traditional battlefields.[197]

Jeh C. Johnson, the General Counsel in the Department of Defense, also gave a series of speeches looking at the IHL question of who counts as a legitimate target. He rejected any inherent distinction between U.S. citizens and noncitizens as to their position as "valid military objectives." Rather, he concluded that so-called lone wolves in the United States ought not be dealt with militarily,[198] while describing who would count as targetable associated forces with al-Qaeda under the AUMF.[199] He clarified that such forces must be both "organized, armed group that has entered the fight alongside al Qaeda" and "a co-belligerent with al Qaeda in hostilities against the United States or its coalition partners.[200]

After detailing the executive's approach to combatant status determinations for targeting purpose, Johnson rejected the need for and competence of judicial involvement in such decision making. This resistance to judicial oversight was echoed in Department of Justice Attorney General Eric Holder's March 2012

---

196 H Koh (May 19, 2011) The lawfulness of the U.S. operation against Osama Bin Laden. Opinio Juris. http://opiniojuris.org/2011/05/19/the-lawfulness-of-the-us-operation-against-osama-bin-laden/. He referenced Bin Laden's leadership position and continuing operational role to support the determination that "he was a legitimate military target in our armed conflict with al Qaeda." He asserted that the operation took "great pains" to follow the principles of distinction and proportionality "even if it meant putting U.S. forces in harm's way" and concluded that U.S. forces would have accepted a genuine offer of surrender as required by IHL. Id at 2. Koh also maintained the self-defense justification.

197 Brennan J (Sept. 16, 2011) Strengthening our security by adhering to our values and laws. Address at Harvard Law School, Cambridge, MA.

198 J Johnson 2011, Speech to the Heritage Foundation, p. 6 Washington D.C.

199 J Johnson 2012, The conflict against Al Qaeda and its affiliates: how will it end? Para 22, Oxford Union, Oxford University, Oxford, England.

200 Ibid. para 34. Brennan 2012b (Brennan continued the conversation regarding who counts as associated force by discussing al Qaeda in the Arabian Peninsula).

address.[201] Holder suggested instead that Congress provides robust oversight as "the Executive Branch regularly informs the appropriate members of Congress about our counterterrorism activities, including the legal framework, and would of course follow the same practice where lethal force is used against United States citizens."[202]

CIA's General Counsel Stephen W. Preston gave the first speech to address the interaction of the CIA and the rules of IHL in April 2012.[203] Placing the CIA's action in the developing legal framework, he suggested the CIA's use of force is governed by the right of self-defense and could be separately justified by the existence of an armed conflict.[204] He asserted that the CIA would take great care to act consistent with IHL principles and in particular to "minimize civilian casualties."[205] In acknowledging limitations on the CIA's transparency in regard to these efforts, he stressed direct supervision of the CIA by the President, the National Security Council, the intelligence oversight committees of the Senate and the House, the Intelligence Oversight Board, and its independent Inspector General.[206]

In April 2012, then Deputy National Security Advisor for Homeland Security and Counterterrorism John Brennan provided a significant amount detail in regard to the process of IHL compliance in a speech to the Woodrow Wilson center.[207] He explicitly acknowledged the practice of drone strikes. Brennan outlined "rigorous standards and process of review" for "considering and authorizing strikes against a specific member of al-Qa'ida outside the "hot" battlefield of Afghanistan."[208] Brennan's speech also delved into the prospective and retrospective assessments of proportionality and civilian casualties. Brennan claims that the U.S. approach exceeds IHL standards as "we only authorize a strike if we have a high degree of confidence that innocent civilians will not be injured or killed, except in the rarest of circumstances."[209] Furthermore, he offered that some strikes were rejected on those grounds. Brennan concluded that civilian deaths are "exceedingly rare." He also referenced review of civilian casualties though it is unclear

[201] E Holder 2012, Address at Northwestern University School of Law. Chicago, IL.

[202] Ibid.

[203] S Preston, Address at Harvard Law School, Cambridge, MA, 2012.

[204] Ibid.

[205] Ibid.

[206] Ibid.

[207] Brennan 2012a. In so doing, he claimed that "the United States government has never been so open regarding its counterterrorism policies and their legal justification."

[208] The speech states that once a name is given, the proposal to consider planning them on a list will "go through a careful review and, as appropriate, will be evaluated by the very most senior officials in our government for decision." He referenced the fact that high grade intelligence was needed to make decisions and stated that operation authorization requires "a high degree of confidence that the individual being targeted is indeed the terrorist we are pursuing. This is a very high bar."

[209] Ibid.

what such review entails, but he suggested that "we constantly work to improve and refine our efforts so that we are doing everything in our power to prevent the loss of innocent life."[210] Brennan concluded with a nod to the importance of congressional oversight and the institutionalization of the administration's standards and processes.[211]

3.6.2 Leaks of Legal Analysis

In addition to speeches and statements, the Obama administration has strategically leaked information in regard to targeted killings and drone strikes.[212] While the administration has leaked many operational and legal details,[213] this chapter will focus on the two most significant legal leaks: the 2011 classified legal opinion regarding al-Aulaqi's targeting and the 2013 Justice Department white paper. Both documents focus on the constitutional issues raised by targeting an American, but they do provide some insight as to how administration attorneys view IHL obligations.

In the wake of al-Aulaqi's death, the Obama administration refused to formally acknowledge its role, but it did covertly leak its legal analysis justifying its authority to target US citizens.[214] The executive branch first revealed the existence of the Justice Department OLC classified legal opinion regarding the targeting of al-Aulaqi[215] and then provided the details to reporter Charlie Savage. In turn, Savage published a New York Times article describing the broad strokes of the OLC's legal analysis.[216] While the memo emphasized the unique questions of targeting U.S. citizens, Savage revealed the memo also reached some factual questions about al-Aulaqi's specific situation. In the memo, the government

[210] Ibid.

[211] Ibid.

[212] B Wittes (Oct. 4, 2011) More on the legal rationale for the al-Aulaqi strike. Lawfare. http://www.lawfareblog.com/2011/10/more-on-releasing-the-legal-rationale-for-the-al-aulaqi-strike/. Simon, R (Oct. 28, 2011) Bill Daley, unplugged. Politico. http://www.politico.com/news/stories/1011/67043.html. (interviewing the White House chief of staff and discussing the overall leakage in the administration).

[213] See e.g., C Whitlock and G Miller (Sept. 20, 2011) U.S. assembling secret drone bases in Africa, Arabian Peninsula, officials say. Washington Post. http://articles.washingtonpost.com/2011-09-20/world/35273162_1_undeclared-drone-wars-seychelles-president-james-michel-unmanned-aircraft.

[214] K Anderson (Oct. 8, 2011) Secret DOJ memo on Awlaki targeting and NYT Public Editor on policy-by-leaks. http://www.volokh.com/2011/10/08/charlie-savage-reads-secret-doj-memo-on-awlaki-targeting/.

[215] P Finn (Sept. 30, 2011) Secret U.S. memo sanctioned killing of Aulaqi. Washington Post. http://articles.washingtonpost.com/2011-09-30/world/35274507_1_qaeda-drone-strike-anwar-al-aulaqi.

[216] Savage 2011, supra n. 104, para 3.

determined both that al-Aulaqi played an operational role in AQAP and that AQAP was a co-belligerent with al-Qaeda. Accordingly, the memo then resolved that the AUMF governed Al-Aulaqi's targeting. Perhaps most interestingly given the U.S. position regarding detainees at Guantanamo, the memo also determined that CIA drone operators commit no war crime, but might be prosecuted in Yemeni courts for murder.[217]

On February 4, 2013, as Congressional criticism of the Obama administration's position on drone strikes was heating up, *NBC News* obtained and posted a confidential Justice Department white paper[218] detailing the Obama administration's legal justification for the targeted killing of American citizens abroad.[219] Unlike the earlier leak, someone provided the legal document itself for public consumption.[220] Like earlier speeches and leaks, the white paper reiterates the dual justification for the use of force. But most notably, it provides the specific legal support used to reach its conclusions. For example, the White Paper provides reasoning and case citations for the determination that the United States is in a non-international armed conflict with al-Qaeda and that no strict geographical limit on force exists in international armed conflicts and by analogy, for non-international armed conflicts.[221] The memo also briefly discusses the content of the four IHL principles. In so doing, the White Paper articulates why an operational leader of al Qaeda who poses an imminent threat of violent attack against the United States is a person taking an active part in hostilities and thus a legitimate target.[222]

3.6.3 Information About External and Internal Oversight

In addition to the administration's speeches and legal leaks, limited information about oversight, institutionalism, and reform efforts have become publicly available. While numerous examples abound, I briefly discuss what I believe to be three significant examples: congressional oversight, the role of the National Counter

[217] Ibid, para 17.

[218] Department of Justice (n.d.) Lawfulness of a lethal operation directed against a U.S. citizen who is a senior operational leader al-Qa'ida or an associated force. http://msnbcmedia.msn.com/i/msnbc/sections/news/020413_DOJ_White_Paper.pdf. Accessed 24 May 2013 (hereafter Department of Justice).

[219] M Isikoff (Feb. 4, 2013) Justice Department memo reveals legal case for drone strikes, para 1, http://openchannel.nbcnews.com/_news/2013/02/04/16843014-justice-department-memo-reveals-legal-case-for-drone-strikes-on-americans?lite.

[220] G Ingersoll (Feb. 4, 2013) Justice Department Memo Details 'Legality' of Drone Strikes on Americans, Bus. Insider. http://www.businessinsider.com/leaked-white-paper-details-legality-of-drone-strikes-on-americans-2013-2.

[221] Dep't of Justice, pp. 3–4.

[222] Dep't of Justice, p. 16.

Terrorism Center (NCTC), and the proposed movement of strike authority away from the CIA. These examples have likely become public as part of the administration's effort to convince others of the existence of an internal accountability architecture.

First, Congress may play a significant role in keeping the Obama administration compliant with IHL. Early on in the drone program, many believed the executive branch acted unilaterally.[223] Yet, this seems not to have been the case, at least not once the Obama administration ramped up the drone program. In 2012, both Republicans and Democrats revealed the longstanding role the intelligence committees play in monitoring the drone strike program. For instance, the monthly Intelligence Committee reviews of CIA strikes include a survey of relevant intelligence, videos of the strikes, and after-action evidence about the victims.[224] Senator Diane Feinstein says that the committee staff has "held 28 monthly in-depth oversight meetings to review strike records and question every aspect of the program including legality, effectiveness, precision, foreign policy implications and the care taken to minimize noncombatant casualties."[225] Obama's recent decision to make the relevant OLC memos available to the Senate Judiciary Committee members and to members of the Senate Intelligence Committee may also serve to enhance this congressional oversight.

Second, the Obama administration has used the NCTC to institutionalize its drone practices. Rather than have the CIA and the Joint Special Operations Command (JSOC) operate independently, the NCTC has been envisioned as a "targeting hub" which integrates inputs from various agencies and streamlines processes. For instance, the NCTC is thought to have developed a database which integrates kill lists from both the Pentagon and the CIA. The database is believed to catalog information about individuals on the list such as "biographies, locations, known associates and affiliated organizations."[226] Apparently, the NCTC has regular meetings in which members of the CIA, State Department and JSOC use this information to determine new listings, review the appropriateness of existing listings and decide about removals.[227] Also thought to be in the hands of the

---

[223] K Ellison (Jan. 13, 2013) Time for Congress to build a better drone policy, Wash. Post, http://articles.washingtonpost.com/2013-01-13/opinions/36311903_1_drone-strikes-drone-program-drone-policy.

[224] K Dilanian (Jun 25, 2012) Congress zooms in on drone killings. LA Times. http://articles.latimes.com/2012/jun/25/nation/la-na-drone-oversight-20120625. See also J Goldsmith (Feb. 12, 2013) Congressman Rogers on congressional (and personal) oversight of the Obama Drone Program and USG involvement in Al-Awlaki strike; and the implications for the ACLU FOIA cases [UPDATED]. Lawfare. http://www.lawfareblog.com/2013/02/congressman-rogers-on-congressional-personal-oversight-of-obama-drone-program-and-usg-involvement-in-al-awlaki-strike-and-the-implications-for-the-aclu-foia-cases.

[225] Dilanian 2012, supra n. 224, para 10.

[226] Ibid.

[227] G Miller (Oct. 23, 2012) Plan for hunting terrorists signals U.S. intends to keep adding names to kill lists. Wash. Post. http://articles.washingtonpost.com/2012-10-23/world/35500278_1_drone-campaign-obama-administration-matrix.

NCTC is the "disposition matrix": an operational menu of whether to extradite, capture, or strike which the administration may have begun drafting as early as 2010.[228]

Third, some believe that the Obama administration has or will transfer strike authority away from the CIA in Afghanistan, Somalia, and Yemen.[229] One reason might be that Congress and the President have more direct oversight over JSOC behavior than over the CIA.[230] Some also suggest that JSOC is also more transparent than the CIA.[231] CIA chief John Brennan is said to favor the move, but no evidence from the administration confirms such a shift is currently underway.[232] It is unclear what to take from this proposed internal reform as it may even be perversely counterproductive if the JSOC ends up being even less transparent than the CIA.[233]

3.6.4 The Underwhelming May Revolution

In 2013, the U.S. President began speaking directly about drone strikes and emphasizing the importance not only of transparency, but also accountability. In February 2013, Obama pledged in his State of the Union address and in a follow up Google "fireside chat,"[234] to continue congressional oversight and make compliance efforts more transparent. In May 2013, he gave a widely touted counterterrorism speech; codified key elements of targeted killing policy standards and procedures;[235] and declassified information regarding strikes on American citizens.[236] This trio of events reiterated several constraints on U.S. behavior that

---

228 Ibid., para 1.

229 DeYoung 2013, supra n. 156; Mazzetti and Shane 2013, infra n. 231.

230 A Entous, et al. (Nov. 4, 2011) U.S. tightens drone rules. Wall Street Journal. http://online.wsj.com/article/SB10001424052970204621904577013982672973836.html.

231 M Mazzetti and S Shane (Mar. 22, 2013) As new drone policy is weighed, few practical effects are seen. NY Times. http://www.nytimes.com/2013/03/22/us/influential-ex-aide-to-obama-voices-concern-on-drone-strikes.html?pagewanted=all (hereafter Mazzetti and Shane).

232 DeYoung 2013, supra n. 156, para 11.

233 Mazzetti and Shane 2013, supra n. 231.

234 A Serwer (Feb. 2, 2013) Here's why Obama won't say whether he can kill you with a drone: because he probably can. Mother Jones. http://www.motherjones.com/mojo/2013/02/why-obama-wont-give-straight-answer-drones.

235 B Obama (2013) U.S. Policy Standards and Procedures for the Use of Force in Counterterrorism Operations Outside the United States and Areas of Active Hostilities (hereafter "Obama 2013").

236 E Holder, 2013, Letter to Patrick J. Leahy, Chairman of the Judiciary Committee, pp. 2–3 (noting al-Aulaqi's senior leadership in AQAP, his intimate involvement in "detailed planning and putting in place plots against U.S. persons" including his instructions to the Christmas day bomber and his role in "numerous other plots").

exceed IHL requirements including: a binding policy preference for capture over kill, the limit of lethal force to targets that pose a continuing, imminent threat to U.S. persons, and "near-certainty that no civilians will be killed or injured" before a strike is cleared. Other notable revelations include the strong rejection of military age males as a legitimate signature for strikes.[237] Both his speech and a contemporaneous letter from the Attorney General explained when U.S. citizens may lawfully be targeted outside the United States and provided a specific justification for why al-Aulaqi was targeted.[238]

Some, including U.N. Special Rapporteur Ben Emmerson believe these May activities indicate a fundamental shift in favor of transparency and accountability.[239] Yet many remain skeptical of this seeming May Revolution in the executive branch's approach to the war on terror.[240] It is not clear that either the goal of transparency or accountability have been significantly advanced. As described above, previous administration speeches had already outlined most of the details. Even the new information is fairly thin in terms of providing any real sense to the public of what the rules are or whether the U.S. complies with them. For instance, the Presidential Policy Guidance only provides key elements of the significantly more detailed legal and policy guidance provided to Congress.[241] Nowhere in that guidance or the speech is there an outline of any post-strike review. While Obama's speech indicated his ongoing consideration of drone courts and an independent oversight board in the executive branch, he provided no detail as to whether the administration would ultimately adopt either of these accountability mechanisms.

So many important questions raised earlier remain unanswered after the May actions. We now know that being a military aged male is an insufficient signature, but what signatures are used for signatures strikes and how are they justified as legally adequate? We now know that there should be a near certainty of no civilian casualties, but what are the government's civilian casualty estimates? Relatedly, how does the United States assess the status of individuals once deceased? What retrospective accountability mechanisms are in place? Has the government determined that any strikes it engaged in violated IHL? Are the enhanced roles of the Congress and the NCTC having specific effects on drone policy? Are they

---

[237] Obama 2013, supra n. 235, p. 2 (Males of military age may be non-combatants; it is not the case that all military-aged males in the vicinity of a target are deemed to be combatants).

[238] Letter of Attorney General Eric H. Holder, Jr., to Senator Patrick J. LeahyMay 2013, pp. 2–3 (noting his senior leadership in AQAP, his intimate involvement in "detailed planning and putting in place plots against U.S. persons" including his instructions to the Christmas day bomber and his role in "numerous other plots").

[239] Emmerson 2013a, supra n. 38. U.N. Special Rapporteur Ben Emmerson credited this speech as "ground breaking" and a "highly significant step toward transparency and accountability."

[240] See e.g. Amnesty International (2013) USA: Words, War, and the Rule of Law. http://www.amnestyusa.org/sites/default/files/words_war__and_the_rule_of__law.pdf. Accessed 25 July 2013.

[241] Obama 2013, supra n. 235.

making the policy more compliant? In addition, the administration has so far declined to provide any meaningful details on casualties from targeted killings or even acknowledge the program of signature strikes. Nor has it released much of the fine grained analysis that reveals its actual interpretation of various IHL principles.

Yet these May activities still matter. For one, they implicate the synergistic relationship between the executive and judicial branch. This chapter has argued that the courts and threat of courts may help spur executive action and that executive action in turn influences and may facilitate the courts' activities. Mere hours after the May acknowledgement of the government's responsibility for the strikes killing al-Aulaqi and other Americans, Judge Collyer ordered the government to file a memorandum explaining the relevance of the information to the Al-Aulaqi v Panetta litigation which it did shortly thereafter.[242] In addition to influencing this suit, a new round of FOIA requests for the fuller version of the Presidential Policy Guidelines and other details referenced during the May activities should be expected. And the back and forth within the transparency ecosystem will continue.

3.7 Conclusion

When the executive branch began deploying drones to engage in targeted killings, the public knew virtually nothing about these activities or how or whether they fit within the IHL framework. In the early stages of the war on terror, both the public and Congress accepted the executive branch's behavior with few questions. But as the number of strikes and fatalities began to mount, calls for transparency and accountability grew louder. The American people wanted assurances that the executive branch was acting consistent with the Constitution and to a lesser extent consistent with IHL.

Journalists and civil rights groups used litigation as part of a larger strategy to force transparency and accountability. Some lawsuits seek a ruling that targeted killings outside of Afghanistan are not part of an armed conflict, while others attempt to force the government to relinquish documents under FOIA. Others threaten to authorize courts to deny listings or provide damages. The evocation of courts in these various ways plays an important role in encouraging greater accountability and transparency. With each FOIA request or damage suit filed, concerned parties can keep public and congressional attention focused on targeted killings. With each denial, they can push back against the lack of transparency and accountability, forcing the executive branch to recalibrate its response. Given the

---

242 Defendant's Response to the Courts May 22, 2013 Order, *Al-Aulaqi v. Panetta* (D.D.C.) No. 1:12-cv-01192 (RMC); L Denniston (May 2013) Constitution Check: Will drone policy be tested in court? Constitution Daily. http://blog.constitutioncenter.org/2013/05/constitution-check-will-drone-policy-be-tested-in-court/.

historically limited role of U.S. courts in the interpretation and application of IHL norms, this ongoing role of the courts is a modest but important one. As shown here, the executive branch has in fact become more responsive. This approach of speeches, leaks, and information about oversight and reforms does mark a step forward. But ultimately, while advocates are using courts to highlight questions about the proper application of IHL, judges themselves seem reluctant to directly apply IHL norms in this area and the future prospect for such rulings seem quite dim.[243]

References

Alston P (2011) The CIA and targeted killings beyond borders. Harv Nat Sec J 2:283

Anderson K (2009) Targeted killings in U.S. counterterrorism strategy and Law. In: Wittes B (ed) Legislating the War on terror: an agenda for reform. Brookings Institution Press, Washington, pp 346–600

Barnidge R (2012) A qualified defense of American drone attacks in Northwestern Pakistan under international humanitarian law. Boston Univ Int Law J 30:409

Ben-Naftali O, Michaeli K (2003) 'We must not make a Scarecrow of the Law:' a legal analysis of the Israeli policy of targeted killings. Cornell Int Law J 36:233

Bergen P, Tiedemann K (2011) Washington's phantom war: the effects of the U.S. Drone Program in Pakistan. For Affs 90.4:12

Blank L (2012) After "Top Gun": how drone strikes impact the law of war. Univ Pa J Int Law 33:675–719

Blum G, Heymann P (2010) Law and policy of targeted killings. Harv Nat Sec J 1:145

Bradley C (2009) The United States, Israel and unlawful combatants. Green Bag 2D(12):397–411

Brennan J (2012a) The ethics and efficacy of the President's counterterrorism strategy. Woodrow Wilson Center, Washington

Brennan J (2012b) U.S. policy toward Yemen. Council on Foreign Relations, New York City

Chesney R (2010) Who may be killed? Anwar al-Awlaki as a case study in the international legal regulation of lethal force. Yearb Int Humanit Law 13:3–60

Chesney R, Goldsmith J (2008) Terrorism and the convergence of criminal and military detention models. Stan Law Rev 60:180

Daskal J (2013) The geography of the battlefield: a framework for detention and targeting outside the 'Hot' conflict zone. Univ Pa Law Rev 161:1165

Eichensehr K (Comment) (2007) On target? The Israeli Supreme Court and the expansion of targeted killings. Yale Law J 116:1873

---

[243] Yet a note of caution is in order. Like in the detention debates, forcing the legal debate may have the counterproductive effect of placing these contested practices on more solid footing. In particular, the ACLU and CCR have both asserted that any strikes off of hot battlefields are not wars and thus not governed by the laws of war. This claim has been made across *al-Aulaqi v. Panetta*, *al-Aulaqi v. Obama*, and their three FOIA requests regarding al-Aulaqi, al Majalah strikes and drones more generally. As they continue to push for more information and damages, the judicial branch may force or the executive branch could explicitly choose to have these targeting practices explicitly governed by IHL and in so doing, lock in IHL applications and interpretations contrary to the substantive preferences of the transparency and accountability advocates.

Foreman M (2013) When targeted killing is not permissible: an evaluation of targeted killing under the Laws of War and morality. J Const Law 15:938
Heller K (2013) One hell of a killing machine: signature strikes and International Law. J Int Crim Justice 11:89–119
Klaidman D (2012) Kill or capture: the war on terror and the soul of the Obama Presidency. Houghton Mifflin Harcourt, Boston
McNeal G (2013) Kill lists and accountability. Forthcoming Geo Law JF
Melzer N (2008) Targeted killing in International Law. Oxford University Press, Oxford
O'Connell M (2011) Seductive drones: learning from a decade of lethal operations. J Law Inf Sci 20:136
Radsan A, Murphy R (2011–2012) The evolution of law and policy for CIA targeted killing. J Nat Sec Law Policy 5:439
Schmitt M (2004) Direct participation in hostilities and 21st century armed conflict. In: Fisher H et al (ed) Crisis management and humanitarian protection. Festschrift fur Dieter Fleck, Berlin, pp 505–529
Schondorf R (2007) The targeted killings judgment: a preliminary assessment. J Int Crim Justice 5:308
Seamon R, Gardner W (2005) The Patriot Act and the wall between foreign intelligence and Law enforcement. Harv J Law Pub Policy 28(319):338–339
Shane S (2013) A court to vet kill lists. New York Times, 9 Feb 2013
Sterio M (2012) The United States' use of Drones in the war on terror: the (Il)legality of targeted killings under International Law, Case W. Res J Int Law 45:146
Vogel R (2010–2011) Drone warfare and the law of armed conflict. Denv J Int Law Policy 39:101

Chapter 4
International Humanitarian Law in the Maritime Context: Conflict Characterization in Judicial and Quasi-Judicial Contexts

Rob McLaughlin and Dale Stephens

Contents

Rob McLaughlin is Associate Professor at the College of Law, The Australian National University, Canberra, ACT, 0200. Dale Stephens is Associate Professor at The University of Adelaide Law School, Adelaide, South Australia, 5005.

R. McLaughlin (✉)
College of Law, The Australian National University, Canberra, ACT, Australia
e-mail: mclaughlinr@law.anu.edu.au

D. Stephens
The University of Adelaide Law School, Adelaide, SA, Australia
e-mail: dale.stephens@adelaide.edu.au

D. Jinks et al. (eds.), *Applying International Humanitarian Law in Judicial and Quasi-Judicial Bodies*, DOI: 10.1007/978-94-6265-008-4_4,

4.1 Introduction

Judicial and quasi-judicial proceedings dealing with 'land-based' incidents of armed conflict are, it is fair to say, an expanding and increasingly detailed source of International Humanitarian Law's ('IHL')[1] interpretation and application—as many of the chapters in this volume attest. The International Court of Justice ('ICJ'),[2] the International Criminal Tribunal for the Former Yugoslavia ('ICTY')[3] and the International Criminal Tribunal for Rwanda (ICTR),[4] for example, have all engaged with IHL in detail across a range of land-based contexts. The International Criminal Court ('ICC')[5] is also now beginning to gain traction as a venue for explicitly IHL-focussed prosecutions, and the outcomes of a recent referral of the Gaza Flotilla incident will be most significant in this regard.[6] The European Court for Human Rights[7] and the Inter-American Commission on Human Rights[8] have likewise engaged with land-focussed IHL contexts, albeit with variable precision and consequences in terms of IHL-related *ratio decidendi*, given their jurisdictional and jurisprudential focus upon constituent Human Rights instruments. UN appointed commissions of inquiry have also engaged with questions of IHL in detail and with great nuance.[9] Certain UN Rapporteurs have likewise contributed

---

[1] For present purposes the terms 'IHL', 'Law of Armed Conflict (LOAC)' and '*Jus in Bello*' will all be used interchangeably.

[2] For example, *Case Concerning Armed Activities on the Territory of The Congo (Democratic Republic of The Congo v. Uganda)* Judgment of 19 December 2005—at http://www.icj-cij.org/docket/index.php?p1=3&k=51&case=116&code=co&p3=4.

[3] For example, *Prosecutor v. Dusko Tadic* (Case No: IT-94-1-A) Appeals Chamber Judgment, 15 July 1999—at http://www.icty.org/x/cases/tadic/acjug/en/tad-aj990715e.pdf.

[4] For example, *Prosecutor v. Jean-Paul Akayesu* (Case No: ICTR-96-4-T) Trial Chamber I Judgment, 2 September 1998—at http://www.unictr.org/Portals/0/Case/English/Akayesu/judgement/akay001.pdf.

[5] As at 11 June 2013, the ICC had before it 18 cases arising from 8 situations (Uganda, Democratic Republic of the Congo, Darfur, Central African Republic, Kenya, Cote d'Ivoire, Libya, Mali). Each of these situations, with the probable exception of Kenya, is characterised by the presence of an armed conflict.

[6] See Referral on behalf of the Union of the Comoros, dated 14 May 2013, available at http://www.icc-cpi.int/iccdocs/otp/Referral-from-Comoros.pdf. See also Solon Solomon and Jackson Nyamuya Maogoto, 'Guest Post: Jurisdictional Aspects of the Article 12(2) Rome Statute Vessel Provision: Some Thoughts on the Provision's Dogma and Implementation in light of the Comoros Referral' at http://opiniojuris.org/2013/07/21/jurisdictional-aspects-of-the-Article-122-rome-statute-vessel-provision-some-thoughts-on-the-provisions-dogma-and-implementation-in-light-of-the-comoros-referral/.

[7] For example, *Case of Al-Jedda v. United Kingdom* (Application No: 27021/08) Grand Chamber Judgment, 7 July 2011—at http://hudoc.echr.coe.int/sites/eng/pages/search.aspx?i=001-105612.

[8] For example, the *Abella and Argentina Case* (Case 11.137) Report, 13 April 1998—at http://www.cidh.oas.org/annualrep/97eng/Argentina11137.htm.

[9] *Report of the Secretary-General's Commission of Experts on Accountability in Sri Lanka*, 31 March 2011—at http://www.un.org/News/dh/infocus/Sri_Lanka/POE_Report_Full.pdf.

to our appreciation of IHL in niche and evolving contexts.[10] Yet there remains within this expanding and deepening body of judgement, assessment, interpretation and scholarship a significant paucity of instances of IHL at sea entering the domain of such courts, tribunals and quasi-judicial commissions of inquiry.

This situation is the logical result of a number of contextually important factors. One is that IHL-governed incidents that take place at sea are less frequent, and in many cases less 'visible' than IHL-governed incidents ashore. Certainly, the advent of social media is changing this. Another factor is that maritime-specific IHL is relatively invisible in the most significant recent 'operationalisations' of IHL accountability. The *Rome Statute of the ICC*,[11] for example, includes no additional specifically maritime IHL offences in Article 8, even though the opportunity to do so is evident on the very face of the detailed offences. The *ICC Statute* makes no reference to those serious violations of the laws and customs applicable in international armed conflict which might be committed against neutral vessels during the implementation of blockade or visit and search regimes, or against enemy vessels in neutral waters. It is evident that Navies are invoking these rights in the operational context, the 2003 Iraq war for example providing a classic example of the US Navy/Coalition relying upon a visit and search regime[12] as well as relying upon legal rights deriving from zones applicable to the immediate area of operations.[13] Hence, it is unclear why this voluminous and long-standing body of law that is being applied in contemporary settings is not picked up within international instruments imposing criminal liability for potential breaches.

Similarly, for example, Article 8(2)(b)(ix)—'intentionally directing attacks against *buildings* dedicated to religion, education, art, science or charitable purposes, historic monuments, hospitals and places where the *sick and wounded* are collected, provided they are not military objectives'—did not grasp the opportunity to incorporate either the exemption from attack afforded to '*vessels* charged

---

[10] For example, several Reports by the Special Rapporteur on extrajudicial, summary or arbitrary executions focus directly upon niche and evolving IHL matters: Christof Heyns 'Lethal Autonomous Robotics' Report (A/HRC/23/47, 9 April 2013) at http://www.ohchr.org/Documents/HRBodies/HRCouncil/RegularSession/Session23/A-HRC-23-47_en.pdf; Philip Alston, 'Study on Targeted Killings' (particularly regarding 'drone' warfare at para 79–86) (A/HRC/14/24/Add.6, 28 May 2010) at http://www2.ohchr.org/english/bodies/hrcouncil/docs/14session/A.HRC.14.24.Add6.pdf.

[11] *Rome Statute of the International Criminal Court*, 17 July 1998—at http://www.icrc.org/applic/ihl/ihl.nsf/Treaty.xsp?documentId=FA328E3CB5C349444125669000039ACBB&action=openDocument.

[12] See for example, MARLO Advisory Bulletin 08-03, March 21, 2003 ('Coalition military forces will conduct a routine boarding …[i]f vessels are used for military purposes, these vessels will be confiscated or destroyed by the Coalition').

[13] See for example, HYDROLANT 602/603 (54, 56) March 21, 2003 ('All Vessels should maintain a safe distance from U.S. Forces so that intentions are clear…Vessels that enter the maritime safety zone…are subject to boarding and visit by US Forces…').

with religious, scientific, or philanthropic missions',[14] or the correlation between sick, wounded *and shipwrecked* that underpins *Geneva Convention II* of 1949.[15] Indeed the initial reference point for assessors of potential maritime IHL offences arguably remains the *San Remo Manual*,[16] rather than the *ICC Statute*. A third factor contributing to this conundrum is that there are no courts or tribunals that have taken on the role of progressive development of maritime-specific IHL. Although some limited opportunities have arisen,[17] the ICJ's record is patchy. The ICTY and ICTR would no doubt have done better, but the necessary fact nexus did not readily arise. The International Tribunal for the Law of the Sea ('ITLOS') does not appear to be likely to deal with maritime armed conflict.[18]

Arguably, this general paucity is due in part to the fact that international courts and tribunals are—to be frank—generally much less adept at dealing with maritime IHL issues, with this capacity generally hostage to the presence of an expert on the bench or at the bar table.[19] It is fair to say, however, that the immediate future prospects for nuanced, specialist maritime IHL application, interpretation and progressive development clearly lay with quasi-judicial commission processes, which do tend to engage fully with relevant maritime IHL issues and to seek out specialist maritime IHL advice.

4.1.1 Outline

This chapter will assess the judicial and quasi-judicial contribution to applying, interpreting and developing IHL in a maritime context by focussing upon the issue

---

[14] *Convention (XI) relative to certain Restrictions with regard to the Exercise of the Right of Capture in Naval War*, The Hague, 18 October 1907, Article 4—at http://www.icrc.org/applic/ihl/ihl.nsf/Treaty.xsp?documentId=97E57C2489CF158CC12563CD002D6848&action=openDocument.

[15] *Convention (II) for the Amelioration of the Condition of Wounded, Sick and Shipwrecked Members of Armed Forces at Sea*, Geneva, 12 August 1949—at http://www.icrc.org/applic/ihl/ihl.nsf/Treaty.xsp?documentId=2F5AA9B07AB61934C12563CD002D6B25&action=openDocument.

[16] Doswald-Beck 1995.

[17] See Infra Sect. 4.2.1.

[18] ITLOS has a potential jurisdiction over such matters—*Law of the Sea Convention* 1982, Part XV, Sections 2 and 3 (but noting the opt out in Article 298(1)(c) for matters before the UNSC); and Annex VI to the Convention (*Statute of the International Tribunal for the Law of the Sea*) Articles 21–22. However it is very difficult to see how or why a maritime armed conflict dispute would be directed towards ITLOS rather that the more 'routine' jurisdictions equipped to deal with armed conflict issues—either the ICJ or ICC.

[19] The addition of Judge Greenwood to the bench entitles us to expect a nuanced maritime IHL analysis should a maritime IHL case find its way onto the ICJ's docket during his tenure. Christopher Greenwood was a participant and rapporteur within the SAN REMO MANUAL drafting process.

of conflict characterisation as considered by two forms of judicial engagement with maritime IHL contexts. We will compare the engagement of a judicial body (the ICJ) with maritime IHL issues, as against the arguably very different levels of response evident in the work of quasi-judicial bodies focussed upon a single incident (the four Gaza Flotilla Commissions of Inquiry). In both contexts, the court/commission was offered the opportunity to engage specifically with IHL in a maritime context, but with remarkably different outcomes. In order to focus our assessment, we will analyse the apparently divergent approaches of the ICJ on one hand, and the Gaza Flotilla Commissions on the other, in respect of characterization of whether an armed conflict was in existence so as to attract IHL, and if so, what was its type. In the course of this analysis it will also be necessary to engage with some of the ancillary *jus in bello* maritime issues exposed in each context. The analysis will thus commence with a brief outline of the two relevant and key ICJ cases—the *Nicaragua*[20] and *Oil Platforms*[21] Cases—as exemplifying the quality of the ICJ's engagement.[22] This will be followed by a similar contextual outline in relation to the Gaza Flotilla Reports, exemplifying the quality of quasi-judicial commission engagement with maritime IHL issues.

Following this contextual assessment, we will then seek to interrogate these sets of analyses. As will become evident, however, we consider it vital that our commentary address the law-policy seams evident in each set of pronouncements, because it is not unknown for judicial and quasi-judicial bodies to conceal what is fundamentally a policy choice behind a veil of legal language and process.[23] All international legal appreciations are to some extent hostage to the particular judicial or quasi-judicial body's need to exert a measure of context control through legal characterisation decisions. These decisions then carry implications as to the applicable law. Thus, while judicial and quasi-judicial legal analyses clearly presage and express legal consequences, they also represent mediated attempts to navigate the contextually fundamental law-policy dialogue that informs and underpins such fact-law interrogations. Thus the most visible and publicly exposed seams will tend to vary according to the nature of the body, its purpose, and its own perception of its place and role in casting an effect into the future.

---

[20] *Case Concerning Military and Paramilitary Activities in and Against Nicaragua (Nicaragua v. United States of America)* Merits Judgment, 27 June 1986. ('Nicaragua' Case).

[21] *Oil Platforms (Islamic Republic of Iran v. United States of America)* Judgments of 12 December 1996, and 6 November 2003. ('Oil Platforms Case').

[22] Some of the many critiques of the occasionally meandering nature of the ICJ's interpretive relationship with national self-defence and use of force—*Nicaragua Case*, *Oil Platforms Case*, *Israeli Wall Advisory Opinion*—include: Wedgwood 2005; Tams 2005; Garwood-Gowers 2004; Taft IV 2004; Bekker 1997, 2004; Hargrove 1987; Moore 1987.

[23] For further background of these issues, see generally Stephens 2010, 2011; also McLaughlin 2012a, b.

4.2 The ICJ and Maritime IHL: The *Nicaragua* and *Oil Platforms* Cases

The ICJ has on rare occasions been invited, via the particular fact nexus before it, to advance the cause of applying, interpreting and progressively developing maritime IHL. The two cases which most clearly have invited this focus—albeit as a discrete set of brush stokes upon a significantly wider canvas of interlinked issues—are the *Nicaragua Case* and the *Oil Platforms Case*. It is important at the outset to note that the ICJ's first case—the *Corfu Channel Case*[24]—also involved issues of use of force at sea, but the fact nexus in that case was clearly and unambiguously determined to reside outside the context of armed conflict.[25]

4.2.1 The Nicaragua *Case*

The Nicaragua Case ostensibly dealt with the interpretation of the Treaty of Friendship, Commerce and Navigation 1956 ('FCN') between Nicaragua and the US.[26] It also dealt with the application of international law relating to national self-defence, armed attack, use of force, issues of attribution and the jurisdictional issues surrounding bringing an unwilling respondent (in this case, the US) to the Court. From a maritime IHL perspective, however, the Nicaragua Case centred upon issues of US accountability for the conduct of anti-Nicaraguan regime 'Contra' forces. The fact nexus included, amongst other maritime issues, a series of attacks from and at sea by 'Contra' forces, with differing degrees of US or US associated involvement, and the mining of three Nicaraguan ports which the Court found attributable to a US Government agency, since they had been carried out by personnel either in the pay of, or acting on the instructions of that agency and with its logistics support.[27] To this end, the ICJ engaged to varying degrees of specificity with two issues of maritime IHL concern—conflict characterisation and the *jus in bello* issues arising from sea attacks and naval mine warfare.

In the Jurisdiction and Admissibility Judgment, the ICJ clearly noted the potential armed conflict characterisation of the use of force context existing between Nicaragua, the Contras and the US. Indeed, at para 94, the Court stated:

---

[24] *Corfu Channel (United Kingdom of Great Britain and Northern Ireland v. Albania)* (Merits Judgment, 9 April 1949) (1949) ICJ Reps 4.

[25] See generally Bannelier et al. 2012, Chaps. 10, 11, 14 and 16, for example.

[26] United States of America and Nicaragua Treaty of Friendship, Commerce and Navigation (21 January 1956, entry into force 24 May 1958) 267 UNTS 3.

[27] *Nicaragua Case* 1986, supra n 20, paras 80–81. The ICJ held, for example, that the mining was carried out 'by persons in the pay and acting on the instructions of [a US Government Agency], under the supervision and with the logistic support of United States agents'.

> This presentation of the matter by the United States treats the present dispute between Nicaragua and itself as a case of armed conflict which must be dealt with only by the Security Council and not by the Court which, under Article 2, para 4, and Chap. 6 of the Charter, deals with pacific settlement of all disputes between member States of the United Nations. But, if so, it has to be noted that, while the matter has been discussed in the Security Council, no notification has been given to it in accordance with Chap. 7 of the Charter, so that the issue could be tabled for full discussion before a decision were taken for the necessary enforcement measures to be authorised. It is clear that the complaint of Nicaragua is not about an ongoing armed conflict between it and the United States, but one requiring, and indeed demanding, the peaceful settlement of disputes between the two States. Hence, it is properly brought before the principal judicial organ of the Organization for peaceful settlement.[28]

Indeed, at this admissibility stage, the ICJ essentially accepted that the characterization of armed conflict was indeed relevant, and recognised that the evidential difficulties associated with proving facts in the context of an armed conflict would be challenging. The Court determined, however, that its ultimate merits judgment would be based upon the law, facts and submissions of the parties, and that the relevance of the existence or otherwise of an armed conflict 'is not to be ruled out as inadmissible *in limine* on the basis of an anticipated lack of proof'.[29] So at this stage, at least, armed conflict and the potential application of maritime IHL was certainly on the table.

In the Merits Judgment, however, the ICJ primarily dealt with the case context in terms of the law relating to national and collective self-defence, armed attack and use of force. The ICJ did find that the conflict was one to which Common Article 3 of the *Geneva Conventions* applied—that is a non-international armed conflict[30]—but did not elaborate on this characterization. However, the Court did recognise and engage with the second set of relevant maritime IHL issues—the clear applicability of key components of IHL (including maritime IHL) in relation to the Contra-Nicaragua conflict—and asserted that specific maritime IHL provisions in relation to attacks at or from the sea, and mine warfare, applied to all parties, including the US.[31] Thus the series of attacks conducted at and from the

[28] *Nicaragua Case* 1986, supra n 20, Jurisdiction and Admissibility Judgment, 26 November 1984, para 94; see also para 97, where the Court explicitly notes the US characterisation of the context as one of armed conflict: 'It is relevant also to observe that while the United States is arguing today that because of the alleged ongoing armed conflict between the two States the matter could not be brought to the International Court of Justice but should be referred to the Security Council…'; and para 99, where the Court deals with the armed conflict based fourth US argument regarding inadmissibility: 'The resort to force during ongoing armed conflict lacks the attributes necessary for the application of the judicial process, namely a pattern of legally relevant facts discernible by the means available to the adjudicating tribunal, establishable in conformity with applicable norms of evidence and proof, and not subject to further material evolution during the course of, or subsequent to, the judicial proceedings'.

[29] Id. at para 101.

[30] *Nicaragua Case* 1986, supra n 20, for example at paras 116–124 (Contra-US accountability nexus in relation to training), and 219 (NIAC determination).

[31] Id. at paras 215–220 (general IHL obligations).

sea (including those upon Potosi Naval Base on 4–5 January 1984, upon patrol boats at Puerto Sandino 28–30 March 1984, and upon San Juan del Norte on 9 April 1984[32]) were held to be governed by the customary principles of IHL. Similarly, the US was held to have failed to fulfil its maritime IHL based obligation to give notice regarding the mining of Nicaraguan ports.[33]

The *Nicaragua Case* is to date the high water mark in the ICJ's engagement with maritime IHL issues. The ICJ accepted from the outset that there was indeed an armed conflict in existence, agreed that it had maritime elements, indicated that IHL applied to attacks perpetrated at and from the sea, and specifically determined that customary maritime IHL on mine warfare applied to US conduct in terms of the obligation to inform States of the presence and location of the mines in Nicaraguan waters. Although the case is based fundamentally upon an analysis of the law of national and collective self-defence, armed attack and use of force, the ICJ saw no problem with integrating specific aspects of applicable IHL into the overall framework of its legal approach to and characterisation of the situation, and its application and interpretation of the law.

4.2.2 The Oil Platforms *Case*

Although dealt with—prima facie—as a case concerning interpretation of the Treaty of Amity, Economic Relations and Consular Rights between the United States and Iran (1955), the Oil Platforms Case[34] is fundamentally another step along the sometimes winding path regarding the ICJ's interpretive approach to UN Charter Article 51, the customary nature of the right to national and collective self-defence. On its face, the case concerned the lawfulness of certain military operations conducted by the US against Iran, within the broader context of the Iran-Iraq War, the associated 'Tanker War', attacks by Iranian and Iraqi forces upon neutral shipping including US flagged shipping in the Gulf area, and the U.S. Iran-attributed damage by naval mines of a US frigate.[35] The case was treated by the ICJ as one of strict treaty interpretation, buttressed by reference to underpinning

---

[32] Id. at para 81.

[33] Id. at para 215 and 254. It is important, however, to differentiate this substantive finding ('that the United States of America, by failing to make known the existence and location of the mines laid by it…has acted in breach of its obligations under customary international law in this respect') at para 292(8), from the national or collective self-defence/use of force focused determination that preceded it ('that, by laying mines in the internal or territorial waters of the Republic of Nicaragua during the first months of 1984, the United States of America has acted, against the Republic of Nicaragua, in breach of its obligations under customary international law not to use force against another State, not to intervene in its affairs, not to violate its sovereignty and not to interrupt peaceful maritime commerce') at para 292(6).

[34] Oil Platforms Case, supra n 21.

[35] See infra, n. 44.

customary international law norms relating to national and collective self-defence, armed attack and use of force.

What is for present purposes most notable about this case, however, is the manner in which the ICJ sidestepped maritime IHL issues. The entire context was dealt with substantively as one of treaty interpretation underpinned by customary international law norms. The option—clearly available on the facts—to examine at least some of incidents in terms of applicable maritime IHL (particularly the Operation Praying Mantis incidents) was excluded at the 'Preliminary Objections' stage in December 1996. This was despite recognition that the overall context was coloured by the Iran-Iraq war and the 'Tanker War', a clear US reference to the armed conflict context, including the lawfulness of 'combat operations', and the targeting of neutral shipping and 'military objectives.'[36] Moreover, in their dissenting opinions, Vice-President Schwebel and Judge Oda, both recognised the conflict context as a separate legal issue to be divorced from the treaty interpretation issue.[37] The ICJ did not consider the threshold question as to the existence or otherwise of an armed conflict between Iran and the US, and thus offered no guidance as to the factors relevant to this assessment, nor of the consequences that would then flow from this fundamental characterisation decision.

With this jurisdictional limitation established, the ICJ's Merits Judgment was thus precluded from examining incidents—such as, *inter alia*, the attack on *USS Samuel B Roberts*, and the 5 days of combat operations from this attack until the cessation of Operation Praying Mantis—in a maritime IHL context involving issues of neutrality, precautions in attack, mine warfare, the definition of military objective and the assessment of military necessity.[38] Despite an even more explicit recognition by the Court, in the main judgement of the armed conflict background,[39] it was nevertheless evident, including in the US counter-claims,[40] that

[36] *Oil Platforms Case*, supra n 21, Preliminary Objection Judgment, 12 December 1996, paras 18–21.

[37] Id. Dissenting opinion of Vice-President Schwebel, at 882; Dissenting opinion of Judge Oda, at paras 21–22.

[38] *Oil Platforms Case*, supra n 21, Merits Judgment, 6 November 2003, para 68 (noting the US characterisation of targets attacked during Operational Praying Mantis as 'legitimate military targets'); and paras 73–77 (the Court's application of the self-defence based forms of the necessity and proportionality criteria, rather than the IHL referenced necessity and proportionality criteria, noting that the emphasis given to the issue of 'military presence' on the platforms was concerned with necessity, not IHL based considerations of status).

[39] Id. at paras 23–26 (Iran-Iraq War and 'Tanker War'); 44–45 (mine warfare and operations affecting neutral shipping).

[40] Id. at paras 19–20—The US counter claim clearly referenced the military conflict fact background, but addressed Iranian military actions primarily in terms of the *1955 Treaty* and, once brought into play, use of force in national self-defence: 'rejecting all submissions to the contrary, that, in attacking vessels in the Gulf with mines and missiles and otherwise engaging in military actions that were dangerous and detrimental to commerce and navigation between the territories of the United States and the Islamic Republic of Iran, the Islamic Republic of Iran breached its obligations to the United States under Article X, para 1, of the 1955 Treaty'.

the Preliminary Objections decision had placed the legal issue of armed conflict, and thus the potential application of maritime IHL, to the side:

> The Court has no jurisdiction to enquire into the question of the extent to which Iran and Iraq complied with the international legal rules of maritime warfare. It can however take note of these circumstances, regarded by the United States as relevant to its decision to take action against Iran which it considered necessary to protect its essential security interests. Nevertheless, the legality of the action taken by the United States has to be judged by reference to Article XX, paragraph 1(d), of the 1955 Treaty, in the light of international law on the use of force in self-defence.[41]

Why, exactly, the issues of naval mine warfare and other forms of interference with neutral shipping—clearly maritime IHL issues, which engage obligations between belligerents and third States—were excluded as a matter of 'jurisdiction,' this is not made clear. At the very least, one party, namely Iran, clearly had maritime IHL obligations, stemming from the law of neutrality, to the other party-the US,[42] so the jurisdictional exclusion cannot have been on the basis of the relevant IHL not applying *de jure* between the parties. Additionally, the adversarial military operations between Iran and the US should—again, at the very least—have put the Court on notice as to the potential existence of an armed conflict between the parties. The consequence of the Court's non-engagement with potentially relevant IHL, however, was that each of the discrete incidents making up this fact matrix were examined separately rather than collectively as indicators of use of force and as insufficient triggers for national self-defence, but not as 'facts on the ground' in terms of maritime conflict characterisation and of conduct amenable to assessment through the application of maritime IHL.

On any realistic reading of these 'facts on the ground' and *Geneva Conventions* Common Article 2,[43] an armed conflict was afoot for at least 5 days throughout Operation Praying Mantis and the context that led to it.[44] The relevant events led to the deaths of nearly 60 military personnel, damage to several oil platforms—described by the US as 'military objectives' as well as the damage and sinking of Iranian and US warships and the loss of a US helicopter. It remains one of the largest US naval combat engagements since 1945. Yet the period between the mining of *USS Samuel B Roberts* and Operation Praying Mantis was never

---

[41] Id. at para 44.

[42] For example, to notify States regarding the location of naval minefields—for example, *Convention (VIII) Relative to the Laying of Automatic Submarine Contact Mines*, The Hague, 18 October 1907, Article 3—available at http://www.icrc.org/applic/ihl/ihl.nsf/Treaty.xsp?documentId=7D389CA23C22337BC12563CD002D67FF&action=openDocument; Doswald-Beck 1995, supra n 16, Rules 87–89.

[43] For example Geneva Convention II, supra n 15, Article 2.

[44] USS Samuel B Roberts struck a naval mine on 14 April 1988, in international waters near Bahrain. The US claimed the mine had been laid by Iran, although the ICJ ultimately did not find this attribution to be sufficiently proven (the evidence was 'highly suggestive' but not 'conclusive'—*Oil Platforms* 2003, supra n 39, para 71). Following the mine strike, the US conducted mine clearance operations, and Operation Praying Mantis followed over the course of 18–19 April 1988.

understood or assessed, in a legal sense, as a single context; rather it was interpreted only as a series of incidents, the examination of which was useful and legally significant only in terms of the sufficiency of each incident to independently meet either the use of force or armed attack thresholds under the broader *jus ad bellum* context. As Judge Simma, in his Separate Opinion, perceptively observed of the Court's different approach in the *Nicaragua Case*:

> ...in the *Nicaragua* case, the Court did not analyse each incident in detail. Rather, it gave a broad picture of the context prevailing at the time, and assessed the nature and the extent of United States involvement and, consequently, its responsibility for the resulting violations of general international law and the FCN Treaty. Nowhere do we find a specific account of what happened to each ship. The Court's approach, in this sense, was more 'generic' than 'specific'.[45]

However, even if the fragmented approach ultimately adopted by the ICJ was followed through in a contextually appropriate manner—even if only specifically in relation to the mining of *USS Samuel B Roberts*—the Court still could have taken the opportunity to refer to clearly applicable maritime IHL. Indeed, given that there was an ongoing armed conflict with maritime dimensions, and it was not seriously disputed that the mines were laid by *either* Iran or Iraq, the conduct of naval mine warfare with foreseeable consequences for neutral shipping is fundamentally an issue of maritime IHL.[46] It is possible that the ICJ reasoned that it was absolved from engaging with maritime IHL obligations because it had determined that the mines could not be conclusively attributed to Iran. But the Court did not say so; if it had, this at least would have constituted some recognition of, and interpretive contribution to, applicable maritime IHL.

The only conclusion one may draw from both the Preliminary Objection and Merits judgments is that the ICJ conspicuously avoided the option of examining either any specific incident, or the context of Operation Praying Mantis more generally and coherently, in terms of maritime IHL. In this respect, and insofar as the ICJ at least chose to explicitly deal with selected *jus in bello* aspects of maritime IHL in the previous *Nicaragua Case*, *Oil Platforms* arguably represents a regression in ICJ engagement with maritime IHL issues.

4.3 The Role of Quasi-Judicial Bodies in Dealing With Maritime IHL Issues: The Gaza Flotilla Incident

The reluctance of the ICJ to deal fully with the obvious maritime IHL issues in the *Nicaragua* and *Oil Platforms* cases, stands in contrast to the manner in which a number of quasi-judicial bodies did directly tackle these issues in the case of the

[45] Id. Separate Opinion of Judge Simma, para 41.

[46] For example, the customary IHL on mine warfare which has been adapted from *Convention (VIII) Relative to the Laying of Automatic Submarine Contact Mines*, 1907, supra n 44, and is now reflected in the mine warfare related rules found in San Remo Manual, Part II and Part VI.

Gaza Flotilla Incident of 31 May 2010, which involved assessment of the actions of the Israeli Defence Force in halting and boarding a number of foreign flagged vessels determined to breach an Israeli imposed blockade on Gaza. Hence, the treatment of these issues in the context of the subsequent Commissions of Inquiry concerning this event provide valuable insight into the manner in which international legal thinking applies to questions of conflict characterization and use of force and also the manner in which the policy-law interface is tackled when confronting such issues. It is pertinent to also note that Comoros, the flag state of one of the vessels involved in this incident has recently sought to refer this matter to the International Criminal Court.[47] Such a referral no doubt will raise jurisdictional issues regarding capacities of flag states to undertake such an action[48] and might, if accepted, provide a useful insight into the interaction of the Rome Statute[49] with maritime IHL. Subject to if, and when, that occurs the respective quasi-judicial Commissions of Inquiry still provide the most authoritative source of legal analysis on this topic.

4.3.1 Gaza Flotilla Incident: The Facts

On 3 January 2009 as a result of continuing armed hostilities with groups in Gaza, Israel declared a blockade, which extended 20 nautical miles from the Gaza coastline.[50] At the same time, Israel expressed its intention to apply the blockade to all maritime traffic and declared that the blockade was in effect until 'further notice'.[51]

On 31 May, 2010, the Israeli Defence Forces (IDF) intercepted and boarded six ships within international waters, approximately 70–100 nautical miles from the Gaza Coast and outside the Israeli declared blockade zone.[52] During the course of the boarding, force was used by the IDF; nine passengers on the largest ship in the

---

47 Supra n 6.

48 For a forceful critique of such capacities see Solomon and Maogoto, supra n 6.

49 *Rome Statute (Statute of the International Criminal Court)*, supra n 11.

50 Advisory Notice (Blockade of Gaza Strip) No. 1/2009 which provided: 'All mariners are advised that as of 03 January 2009, 1700 UTC, Gaza maritime area is closed to all maritime trafic [sic] and is under blockade imposed by Israeli Navy until further notice', found at: http://un-truth.com/israel/here-it-is-naval-blockade-notice; The Notice was also originally posted on the Israeli Ministry of Transportation website at http://he.mot.gov.il; see also http://www.mag.idf.il/592-4071-en/patzar.aspx.

51 Id.

52 The Public Commission to Examine the Maritime Incident of 31 May 2010—The Turkel Commission Report (Part 1) of January 2011, found at: http://www.turkel-committee.com/files/wordocs//8707200211english.pdf ('The Turkel Commission Report') at para 172, 220.

flotilla, the MV *Mavi Marmara*, were killed, and 55 passengers from all ships were wounded, including nine Israeli soldiers.[53]

Following this incident, Secretary General of the UN, Ban Ki-Moon issued a press statement at the time of the event claiming that '[i]t is vital that there is a full investigation to determine exactly how this bloodshed took place. I believe Israel must urgently provide a full explanation'.[54]

4.3.2 The Establishment of the Commissions of Inquiry

In a cascade of national and international announcements following the incident, four separate quasi-judicial bodies were established to review the operation. These, in chronological order, were sponsored by the UN Human Rights Council ('The HRC Fact Finding Mission'), The Israeli Government ('The Turkel Commission of Inquiry'), the Secretary-General of the United Nations (The United Nations Panel of Inquiry), and the Turkish Government ('The Turkish National Commission of Inquiry').

The Human Rights Council Fact-Finding Mission was established on 1 June 2010 pursuant to resolution 14/1 of the Council, where it was decided 'to dispatch an independent international fact-finding mission to investigate violations of international law, including international humanitarian law and human rights law, resulting from the Israeli attacks on the flotilla of ships carrying humanitarian assistance' to Gaza.[55]

The Turkel Commission was established on June 14, 2010 by Resolution 1796 of the 32nd Government authorising the 'appointment of a independent public Commission, chaired by the supreme court judge (ret.), Jacob Turkel, to examine the maritime incident of May 31, 2010'.[56]

The UN Secretary General on 2 August 2010, established a UN Panel of Inquiry headed by former New Zealand Prime Minister, Sir Geoffrey Palmer.[57] The panel was tasked to, inter alia, receive and review interim and final reports of national

[53] These facts are uncontested in all the Investigations/Inquiry Reports that are canvassed in this Chapter.

[54] 'Secretary-General 'shocked' by deadly raid on Gaza aid flotilla', found at http://www.un.org/apps/news/story.asp?NewsID=34863#.UaqaypUbY04 (Last Accessed 1 June 2013).

[55] General Assembly, Human Rights Council, *Report of the International Fact-Finding Mission To Investigate Violations of International Law, Including International Humanitarian and Human Rights Law, Resulting From The Israeli Attacks On The Flotilla Of Ships Carrying Humanitarian Assistance*, A/HRC/15/21 of 27 September 2010, found at: http://www2.ohchr.org/english/bodies/hrcouncil/docs/15session/A.HRC.15.21_en.pdf ('The HRC Report').

[56] The Turkel Commission Report, supra n 52, 16–17.

[57] Including also, Mr Alvaro Uribe (outgoing President of Colombia) with two additional members coming from Turkey and Israel: Report of the Secretary-General's Panel of Inquiry on the 31 May 2010 Flotilla Incident, September 2011; found at http://unispal.un.org/UNISPAL.NSF/0/1922B40C9F45755985257903004571 32 ('The UN Panel Report').

investigations into the incident; request such clarifications and information as it may require from relevant national authorities, examine and identify the facts, circumstances and context of the incident and to consider and recommend ways of avoiding similar incidents in the future. The panel was charged with preparing a report including its findings and recommendations and submit it to the Secretary-General.[58]

The Turkish National Commission of Inquiry was established on 11 August 2010, 'to examine the Israeli military attack in international waters against the international aid convoy on 31 May 2010 which resulted in the killing of nine civilians and injury of many others'.[59] The Commission was tasked with assessing the facts and the law and was to prepare a report for consideration by the UN Panel of Inquiry.[60]

Each of these quasi-judicial bodies issued its own report.[61] The reasoning employed and the conclusions reached by this fusillade of reports were largely divergent and hard to reconcile. While more fully discussed below,[62] it is clear that law and policy considerations were intermixed and the legal outcomes reached were a product of these mixed considerations as well as an example of employment of justificatory discourses directed at relevant constituencies. What makes this experience so illuminating is the relatively agreed set of facts that provided the basis for use of particularised techniques of analysis, but the widely divergent set of outcomes that were reached in terms of the application and interpretation of IHL in a maritime context.

4.3.3 The Gaza Flotilla Commissions and Their Findings

In the four Gaza Flotilla Reports, the various quasi-judicial bodies engaged consciously, directly and in great detail with the issue of conflict characterisation. The nature of this designation, while producing specific and therefore satisfying results, nonetheless produced outcomes with differing trajectories. Such consequences say much about the nature of legal analysis as well as the liberal promise of neutral legal resolution of contentious political facts. Given that the facts of the case are generally agreed, this incident provides a useful case study into the nature of the legal

---

[58] Id. at 7.

[59] Report On The Israeli Attack On The Humanitarian Aid Convoy To Gaza on 31 May 2010, February 2011 found at: http://www.mfa.gov.tr/data/Turkish%20Report%20Final%20-%20UN%20Copy.pdf ('The Turkish Commission Report') 10.

[60] Id.

[61] The HRC report, n 55; The Turkel Commission Report n 52; The UN Panel Report n 57; The Turkish National Commission Report Id.

[62] Infra Sect. 4.4.2.

reasoning and the nature of the policy/legal assimilation. Accordingly, a relatively detailed outline of the key findings in each inquiry will be outlined below, followed by an analysis of the mechanisms that can lead to such divergent results.

4.3.3.1 Human Rights Council

The first report submitted was by the Human Rights Council ('HRC')[63] and was presented at the fifteenth session of the Council 27 September 2010. The report concluded that the law of blockade survived the 1982 UN Convention on the Law of the Sea[64] and remained a viable tool applicable as a legitimate measure of the Law of Naval Warfare. Notably, the report also endorsed the *San Remo Manual on the Law of Naval Warfare*.[65] It determined that the blockade imposed by Israel inflicted disproportionate damage to civilian population and hence was unlawful.[66] The Report acknowledged that damage in this context, usually correlated to 'deaths, injuries and property damage' but here linked this requirement to 'destruction of the civilian economy and prevention of re-construction'.[67] Strikingly, the report also equated starvation with 'causing hunger'.[68] Hence on these grounds, the HRC report determined that the blockade was illegal.[69] The mission also determined that, despite the Israeli disengagement in 2005, Israel is still occupying Gaza by exercising constructive 'effective control',[70] and that the blockade was a collective punishment, violating Article 33 of the Fourth Geneva Convention.[71] As the blockade was unlawful, the legal framework for the application of any force was to be governed entirely by international human rights standards. This proposition is correct in that the law does not conceive of a mixed framework of the law of peace and the law of war. Dinstein succinctly notes, for example, that it is not justified 'to speak loosely of a *status mixtus* in the sense of a

---

[63] The HRC Report, n 55.

[64] Id at para 50.

[65] Id.

[66] Id. para 53.

[67] Id. para 52.

[68] Id.

[69] Id. at para 53.

[70] This view is also shared by others who regard the Israeli occupation to be a virtual one through control of airspace and maritime areas of Gaza as well as the entry and exit of persons and goods into the territory. Some support for this proposition might be found in the ICTY case of *Prosecutor v. Naletilić*, IT-98-34-T, Decision of 31 March 2003, at paras. 219–222, where the ICTY determined that an occupying power for the purposes of the Fourth Geneva Convention need not have 'actual authority' to attract the operation of the Convention see also generally: http://www.opendemocracy.net/opensecurity/federico-sperotto/virtual-occupation-of-gaza#ftn6. This position has been rejected by the Israeli Supreme Court in HCJ 9132/07 *Al-Bassiouni v. Prime Minister* (unpublished, Jan. 30, 2008) noted in The Turkel Commission Report supra n 52 at para 45.

[71] Id. para 54.

twilight zone between war and peace. Legally speaking, there are only two states of affairs in the relations between States—war and peace—with no undistributed middle ground'.[72] Accordingly, in the absence of a lawfully imposed blockade, namely a law of war concept, peacetime rules regarding the application of force applied and they are based upon human rights considerations.[73] The report determined, accordingly, that the force applied by the IDF was 'unnecessary, disproportionate, excessive and inappropriate'.[74] As the legal regime governing the boarding was the generally applicable maritime law, only flag state authority applied within international waters. As such, there was no right to board the vessel.[75] The arrests were therefore unlawful and the passengers were subjected to unlawful detention and abuse by the Israeli authorities.[76]

4.3.3.2 The Turkel Commission

The Israeli Government Turkel Commission Report[77] concluded that the law of naval warfare was applicable and while mostly having customary status, reliable reference could be made to the San Remo Manual for clarification of specifics.[78] The Commission concluded that a blockade was a legitimate measure of naval warfare applicable in an international armed conflict but also found evidence that it had and could be applied in a non-international armed conflict.[79] It determined that the conflict between Israel and non-state parties in Gaza was an international armed conflict.[80] Significantly however, it stated that a blockade could also apply in the context of a non-international armed conflict.[81] The fact that the interception took place beyond the blockade zone was acceptable on the basis of evidence of an express stipulated intention to enter the blockade zone by the flotilla.[82] The Commission rejected the notion that Israel was an occupying power of Gaza, observing that there was no effective control exerted given the lack of physical Israeli presence, hence the Fourth Geneva Convention simply did not apply.[83]

---

[72] Dinstein 2001, p. 16

[73] Two operative international codes in play include *Basic Principles on the Use of Force and Firearms by Law Enforcement Officials;* UN Congress on the Prevention of Crime and the Treatment of Offenders 1990 and the *Code of Conduct for Law Enforcement Officials*; General Assembly Resolution 34/169 of 17 Dec 1979.

[74] The HRC Report, supra n 55, para 172.

[75] Id. paras 159 and 163.

[76] Id. at para 174.

[77] The Turkel Commission Report, supra n 52.

[78] Id. at para 33.

[79] Id. at paras 41–45.

[80] Id. at paras 38 and 44.

[81] Id. at paras 39 and 42.

[82] Id. at para 175.

[83] Id. at paras 46 and 47.

In relation to the constituent elements of a blockade, the Commission concluded that Israel had provided sufficient notice, and that the duration requirements of 'until further notice' made by Israel were adequate.[84] In responding to the HRC report, the Turkel Commission concluded that starvation is not hunger for the purposes of IHL requirements for the validity of a blockade and also that food insecurity does not equate to starvation.[85] In relation to the proportionality assessments of the blockade, the Commission noted that the San Remo Manual linked damage to starvation.[86] Moreover, in this instance, Israel did not prevent food and other objects essential for survival from entering Gaza through land crossings and hence was not in violation of this requirement of IHL.[87] The Turkel Commission also rejected the notion that the prohibition against Article 33 collective punishments was effectively violated by virtue of the blockade as being an obligation with an entirely different character.[88]

The Turkel Commission did establish that in relation to the use of force authority, the IDF had restrictive Rules of Engagement that were predicated upon a self-defence regime.[89] It is clear that planners had anticipated low-level resistance, or alternatively, had made some kind of differentiation between *jus in bello* rights against the vessels as opposed to the passengers.[90] There was a reference to the requirement of 'effectiveness' as an element of blockade, and an implication that the IDF were compelled to intercept, capture and/or divert the vessels.[91] In respect of the resort to the lethal use of force against the passengers, the Commission determined that such resort was consistent with both with the right to self-defence as well as with broader notions of force permitted under IHL in relation to the concept of direct participation in hostilities.[92]

There was discussion within the report of the application of international human rights law ('IHRL') and the question of effective control.[93] The Commission did in fact examine traditional views about the extraterritorial application of IHRL to effectively determine that this was not the governing regime to the fact scenario in the particular case.[94] Despite this, there was considerable ambivalence within the report to the question of the use of force. While asserting that IHL rather than IHRL governed the 'take-over',[95] most analysis on the use of force was based upon

---

[84] Id. at para 59.

[85] Id. at paras 76–77.

[86] Id.

[87] Id. para 80.

[88] Id. at para 107.

[89] Id. at paras 206–208.

[90] Id.

[91] Id. at paras 57 and 100.

[92] Id. at para 201.

[93] Id. at paras 185 and 186.

[94] Id. at para 187.

[95] Id. at para 188.

a self-defence paradigm. This was done notwithstanding repeated emphasis throughout the report on the 'combat' nature of the resistance,[96] the use of firearms and other weapons, threats of mortal danger and the determination for hostile confrontation exhibited by some of the passengers involved.

In relation to each instance of the use of lethal force, there was recognition that each death needed to be reviewed on a case-by-case basis. The Commission examined 133 incidents of the use of force and determined that 127 incidents were in conformity with international law.[97] In remaining 6 cases there was a statement of insufficient information.[98] In 5 of the 127 incidents, there was a statement that there was insufficient evidence to conclude that the use of force was also in conformity with law enforcement.[99] Hence, the implication deriving from this conclusion was that the paradigm used to assess the lawfulness of those incidents derived from a direct participation in hostilities (DPH) framework that exists under IHL and not under the auspices of any discussion on the right to self-defence. Despite this, the Commission did not provide a detailed analysis of DPH in this context and the reasoning behind a retrospective analysis of the facts under the DPH formula. Although as outlined above, the Turkel Commission also notes that if a law enforcement regime alone had been applicable, then self-defence under peacetime rules relating to the use of force was justified in the majority of the incidents (122 of 127 incidents).

4.3.3.3 The Turkish Government National Commission

Similar to the other Reports canvassed above, the Turkish Government national commission determined in its report[100] that the *San Remo Manual on the Law of Naval Warfare* reflects existing customary international law,[101] and is therefore a recognised restatement of this body of law. It noted that a blockade was only applicable as a lawful means of war in an international armed conflict.[102] In this regard, the Commission concluded that Israel was inconsistent with its characterization of the conflict with Hamas in Gaza as being both non-international and international.[103] Accordingly, to the extent that this was in fact a non-international armed conflict, the Commission concluded that the blockade was unlawful in its entirety.[104] Moreover, the Commission concluded that it was also unlawful in

---

[96] Id. at paras 197 and 200.

[97] Id. at para 239(d).

[98] Id.

[99] Id. at para 239(e).

[100] The Turkish Commission Report, supra n 59.

[101] Id. at 61.

[102] Id. at 61.

[103] Id. at 62.

[104] Id. at 63.

relation to its specific constituent elements, since an insufficient notification of duration was provided (the 'until further notice' issue which was canvassed above) and Israel was not clear regarding the products forbidden to enter and exit Gaza and no list was provided.[105] There was also an insightful reference to Israeli testimony within the Turkel Commission to the desire to 'delegitimize Hamas' as a strategic goal of the blockade, which the Turkish commission concluded was not a military objective for the purposes of establishing the validity of the said blockade.[106] As with the Human Rights Council, the Turkish Commission determined that that the blockade was not proportionate to the suffering of the Gaza population, threatened with an inadequate food supply,[107] and that it also violated Article 33 of the Fourth Geneva Convention.[108] In relation to the issue of the use of force, the Turkish Commission concluded that the force that was used was excessive and not consistent with IHRL, which was determined to be the applicable normative regime.[109]

4.3.3.4 The UN Panel of Inquiry

The UN Panel of Inquiry[110] determined that the naval blockade was a legitimate security measure that was available to Israel.[111] The Palmer Report, named after the head of the Panel, noted that over 5000 rocket/mortar attacks on Israel had originated from Gaza between 2005 and 2009.[112] Decisively, the UN Inquiry determined that the armed conflict with Gaza was unique, finding that the conflict may be characterised as an international armed conflict.[113] Yet, at the same time the Panel also noted that the conclusion reached regarding the conflict's legal character was not to be generally applied, but only in the realm of the particular circumstances arising out of the blockade.[114] The Panel determined that the interception of the flotilla outside the blockaded zone was lawful given the expressed flotilla participants' intention to breach the blockade.[115] Moreover, the stipulated duration of the blockade being 'until further notice' was determined to be satisfactory for the purposes of the constituent elements of a lawful blockade.[116]

---

105 Id. at 66.
106 Id. at 66–7.
107 Id. at 68.
108 Id. at 78 and 80.
109 Id. at 105.
110 The UN Panel Report, n 57.
111 Id. at para 81.
112 Id. at para 71.
113 Id. at para 73.
114 Id. ('This conclusion goes no further than is necessary for the Panel to carry out its mandate').
115 Id. at para 108.
116 Id. at para 75.

While it was conceded that it was necessary for the flotilla to be intercepted in order to maintain the element of 'effectiveness'[117] and thus lawfulness, the application of force was given close scrutiny by the Panel. In relation to the issue of the use of force, the Panel determined that Israel's decision to board the vessels with such substantial force at a great distance from the blockade zone was excessive and unreasonable.[118] Notwithstanding this determination, the Palmer Report also concluded that the IDF soldiers faced significant, organised and violent resistance requiring force in self-defence.[119] Despite this, there was no adequate account or explanation of the circumstances of the deaths of nine passengers.[120]

Strikingly, the Panel provided a comprehensive and thoughtful analysis of the intersection between IHL and IHRL in a remarkable recitation within an enclosed Appendix to the Report.[121] It characterised the relationship between these two bodies of law as being one of dynamic divergence, convergence, assimilation and complementarity, although observing that 'it is important to stress that it is difficult to make generalised statements on the exact nature of the relationship between human rights law and international humanitarian law'.[122] Despite the comprehensive description of the respective bodies of law and their intersection, there was a frustrating inadequacy of application of this framework to the facts in question. The Palmer Report refrained from any discussion of the 'Direct Participation in Hostilities' concept and chose to review the application of force issue largely through a human rights framework for assessing the lawfulness of the application of force questions.[123] There seemed no conclusive determination on this point, other than an acknowledgement that Israeli operational choices inflamed the situation.[124]

4.4 Construction and Contestation in Legal Argument: Maritime IHL

4.4.1 The ICJ and Conflict Characterisation in the Maritime Domain

In the *Nicaragua Case*, the ICJ clearly recognised the issue of conflict characterisation, specifically noting the applicability of Common Article 3 (thus implying it was a Non-International Armed Conflict (NIAC) between Nicaragua and the

[117] Id. at para 109.
[118] Id. at para 117.
[119] Id. at para 124.
[120] Id. at para 127.
[121] Id. at pp. 76–102.
[122] Id. at para 64.
[123] Id. at paras 117 and 134.
[124] Id. at Panel Finding vi at 3.

Contras), and assessing the mining incidents in terms of applicable maritime IHL by reference to customary norms.

Indeed, the Court exhibited no inherent difficulty with recognising the armed conflict context, and integrating it within the broader legal architecture of the judgment. The Court opted to take as evident the existence of an armed conflict without further detailed judicial inquiry—essentially, without taking judicial notice of the broad political and operational context. It further accepted that this situation of armed conflict carried with it obligations upon the US, the third party in the armed conflict context.[125] But there can be no doubt that the Court primarily wished to deal with national and collective self-defence and use of force, specifically developing the idea of parallel streams of legal obligation and rule content.

Perhaps as a result of this desire to focus upon the more pressing issue of judicial interpretation of the law of national and collective self-defence and use of force, the Court appeared to accept that it was not in the best position to adjudicate on armed conflict, recognising both the political issues and evidential difficulties.[126] The decision thus reflects a retreat into an area of greater familiarity and direct interpretive endeavour for the ICJ—the *UN Charter*, Article 51, and parallel customary international law. Those aspects of maritime IHL with which the Court did directly engage were the relatively straightforward *jus in bello* issues of attack, mine warfare and customary international law IHL obligations.[127] The Court examined conflict characterisation only to the extent of determining that a NIAC existed, but did not engage with the threshold question about how and why it reached this non-international conflict characterisation. Nor did the Court analyse the internationalising effect-if any- of US involvement, or carry out an assessment of the thresholds between IAC and NIAC, which, given the nature of the conflict, would have been of significance in assessing conflict characterisation in maritime contexts. The sense one takes from the *Nicaragua Case* decision is that the ICJ primarily wanted to say something about national and collective self-defence, and this case provided the foundation to do so. As a consequence, maritime IHL was present, but more as an incident, rather than a driver, of the legal context.

In the *Oil Platforms Case*, the ICJ sidestepped a clear opportunity—indeed, arguably a requirement—to deal with the issue of maritime IHL applicability. Even if the Court had engaged with the maritime IHL context just long enough to determine that there was no armed conflict afoot between Iran and the US, and thus that maritime IHL was not applicable, this would have been of fundamental importance and value in and of itself. It would have provided useful jurisprudence on essential considerations when analysing the issue of conflict threshold and characterisation in a maritime context, and why this specific context did not cross

[125] For example, as noted previously, the obligations attaching to belligerents in respect of naval mine warfare.

[126] *Nicaragua* 1986 n 22 at paras 32–35, 57–74.

[127] Although it is important not to underestimate the importance of the ICJ's express, and timely, characterisation of the core principles of IHL as CIL.

that threshold. This decision to sidestep maritime IHL issues, and to focus exclusively on interpreting the treaty—along with supplementary exegesis concerning national and collective self-defence, armed attack and use of force—meant that clearly relevant maritime IHL issues such as neutrality and interference with neutral shipping, mine warfare, IHL proportionality and defining military objectives in terms of the *jus in bello* applicable in maritime armed conflicts, were deprived of a prime opportunity for ICJ application, interpretation and development.

One reading of the *Oil Platforms* Merits Judgment is, consequently, that the ICJ wanted to send a message to the US, and others, in the wake of the invasion of Iraq, which according at least to the US, was partially based on the law of national and collective self-defence. Indeed, as Judge Simma noted, the case provided the ICJ an opportunity to opine upon the legal limits of the use of force 'precisely at a time when the effectiveness of these rules is being challenged to the breaking-point', and 'in a context and at a time when such a reconfirmation is called for with the greatest urgency'.[128] Other Judges indicated that there was a degree of incoherence in restricting the jurisdictional scope of the case strictly to the relevant treaty, and then embarking upon what was fundamentally an examination of customary international law on the use of force.[129]

Indeed, if this expansive review was in fact justified under a jurisdiction based in the treaty provisions at issue, it is difficult to see why maritime IHL was not also a relevant implied legal context. Again, it was Judge Simma who explicitly observed that the question as to whether the military operations carried out by Iran and Iraq against neutral shipping were legitimate, was indeed a valid and relevant one.[130] Perhaps the core of this criticism is simply that the ICJ spent no—or at least insufficient—intellectual capital explaining why, from the very outset, they discarded IHL as a means of imposing a legal characterisation upon the situation, and maritime IHL as a tool for legal analysis of incidents and series of incidents. Clearly, the incidents—particularly the 5 days linking the mining of *USS Samuel B Roberts* and Operation Praying Mantis—were capable of characterisation as a set of linked engagements within an armed conflict, just as the series of maritime and other engagements in the *Nicaragua Case* were considered, from a holistic perspective, as incidents of maritime armed conflict susceptible to analysis using maritime IHL.

From a legal perspective, the fact-law contexts in both cases were remarkably similar. An international or non-international armed conflict between two parties provided the background for a third state-the US-to engage in military operations at sea. Both sets of military operations involved mine warfare and attacks at and

---

[128] *Nicaragua* 1986 supra n 20, Separate Opinion of Judge Simma, paras 6, 8.

[129] *Nicaragua* 1986 supra n 20, for example: the Separate Opinions of Judges Higgins (at, for example, para 47), Kooijmans (at, for example, paras 24–29, 42–43), and the Dissenting Opinions of Buergenthal (at, for example, paras 45–46), and Owada (at, for example, paras 9–13).

[130] *Nicaragua* 1986 supra n 22, Separate Opinion of Judge Simma, paras 59–64.

from the sea, and are discussed in the language of maritime IHL. From a maritime IHL perspective, what perhaps most notably distinguished these two situations was that even though both sets of facts involved questions as to attribution in opaque circumstances—the degree to which the US exerted control over the Contras and the agents laying naval mines; the degree to which the Iranians could be attributed responsibility for the naval mines—the ICJ was not satisfied as regards sufficiency of evidence for attribution in the *Oil Platforms Case*. It is interesting that in not dissimilar circumstances in the *Corfu Channel Case*, the ICJ had been satisfied that the presence of mines could be attributable to the coastal State.[131]

This observation is not to understate the importance of the ICJ's conscious recognition of the attribution issue. But attribution of responsibility for the mines was only one potential factor in assessing the conflict characterisation of the situation—there were certainly sufficient other indicators of a short, sharp maritime armed conflict between Iran and the US which the Court could have explored. Yet only in the *Nicaragua Case* did the Court make the logical, legally appropriate leap from recognising the context of such maritime incidents, to then analysing at least some of the relevant facts within this maritime IHL framework. As the ICJ has progressed in its appreciation and application of IHL on land, it has arguably regressed in its appreciation and application of IHL at sea.[132]

4.4.2 The Gaza Flotilla Reports

In contrast to the reluctance of the ICJ to grapple comprehensively with issues of maritime IHL, the respective reports relating to the Gaza flotilla incident do provide some illumination of key issues. While there was some internal effort in some of the reports to reconcile the divergence of findings, it is clear that the disparity of results renders such a task illusory.

The themes and styles of each report around the incident reflect the essential struggle between sovereignty (apology) and normativity (utopia) as described by well-known international legal theorist Martii Koskenniemi.[133] There is a strict construction of the technical requirements of a blockade with issues such as duration and geographic scope and 'effectiveness' all being carefully parsed but at the same time, the invocation of the law of blockade being predicated upon broad policy choices of whether these facts constituted an international armed conflict.

---

[131] *Corfu Channel Case*, supra n 24.

[132] Whether the Judges of the ICJ perceived a need to send a message to the US, but were concerned that recognising and assessing the context as an armed conflict may have watered down their jurisdiction, or blunted their message, is in many ways not the issue. The decision to treat the context as one of treaty interpretation and interpretation of a fundamental underpinning norm, to the exclusion of a IHL appreciation was effectively made at the Preliminary Objection Judgment stage in 1996, well before the events of 2003.

[133] See generally Koskenniemi 2005

The Human Rights Council and the Turkish Governments reports conclude in the negative, the Israeli Commission's report takes the opposite stance and the UN Palmer report develops a highly contextual, *sui generis* conclusion. That such determinations equated with divergent national and international preferences might just be a coincidence.

Alternatively, this fits in with our suggested taxonomy of identifying the exposed seams of the law-policy intercessions in accordance with context control preferences. Establishing material facts, navigating constructive ambiguity in terminology and dealing with the inevitable uncertainty of observed violence all factor into determinations of legal characterization. In structuring a policy framework that deals with these variables States are invariably grappling with questions of legal defensibility, facilitating preferred courses of action, attributing status to the 'other' and most significantly managing context control.[134]

Such a framework establishes a useful topology for understanding the manner in which facts and law interrelate, especially in the context of assessing the risks and benefits of whether the existence of an armed conflict allows realisation of broader State preferences. Hence, in the face of these variables, Governments are able to determine the bounds of social reality by their choice of factors that are deemed relevant in any characterization process. Analogical, inductive and deductive reasoning techniques are all employed to find the right answer, but much turns on the premises and selected facts that underpin such reasoning. Broader policy goals of coalition building, maintaining credibility and reputation costs, along with capacities for military, political and economic commitments and escalatory consequences, all act to shape the imprint of mission planning and execution. In such a combination, the role of law loses much of its assumed operative independence. Legal choices are made somewhat redundant or inevitable, depending upon the manner in which the precursors to the exercise of legal judgment are ordered.

The test for whether an international armed conflict exists is remarkably succinct. According to the standard reference point provided by the ICTY in the Tadic case,

> [A]n armed conflict exists whenever there is a resort to armed force between States or protracted armed violence between governmental authorities and organised armed groups or between such groups within a State[135]

The open-ended nature of this test allows for considerable allocation of factual and legal values. In these circumstances, it is not altogether surprising that there were divergent conclusions given the questions of status of non-state actors, the significance of the *de facto* control of Gaza and of course the perennially variable issue of establishing attribution. Given such discretion it is not surprising that the

[134] McLaughlin 2012a, b.

[135] *Tadić v. Prosecutor (Decision on the Defence Motion for Interlocutory Appeal on Jurisdiction)* (International Criminal Tribunal for the Former Yugoslavia, Appeals Chamber, Case No IT-94-1-A, 2 October 1995) at [70].

respective national inquires opted for a conclusion that favoured their national perspectives and the UN Panel of Inquiry was careful to restrict its finding of an international armed conflict in a highly context-specific manner. The UN Panel of Inquiry was able discern an international armed conflict based on the facts before it, and so reinforced the law of blockade in a modern guise. While necessarily providing a measure of certainty, the *sui generis* nature of its analysis restricts the precedential value of its conclusions.

The finding of collective punishment was an extraordinary conclusion reached by both the UN Human Rights Council and the Turkish Commission reports. It is a stretch to argue that Article 33, which prohibits the indiscriminate punishment of protected persons, can apply to the law of blockade. Article 33 is concerned with ensuring that penal liability is incurred individually and that collective punishments are prohibited.[136] Such a focus does not have application to the law of blockade, which is an established method of legitimate warfare. While a blockade necessarily results in hardship for the civilian population being blockaded, its imposition does not exclude the importation of food and medicine[137] and it has never been equated to a collective punishment as is the case with any other legitimate measure of warfare that causes hardship on a civilian population. In the case of the Gaza blockade, food and medicine were allowed into Gaza.[138] It is perhaps symptomatic of the increasing assimilation of international human rights norms within the IHL framework, that such humanitarian priorities are sought to be given such prominence within an operative rule of the Law of Naval Warfare. This point does not seem to have gained traction within the broader 'invisible college' of commentators[139] or States.[140]

The paucity of analysis by the Turkel commission regarding direct participation in hostilities and the equivocal stand on what was lawfully acceptable regarding the application of force, again reflects the fragmented nature of the international legal interpretative structure. The relatively recent International Law Commission Fragmentation study[141] determined that both IHL and IHRL represented archetypes of normative commitment under international law, at least in relation to their humanitarian features that belied the application of traditional interpretative

136 Pictet 1958, pp. 225–226.

137 Doswald-Beck 1995, rule 103 'If the civilian population of the blockaded territory is inadequately provided with food and other objects essential for its survival, the blockading party must provide free passage of such foodstuffs…' and Rule 104 'The blockading belligerent shall allow the passage of medical supplies for the civilian population…'.

138 The Turkel Commission, supra n 52, para 73.

139 See generally Schachter 1977–1978.

140 Following this assertion, there is no evidence in State practice, through promulgation of military manuals or statements by State Governments that Article 33 of the Fourth Geneva Convention applies in the manner advocated by the HRC or Turkish Commission reports.

141 Fragmentation of International Law: Difficulties Arising from the Diversification and Expansion of International Law: Report of the Study Group of the International Law Commission, General Assembly, A/CN.4/L.682, 13 April 2006.

mechanisms.[142] While that may be a reflection of their contemporary status, there has been little attempt to reconcile the two areas in their joint application to a given set of facts within the battle space. The UN Panel of Inquiry observes in its Annex that when effective control is exercised over a boarded ship, even one seeking to breach a blockade, then:

> The human rights obligations of the State enforcing the blockade would therefore come into play once it asserts physical control over the vessel and its passengers, regardless of the ship's position on the high seas. In such a case, the relevant human rights obligations are those of the State exercising effective control over the vessel, rather than the flag State.[143]

While such a legal position is mandated, there is precious little examination of the operational factors that would establish when effective control is manifested and at which stage during the ship's interception. Moreover, what is the role of those members on board who take a direct part in hostilities? Do their ongoing actions undermine a conclusion of 'effective control', or is there a sliding scale? The answers to these queries raise fundamental and grave issues of lawfulness. Proportionality and distinction in a law of armed conflict context is a profoundly different concept than in a law enforcement context. Understanding the indicia of the transition between regimes and operationalizing them requires a high calibration of factual–legal assessment. The generalisations emanating from learned commentators or from the rarefied considerations of Courtrooms are usually frustrating to operational commanders and lawyers due to the abstract renderings of the law they contain. They are invariably difficult to apply in a highly contingent and dangerous set of operational facts.

Significantly, the UN Inquiry makes a pointed reference to legal analysis in general, noting 'The Panel will not add value for the United Nations by attempting to determine contested facts or by arguing endlessly about the applicable law. Too much legal analysis threatens to produce political paralysis'.[144] Such a conclusion is striking in what it says about the legal–policy interface. In this context, it is ironic that the law of naval blockade requires 'effective' responses as part of its constituent elements thus seemingly mandating forceful action. Yet at the same time, the law of blockade does not readily anticipate that a vessel would seek to breach a blockade for protest/political reasons alone. Moreover, the rise of human rights law, were hardly contemplated within the law of naval warfare regime that was largely formulated in the late nineteenth/early twentieth centuries.[145] Such a

---

[142] Id. at para 493 ('Moreover, nothing has undermined Fitzmaurice's original point that for example, human rights and humanitarian law treaties, ... form a special class of non-bilateral ("integral" or "interdependent") instruments that cannot be operated through the same techniques as "ordinary" treaties creating bilateral relationships).

[143] The UN Panel Report, supra n 57, at para 69.

[144] Id. at para 15.

[145] See generally, *Convention (VI) Relating to the Conversion of Merchant Ships into Warships*, The Hague, 18 October 1907; *Convention (VIII) Relative to the Laying of Automatic Submarine Contact Mines*, The Hague, 18 October 1907; *Convention (IX) Concerning Bombardment by*

mix plainly invokes an assessment of the efficacy of a strict legal interpretation to political realities.

More fundamental are the implications of this statement to the grand promise of a liberalist commitment to law. The development of an international legal regime regulating warfare and an allied machinery to enforce such normative standards is the realisation of such a cosmopolitan dream. This derives from the nineteenth century movement to ameliorate the excesses of warfare through law, or even obtain its abolition.[146] Within liberal conceptions of politics, law acts to counterpoise violence to politics rather than allowing it to be consumed by it.[147] The recognition of the limits of law made by the UN panel in this instance is refreshingly honest and suggests that law's liberating and—slightly more negatively—colonising promise is not yet complete. It does also reflect, however, the tendency to equate law with legitimacy and points to the need for a growing sophistication for understanding the significance of law and its political role in adjudicating conflict.

What then is the enduring significance of the Gaza flotilla quasi-judicial reports? They did establish that the law of blockade exists as a key and enduring element of IHL in the contemporary environment. The reliance upon the *San Remo Manual* reinforces the notion that this is 'the age of the manual', not because it is a formally authoritative,[148] but rather because such manuals are useful, available and persuasive references. Even in their disagreements, it was extremely insightful to observe the interpretative approaches taken by the instituted quasi-judicial bodies. In this latter regard, the respective Reports confirmed, yet again, that assimilation and differentiation between IHL and IHRL is a complicated and elusive exercise, but one which is nonetheless doctrinally necessary. Moreover they illuminated clearly the limits and capacities of law and recognised, implicitly at least, the connections between legal validity and political legitimacy.[149] That the various Reports relied upon a largely agreed set of facts enables this event to be a useful case study for understanding the relationship between law and policy.

(Footnote 145 continued)
Naval Forces in Time of War, the Hague, 18 October 1907; *Convention (XI) Relative to certain Restrictions with regard to the Exercise of the Right of Capture in Naval War*, The Hague, 18 October 1907; *Convention (XIII) Concerning the Rights and Duties of Neutral Powers in Naval War*, The Hague, 18 October 1907—available at http://www.icrc.org/ihl.

146 See generally Meyer 2002.

147 Luban 2004, p. 119.

148 The San Remo Manual was the product of a group of experts in the field. It does not represent a Treaty or restatement of the Law by Governments; its persuasiveness depends entirely on the force of its arguments and conclusions. Hence its significance lies in the nature of its methodological approach to locating and stating the applicable law.

149 Kennedy 2006, p. 96 ('In the court of world public opinion, the laws in force are not necessarily the rules that are valid, in some technical sense, but the rules that are persuasive to relevant political constituencies. Whether a norm is or is not legal is a function not of its origin or pedigree, but of its effects. Law has an effect—is law-when it persuades an audience with political clout that something someone else did, or plans to do, is or is not legitimate …)'.

4.5 Conclusion

After promising signs in the *Nicaragua Case*, the ICJ appears to have become more reluctant to engage with the detailed application, analysis and interpretation of maritime IHL issues, including the threshold issue of conflict characterisation in a maritime context. This stands at odds with its more recent willingness to deal with conflict characterisation in land-based contexts, as exemplified in the *Armed Activities on the Territory of the Congo Case*.[150] Perhaps it is a consequence of a lack of opportunity, but the institutional retreat from even considering the potential applicability of maritime IHL, evident in the *Oil Platforms* judgements, is indisputable.

Perhaps more recent forays into land-based IHL contexts, along with the presence on the Court of a noted expert in maritime IHL, presage a different approach should a similar fact nexus presents itself in the near future. Until that opportunity arises, however, we will need to look to the reports of quasi-judicial bodies charged with inquiring into specifically maritime IHL contexts—such as with the case of the various Gaza Flotilla Reports—to provide the necessary lightening rods for detailed contextual application, analysis and debate in terms of maritime IHL. The preparedness of quasi-judicial bodies, through such reports, to grapple with constituent elements of the law of blockade such as duration, geographical extent, humanitarian requirements and even the vexed issue of effectiveness, is welcome. Additionally, in a number of reports there was a courageous attempt to outline the distinctions between IHL and IHRL and differentiate their relevance under the now talismanic 'effective control' test of application. This, in itself, is useful even if the details of such application were left vague and probably impossible to 'operationalize' given the paucity of tactical clarification. Issues such as starvation and collective punishments were also usefully raised and their relevance now subject to broader assessment by engaged constituencies. It does seem very unlikely that these factors will be convincingly embraced in the context of blockade—as advocated in some of the reports—but it was intriguing to observe such arguments being advanced.

It was useful to note that all of the various reports were able to identify the issue of whether or not this was an international armed conflict as a key point of application, and yet frustrating that analysis of this issue largely revolved around mere public statements as to the correct characterisation. While it is conceded that these quasi-judicial bodies are not courts, a prime opportunity to clarify this issue in a meaningful way was not taken up. Nevertheless, the various reports themselves provide a useful external insight into how law and policy interrelate, allowing for a more sophisticated understanding of the manner in which the

[150] *Armed Activities on the Territory of The Congo*, supra n 2.

international community will likely weigh invocation of 'classic' maritime IHL arguments within the dynamic and contested terrain of maritime military operations and their legal framework.

The distinctions between policy and law, and between legal validity and legitimacy, are key to understanding the normative force of legal discourse. Yet such distinctions are rarely acknowledged, let alone embraced. The modes of analysis and the choices made in the respective inquiries do offer insight into the manner in which these fundamental questions are both avoided and engaged. In this respect, it has unarguably been quasi-judicial bodies, such as those stemming from the Gaza flotilla incident, which have to date provided the most useful platform for the application, interpretation and development of maritime IHL.

References

Bannelier K, Christakis T, Heathcote S (eds) (2012) The ICJ and the evolution of international law: the enduring impact of the Corfu channel case. Routledge, London

Bekker P (1997) Oil platforms (Iran vs. United States), preliminary objection, judgment. Am J Int'l L 91:518

Bekker P (2004) Oil platforms (Iran vs. United States). Am J Int'l L 98:550

Dinstein Y (2001) War, aggression and self-defence, 3rd edn. Cambridge University Press, Cambridge

Doswald-Beck L (ed) (1995) San Remo manual on international law applicable to Armed conflicts at sea. Cambridge University Press / International Institute of Humanitarian Law, Cambridge

Garwood-Gowers A (2004) Case concerning oil platforms (Islamic Republic of Iran vs. United States of America): did the ICJ miss the boat on the use of force? Melb J Int'l L 5:241

Hargrove J (1987) The Nicaragua judgment and the future of the law of force and self-defence. Am J Int'l L 81:135

Johnstone I (2008) Law-making through operational activities of international organizations. Geo Wash Int'l L Rev 40:87

Kennedy D (2006) Of war and law. Princeton University Press, Princeton

Koskenniemi M (2005) From apology to utopia. Cambridge University Press, Cambridge

Luban D (2004) A theory of crimes against humanity. Yale J Int'l Law 29:85

McLaughlin R (2012a) Legal-policy considerations and conflict characterisation at the threshold between law enforcement and non-international armed conflict. Melb J Int'l L 13:94

McLaughlin R (2012b) An Australian perspective on non-international armed conflict: Afghanistan and East Timor. In: Watkin K, Norris A (eds) A non-international armed conflict in the 21st century, vol 88. U.S. Naval War College International Law Studies Series, New Port, p 293

Meyer H (2002) The World Court in Action. Rowman and Littlefield Publishers, New York

Moore JN (1987) The Nicaragua case and the deterioration of world order. Am J In'l L 81:151

Pictet J (1958) Commentary on the Fourth Geneva Convention. International Committee of the Red Cross, Geneva

Schachter O (1977–1978) The invisible college of international lawyers. Northwestern U. L. Rev 72:217

Stephens D (2010) Counterinsurgency and stability operations: a new approach to legal interpretation. In: Pedrozo R (ed) The war in Iraq: a legal analysis, vol 86. U.S. Naval War College International Law Studies Series, New Port, p 289

Stephens D (2011) The age of lawfare. In: Pedrozo R, Wollschlaeger D (eds) International law and the changing character of war, vol 87. U.S. Naval War College International Law Studies Series, p 327

Taft W IV (2004) Self-defence and the oil platforms decision. Yale J Int'l L 29:295

Tams C (2005) Light treatment of a complex problem: the law of self-defence in the wall case. EJIL 16:963

Wedgwood R (2005) The ICJ advisory opinion on the Israeli security fence and the limits of self-defence. Am J Int'l L 99:52

Chapter 5
Domestic Humanitarian Law: Developing the Law of War in Domestic Courts

Ashley Deeks

Contents

Ashley Deeks is Associate Professor at the University of Virginia Law School, 580 Massie Road, Charlottesville, Virginia.

A. Deeks (✉)
University of Virginia Law School, Charlottesville, VA 22903, USA
e-mail: adeeks@virginia.edu

D. Jinks et al. (eds.), *Applying International Humanitarian Law in Judicial and Quasi-Judicial Bodies*, DOI: 10.1007/978-94-6265-008-4_5,

5.1 Introduction

The United States is in its twelfth year of its struggle against al Qaeda. This situation, which the United States has treated as an extra-territorial armed conflict with a non-state actor,[1] has implicated a wide array of thorny questions related to international humanitarian law ('IHL'). For structural and political reasons, however, the international community has not attempted to craft a new treaty to regulate this type of armed conflict, which does not fit the standard armed conflict paradigms. Nor has there been state practice of sufficient generality and uniformity to establish new customary IHL. A dozen years in, we have no new *international* rules to guide states' conduct in this and similar contexts.

But that is not to say that we have *no* new rules at all to regulate these types of armed conflict: the new rules simply stem from non-international sources. The domestic legislatures and, importantly for the purposes of this chapter, domestic courts of certain states have played a significant role in setting forth new rules to govern how those states must conduct themselves during these armed conflicts.[2] We might attribute this newly expanded role for courts in the armed conflict context to several factors, including a shift from collectivism to individualism in armed conflict[3] and, relatedly, a growing ability of individuals to bring before courts allegations of unlawful state conduct during wartime. Regardless of the cause, these domestic courts and on a transnational level, courts like the European Court of Human Rights,[4] have stepped in to interpret, extend, and craft laws applicable in armed conflict, producing what this chapter terms 'domestic humanitarian law' ('DHL'). On occasion DHL simply reflects treaty interpretation by domestic courts, but often DHL represents court decisions that effectively create new rules, the sources of which cannot be traced back to treaties alone.[5] These court decisions help answer previously unanswered questions in IHL about who may be detained; the type of detention review to which individuals are entitled; what groups count as co-belligerents; whether there are *non-refoulement*-type limits on certain detainee transfers; and what the nature of these conflicts is.

DHL is important for two reasons. First, by definition it establishes detailed, legally binding rules by which particular states' militaries must conduct themselves in extra-territorial conflicts. Second, DHL has a significant effect on future IHL developments—affecting the likelihood of a future international agreement on those rules; the substance of those future rules in the event such an agreement emerges; the way in which states interpret certain existing treaty provisions; and

---

[1] U.S. Department of Justice White Paper, Lawfulness of a Lethal Operation Directed Against a U.S. Citizen Who Is a Senior Operational Leader of Al-Qaida or an Associated Force, pp. 2–3.

[2] See infra part 4.

[3] Blum 2013.

[4] As discussed below, case law emerging from the European Court of Human Rights must be distinguished in certain ways from the decisions emerging from domestic courts.

[5] See infra part 5.1.

the content of state practice that contributes to the formation of new rules of customary international law. One goal of this chapter is to examine the nature and character of DHL, in order better to understand its relationship to and effect on IHL. A second goal is to assess whether the increasing role of domestic courts in producing rules governing armed conflict is a salutary development.

This chapter proceeds as follows. First, it briefly describes the assertions by the United States and other states that gaps exist in IHL, such that current IHL offers only partial guidance as to how to conduct certain military operations in an extraterritorial conflict against non-state actors. Second, it highlights the international community's inability to negotiate and conclude an international agreement to fill in those gaps, drawing on international relations literature about when issues are suitable for negotiation. Third, it turns to an alternative outlet for resolving some of these challenging IHL issues: domestic courts. It explores some of the doctrinal conclusions emerging from these courts and identifies tensions between different states' DHL. The chapter then considers the precise nature of DHL and concludes by identifying some costs and benefits of amplifying the meaning of IHL in domestic court settings. The chapter focuses primarily on U.S. practice and institutions, but draws on comparable practices in other states where relevant.

5.2 Gaps in IHL

One of the most contentious issues to emerge in the international community in the wake of the September 11 attacks is the extent to which the United States appropriately resorted to military force and an 'armed conflict' paradigm to suppress the security threat posed by al Qaeda. One school of thought asserted that the United States should have relied on a law enforcement model to arrest and prosecute those responsible for those attacks.[6] Another school accepted the idea that the United States lawfully could use military force against al Qaeda but believed that existing IHL provided sufficient guidance to direct U.S. detention, treatment, and transfer practices.[7] A third school accepted that there might be gaps in IHL but sought to fill those gaps with international human rights law.[8] A fourth school, to which the United States, Israel, and some European states subscribe,

---

[6] See Bellinger and Padmanabhan 2011, p. 209 (discussing this view); Pearlstein 2008 (considering reasons why international law should not be applied in current U.S. terrorist-detention situations).

[7] See generally Henckaerts and Doswald-Beck 2005 (concluding that 'the gaps in the regulation of the conduct of hostilities in Additional Protocol II have largely been filled through State practice, which has led to the creation of rules parallel to those in Additional Protocol I, but applicable as customary law to non-international armed conflicts').

[8] International Commission of Jurists, The Eminent Jurists Panel on Terrorism, Counter-terrorism and Human Rights (2009) Assessing Damage, Urging Action. http://www.icj.org/dwn/database/EJP-Report.pdf. Accessed 2 July 2013.

believes that these extra-territorial armed conflicts against armed, non-state groups constitute conflicts for which the governing international law is non-existent, unclear, insufficiently detailed, or, at best, an awkward fit with the facts.[9] Even the International Committee of the Red Cross (ICRC) has conceded that the rules governing detention in non-international armed conflict contain 'gaps and weaknesses' that should be strengthened and that the question of who may be targeted in such conflicts required clarification.[10]

Much has been written in defense of each of these schools.[11] This chapter focuses on the fourth school, because the Executive branches' approach in those countries that adhere to this view has led to a wide range of litigation contesting the rules that these states have applied (or not applied) in the face of those gaps. It also considers DHL that adopts the third school's view—that international human rights law provides rules applicable in armed conflict—because certain courts have taken this position in their case law.

5.3 International Stasis

Given the wide range of views on and intense attention paid to U.S., Israeli, and NATO practices in extra-territorial armed conflicts against non-state actors such as al Qaeda, the Taliban, Hezbollah, Hamas, and Iraq's Jaish al Mahdi, we might have expected to see states convene international conferences to craft new rules to regulate these conflicts. Despite an endless array of multilateral, regional, and transatlantic conferences, panels, debates, and reports on the disputed issues, however, we have seen no attempts on the international stage to negotiate new

---

[9] Blum and Heymann 2010 ('The killing on the basis of blame rather than status, the difficulties in ensuring the accurate identification of the target, and the fact that operations take place outside of a defined battlefield—all make the war paradigm at best a proximate, but by no means a perfect, fit.'); Rona 2007, p. 241; The Guardian, Reid calls for changes to Geneva Convention, 3 April 2006, http://www.theguardian.com/uk/2006/apr/03/politics.terrorism. It is beyond the scope of this chapter to delineate the complicated interplay between domestic and international law; IHL and international human rights law; the armed conflict and law enforcement paradigms; and questions related to extraterritorial application of domestic laws.

[10] Vite S, ICRC Legal Expert, Interview, 28 Nov. 2011, http://www.icrc.org/eng/resources/documents/interview/2011/ihl-development-interview-2011-11-28.htm. Accessed 2 July 2013; International Committee of the Red Cross, Resource Center, 'Direct participation in hostilities: questions & answers', 2 June 2009. http://www.icrc.org/eng/resources/documents/faq/direct-participation-ihl-faq-020609.htm#a3. Accessed 22 July 2013.

[11] See Bellinger and Padmanabhan 2011 (listing literature).

binding IHL rules.[12] This absence of negotiations may be part of a larger trend in international law away from treaty-making more generally. Joost Pauwelyn, Ramses Wessel, and Jan Wouters have argued that traditional forms of international law—such as multilateral treaties—are stagnating in both quality and quantity.[13] They attribute this phenomenon in large part to societal changes: an increasingly transnational set of networks and an increasingly complex society in which authority derives not only from public sources but also private ones.[14] The fact that all actors interested in and affected by IHL are increasingly interconnected and that actors other than states may serve as sources of legal legitimacy surely is relevant to what the next stage of IHL will look like. But there are other factors unique to IHL that also have contributed to this inaction on the international plane.

5.3.1 Politics

Treaty-based IHL faces a persistent irony: major legal developments tend to address problems that arose in the last war, for reasons of human nature and the limits of imagination. The related irony is that it is usually during a conflict that gaps in the law become apparent and that new gap-filling IHL rules would be most helpful. But it is virtually impossible to negotiate rules during a conflict, for reasons of politics and logistics. Afterwards, when it becomes more feasible to craft new rules, the impetus to do so wanes.[15]

That irony has borne itself out in the current conflict between the United States and al Qaeda. At several points during the Bush Administration, many states presumably would have liked to have established a clear set of international rules governing the U.S. conflict with al Qaeda. One even could imagine that the Bush Administration would have welcomed the increased legitimacy that those rules could have delivered. But the atmosphere was so poisonous politically that states

---

[12] At the 31st International Conference of the Red Cross and Red Crescent, states invited the ICRC to 'pursue further research, consultation and discussion in cooperation with States . . . to identify and propose a range of options and its recommendations to: (i) ensure that international humanitarian law remains practical and relevant in providing legal protection to all persons deprived of their liberty in relation to armed conflict.' International Conference of the Red Cross and Red Crescent Resolution. http://www.icrc.org/eng/resources/documents/resolution/31-international-conference-resolution-1-2011.htm. Accessed 2 July 2013. As a result, the ICRC has consulted with various states on detention in NIACs, with the apparent goal of producing a 'soft law' or 'best practices' document.

[13] Pauwelyn et al. 2012.

[14] Id., pp. 10–12.

[15] At least one counter-example exists. Francis Lieber developed and the U.S. military issued General Order 100 after the Civil War had begun, though the Order was a unilateral proclamation, not an international treaty. The War Department issued the Order on April 24, 1863.

never could have reached consensus on a set of new legal rules, even if some states might privately have agreed with the United States that existing IHL was incomplete.[16] Other states were loath to bless the notion that a state could be in an armed conflict with terrorist groups.[17] These states would have resisted the exercise in its entirety. And the United States had good reason to fear that it would have a very hard time garnering support for the approaches it had taken toward members of al Qaeda. Further, U.S. domestic politics were such that the Executive did not want to be seen as providing robust individual protections for members of a group such as al Qaeda, which was reviled in the United States. Politics therefore played a significant role in curtailing any efforts to assemble states to discuss new IHL rules.

5.3.2 Non-reciprocal Incentive Structures

IHL traditionally has been undergirded by symmetrical legal obligation between the conflict's participants and an expectation of roughly reciprocal treatment between the warring parties.[18] As IHL rules have expanded to conflicts with non-state actors who employ terrorist tactics to achieve their objectives, those foundations have been challenged. One thorny problem in crafting a new treaty regulating the treatment by states of transnational non-state groups during armed conflict is that states—reasonably—do not expect to receive reciprocal treatment by those non-state armed groups. This anticipated lack of reciprocity diminishes a state's will to negotiate these treaties, notwithstanding perceived reputational and moral benefits to establishing IHL rules that regulate states' behavior.[19] Even the two core sets of rules in NIAC—Common Article 3 of the Geneva Conventions

[16] New legal rules tend to emerge when, among other factors, trust is high among the relevant players and consensus exists about foundational values. Glennon 2013, p. 563. In the 2002–2008 time frame, trust was low among the United States and many other countries, and there was a patent lack of consensus about the foundational values reflected in U.S. military and intelligence strategies and tactics. See also Keohane 1982, pp. 335–336 ('The condition for [regimes to be formed] is that sufficient complementarity or common interests exist so that agreements benefiting all essential regime members can be made.').

[17] See, e.g., Bellinger 2007 ('Now, I am aware that many Europeans do not agree that we are in a war with al Qaida at all . . . .').

[18] Kretzmer 2009, p. 31.

[19] As Michael Glennon notes, laws emerge when certain conditions are present, including when actors within the system are relatively equal. Glennon 2013, p. 563. Here, one set of affected actors (states) is unequal to the other set of actors (non-state actors). In addition, states with powerful militaries that are currently engaged in conflicts against transnational non-state actors are very differently situated from states with weak militaries and no potential conflicts on the horizon.

and Additional Protocol II—envision some possibility of reciprocal treatment.[20] States that decided to negotiate a new treaty regulating armed conflicts against groups such as al Qaeda would hold little hope for such reciprocal treatment. The structure of negotiations therefore is such that states effectively would be negotiating against themselves. In addition, studies suggest that actors are more likely to comply with norms that embed concepts of reciprocity than with those that do not.[21]

5.3.3 Systemic Diversity

Another reason that states may have been unable to make progress on the international plane is that they have different perceptions of the threat, the relevant adversaries, and the appropriate legal baseline from which to work. This systemic diversity means that states often talk past each other when debating the size of the problem and the rules that should apply to these NIACs.

States face, or envision facing, different kinds of adversaries in these non-international armed conflicts.[22] Groups such as Hamas and Hezbollah, for instance, though often viewed as terrorist groups, have 'civil' or governmental roles in their respective communities in Gaza and Lebanon.[23] Groups such as the ETA in Spain and the FARC in Colombia have political goals that involve participation in the government or greater autonomy for geographic regions of the state in which they operate.[24] Groups such as al Qaeda have far broader and more unattainable goals, including re-creating the Islamic caliphate, destroying Israel,

---

20 Kretzmer 2009, p. 32; 1949 Geneva Convention III, Article 3; Additional Protocol II to the Geneva Conventions, Article 1 (envisioning that non-state actor party to conflict has capacity to comply with IHL).

21 Provost 2012, p. 29 (Empirical analysis suggests that 'norms that do not attract reciprocity have a weaker compliance pull than norms that do'.).

22 For a discussion of the diversity of terrorist groups that may conduct armed activities against states, see generally Waxman 2010.

23 See Civil Military Fusion Centre, Blowback: The Unintended Consequences of Hezbollah in Syria, p. 2, Sept. 2013, https://www.cimicweb.org/cmo/ComplexCoverage/Documents/Reports/20130915_Hezbollah_Final.pdf (describing Hezbollah's provision of social services); Council on Foreign Relations, Backgrounder: Hamas, 27 Nov. 2012, http://www.cfr.org/israel/hamas/p8968 ("Hamas's local support, in many ways, can be traced to its extensive network of on-the-ground social programming, including food banks, schools, and medical clinics."). The Government of Israel has given Hezbollah fighters POW protections in some cases, in hopes of obtaining reciprocal treatment for captured Israeli soldiers.

24 Terrorist Organization Profile, Basque Fatherland and Freedom (ETA), Study of Terrorism and Responses to Terrorism, http://www.start.umd.edu/start/data_collections/tops/terrorist_organization_profile.asp?id=96. Accessed 2 July 2013 (stating that ETA is 'dedicated to a separate nation-state for the Basque people'); id., Revolutionary Armed Forces of Colombia (FARC) ('The FARC's stated goal is to overthrow the current democratic government of Colombia and replace it with a Communist government.').

and forcing U.S. troops out of all Muslim nations, including Saudi Arabia.[25] As a result of these distinctions among groups, the way in which states conceive of these groups and the relevant strategies to defeat them will be different.[26] Legal structures that are appropriate for a conflict against one adversary may make less sense against a very different type of adversary.

In addition to the nature of the threat, states perceive the magnitude of the threat differently. As Robert Kagan put it:

> Strong powers naturally view the world differently than weaker powers. They measure risks and threats differently, they define security differently, and they have different levels of tolerance for insecurity. Those with great military power are more likely to consider force a useful tool of international relations than those who have less military power. The stronger may, in fact, rely on force more than they should.[27]

European states (with the UK as an exception) originally viewed al Qaeda as a threat manageable by law enforcement, though their perceptions of the threat presumably changed somewhat after the Madrid and London bombings by al Qaeda.[28] Even after those attacks, however, the United States and Europe retain different overall assessments of how potent the threat of al Qaeda remains.[29]

5.3.4 Issue Complexity

The sheer complexity and intertwined nature of the various IHL, *jus ad bellum*, and international human rights law questions implicated by transnational armed conflicts may have contributed to the failure of the international community or some sub-set thereof to produce new IHL rules. Even IHL legal experts, both practitioners and academics, have had immense difficulty sorting out the various inter-connected

---

[25] Colucci L (2013) 'Don't Underestimate the al Qaeda Threat', U.S. News (14 March 2013). http://www.usnews.com/opinion/blogs/world-report/2013/03/14/dont-underestimate-the-al-qaeda-threat. Accessed 2 July 2013. As former CIA Director James Woolsey put it, 'Al Qaeda does not want a seat at the table; they want to blow the table up.'.

[26] Waxman 2010, pp. 442–443 ('[T]he structural heterogeneity of transnational terrorist threats means the development of customary international law on the use of force in self-defense against 'terrorism' or even 'state-sponsored terrorism' is likely to be slow and methodologically more challenging than typical interstate issues.'); Transatlantic Threat Perceptions (2002) 8 Strat. Comments, International Institute for Strategic Studies (hereafter 'Transatlantic Threat Perceptions') ('The ethnonationalist groups that have tended to plague Europe used violence with restraint to preserve or secure a place at the negotiating table and to an extent could be politically tamed. Al-Qaeda, by contrast, has no interest in bargaining and seeks to debilitate the US by inflicting mass casualties.').

[27] Kagan 2003, pp. 27–28. With regard to the threat posed by al Qaeda, Kagan argues that Europeans have never really believed that they will be a primary target of that group. Id. at 36.

[28] Phillips J 2006 The Evolving Al-Qaeda Threat. Heritage Foundation (17 March 2006). www.heritage.org/research/lecture/the-evolving-al-qaeda-threat. Accessed 2 July 2013.

[29] Transatlantic Threat Perceptions ('Transatlantic differences in terrorist threat perceptions are, to a degree, justified. The United States is al-Qaeda's *bête-noire* and its preferred target.').

strands of IHL that are implicated by a conflict against a group such as al Qaeda.[30] It is no exaggeration to say that fifteen IHL and human rights experts in a room will have fifteen opinions on the issues. This suggests that states must find some way to disentangle the sub-issues before there can be hope of international agreement on any of the issues—and that states have not yet found a way to achieve this.

5.3.5 Other Factors

A few other factors are worth mentioning. The absence of one or more focal points in the international community for IHL discussions may have made it somewhat more difficult for states to come together to discuss IHL issues, at least in an inclusive forum. In fact, international human rights bodies, including a UN Special Rapporteur, have pursued mandates related to targeted killings and drone use, in part because there is no IHL-specific body to do so.[31] Additionally, notwithstanding continued disagreements about the rules to apply in these NIACs, states do not appear to have withheld significant intelligence and other assistance to the United States as a way to express legal or policy objections. As a result, the United States has a reduced incentive to resolve these differences, because there are limited tangible costs to not doing so. Third, European and other states may believe that the 'al Qaeda paradigm' of armed conflict is unlikely to recur and will run its course in the next few years. If states view the conflict with al Qaeda as sui generis (or as a close cousin of the relatively unique Israeli conflicts with Hamas and Hezbollah), they may perceive the costs of crafting new rules as exceeding the benefits of doing so.

All of these factors have contributed to a situation in which the international community failed to come together to craft new rules for these extraterritorial armed conflicts against non-state actors. Yet nature and courts abhor a vacuum, as the past 10 years amply illustrate. Where IHL has proven insufficiently thick, domestic courts often proved to be the lowest cost, most readily available forum in which individuals who are subject to state military action can seek protection. That is why some of the thorniest IHL issues in the past 10 years have ended up in domestic courts, even in the face of legislative and executive hostility to the idea.[32]

---

[30] See generally Bellinger and Padmanabhan 2011.

[31] See UN Human Rights Council (2010) Report of the Special Rapporteur on Extrajudicial, Summary or Arbitrary Executions, Addendum: Study on Targeted Killings. U.N. Doc. A/HRC/14/24/Add.6.

[32] In the wake of September 11, the U.S. government repeatedly objected to judicial involvement in detention cases. See *Hamdi* v. *Rumsfeld*, 542 U.S. 507 (2004); *Rasul* v. *Bush*, 542 U.S. 466 (2004); Respondents' Motion To Dismiss for Lack of Jurisdiction, *Hamdan* v. *Rumsfeld*, No. 05-184 (Jan. 2006). See also Resnik 2006, p. 1573 ('[T]he Bush Administration has consistently opposed judicial oversight of the treatment of detainees alleged to be threats to national security.').

5.4 Conflict Paradigms in IHL: The Emergence of the DHL Phenomenon

This section explores the role of domestic courts in creating DHL, a body of law that likely will constitute an important building block in the next stage of IHL.[33] It considers the specific law of war issues that domestic courts have taken up and discusses the holdings of those cases.

The conflict paradigm that has produced this DHL is a conflict between states and non-state actors, in which non-state actors, operating from outside the territory of victim states, launch attacks that rise to the level of 'armed attacks' under the UN Charter. Neither the Geneva Conventions nor the 1977 Additional Protocols squarely regulate this kind of conflict; this is one reason why many have looked to international human rights law to fill the gaps.[34] John Bellinger and Vijay Padmanabhan have delineated four key questions that IHL and other existing bodies of international law do not answer in this new kind of conflict. Those and other categories of questions have come before domestic courts: (1) What is the nature of an armed conflict between a state and a non-state actor operating outside that state's territory? (2) Who may a state detain or target in this type of conflict? (3) To what kind of review processes are detainees in this conflict entitled? (4) Are there limits on a state's ability to transfer detainees to other states?[35] As noted earlier, a number of states, scholars, and non-governmental actors agree that international law does not currently provide clear answers to these questions. The various domestic court analyses discussed below support that conclusion.

[33] Although this chapter focuses on domestic court decisions, other domestic state practice obviously has emerged in and as a result of the current conflicts. Examples include legislation (including, in the United States, the Detainee Treatment Act, the Military Commissions Act, and the National Defense Authorization Act of 2012, and in Israel the Unlawful Enemy Combatants Law); US military policies (including review boards for detention such as Combatant Status Review Tribunals, Administrative Review Boards, and Detainee Review Boards in Afghanistan); UK detention review procedures in Iraq; and several US Executive Orders (including one establishing a periodic review of the need to retain at Guantanamo detainees who lost their habeas cases). This type of state practice raises fewer novel institutional questions, however, because the executive branch and particularly the military traditionally have been the domestic actors who develop those rules and policies.

[34] Bellinger and Padmanabhan 2011, pp. 209–212.

[35] One might include a fifth category: for what acts may individuals fighting in this conflict be tried criminally? For reasons of space, I do not take on this category. It is certainly possible, however, that decisions in various U.S. military commissions and federal cases will shed light on this question.

5.4.1 Nature of the Armed Conflict

One perplexing aspect of the type of conflict between the United States and al Qaeda is how to characterize it. Is it more like an international armed conflict because it includes a state that is fighting a conflict outside of its own territory? Is it more like a non-international conflict because it is a struggle between a state and non-state actors? A key reason that it matters how one characterizes the conflict is that the rules for each type of conflict are different.[36] In the *Targeted Killings* case, the Israeli Supreme Court concluded that 'the law that applies to the armed conflict between Israel and the terrorist organizations in the [occupied territories] is the international law dealing with armed conflicts. According to that view, the fact that the terrorist organizations and their members do not act in the name of a state does not turn the struggle against them into a purely internal state conflict.'[37] Having reached that conclusion, however, the Court still had to determine whether members of terrorist organizations should be viewed as combatants, civilians or something else. In effect, the determination that the conflict was of an 'international' nature did not resolve for the Court the ultimate question about whether and when Israel lawfully could use force against the individuals at issue. Nevertheless, it reflects one court's assessment of how to conceive of a conflict between these types of actors.

The U.S. Supreme Court conceived of it differently, effectively creating an international 'circuit split' between supreme courts. In *Hamdan* v. *Rumsfeld*, the Court stated,

> 'We need not decide [whether the full set of Geneva Conventions protections apply to the conflict between the United States and al Qaeda] because there is at least one provision of the Geneva Conventions that applies here even if the relevant conflict is not one between signatories[...] The term 'conflict not of an international character' is used [in Common Article 3] in contradistinction to a conflict between nations.'[38]

Thus, in a comparable factual context, the Supreme Court appears to have concluded that the conflict in which the United States detained Mr. Hamdan—the conflict with al Qaeda—was non-international.[39]

---

[36] Even if one concludes that neither the laws of international or non-international armed conflict is a perfect fit, deciding that the transnational armed conflict looks more like one or the other will dictate one's starting point for modifying the rules.

[37] *Public Committee Against Torture in Israel* v. *Government of Israel* (Targeted Killings), HCJ 769/02 (IsrSC 2006), para 21, available at http://elyon1.court.gov.il/files_eng/02/690/007/a34/02007690.a34.pdf.

[38] *Hamdan* v. *Rumsfeld*, 548 U.S. 557, 629 (2006) (concluding that a conflict between individuals and states is distinguishable from a Common Article 2 conflict chiefly because it does not involve a clash between nations).

[39] Although it technically may have reserved the issue of whether the conflict was international, the Court determined that, as a matter of treaty law, Common Article 3 applied. It is impossible for a conflict to be both international and non-international, at least under a plain language

If this issue makes its way into treaty negotiations, the way that states decide to characterize or denominate the conflict almost surely will be less important than what they decide about the rights and obligations that attach to states fighting those conflicts. This inter-state divide merits several comments, though. First, it further supports arguments by the United States and others that the existing baskets of rules are an imperfect fit with this conflict: if the fit were clear, the respective Supreme Courts would have agreed on how to characterize the basket. Second, these cases gesture toward a likely substantive outcome that accords a quantity of protections that falls somewhere between those the law currently accords in international armed conflicts and those it accords in non-international armed conflicts. Third, it may bolster the views of those who argue for eliminating distinctions between types of conflicts entirely.[40]

5.4.2 *Who a State Lawfully May Detain or Target During Armed Conflict*

Traditionally, decisions about which individuals a state may detain or target during armed conflict have fallen almost exclusively to that state and its military officials. The Geneva Conventions give states parties significant discretion to decide in international armed conflicts whether a detainee is entitled to prisoner of war status and whether a civilian poses an imperative threat to security such that he is subject to internment. Much has been written about the ways in which the 'new' conflicts press on those existing categories, leaving states to analogize to existing categories of detainability.[41] In part because the treaties regulating both international and non-international armed conflict accept that a state may target and, by deductive reasoning, detain civilians who take direct part in hostilities, states have been forced to assess, through an iterative process, what activities fall within that description.[42] At the same time that the executive branches of the United States, Israel, Australia, and many NATO countries have wrestled with that issue, the inquiry also has found its way to U.S. and Israeli courts.

U.S. courts have waded deeply into this question—at least as it relates to detention—through the vehicle of habeas cases brought by Guantanamo detainees. These cases interpret whether a particular individual's detention is consistent with a U.S. statute, the 2001 Authorization for Use of Military Force (AUMF), as

(Footnote 39 continued)
reading of those terms. Therefore, if Common Article 3 applied, the bulk of the Geneva provisions applicable to international armed conflicts did not.

40 Brooks 2004, pp. 755–756.

41 Goodman 2009.

42 See Additional Protocol I, Article 50(3); Additional Protocol II, Article 13(3).

informed by the laws of war.[43] In practice, these cases have required courts to interpret specific language from existing IHL treaties and concepts, to reason by analogy from international armed conflict to non-international armed conflict, and to create DHL. Specifically, these courts have considered what it means to take 'direct part in hostilities';[44] whether *only* those who take direct part in hostilities in non-international armed conflicts may be targeted or detained;[45] what it means to be a member of (or part of) an organized armed group;[46] whether a non-member of an armed group nevertheless is detainable based on his support to that group;[47] and what relationship between armed groups constitutes 'co-belligerency'.[48] While these cases have focused exclusively on detainability, scholars have pointed out that these holdings will affect targeting questions as well.[49]

The Israeli Supreme Court also has stepped into the breach, parsing on the merits legal issues related to detention and targeting. In a situation redolent of the U.S. courts' work interpreting the AUMF against the background of the laws of war, the Israeli Supreme Court has considered whether Israel's Unlawful Combatants Act is constitutional and consistent with Israel's law of war obligations.[50] That statute allows Israeli security authorities to detain unlawful combatants, a category of people defined as persons who participate in hostilities directly or indirectly or are members of forces that carry out hostilities against Israel and who do not qualify for prisoner of war status.[51] The statute establishes detention review procedures, including initial and periodic judicial review, the right to meet with a lawyer no more than 7 days after first being brought before the district court, and a right of appeal to the Supreme Court.[52] The Court concluded that there was some

---

43 See Respondents' Memorandum Regarding the Government's Detention Authority Relative to Detainees Held at Guantanamo Bay, In re Guantanamo Bay Litigation, Misc. No. 08-442 (JDB) (13 March 2009) (arguing that the United States and courts should reason by analogy to those detainable in international armed conflict).

44 *Gherebi* v. *Obama*, 609 F. Supp.2d 43, 63–66 (D.D.C. 2009) (discussing proper interpretation of 'direct participation in hostilities').

45 Id.

46 *Bensayah* v. *Obama*, 610 F.3d 718, 725 (D.C. Cir. 2010) (holding that position in the command structure of the armed group is sufficient, but not necessary, to show detainability).

47 *Hatim* v. *Gates*, 632 F.3d 720 (D.C. Cir. 2011) (holding that the government may detain those who purposefully and materially support al Qaeda or the Taliban).

48 *Hamlily* v. *Obama*, 616 F. Supp.2d 63, 75–77 (D.D.C. 2009) (interpreting 'associated forces' to be equivalent to 'co-belligerents' and defining the concept as a 'fully fledged belligerent fighting in association with one or more belligerent powers').

49 R. Benhalim, R. Chesney and B. Wittes, The Emerging Law of Detention. Brookings Institution, Washington, (2010) p. 22 ('[A] conclusive judicial determination adopting a narrow understanding of the range of groups and individuals subject to detention under the AUMF may raise comparable questions regarding the range of groups and individuals subject to targeting or other military measures.').

50 *A&B* v. *State of Israel* 2007.

51 Incarceration of Unlawful Combatants Law, 5762–2002, sec 2.

52 Id.

tension between the definition and the laws of war, but ameliorated that difference by interpreting the Unlawful Combatants Act law to require that the person's contribution to hostilities not be negligible and, for those individuals who were members of the force carrying out hostilities, that those individuals have real connections with the relevant organization.[53]

The European Court of Human Rights also has evaluated targeting in non-international armed conflict. In a series of cases adjudicating Russia's use of force in Chechnya, the ECtHR used human rights law, rather than IHL, as the yardstick by which it evaluated Russia's conduct.[54] Its conclusions—which allowed Russia to target insurgent groups only when 'absolutely necessary'—stand in tension with the standard understanding of IHL and targetability in NIAC.[55] Although ECtHR case law, which emerges from an international tribunal, has a different character than DHL, that case law almost certainly influences the DHL that emerges from the courts of Council of Europe member states, which know that their decisions may face ECtHR review.

In addition to evaluating detention questions, the Israeli Supreme Court also has considered targeting issues, most notably in its *Targeted Killings* case.[56] There, in great detail, it wrestled with what it means to 'take direct part in hostilities', such that a state lawfully may target someone who was doing so. The Court not only parsed what it means to 'take part… in hostilities', but also what it means to do so 'directly', and what period of time is relevant to that determination.[57] The Court then rolled up its sleeves and listed activities that fall on one side of the line or the other. Direct participation, in its view, includes collecting intelligence on a foreign army; transporting unlawful combatants to or from the site of hostilities; operating or supervising the operation of weapons that those combatants use, even if distant from the battlefield; driving ammunition to the place it will be used to conduct hostilities; and voluntarily serving as a human shield. Those who enlist and send others to the fight also are taking direct part.[58] In contrast, those who interface with unlawful combatants by selling them food or medicine; providing them general strategic analysis or logistical support (including financial support); or distributing their propaganda are not taking direct part in hostilities.[59]

---

[53] *A&B*, para 21 ('[W]e are drawn to the conclusion that in order to detain a person it is not sufficient for him to have made a remote, negligible or marginal contribution to the hostilities against the State of Israel.'); id. ('[I]t is insufficient to show any tenuous connection with a terrorist organization in order to be included within the cycle of hostilities in the broad meaning of this concept.').

[54] *Isayeva, Yusupova and Bazayeva* v. *Russia*, ECtHR, App Nos 57947–49/00 (24 Feb. 2005); *Isayeva* v. *Russia*, ECtHR, App No 57950/00 (24 Feb. 2005).

[55] Abresch 2005, p. 742, 758.

[56] See supra note 37.

[57] Id., paras 30, 34, and 38.

[58] Id., paras 35–37.

[59] Id., para 35.

There is a sub-issue with which several courts have wrestled: need a state attempt to detain someone taking a direct part in hostilities before resorting to lethal force against him? The Israeli Supreme Court in the *Targeted Killings* case concluded that Israel may not carry out a targeted killing 'when it is possible to arrest a terrorist taking a direct part in hostilities, without significant risk to the lives of soldiers'.[60] Similarly, the ECtHR concluded that the ECHR 'permits the use of lethal force only where capture is too risky, regardless of whether the target is a "combatant" or a "civilian"'.[61]

This category of decisions—perhaps more than any other discussed here—almost certainly will play an important role in future international discussions about who is detainable and targetable in these conflicts.[62] It is possible that the executive branches in states whose courts have created DHL might seek to create international rules different from those contained in their domestic court decisions. However, there is reason to think that these affected states may prefer to preserve the rules that their courts have developed for them, because they may have become accustomed to operating under those rules or because they see substantive merit in those rules. The courts have had before them a wide variety of fact patterns, have sought internally to develop a coherent and categorical approach across facts, and have been informed in their considerations by input from state militaries, intelligence services, NGOs, and the detainees themselves. While the courts' judgments are not binding on any state other than their state of nationality, their influence likely will reach beyond the borders of those states.

5.4.3 Detention Review Processes

Before September 11, 2001, there were very few situations in which civil courts considered whether wartime detainees were entitled to judicial or other procedural review of their military detentions.[63] The Third Geneva Convention and the Additional Protocols quite clearly do not anticipate that detainees will receive direct judicial or administrative review of the lawfulness of their detention. The Fourth Geneva Convention requires states to provide protected persons with

---

[60] Id., Beinisch concurrence.

[61] See Abresch 2005, p. 742. This approach stems in large part from the simultaneous application by the European Court of Human Rights of international human rights law and IHL, where the former provides that a state may use lethal force only where it is 'absolutely necessary.' ECHR Article 2(2). The ICRC DPH Study also took this position, although the inclusion of this section of the Study caused several expert participants to withdraw their names from the final Study.

[62] Studies such as the ICRC's DPH study (and certain participants' reactions thereto) also will play an important role in future discussions.

[63] US Supreme Court cases such as *Johnson* v. *Eisentrager*, 339 U.S. 763 (1950); *In re Yamashita*, 327 U.S. 1 (1946); and *Ex Parte Quirin*, 317 U.S. 1 (1942) were about the review of criminal convictions during wartime.

review of their internment by a court or administrative board, but does not require those states to provide habeas-type judicial review of the detention determinations that the state established pursuant to the Convention.[64]

Yet, the U.S. Supreme Court in *Boumediene* held that U.S. detainees at Guantanamo Bay are constitutionally entitled to a writ of habeas corpus.[65] By definition, that entails review of the lawfulness of their detention by an Article III court. More recently, the D.C. Circuit in *Maqaleh* v. *Gates* held that three non-Afghan nationals held by the United States in Afghanistan were not entitled to habeas corpus, and thus were not entitled to have the legality of their detentions reviewed by a court.[66] Among the *Maqaleh* court's considerations were the fact that the detainees were held in an active theater of war that was not under the *de jure* sovereignty of the United States and that there would be significant practical problems in applying the writ to those detainees held in Afghanistan.[67] Thus, for now, only detainees held at Guantanamo or within the United States are entitled to habeas review.

In the case of *Al Jedda*, which also related to the legality of a detention during an armed conflict between a state (the United Kingdom) and non-state actor (a member of a terrorist group in Iraq) outside the state's territory, the UK Supreme Court concluded that, although a UN Security Council Resolution authorized Al Jedda's detention in broad sense, the United Kingdom nevertheless was required to 'ensure that the detainee's rights under Article 5 [of the European Convention on Human Rights] are not infringed to any greater extent than is inherent in such detention'.[68] ECHR Article 5 includes a requirement that everyone deprived of his liberty by detention 'shall be entitled to take proceedings by which the lawfulness of his detention shall be decided speedily by a court'.[69] On appeal, the ECtHR rejected the idea of trying to reconcile the Security Council Resolution and ECHR Article 5. It held that the UK simply violated its ECHR obligations in detaining Al Jedda 'without charge and without judicial guarantees',[70] effectively foreclosing ECHR states parties from conducting long-term security detentions during armed conflict, with the possible exception of detention cases that have obtained an explicit UN Security Council approval.

---

[64] Fourth Geneva Convention of 1949, Articles 43, 78.

[65] *Boumediene* v. *Bush*, 553 U.S. 723 (2008). The *Hamdi* case, decided well before *Boumediene*, required the U.S. government to provide an American citizen detainee with notice of the reasons for his detention and an opportunity to rebut those reasons before a neutral decision-maker. Even if future law of war discussions do not mandate judicial review for most cases, it seems likely that decisions such as *Hamdi* would, in conjunction with provisions such as those found in the Fourth Geneva Convention and Article 75, influence other types of process to which detainees would be entitled. See Deeks 2009.

[66] *Maqaleh* v. *Gates*, 605 F.3d 84 (D.C. Cir. 2010).

[67] Id. at 97–98.

[68] *R (Al Jedda)* v. *Secretary of State for Defence*, [2007] UKHL 58, para 39.

[69] ECHR Article 5.

[70] *Al Jedda* v. *United Kingdom*, Grand Chamber, 27021/08, para 105 (2011).

In addition to decisions granting detainees access to civilian courts so that those courts could review their detentions, those courts have had to determine the procedures by which to conduct those reviews and what the standard of proof should be to uphold detention. The Israeli Supreme Court has demanded 'clear and convincing evidence' that the detainee poses a security threat.[71] The U.S. D.C. Circuit has suggested that it would accept a lower, 'some evidence' standard.[72] The U.S. courts also have established procedures by which detainees' counsel are permitted access to classified material,[73] and have determined when it is appropriate to take into account a detainee's involuntary statements when assessing his detainability.[74]

Now that some courts have concluded that judicial review of detention is required in some circumstances, even if they have not relied on IHL directly to reach that decision, their conclusions are very likely to color future international conversations both about what protections future IHL treaty rules should mandate and about what is operationally practical in particular circumstances. The various U.S. decisions stake out different places on the spectrum for judicial review, depending on the nature and location of the detention facilities; that seems likely to frame the issue and highlight the interplay between the logistics of court review and operational realities.[75] The ECtHR jurisprudence, in contrast, cedes no ground to operational complexities. As a result, the state practice that will result if and as ECHR member states implement this decision undoubtedly will look different from that of the United States.

5.4.4 Limits on Transfers

No IHL treaty provisions regulate the transfer of detainees in non-international armed conflicts, in large part because traditional non-international armed conflicts took place within one state and did not involve transfers of detainees from one state's custody to another. These new conflicts regularly raise that prospect, however, including in the complicated situation in which the detaining state is operating on foreign soil and seeks to — or is asked to — transfer a person back to

---

[71] *A&B* v. *Israel*, para 22.

[72] *Bihani* v. *Obama*, 590 F.3d 866, 878 n.4 (D.C. Cir. 2010).

[73] *In re Guantanamo Detainee Litigation*, 577 F.Supp.2d 143 (D.D.C. 2008) (protective order). Israel's statute governing preventive detention of security threats allows the Israeli courts to admit evidence without disclosing it to the detainee or his counsel if the disclosure were likely to harm state security. Incarceration of Unlawful Combatants Law, 5762–2002, sec 5(e).

[74] See R. Chesney, L. Reynolds and B. Wittes, The Emerging Law of Detention 2.0, p. 82, Brookings Institution, Washington (2012) (hereafter 'Emerging Law 2.0') ('A statement will not be discredited merely because it was given in a custodial context without access to counsel or the benefit of a *Miranda*-style statement of rights . . . and no one has suggested the admissibility of the fruits of coercion rising to the level of torture.').

[75] See supra notes 65–67.

the territorial state's custody.[76] While all states seem to agree that a state may not transfer any detainee to another state's custody if it believes that he faces a real risk of torture, the agreement ends there. Some states take that position as a matter of law; others adopt it as a matter of policy; and some believe that the obligations extend much further than that basic proposition.[77]

To date, U.S. courts hearing disputes about this proposition have not reached the merits of particular transfer decisions during armed conflict. Instead, the courts have focused on whether judicial review is available pre-transfer and have concluded that it is not. In 2006, two U.S. nationals held by the Multi-National Forces—Iraq (MNF-I) petitioned for habeas corpus in U.S. court, asking the court to block their transfer by MNF-I to the government of Iraq (which had issued arrest warrants for them).[78] The Supreme Court, hearing their consolidated cases as *Munaf v. Geren*, considered 'whether United States district courts may exercise their habeas jurisdiction to enjoin our Armed Forces from transferring individuals detained within another sovereign's territory to that sovereign's government for criminal prosecution'.[79] The Court concluded that the courts had statutory habeas jurisdiction over the individuals (presumably because they were U.S. citizens), but could not enjoin U.S. forces from transferring individuals within Iraq's territory to the Iraqi government for prosecution.[80]

Guantanamo detainees have been no more successful in suing to block their transfers from Guantanamo Bay to other countries. In a case known as *Kiyemba II*, the D.C. Circuit held that *Munaf* controlled to bar courts from granting writs of habeas corpus to block U.S. transfers of Guantanamo detainees to foreign countries, even when the individuals being transferred would face continued detention or prosecution under the receiving country's laws.[81] The Supreme Court denied certiorari in 2010.[82] U.S. judges thus lack the authority to block the transfer of a

[76] Deeks 2008.

[77] See Bellinger and Padmanbhan 2011, pp. 41–42 (describing lack of guidance in law of war treaties) and 46 (noting that the United States and UK believe that non-refoulement protection does not apply to in-country transfers as a matter of law); *Amnesty Int'l Canada* v. *Att'y Gen. of Canada*, 2008 FC 336 (12 March 2008), para 64 ('Before transferring a detainee into Afghan custody, General Laroche must be satisfied that there are no substantial grounds for believing that there exists a real risk that the detainee would be in danger of being subjected to torture or other forms of mistreatment at the hands of Afghan authorities.').

[78] *Omar* v. *Harvey*, 410 F. Supp.2d 19 (D. D.C. 2006); *Mohammed* v. *Harvey*, 456 F. Supp.2d 115 (D.D.C. 2006).

[79] *Munaf* v. *Geren*, 553 U.S. 674 (2008).

[80] Id.

[81] *Kiyemba v. Obama*, 561 F.3d 509 (D.C. Cir. 2009).

[82] *Kiyemba v. Obama*, 559 U.S. 1005 (2010).

detainee from Guantanamo to another country, as long as the United States acts consistently with its stated policy not to transfer a detainee to a place where he is more likely than not to face torture.[83]

Canada's courts have been similarly cautious about blocking transfers of detainees from Canadian custody to the custody of Afghanistan, at least when conducted pursuant to an agreed bilateral framework. In 2007, Amnesty International sued Canada, seeking to block Canada's detainee transfers to Afghanistan. The Canadian Court of Appeals concluded that Canada lacked effective control over Afghan territory, such that the Canadian Charter and its prohibition on cruel and unusual treatment did not apply to that territory.[84] Instead, Canada and Afghanistan had agreed that international law would govern the treatment of detainees in Canadian custody and their transfer to Afghanistan. That agreement provided that they were entitled to the 'same treatment as Prisoners of War'.[85] Further, Canada's policy was to transfer detainees only when satisfied that there were no substantial grounds for believing that the detainee would be in danger of being subjected to torture.[86] The Canadian Court of Appeals thus declined to halt detainee transfers to Afghanistan, even in the face of torture allegations.[87]

The ECtHR has taken a more detainee-protective approach. In *R (Al Saadoon & Mufdhi)*, the facts of which are similar to *Munaf*, the UK military sought to transfer two Iraqi murder suspects to the Iraqi government for trial.[88] The individuals, who faced the death penalty under Iraqi law, sued to block their transfer as violative of the ECHR. Although the UK courts concluded that the detainees were not within the UK's jurisdiction for purposes of application of the ECHR, the ECtHR disagreed. That Court concluded that the applicants were within the jurisdiction of the ECHR and that the UK lawfully could not transfer the applicants, given the real risk that they would be sentenced and executed.[89] For states parties to the ECHR, then, the rule for transfers—including transfers of detainees held in transnational armed conflicts—is that the state may not transfer a person where there is a real risk that the person will receive the death penalty or be subject to ill-treatment.

A UK divisional court has applied that standard to UK transfers to specific Afghan detention facilities. The UK court concluded that certain transfers were lawful, but only when they met several stringent conditions, including a requirement that the UK be given access to each detainee on a regular basis; have the opportunity for private interviews with the transferees; actually visit and interview

[83] *Munaf*, 533 U.S. at 702 (appearing to reserve the 'extreme case' in which the Executive determines that a transferee is likely to face torture but chooses to transfer him anyway).

[84] *Amnesty International Canada* v. *Canada (Chief of the Defence Staff)*, 2008 FCA 401, [2009] 4 F.C.R. 149.

[85] Id., para 30.

[86] Id., para 36.

[87] Id.

[88] *R (Al Saadoon & Mufdhi)*, 61498/08 (Merits and Just Satisfaction) (2010).

[89] *Al Saadoon & Mufdhi* v. *United Kingdom*, Admissibility Decision (2009), para 88.

each transferee regularly; and consider suspending transfers if the Afghan National Directorate of Security facility in Kandahar denied the UK access without good reason.[90] This detailed decision further lays down possible parameters for transfers of detainees during armed conflict, and, along with UK state practice pursuant to that decision, will influence future negotiations about IHL rules regarding detainee transfers.[91]

5.5 Implications for the Future of IHL

5.5.1 The Nature of DHL

Having seen what DHL looks like doctrinally, we must ask: What, exactly, is this law emerging from domestic courts? The precise nature of these court decisions is a matter for debate. Are the decisions best thought of as purely domestic law? Treaty interpretation? "Subsequent practice" that guides later treaty interpretation? A 'common law of war'? Hybrid domestic/international law?[92] It is difficult to reach definitive conclusions on this point; indeed, specific domestic judicial decisions will have different characters, depending on the extent to which the court is (i) interpreting international law directly; (ii) interpreting domestic law through the lens of international law; or (iii) crafting new domestic law in a field of interest to international law, reasoning by analogy from related bodies of international law.[93] This chapter does not resolve how best to characterize DHL. Nevertheless, it is useful to have a general understanding of DHL's forms and characteristics to guide normative assessments of its existence and further development.

The first category of DHL is the least controversial from an international law perspective. This DHL is nothing more than interpretations and applications by domestic courts of the international legal obligations to which their states are bound.[94] The Israeli Supreme Court's decision in the *Targeted Killings* case is, at least in part, a direct interpretation of an IHL treaty term.

---

90 *R (Evans)* v. *Secretary of State for Defence*, [2010] EWHC 1445 (Admin), para 320.

91 Several cases related to transfers during armed conflict are pending in Danish courts. See *Ghousouallah Tarin* v. *Ministry of Defence*, Case No. 180/2011 (transfer to Afghanistan); *Brak & Others* v. *Ministry of Defence*, Case No. B3421-11 (Iraq), *Shahel & Others* v. *Ministry of Defence*, Case No. B-397-12 (Iraq), *Saadoun & Others* v. *Ministry of Defence*, Case No. B-1162-12 (Iraq), *Al Albarrak & Others* v. *Ministry of Defence* (unnumbered) (Iraq).

92 Roberts 2011, p. 60 (discussing 'hybrid international/national norms').

93 See Tams and Tzanakopoulos 2013, pp. 4–5.

94 In the language of Article 31 of the Vienna Convention on the Law of Treaties, this is 'subsequent practice', though not subsequent practice that necessarily establishes the agreement of the parties regarding the treaty's interpretation. The World Trade Organization's Appellate Body has stated that for an act to count as 'subsequent practice' for purposes of Article 31(3)(b) of the Vienna Convention on the Law of Treaties, there must be a 'concordant, common, and

The second category of DHL is harder to pin down. Where a state's domestic law incorporates international law by reference—as the U.S. Executive branch believes that the 2001 AUMF does—and therefore requires the domestic court adjudicating the issue to opine on the parameters of that international law through the lens of a domestic statute, what is the nature of the decision that emerges? Is it a domestic legal decision that binds the state but has no implications for international law? Is it a more diluted form of 'subsequent practice' interpreting a treaty than we saw in the first category? Will that judicial decision bear some weight in future consideration (by other states, other states' domestic courts, or other international bodies) of the meaning of that international law provision?

At the very least, the decisions in the second category constitute state practice, and thus may contribute at an early stage to the formation of new customary IHL rules. Nevertheless, whether the decisions are accompanied by opinio juris is a difficult question.[95] Indeed, these cases may stimulate multiple examples of state practice, in the form of briefs by the U.S. government asserting what it believes international law requires; amicus briefs by other states providing their own interpretation of IHL; and the domestic court decisions, which serve as a different form of state practice and which may represent a rule somewhat different from that proffered by the U.S. Executive branch.[96] The existence of this DHL—given its transparent and relatively accessible nature—may inspire the production by other states of state practice in the form of public rejection of or praise for these DHL decisions. As a practical matter, too, U.S. and European practice on the battlefield often takes place in the context of coalitions; to the extent that those coalitions attempt to harmonize their rules, domestic judicial decisions have indirect impacts on the practice of other states in the coalition. The need to operate as a coalition produces additional state practice by these coalition members, practice that may be roughly consistent among the involved states.

The third category of decisions is least likely to garner traction on the international plane or be viewed as having international 'weight.' Yet this category of law is quantitatively significant. Much of the work of the domestic courts in this area arguably is not just 'prescription and application of international law',[97] but

(Footnote 94 continued)
consistent' set of acts or pronouncements. Appellate Body Report, Japan-Taxes on Alcoholic Beverages, 10, WT/DS8/AB/R, WT/DS10/AB/R, WT/DS11AB/R (Oct. 4, 1996) at 12. With a small (though growing) set of examples of DHL from a limited number of states, it is hard to argue that DHL meets the Appellate Body's test.

95 See Henckaerts and Doswald-Beck 2005, p. xxxii ('Both physical and verbal acts of States constitute practice that contributes to the creation of customary international law. . . . Verbal acts include military manuals, national legislation, national case-law . . . [and] executive decisions and regulations.'). In the view of some states and scholars, this would constitute practice by 'specially affected' states. North Sea Continental Shelf [1969] ICJ 4, 43.

96 Wuerth 2012, p. 826 (describing possibility of conflicts between judicial and executive state practice).

97 Lillich 1970–1971, p. 9.

also the creation and development of that law.[98] Many of these domestic cases require judges to reason by analogy from existing IHL, and then to apply those analogies to new circumstances that most players agree should be covered by some form of IHL. For instance, in March 2009, the Obama Administration argued to the D.C. District Court that the AUMF gives the Executive branch the authority to detain individuals whose relationship with the Taliban or al Qaeda 'would, in appropriately analogous circumstances in a traditional international armed conflict, render them detainable.'[99] This suggests that the courts must first interpret traditional IHL principles and then apply those principles analogically to a new conflict, thus effectively creating new DHL.[100]

Judges have been surprisingly frank about their law-creating roles here. In a 2011 speech, D.C. District Court Judge Lamberth stated:

> [W]e really have come to a very broad consensus on the way we would make up this law, which we've made up. We had no guidance from Congress. We had four different definitions from President Bush. We got two words in it changed by President Obama, and other than that we've been off and running doing the best we could with adjudicating these cases with very little political differences among the judges.[101]

In similar language, the Israeli Supreme Court has written:

> The legal difficulties with which we must contend stem primarily from the fact that international law has not yet developed the laws of armed conflict to respond to combat against terrorist organizations, as opposed to a regular army. Therefore, we must use interpretational tools in order to adapt the existing humanitarian laws to the difficult reality which the State of Israel confronts.[102]

Where a domestic court undertakes overt law-creation—as when the UK court establishes procedural requirements that the UK military must meet before it may transfer detainees in Afghanistan to certain facilities,[103] or when U.S. courts select a standard of proof by which a state must persuade those courts that the Executive is detaining someone lawfully in a NIAC—it feels as though we are far from

---

[98] Tams and Tzanakopoulos 2013, p. 1.

[99] See Brief of Respondent, *Hamlily* v. *Obama*, 616 F. Supp. 2d 63 (D.D.C. 2009) (No. 05-0763).

[100] Eric Posner suggests that judges often do both things at once. Posner 2009, p. 20 ('Like priests in an ancient society who know that their magic is just an illusion, judges purport to find law—that is, apply the rules—even as they make it. They make law by appealing to vague or conflicting rules that do not indicate a determinate outcome while making a policy choice on the sly.').

[101] Emerging Law 2.0, p. 25. Judge Lamberth also said, 'I think the number of difficult questions presented by the Guantanamo cases is unprecedented in our court. . . . In our court, mostly settled law applies. It makes it interesting. But it really is time-consuming because of the need to proceed carefully' and decide 'precedents for future wars as well as this war.' Rosenberg C (2009) 'Judges siding with detainees in Guantanamo habeas cases'. Miami Herald, 7 Sept 2009. http://www.mcclatchydc.com/2009/09/07/74970/judges-siding-with-detainees-in.html. Accessed 3 July 2013.

[102] *Public Committee* v. *Israel* (Targeted Killings), Pres Beinisch concurrence.

[103] *R (Evans)* v. *Secretary of State for Defence*, [2010] EWHC 1445 (Admin).

international law. And yet the source of the law being created is not entirely domestic: it has roots and analogues in international concepts, not just domestic ones. And it speaks to matters of the sort on which we would expect international regulation. Like the DHL in category two, this category of DHL also should count as state practice, though it would be surprising to find opinio juris attached to such practice.

In addition to DHL's potential to contribute directly to the future shape of IHL in the form of treaty interpretation and customary international law formation, DHL has the potential to affect IHL's future indirectly too. That is, DHL will set the stage for additional international discussions about what the future IHL treaty rules for this kind of conflict will be. DHL decisions offer a diversity of approaches to operational problems confronted by the militaries fighting these conflicts. States bound by DHL decisions will come to the negotiating table having implemented these decisions during conflict and having determined what aspects of the DHL rules are most and least conducive to implementation. DHL decisions also may draw the attention of NGOs and other actors with a stake in the future of IHL, and will prompt those actors to lobby governments in favor of or against the adoption of DHL-derived rules at future international negotiations.

5.5.2 Is DHL Normatively Desirable?

Having reviewed the process by which DHL is forming and considered some of its substantive contours, it is useful to consider whether the development of DHL— and its influence on future IHL—is salutary. This part considers the advantages and disadvantages of this phenomenon, measured against prior decades in which domestic courts played a sharply limited role in evaluating and developing rules applicable during armed conflict.

5.5.2.1 Advantages

Legally Binding Review by a Respected Institution

When a court adjudicates the legality of the rules that a state is applying in an armed conflict, it provides a second layer of review of those rules. Assuming the court is independent, it has the authority to strike down, amend, or uphold the Executive's rule—in short, to have the final say on what a particular rule looks like and how it is interpreted. Independent review, though not cost-free, bears a number of advantages, including error-correction and an ability to force the Executive to consider additional information that it may not have had when first establishing the policy.[104] Court review also can counteract cognitive biases to which the Executive is susceptible, such as the propensity to overreact to perceived threats during times of crisis.[105]

This oversight of the Executive carries particular weight—both domestically and internationally—because it comes from one of the more trusted institutions within a democracy.[106] The Executive branches, including state militaries, are more directly self-interested in the rules by which they fight armed conflicts. The courts operate at a greater remove from the conflicts themselves, and thus may be more objective in their application of existing legal rules and in their ability to reason by analogy from those rules to new situations.[107]

Individual Rights Perspective

As a related matter, Executive branches in many states have strong incentives to prioritize national security at the expense of individual rights protections, and are rewarded for doing so by their constituents.[108] By virtue of the way that cases come before them, courts have the opportunity and ability to focus on individuals.[109] As the U.S. Supreme Court put it in *Hamdi* v. *Rumsfeld*, 'Whatever power the United States Constitution envisions for the Executive in its exchanges with other nations or with enemy organizations in times of conflict, it most assuredly

---

[104] See Pearlstein 2009, p. 1617 ('Beyond simple error correction, some form of independent review or monitoring with full information and incentive-creating capacity could function to check an organization's tendencies to exclude relevant information in decision-making, help decisionmakers avoid capture by narrow conceptions of self-interest, correct decision-making tendencies to miss the strategic forest for the tactical trees, and afford opportunities for organizational learning over time.').

[105] Wells 2004, p. 907.

[106] Kumm 2004, p. 925 ('[C]onstitutional courts have engaged in [the practice of striking down laws generated by the legislative process on grounds of constitutional principle] more or less aggressively in many jurisdictions. In many jurisdictions, they enjoy more public support than any other political institution as a result.'); Grosskopf 2008 (arguing that citizens of democratic governments place the highest levels of trust in unelected constitutional courts over elected institutions).

[107] See Martin 2007, p. 358 (arguing that increased legal review by courts can increase fact-finding accuracy in the Executive Branch). The counter-argument, of course, is that this remove makes it more likely that courts will issue judgments that are insensitive to true military needs and will undercut the security of the state in which they sit. See *U.S.* v. *Hamdi*, 542 U.S. 507 (2004) (Thomas, J., dissenting).

[108] Cole 2008, p. 1335 ('Precisely because we rely so heavily on the executive to maintain our security, we should be skeptical of its ability to give sufficient weight to the liberty side of the balance.'); Sunstein 2004, pp. 52–53 ('A primary task of the President is to keep the citizenry safe, and any error on that count is likely to produce extremely high political sanctions. As a result, the President has a strong incentive to take precautions even if they are excessive and even unconstitutional.').

[109] Sunstein 2004, p. 53 (describing courts' 'historic mission' to 'protect individual liberty').

envisions a role for all three branches when individual liberties are at stake'.[110] This is not to suggest that Executive branches are immune to individual rights perspectives when crafting national security policies. However, Executive decision-making may not give adequate weight to the liberty side of the equation in the face of domestic pressure to 'do something' to diminish real or perceived security threats.

Transparency and Participation

Inserting courts into the process of evaluating a state's war-fighting rules increases the transparency of those rules. First, litigation provides a forum in which—in most cases—the Executive must identify its policies and defend their legality.[111] Second, these kinds of cases tend to attract media attention, further distributing information about the policies and how they have been applied. Third, litigation sometimes may prompt the U.S. Executive branch to declassify information in a way that the usual process of international law creation does not.[112] For instance, litigation surrounding detainee transfers from Guantanamo led the U.S. government to disclose information about the process and standards by which it evaluated potential detainee transfers, information that it had not previously revealed.[113] As such, the relevant debate about proper war-fighting rules opens up more widely than had it been constrained to an Executive-only process.[114]

The fact that war-fighting rules may be litigated in court gives outsiders an opportunity to express views about the rules' legality. For example, the amicus process, at least in the United States, allows for transparent and varied input from a wide range of groups with an interest in IHL, including foreign governments and legislatures; NGOs; international organizations; scholars; and the detainees themselves. Amicus briefs help increase the total quantity of information and legal analysis available to the court; give courts information about the potential consequences and policy implications of different outcomes; and increase the legitimacy of the subsequent decision, inter alia through their influence on the decision

---

[110] *Hamdi* v. *Rumsfeld*, 542 U.S. 507, 535–36 (2004).

[111] In some set of cases, the United States government may invoke and a court may accept the applicability of doctrines such as the state secrets or political question doctrine, pursuant to which the court concludes that a particular issue is not justiciable.

[112] Deeks 2013 (discussing ways in which national security litigation has led the U.S. Executive branch to reveal previously classified policies on detainee transfers).

[113] See, e.g., Declaration of Matthew C. Waxman, para 7, *available at* www.state.gov/documents/organization/55820.pdf.

[114] See Pearlstein 2009, pp. 1575–1578 ('It is precisely because security sometimes requires secrecy that the involvement of more than one branch may be required to make popular accountability possible at all.'); Benvenisti and Downs 2009, p. 69 (noting that national courts 'become venues for public participation through NGOs and other representatives of civil society acting either as claimants or *amici*').

itself.[115] The Supreme Court in *Hamdan* v. *Rumsfeld* received dozens of amicus briefs, including a brief by 422 UK and EU parliamentarians.[116]

International Federalism

Justice Brandeis famously once described U.S. states as social and economic 'laboratories'[117] and celebrated their ability to conduct novel experiments without adversely affecting the rest of the country. Experimentation in different nations may produce a similarly salutary effect on the development of IHL. As John Bellinger and Vijay Padmanabhan note, the lack of clear guidance in existing IHL may give 'States the appropriate room required to experiment with potential alternative responses to the problems discussed. The laboratory of ideas of the different States[...] could suggest different solutions to these questions that over time could end in an international consensus'.[118] This concept echoes the idea of global legal pluralism. As Paul Berman put it:

> [T]he important point is to see jurisdictional overlap in the state and supranational spheres as a plural legal space where alternative norms are proposed and contested. Sometimes, instead of one jurisdiction ultimately adopting the other's norms, we may see the existence of jurisdictional redundancy open up space for the creation of hybrid substantive norms.[119]

Particularly where the states whose courts are issuing DHL are actually fighting conflicts, the rules being litigated have been forged in the fire of the battlefield and thus have been determined to be operationally functional, if not sufficiently protective of individual rights.[120]

---

[115] Abramowicz and Colby 2009, p. 987; Vagts 1993, p. 483 ('Non-government parties too have functions in the [treaty interpretation] process. Private attorneys confronted with executive agents or private adversaries in litigation tell their clients their version of what the treaties mean and argue their position before courts. Law professors find their place in this complex network; through teaching or writing they inform the other actors in this system about their authoritative views on meaning. And in the absence of other powerful assigners of meaning, their role here looms larger than that traditionally assigned to professors in domestic legal processes.').

[116] *Hamdan* v. *Rumsfeld* Supreme Court Files, available at http://www.oyez.org/node/61175 (listing 51 amicus briefs, including briefs filed by former ICRC officials; 300 detainees; the Yemeni National Organization for Defending Rights and Freedoms; retired U.S. generals and admirals; and law professors).

[117] *New State Ice Co.* v. *Liebmann*, 285 U.S. 262 (1932).

[118] Bellinger and Padmanabhan 2011, p. 51 (noting that this approach does not resolve the international community's concern that this policy freedom may be abused). Compare Osofsky 2009, p. 588 (noting that focusing attention only on international solutions to climate change will cause people to 'miss opportunities for much needed innovation and emissions reduction' that occur on national and local levels).

[119] Berman 2008, p. 1165. See also Dinwoodie 2000, p. 515 ('[E]xperimentation enables the common understanding (the international standard) to be forged by experience, which should assist in identifying an appropriate standard.').

[120] There is a disadvantage to this as well, which is that the rules may skew consistently toward state security, which they might not do if the states crafting them fought fewer armed conflicts.

Several factors complicate the optimism of global legal pluralism. First, the fact that the different courts considered in section 4 start their analyses from different legal baselines (constitutional law, IHL, human rights law) has led to different substantive outcomes in some cases.[121] Second, because DHL often develops in a state-specific manner, there is little reason to expect short-term international buy-in to specific DHL rules. Third, DHL forecasts a long period of uncertainty about the ultimate content of IHL.[122]

Depth of Rule Explication

A significant advantage of DHL is the fact that many of the court cases parsing IHL concepts and gaps delve deeply into the hard questions and offer concrete examples and procedures relevant to detention and transfer. This level of detail almost certainly is significantly greater than what an international conference could produce if tasked with negotiating consensus rules on detention. Especially when courts have the opportunity to consider a series of related cases, that repeated consideration of the law, and the application of the law to different facts, can deepen a state's understanding of the rule and smooth out bumps that may arise as the Executive attempts to implement judicial decisions.

Consider, for example, the Israeli Supreme Court's opinion in the targeted killings case. The Court discussed in great depth what it meant to take 'direct part in hostilities'. The opinion identified a large number of examples of activity that would or would not constitute direct participation.[123] Whether or not one agrees with the way the Court categorized each example, such a list allows future conversants to base their conversations in concrete examples, and to identify the specific characteristics of the example group that they find compelling.

This level of detail stands in some contrast to the Copenhagen Principles, one of the few exercises on the international plane that has produced a document that purports to identify generally acceptable principles, rules, and standards for detainee treatment.[124] While a laudable exercise and one committed to preserving — at a minimum — existing legal standards, the resulting principles are written at a high level of generality. For example, the principle summarizing the

---

[121] See Roberts 2011, p. 79 (describing how international law may assume different qualities as it is 'domesticated').

[122] Berman mentions downsides to a pluralist approach to rule-creation. He notes, 'Of course, all of these jurisdictional redundancies might be seen as perhaps necessary but regrettable concessions to the realities of a world of normative disagreement. Such a view would focus on encroachments upon sovereignty, concerns about forum shopping, uncertainty about applicable rules, litigation costs, and so forth.' Berman 2008, p. 1167.

[123] See supra note 37, paras 34–37.

[124] The Copenhagen Process on the Handling of Detainees in International Military Operations, available at http://um.dk/en/politics-and-diplomacy/copenhagen-process-on-the-handling-of-detainees-in-international-military-operations/ (click through to download).

requirement for review of detention states, 'A detainee whose liberty has been deprived for security reasons is to, in addition to a prompt initial review, have the decision to detain reconsidered periodically by an impartial and objective authority that is authorized to determine the lawfulness and appropriateness of continued detention'.[125] These principles, which largely track language found in existing IHL treaties, do not produce the level of detail that the DHL cases do.

Finally, if one takes the view that the current issues in IHL are not susceptible to international regulation at all, DHL offers a critical substitute for international constraints on states.

5.5.2.2 Disadvantages

Framing

Most courts are limited to adjudicating the case before them on the facts presented. Except for the U.S. Supreme Court, U.S. courts have a very limited capacity to select the frame within which they must resolve the legal issue presented.[126] U.S. courts may employ a range of non-justiciability doctrines, which offers a way to avoid deciding cases on the merits, but may not reach out to adjudicate issues that parties do not bring before them.[127] As a result, there may be a range of IHL-related issues that never come before domestic courts for consideration. DHL coverage is likely to be patchwork, though we might expect that it will produce decisions about at least some of the most contentious and difficult issues, as those are the ones that tend to be litigated.

Structural Weaknesses

One reason that U.S. courts tend to defer quite extensively to the Executive on national security issues is that the courts perceive themselves as less competent than the Executive to make national security decisions. The Executive has greater policy expertise and can act with greater speed and secrecy than courts can.[128] Courts tend to lack access to important information that would affect the disposition of the case, and also have difficulty assessing the foreign policy and military

125 Id., principle 12.

126 U.S. Const. Article III, sec. 2, cl. 1 (limiting exercise of judicial review to "cases or controversies").

127 These include doctrines related to ripeness, mootness, standing, "political questions," and the protection of state secrets.

128 Deeks 2013, pp. 51–52.

implications of their judgments.[129] For this reason, some commentators have called on Congress to provide statutory guidance to courts in the detention cases, rather than force the courts to craft the rules themselves.[130]

Two things follow from this real or perceived structural weakness. First, courts may defer more than they should to the Executive branch's war-fighting policies. Second, when courts do not defer, they may miscalculate the proper balance between security and liberty.[131] As a result, the DHL the courts produce may be systematically flawed. Of course, legislatures may react to DHL by overriding non-constitutional decisions by statute, though the legislative activity to date in this area has been modest.

Precedent as Limiter

When an Executive branch's detention and transfer policies have come under extensive judicial scrutiny, that Executive will come to future international negotiations with its flexibility reduced. In other words, DHL may foster premature entrenchment of the norm in question, making it harder for the state bound by that DHL to agree to a new rule. This is the case especially where the DHL implicates constitutional requirements. On the other hand, some of the DHL in question represents statutory interpretation. For states that follow a later-in-time rule regarding treaties and statutes, a new treaty obligation would trump the existing statute that binds the Executive.[132]

Some of the states whose courts are producing DHL may view the existence of DHL as advantaging them in negotiations. DHL states may use the fact that their hands are tied by court decisions as negotiating leverage, assuming those states view their own DHL favorably. As Graham Dinwoodie has noted, 'National laws

---

[129] Id. at 52; Sunstein 2004, p. 53 ('Worst of all, they lack relevant information and hence they may not know whether an interference with liberty is actually justified. Because their historic mission is to protect individual liberty, they may give insufficient attention to the variables on the other side.').

[130] Emerging Law. To date, Israel's parliament has enacted the Unlawful Enemy Combatants Law, which addresses who may be detained during armed conflicts, but which lacks detail. The U.S. Congress has enacted several relevant statutes, including the Detainee Treatment Act of 2005 (effectively incorporating into law the Executive's combatant status review tribunals) and the 2012 National Defense Authorization Act (incorporating into law the Executive's claimed detention authority under the 2001 Authorization for Use of Military Force).

[131] Making an empirical assessment of the 'right' balance between liberty and security is virtually impossible. See, e.g., Goldsmith 2013, p. 193 ('The optimal level of presidential constraint—in national security and other contexts—is elusive because it depends on ever-changing and sometimes unknowable facts (about, for example, the nature of the threat or the efficacy of particular counterterrorism policies), as well as contested normative judgments (about, for example, what the Constitution permits or what morality requires).').

[132] See, e.g., *Whitney* v. *Robertson*, 124 U.S. 190 (1888); Hollis 2005, p. 48 (describing phenomenon in other states).

become cards to play in forthcoming negotiations.'[133] If too many states come to the negotiating table with competing DHL provisions structuring their behavior, however, it may complicate the negotiations and pose compliance challenges if and when states conclude a new agreement.

Small Group of Contributors

One might be skeptical about DHL's value because it is emerging from the courts of a very small number of states. There are, in other words, only a few laboratories of experimentation in play at this point and many in the international community view several of those states with deep skepticism. The role of DHL would be both more potent and more legitimate if a larger number of domestic courts were shaping these norms. There are cases in which a handful of states developed an international regime that ultimately garnered widespread acceptance, including the Financial Action Task Force and the Proliferation Security Initiative.[134] In general, though, the greater number of states involved at the outset, the greater the acceptance of the international legal project being undertaken.

On the other hand, the states whose courts are producing DHL are highly sophisticated war-fighting states, and the courts developing DHL are respected and credible. As a result, the rules set by the courts will be keyed at a high level of military sophistication and legal rigor. Further, even among this small group of states, not all case law has reached the same result, so the rules very much remain open for debate. And to the extent that European domestic courts as well as the ECtHR are issuing a larger number of decisions on the merits (rather than using abstention-like doctrines), those courts ultimately will product more DHL in this area than those courts that abstain on the merits more frequently, as is the case with U.S. courts.

5.6 Conclusion

Domestic court decisions governing war-fighting have reduced—though not eliminated—what previously was seen as a huge legitimacy gap in U.S. practice. This lack of legitimacy flowed both from the substance of the policies the United States adopted and from the fact that in the wake of September 11 the U.S. executive branch was able to establish its policies unilaterally, with little oversight

[133] Dinwoodie 2000, p. 501; Benvenisti and Downs 2009, pp. 72–73 ('Pressure exerted on a certain government by its disapproving court can, in fact, result in greater bargaining leeway for that government, as it uses that pressure as an explanation of its inability to bow to the pressure of the foreign negotiators.').

[134] For the goals and roles of these organizations, see http://www.fatf-gafi.org (FATF); and http://www.state.gov/t/isn/c10390.htm (PSI).

from either co-equal branch of government or from the international community. As the content of DHL grows broader and deeper, one of the chief impetuses for a new treaty—as a tool to constrain the states fighting these new conflicts—weakens. Ironically, then, the very proliferation of DHL may reduce the likelihood that this DHL will ever have the chance to serve as an important basis for the next stage of treaty-based IHL development.

States continue to face serious challenges in developing new IHL treaty norms on the international stage. As a result, the production of new interpretations and norms in U.S. and other domestic courts represents a potentially important but little-considered phase in the development of IHL. Just as importantly, the phenomenon of DHL may prove to be an area in which fruitfully to explore the nature of internationally-inflected domestic court decisions more generally in the project of international law construction.

References

Abramowicz M, Colby T (2009) Notice-and-comment judicial decisionmaking. Univ Chicago Law Rev 76:965

Abresch W (2005) A human rights law of internal armed conflict. EJIL 16:741

Bellinger J (2007) Lecture at the University of Oxford, 10 December 2007. http://2001-2009.state.gov/s/l/rls/96687.htm. Accessed 11 Feb 2014

Bellinger J, Padmanabhan V (2011) Detention operations in contemporary conflicts: four challenges for the Geneva Conventions and other existing law. AJIL 105:201

Benvenisti E, Downs G (2009) National courts, domestic democracy, and the evolution of international law. EJIL 20:59

Berman P (2008) Federalism and international law through the lens of legal pluralism. Mo Law Rev 73:1151

Blum G (2013) The individualization of war: from collectivism to individualism in the regulation of armed conflicts. In: Sarat A, Douglas L, Umphrey M (eds) Law and war. Stanford University Press, Stanford

Blum G, Heymann P (2010) Law and policy of targeted killing. Harvard Nat Secur Law J 1:145

Brooks R (2004) War everywhere: rights, national security law, and the law of armed conflict in the age of terror. Univ Pennsylvania Law Rev 153:675

Cole D (2008) No reason to believe: radical skepticism, emergency power, and constitutional constraint. Univ Chicago Law Rev 75:1329

Deeks (2008) Avoiding transfers to torture. Council on Foreign Relations, New York

Deeks A (2009) Administrative detention in armed conflict. Case Western Res J Int Law 40:403

Deeks A (2013) The observer effect: national security litigation, executive policy changes, and judicial deference. Fordham Law Rev 82:827

Dinwoodie G (2000) A new copyright order. Univ Pennsylvania Law Rev 149:69

Glennon M (2013) The dark future of international cybersecurity regulation. J Nat Secur Law Policy 6:563

Goldsmith J (2013) A reply to professor Katyal. Harvard Law Rev Forum 126:188

Goodman R (2009) The detention of civilians in armed conflict. AJIL 103:48

Grosskopf A (2008) Explaining the democratic trust conundrum. Int Soc Sci Rev 83:3–26

Henckaerts JM, Doswald-Beck L (2005) Customary international humanitarian law. Cambridge University Press, Cambridge

Hollis D (2005) A comparative approach to treaty law and practice. In: Hollis D et al (eds) National treaty law and practice. Martinus Nijhoff, Ch, p 1

Kagan R (2003) Of paradise and power. Knopf, New York

Keohane R (1982) The demand for international regimes. Int Org 36:325

Kretzmer D (2009) Rethinking the application of IHL in non-international armed conflicts. Israel Law Rev 42:8

Kumm M (2004) The legitimacy of international law: a constitutionalist framework of analysis. EJIL 15:907

Lillich R (1970–1971) The proper role of domestic courts in the international legal order. Virginia JIL 11:9

Martin D (2007) Judicial review and the military commissions act: on striking the right balance. AJIL 101:344

Osofsky H (2009) Is climate change 'International'? Litigation's diagonal regulatory role. Virginia JIL 49:585

Pauwelyn J, Wessel R, Wouters J (2012) The stagnation of international law, Leuven center. http://papers.ssrn.com/abstract=2271862. Accessed 2 July 2013

Pearlstein D (2008) Avoiding an international law fix for terrorist detention. Creighton Law Rev 41:663

Pearlstein D (2009) Form and function in the national security constitution. Connecticut Law Rev 41:1549

Posner E (2009) The perils of global legalism. Univ Chicago, Chicago

Provost R (2012) Asymmetrical reciprocity and compliance with the laws of war. In: Perrin B (ed) Modern warfare: armed groups, private militaries, humanitarian organizations, and the law. University of British Columbia Press, Vancouver

Resnik J (2006) Law's migration: American exceptionalism, silent dialogues, and federalism's multiple points of entry. Yale Law J 115:1564

Roberts A (2011) Comparative international law? The role of national courts in creating and enforcing international law. ICLQ 60:57

Rona G (2007) An appraisal of U.S. practice relating to 'Enemy Combatants'. Yearb Int'l Humanitarian Law 10:232

Sunstein C (2004) Minimalism at war. Supreme Court Rev 2004:47

Tams C, Tzanakopoulos A (2013) Domestic courts as agents of development of international law. Leiden JIL 26:531

Vagts D (1993) Treaty interpretation and the new American ways of law reading. EJIL 4:472

Waxman M (2010) The structure of terrorism threats and the laws of war. Duke J Comp Int Law 20:429

Wells C (2004) Questioning deference. Mo Law Rev 69:903

Wuerth I (2012) International law in domestic courts and the jurisdictional immunities of the state case. Melbourne J Int Law 13:819

Chapter 6
The Interaction of the International Terrorism Suppression Regime and IHL in Domestic Criminal Prosecutions: The UK Experience

Kimberley N. Trapp

Contents

6.1 Introduction

'Terrorism' is not only a phenomenon affecting the security interests of the international community. It is also a label—and one at the centre of a war of rhetoric. To label conduct as terrorist, and more importantly, to make that label stick as a matter of law, is a powerful rhetorical tool indeed. While States largely agree on what 'terrorism' looks like in its *actus reus* and *mens rea* elements, they

Kimberley N. Trapp is Lecturer in International Law, University College London, Faculty of Laws.

K. N. Trapp (✉)
Faculty of Laws, University College London, London, UK
e-mail: k.trapp@ucl.ac.uk

D. Jinks et al. (eds.), *Applying International Humanitarian Law in Judicial and Quasi-Judicial Bodies*, DOI: 10.1007/978-94-6265-008-4_6,

cannot agree on who is entitled to use violence[1] and for what purposes.[2] One manifestation of this disagreement is the seemingly interminable debate on the distinction, if any, to be drawn between acts of terrorism and acts carried out in the course of a struggle for self-determination[3] (which struggles can be situated within the framework of international humanitarian law ('IHL')[4]). Another is whether States can be terrorist actors.[5] The war of rhetoric regarding the 'terrorist' label certainly shapes these debates, but saying so should not obscure what else is at stake. Both the 'self-determination vs. terrorism' and 'States as terrorist actors' debates are as much about labels as they are about regime interaction—in particular, the appropriate interaction between the terrorism suppression regime and each of the *jus in bello* and *jus ad bellum*.

This chapter will focus on the former—the interaction between the terrorism suppression regime and the *jus in bello*—in the context of domestic terrorism prosecutions. It will do so first by situating efforts to suppress transnational terrorism within their historical context, one which has swung between the international and the domestic and is now firmly settled in a hybrid space of domestic law, which implements and is limited by international law. Within such historical context, this chapter will set out the relevant international terrorism suppression treaty regime, and explore the way in which that regime addresses its interaction with IHL. Negotiations on the interaction between relevant regimes have been

---

1 See Saul 2006, p. 4.

2 See e.g. summary record of the 5th meeting of the Ad Hoc Committee on International Terrorism, UN Doc. A/AC.160/SR.5 (1977), [10] (Algeria); summary record of the 8th meeting of the Ad Hoc Committee on International Terrorism, UN Doc. A/AC.160/SR.8 (1977), [35] (Tanzania).

3 See generally UNGA 56th Session, 12th meeting, UN Doc. A/56/PV.12 (2001), 3; Report of the Ad Hoc Committee established by General Assembly Resolution 51/210 of 17 December 1996, UN Doc. A/59/37 (2004), Annex I, [15]–[17]. See in particular proposals that self-determination be excluded from the definition of terrorism, UNGA, Sixth Committee, UN Doc. A/C.6/55/SR.27 (200), [41]–[45] (Qatar and Egypt); UNGA, Sixth Committee, UN Doc. A/C.6/55/L.2 (2000), Annex III, [30] (Malaysia). See also UNGA, Sixth Committee, UN Doc. A/C.6/60/L.6 (2005), Annex, [2]–[17]; Reports of the Ad Hoc Committee established by General Assembly Resolution 51/210 of 17 December 1996, UN Doc. A/61/37 (2006), Annex I, [2]; UN Doc. A/62/37 (2007), Annex, [5] and [11]–[21]; UN Doc. A/63/37 (2008), Annex I, [5]–[6]; UN Doc. A/64/37 (2009), [6]; UN Doc. A/65/37 (2010), [3] and [11].

4 Conflicts in which a people are fighting in exercise of their right of self-determination have long been recognized as armed conflicts to which humanitarian law applies. Article 1(4) of the Protocol Additional to the Geneva Conventions of 12 August 1949, and Relating to the Protection of Victims of International Armed Conflicts, 8 June 1977, 1125 UNTS 3 ('API') incorporates factually non-international armed conflicts in which a people is fighting in exercise of their right of self-determination into the legal definition of international armed conflict. The circumstances under which a non-international armed conflict will amount to an international armed conflict because a people is fighting in exercise of a right of self-determination, as envisioned in Article 1(4) of API, is not defined clearly in API, but the Commentary suggests (rather optimistically) that it is a question of 'common sense'. See Sandoz et al. 1987, p. 56.

5 See Trapp 2011, Sect. 6.4, for a discussion of efforts to define terrorism as a crime committed uniquely by State agents.

heavily influenced by the power of the 'terrorism' label and the cause in support of which that power might be unleashed. This is no more evident than in the recent UK case of *R v. Mohammed Gul*[6]—which raises *par excellence* the interaction between terrorism suppression and IHL and the power of the 'terrorist' label. Mr. Gul was convicted of supporting terrorism in virtue of his support for the military activities of non-State actors against Coalition forces in the non-international phase of the armed conflict in Afghanistan. This chapter will conclude by examining the *Mohammed Gul* case and what it might tell us about the interaction of the international terrorism suppression regime and IHL in domestic criminal prosecutions.

6.2 From the International to the Domestic and Back Again

The international community has long addressed transnational terrorism as a criminal law enforcement challenge through the adoption of treaties, which aim to secure individual responsibility. The first such treaty was adopted under the auspices of the League of Nations in response to the assassination of King Alexander of Yugoslavia and Mr. Louis Barthou, Foreign Minister of the French Republic, in Marseilles on 9 October 1934, by Yugoslav *émigrés* operating from Hungary.[7] The League of Nations Terrorism Convention required States to criminalise and prosecute acts of terrorism, but equally provided for the possibility of terrorism prosecutions before an International Criminal Court.[8] The creation of an international criminal jurisdiction was intended to ensure that there was no impunity for terrorist crimes, even in situations where the custodial State was unable to prosecute (because the conduct had not been criminalised domestically for lack of any connection with the criminal, victims or crime) and there were asylum or political offence exception bars to extradition.[9] In part due to the political situation in Europe in the late 1930s, the League of Nations Terrorism Convention never entered into force.[10] International efforts to suppress terrorism through the creation of an international criminal jurisdiction were side-lined following the end of WWII, with attention focused on war crimes prosecutions.

---

[6] EWCA Crim 280 (22 February 2012). The Supreme Court granted permission to appeal on 13 June 2012 (www.supremecourt.gov.uk/docs/PTA-1206.pdf).

[7] League of Nations, Convention for the Prevention and Punishment of Terrorism, 16 November 1937 (never entered into force), *reprinted in* Ferencz 1980.

[8] League of Nations, Convention for the Creation of an International Criminal Court, 16 November 1937 (never entered into force), *reprinted in* Ferencz 1980.

[9] League of Nations, Records of the Seventeenth Ordinary Session of the Assembly, Plenary Meetings (1936), *reprinted in* Friedlander 1979, Volume 1, p. 135. See also Hudson 1938, pp. 553–554.

[10] Lambert 1990, p. 29.

Following the close of the Nuremberg trials, terrorism was again included in the (r)evolution of a permanent international criminal jurisdiction as a crime in the Draft Code of Offences against the Peace and Security of Mankind.[11] Work on the Draft Code was suspended, however, between 1954 and 1981 as a result of the impasse on a definition of aggression.[12] In the meantime, the international community's concern over transnational terrorism sharpened as a result of the alarming increase in hijackings for political purposes in the late 1960s and early 1970s.[13] These hijackings and other acts of transnational terrorism posed criminal law enforcement challenges in that the crimes and criminals crossed jurisdictional boundaries. To address these challenges, States adopted a series of terrorism suppression conventions which oblige them to criminalise the defined terrorist conduct on a variety of jurisdictional bases (including territoriality, nationality, passive personality and universality) and to extradite or submit alleged offenders to prosecution in the event such persons are within that State Party's territory (*aut dedere aut judicare*).[14] The aim was to ensure that transnational terrorists could not exploit the limitations of any one State's jurisdictional capacity, and were subject to criminal law enforcement without recourse to safe havens. The terrorism suppression treaty regime served to fill the same jurisdictional gap that an international criminal court might have filled.

When the Draft Code project was revived, terrorism was left out as a result of long-standing disagreement over the general definition of terrorism and whether it should cover the conduct of non-State actors, State actors, or both.[15] This was not, however, the end of the story linking an international criminal jurisdiction with terrorism prosecutions, in that terrorism was included as a crime within the jurisdiction of the International Law Commission's (ILC) proposed international criminal court in 1994. To avoid the continuing debates about self-determination

---

[11] Article 2(6) of the Draft Code adopted in 1954 defined the offence of terrorism as "[t]he undertaking or encouragement by the authorities of a State of terrorist activities in another State, or the toleration by the authorities of a State of organized activities calculated to carry out terrorist acts in another State." Report of the International Law Commission covering the work of its sixth session, UN Doc. A/2693 (1954), 151.

[12] See UNGA Resolution 36/106 (1981).

[13] See generally Evans 1978.

[14] There are currently 13 international conventions and protocols addressing various manifestations of terrorism (including hijackings, shipjackings, hostage takings, crimes against internationally protected persons, terrorist bombings and acts of nuclear terrorism). A full list of the international terrorism suppression conventions and protocols can be found at http://www.un.org/terrorism/instruments.shtml, and are referred to in this chapter as the 'Terrorism Suppression Conventions' or 'TSCs'. This chapter will focus on the International Convention on the Suppression of Terrorist Bombings, 15 December 1997, UN Doc. A/RES/52/164 (1997) ('Terrorist Bombing Convention') and will also have regard for the International Convention against the Taking of Hostages, 17 December 1979, 1316 UNTS 205 ('Hostages Convention').

[15] See Report of the International Law Commission on the work of its forty-fifth session, UN Doc. A/48/10 (1993), 28, [105]; Report of the International Law Commission on the work of its forty-eighth session, UN Doc. A/51/10 (1996), 16, [46]. See further Trapp 2011, Sect. 6.4.2.

and State terrorism, the ILC incorporated certain terrorist crimes by reference in its draft Statute for an International Criminal Court (ICC)—relying on existing Terrorism Suppression Conventions as the vehicle for defining the *actus reus* and *mens rea* elements of crimes, which would be subject to international prosecution.[16] The idea was to provide for international criminal jurisdiction for the particular terrorist crimes over which States had already agreed, while leaving aside the difficult question of a general definition of terrorism.

This pragmatic yet evasive approach was not adopted by States negotiating the Rome Statute, and the time pressure of the Rome Conference did not allow for agreement to be reached on a general definition of terrorism as a crime within the ICC's jurisdiction. Nevertheless, as a concession to States supporting the creation of international criminal jurisdiction for terrorist offences, a resolution was included in the Final Act of the Rome Conference recommending that the Review Conference consider defining terrorism and including it within the ICC's jurisdiction.[17] Given the 2010 Review Conference was focused on the crime of aggression, terrorism was not discussed at any length and has not yet been (if ever it will be) included within the International Criminal Court's jurisdiction.

Situating terrorism within the broader framework of international criminal law—particularly with its focus on crimes committed during the course of armed conflicts—would have ensured that terrorism prosecutions were carried out in a context that was sensitive to the interaction between the criminalisation of transnational crime and international humanitarian law. Instead of such institutional sensitivity to regime interaction issues, however, the matter has been left to the appreciation of domestic courts. While the idea of international terrorism prosecutions has not yet been fully abandoned, as things stand, States bear principal responsibility for suppressing transnational terrorism through the exercise of domestic jurisdiction.[18] As discussed above, the TSCs which impose this responsibility are modelled on the League of Nations Terrorism Convention, each addressing a particular manifestation of transnational terrorism and imposing criminal law enforcement obligations on States.[19]

Despite this movement away from international prosecutions in favour of relying on domestic criminal law enforcement, terrorism prosecutions remain very much a creature of international law. Unlike most exercises of domestic criminal jurisdiction, which States exercise as a matter of right and discretion driven by national policy, the exercise of jurisdiction in regard to transnational

---

[16] See Report of the International Law Commission on the work of its forty-sixth session, UN Doc. A/49/10 (1994), Article 20(e) and Appendix II.

[17] Final Act of the United Nations Diplomatic Conference of Plenipotentiaries on the Establishment of an International Criminal Court, done at Rome on 17 July 1998, UN Doc. A/CONF.183/10 (1998), Resolution E.

[18] There are of course hybrid international / domestic courts which have been created purely for the purposes of prosecuting acts of terrorism, but these are exceptional. See for instance the Special Tribunal for Lebanon, http://www.stl-tsl.org/en.

[19] Supra note 14 and accompanying text.

terrorism is an obligation,[20] and the modalities and extent of the exercise of that jurisdiction are prescribed by international law. In particular, the TSCs dictate both a floor and potentially a ceiling for the exercise of domestic criminal jurisdiction. The floor is expressed in terms of the basic obligation to criminalise on a variety of jurisdictional bases and to actualise that exercise of prescriptive jurisdiction through an *aut dedere aut judicare* obligation. The potential ceiling is expressed through exclusion clauses which carve out conduct otherwise meeting the *actus reus* elements of the defined terrorist crime from the treaty obligation to criminalise. These exclusion clauses define the relationship between the criminalisation of transnational terrorist crimes and other sources of criminal responsibility under international law—including, of interest for present purposes, international humanitarian law. This chapter will address in particular bombings carried out in the course of an armed conflict and the extent to which they should be subject to domestic prosecution for terrorism, in order to best speak to the case study (examined in Sect. 6.4) of the prosecution of Mohammed Gul before the English courts.

6.3 Models of Terrorist Suppression: IHL Regime Interaction

Of the thirteen Terrorism Suppression Conventions adopted to date, several address conduct that might take place within the context of an armed conflict. If the TSCs failed to address the overlap in applicable legal regimes, they might well be a vehicle for criminalising conduct during an armed conflict that would otherwise be subject to combatant's immunity under the more directly applicable regime of IHL. Indeed, not only would a TSC *permit* criminalisation of conduct in such cases, it would *require* States to exercise such domestic criminal jurisdiction. The result would be to undermine combatant's immunity and to require States to prosecute (for instance) the proportionate targeting of military objectives during an international armed conflict. To avoid this possibility, a number of the TSCs contain clauses that attempt to manage their interaction with other regimes of international law through exclusion clauses. There are two models for excluding conduct that would otherwise meet the definition of the relevant terrorist offence (and thereby be subject to the criminal law enforcement obligations of the terrorism suppression regime) under the current TSCs, each as discussed below.

---

[20] See Mills 2012.

6.3.1 *Exclusion Triggered by the Applicability of an Alternative Criminal Law Enforcement Regime*

The first model of exclusion, of which the Hostages Convention is an example, is triggered by the availability (and applicability) of an alternative criminal law enforcement regime. Article 12 of the Hostages Convention reads:

> In so far as the Geneva Conventions of 1949 for the protection of war victims or the Additional Protocols to those Conventions are applicable to a particular act of hostage-taking, and in so far as States Parties to this Convention are bound under those conventions to prosecute or hand over the hostage-taker, the present Convention shall not apply to an act of hostage-taking committed in the course of armed conflicts as defined in the Geneva Conventions of 1949 and the Protocols thereto, including armed conflicts mentioned in Article 1, para 4, of Additional Protocol I of 1977, in which peoples are fighting against colonial domination and alien occupation and against racist regimes in the exercise of their right of self- determination, as enshrined in the Charter of the United Nations and the Declaration on Principles of International Law concerning Friendly Relations and Co-operation among States in accordance with the Charter of the United Nations.

Hostage taking is unlawful under most domestic legal systems and is also prohibited in the context of armed conflicts.[21] As such, criminalising conduct under the terrorism suppression regime that would otherwise be lawful (or at least not unlawful) under IHL was not a concern. Hostage taking is unlawful under both regimes. Instead, the exclusion clause as finally agreed ensures that there is no impunity for hostage taking and manages the rhetorical power of the 'terrorist' label in the context of struggles for self-determination.

As a starting point, a number of Non-Aligned Movement ('NAM') delegates proposed that the definition of the offence 'taking of hostages' exclude "any acts carried out in the process of national liberation against colonial rule, racist and foreign regimes, by liberation movements recognized by the United Nations."[22] Western States opposed the proposal on the basis that that such an exclusion amounted to revisiting questions which had already been settled in the context of the Geneva Conventions and negotiations on API—under which treaties hostage taking was prohibited in international armed conflicts, including conflicts in which a people were fighting in exercise of their right of self-determination.[23] In

---

[21] See Article 75(2)(c), API; Article 3(1)(b), Geneva Convention Relative to the Protection of Civilian Persons in Time of War of August 12 1949, 7 UNTS 287 ('GCIV').

[22] Report of the Ad Hoc Committee on the drafting of an International Convention against the Taking of Hostages, Proposal by Lesotho, Tanzania, Algeria, Egypt, Libya and Nigeria, UN Doc. A/AC.188/L.5 (1978), [11]. See also Tanzania's comment "[t]he oppressed peoples and colonial peoples who were held in perpetual bondage could not be stopped from taking their oppressors hostage, if that became inevitable." Report of the Ad Hoc Committee on the drafting of an International Convention against the Taking of Hostages, UN Doc. A/32/39 (1977), Annex, [28–29]. See further Report of the Ad Hoc Committee on the drafting of an International Convention against the Taking of Hostages, UN Doc. A/33/39 (1978), 58.

[23] Article 34 GCIV and Article 1(4) API.

response, NAM's principal negotiating objective became to ensure that hostage takings committed in furtherance of a people's right of self-determination were qualified as war crimes and not as 'terrorism' falling within the scope of the Hostages Convention.[24] The result of these negotiations is the Article 12 exclusion clause whereby hostage takings committed in peace time will be characterised as terrorist and subject to the criminal law enforcement framework of the Hostages Convention, while hostage takings committed during armed conflicts, including Article 1(4) API self-determination conflicts, will be excluded from the terrorism suppression regime and qualified as war crimes, subject only to applicable IHL criminal law enforcement regimes.

6.3.2 Exclusion Triggered by the Applicability of Any Alternative Legal Regime

The second model for exclusion under the TSCs is triggered by the applicability of an alternative legal regime, irrespective of whether that regime criminalises or imposes individual criminal responsibility for the relevant conduct. The regime interaction clause in the Terrorist Bombing Convention exemplifies this approach:

> The activities of armed forces during an armed conflict, as those terms are understood under international humanitarian law, which are governed by that law, are not governed by this Convention [...].[25]

For present purposes, the relevant question is whether Article 19(2) should be interpreted as (i) permissive, in the sense that States *may* exclude the activities of armed forces during an armed conflict from the scope of application of their legislation criminalising terrorist bombings (adopted in implementation of the obligations under the Terrorist Bombing Convention), but *need not*, or (ii) imposing a limitation on States' power to prescribe terrorist conduct (a ceiling on the exercise of domestic criminal jurisdiction). What hangs in the balance is the extent to which States *can*, consistently with their international obligations, criminalise and prosecute bombings carried out by armed forces during an armed conflict as terrorism.

The exclusion clause under Article 19(2) of the Terrorist Bombing Convention draws on the definition of 'armed conflict' and 'armed forces' under international humanitarian law. 'Armed conflict' includes, both as a matter of customary international law and the relevant treaties, international and non-international

---

[24] Despite the shift in NAM's objective, from legitimising hostage taking in the context of struggles for self-determination to shifting the source of condemnation, some commentators have nevertheless interpreted Article 12 of the Hostages Convention as legitimising hostage takings committed in furtherance of a struggle for self-determination. See Wardlaw 1982, p. 113; Aston 1982, p. 156.

[25] Article 19(2), Terrorist Bombing Convention, supra note 14.

armed conflicts. And while early definitions of 'armed forces' were restricted to the forces of a State, therefore excluding freedom fighters fighting against the State,[26] the International Committee of the Red Cross (ICRC) has treated the expanded definition of 'armed forces' in Article 43 API, including organised armed forces, groups and units,[27] as having reached customary status.[28] The definition is not dependent on state organ or agent status and applies to non-state armed groups, including, but not limited to, peoples exercising their right of self-determination, as long as they are organised and operate on the basis of command responsibility.

The exclusion clause in the Terrorist Bombing Convention is broad—in that it excludes bombings by armed forces that are *governed* by IHL—whether lawful or unlawful under IHL. The exclusion is framed in these terms because States were principally concerned with preserving the integrity of IHL—ensuring that States do not make unlawful otherwise lawful acts of war, for example the targeting of military objectives, under the guise of terrorism.[29] Unlike the Hostages Convention, the regime interaction clause in the Terrorist Bombing Convention does not condition exclusion from its scope on the availability of an alternative criminal law enforcement framework. Given the definition of the offence of terrorist bombing, which includes detonating an explosive in or against a state or government facility,[30] such acts will often be lawful acts of war under IHL to the extent that the state or government facility makes an effective contribution to military action, the bombing is justified by military necessity,[31] and any incidental loss of civilian life is not excessive in relation to the concrete and direct military advantage anticipated from the bombing.[32] As a result, bombing such targets during an armed conflict is not prohibited under IHL, does not amount to a grave breach of the

[26] See Pictet 1958, p. 35; ICRC 1960, p. 51.

[27] Article 43(1), API. The principal effect of the expanded definition of 'armed forces' was on combatant status, and therefore entitlement to prisoner of war treatment. On the compromise reached in regard to these issues during the negotiation of Protocol I, see Greenwood 2007, pp. 216–18.

[28] ICRC 2005, Vol. I, Rule 4, 14–17. See also ICRC 2005, Vol. II, 86–100. Article 43 of API goes on to stipulate that '[s]uch armed forces shall be subject to an internal disciplinary system which, inter alia, shall enforce compliance with the rules of international law applicable in armed conflict'. Article 44(3) of API further provides that '[w]hile all combatants are obliged to comply with the rules of international law applicable in armed conflict, violations of these rules shall not deprive a combatant of his right to be a combatant or, if he falls into the power of an adverse Party, of his right to be a prisoner of war'. Article 44(3) of API strongly suggests that the mention of compliance with international humanitarian law in the Article 43 of the API definition of 'armed forces' is not an element of that definition, but rather a statement of the obligations by which such armed forces are bound.

[29] See Report of the Ad Hoc Committee established by General Assembly Resolution 51/210 of 17 December 1996, UN Doc. A/65/37 (2010), [5].

[30] Article 2(1), Terrorist Bombing Convention, supra note 14.

[31] Article 147, GCIV.

[32] Articles 50(4), 52(2), and 85(3)(b), API.

Geneva Conventions or Additional Protocols, and would therefore not be subject to an extradite or prosecute obligation under IHL.[33]

Were exclusion from the scope of the Terrorist Bombing Convention conditioned on the applicability of the Geneva Convention or API criminal law enforcement framework (using an exclusion clause like that found in the Hostages Convention), the very fact that the conduct is *not* prohibited as a matter of IHL (and therefore not subject to the IHL criminal law enforcement framework) would result in its falling within the scope of the Terrorist Bombing Convention—requiring the criminalisation and punishment of conduct committed during the course of an armed conflict that is perfectly lawful under the more directly applicable laws of war. In not requiring the applicability of an alternative criminal law enforcement framework, Article 19 of the Terrorist Bombing Convention better respects the balance between military necessity and humanitarian considerations achieved by IHL.

In focusing on preserving the integrity of IHL, however, the model of exclusion under Article 19(2) of the Terrorist Bombing Convention might be criticised for being too broad. The danger is that conduct which is prohibited by humanitarian law, for instance intentionally attacking civilians,[34] but not subject to its criminal law enforcement regime, will go unpunished because it is excluded from the scope of the Terrorist Bombing Convention merely in virtue of its being 'governed' by IHL. This problem could arise in International Armed Conflicts ('IACs') due to incomplete ratification of API (in that the universally ratified Geneva Conventions and their criminal law enforcement obligations do not govern the conduct of hostilities, and therefore only State parties to API will be subject to an *aut dedere aut judicare* obligation in regard to unlawful bombings under IHL)[35] and, in Non-International Armed Conflicts ('NIACs'), due to the absence of an international criminal law enforcement framework in Protocol Additional to the Geneva Conventions of 12 August 1949 and Relating to the Protection of Victims of Non-International Armed Conflicts.[36] It is not, however, for the terrorism suppression

---

[33] Article 147, GCIV; Articles 50(4), 52(2), and 85(3)(b), API.

[34] See Article 51(2), API.

[35] While bombings which are grave breaches of API can be prosecuted on a universal basis as a matter of right under customary international law, the question of whether States are *obliged* to exercise such jurisdiction (or to extradite or prosecute) absent a treaty obligation to that effect is still much debated. See Report of the International on the work of the sixty-fourth session, UN Doc. A/67/10 (2012), [211]: "It was suggested by some members that the main stumbling block in the way of the progress on the topic had been the absence of basic research on whether or not the [*aut dedere aut judicare*] obligation had attained customary law status."

[36] 8 June 1977, 1125 UNTS 609 ('APII'). While there is increasing evidence that states claim a right to prosecute breaches of IHL committed during NIACs (see Graditzky 1998), there is as of yet no customary international law *obligation* to exercise universal jurisdiction or to extradite or prosecute war crimes committed in the context of non-international armed conflicts. See *Tadić* (ICTY-94-1-A), Decision on the Defence Motion for Interlocutory Appeal on Jurisdiction, 2 October 1995, [48]; Zegveld 2002, p. 175; Moir 2002, p. 235; Moir 2009.

regime to remedy gaps in IHL criminal law enforcement. Thus, quite rightly, States negotiating the Terrorist Bombing Convention focused their attention on the integrity of international humanitarian law.

6.4 Regime Interaction and the Case of *Regina v. Mohammed Gul*[37]

This focus on the integrity of IHL brings us back to the question of whether Article 19(2) of the Terrorist Bombing Convention imposes a floor or a ceiling in the exercise of domestic criminal jurisdiction. The following sections will attempt to provide an answer by examining the relative normative status of the Article 19(2) exclusion clause from the perspective of IHL and its non-implementation in the *Mohammed Gul* case.

Mohammed Gul graduated with a law degree from Queen Mary, University of London. During his law studies, Mr. Gul posted videos on YouTube that "showed attacks by Al Qaeda, the Taliban and other proscribed groups on *military targets*, including those in Chechnya and Coalition forces in Iraq and Afghanistan, [and] the use of [improvised explosive devices] against Coalition forces [...]."[38] He was prosecuted for supporting terrorism as defined under Section 1 of the UK Terrorism Act 2000[39] and found guilty—sentenced to five years in prison.[40] His conviction was appealed to the Court of Appeal (CA).[41] One of the principal issues before the CA was whether the trial judge's response to jury questions had been correct in law. After having retired, the jury asked whether "an explosives attack on Coalition forces in Iraq is a terrorist attack" within the meaning of the Terrorism Act 2000.[42]

'Terrorism' is defined under Section 1 of the UK Terrorism Act 2000 as "the use or threat of action [...] designed to influence the government or an international organisation or to intimidate the public,[43] and [...] made for the purpose of advancing a political, religious, racial or ideological cause[,...] if it (a) involves serious violence against a person (b) involves serious damage to property (c) endangers a person's life [...] (d) creates a serious risk to the health or safety of the public [...], or (e) is designed seriously to interfere with or seriously to disrupt an

---

[37] Supra note 6.

[38] Emphasis added, *R v. Mohamed Gul*, supra note 6, [6].

[39] Terrorism Act 2000 c. 11, available at http://www.legislation.gov.uk/ukpga/2000/11.

[40] *R v. Mohamed Gul*, supra note 6, [5].

[41] *R v. Mohamed Gul*, supra note 6.

[42] *R v. Mohamed Gul*, supra note 6, [19].

[43] This element of the definition of terrorism is referred to as a 'terrorist purpose'. Terrorist purpose is expressly excluded from the definition of an act of terrorism where that act of terrorism "involves the use of firearms or explosives". Terrorism Act, supra note 39, s. 1(3).

electronic system."[44] The judge told the jury that an explosives attack on Coalition forces in Iraq was indeed an act of terrorism within the meaning of the Act, and the Court of Appeal agreed.

It is certainly true that there is no language in Section 1 of the UK Terrorism Act, or under UK domestic criminal law more broadly, which suggests that attacks against military objectives in the course of an armed conflict ought to be treated differently from, for instance, a bomb attack against civilians in peacetime.[45] The UK Terrorism Act is, however, domestic criminal legislation which gives effect to obligations under international law.[46] The Court of Appeal (CA) therefore quite rightly looked to international law to guide its interpretation, and held that "there is nothing in international law which would exempt those engaged in attacks on the military during the course of an insurgency from the definition of terrorism."[47]

The CA focused its reasoning on *customary* international law as the source of a potential military exclusion from the definition of terrorism. It examined what it referred to as state practice (some of it in the form of treaty practice of the Organization of the Islamic Conference and the Organization of African Unity, plus the criminal codes of Canada and Australia) and concluded—despite the fact that three out of the four sources examined exclude military conduct from the definition of terrorism—that the "necessary widespread and general state practice or the necessary *opinio juris* to that effect has not yet been established."[48] The CA was of course correct to conclude that a few regional treaties and the practice of two other commonwealth countries is not a sufficient basis for concluding the existence of customary international law.

But it is unclear how the CA jumped from its conclusion that *customary international law* does not exclude acts of war from the definition of terrorism (accepting for argument's sake that custom does indeed define terrorism as an international crime) to its conclusion that "there is nothing in *international law* which would exempt those engaged in attacks on the military during the course of an insurgency from the definition of terrorism."[49] The Terrorism Act was adopted in part to give effect to the Terrorist Bombing Convention;[50] the Convention is

---

[44] Terrorism Act, supra note 39, s. 1(2).

[45] The CA notes that "the definition [of terrorism] in Sect. 6.1 is clear. Those who attacked the military forces of a government or the Coalition forces in Afghanistan or Iraq with the requisite intention set out in the Act are terrorists." *R v. Mohammed Gul*, supra note 6, [60].

[46] Infra note 50.

[47] *R v. Mohammed Gul*, supra note 6, [49].

[48] *R v. Mohammed Gul*, supra note 6, [47].

[49] Emphasis added. *R v. Mohammed Gul*, supra note 6, [49].

[50] The UK signed the Terrorist Bombing Convention before adoption of the Terrorism Act 2000 (on 12 January 1998) and the Act clearly gives effect to obligations under the Terrorist Bombing Convention. In particular, s. 62 of the Terrorism Act (establishing universal jurisdiction over terrorist bombings) gives effect to obligations under Article 6(4) of the Terrorist Bombing Convention, and the definition of terrorism under the Act (which excludes the requirement of a terrorist purpose from the definition of terrorism *as it applies to bombings*, supra *note* 43) gives

clearly applicable to the facts of the case (in that the videos Mr. Gul posted were of attacks by explosive device); and as discussed further below Article 19(2) of the Convention speaks directly to the issue of whether bombings carried out by insurgent groups in the context of an armed conflict amount to an act of terrorism under international treaty law.

In the UK, there has long been a presumption in favour of consistent interpretation where a statute is intended to give effect to a treaty.[51] If Article 19(2) of the Terrorist Bombing Convention should be read as prohibiting the exercise of domestic criminal jurisdiction in cases where the relevant act is governed by IHL, then the only way for the UK or any other State Party to remain in compliance with its international obligations is if it defines terrorist crimes subject to domestic criminal jurisdiction so as to exclude conduct that is expressly excepted from the scope of the Terrorist Bombing Convention. The question remains: Does Article 19(2) of the Terrorist Bombing Convention create a ceiling in regard to the criminalisation of terrorism (prohibiting States from criminalising conduct as 'terrorist' where acts are otherwise governed by international humanitarian law)?

6.4.1 International Armed Conflicts (IAC)

In the context of an IAC, the armed forces of a State are immune from prosecution by foreign powers for taking part in hostilities.[52] The immunity is commonly referred to as combatant's immunity and gives effect to the right of a State's armed forced to fight on its behalf.[53] The flipside of this immunity is that it is unlawful, as a matter of international law, for a foreign power to exercise its domestic prescriptive or enforcement jurisdiction against members of the armed forces of an enemy state for conduct that does not amount to a grave breach of the Geneva Conventions (or API for State parties thereto). In regard to IACs at least, Article 19(2) of the Terrorist Bombing Convention ensures that domestic terrorism legislation (giving effect to obligations under the Convention) is not a vehicle for breaching combatant's immunity and the prohibition against criminalising conduct that is lawful under IHL. If the conduct of the armed forces during an armed conflict (as governed by IHL) was not excluded from the scope of the Terrorist

(Footnote 50 continued)
effect to the broader definition of terrorism (which has no terrorist purpose element) under the Terrorist Bombing Convention. See also the Home Secretary's comments regarding ss. 60–61 of the Terrorism Act: "I want to emphasise that clauses 60 and 61 will enable the United Kingdom to ratify the United Nations convention on the suppression of terrorist bombings and, therefore, to meet our international obligations." HC Deb 14 December 1999, vol. 341, col. 230.

[51] See *Salomon v. Commissioners of Customs and Excise* [1967] 2 QB 116.

[52] Fleck 2008, §312.

[53] See Article 43(2), API, which reflects customary international law, to the effect that members of the armed forces are combatants and have "the right to participate directly in hostilities.".

Bombing Convention, States Parties would in effect be obligated, under the terrorism suppression regime, to criminalise and punish (through the *aut dedere aut judicare* obligation) conduct that they would otherwise be prohibited from criminalising and punishing under IHL. As a result, Article 19(2) of the Terrorist Bombing Convention can only be understood as a ceiling – prohibiting States from criminalising the conduct of armed forces during an IAC as terrorism. To the extent that domestic legislation giving effect to the Terrorist Bombing Convention is not explicit on the matter, consistent interpretation would dictate that the definition of the terrorist crime, however broad, be interpreted so as to exclude the conduct of armed forces during an IAC.

6.4.2 Non-international Armed Conflicts

In the case of *R v. Mohammed Gul*, however, the Secretary of State certified that the conflicts in Afghanistan and Iraq are non-international (in which UK troops are fighting with the consent and at the behest of those States' governments).[54] While it is clear as a matter of international law why Article 19(2) of the Terrorist Bombing Convention must be read as a ceiling in regard to the exercise of domestic criminal jurisdiction over conduct carried out in the context of IACs, the issue is more complicated in the context of NIACs. There is nothing in IHL, including the Protocol Additional to the Geneva Conventions of 12 August 1949, and Relating to the Protection of Victims of Non-International Armed Conflicts[55] (to which the UK is a State Party[56]), which prohibits States from criminalising and punishing participation in hostilities by insurgent armed forces during a NIAC. Insurgents, unlike the armed forces of a State, do not fight as a matter of right. As a result, while APII sets out rules governing hostilities (including rules prohibiting attacks against civilians[57]), it does not create a criminal law enforcement regime with respect to the breach of those rules. Instead, APII leaves States free to criminalise any and all conduct during the course of a NIAC, including attacks against military objectives (which are not prohibited under APII).

[54] While there remains some academic controversy over the qualification of the conflicts in Afghanistan and Iraq as non-international, the Secretary of State's certificate "was accepted by the appellant as highly persuasive". *R v. Mohammed Gul*, supra note 6, [22]. The Court of Appeal's provisional view was that the certificate was conclusive on the matter, but the appellant had also argued that the qualification of the conflict was a question of fact for the jury. As a result, the Court of Appeal held that "it was unnecessary [...] to express a final view" on whether the certificate was conclusive or not, but proceeded with its decision on the basis of the Secretary of State's non-international armed conflict designation. Ibid., [22–23].

[55] 8 June 1977, 1125 UNTS 609 (APII).

[56] State parties to APII available at http://www.icrc.org/ihl.

[57] Article 13(2), APII.

That said, there are strong policy reasons for restraint in criminalising mere participation in hostilities (to be distinguished from prohibited behaviour like direct attacks against civilians) during a NIAC—most particularly that such restraint encourages compliance with the rules governing hostilities in APII. If insurgents are subject to domestic criminal law whether they respect APII or not, they are not properly incentivised to comply with humanitarian law.[58] Indeed, Article 6(5) of APII calls on States "[a]t the end of hostilities, [...] to grant the broadest possible amnesty to persons who have participated in the armed conflict, or those deprived of their liberty for reasons related to the armed conflict [...]." The amnesty called for is of course intended only for acts of mere participation in hostilities (that is to say participation in compliance with the laws of war, including the rules set out in APII).

The policy reasons for exercising such restraint are perhaps stronger in the terrorism context. The ICRC puts the concern thusly:

> A crucial difference between IHL and the legal regime governing terrorism is that IHL is based on the premise that certain acts of violence in war—against military objectives and personnel—are not prohibited. Any act of "terrorism", however, is by definition prohibited and criminal. The two legal regimes should not be blurred given the different logic and rules that apply. This is particularly important in situations of non-international armed conflict, where a "terrorist" designation may act as an additional ***disincentive*** for organized armed groups to respect IHL (they are already subject to criminal prosecution under domestic law).[59]

The bombings carried out by insurgents portrayed in the videos posted by Mr. Gul were against military objectives and were therefore not unlawful under IHL, even though not subject to combatant's immunity. Had the conflicts been designated as international, and had the insurgents been deemed to have been acting on behalf of a State, their conduct would have been subject to combatant's immunity. In their formulation of Article 19(2) of the Terrorist Bombing Convention, however, States do not distinguish between IACs and NIACs—conduct governed by IHL in both types of conflict is excluded from the scope of the terrorism suppression regime. In regard to IACs, part of the reason for this is that compliance with the Terrorist Bombing Convention would otherwise put States in breach of IHL and combatants' immunity. In regard to NIACs, where combatant's immunity does not apply, there is no direct legal conflict between the obligations under the Terrorist Bombing Convention and obligations under IHL—but there are strong policy reasons (as discussed above) for maintaining the approach adopted in regard to IACs. And given the lack of distinction between IACs and NIACs in Article 19(2) of the Terrorist Bombing Convention, States appear to have expressed those policy reasons in the form of a prohibition: no criminalisation of conduct during NIACs as terrorism.

[58] ICRC 2008, p. 28.

[59] Emphasis added. ICRC 2010.

Given that the Terrorism Suppression Conventions require States to criminalise the conduct defined therein on a universal basis, there are also further policy reasons (and indeed legal reasons) for reading Article 19(2) of the Terrorist Bombing Convention as a ceiling on the exercise of domestic criminal jurisdiction in regard to NIACs. In particular, States would otherwise be obligated to criminalise as terrorism the conduct of foreign nationals against foreign States during NIACs, even if that conduct respected the applicable rules of IHL (which is to say hostilities were limited to military objectives and were protective of civilians). Such a legal obligation would interfere with the territorial State's capacity to effectively grant amnesties in regard to insurgent conduct which respected the laws of war (which amnesties are strongly encouraged by the ICRC[60]), and could thereby undermine efforts at truth and reconciliation following a civil conflict. International law does not require States to prioritise their own evaluation of facts on the ground and appropriate legal measures in regard to foreign NIACs over that of the territorial State—which prioritisation would in any event be inconsistent with the principle of non-intervention.[61]

6.5 Conclusion

The above analysis strongly suggests that Article 19(2) of the Terrorist Bombing Convention imposes both a floor and a ceiling on the exercise of domestic criminal jurisdiction in regard to bombings carried out in the course of armed conflicts that might otherwise meet the definition of terrorist bombings under the Convention. The floor is that such conduct (at least when committed in peacetime or by unorganised armed groups during NIACs) has to be criminalised, including on a universal basis. The ceiling is expressed in terms of regime interaction, prohibiting States from exercising their domestic criminal jurisdiction in regard to bombings governed by the more directly applicable body of IHL. The purpose of the ceiling is to (i) preserve the integrity of IHL (so as not to criminalise as 'terrorism' conduct that is otherwise permissible under IHL); (ii) to avoid conflict with other international legal obligations (for instance the obligation to respect combatant's immunity or not to interfere in the domestic affairs of other States) and (iii) to preserve the policy options of States in whose territory NIACs are being fought (for instance through the granting of amnesties). In the circumstances, the UK Court of Appeal was quite simply wrong to conclude that there is "nothing in international law which would exempt those engaged in attacks on the military during the course of an insurgency from the definition of terrorism"[62] in the *Mohammed Gul* case.

[60] ICRC 2008, pp. 28–29.

[61] UN Declaration on Friendly Relations, UNGA Resolution 2625 (1970).

[62] *R v. Mohammed Gul*, supra note 6, [49].

This is not to say, however, that the regime interaction clause in the Terrorist Bombing Convention is perfect—but much of the imperfection is perhaps the mirror reflection of imperfections in the other applicable regimes of international law. In particular, the criminal law enforcement regime for breaches of IHL has a number of gaps through which impunity might slip. Exclusion from the scope of the terrorism suppression regime will therefore sometimes result in there being no applicable obligation to extradite or submit to prosecution, even for conduct that is also unlawful as a matter of IHL. As discussed above, this will be the case in regard to States that are not party to API, but equally in regard to breaches of IHL committed during NIACs—where there is no international legal obligation to exercise domestic criminal jurisdiction on a universal basis.[63] Such imperfections, however, are for humanitarian law to address. The terrorism suppression regime should not be the vehicle for plugging gaps in the IHL criminal law enforcement regime.

While States have decided on a division of labour between IHL and terrorism suppression as a matter of international law (through regime interaction clauses like Article 19(2) of the Terrorist Bombing Convention), they are not always content with that division of labour as a matter of rhetoric and domestic law. The legal power to label Mr. Gul a terrorist is one example. Given that terrorism suppression is principally carried out through domestic exercises of jurisdiction, and is not yet subject to international criminal jurisdiction, it will fall on domestic courts to safeguard the principled distinction between acts of terrorism and acts of war which States have committed themselves to in the Terrorist Bombing Convention. Failure to do so will amount to an internationally wrongful act—not only for breaching the ceiling on the exercise of domestic criminal jurisdiction created by Article 19(2) of the Terrorist Bombing Convention, but also for failing to respect the integrity and distinct logic of two separate but overlapping legal regimes.

References

Aston CC (1982) The United Nations Convention against the Taking of Hostages: realistic or rhetoric? Terror J 5:139

Evans AE (1978) The apprehension and prosecution of offenders: some current problems. In: Evans AE, Murphy JF (eds) Legal aspects of international terrorism. American Society of International Law. D.C. Heath, Toronto, p 493

Ferencz BB (1980) An international criminal court; a step toward world peace. Oceana Publications, Dobbs Ferry

Fleck D (ed) (2008) The handbook of international humanitarian law. Oxford University Press, Oxford

Friedlander RA (1979) Terrorism; documents of international and local control. Oceana Publications, Dobbs Ferry

[63] Supra note 36.

Graditzky T (1998) Individual criminal responsibility for violations of international humanitarian law committed in non-international armed conflicts. Int Rev Red Cross 322:29
Greenwood C (2007) War, terrorism and international law. In: Greenwood C (ed) Essays on war in international law. Cameron May Ltd, London, p 409
Hudson MO (1938) The proposed International Criminal Court. AJIL 32:549
International Committee of the Red Cross (1960) Commentary to Geneva Convention Relative to the Treatment of Prisoners. ICRC, Geneva
International Committee of the Red Cross (2008) Increasing respect for International Humanitarian Law in non-international armed conflicts. ICRC, Geneva
International Committee of the Red Cross (2010) Challenges for IHL—terrorism. www.icrc.org/eng/war-and-law/contemporary-challenges-for-ihl/terrorism/overview-terrorism.htm
International Committee of the Red Cross, Henckaerts J-M, Doswald-Beck L (2005) Customary international humanitarian law. Cambridge University Press, Cambridge
Lambert JL (1990) Terrorism and hostages in international law: a commentary on the Hostages Convention 1979. Grotius Publications Ltd, Cambridge
Mills A (2012) Normative individualism and jurisdiction in public and private international law: toward a 'cosmopolitan sovereignty'? Available at SSRN: http://ssrn.com/abstract=2055295 or http://dx.doi.org/10.2139/ssrn.2055295
Moir L (2002) The law of internal armed conflict. Cambridge University Press, Cambridge
Moir L (2009) Grave breaches and internal armed conflicts. J Int Crim Justice 7:763
Pictet J (1958) Commenrary on the Geneva Conventions of 12 August 1949, vol. III. ICRC, Geneva
Sandoz V, Swinarski C, Zimmerman B (eds) (1987) Commentary on the additional protocols of 8 June 1977 to the Geneva Conventions of 12 August 1949. Martinus Nijhoff / International Committee of the Red Cross, Geneva
Saul B (2006) Defining terrorism in international law. Oxford University Press, Oxford
Trapp K (2011) State responsibility for international terrorism. Oxford University Press, Oxford
Wardlaw G (1982) Political terrorism: theory, tactics, and counter-measures. Cambridge University Press, Cambridge
Zegveld L (2002) Accountability of armed opposition groups in international law. Cambridge University Press, Cambridge

Part II
The Thematic Expansion of International Humanitarian Law

Chapter 7
Beyond Life and Limb: Exploring Incidental Mental Harm Under International Humanitarian Law

Eliav Lieblich

Contents

Eliav Lieblich is Lecturer (Assistant professor), Interdisciplinary Center Herzliya (IDC), Radzyner Law School. JSD, LLM, Columbia Law School; LLB, Hebrew University of Jerusalem.

E. Lieblich (✉)
Interdisciplinary Center Herzliya, Herzliya, Israel
e-mail: elieblich@idc.ac.il

D. Jinks et al. (eds.), *Applying International Humanitarian Law in Judicial and Quasi-Judicial Bodies*, DOI: 10.1007/978-94-6265-008-4_7,

7.1 Introduction

In late 2012, an inclusive report drawn up by legal clinics at Stanford and NYU—entitled Living under Drones—addressed the effects of US drone strikes in Pakistan on civilians.[1] Among other calamities, the report discussed the "trauma" caused to civilians living in operational theaters of drones, thoroughly describing the stress they suffer, and its effects over their mental health. Interviewee after interviewee described the constant state of fear that came to characterize, in the words of the report, the day-to-day of those "living under drones."[2] However, in its legal analysis of the situation, the issue of mental harm seems to have faded, as if not playing any part beyond a factual exposition.

Instead, the report outlined a set of rather conservative concerns emanating from the use of drones, such as the possible violation of Pakistani sovereignty; questions regarding the legality of targeting killings under international humanitarian law (IHL) (and international human rights law); issues of transparency, accountability, and problems relating to domestic US law.[3] The psychological trauma, so thoroughly discussed earlier in the Report, was simply set aside when push came to legal shove: the report simply did not follow up with regard to the legal effects of such trauma, leaving it hanging in limbo. Living under Drones is hardly alone in this omission. Indeed, as we shall see, IHL discourse—across the board—has not been remotely clear concerning this issue.

This is particularly true concerning *incidental* mental harm. Indeed, as we shall see, the illegality of acts *intentionally* meant to spread "terror" among civilians is unchallenged, even if not elaborated upon in practice and literature. This is not too surprising: the prohibition on such acts does not raise complex fundamental questions—since it can be viewed as a straightforward corollary of the principle of distinction,[4] the principles of necessity and humanity,[5] and perhaps also of traditional notions of chivalry.[6] It is indeed easy to grasp the normative pull of a rule that prohibits armed forces from callously spreading terror among the civilian population, however such terror is defined. Conversely, how mental harm plays out in the context of the principle of *proportionality* remains unaddressed. The principle of proportionality in IHL, as is well known, prohibits attacks—even against otherwise legitimate targets—that cause excessive incidental harm to civilians,

---

[1] Living under drones: death, injury and trauma to civilians from US drone practices in Pakistan, Stanford Law School and New York U Law School, 2012, pp. 103–117.

[2] ibid., pp. 80–88.

[3] ibid., pp. 103–124.

[4] Protocol Additional to the Geneva Conventions of 12 August 1949, and Relating to the Protection of Victims of International Armed Conflicts (Protocol I), 8 June 1977 (hereinafter API), Article 48.

[5] See generally Dinstein 2010, pp. 4–6.

[6] On chivalry see Solis 2010, pp. 5–6.

in relation to the concrete and direct military advantage gained from the attack.[7] This chapter, thus, seeks to offer a preliminary discussion of an uncharted question: should *incidental* mental harm to civilians be taken into consideration by states, commanders, judges and fact-finding missions in their analyses?

Any consideration of this question quickly reveals the urgent need to clarify the modalities of civilian harm: the problem of mental harm being just one of the unsettled issues of the larger question. Indeed, while much work has been done, in recent years, to define and elucidate some of IHL's vaguer terms,[8] scant attention has been given to the nature of harm. This is a striking realization, considering that civilian harm is one of the main calamities that IHL seeks to prevent.[9] In other words, while positive IHL is unequivocal about the need to prevent or at least minimize civilian harm, it does not tell us—beyond the obvious—what this harm is. How far, temporally, is harm measured? Where does the causal chain of harm end? To what extent does harm transcend the purely physical into the economical and emotional? While questions of this order troubled torts lawyers for centuries,[10] they are virtually absent from the discussion of proportionality in the realm of *jus in bello*. As we shall see, it is in the context of *jus in bello* proportionality that this absence is especially troubling, since the latter requires quantifying, to the extent possible, opposing values and striking a balance between them. This is an exercise in futility, unless both parts of the equation are adequately circumscribed.[11]

Like many problems relating to proportionality, the question of incidental mental harm is of special significance in the context of non-international armed conflicts, which constitute the vast majority of contemporary struggles.[12] The problem is exacerbated in such conflicts, since many of them involve asymmetrical warfare.[13] In warfare of this type, uninvolved civilians and legitimate targets often intermingle, enhancing the risk of collateral damage.[14]

In this context, inclusion of incidental mental harm in the proportionality equation can have various practical implications. For instance, it can affect the

---

[7] API, Article 51(5)(b).

[8] See eg Talinn Manual 2013, rule 30; Ferraro 2012; Melzer 2009; Henckaerts and Doswald-Beck 2005.

[9] See generally Meron 2000a.

[10] See eg Addison et al. 1870, pp. 4–7, 2–22

[11] Indeed, understanding proportionality requires the clarification, for instance, of the temporal scope of harm (whether only short-term, or rather long-term harm is addressed) and its separate or cumulative nature. See, respectively, McCormack and Mtharu 2006, pp. 9–10 (addressing the question in the context of explosive remnants of war); ICTY *Prosecutor v. Kupreskic* (Judgement) [2000] IT-95-16-T, p. 526 (resorting to the residual Martens Clause in the context of this question).

[12] See UCDP/PRIO 2009.

[13] For instance, asymmetry is a common characteristic of counterinsurgency scenarios. US Army and Marin Corps 2006, pp. 1–2.

[14] See eg, Schmitt 2007, pp. 22–23. This is not to say that the question does not have possible implications in the context of *international* armed conflicts—to the extent that the latter are conducted in the proximity of civilian population. For an example see ibid., pp. 23–39.

timing or method of an attack. A simplified example is in order: assume that a state, involved in an armed conflict against a non-state actor, has positively identified a squad of militants on its way to launch a rocket, or to plant an explosive device. Undoubtedly, the squad is a legitimate target under IHL.[15] On its way, the squad passes nearby a school, where children are playing in the yard. Now, our state has sophisticated armed forces, capable of attacking the squad without causing any physical harm to the children in the school; however, hearing and witnessing the attack could cause them significant mental trauma. Does the state have a legal duty to wait until the squad moves on to a less "sensitive" area? Consider the same scenario, in which it is expected that some children will be physically harmed during the attack. When considering proportionality, should this element of mental harm be "added" to the physical harm incurred?

Whenever discussing questions related to mental harm, an easy way out exists—which I shall nevertheless avoid. By denying any substantive difference between "physical" (or bodily) and "mental" (or emotional) harm, it is possible to immediately quash the conversation. Such claims could rely on contemporary critical approaches which negate the concept of "mind-body dualism" to begin with[16]; or, perhaps, highlight the predominant trend in psychology to address mental disorders in biological terms.[17] Therefore, the argument would go, mental harm is bodily harm and vice versa, and, accordingly, whenever IHL—or any legal arrangement, for that matter—protects persons from "injury" the term *per se* includes also mental harm.[18] However, since the purely biological approach to psychology, while widespread, is still contested;[19] and because, in any case, there are differences between these spheres of harm *at least* with regard to their methods of identification[20]—and certainly in their everyday understanding—[21] there is still merit in discussing these types of harm separately.

A further important distinction must be made. In recent years, there is an explosion of literature and jurisprudence discussing the interplay between international human rights law (IHRL) and IHL, whether during occupation or during active hostilities.[22] Most authorities are nowadays in agreement that IHL and

---

[15] See Melzer 2009, p. 15.

[16] See Tirosh 2012, pp. 295–300.

[17] For a basic discussion see Brain 2002, pp. 15–17.

[18] Comparable claims are made in tort law, with regard to the traditional distinction between physical and emotional harm in some jurisdictions for the purpose of tort liability. See Grey 2011.

[19] Brain 2002, pp. 17–18.

[20] For instance, most (if not all) "bodily" harm can be identified by simple visual analysis conducted even by non-specialized personnel. Identifying mental harm, conversely—and as we shall discuss later on—requires expertise and time; it could be thus argued that mental harm is harder to attribute to a specific event. Compare Restatement (Third) Ch. 2, §4 Comment (b).

[21] See Luban and Shue 2012, pp. 829–830 ("we doubt that asking what pain is 'at root' will shed light on the law, which operates in theoretical shallows, using ordinary language categories").

[22] See eg, Watkin 2004; Lubell 2012; see generally Arnold and Quénivet 2008, p. 1, 2, pp. 10–11.

IHRL apply both, in some form, during armed conflict.[23] This means that state-obligations, under IHRL, to protect the mental health of those under the state's control[24] continue to apply during armed conflict. Moreover, according to some, IHRL protects not only those under the effective control of the state, but also those *affected* by state power.[25] In cases where control is not full and complete, IHRL norms concerning the protection of mental health can be, perhaps, applied functionally, in line with the level of control or power exercised over the individual in the specific case.[26] Be it as it may, for the sake of discussion, this chapter assumes situations where effective control is absent, as will be the case in most targeting scenarios occurring during active hostilities. In such situations IHL's rules of targeting—and particularly those that recognize that some incidental harm could be acceptable when measured against a valid military advantage—generally prevail as the *lex specialis*.[27] It is in this context in which possible obligations relating to mental harm give rise to especially challenging questions.

In sum, this chapter seeks to raise the issue of incidental mental harm within IHL's proportionality paradigm. It does not presume to provide definite answers to all possible questions, but rather to spark a discussion. It attempts to demonstrate that incidental mental harm cannot be brushed aside—both by decision makers and by assessing bodies—if IHL is to maintain its integrity as a legal body aiming to minimize civilian harm. The chapter starts, in Sect. 7.2, with a brief policy discussion, arguing that the inclusion of incidental mental harm does not launch IHL into utopia, nor does it upset its internal balance. On the contrary, as I claim, IHL's integrity *demands* a substantive treatment of the question. Section 7.3 proceeds to exemplify the blind-spot, towards the issue, in contemporary IHL discourse—which is particularly intriguing considering that modern IHL indeed aims to protect the *person* not only on a physical but also on a mental and emotional basis.

---

[23] See eg ICJ, Legality of Threat or Use of Nuclear Weapons (Advisory Opinion), 1996 ICJ Reports 226, para 25; ICJ, Legal Consequences of the Construction of a Wall in the Occupied Palestinian Territory (Advisory Opinion) 2004 ICJ 136, para 106; ICJ, Armed Activities on the Territory of the Congo (DRC v. Uganda) 2005 ICJ Reports 168, paras 216–220; Human Rights Committee (2004) General Comment 31, CCPR/C/21/Rev.1/Add.13, para 11; ECtHR, *Al-Skeini v. UK* App No 55721/07 [2011].

[24] International Covenant on Economic, Social and Cultural Rights 1966, Article 12(1); see also Committee on Economic, Social and Cultural Rights 2000, General Comment 14, UN Doc E/C.12/2000/4 (Aug. 11, 2000); GA Res 46/119 (1991) The Principles for the Protection of Persons with Mental Illness and for the Improvement of Mental Health Care, UN Doc A/RES/46/119.

[25] General Comment 31, para 10.

[26] Compare *Al-Skein v. UK* 2011 (Concurring Opinion of Judge Bonello).

[27] These are generally the rules found in API, Articles 48–59, and their counterparts under customary international law. One of the key distinctions between IHRL and IHL has to do with the acceptability of collateral damage, a concept which is all but absent from the IHRL paradigm. See Meron 2000b, p. 240; but see Hakimi 2012, p. 1371 note 18. On the concept of IHRL/IHL *lex specialis* see Solomon 2011, pp. 79–80.

As I demonstrate, this legal blind-spot can be constructed either as obliviousness to incidental mental harm, or as implicit disapproval of its inclusion in the proportionality analysis. I conclude that since this is a question of interpretation, the answer must be given in accordance with IHL's object and purpose. Section 7.4 critically analyzes some possible challenges to the inclusion of incidental mental harm. Such challenges can emanate from the presumption that mental harm is not tangible enough for legal application; from problems of ex-post identification and attribution; and from concerns regarding mental harm's foreseeability. Essentially, I ask whether these challenges are convincing enough to reject the inclusion of incidental mental harm, as an idea incompatible with IHL's objectives. Drawing a rough analogy from developments in common-law torts, and from recent research on Posttraumatic Stress Disorder (PTSD), I conclude that challenges of this order are not strong enough to negate incidental harm altogether and that it is high time that the question be seriously considered by states, commentators and the international legal community at large.

7.2 The Policy Analysis: Utopianism, Adverse Incentives and the Argument from Integrity

Inclusion of mental harm in the proportionality analysis might seem, on its face, as a radical suggestion. Therefore, before delving into the legal question, a brief discussion of policy is required. Namely, it is worthwhile to ask whether the inclusion of mental harm would skew the basic balance sought by IHL—that between military necessity, on the one hand, and humanitarian considerations on the other.[28] Indeed, conservative interpreters of IHL might reject out of hand the idea of incidental mental harm, labeling it as a naïve, utopian, and ultimately futile attempt to sterilize the harsh realities of war. Claiming that mental harm should be taken into account is really an act of concealed pacifism, they would argue, since anguish is an integral part of war's reality and cannot be avoided unless military action is totally banned.[29] Moreover, imposing extra-burdens on states is especially problematic in contemporary conflicts involving unaccountable non-state actors,[30] which bluntly violate even the most basic of international norms.[31] In such conflicts, the argument goes, any additional burden on states will adversely incentivize non-state actors to take advantage of these enhanced obligations, rather than induce them to comply.[32]

---

[28] See Schmitt 2010.

[29] Walzer argued, for instance, that imposing radical limitations on the use of force in *jus in bello* can essentially amount to pacifism. Cf Walzer 2004, pp. 13–14.

[30] See eg Lamp 2011, pp. 225–226; Zegveld 2011, pp. 133–163.

[31] See eg Richemond-Barak 2011, p. 106, 119.

[32] Cf Schmitt 2007, p. 22, 27.

The argument concerning utopianism does not carry much weight. This is because physical suffering, injury and death also form an inherent part of war—perhaps even its key characteristic—but the general perception is that IHL *still* seeks to minimize them;[33] it is unclear, therefore, why the minimization of *other* inherent parts, such as mental anguish, would launch IHL into the realm of utopia.

Moreover, IHL's inner mechanism is arguably utopia-resistant, being based, in its essence, on compromise.[34] Indeed, IHL does in fact recognize that all proportional types of harm can be justified in light of a military advantage,[35] which is in itself hardly a utopian concept. In this sense, the inclusion of mental harm in the equation would not render IHL utopian and less prone to compromise. Mental harm would have to be considered when planning and launching an attack, but it would not be *a priori* excluded as lawful collateral damage, in a manner that would negate any possible military operation.

Furthermore, the claim that since anguish, pain, and overall negative emotions are integral to warfare, the inclusion of mental harm in the proportionality equation would inhibit every military action is essentially an *ad absurdum* argument. When we discuss mental harm, we naturally refer to the most serious, well studied forms of such harm, such as post-traumatic stress disorder (PTSD).[36] Inclusion of negligible forms of discomfort, or vague notions such as "civilian morale"[37] would not only be impractical, but would also result in an uncontrollable "ripple effect," extending far beyond the battlefield into spheres which IHL was never intended to regulate.[38]

The challenges posed by non-state actors—and the possible problem of adverse incentives caused by any extension of the notion of harm—cannot be cast-off without serious consideration. Indeed, in many contemporary conflicts involving armed groups, civilians and fighters intermingle in a manner that significantly strains IHL's core principles, such as distinction and proportionality.[39] In some instances, non-state actors make use of this fact by intentionally operating from civilian areas—a tactic that damages states both operationally and in the court of international legitimacy.[40] It could be argued therefore that increasing the burden on militaries, by adopting a wide perception of civilian harm, will push non-state actors to further abuse the proximity of civilians, while shifting to states the increased costs of prevention. If international law, the argument goes, will

---

33 Namely through the prohibition on causing unnecessary suffering and the general principle of necessity. See API, Articles 35(2); Sassòli et al. 2011, pp. 32–34; Ohlin 2013, pp. 1297–1299.

34 See Muzenović Larsen 2012, p. 124.

35 API, Article 51(5)(b).

36 See discussion, at Sect. 7.4.1.

37 See Schmitt 2013, p. 33 ("a decline in civilian morale is not to be considered collateral damage in the context of … the rule of proportionality.").

38 Compare the "ripple effect" concern as grounds for limiting liability for pure economic loss resulting from negligence. See Rabin 2006, p. 862.

39 See Schmitt 2007, pp. 22–23.

40 See eg Banks 2011, pp. 1–2.

overlook this phenomenon—and be therefore understood by state actors as unbalanced, it would eventually be disregarded altogether, in light of its weak enforcement mechanisms.[41] Recognizing incidental mental harm will only result, ultimately, in reduced compliance by all involved parties.

While such dynamics give rise to real concerns, they are not sufficient in themselves to tilt the scale. Simply put, this is because accounting for mental harm goes *both ways*. Recognizing the importance of mental harm does not necessarily weaken the position of states confronting non-state actors—in particular when the latter are involved in attacks against civilians. It suffices to look at the tactics employed by some of these actors: many involve attacks that result in significant fear and terror,[42] if not directly aimed to that end altogether. Indeed, spreading fear much wider than the direct physical outcome of the attack is an essential characteristic of terrorism.[43] Accordingly, in its definition of the term, the Special Tribunal for Lebanon ruled that "the intent to spread fear among the population" is a key element of the crime of terrorism under customary international law.[44]

In this context, if mental harm, in any constellation, can be accounted for under relevant international law, it may grant states more leeway when acting against attackers. This additional flexibility stems from the fact that it is not only the physical harm inflicted by the attack, but also its effects on the mental well being of the civilian population that will be taken into consideration in any assessment of state action.[45] The implications of such an understanding can be easily exemplified. For instance, in the 2011 UN Secretary General's Panel Report on the Gaza Flotilla incident, widely known as the Palmer Report, it was implied that the "psychological toll" of rocket attacks launched against civilians might play a role in the *jus ad bellum* assessment of states' right to self-defense.[46] Moreover, in its Guidelines on Direct Participation in Hostilities (DPH), the International

[41] See Schmitt 2004, p. 510.

[42] See Gelkopf et al. 2008.

[43] See eg Schmid 2011, pp. 1–3.

[44] Interlocutory Decision on the Applicable Law: Terrorism, Conspiracy, Homicide, Perpetration, Cumulative Charging [2011] STL-11-01/I/AC/R167bis , paras 85, 88–100; cf Ambos 2011, pp. 665–675.

[45] For instance, even the Goldstone Report recognized that the wide psychological trauma caused to Israeli civilians by rockets launched from Gaza must be accounted for as a possible war crime; however this fact did not seem to play a part in its analysis of the Israeli military response. See Human Rights Council (2009) Report of the United Nations Fact-Finding Mission on the Gaza Conflict, UN Doc A/HRC/12/48, paras 1653–1658 (hereinafter Goldstone Report).

[46] Report of the Secretary-General's Panel of Inquiry in the 31 May 2010 Flotilla Incident (2011), para 71 ("[t]he enormity of the psychological toll on the affected population cannot be underestimated … It seems obvious that stopping these violent acts was a necessary step for Israel … "). For this understanding of the Palmer Report see Solomon (2012) The Recent European Court of Human Rights Judgment in the Finogenov Case: Towards an Esoteric Humanization of Warfare. 11 Berkeley Journal of International Law PUBLICIST at http://bjil.typepad.com/publicist/2012/04/the-recent-european-court-of-human-rights-judgment-in-the-finogenov-case-towards-an-esoteric-humanization-of-warfare.html.

Committee of the Red Cross (ICRC) has suggested that for civilians to be deemed as directly participating in hostilities and thus be deprived of protection from attack under IHL, their act must, *inter alia*, cross a "threshold of harm." For this threshold to be crossed, the act must be likely to cause harm of a specifically military nature; *or* to inflict death, injury, or destruction on those protected against direct attack—namely civilians.[47] When constructing direct participation in hostilities in terms of harm to civilians, two preliminary suggestions can be made.[48] First, taking mental harm seriously within IHL could, perhaps, broaden the "threshold of harm" criterion in the determination of direct participation in hostilities. This could hypothetically result in wider targetability of certain individuals. Even if the latter suggestion goes too far, a second possible argument is that protecting one's "own" civilians from mental harm could *at least* be calculated as part of a valid military advantage emanating from a specific attack—which could be balanced, under IHL, against collateral damage.[49]

In sum, inserting considerations of mental harm into the IHL discourse would not only serve to constrain states, but can equally restrict actions of non-state actors. The inclusion of mental harm, thus, does not *a priori* benefit one side over the other. In other words, placing the additional burden of mental harm on the "military advantage" part of the proportionality equation can perhaps be offset by the concept's benefits for state actors in other contexts.

A further argument for the inclusion of incidental mental harm is derived from the concept of integrity. As any legal system, IHL must maintain its coherency and integrity, and strive to avoid arbitrary results, in order to ensure its legitimacy.[50] Rejecting the idea of incidental mental harm, without serious consideration, would lead to an anomaly that might discredit one of IHL's main ideas: minimizing civilian harm. Assume that a state conducts an otherwise lawful targeted killing operation, destroying, as collateral damage, a car. Children in a nearby kindergarten, however, become traumatized, perhaps for the rest of their lives. A conservative approach towards the analysis of harm, in such a situation, results in a stark paradox: the expected damage to the car should have been considered when deciding on the attack; while the potential lifelong mental trauma caused to the children could be disregarded. Obviously, such a legal outcome is absurd, unless there is something inherent in mental harm that merits its exclusion from the proportionality analysis. It becomes crystalized at once that if we take civilian harm seriously, we cannot gloss over its mental aspects.

[47] Melzer 2009, p. 47, pp. 49–50.

[48] These suggestions are worthy of further exploration, beyond the scope of this chapter. Therefore, they are mentioned here only in a non-exhaustive manner.

[49] I specifically reserve the complex question of protection of one's "own" civilians as a valid military advantage, in particular when balanced against civilian harm to "enemy" civilians. See generally Luban 2011.

[50] For the classic statement of this idea see Dworkin 1986, pp. 176–224.

7.3 Incidental Mental Harm as a Blind-Spot of International Humanitarian Law

7.3.1 *From Protection of Life and Limb to Protection of the Mental?*

The question of incidental mental harm must be analyzed in light of the general development of the concept of "harm" under IHL. As we shall see in this section, provisions for the protection of civilians from arbitrary bodily or property harm can be already found in the earliest instruments of IHL. However, IHL's approach towards mental harm is more complex.[51] As detailed below, *intentional* infliction of mental harm has been outlawed in line with IHL's increasing concern for individuals. The idea of *incidental* harm, conversely, has yet to be explicitly addressed, and therefore requires in-depth discussion. Since, as this section demonstrates, the general perception of harm in IHL has moved beyond the strictly physical also to include the concept of the "person" in the wide sense, the recognition of incidental mental harm is plausibly the next evolutionary stage in IHL's regime of civilian protection.

Indeed, early rules of armed conflict did not expressly refer to any form of mental harm, whether intentional or incidental. The Lieber Code of 1863—perhaps the earliest blueprint of modern IHL[52]—permitted the destruction of *life* and *limb* of "armed enemies," and by way of negation, prohibited the "destruction" of those of non-armed "persons" unless "incidentally unavoidable."[53] Other types of harm, such as destruction of civilian property or "withholding of sustenance" from the "enemy,"[54] were at large tolerated even if intentional, as long as they could be reconciled with some vague notion of military necessity. Indeed, the civilian population, as a whole, was considered part of the "enemy," and as such could be "subjected to the hardships of the war."[55] The protection of mental well-being, obviously, was utterly beyond the scope of this paradigm. The 1907 Hague Regulations added little to our understanding in this context, as their provisions for the protection of civilians during active hostilities, were mainly manifested in the prohibition on the "bombardment" of undefended localities.[56]

---

[51] As we shall later detail, it is unsurprising that mental harm was not clearly addressed in early IHL, considering that the idea of mental harm, as a concrete phenomenon, has developed in a later period.

[52] See Kolb 2012, p. 25.

[53] General Orders No. 100 (1863) Instructions for the Government of Armies of the United States in the Field, Article 15 (emphasis added).

[54] Ibid. See also ibid., Articles 16, 17. 22.

[55] At the time, the notion of "enemy" included the civilian population of the hostile state/belligerent, which as such could be "subjected to the hardships of the war." Ibid., Article 21.

[56] Convention (IV) Respecting the Laws and Customs of War on Land. The Hague, 18 October 1907, Articles 23(g), 25.

A wider perception of the concept of harm, even if not explicitly phrased as such, has been a natural product of IHL's consistently increasing focus on the protection of individuals.[57] This widening perception is chiefly reflected in the recognition, in the Fourth Geneva Convention of 1949 (GCIV), of the "person" as a distinct protected value.[58] For instance, Article 27 of the Fourth Geneva Convention provides that "[p]rotected persons are entitled, in all circumstances, to respect for their *persons*, their honour, their family rights, their religious convictions and practices, and their manners and customs."[59]

Moreover, Article 33 of GCIV, which prohibits, in the general context of collective punishment, measures of "intimidation" and "terrorism" against protected individuals, also implies the protection of the person beyond the purely physical.[60] The protection of the person is furthermore entrenched in Article 3 Common to the Geneva Conventions, the main normative framework regulating non-international armed conflicts.[61]

The concept of the person as a distinct value, according to the authoritative commentaries on the Geneva Conventions, must be understood in "its widest sense,"[62] alluding to "the rights and qualities which are inseparable from the human being by the very fact of his existence and his mental and physical powers; it includes, in particular, the right to physical, moral and intellectual integrity."[63] Indeed, these developments clearly reflect the emerging recognition at the time that damage to civilians, during hostilities, can transcend the strictly bodily.

A further development in this context can be found in Additional Protocol I (API) of 1977. As part of its civilian protection regime, API prohibits, in Article 51(2), all "acts or threats of violence the primary purpose of which is to spread terror" among civilians.[64] This provision, thus, disallows violent acts, as well as threats of such, which are *meant* to cause the subjective sensation of "terror."[65] API does not provide a definition of "terror;" however, since the term is quite wide, any reasonable conception of it would include mental trauma.[66]

---

57 See Meron 2000b.

58 Respect for the person has been already laid down, in the context of prisoners of war, in the 1929 Geneva Convention on prisoners of war. See Pictet 1958, p. 201.

59 Convention (IV) Relative to the Protection of Civilian Persons in Time of War. Geneva, 12 August 1949, Article 27 (hereinafter GCIV) 27 (emphasis added). Article 27, arguably, applies to all instances of hostilities, not only during occupation. See ICRC 2012 p. 10. 12.

60 Ibid, Article 33.

61 GCIV Article 3 (common to the Geneva Conventions) (prohibiting, *inter alia*, violence "to life and person" and "outrages upon personal dignity").

62 Pictet 1958, p. 201.

63 Ibid., p. 201.

64 API, Article 51(2).

65 The ICTY in the Galić case ruled that "acts or threats of violence," in this context, means "attacks or threats of attacks." ICTY, *Prosecutor v. Galić* (Judgement) [2006] IT-98-29-A, para 102 (hereinafter Galić).

66 Ibid., For a similar approach see Schmitt 2013, p. 108.

Essentially, therefore, Article 51(2) can be viewed as the first major provision in IHL to explicitly prohibit acts intended to inflict mental harm.[67]

However, Article 51(2) does not prohibit acts which *result* in terror, if this is not their "primary purpose." Indeed, as conceded in the Commentary on API, "some degree of terror among the population" is almost a given consequence of armed conflict, and is accordingly not "envisaged" in this provision.[68] The provision merely prohibits acts primarily meant to spread terror among civilians, when the acts do not offer a "substantial military advantage."[69] The same understanding was articulated by Dinstein:

> There is no legal blemish in a 'shock and awe' air offensive (like the one undertaken in the hostilities against Iraq in 2003), designed to pound military objectives and break the back of the enemy armed forces. A large-scale aerial bombardment — inflicting extensive destruction on military units and objectives — is liable to terrify civilians, and may be inimical to their morale, but it does not *per se* taint such an attack with illegality.[70]

This construction of the law, in turn, leaves open the question whether there are any legal limitations on the *incidental* "terror" caused by attacks that *do* offer a valid military advantage, or rather that military exigencies immediately quash the discussion.

While the prohibition on intentionally terrorizing the civilian population does not require a set-definition of "terror,"[71] in the context of the principle of proportionality, such an abstract understanding simply does not do the work. Indeed, prior to the introduction of proportionality in API, all harm was allowed, more or less, when military necessity could be invoked.[72] Proportionality, conversely, introduced a regime in which the element of military necessity—coined as a "concrete and direct military advantage"—must be scrutinized in light of the expected incidental harm to civilians.[73] Such an assessment, naturally, requires at least a basic definition of both the military advantage sought and of the "harm"

---

[67] Note, however, that the ICTY Appeals Chamber concluded that Article 51(2) in its entirety reflected customary international law at the time of API's adoption. The Appeals Chambers found evidence for this perception, for instance, in Article 22 of the non-binding Rules Concerning the Control of Wireless Telegraphy in Time of War and Air Warfare (1923); the 1938 Draft Convention for the Protection of Civilian Populations against new Engines of War; and Article 33 of GCIV. *Galić*, paras 87–90. It further found evidence for the criminalization of intentional terror as early as 1919. See ibid., para 93.

[68] Sandoz et al. 1987, p. 618.

[69] Ibid. Note, however, that the requirement that an act offer a "substantial military advantage" in order to justify "spreading terror" actually alludes, albeit vaguely, to a proportionality-based approach: the military advantage must be "substantial" for the act not to be considered as one "primarily" meant to spread terror.

[70] Dinstein 2004, p. 119. Interestingly, in a later edition of his book, Dinstein seems to have tempered, somewhat, the language with regard to incidental terror. See Dinstein 2010, p. 126.

[71] See infra, Sect. 7.4.1.

[72] See supra, text accompanying notes 53–57.

[73] API, Article 51(5)(b).

against which it is measured. In this context, the wording of API seems, on its face, rather conservative: it refers to "incidental loss of civilian life, injury to civilians, damage to civilian objects, or a combination thereof."[74] The same formula is used in the context of the duty to take precautionary measures in the choice of means and methods of attack.[75] The Commentary on API does not assist us much in determining whether these provisions can be read so as to include also mental harm; on the contrary, it seems to focus on the more obvious types of harm occurring when civilians are "hit" incidentally.[76]

7.3.2 Overview of Practice: Silence or Disapproval?

Much like the Commentary on API, international practice seems to gloss over the meaning of civilian harm in the context of proportionality, leaving open the question whether it is simply oblivious to incidental mental harm, or tacitly disapproving of is inclusion. For instance, the ICRC's study on customary IHL does not at all elaborate on the nature of civilian loss.[77] Likewise, military manuals are also inconclusive in this context: some follow the wording of API[78]; others use narrow language such as "loss of life and damage to property,"[79] or refer to generic "collateral damage,"[80] "injuries" or "casualties."[81] Occasionally, wider language such as "adverse effect upon civilians" or "possible harmful effects" is used.[82] The UK military Manual, for instance, refers to a rather inclusive category of *foreseeable* effects as those that must be considered when assessing incidental harm, but proceeds to exemplify them only in the context of physical injuries.[83]

In the same vein, a 2009 US Joint Chiefs of staff instruction, providing detailed and technical instructions regarding US collateral damage estimation methodology, also demonstrates the blind-spot regarding incidental mental harm. When outlining the "dominant hazard" for collateral damage emanating from different

---

74 Ibid.

75 API, Article 57(2)(ii)–(iii).

76 Sandoz et al. 1987, p. 684.

77 Henkaerts and Doswald Beck 2005, Rule 14.

78 Germany, Bundesminsterium der Verteidigung (2013) Humanitäres Völkerrecht in bewaffneten Konflikten—Handbuch, paras 512–513.

79 US Army (1956) The Law of Land Warfare, para 41.

80 Royal Australian Air Force (2004) Operations Law for RAAF Commanders , pp. 50–51.

81 Australian Defense Force (2006) Law of Armed Conflict, para 2.8; Canada, Office of the JAG (2003) Law of Armed Conflict at the Operational and Tactical Levels, para 413 (hereinafter Canada); US Navy 2007, Marine Corps and Coast Guard (2007) The Commander's Handbook on the Law of Naval Operations, para 8.3.1.

82 Canada, para 4.

83 UK Chiefs of Staff (2004), The Joint Service Manual on the Law of Armed Conflict, para 5.33.4.

types of weapons, the instruction refers to conventional effects such as "fragmentation" and "debris" which may spawn a probability of "serious or lethal injury" to personnel or "structural damage" to objects.[84]

A similar blind-spot can be found in the Israeli debate on the practice of causing intentional sonic booms over densely populated areas. In the years 2005–2006, in several instances, the Israeli Air Force deliberately caused sonic booms above the Gaza Strip, in the context of the ongoing conflict between Israel and Gaza based armed groups.[85] Challenging this practice in front of the Israeli Supreme Court,[86] petitioners argued—among other claims—that the sole purpose of the booms was to "prevent the residents from sleeping and to create an ongoing sense of fear and anxiety." As such, they argued that the practice violated Article 33 of GCIV, which prohibits measures of intimidation.[87]

The State, in its response, argued that the measure was not meant to intimidate the civilian population, but rather "to cause disinformation and confusion among terrorists concerning the type, character and scope of IDF operations."[88] As such, it claimed, the sonic booms were not *primarily* meant to spread terror: the anxiety and fear caused to the civilian population were merely a secondary, incidental effect in relation to the legitimate military necessity.[89] However, when the State moved to defend its position under the principle of proportionality,[90] it discussed only the possible *physical* effects of sonic booms: meaning, their potential to shatter glass windows. This discourse allowed the State to reduce any perception of harm caused by sonic booms to the point of *de minimis*.[91] Indeed, this is a prime example of the paradox mentioned earlier: it is peculiar, to say the least, that shattered windows are mentioned as potentially relevant harm, while mental health is not even discussed. In any case, the Court did not decide the merits of the question, as Israel ceased from this practice by the time the decision was rendered.

In this context, the 2013 Tallinn Manual, written by independent experts commissioned by NATO to analyze the application of international law to cyber warfare, is also telling. While "inconvenience, irritation, stress, of fear" caused to civilians by cyber operations were, according to the experts, excluded from the proportionality analysis, "deprivation of functionality" from civilian *objects*—meaning, rendering them useless without causing them substantial physical

---

84 US Chairman of the Joint Chiefs of Staff 2009, p. D-C-1.

85 B'Tselem, 2013, The Sonic Booms in the Sky over Gaza. www.btselem.org/gaza_strip/supersonic_booms. (Accessed June 3 2013).

86 HCJ, Case 10265/05 Physicians for Human Rights v. Minister of Defense [2008].

87 For this position, see B'Tselem, supra n. 85.

88 *Physicians for Human Rights,* State's Response paras 69–71 (in Hebrew).

89 Ibid., paras 96–102.

90 The State discussed this issue assuming *arguendo* that causing sonic booms can be qualified as an "attack" and thus subjected to proportionality analysis, although this was not its position. Ibid., para 152.

91 Ibid., paras 118–144.

damage—could, in some cases, be calculated as civilian harm within the proportionality balance.[92] Again—the paradox emerges: if law is generous enough to recognize the proportionality significance of deprivation of functionality of objects, why does it not recognize comparable harm—deprivation of a fully functioning life, comprising of all cognitive and sentimental abilities—when caused to persons? Indeed, this challenge to IHL's integrity, unresolved, strains its basic premises to the core.

Interestingly, a May 2013 decision by a Pakistani court demonstrates that this blind-spot is also shared by states at the receiving end of military operations.[93] The Peshawar High Court was called upon by petitioners to order the State to act against US drone strikes, allegedly violating Pakistani sovereignty and international law—and so it did.[94] However, of interest to us is the Court's account of the harm caused by drone strikes. This harm includes, as per the Court, death and physical injuries, and also damage to property such as "vehicles of different category, make and model" and "many cattle heads of different kinds."[95] It is worthwhile to point out that the Court went as far as to note that the harm to cattle, beyond its economic aspects, amounts to "the worst kind of cruelty to animals."[96] However, the possible infliction of mental harm on Pakistani civilians—such as described in Living under Drones—[97] was completely omitted from the Court's assessment.

The blind-spot regarding incidental mental harm is hardly unique to military lawyers or national courts. In addition to its absence from non-governmental reports such as Living under Drones, as discussed in this chapter's introduction, a normative analysis of incidental mental harm is also absent from the findings of international fact-finding missions.

For instance, the 2009 Report of the Independent Fact-Finding Mission on the Conflict in Georgia followed the wording of API, strictly referring to incidental loss of life, injury, or damage to objects, without explaining the meaning of these terms.[98] Even the controversial Goldstone Report, which referred extensively to the psychological trauma suffered by civilians in Israel and Gaza,[99] restricted its legal analysis, if at all, to trauma emanating from attacks primarily meant to spread terror (intentional mental harm), or to mental health as a human rights concern.[100]

[92] Schmitt 2013, pp. 160–161. Note, however, that the Manual did not expressly exclude serious cases of mental harm. On deprivation of functionality see ibid., pp. 108–109.

[93] Writ Petition No. 1551-P/2012 (2013) Peshawar High Court, Judgment of 11 April 2013.

[94] Ibid. para 22.

[95] Ibid., para 3.

[96] Ibid., para 14.

[97] Living Under Drones, supra n. 1.

[98] Independent International Fact-Finding Mission on the Conflict in Georgia (2009) Report, p. 322.

[99] Goldstone Report, paras 1252–1267, 1653–1658.

[100] Ibid., paras 1300–1335, 1598, 1689.

It did not discuss the question under proportionality. Likewise, the UN Human Rights Council's 2013 Report on the Syrian conflict too alleged that parties to the conflict conduct acts aimed at spreading terror among civilians, but did not discuss the notion of "incidental terror."[101]

In sum, the analysis above paints a complex picture. On one hand, it is possible to identify a general process in which respect for the "person," beyond the purely physical realm, has become a distinct protected value under IHL. In line with this trend, intentional infliction of mental harm—as a distinct type of terror—has been explicitly outlawed. On the other hand, most sources neither expressly accept nor manifestly reject the notion of *incidental* mental harm as relevant in the context of proportionality. This could either mean that international lawyers consider it obvious that the term "injury" is limited to "pure" bodily harm or, conversely, that they take the notion of incidental mental harm for granted, and accept it without reservations. The latter possibility is rather far-fetched, since if this was the case, at least some discussion of the issue's complexities would have been expected. Another explanation, perhaps, for the silence on the issue could be that incidental mental harm remains "under the radar," due to plain lack of awareness. Be it as it may, the consequences of law's inconclusiveness are a matter of interpretation, which is always a normative exercise.[102]

7.3.3 Setting Aside Textual Misgivings

A simple textual solution to the question of incidental mental harm is unavailable, because of the indeterminacy of the language found both in treaty rules and in practice. Indeed, a conservative textual reading could lead to the conclusion that proportionality's reference to "loss of life" and "injury" should be understood in accordance with their ordinary meaning,[103] as restricted to pure physical harm. However, this is not the only possible conclusion. Indeed, the meaning of the term "injury" is not necessarily limited to bodily harm, and could be reasonably understood to encompass also *psychological* harm.[104] Furthermore, the term "casualties," as frequently used in military manuals when describing harm in the context of proportionality, is also regularly used, in other contexts, with regard to those affected by combat stress. These are commonly described as "stress casualties" or "mental health casualties".[105]

---

[101] Human Rights Council (2013) Report of the Independent International Commission of Inquiry on the Syrian Arab Republic, UN Doc A/HRC/22/59, para 127, paras 134–135.

[102] See eg Barak 2005, pp. 88–90.

[103] Vienna Convention on the Law of Treaties 1969 (hereinafter VCLT), Article 31(1).

[104] See eg Desmond 2006.

[105] See eg Peterson et al. 2008, p. 152.

It follows that the relevant language covers a wide enough semantic spectrum[106] to encompass mental harm within the damage envisioned in proportionality. Within this spectrum, the normative meaning of international law is extracted through *teleological* interpretation.[107] This is not least true in IHL, where the promotion of humanitarian principles, beyond the purely "written" text, bears key interpretational power.[108] Thus, the challenge in determining whether IHL should be interpreted to recognize the concept of "incidental mental harm" involves a value judgment: whether the object and purpose of IHL, namely, striking a balance between humanitarian considerations and military necessity, call for this conclusion. The 2013 Tallinn Manual clearly takes this interpretational approach towards the legal meaning of "injury," when in defining acts constituting *intentional* cyber-attacks against civilians, it states that

> While the notion of attack extends to injuries and death caused to individuals, it is, in light of the law of armed conflict's underlying humanitarian purposes, reasonable to extend the definition to serious illness and severe mental suffering that are *tantamount to injury* ...[109]

The next sections critically assess possible explanations for the blind-spot discussed above. As they demonstrate, none of these reflect negatively on the object or purpose of IHL so as to reject the notion of incidental mental harm altogether and to justify the anomalies and paradoxes emanating from its exclusion.

7.4 Incidental Mental Harm: A Critical Analysis of Possible Challenges

7.4.1 Challenging the Intangibility Presumption

As discussed above, IHL has gradually developed from setting out to protect the "life and limb" of civilians, to explicitly banning threats or acts of violence intentionally meant to spread "terror." The latter must be construed, of course, to include a prohibition on causing mental harm.[110] However, when addressing the question of *incidental* mental harm, the interpretation of modern IHL has remained silent. This seems, at first glance, as an inconsistency: how can a type of harm

---

[106] See Barak 2005, p. 106 (the range of semantic possibilities "includes the language's totality of meanings").

[107] VCLT, Article 31 ("[a] treaty shall be interpreted in good faith in accordance with the ordinary meaning to be given to the terms of the treaty in their context and in the light of its object and purpose.").

[108] See eg Meron 2000a.

[109] Schmitt 2013, p. 108 (emphasis added).

[110] *Galić*, para 102.

which we seek to prohibit when inflicted intentionally, be completely disregarded—not surfacing even as a remote consideration—as something we seek to *minimize* incidentally? After all, harm is harm, whether intentionally caused or not.

One possible explanation for this phenomenon could relate to the question of tangibility, in other words, whether the harm can be perceived, identified or appraised at an actual or approximate value.[111] Tangible harm, thus, must be *definable*. The challenges mental harm poses stem from the fact that its mere perception as a tangible possibility is a relatively new concept. As demonstrated below, until recent decades mental harm was not perceived as something "real."[112] Rather, it was viewed as subjective by nature: a slippery concept that could never be addressed as a concrete phenomenon.[113] How is it possible, then—if mental harm was indeed perceived, until recently, as intangible—that intentionally spreading terror was still expressly prohibited?

The answer seems to lie in the simple fact that that the notion of terror, which traditional IHL sought to prevent, did not presume the existence of "terror" as a tangible, definable harm to begin with. It alluded, rather, to a wide, ambiguous, fluid sensation of fear that civilians should be spared of, and that armed forces should not endeavor to inflict. It is for this reason, perhaps, that the prohibition on spreading terror refers to the *intention* to do so, rather than to the actual results of the act in question.[114] As ruled by the ICTY, "the actual terrorization of the civilian population" is not an element of the prohibition.[115]

The methods usually employed to determine the existence of such intent, augment the assumption of intangibility towards the concept of "terror." As evident from the practice of international tribunals, intent to spread terror is generally deduced from circumstantial evidence, namely the actual infliction of "regular" physical harm,[116] or the use of indiscriminate means or methods of attack without a discernible military advantage.[117] For instance, in the Galić case, the ICTY based its finding of intent to spread terror by first determining that the Sarajevo Romanija Corps (SRK), commanded by Galić, deliberately targeted civilians in Sarajevo by sniper-fire and shelling;[118] thereafter, the Tribunal drew the intent from the *manner* in which these methods of attacks were carried out by

---

[111] The Merriam-Webster Dictionary.

[112] In another (related) context, Luban and Shue call this bias against mental pain and suffering "the materialist bias." Luban and Shue 2012, p. 842.

[113] Ibid., p. 850.

[114] API, Article 51(2); Dinstein 2010, p. 126; see also *Galić*, para 104.

[115] Ibid.

[116] See discussion infra Sect. 7.4.2; likewise, the ICRC Study on Customary IHL, when exemplifying acts that amount to spreading terror, refers to conducts that also cause direct physical harm such as "rape" and "mass killing." Henckaerts and Doswald Beck 2005, rule 2. On the bias reflected in tying mental harm with physical harm see Luban and Shue 2012 pp. 844–845.

[117] *Galić*, para 107.

[118] Ibid.

the SRK.[119] As the ICTY held, thus, intent is inferred casuistically from the nature, manner, timing and duration of the acts or threats,[120] but "terror" itself remained an abstract concept. Indeed, the focus on intent rather than on results, in conjunction with reliance on physical harm as a prime indication for such intent, sidesteps, to a large extent, the need to elaborate on the concept of "terror" itself—which could safely remain, in turn, in the zone of intangibility.

However, this luxury is unavailable—whether to commentators, states, fact-finding missions or tribunals—when dealing with *incidental* harm in the context of the principle of proportionality. This is because proportionality is in essence a formula in which expected adverse *consequences* to civilians are measured against a concrete and military advantage. When in the business of measurements, the pull towards tangibility is understandable, since after all, it is impossible to quantify the indefinable. Accordingly, the implied exclusion of mental harm from the proportionality equation might be accredited to its perception as not being tangible enough as a measurable incidental loss.

The presumption of intangibility with regard to mental harm, as is perhaps reflected in traditional IHL, is rather unsurprising. IHL, at large, is a product of mid-late nineteenth century thinking.[121] Risking oversimplification, modern psychology roughly originates from the same period.[122] The fact that these two distinct fields have developed in parallel, could account at least as one explanation for the unclear treatment of incidental mental harm under IHL. For instance, API—the most recent substantial legal development of IHL—was adopted in 1977, whereas significant consolidation of mental harm as a tangible concept has only solidified in the decades since.[123] Importantly, the chief mental harm relevant to effects of warfare—Post Traumatic Stress Disorder (PTSD)—was only authoritatively incorporated into psychological nomenclature in 1980.[124] It is telling that an analogous process has occurred in the law of torts in some jurisdictions. For instance, while the American Second Restatement on Torts—published in 1965—failed to recognize as recoverable negligence resulting in mental harm alone,[125] the recent Third Restatement adopted a different approach.[126]

---

[119] Ibid. The Tribunal noted that the attacks were numerous, but not consistently intensive enough to suggest an attempt to destroy or "deplete" the civilian population. The random nature of the attacks, combined with the absence of a discernible military advantage, led the Tribunal to the "reasonable" conclusion that the primary purpose of the SRK's actions was to spread terror.

[120] Ibid., para 104.

[121] See Kolb 2012, pp. 25–40.

[122] See eg Wertheimer 2012, p. 19.

[123] This process might parallel, for instance, traditional IHL's minimal attention to sexual violence, as noted in feminist critiques. See Cahn 2005, p. 238; such violence was sometimes treated as a violation of "family honor." See Askin 2003, pp. 294–296.

[124] Keane et al. 2009, p. 2.

[125] Restatement (Second) §436A.

[126] See infra, Sect. 7.4.4.

Of course, beyond the latter development of positive tort law—and perhaps reflecting its logic—the presumption of intangibility of mental harm can be substantively challenged by deconstructing the different categories of harm. For instance, it could be argued that some cases of mental harm are actually more tangible than some types of conditions which are usually thought of as reflecting physical harm, such as chronic pain.[127] Similarly, recall the argument that the separation between physical and mental is in any case an artificial construction.[128]

Other critical responses to the tangibility challenge can emanate from within the principle of proportionality itself. For example, any claim that this or that type of harm is intangible, and therefore cannot be included in the proportionality calculus, must account for the fact that the other side of the equation—that of the concrete and direct military advantage—too suffers from vagueness and intangibility.[129]

Granted, a possible answer to this critique would be that precisely for this reason, the notion of legitimate military advantage is narrowly concretized as "ground gained" or weakening of the enemy's armed forces.[130] However, closer analysis reveals the term in its immense complexity. For instance, is the expected military advantage, in light of which collateral damage is assessed, measured in relation to a single attack, or to the operation as a whole? Can it be extended to encompass the goals of the entire campaign?[131] Can the protection of one's own forces be considered as a military advantage?[132] What role, if at all, do considerations of deterrence play in assessing such an advantage? How does a military advantage measure when confronting non-state actors in asymmetric conflicts? Indeed, if the military advantage part of the equation is open-textured, the same must be acceptable also for the equation's other part, that of civilian harm.

Proportionality's inherent intangibility does not end here. Significantly, the proportionality analysis requires those planning or authorizing an attack to measure a military advantage—intangible as that concept may be—versus civilians' *lives*. Doing so, proportionality assumes, in practice, that *life itself* is quantifiable. Needless to say, such presumption is itself morally controversial and is arguably at odds with Kantian perceptions of human dignity.[133] If proportionality can be

---

[127] Chronic pain is an especially vexing phenomenon, since it is not a "reliable indicator of tissue damage." See Lumley et al. 2011 p. 943.

[128] See supra, text accompanying notes 17–19.

[129] See eg Blum 2013, pp. 419–420.

[130] Sandoz et al. 1987, p. 685.

[131] Henckaerts and Doswald-Beck 2005, Practice, Ch. 4, paras 16 –162, 184; see also Hays-Parks 1990, p. 172.

[132] See eg Geiss 2012; Ziegler and Otzari 2012.

[133] Compare eg Lepsius 2006, pp. 766–772 (discussing the annulment, by the Federal Constitutional Court of Germany, of a law which allowed the German executive to shoot down a hijacked jet in order to save lives in light of violations of the right to life and human dignity); See BVerfg, 1 BvR 357/05 [2006].

reconciled with something as intangible as quantification of lives, any intangibility claims against the inclusion of this or that harm within the proportionality analysis, lose their vigor across the board.

However, it is also possible to challenge the intangibility presumption of mental harm in itself. For this purpose it suffices to point out—by no means exhaustingly—that nowadays, we possess a clear conceptual framework within which to discuss such harm. The developing understanding of PTSD has been paramount in this context[134] — as expressed, for instance, in the diagnostic criteria established by the American Psychiatric Association (APA).[135]

The first criterion relates to exposure to a traumatic event involving actual or threatened death, serious injury, or sexual violence, namely by directly experiencing the event or witnessing it in person as it occurred to others.[136] Military attacks—even if directed against legitimate targets—can clearly amount to such traumatic events.[137] Further criteria require that the traumatic event causes "intrusion" symptoms, such as recurrent and intrusive recollections of the event;[138] "avoidance" symptoms, meaning, for instance, avoiding certain situations which remind of the traumatic event;[139] negative alterations in cognition and moods, such as inability ro remember important aspects of the traumatic event or persistent negative emotions such as horror and anger;[140] and alterations in arousal, such as irritable behavior or exaggerated startle response.[141] Finally, PTSD requires that the symptoms occur for more than one month and that the disturbance causes significant difficulties in the individual's life.[142]

PTSD is by no means an esoteric syndrome; on the contrary, it is viewed nowadays as a "major public health challenge" for the world, being a common reaction to traumatic events.[143] It is not a random, theoretical grouping of symptoms. Rather, it represents a real-world, "touchable" phenomenon, which is also addressed by international organizations such as the UN, when planning

---

[134] As noted later on, while the role of PTSD in the determination of mental harm would not appear novel to tort lawyers, it has not yet trickled to the IHL discourse. See Restatement (Third) Ch. 8 §47 Reporters' Note on Comment b. ("Greater rigor in diagnosing emotional harm can be traced to 1980 when the Diagnostic and Statistical Manual of Mental Disorders (DSM-II) recognized post-traumatic stress disorder ("PTSD") and provided diagnostic criteria for it.").

[135] American Psychiatric Association 2013, pp. 271–280 (hereinafter DSM-5).

[136] Ibid. p. 271.

[137] Ibid. p. 274.

[138] Ibid. p. 271.

[139] Ibid.

[140] Ibid. pp. 271–272.

[141] Ibid. p. 272.

[142] Ibid, Note that PTSD also requires that the condition is not attributable to physiological effects of a substance (such as medication) or another medical condition. See ibid. Moreover, DSM-5 introduced specific criteria for PTSD among children 6 years old and younger. Ibid. 272–274.

[143] Keane et al. 2009. p. 3; see also DSM-5, p. 276.

responses to conflict and natural disasters.[144] Accordingly, as the main form of mental harm relevant to armed conflict,[145] PTSD cannot be looked upon as an abstract intangible. As such, it cannot be rejected offhand as irrelevant even when caused incidentally.

It follows from all of the above that arguments from intangibility are not entirely convincing. This is chiefly because they overlook the fact that proportionality involves inherent intangibilities to begin with, and that the notion of mental harm has indeed been concretized in recent decades.

7.4.2 Tangibility of Mental Harm Under International Criminal Law

One can argue, in response, that although mental harm might not be intangible in absolute terms—for instance, for the purpose of psychological diagnostics—it might still not be tangible enough for legal application, which requires clarity of a higher order.[146] However, beyond the fact that, as aforementioned, the common law of torts challenges this proposition, international law, too, views mental harm as tangible enough in other contexts. Significantly, this is not only true with regard to state responsibility,[147] but also in the field of international *criminal* law, in which determinacy is of paramount importance.[148] If mental harm is concrete enough to result in criminalization—and, in turn, in the deprivation of liberty—*a fortiori* that it is solid enough to matter in the proportionality equation. Although the treatment of such harm by international criminal tribunals leaves much ambiguity,[149] it still clearly demonstrates that intentional infliction of serious mental harm, such as PTSD, is tangible enough to trigger criminal liability.

The issue of mental harm is addressed, in international criminal law, chiefly in the context of genocide, torture and crimes against humanity.[150] The crime of genocide explicitly includes causing, besides bodily harm, serious *mental* harm to

---

144 See Lykes and Mersky 2006, p. 594.

145 For instance, in 1989 the US Department of Veterans Affairs established the National Center for PTSD, http://www.ptsd.va.gov/about/mission/history_of_the_national_center_for_ptsd.asp.

146 See eg Fuller 1969, pp. 63–65.

147 See eg IACtHR, *Velásquez Rodríguez v. Honduras*, Compensatory Damages [1989] (Ser. C) No. 7 (1990), paras 50–51.

148 See eg Heller 2011, pp. 326–327, p. 377 2002, p.56.

149 See infra.

150 Wes shall discuss here only the former two, since there is significant overlap with the latter. It is also worthwhile to mention that when violations of Article 3 Common to the Geneva Conventions were placed within the jurisdiction of the ICTR, the wording of that article was extended to include "violence to life, health and physical or *mental* well-being" of persons rather than just "violence to life and person" as is in the original phrasing. Statute of the International Criminal Tribunal for Rwanda 1994 (hereinafter ICTR Statute), Article 4(a).

members of a national, ethnical, racial or religious group, with intent to destroy it in whole or in part.[151] While the notion of "mental harm" is defined neither in the Genocide Convention nor in relevant statutes of international tribunals,[152] plain reading of the text suggests that such harm can be independent from any accompanying "bodily" harm.[153] Granted, the reference to mental harm in the Convention—a product of the 1940s—originally envisioned a narrow understanding of such harm, alluding to the injection of pharmacological substances that seriously impair mental faculties,[154] or to the use of narcotics.[155] However, international jurisprudence subscribed to a wider, case-by-case approach to the question, emphasizing that mental harm generally refers to lasting, albeit not necessarily permanent, impairment of mental faculties.[156]

International tribunals—namely, the ICTY and the ICTR—scantly elaborated more than that on the notion of mental harm. A plausible explanation for this tendency is that in practice, tribunals virtually always deal with cases that involve bodily harm, and therefore do not find it necessary to address mental harm independently. Not unlike the notion of "terror" under IHL, mental harm has been treated, if at all, as an extension of physical harm, which relieved tribunals of the need to discuss it extensively.[157] Moreover, rather than elaborating on the essence of mental harm, tribunals generally prefer to enumerate acts that might *cause* such harm, which are, unsurprisingly, acts that can also cause physical harm.[158]

Beyond these intricacies, the ICTR's and the ICTY's treatment of the concept of mental harm sets forth a standard of severity: such harm must be "more than minor or temporary impairment of mental faculties such as the infliction of strong

---

[151] Convention on the Prevention and Punishment of the Crime of Genocide Convention 1948 (hereinafter Genocide Convention), Article II(b); Statute of the International Criminal Tribunal for the Former Yugoslavia (1993) (hereinafter ICTY Statute), Article 4(2)(b); ICTR Statute, Article 2(2)(b); Rome Statute of the International Criminal Court (1998) (herinafter ICC Statute), Article 6(b).

[152] Nor is it elaborated upon in the ICC's Elements of Crimes. International Criminal Court, Elements of Crimes 2000, p. 6.

[153] Jessberger 2009, p. 98.

[154] See ICTY *Prosecutor v. Krstic* [2001] IT-98-33 (hereinafter *Krstic*), para 510.

[155] Gorove 1951, pp. 176–178 (discussing Chinese allegations, during the drafting of the Convention, that Japan committed genocide in China by spreading opium). It should be noted that some states saw the inclusion of mental harm as redundant since physical integrity included also mental integrity, which of course supports the argument of this chapter. Ibid., p. 180.

[156] *Krstic*, paras 510–513; ICTR *Prosecutor v. Kajelijeli* [2003] Case No. ICTR-98-44A-T, para 815; ICTR, *Prosecutor v. Kayishema* [1999] Case No. ICTR-95-1-T, para 113.

[157] Compare Jessberger 2009, p. 99.

[158] See eg *Prosecutor v. Akayesu* [1998] Case No. ICTR-96-4-T, paras 503–504; ICTR, *Prosecutor v. Musema* [2000] Case No. ICTR-96-13-A para 156; ICTR, *Prosecutor v. Rutaganda* [1999] Case No. ICTR-96-3-T, para 50.

fear or terror, intimidation or threat."[159] A vague "state of anxiety"—as phrased by the ICTR—would be insufficient to establish serious mental harm.[160] As per the ICTY, any serious mental harm has to go beyond "temporary unhappiness, embarrassment or humiliation," it must cause "grave and long-term disadvantage to a person's ability to lead a normal and constructive life."[161] The extent to which these definitions resemble the APA's criteria for PTSD is striking.

Similarly, the Convention against Torture (CAT) defines torture as including "severe pain or suffering, whether *mental* or physical."[162] As such, mental torture is criminalized both as an international crime giving rise to mandatory universal jurisdiction,[163] and as a crime under the jurisdiction international tribunals.[164] Without elaborating on the modalities of mental torture, it seems obvious that the latter captures a wider set of conducts than the crime of genocide, since it refers to the mental pain or suffering in itself—without requiring additional, prolonged *harm*.[165] This wide criminalization of mental torture augments the conclusion that international law does not, in principle, shy away from assigning responsibility with regard to mental harm, even in the more conservative context of criminal liability. It is thus clear that mental harm is in principle tangible enough for legal consideration, in all of its manifestations.

7.4.3 Ex-Post Identification and Attribution

Another possible challenge to the concept of incidental mental harm concerns the problem of identification, which complicates assessing the outcomes of an attack *ex post*. While a simple visual examination, in most cases, is sufficient to validate

159 ICTR, *Prosecutor v. Seromba* (Appeals Chamber Judgement) [2008] Case No. ICTR-2001-66-A (hereinafter *Seromba*), paras 45–47 (overruling the Trial Chamber's conclusion that Seromba caused serious mental harm to Tutsi refugees in a church by prohibiting them from accessing a banana plantation, refusing to celebrate mass for them, and expelling them from a parish); see also ICTR, *Prosecutor v. Ntawukulilyayo* [2010] Case No. ICTR-o5-82-T, para 452. This understanding of mental harm corresponds with the view of the Preparatory Committee of the International Criminal Court; Report of the Preparatory Committee on the Establishment of an International Criminal Court 1998, Part 2: Jurisdiction, Admissibility and Applicable Law, UN Doc A/CONF. 183/2/Add.1, p. 11; see also ICTY, *Prosecutor v. Blagojevic* [2005] IT-02060-T, para 645.

160 *Seromba*, paras 47–48.

161 ICTY, *Prosecutor v. Tolimir* [2012] IT-05-88/2-T, para 738.

162 Convention Against Torture and Other Cruel, Inhuman or Degrading Treatment or Punishment 1985 (hereinafter UNCAT) Article 1.

163 Ibid., Articles 5–7; for a recent application see ICJ, Questions Relating to the Obligation to Prosecute or Extradite (Belgium vs. Senegal) ICJ (Judgment of Jul. 20, 2012).

164 See eg ICC Statute, Article 7(2)(e).

165 See Luban and Shue 2012, pp. 840–841 (challenging the Bush Administration's perception that conduct must result in long term psychological harm in order to count as mental torture).

whether incidental physical harm has occurred, prognosis of mental harm—as well as its attribution to a certain event—are time consuming and require significant expertise. Moreover, while physical harm, in the vast majority of cases, occurs immediately after an attack, lasting mental harm—such as PTSD—can only be measured after several weeks.[166] This makes difficult the identification and attribution of mental harm, in particular when an individual has been exposed to several attacks over time.[167]

Indeed, the proportionality principle on the level of *state-responsibility* does not require such an *ex post* assessment.[168] However, since in reality international reaction to events is consequence-based, difficulties in fact-assessment can be abused and manipulated, in the public sphere, by interested parties. Arguably, this potential for abuse merits a careful approach towards the inclusion, within the proportionality analysis, of any type of harm that is difficult to identify and attribute *ex post*.

Nonetheless, it is doubtful whether this difficulty, stemming from the unsatisfactory state of IHL's secondary norms,[169] justifies in itself dropping the idea of mental harm altogether. Indeed, such difficulties are not foreign to other fields of international law[170] and should not *per se* impede the development of necessary primary norms. Instead, a more constructive approach would be to look for ways to enhance the efficiency and credibility of international fact-finding, and other methods of enforcement.

In this context, it should be borne in mind that "conventional" physical harm is also subject to ambiguities and potential abuse, perhaps no less that mental harm. The mere determination of which individuals and objects constitute legitimate targets is increasingly difficult in contemporary armed conflict, yet no one has seriously suggested abandoning the principle of distinction because of this. Moreover, experience shows that in any case, the mere occurrence of incidental or even intentional *physical* harm can be hotly contested. For instance, it suffices to

---

[166] See supra Sect. 7.4.1.

[167] This is not to imply that mental harm is never attributable to a certain event. Indeed, while the origins of many specific phobias are difficult to identify, PTSD, for instance, generally emerges from "one special chain of events," and thus can be attributed to a certain occurrence. Keane et al. 2009, p. 6.

[168] As opposed to state-responsibility, the problem of *ex post* assessment could be acute with regard to *individual* responsibility. For instance, the crime of disproportionate attack, as part of API's supplement to the Grave Breaches regime, requires actual "death or serious injury to body or health" for the crime to materialize. See API, Article 85(3)(b). Note that such a requirement seems to be absent from the parallel provision in the Rome Statute. See ICC Statute, Article 8(2)(b)(iv)—be it as it may, it is highly unlikely that a person be indicted for such an act if harm was not in fact caused, for obvious reasons.

[169] Secondary norms are norms that are meant to ensure the operation of the primary norms regulating the behavior of the legal subject. Norms regulating the determination of violations, for instance, are such. See in general and in the context of international law specifically Hart 2012, pp. 79–91, 214.

[170] For a general discussion see Koh 1997.

look at the differing numbers of casualties reported by Israel, the Palestinians and international bodies following the late 2008–early 2009 Operation Cast Lead in Gaza,[171] as well as after Operation Pillar of Defense of 2012.[172]

Furthermore, it is telling that violations of the principle of proportionality that amount to war crimes—as circumscribed in the ICC Statute—include excessive "widespread, long-term and severe damage to the natural environment."[173] Of course, such harm could pose identification and attribution problems, significant no less—if not more—than those relating to incidental mental harm. Indeed, the ICC Statute mitigates this problem by requiring that the harm be "clearly excessive" in relation to the overall military advantage.[174] Nevertheless the principle remains. It follows from all of the above that the identification and attribution problems of incidental mental harm and their potential abuse and manipulation, are not sufficient *per se* to negate the plausibility of the concept.

However, as implied above,[175] the key argument to counter these problems, in the legal realm, has more to do with the temporal nature of the proportionality obligation itself, which is closer to a discretion-guiding administrative standard than to a corrective-minded rule of private or criminal law. Thus, while the problems of identification and attribution certainly challenge the ability to assign responsibility *ex post*, this is less of an issue in the normative sphere of proportionality. This is because the proportionality analysis aims to set a *forward* looking standard, according to which the discretion of the reasonable commander is assessed in light of the information available prior to the attack.[176] She is required to take all feasible precautions "with a view" to avoid or minimize collateral damage,[177] and to refrain, cancel or suspend any attack which may be *expected* to cause excessive harm.[178] Hypothetically, then—and although such situations

---

[171] According to the Israeli Defense Forces, there were 1,166 fatalities in Gaza, among them 295 civilians. *See* IDF IDF (2009) Operation Cast Lead: Humanitarian Aspects. www.mfa.gov.il/MFA_Graphics/MFA%20Gallery/Documents/CastLeadHumanitarianReport.pdf., p.3 (Accessed 6 June 2013). Hamas authorities in Gaza reported 1,444 fatalities, while NGOs reported 1,387 fatalities. See Goldstone Report, para 30.

[172] Israel claimed that 68 civilians were killed in Gaza, while Palestinian sources claimed 105 fatalities. See respectively Intelligence and Terrorism Information Center (2012) Findings of Analysis of Names of Terrorists Killed in Operation "Pillar of Defense" and the Relations between them and Uninvolved Civilian Deaths. www.terrorism-info.org.il/he/article/20444. (Accessed 6 June 2013); PCHR (2012) The Total Numbers of Victims of the Israeli Offensive on the Gaza Strip. www.pchrgaza.org/portal/en/index.php?option=com_content&view=article&id=9052:1&catid=145:in-focus. Accessed 6 June 2013.

[173] ICC Statute, Article 8(2)(b)(iv).

[174] Ibid.

[175] See supra, text accompanying note 171.

[176] McCormack T and Mtharu P (2006), Expected Civilian Damage and the Proportionality Equation. www.apcml.org/documents/un_report_exp_civilian_damage_1106.pdf. (Accessed 2 June 2013).

[177] API, Article 57(2)(a)(ii).

[178] Ibid., Articles 57(2)(a)(iii), 57(2)(b).

might only be of academic interest—an attack in violation of these duties would be unlawful even if by some miraculous twist of events, it does not cause incidental harm at all. In other words, actual harm is not a constitutive element of the internationally wrongful act of launching a disproportionate attack.[179] The forward-looking nature of proportionality means that its application, in itself, is by no means contingent upon—albeit it can greatly benefit from—the ability to identify and attribute specific harm to a specific attack *ex post*. It suffices that the harm is foreseeable according to the standard of the reasonable commander, in light of the information available to her at the time.[180]

It follows that difficulties in assessing incidental or intentional harm during armed conflicts are ever-present, be it mental or physical harm. These challenges should be addressed by improving monitoring mechanisms, rather than by eliminating types of harms from consideration.

7.4.4 Foreseeability

A problem related to but at the same time differing from the issue of mental harm's tangibility and identification, concerns the question of its foreseeability. This question can arise in two distinct contexts. The first concerns the practicality of the concept during hostilities. As the argument goes, the proportionality standard is infamously vague enough to begin with, imposing a significant burden on commanders as it is.[181] It could be claimed, therefore, that due to the complexity of its prediction, the inclusion of incidental mental harm within the proportionality equation would require every commander to become a psychiatrist, or at least to consult with one before each attack. This claim relates to our policy discussion earlier on: if IHL will over-complicate warfare, it would eventually implode due to pressure from chronic non-compliance.

However, concerns of such type reflect a common misunderstanding of proportionality under IHL. It is imperative to emphasize that proportionality is intrinsically woven with the notion of "feasibility:" it certainly does not require commanders to take every technically possible precaution—both in the planning

---

[179] In international law, state responsibility does not necessarily require actual harm, unless the primary rule provides so. See International Law Commission 2001, p. 3. In this, the proportionality principle differs from the common law tort of negligence, which requires actual materialization of harm. This difference seems rooted in IHL's nature as public, rather than private law.

[180] See eg Final Report to the Prosecutor by the Committee Established to Review the NATO Bombing Campaign Against the Federal Republic of Yugoslavia (2000), para 50; McCormack and Mtharu 2006, p. 4.

[181] Sandoz et al. 1987, p. 679 "[t]he differences of opinion [regarding the proportionality standard] were mainly related to the very heavy burden of responsibility imposed by this article on military commanders, particularly as the various provisions are relatively imprecise and are open to a fairly broad margin of judgment).

and execution stage—in order to minimize incidental harm. It only requires what is *feasible*.[182] Feasibility is manifested in the standard of the "reasonable" commander, which guides the assessment of proportionality.[183] Feasibility, thus, is context-sensitive.[184] In the view of some, it is even affected by militaries' relative capabilities.[185] Accordingly, precautions that could be feasible for a division commander, with access to an entire range of intelligence capabilities, might not be practicable on the platoon level. Likewise, what might be feasible during early planning becomes impossible under fire. Thus, while it can be expected of high-level commanders to conduct complex collateral damage estimations, including by using sophisticated software to predict such damage,[186] field commanders during active combat might be granted more leeway.[187]

A second challenge is substantive—doubting the foreseeability of mental harm to begin with. For instance, while physical harm is more or less universal in its occurrence, those holding this view would claim that mental harm is sensitive to individuals' characteristics, as well as to cultural, social and political circumstances of a specific conflict.[188]

If mental harm is indeed unforeseeable, it makes no sense to require commanders to take it into consideration when planning or authorizing an attack. However, a simple analogy to common-law torts reveals that mental harm and foreseeability are not mutually exclusive in modern legal systems.[189] This analogy should not be overstated. I do not suggest that IHL should be analyzed according to the principles of tort law, but merely seek to demonstrate that mental harm has been treated as relevant in contexts not far removed, in their essence, from the

182 API, Article 57(2)(a)(ii).

183 And not according to the outcome in practice. See Dinstein (2010) pp. 132–133.

184 See eg Schmitt 2005, p. 460.

185 Blum 2011.

186 See Mcneal 2013, p. 54, pp. 64–78 (detailing the CDM process employed by US forces).

187 See ibid., at p. 66.

188 See eg Perilla et al. 2002. Nonetheless, this difference between the types of harm should not be taken at face value. First, physical effects also vary in different environments. See US Chairman of the Joint Chiefs of Staff 2009, p. D-5. Second, some persons are more sensitive than others also with regard to *physical* harm. Be it as it may, it is helpful to mention the famous "thin skull" rule in torts which recognizes that differential sensitivity in itself does not preclude liability. Moreover, the Restatement (Third) of Torts acknowledges that the thin skull rule applies also to *emotional* harm of an unforeseeable magnitude. It suffices that the *type* of harm that occurs is unexceptional. Restatement (Third), Ch. 6. §31.

189 On the contrary: some view foreseeability of mental harm as rather obvious, in the sense that it results in too-wide liability. *Thing v. La Chusa*, 771 P..2d 814, 826–827 (Cal. 1989). This seems to be the view of the Third Restatement of Torts. See Restatement (Third) Ch. 8§47, Reporters' Notes Comment (i); see also The Law Commission 1997, paras 2.4–2.9. It should be added that resort to international authorities in this context is less helpful, since these are more concerned with remedies in relation to intentional harm such as torture and forced disappearances, and less with the issue of negligence. For a survey see Evans 2012, pp. 44–85.

proportionality analysis. For our illustrative purposes, it suffices to draw, in a preliminary manner, from the Restatement (Third) of Torts.[190]

With some simplification, it could be said that the proportionality principle roughly resembles, in some aspects, the common law tort of negligence. Like negligence, it is based on a standard of reasonableness; like negligence, it requires objective foreseeability at the time of conduct (which might be translated to an obligation to gather more information); like negligence, proportionality's reasonableness is built upon some form of cost-benefit analysis.[191] A disproportional attack can be labeled as "negligent," for our purposes, when the incidental harm it is expected to cause is excessive in relation to the military advantage sought.

US negligence law, thus, traditionally differentiated between "emotional" harm accompanying physical harm—which was usually recoverable—and "stand alone" emotional harm, regarding which courts were generally restrictive.[192] The analogue of the former, in the context of proportionality, can be found in instances where an attack is expected to cause incidental mental harm in addition to physical injury—not an uncommon occurrence by far. In this context, just as in torts, it seems that there are no convincing grounds to disregard, when planning or authorizing an attack, the mental harm caused to those expected to incur incidental physical harm. This harm can be accounted for prior to the attack by relying, for instance, on prediction models concerning the risk of PTSD among injured persons.[193]

The reasons for the historically cautious approach towards "stand alone" emotional harm correspond to some of the concerns already discussed in this chapter, such as problems relating to tangibility, excessive liability and potential abuse.[194] In recent years, however, the approach towards negligently inflicted emotional harm, even when standing alone, has been relaxed.[195] This could be explained, to some extent, by the increasing understanding and concretization of serious mental harm such as PTSD.[196] Accordingly, the Restatement has recently acknowledged that serious "stand alone" emotional harm would be recoverable in two cases.[197] The first relates to scenarios where the conduct places a person in danger of immediate bodily harm. In other words, the person is in a "zone of

[190] Comparable conclusions could also be drawn from the development of UK law in this context. See generally The Law Commission 1997.

[191] Restatement (Third) Ch. 1§3. A key difference is that the benefit in *in bello* proportionality is measured according to an attacker's military advantage, while in torts the benefit considered is societal.

[192] Ibid., Ch. 2§4 Comments c–d.

[193] See eg Zatzick et al. 2002.

[194] Restatement (Third) Ch. 8 Scope Note.

[195] Ibid.

[196] See Grey 2011. It should be noted that other jurisdictions, such as the UK, do not use the term "serious emotional harm" but specifically demand a "recognizable psychiatric illness." See The Law Commission 1997 para 2.3. For a critique see Mulheron 2012.

[197] Restatement (Third) Ch. 8§47.

danger"[198] and that specific danger causes the emotional harm. The second case arises when the negligent conduct occurs in circumstances where it is "especially likely to cause serious emotional harm" *even* if no risk of bodily harm exists.[199]

Importing this logic to IHL proportionality is rather straightforward. The first situation relates to instances where the risk of mental harm is built upon the danger of actual *physical* injury caused by the attack. This would require accounting for possible mental harm among those in the zone of bodily danger expected from the attack, even if actual physical harm is not certain. As modern collateral damage estimation methodologies are able to demarcate the zone of physical danger, PTSD prediction models can be implemented on top of this delineation.

The second situation relates to incidents where actual physical danger is absent, but the activities undertaken are of the type in which serious mental harm is especially likely. Engaging in hostilities during armed conflict is a clear cut example of such an activity. Indeed, PTSD has been documented as a major mental harm among civilians generally exposed to war in various contexts. Without elaborating on the nuances of these studies, research suggests that such is the case, for instance, in Kosovo,[200] Kashmir,[201] Israel[202] and in the Palestinian territories.[203] In the context of proportionality, this means that consideration would have to be given also to risk of serious mental harm, such as PTSD, *beyond* the immediate zone of physical danger.

As is evident from the latter suggestion, accounting for mental harm within the proportionality analysis is not an easy task, leaving many questions open for future debates. It is beyond the scope of this chapter to elaborate on the technicalities of such questions. It suffices to suggest that sophisticated militaries could embed available PTSD prediction models, which account statistically for suspected risk factors,[204] in the collateral damage assessment algorithms which they apply during the planning stage, to the extent these are feasible in the situation at hand.[205]

---

198 ibid., comment e.

199 Restatement (Third) Ch. 8§47.

200 Eytan et al. 2011, p. 954.

201 Yaswi and Haque 2008, pp. 479–480.

202 Although some speculate that ongoing violence has immunized Israelis, to some extent, from PTSD, at least in the long-run. See Neria et al. 2010, pp. 329–330 (noting the possible implications of ongoing trauma exposure as a mitigating or aggravating factor in the development of PTSD).

203 See Thabet et al. 2008, pp. 196–197.

204 It is of course beyond this chapter to assess such models, but these are abound. For a survey of epidemiology of PTSD see Vasterling and Brewin 2005, pp. 7–11. See also Z Steel et al. 2009; Charlson et al. 2012.

205 Such algorithms, currently used to predict physical harm, "are based on empirical data gathered in field tests, probability, historical observations from weapons employed on the battlefield, and physics-based computerized models for collateral damage estimates." See Mcneal 2013. p. 65. It is not implausible, therefore, that PTSD prediction models, based on complex variables—some sensitive even to wider political contexts—could be applied within these algorithms.

7.5 Conclusion

The fact that incidental mental harm has largely been neglected in international discourse can be explained, perhaps, mainly due to lack of awareness or lack of interest. After all, mental harm does not result in immediate clips of carnage uploaded to YouTube—and is thus much easier to underestimate or to disregard altogether. In the legal realm, the question whether this blind-spot amounts to a total rejection of the concept is a matter of interpretation, in itself a normative exercise. As this chapter argued, the possible challenges to the inclusion of incidental mental harm within the proportionality analysis are not convincing enough to support such a rejection. In particular, they lose much ground when juxtaposed with one of IHL's key objectives, that of minimizing civilian harm.

Indeed, mental harm should be taken seriously, even when occurring incidentally, if IHL is to maintain its integrity as a coherent legal body. As this chapter has demonstrated, many of the possible gut-reactions against such a notion do not withstand deeper scrutiny. The concept is not utopian, nor will it skew the balance in favor of non-state actors, since it highlights also the mental harm caused by terrorist tactics. Furthermore, arguments regarding mental harm's tangibility, identification, attribution and feasibility are not strong enough to negate its plausibility as a legal construct.

This is not to suggest that the concept of incidental mental harm, even if normatively sound, is easy to apply. As noted repeatedly in this chapter, many questions are left open for further discussion. Perhaps, as a first stage, conflicting parties should start by enhancing their awareness to the incidental mental effects of their actions, and seek to reduce them. Over time, methodology to account for such harm can be developed within collateral damage assessments. In recent decades, immense technological advancements have been made in all aspects of warfare. Mechanisms for collateral damage control that were once unimaginable are nowadays applied routinely. Accounting for mental harm, therefore, cannot be dismissed only because it has not yet been done, or simply because it raises difficult questions.

References

Addison CG et al (1870) Wrongs and their remedies: being a treatise on the law of torts, 3rd edn. Banks and Brothers, New York

Ambos K (2011) Judicial creativity at the Special Tribunal for Lebanon: is there a crime of terrorism under international law? Leiden J Int Law 24:655

American Law Institute (1965) Restatement second, torts. American Law Institute, Philadelphia

American Law Institute (2012) Restatement third, torts: liability for physical and emotional harm. American Law Institute, MN

American Psychiatric Association (2013) Diagnostic and statistical manual of mental disorders, 5th edn. (DSM-5). American Psychiatric Publishing, Arlington

Arnold R, Quénivet N (eds) (2008) International humanitarian law and human rights law: towards a new merger in international law. Brill, Leiden
Askin KD (2003) Prosecuting wartime rape and other gender-related crimes under international law: extraordinary advances, enduring obstacles. Berkeley J Int Law 2:288
Banks WC (2011) Toward an adaptive international humanitarian law: new norms for new battlefields. In: Banks WC (ed) New battlefields/old laws: critical debates on asymmetric warfare. Columbia University Press, New York, pp 1–22
Barak A (2005) Purposive interpretation in law. Princeton University Press, Princeton
Blum G (2011) On a differential law of war. Harv J Int Law 52:164
Blum G (2013) The fog of victory. EJIL 24:391
Brain C (2002) Advanced psychology: applications, issues and perspectives. Nelson Thornes, Bolton
Cahn N (2005) Beyond retribution and impunity: responding to war crimes of sexual violence. Stanf J Civil Rights Civil Lib 1:217
Charlson FJ et al (2012) Prediction the impact of the 2011 conflict in Libya on population mental health: PTSD and depression prevalence and mental health service requirements. PLoS ONE 7:1–11
Desmond JM (2006) Mental and physical examinations in cases involving brain injuries and psychological injuries. Mass Law Rev 90:2
Dinstein Y (2004) The conduct of hostilities under the international law of armed conflict, 1st edn. Cambridge University Press, Cambridge
Dinstein Y (2010) The conduct of hostilities under the law of international armed conflict, 2nd edn. Cambridge University Press, Cambridge
Dworkin RM (1986) Law's empire. Harvard University Press, Cambridge
Evans C (2012) The right to reparation in international law for victims of armed conflict. Cambridge University Press, Cambridge
Eytan A et al (2011) Mental and physical health of kosovar albanians in their place of origin: a post-war 6-year follow-up study. Soc Psychiatry Psychiatr Epidemiol 46:953
Ferraro T, ICRC (2012) Expert meeting: occupation and other forms of administration of foreign territory. ICRC, Geneva
Fuller LL (1969) The morality of law. Yale University Press, New Haven
Geiss R (2012) The principle of proportionality: "force protection" as a military advantage. Isr Law Rev 45:71
Gelkopf M et al (2008) The mental health impact of terrorism in Israel: a repeat cross-sectional study of Arabs and Jews. Acta Psychiatr Scand 117:369
Gorove S (1951) The problem of "mental harm" in the Genocide Convention. Wash Univ Law Q 1951:174
Grey BJ (2011) Neuroscience and emotional harm in tort law: rethinking the American approach to free-standing emotional distress claims. Curr Leg Issues 13:203
Hart HLA (2012) The concept of law, 3rd edn. Oxford University Press, Oxford
Hakimi M (2012) A functional approach to targeting and detention. Mich Law Rev 110:1365
Hays-Parks W (1990) Air war and the law of war. Air Force Law Rev 32:1
Heller KJ (2011) The Nuremberg military tribunals and the origins of international criminal law. Oxford University Press, Oxford
Henckaerts JM and Doswald-Beck L, ICRC (2005) Customary international humanitarian law. Cambridge University Press, Cambridge
Independent International Fact-Finding Mission on the Conflict in Georgia (2009) Report
International Human Rights and Conflict Resolution Clinic, Stanford Law School and Global Justice Clinic, New York University School of Law (2012) Living Under Drones: Death, Injury and Trauma to Civilians From US Drone Practices in Pakistan
International Law Commission (2001) Draft Responsibility of States for Internationally Wrongful Acts, with Commentaries
Jessberger F (2009) The definition and the elements of the crime of genocide. In: Gaeta P (ed) The UN Genocide Convention: a commentary. Oxford University Press, Oxford, pp 87–111

Keane TM et al (2009) Post-traumatic stress disorder: definition, prevalence, and risk factors. In: Shiromany PJ et al (eds) Post-traumatic stress disorder: basic science and clinical practice. Humana Press, New York, pp 1–22
Koh HH (1997) Why do nations obey international law? Yale Law J 106:2599
Kolb R (2012) The main epochs of modern international law since 1864 and their related dominant legal constructions. In: Muzenović Larsen et al (eds) Searching for a "principle of humanity" in international humanitarian law. Cambridge University Press, Cambridge, pp 23–71
Lamp N (2011) Conceptions of war and paradigms of compliance: the "new war" challenge to international humanitarian law. J Confl Secur Law 1:225
Law Commission (1997) Liability for psychiatric illness
Lepsius O (2006) Human dignity and the downing of aircraft: the German federal constitutional court strikes down a prominent anti-terrorism provision in the new air-transport security act. Ger Law J 7:761
Luban D (2011) Risk taking and force protection. Georgetown Public Law Research Paper No. 11-72
Luban D, Shue H (2012) Mental torture: a critique of erasures in US law. Georget Law J 100:823
Lubell N (2012) Human rights obligations in military occupation. Int Rev Red Cross 94:317
Lumley MA et al (2011) Pain and emotion: a biopsychosocial review of recent research. J Clin Psychol 67:942
Lykes MB, Mersky M (2006) Reparations and mental health: psychological interventions towards healing, human agency and rethreading social realities. In: De Greiff (ed) The handbook of reparations. Oxford University Press, Oxford, pp 589–622
McCormack T and Mtharu P (2006) Expected civilian damage and the proportionality equation. www.apcml.org/documents/un_report_exp_civilian_damage_1106.pdf. Accessed 2 June 2013
Mcneal GS (2013) Kill-lists and accountability. Georget Law J (forthcoming), Available at SSRN: papers.ssrn.com/sol3/papers.cfm?abstract_id=1819583
Melzer N, ICRC (2009) Interpretive guidance on the notion of direct participation in hostilities under international humanitarian law. ICRC, Geneva
Meron T (2000a) The Martens Clause, principles of humanity, and dictates of public conscience. Am J Int Law 94:78
Meron T (2000b) The humanization of humanitarian law. Am J Int Law 94:239
Mulheron R (2012) Rewriting the requirement for a "recognized pyschiatric injury" in negligence claims. Oxf J Leg Stud 32:77
Muzenović Larsen K (2012) A "principle of humanity" or a "principle of human-rightism"? In: Muzenović Larsen et al (eds) Searching for a "principle of humanity" in international humanitarian law. Cambridge University Press, Cambridge, pp 124–148
Neria et al (2010) A longitudinal study of posttraumatic stress disorder, depression, and generalized anxiety disorder in israeli civilians exposed to war trauma. J Trauma Stress 23:322
Ohlin JD (2013) The duty to capture. Minn Law Rev 97:1268
Perilla JL et al (2002) Ethnicity, culture and disaster response: identifying and explaining ethnic differences in PTSD six months after hurricane Andrew. J Soc Clin Psychol 21:20
Peterson AL et al (2008) Combat stress casualties in Iraq. Part 1: behavioral health consultation at an expeditionary medical group. Perspect Psychiatr Care 44:146
Pictet JS (ed) (1958) Geneva Convention IV: commentary. ICRC, Geneva
Rabin RL (2006) Respecting boundaries and the economic loss rule in tort. Ariz Law Rev 48:857
Richemond-Barak D (2011) Nonstate actors in armed conflicts: issues of distinction and reciprocity. In: Banks WC (ed) New battlefields/old laws: critical debates on asymmetric warfare. Columbia University Press, New York, pp 106–132
Sandoz Y et al. (eds) (1987) Commentary on the Additional Protocols of 8 June 1977. Kluwer, Dordrecht
Sassòli M et al. (2011) How does law protect in war, vol I. ICRC, Geneva

Schmid AP (2011) Introduction. In: Schmid AP (ed) The Routledge handbook of terrorism research. Routledge, Abingdon, pp 1–37
Schmitt MN (2004) "Direct participation in hostilities" and 21st century armed conflict. In: Fischer H et al (eds) Crisis management and humanitarian protection: Festschrift für Dieter Fleck. BWV, Berlin, pp 505–529
Schmitt MN (2005) Precision attack and international humanitarian law. Int Rev Red Cross 87:445
Schmitt MN (2007) Asymmetrical warfare and international humanitarian law. In: Heintschel von Heinegg W, Epping V (eds) International humanitarian law facing new challenges: symposium in honour of Knut Ipsen. Springer, Berlin, pp 11–48
Schmitt MN (2010) Military necessity and humanity in international humanitarian law: preserving the delicate balance. Va J Int Law 50:795
Schmitt MN (ed) (2013) Tallinn Manual on the International Law Applicable to Cyber Warfare. International group of experts at the invitation of the Nato Cooperative Cyber Defence Centre of Excellence. Cambridge University Press, Cambridge
Solis GD (2010) The law of armed conflict: international humanitarian law in war. Cambridge University Press, Cambridge
Solomon S (2011) Occupied or not: the question of Gaza's legal status after the Israeli disengagement. Cardozo J Int Comp Law 19:59
Solomon S (2012) The recent European court of human rights judgment in the finogenov case: towards and esoteric humanization of warfare. Berkeley J Int Law PUBLICIST 11
Steel Z et al (2009) Association of torture and other potentially traumatic events with mental health outcomes among populations exposed to mass conflict and displacement. JAMA 302:537
Thabet AA et al (2008) Exposure to war trauma and PTSD among parents and children in the Gaza strip. Eur Child Adolesc Psychiatry 17:191
Tirosh Y (2012) The right to be fat. Yale J Health Policy Law Eth 12:264
UCDP/PRIO (2009) Armed conflict dataset. www.prio.no/Data/Armed-Conflict/UCDP-PRIO/Armed-Conflicts-Version-X-2009/. Accessed 2 June 2013
US Army and Marine Corps (2006) Counterinsurgency field manual
US Chairman of the Joint Chiefs of Staff (2009) Instruction: no-strike and the collateral damage estimation methodology. CJCSI 3160:01
Vasterling J, Brewin CR (eds) (2005) Neuropsychology of PTSD: biological, cognitive, and clinical perspectives. Guilford Press, New York
Walzer M (2004) Arguing about war. Yale University Press, New Haven
Watkin K (2004) Controlling the use of force: a role for human rights norms in contemporary armed conflict. AJIL 98:1
Wertheimer M (2012) A brief history of psychology. Taylor and Francis, New York
Yaswi A, Haque A (2008) Prevalence of PTSD symptoms and depression and level of coping among the victims of the Kashmir conflict. J Loss Trauma 13:471
Zatzick F et al (2002) Predicting posttraumatic distress in hospitalized trauma survivors with acute injuries. Am J Psychiatry 159:941
Zegveld L (2011) The accountability of armed opposition groups in international law. Cambridge University Press, Cambridge
Ziegler R, Otzari S (2012) Do soldiers' lives matter? A view from proportionality. Isr Law Rev 45:53

Chapter 8
Armed Conflict and the Inter-American Human Rights System: Application or Interpretation of International Humanitarian Law?

Shana Tabak

Contents

8.1 Introduction

Protection of human rights is the ultimate goal of the Inter-American Human Rights System (IAHRS). Yet, the instruments of this system, the Inter-American Commission of Human Rights (IACHR or the Commission) and the Inter-American Court of Human Rights (IACtHR or the Court) are oftentimes confronted with human rights allegations that occur in countries where brutal armed conflict

S. Tabak (✉)
Washington College of Law, American University, Washington, USA
e-mail: tabak@wcl.american.edu

D. Jinks et al. (eds.), *Applying International Humanitarian Law in Judicial and Quasi-Judicial Bodies*, DOI: 10.1007/978-94-6265-008-4_8,

occurs, such as El Salvador, Colombia, Guatemala, Mexico, and Peru, among others.[1] The system has also been confronted with allegations of human rights violations committed by the United States in its treatment of detainees in Guantanamo Bay.[2] In these types of cases, human rights bodies apply human rights law (HRL), but these circumstances may also give rise to the application of international humanitarian law (IHL), which is applied in situations of armed conflict or occupation. Thus, on multiple occasions both the Court and the Commission have grappled with the intersections between HRL and humanitarian law.[3] These intersections are complicated and, according to some, problematic, because the bodies of the IAHRS, are charged specifically with enforcing HRL in the Americas, not humanitarian law.

This chapter explores the way in which the instruments of the IAHRS have reached their current approach to the intersection of these two areas of law. Although numerous important factors may be considered in determining the appropriate balance between IHL and HRL in any given context, the current approach can be attributed largely to jurisdictional constraints imposed within the system. Specifically, jurisdiction *ratione materiae* has played a crucial role in this interaction. When these two areas of law intersect in the IASHR, the primary challenge is jurisdictional because jurisdiction *ratione materiae* in the Inter-American System does not explicitly include IHL.

HRL and IHL are distinct, yet complementary bodies of law.[4] Although they are certainly not mutually exclusive, the scope of their application creates distinct challenges.[5] In situations of conflict, facts on the ground may give rise to the application of both these sets of rules within international law, raising the question of how these two areas should intersect. The jurisprudence of the International Court of Justice (ICJ) demonstrates that it is well established that HRL is not

---

[1] See Parada Cea v. El Salvador [1999] Report No. 1/99, OEA/Ser.L./V/II.102 doc. 6 rev. 165; IACHR Case 11.142 Avilan v. Colombia [1998] Report No. 26/97, OEA/Ser.L./V/ 11.98, doc. 6 rev.; IACtHR Judgment [2000] Bámaca Velásquez v. Guatemala Series C No. 70; IACHR Case 11.565 Gonzalez Perez v. Mexico [2001] Report No. 53/01, OEA/Ser.L/V/I11.I doc. 20 rev.; IACHR Case 10.548 Hugo Bustios Saavedra v. Peru [1997] Report No. 38/97.

[2] IACHR Press Release, 10 Years After Detentions in Guantanamo Began, the IACHR Repeats its Call to Close the Detention, 11 January 2012, http://www.oas.org/en/iachr/media_center/PReleases/2012/003.asp (last accessed on 31 June 2013); IACHR (2011) Resolution No. 2/11 Regarding the Situation of Detainees at Guantanamo Bay. http://www.cidh.oas.org/pdf files/Resolution 2-11 Guantanamo.pdf. Accessed 31 June 2013; IACHR (2002) Report on Terrorism and Human Rights, paras 61, 146. http://www.cidh.org/Terrorism/Eng/toc.htm. Accessed 31 June 2013.

[3] IACHR, Case 11.137 Abella v. Argentina [1997] Report No. 55/97, 271, OEA/ Ser.L/V/II.98, doc. 6 rev., paras 160, 164 ("during situations of internal armed conflict that these two branches of international law most converge and reinforce each other" … "in those situations where the American Convention and humanitarian law instruments apply concurrently, Article 29(b) of the American Convention necessarily require the Commission to take due notice of and, where appropriate, give legal effect to applicable humanitarian law rules.").

[4] Moir 2003.

[5] Droege C 2008.

displaced entirely by humanitarian law during conflict.[6] Yet, the relationship between these two sets of rules has oscillated from complicated to controversial in recent years as some human rights bodies and activists have advocated that human rights bodies are an appropriate venue in which to adjudicate claims under IHL.[7]

This chapter describes the IAHRS's treatment of questions arising under IHL, claiming that despite a variety of important arguments regarding the application of IHL, the key to understanding this approach lies in the court's *ratione materiae* competence. Although this system derives its authority from treaties and political declarations that grant jurisdiction on human rights questions, these organs have utilized, interpreted, and in some cases, even applied IHL.[8] This chapter first offers an overview of the intersections between IHL and HRL. Next it describes the jurisdictional restraints within the Inter-American System of Human Rights. Third, it explores the jurisprudence of both the Commission and the Court, observing that institutional and procedural constraints within the human rights system have led to a favoring of HRL over humanitarian law.

In contributing a framework to understanding the IAHRS's jurisprudence, this chapter highlights the distinction between (1) IHL as interpretive reference and (2) direct application of IHL. IHL serves as an interpretive reference when it is employed to provide contextual interpretation, and is used to clarify how HRL should be interpreted in situations of armed conflict.[9] Meanwhile, direct application of IHL occurs in cases where it is directly applied by the body to find a violation thereof.[10] After discussing the patterns within findings of the Commission and the Court, this chapter weighs a number of positive and negative factors that should be considered in evaluating whether these regional human rights organs are appropriately involved in the application, interpretation or reference of IHL.

Conversations exploring the overlap between IHL and HRL may occasionally rely on intellectual debates; the IACHR provides fertile ground in which to

---

6 ICJ Reports (2004) Legal Consequences of the Construction of a Wall in the Occupied Palestinian Territory. http://www.icj-cij.org/docket/files/131/1671.pdf, p. 178. Accessed 31 June 2013; see infra Sect. 8.2 discussion of ICJ jurisprudence.

7 Happold 2010.

8 American Declaration of Rights of Man, Organization of American States, American Declaration of the Rights and Duties of Man, Apr. 30, 1948, Hein's No. KAV 7225; American Convention on Human Rights Article 44. http://www.oas.org/dil/treaties_B-32_American_Convention_on_Human_Rights.pdf.

9 IACHR, Case 11.137 Abella v. Argentina [1997] Report No. 55/97, 271, OEA/ Ser.L/V/II.98, doc. 6 rev., paras 158, 161 ("human rights instruments do not govern the means and methods of warfare…[t]herefore, the Commission must necessarily look to and apply definitional standards and relevant rules of humanitarian law as sources of authoritative guidance in its resolution of this and other kinds of claims alleging violations of the American Convention in combat situations.").

10 For example, IACHR, Case 11.137 Abella v. Argentina [1997] Report No. 55/97, 271, OEA/ Ser.L/V/II.98, doc. 6 rev.

examine the practical implications of the intersections between these two areas of law. In comparison with other regional systems of human rights, the IACHR has been much more liberal in its application of IHL than other systems.[11] Further, an exploration of this jurisprudence prompts other important questions: If the IAHRS does not enforce IHL in the Americas, what body exists to ensure that these perpetually under-enforced norms will continue to inform state behavior during conflict? Is the system obligated to examine this law? Is the IAHRS inherently flawed if it cannot be utilized to seek accountability for humanitarian law violations? Jurisprudential trends within the Americas may also inform the normative content of humanitarian law globally. Theodore Meron claims that the law of war has gradually evolved from its militaristic origins, acquiring a more humane face over the years.[12] Others argue that the application of IHL by human rights bodies may be breaking down the boundaries between these areas of the law, undermining crucial distinctions between human rights and humanitarian law.[13] If these descriptions of the state of IHL are accurate, much debate remains as to whether these trends benefit or endanger protections available under each framework.

8.2 IHL and HRL: Challenges of Fragmentation of International Law

The debate over the appropriate application of and interplay between IHL and HRL reflects a phenomenon of international law known as fragmentation. Fragmentation, deemed by some to be problematic and by others to be crucial,[14] can be understood as "splitting up the law into highly specialized boxes that claim autonomy from one another."[15] Antonio Cassese discussed this overlap between different areas of law, stating that "tight legal compartments" are "gradually tending to influence one another... and international courts are tending to look at them as parts of a whole."[16] This trend has only increased with the proliferation of tribunals and the multiple sets of rules that they interpret. The Inter-American system has struggled to determine the appropriate role of two specialized branches of international law: IHL and HRL. Thus, the jurisprudence addressing a human rights organ's attempts to integrate IHL offers a fitting example of the concerns that fragmentation can raise.

Especially by those who are not well versed in the intricacies of international law, it is common to conflate HRL and humanitarian law. This confusion is easily

[11] Zegveld 1998; Moir 2003.

[12] Meron 2000.

[13] Byron 2006–2007.

[14] For a detailed analysis of fragmentation, international human rights law, and international humanitarian law, see Orakhelashvili 2008.

[15] Koskenniemi 2006, pp. 13–14.

[16] Cassese 2001, p. 45.

understood, considering that the commonalities and distinctions between the two areas are the subject of much scholarly debate.[17] Indeed, there is significant overlap in these two bodies of law, and these intersections are haphazard and difficult to untangle.[18] As articulated by the President of the International Commission for the Red Cross (ICRC), "the common underlying purpose of IHL and international HRL is the protection of the life, health and dignity of human beings."[19] Both branches of law seek to protect basic rights of individuals whose rights may be threatened, either by a state or by an armed group in times of conflict.

This common goal is not universally agreed upon, however.[20] Instead of considering the commonality of protection of life, other commentators argue that these branches of law are intrinsically incompatible.[21] HRL, as demonstrated by the Commission in its holding in the famous *Abella* case, is fundamentally hostile to war; one of its central purposes is to prevent warfare.[22] Meanwhile, IHL is agnostic on the topic of warfare and seeks to regulate it as a social activity within international law.[23] As Meron explains, humanitarian law is aimed at inserting a modicum of fair play into conflict.[24]

HRL applies universally, during times of war and times of peace, through systems of international and regional treaties that lay out the standards by which humans can expect to be treated by states.[25] These norms are dedicated to protecting the physical

---

[17] See for example, Happold 2010, a symposium of authors dedicated to exploring the intersections between the two, including Cryer 2010 as well as Droege 2008; Hathaway 2012.

[18] Hampson 2008, p. 559; Orakhelashvili 2008, p. 168 ("...[states] are expected, at least by implication, to consider the impact of both human rights law and humanitarian law, to reach the outcomes permissible at the level of international law" during armed conflict).

[19] Kellenberger, Address at the 27th Annual Round Table on Current Problems of International Humanitarian Law. 2003 http://www.icrc.org/eng/assets/files/other/irrc_851_kellenberger.pdf. Accessed 12 July 2013.

[20] Bowring 2009.

[21] Scobbie 2009, indicating that although some overlap exists, "there is a fundamental incompatibility in what the two systems set out to achieve. There is no over-reaching axiology, no value system that unifies the objectives of these fields of international law." See also Schindler 1979 articulating the separatist view that the two legal regimes have evolved "along entirely different and totally separate lines", p. 5.

[22] IACHR, Case 11.137 Abella v. Argentina [1997] Report No. 55/97, 271, OEA/ Ser.L/V/II.98, doc. 6 rev., para 158. (indicating that one of the primary purposes of human rights instruments is to prevent warfare).

[23] Escorihuela 2011, p. 362.

[24] Meron 2000.

[25] See for example, American Convention on Human Rights (November 22, 1969) http://www.oas.org/dil/treaties_B-32_American_Convention_on_Human_Rights.pdf. Accessed 28 Sept. 2013; African Charter on Human and Peoples' Rights, OAU Doc. CAB/LEG/67/3 rev. 5, 21 I.L.M. 58 (June 27, 1981) http://www.achpr.org/files/instruments/achpr/banjul_charter.pdf Accessed 28 Sept. 2013; European Convention for the Protection of Human Rights and Fundamental Freedoms (Nov. 4, 1950) http://www.echr.coe.int/Documents/Convention_ENG.pdf Accessed 28 Sept. 2013, UN Charter http://www.un.org/en/documents/charter/, Universal Declaration of

safety and human dignity of all peoples in all circumstances.[26] They protect individuals from state behavior, regulating behavior between parties in an unequal relationship of power. International and regional enforcement mechanisms exist which offer individuals, groups, and their advocates the opportunity to seek accountability against governments who may violate their human rights. Further, domestic states' incorporation of human rights guarantees within domestic law provides an additional means for accountability. Thus, HRL, with its origins rooted in eighteenth century democratic thought, has often been perceived as a threat to state order.[27] The Inter-American System of Human Rights is one such regional system of instruments dedicated to enforcing and protecting human rights as defined in the treaties and declarations that create these instruments.[28]

IHL, also known as the law of war or *jus in bello,* applies during armed conflict and during occupation[29] between parties who operate on the basis of a formally equal relationship. IHL was codified in the Hague Conventions (Hague Law) which address the treatment of the laws of war, including such topics as proportionality within retaliation and military objectives regarding the means and methods of warfare.[30] IHL is also comprised of the Geneva Conventions, which address the treatment of civilians and non-combatants during armed conflict.[31]

Despite its long history and developed ideology, one of the major challenges of humanitarian law has historically been its enforcement, or lack thereof. No

(Footnote 25 continued)
Human Rights, G.A. Res. 217 (III) A, U.N. Doc. A/RES/217(III) (Dec. 10, 1948), Convention on the Rights of the Child, G.A. Res. 44/25, U.N. Doc. A/RES/44/25 (Nov. 20, 1989).

[26] Ibid.

[27] Bowring 2009.

[28] Specific features of the IACHR will be discussed in Sect. 8.3.1 infra.

[29] Occupation for the purposes of application of IHL is defined as "effective control" of a region, as determined by Article 42 of 1907 Hague Regulations. Definitions of the limits of effective control have been discussed by scholars extensively. See Hathaway et al. 2012, pp.1883, 1893, 1920 ("…there is growing consensus among international bodies and foreign States that human rights law obligations apply abroad wherever a State exercises "effective control" over territory or individuals outside its borders" "…the scope of States' human rights obligations is limited during battlefield hostilities because the States lack effective control…"); Le Mon 2002–2003, pp. 741, 743, 793 (2002–2003) (discussing the "dissonance within the law" created by the acceptance of unilateral intervention while upholding standards of effective control and the questionable legitimacy of the legitimacy of invited external government intervention); Holland 2011, p. 165 (addressing the ICJ's articulation and application of the "effective control test" regarding US activities in Military and Paramilitary Activities in and against Nicaragua); Military and Paramilitary Activities in and Against Nicaragua (Nicar. vs. U.S.), 1986 I.C.J. 14, 181 paras 123–124 (June 27) (finding that while the US closely collaborated with the *contra* force providing intelligence and logistic support the US' "operational support" did not "justify treating the *contras* as acting on its behalf" precluding the claim of effective control).

[30] Convention (IV) respecting the Laws and Customs of War on Land and its annex: Regulations concerning the Laws and Customs of War on Land. (Oct. 18, 1907) http://www.icrc.org/applic/ihl/ihl.nsf/INTRO/195 Accessed 28 Sept. 2013.

[31] Geneva Convention Relative to the Protection of Civilian Persons in Time of War, Aug. 12, 1949, 6 U.S.T.3516, 75 U.N.T.S. 287 [hereinafter Geneva Convention IV].

international adjudicative body is charged with enforcement of IHL, and as such, it generally lacks authoritative methods for interpretation.[32] This task has been largely left to the state parties who have signed onto these agreements, and more recently, to international criminal tribunals and UN bodies. Traditionally, multiple methods have been utilized to enforce IHL, but none of these are seen as particularly effective. Available enforcement mechanisms include belligerent reprisals,[33] which have been long considered to be counter-productive, and have been significantly curtailed by the Geneva Conventions.[34] The Protecting Powers Doctrine was also set up by the Geneva Conventions to account for violations of IHL, however, these have only been used in four instances and without much success.[35] Other means include state action and the work of the ICRC, a non-judicial body located in Geneva with a mandate to protect individual victims of international and internal armed conflict from violations of humanitarian law. The Geneva Conventions provide for the ICRC to take a role in enforcement of IHL, as it is charged with intervening and accounting for violations if no protecting powers are appointed, and with visiting prisoners of war.

Thus, despite the numerous treaties codifying the obligations of states under humanitarian law, a lack of viable means to enforce this law is widely blamed for its lack of practical meaning within conflict. Some scholars have proposed the creation of an IHL adjudicative body to remedy this concern,[36] though others find this impracticable.[37] As a result of the weaknesses of each of these potential enforcement mechanisms, activists and jurists have increasingly turned to international and regional human rights tribunals to resolve violations of humanitarian law.[38] It is commonly argued that the void of enforcement of IHL should be filled through utilization of HRL at human rights tribunals.[39]

---

[32] Weissbrodt 2009–2010; see *also* Caceres 2003.

[33] Greenwood 1989, p. 38.

[34] Geneva Convention for the Amelioration of the Wounded and Sick in Armed Forces in the Field Article 46, Aug. 12, 1949, 6 U.S.T. 3114, 75 U.N.T.S. 31 [hereinafter Geneva Convention I]; Geneva Convention for the Amelioration of the Condition of the Wounded, Sick, and Shipwrecked Members of Armed Forces at Sea Article 47, Aug. 12, 1949, 6 U.S.T. 3217, 75 U.N.T.S. 85 [hereinafter Geneva Convention II]; Geneva Convention Relative to the Treatment of Prisoners of War Article 13, Aug. 12, 1949, 6 U.S.T.3316, 75 U.N.T.S. 135 [hereinafter Geneva Convention III]; Geneva Convention Relative to the Protection of Civilian Persons in Time of War Article 33, Aug. 12, 1949, 6 U.S.T.3516, 75 U.N.T.S. 287 [hereinafter Geneva Convention IV]; Protocol Additional to the Geneva Conventions of 12 August 1949, and Relating to the Protection of Victims of International Armed Conflicts Articles 20, 51(6), 52(1), 53(4), 55(2), 56(4), June 8, 1977, 1125 U.N.T.S. 3 [hereinafter Additional Protocol I]; see Darcy 2003, pp. 199–216; Mitchell 2001, pp. 164–170.

[35] Established by Geneva Convention I, *supra* note 12, Articles 8, 10; Geneva Convention II, *supra* note 12, Articles 8, 10; Geneva Convention III, *supra* note 12, Articles 8, 10; Geneva Convention IV, *supra* note 12, Articles. 9, 11. See generally Pierce 1980.

[36] Kleffner and Zegveld 2000.

[37] Heintze 2004, p. 797.

[38] Byron 2006–2007, p. 847.

[39] Gardam 2001, p. 353.

In addition to a comparison of the intrinsic goals of IHL and HRL, of the application, and of the differences in enforcement, a last important area of examination between these two branches of law involves the question of derogation. Human rights treaties have essentially all developed a regime in which some derogation is possible, but only in circumstances which pose extreme danger to self or to the nation and for certain rights, whereas IHL is never derogable. In order to demonstrate how critically these divergences play out when IHL and HRL are both applicable to a set of facts, we examine one right that is never derogable under HRL, the right to life, and another which is derogable, the right to personal liberty, exploring parallel and integrated treatment under both IHL and HRL.

Even the human right to life, which is never derogable, may receive distinct treatment when it is explored within a context in which IHL is considered. The human right of right to life, protected in Article 4 of the American Convention of Human Rights (ACHR), may never be derogated from. Yet, IHL and HRL treat the right to life differently. While HRL protects the right to life under all circumstances, under IHL, deadly force is permitted against combatants until they have been captured. Furthermore, civilians lose their immunity under IHL as soon as they participate in attacks. Therefore, a key determination when an individual has been killed is whether the individual can be characterized as a combatant. If so, then IHL is triggered and presumably, the right to life would not have been violated by the state. Thus, if a killing is sanctioned under IHL as against a combatant, then this killing would not constitute a violation of the non-derogable right to life under the American Declaration or Convention.[40]

Another example that demonstrates the divergent treatment under IHL and HRL is the right to personal liberty, which includes an individual's right to freedom from arbitrary arrest and detention. Any derogation must be exceptional and temporary (under Article 27 of the ACHR), and the state's power to suspend this right during times of armed conflict has been strictly defined. The interplay between IHL and HRL here is relevant, for example, when considering the position of Prisoners of War (POWs) who are interned for reasons of military necessity. Under IHL, POWs may be detained as an incidence of war, and therefore are not afforded procedural protections under General Convention III, as they would have been granted as non-combatants under HRL, such as judicial review, and freedom from arbitrary arrest or detention. Again, the complicated interaction between HRL and IHL is demonstrated with regard to the right to personal liberty. A state may be able to treat POWs one way under IHL, and civilians another under HRL, however, in circumstances during which the existence of armed conflict mandates the consideration of both.

Because a number of significant divergences between IHL and HRL exist, the use of IHL in interpretation at HRL tribunals is controversial. In addressing this issue, a central question has long been that of applicability: it is clear that

[40] *Juan Carlos Abella v. Argentina,* IACHR, Case 11.137, Report No. 355/97, 18 November 1997.

humanitarian law applies during armed conflict, yet, does HRL continue to apply in those instances? How should an adjudicative body address this overlap?[41] The International Court of Justice (ICJ) has addressed this question, finding that indeed, HRL does continue to apply conterminously with IHL.

The ICJ's discussion of the convergence between these two areas of law reflects a classic solution to the concern of fragmentation of international law. The Court relies on the interpretive principle of *lex specialis.* As explained by the ILC, "the maxim *lex specialis derogat legi generali* is a generally accepted technique of interpretation and conflict resolution in international law. It suggests that whenever two or more norms deal with the same subject matter, priority should be given to the norm that is more specific."[42] As is discussed below, although the ICJ has relied on this principle, application of the rule is oftentimes more complicated than the ICJ may have indicated in its holdings.[43]

In a series of three cases addressing the intersection between humanitarian law and HRL, the ICJ held that HRL continues to apply as *lex specialis* during armed conflict, stating that "the protection offered by human rights conventions does not cease in the case of armed conflict."[44] In its Advisory Opinion on the *Legality of Threat of Nuclear Weapons*, the ICJ examined whether the use of nuclear weapons violate the International Covenant on Civil and Political Rights Article 6 prohibition of the arbitrary deprivation of right to life. There, the Court found that since Article 6 was non-derogable, it could not cease to apply, even within armed conflict. Because in this context both IHL and HRL were applicable, IHL was deemed to be *lex specialis*, and therefore the term "arbitrary" was to be defined according to IHL.[45] In later cases, the ICJ reiterated that HRL continues to apply during armed conflict. In its *Advisory Opinion on the Legal Consequences of the Construction of a Wall in the Occupied Palestinian Territory*, the Court's holding demonstrates even more clearly that the right to life is to be interpreted only according to IHL, because norms developed for peacetime cannot be applied in "an unqualified manner" during conflict.[46]

---

[41] Heintze 2004, p. 797.

[42] Koskenniemi 2006, para 5.

[43] Hampson 2008, indicating that the decisions at the ICJ have not fully resolved questions about the relationship of the two bodies of law.

[44] ICJ Reports (2004) Legal Consequences of the Construction of a Wall in the Occupied Palestinian Territory. http://www.icj-cij.org/docket/files/131/1671.pdf, p. 178. Accessed 31 June 2013; see ICJ Reports (1996) Legality of the Threat or Use of Nuclear Weapons, Advisory Opinion, ICJ 226, p. 240. http://www.icj-cij.org/docket/files/95/7495.pdf. Accessed 31 June 2013; ICJ Reports (2005) Armed Activities on the Territory of the Congo (DRC v. Uganda) p. 69, para 216. http://www.icj-cij.org/docket/files/116/10455.pdf. Accessed 7 July 2013.

[45] ICJ Reports (1996) Legality of the Threat or Use of Nuclear Weapons, Advisory Opinion, ICJ 226, p. 240, para 25. http://www.icj-cij.org/docket/files/95/7495.pdf. Accessed 28 Sept. 2013.

[46] ICJ Reports (2004) Legal Consequences of the Construction of a Wall in the Occupied Palestinian Territory. http://www.icj-cij.org/docket/files/131/1671.pdf, p. 178. Accessed 31 June 2013. See also ICJ, Case concerning armed activity on the territory of the Congo (Democratic Republic of the Congo vs. Uganda), Judgment of 19 December 2005, paras 216–220.

Although the ICJ has made an unambiguous assertion that HRL does indeed continue to apply during times of conflict, it remains unclear how courts should specifically adjudicate when these two bodies of law may both be applicable. One scholar explains that the ICJ appears to have meant,

> "first, that where both IHL and HRL are applicable, priority should be given to IHL. Second, given the ICJ's view that HRL remains applicable at all times, by necessary implication the ICJ also meant that the human rights body should make a finding based on IHL expressed in the language of HRL."[47]

Yet others claim that the ICJ's resolution on this question was so ineffectual that in a later holding, it neglected to use the term *lex specialis* which it had previously relied so heavily upon.[48]

Even if the ICJ's position on the matter of how to apply IHL and HRL were crystal clear, regional systems of human rights still confront additional concerns separate from the substantive question of what law to apply. The Statute of the ICJ permits that Court to hear claims stemming from violations of nearly any type of international law.[49] Further, the ICJ does not face the procedural challenges confronting regional bodies, where judges are aware that both IHL and HRL do apply, yet may not be permitted to consider both branches of law equally under their statutes. Regional systems, however, are limited in their jurisdiction and may only consider breaches of law as specifically permitted by their constitutive instruments.[50] In the IAHRS the Commission and the Court must first consider whether they are competent to hear such claims, a jurisdictional hurdle that the ICJ need not address due to its general jurisdiction under Article 38.

8.3 Interplay of IHL and HRL in the Americas: Jurisdiction *Ratione Materiae* Rules

Regional human rights systems offer practical fora in which states' compliance with IHL and HRL may be examined. Although the IAHRS offers tangible evidence of the interplay between these laws,[51] this exchange has been largely governed by the jurisdictional constraints of the statutes that create the system itself.[52] As a result, in recent years the system has been less and less capable of a pure examination of the

---

47 Hampson 2008.

48 ICJ Reports (2005) Armed Activities on the Territory of the Congo (DRC vs. Uganda), p. 69, para 216. http://www.icj-cij.org/docket/files/116/10455.pdf. Accessed 7 July 2013.

49 ICJ Statute, Article 38.

50 Lorite Escorihuela 2011, at p. 377.

51 IACHR, Case 11.137 Abella v. Argentina [1997] Report No. 55/97, 271, OEA/ Ser.L/V/II.98, doc. 6 rev., para 161.

52 Rules of Procedure of the Inter-American Court of Human Rights, Annual Report of the Inter-American Court of Human Rights, 1991, O.A.S. Doc. OEA/Ser.L/V/III.25 doc. 7 at 18 (1992) http://www1.umn.edu/humanrts/oasinstr/zoas7ctr.htm Accessed Oct. 8, 2013.

substantive legal issues involved in the interplay between the two bodies of law, because jurisdictional restraints in its constitutive statues permit adjudication only of HRL. Although the Commission applied IHL in several early cases, direct application of IHL has been undermined by the Court's admonition that the IAHR System may consider IHL as an interpretive device for the application of HRL only, but may not explicitly find IHL violations to have been committed by member states. These patterns in the jurisprudence result directly from the particularities of the IAHR System and its instruments as created by its constitutive charter.

8.3.1 The Evolution of the IAHRS

The IAHRS has developed over the past fifty years into a complex mechanism of bodies aimed at supporting states and individuals in the protection of human rights throughout the Western Hemisphere. The system, created by the Organization of American States (OAS) consists of the Inter-American Commission of Human Rights in Washington D.C., the seat of the OAS, and the Inter-American Court of Human Rights, located in San José, Costa Rica. Over a half-century of work, these instruments have held up mirrors to state behavior during an era characterized by military dictatorships, forced disappearances, and mass displacement. Despite these challenges, this era has also been characterized by the emergence of a Latin American human rights revolution seeking accountability for past abuses, as well as increased global attention to improvement and implementation of standards that prevent and account for violations when they do occur.[53]

Because of its gradual development and acceptance over several decades, the body of legal mechanisms within the IAHR System is somewhat complex. In 1949, the member states of the OAS passed *The Declaration on the Rights and Duties of Man,* becoming the first regional human rights resolution, coterminous with the creation of the Universal Declaration of Human Rights and the Genocide Convention.[54] The Declaration was not at the time considered to be a binding treaty, because it emerged as a resolution from the OAS conference that adopted the Charter of the OAS. The Declaration was later incorporated by reference into the OAS Charter by the Protocol of Buenos Aires.[55] The Commission was created eleven years later as an autonomous and permanent organ of the OAS, created to promote the observance

[53] Dulitzky 2011, p.135

[54] Universal Declaration of Human Rights, G.A. Res. 217 (III) A, U.N. Doc. A/RES/217(III) (Dec. 10, 1948); Convention on the Prevention and Punishment of the Crime of Genocide, Jan. 12, 1951, 78 U.N.T.S. 277.

[55] University of Minnesota Human Rights Library (1970) Protocol of Amendment to the Charter of the Organization of American States, "Protocol of Buenos Aires," O.A.S. Treaty Series No. 1-A. http://www1.umn.edu/humanrts/oasinstr/buenosaires.html. Accessed 2 July 2013.

and defense of human rights.[56] The Commission, though it is not a juridical body, was granted authority by the OAS to apply the ADHR, and in 1968 began evaluation of individual petitions alleging violations of human rights within the member states of the OAS.[57] The existence and mandate of the Commission, created with the Statute, breathed new life into the Declaration and multiplied its normative value within the Americas as a mechanism for protecting human rights.[58]

In 1979 the Court was created with the passage of the *American Convention of Human Rights* (ACHR or the Convention), a binding treaty that laid out obligations with which signing states must comply.[59] Because of the binding nature of the ACHR, only cases against state parties to the Convention are adjudicated by the Court. Thus the Commission lacks an express jurisdictional scope, while the Court's jurisdictional scope is clearly outlined in the ACHR.[60] As a result, matters concerning human rights violations by the United States, a signatory to the American Declaration but not to the Convention, are heard by the Commission, not by the Court. As Christina Cerna, a former human rights specialist at the IACHR, has explained,

> "this lack of an express jurisdictional scope is relevant since most of the examples from the Inter-American system, involving the extraterritorial application of its human rights instruments, concern the United States, which has not ratified the American Convention and which is considered by the Inter-American Commission to be subject to the American Declaration."[61]

8.3.2 *Competence Ratione Materiae*

Thus, in referring to human rights within the IASHR, we refer to those rights outlined within the constitutive instruments that created the system: the OAS

---

[56] IACHR Statute, Adopted by the OAS General Assembly, 9th Regular Session, La Paz, Bolivia, 1979, Res. No. 448.

[57] Id. Article 1(2)(a).

[58] Buergenthal 1975, pp. 828–829, 835.

[59] O.A.S. Resolution XXX, Chap. 2, Articles XXIX–XXXVIII, Adopted by the Ninth International Conference of American States. http://www.hrcr.org/docs/OAS_Declaration/oasrights5.html. Accessed 14 July 2013. The ACHR incorporated the rights that had previously been included in the ADHR, and thus the Commission's mandate was redefined with this passage of the ACHR, although its existence formally predates the ACHR.

[60] Convention for the Protection of Human Rights and Fundamental Freedoms, Adopted 4 November 1950. Article 1(1) states "The States Parties to the Convention undertake to respect the rights and freedoms recognized herein and to ensure to all persons subject to their jurisdiction the free and full exercise of those rights and freedoms, without any discrimination for reasons of race, color, sex, language, religion, political or other opinion, national or social origin, economic status, birth, or any other social condition."

[61] Cerna 2006. The unique relationship between the Commission and the U.S. becomes particularly significant in light of ongoing adjudication surrounding detention at the Guantanamo Bay Detention facility, discussed infra, at pp. 19–22.

charter, the ADHR, and the ACHR.[62] If a regional human rights body, such as the IAHR System, seeks to enforce legal rights, in order to evaluate its subject-matter jurisdiction, it must rely upon the jurisdictional competence authorized that body in its constitutive instrument. In the case of the IACtHR, the statute clarifies that "only denunciations or complaints of violations to the treaty itself by state parties can be dealt with and can provide a basis for proceedings."[63] Therefore, only breaches of the constitutive instrument may be addressed in this setting. The Court has read this provision as indicating that examination of claims under law other than the ACHR would violate the principle within the Vienna Convention on the Law of Treaties (VCLT) of express consent, which provides that a state can only be evaluated against a particular treaty if that state has consented to the treaty.[64]

The convergence of IHL and HRL within the Inter-American System raises several challenges. In certain cases before the IACHR, it is clear that both IHL and HRL apply in parallel, yet proscribe different outcomes with regard to the same subject matter. First, it is not always clear how these two areas of law should intersect, substantively. For example, the term "arbitrary" is referenced in the human rights prohibitions against the arbitrary deprivation of life, and arbitrary arrest or imprisonment. Yet, whether a state's action during an armed conflict is arbitrary or not revolves on a judicial body's interpretation of the term "arbitrary" under IHL. These situations result in numerous practical challenges.

Second, procedural and, or, institutional impediments may block the parallel application of both of these bodies of law within certain adjudicative bodies. The former has presented challenges of interpretation within the jurisprudence of the IACHR, but these substantive problems have proved less of a stumbling block than the latter procedural question regarding the IA system's capacity to enforce IHL.[65]

In order to best understand these procedural and institutional impediments, we must look to the constitutive documents of the instruments themselves. Jurisdiction *ratione materiae* (or subject-matter jurisdiction) refers to a tribunal's authority to decide a particular case.[66] At the Inter-American Court, the scope of jurisdiction

[62] Convention for the Protection of Human Rights and Fundamental Freedoms, Adopted 4 November 1950. Article 1, 'Nature and Purposes', of the Statute.

[63] American Convention on Human Rights Article 44. http://www.oas.org/dil/treaties_B-32_American_Convention_on_Human_Rights.pdf. Accessed 13 July 2013.

[64] Vienna Convention on the Law of Treaties. 1115 UNTS 331, entry into force 1980. http://untreaty.un.org/ilc/texts/instruments/english/conventions/1_1_1969.pdf. Accessed 13 July 2013.

[65] IACHR Report on Terrorism and Human Rights (2002), para 116. http://www.cidh.org/Terrorism/Eng/toc.htm. (discussing to the right to life and terrorism, the IACHR Report on Terrorism states "additional procedural requirements, such as the notification of Protecting Powers, may apply based upon the lex specialis of international humanitarian law governing international armed conflicts").

[66] American Convention on Human Rights Article 62(3), July 18, 1978, O.A.S.Treaty Series No. 36, 1144 U.N.T.S. 123 ("The jurisdiction of the Court shall comprise all cases concerning the interpretation and application of the provisions of this Convention that are submitted to it, provided that the States Parties to the case recognize or have recognized such jurisdiction, whether by special declaration pursuant to the preceding paragraphs, or by a special agreement").

ratione materiae is determined by Article 62(3) of the ACHR, which states that "[t]he jurisdiction of the Court shall comprise all cases concerning the interpretation and application of the provisions of this Convention that are submitted to it, provided that the States Parties to the case recognize or have recognized such jurisdiction, whether by special declaration pursuant to the preceding paragraphs, or by a special agreement."[67] Although the ACHR Article 62(3) dictates jurisdiction, the Court's case law has determined where the outer limits of this scope lie with regard to a number of different specific questions, one of which is the interplay between IHL and HRL.[68]

As a result, a clear bias in favor of HRL exists when human rights bodies within the Inter-American system examine legal claims to which IHL and HRL could apply. Oona Hathaway explains that this bias is due to jurisdictional restraints imposed in the instrument creating the Court.[69] For many years, however, this bias remained unconfirmed until the Court ultimately imposed this restriction upon itself in *Las Palmeras*. There, it explained that in order to carry out an evaluation of legal norms not enshrined in the Convention, such as the Geneva Conventions, these norms must be interpreted vis-à-vis the Convention.[70] According to the Court, "the American Convention…has only given the Court competence to determine whether the acts or norms of the State are compatible with the Convention itself, and not with the 1949 Geneva Conventions."[71]

8.4 Cases Reflecting the Intersection of HRL and IHL in the Inter-American System of Human Rights

The Court's and Commission's respective approaches to legal questions arising under armed conflict, despite initial significant differences, have developed a more unified approach over recent years. The Commission's current position is that HRL is not displaced by IHL during armed conflict and remains fully applicable save for permissible derogations.[72] The Court has also held that IHL and HRL share a common origin of non-derogable rights.[73] Although the two bodies share a

[67] American Convention on Human Rights Article 44. http://www.oas.org/dil/treaties_B-32_American_Convention_on_Human_Rights.pdf. Accessed 13 July 2013.

[68] Burgorgue-*Larsen and Ubeda* de Torres 2011, p. 67.

[69] Hathaway 2012.

[70] IACtHR (2000) Las Palmeras Case, Judgment on Preliminary Objections of February 4, 2000, Inter-Am. Ct. H.R. (Ser. C) No. 67. paras 32–33.

[71] Ibid.

[72] See IACHR Report on Terrorism and Human Rights (2002), paras 57–62. http://www.cidh.org/Terrorism/Eng/toc.htm. Accessed 31 June 2013.

[73] IACHR, Case 10.951 Coard v. United States [1999] Report No. 109/99, OEA/Ser.L./V/II.106, doc. 6 rev. 39.

common theoretical basis, and currently appear to adopt the same perspective with regard to the application of IHL, for several years, they diverged significantly in their approach to IHL.

The Commission's utilization of IHL is characterized by two central approaches. First, in several early cases, the Commission invoked the direct application of IHL, and found that it was competent to determine whether states had committed violations thereof.[74] Second, in situations in which provisions of the ACHR benefitted from clarification of IHL standards, the Commission utilized IHL as an interpretive reference.[75] This usage of IHL rules as authoritative guidance when interpreting the American Convention and Declaration during armed combat follows the ICJ's recommended use of IHL as *lex specialis* when two bodies of law apply simultaneously.[76] The Commission continues to apply IHL as *lex specialis* in an interpretive capacity, but as its jurisprudence demonstrates, has essentially ceased to directly apply IHL.[77]

The Court has consistently taken a more orthodox, formalist approach than the Commission, and has never advocated direct application of IHL by the instruments of the IAHR System. This position was forcefully articulated in *Las Palmeras*, in which the Court found that the Commission was overreaching in its finding that Colombia had breached its obligations under IHL. In the words of the Court, "[t]he American Convention has only given the Court competence to determine whether the acts or norms of the States are compatible with the ACHR."[78]

Despite its reticence to find states directly in breach of IHL, the Court has acknowledged that IHL may and should be utilized as an interpretive reference of human rights norms during times of conflict. The Court has rejected the *lex specialis* direct application of IHL on jurisdictional grounds, but refers to IHL and considers it in an advisory capacity.[79] These trends are best demonstrated in a chronological overview of some of the most relevant cases within the IAHR System.

---

74 IACHR Case 11.142 Avilan v. Colombia [1998] Report No. 26/97, OEA/Ser.L./V/ 11.98, doc. 6 rev. para 202; IACHR Case 10.548 Hugo Bustios Saavedra v. Peru [1997] Report No 38/97, para 61; IACHR, Case 11.137 Abella v. Argentina [1997] Report No. 55/97, 271, OEA/ Ser.L/V/ II.98, doc. 6 rev., para 178.

75 Abella v. Argentina, para 16.

76 Goldman 2013, p. 14.

77 Moir 2003

78 IACtHR (2000) Las Palmeras Case, Judgment on Preliminary Objections of February 4, 2000, Inter-Am. Ct. H.R. (Ser. C) No. 67.

79 Weissbrodt 2009–2010.

8.4.1 The Commission: IHL Applied Directly and Employed as Interpretive Reference

The Commission first confronted IHL in several cases where it demonstrated a proactive stance in its willingness to directly apply the law of armed conflict. In 1997 a Commission Report discussed three cases in which the Commission evaluated whether states had committed direct violations of IHL[80]: *Avilán v. Colombia,*[81] *Hugo Bustios Saavedra v. Peru,*[82] and *Abella v. Argentina.*[83] Each of these cases involved state violence in situations classified as internal armed conflict, and through jurisprudence in these cases, the Commission applied IHL and articulated its evolving defense of why it was competent to apply IHL in such a manner.

In *Avilán v. Colombia*, the Commission found that eleven individuals had been extra-judicially executed during a confrontation between the Colombian army and an armed dissident group. In its report, the Commission found that the state had violated multiple articles of the ACHR, but also found violations of Common Article 3 of the Geneva Conventions. Interestingly, the petitioners' request did not allege such violations, and thus the Commission raised this issue *sua sponte*.[84] It defended this move, explaining that the facts of the case required the application of IHL if the facts of the case were to be analyzed in their proper context of armed conflict. Further, it relied on the Court's previous position that the "Commission had the power and duty to apply the judicial provisions relevant to the proceedings, even where the parties do not expressly invoke them."[85] The Commission reasoned further that "[i]t is precisely in situations of internal armed conflict that human rights and humanitarian law converge most precisely and reinforce one another."[86] Thus, it found Colombia to have violated Common Article 3.

---

[80] IACHR 1997 Annual Report of the Inter-American Commission of Human Rights, C.H.R. OAS/Ser L./V/ II.98 doc. 7 rev. (1998).

[81] IACHR Case 11.142 Avilán v. Colombia [1998] Report No. 26/97, OEA/Ser.L./V/ 11.98, doc. 6 rev.

[82] IACHR Case 10.548 Hugo Bustios Saavedra v. Peru [1997] Report No 38/97 para 88. In this case against Peru, the Commission found state violations of IHL: "With respect to the right to life of Hugo Bustíos Saavedra and the personal integrity of Eduardo Rojas Arce, the Peruvian State has also violated common Article 3 of the 1949 Geneva Conventions."

[83] IACHR, Case 11.137 Abella v. Argentina [1997] Report No. 55/97, 271, OEA/ Ser.L/V/II.98, doc. 6 rev.

[84] IACHR 1997 Annual Report of the Inter-American Commission of Human Rights, C.H.R. OAS/Ser L./V/ II.98 doc. 7 rev. (1998), para 202. "The state of Colombia did not carry out its obligation to respect and guarantee the rights of persons who are placed in hors de combat in an internal armed combat. The extrajudicial execution of 11 victims constituted a flagrant violation of Common Article 3 of the Geneva Conventions in that state agents were absolutely required to treat humanely all of the persons within their power due to injury, surrender or detention, whether or not they had previously participated in hostilities."

[85] IACtHR Velasquez Rodriguez Case [1988] (ser. C) No. 4, para 163.

[86] IACHR Case 11.142 Avilán v. Colombia [1998] Report No. 26/97, OEA/Ser.L./V/ 11.98, doc. 6 rev., para 174.

The *Abella* case marks the most celebrated occasion in which the Commission took the ultimately controversial choice to apply IHL, although its statute normally only provided competence under the ADHR. After the attackers of a military base took 42 people there hostage, the Argentine military re-captured the base. The subsequent confrontation resulted in the death of 29 of the attackers. The surviving attackers alleged that Argentina was responsible not only for violations of the ACHR, in particular the Article 4 right to life, but also of IHL. They alleged that the military (1) refused offers to surrender and (2) used arms designed to inflict superfluous injury.[87] On the merits, the Commission examined whether or not it could apply IHL directly, and it found that it was competent to do so. Its decision determined that killings sanctioned by IHL did not constitute arbitrary deprivations of life under the American Declaration or Convention.[88]

These cases highlight the Commission's direct application of IHL to find state violations thereof, and use of IHL as an interpretive device. It rationalized its capacity to apply IHL on numerous grounds which are discussed below: on the overlapping scope of HRL and IHL, and on Articles 25, 27, 29(d), and 64(1) of the Convention.[89] Aside from the Commission's defense of IHL due to its overlapping scope with HRL, the Commission's reliance on each of these articles focused on its utilization of IHL as an interpretive reference for application of HRL, not on direct application of IHL.

First, the Commission explained that due to the overlapping of the scope of application of HRL and IHL, the application of IHL was no more burdensome upon a state than it was to only apply HRL.[90] It explained that the "integral linkage between the law of human rights and humanitarian law which share a common nucleus of non-derogable rights and a common purpose of protecting human life and dignity result in in a substantial overlap in the application of these bodies of law."[91] This rationale is echoed by advocates who claim that human rights mechanisms should be used to fill the void of enforcement of IHL. Because of human rights' common philosophy with IHL, some scholars argue that it may also be used to compensate for the deficits of IHL.[92]

In defending its use of IHL as *lex specialis*, or as an interpretive device, the Commission explained that Article 29(d) of the Convention precludes the

[87] para 180.

[88] IACHR, Case 11.137 Abella v. Argentina [1997] Report No. 55/97, 271, OEA/ Ser.L/V/II.98, doc. 6 rev., p. 92, para 327; p. 93, para 328. The Commission concluded that Argentina did *not* violate the applicable provisions of international humanitarian law.

[89] For an in-depth analysis of each of these defenses as discussed by the Commission, see Moir 2003, p. 194.

[90] IACHR, Case 11.137 Abella v. Argentina [1997] Report No. 55/97, 271, OEA/ Ser.L/V/II.98, doc. 6 rev.; IACHR Case 11.142 Avilán v. Colombia [1998] Report No. 26/97, OEA/Ser.L./V/ 11.98, doc. 6 rev.

[91] IACHR, Case 10.951 Coard v. United States [1999] Report No. 109/99, OEA/Ser.L./V/II.106, doc. 6 rev. 39.

[92] Gardam 2001, p. 353.

Commission from interpreting the Convention in a manner that is inconsistent with the other international law obligations of a member state.[93] In *Abella*, for example, the Commission explained that in order to evaluate whether the state's killing of the *Tablada* attackers was a violation of Article 4's right to life, reference to the ACHR was insufficient. Because the American Convention provides no guidance for distinguishing between civilians and legitimate military targets, IHL provided the Commission with invaluable authoritative guidance.[94] Here, the Commission found that the attackers did in fact qualify as combatants, and that "despite the brief duration of the clash between the attackers and the Argentine military, the activity triggered the application of the provisions of Common Article 3."[95] Because IHL was triggered, the Commission evaluated Argentina's acts applying humanitarian law and adjudicated the matter categorizing the attackers as combatants, not as civilians. As combatants, the attackers were not fully protected under IHL, and thus the Commission determined that Argentina was not in violation of IHL.[96]

In these instances, in order to respect Article 29, and not offer judgment in violation of other IHL obligations, the Commission chose to employ IHL as an interpretive device, due to its evaluation that IHL provided a higher standard of protection for these individuals than did HRL. Ironically, most often it is perceived that HRL offers a higher degree of protection for victims, but it depends who seeks protection—in this case, the enemy combatants themselves were in need of the "higher" level of protection afforded them under IHL.[97] Unexpectedly, perhaps, to petitioners in the *Abella* case, IHL did not benefit the claimants because it permitted the government's acts to be evaluated vis-à-vis combatants, not civilians.[98] Thus, once it was determined that the situation qualified as armed conflict, this triggered application of IHL. Argentina's

---

[93] Article 29 of the American Convention on Human Rights Article states, "No provision of this convention shall be interpreted as … restricting the enjoyment or exercise of any right or freedom recognized by virtue of the laws of any State Party or by virtue of another convention to which one of the said states is a party." http://www.oas.org/dil/treaties_B-32_American_Convention_on_Human_Rights.pdf. Accessed 13 July.

[94] IACHR, Case 11.137 Abella v. Argentina [1997] Report No. 55/97, 271, OEA/ Ser.L/V/II.98, doc. 6 rev., p. 161; IACHR Case 10.480 Parada Cea v. El Salvador [1999] Report No. 1/99, OEA/ Ser.L./V/II.102 doc. 6 rev. 165; IACHR Case 11.142 Avilán v. Colombia [1998] Report No. 26/ 97, OEA/Ser.L./V/ 11.98, doc. 6 rev., p. 173.

[95] IACHR, Case 11.137 Abella v. Argentina [1997] Report No. 55/97, 271, OEA/ Ser.L/V/II.98, doc. 6 rev., para 156.

[96] IACHR, Case 11.137 Abella v. Argentina [1997] Report No. 55/97, 271, OEA/ Ser.L/V/II.98, doc. 6 rev., para 437. Similarly, in *Coard*, the Commission utilized the *lex specialis* argument, where it was asked to adjudicate on the right to liberty during an international armed conflict, and again, it interpreted this right (under the ACHR) in the context of armed conflict with the benefit of definitional guidance from IHL. IACHR, Case 10.951 Coard v. United States [1999] Report No. 109/99, OEA/Ser.L./V/II.106, doc. 6 rev. 39.

[97] Orakhelashvili 2008, p. 167.

[98] In retrospect, it is difficult to understand why petitioners chose to invoke IHL considering the outcome, but it is possible that counsel for the victims (the armed attackers of the military compound) were emboldened by the Commission's holding in *Avilán* that Colombia had violated IHL, resulting in their petition that the Commission find that Argentina had also violated IHL.

actions were held to a lower standard than they would have been had the individuals not been classified as combatants, under HRL alone. The Commission observed that petitioners had misunderstood the impact of their request to have IHL considered.[99] Thus, the government benefited from the Commission's decision that the situation qualified as armed combat and that petitioners qualified as combatants.

The Commission also based its application of IHL on Article 25, which grants every individual the right to a suitable legal remedy for violation of his or her basic rights. Thus, if Colombian law grants protection under IHL, and if the government does not enforce this protection, then the Commission is obligated to evaluate whether there exists an adequate legal remedy to those rights within Colombia. In *Avilán*, for example, the Commission explained that

> "[t]he right to the protection of humanitarian law is recognized in the Colombian legal regime.... Therefore, given that Colombian domestic law provides for the application of humanitarian law, the Convention itself authorizes the Commission to analyze humanitarian law in cases such as this one, where a violation of Article 25 has been alleged."[100]

This rationale thus posits that the Commission is obligated to enforce IHL in order to comply with Article 25 and not violate domestic law.

Article 27, which states that derogations from duties entrenched in the Convention during times of national emergency may not stand in the way of other international legal duties, also provided the Commission with defense in its interpretation of IHL.[101] The Commission explained that, for example, in the situation of a public emergency, even if human rights obligations are derogated from, then IHL still remains in force, and is a useful tool to protect individuals since its provisions can never be derogated from.[102] Therefore, the Commission explained, recourse to IHL during times of national emergency might be imperative, since if it could not evaluate a state's actions during these times in light of IHL, there may be no applicable standard if certain provisions HRL were to be found inapplicable.

Lastly, as rationale for its decision to consider IHL, the Commission cited an Advisory Opinion of the Inter-American Human Rights Court, which declared that the Commission may use treaties that do not emerge from the Inter-American system.[103] In that decision, Peru had requested that the Court clarify the scope of Article 64 of the ACHR, which allows the Court to give opinions on the

---

[99] IACHR, Case 11.137 Abella v. Argentina [1997] Report No. 55/97, 271, OEA/ Ser.L/V/II.98, doc. 6 rev., para 178. "The Commission believes that petitioners misperceive the practical and legal consequences that ensued with respect to the application of these rules to those MTP members who participated in the Tablada attack."

[100] IACHR Case 11.142 Avilán v. Colombia [1998] Report No. 26/97, OEA/Ser.L./V/ 11.98, doc. 6 rev., paras 177–178.

[101] American Convention on Human Rights Article 27. http://www.oas.org/dil/treaties_B-32_American_Convention_on_Human_Rights.pdf. Accessed 29 Sept. 2013.

[102] IACHR Case 11.142 Avilán v. Colombia [1998] Report No. 26/97, OEA/Ser.L./V/ 11.98, doc. 6 rev., para 135.

[103] "Other Treaties" Subject to the Consultative Jurisdiction of the Court (Article 64 of the American Convention on Human Rights), Advisory Opinion OC-1/82, September 24, 1982, Inter-

interpretation of "other treaties concerning the protection of human rights in the American states."[104] The Court found that the ambit of Article 64 included treaties that were not adopted under the Inter-American System, and included treaties to which other states were party.[105] Thus, the Commission held that this opinion validated its choice to utilize IHL in its interpretation of facts arising during armed conflict.

8.4.2 The Court: A Legalist Interpretation of the Statute

As the Commission adjudicated cases in which it directly applied IHL and found states in breach of these norms, it became clear that before long, the Court would opine on this controversial topic.[106] The *Las Palmeras* case, decided in 2000, is heralded as the first case in which the Court articulated clear subject-matter jurisdiction limitations in the area of IHL.[107] As such, it has also been critiqued as the decision that essentially deprived victims of humanitarian crimes the option of binding recourse within the Inter-American System. The Court's aforementioned Advisory Opinion on Article 64 left open the possibility that the Court could directly apply IHL, finding that "the Commission has properly invoked in some of its reports and resolutions 'other treaties concerning the protection of human rights in the American States', regardless of … whether they have been adopted within the framework or under the auspices of the Inter-American system."[108] Perhaps because this approach was described in an advisory opinion and not in a case

(Footnote 103 continued)
Am. Ct. H.R. (Ser. A) No. 1 (1982), para 42. http://www1.umn.edu/humanrts/iachr/b_11_4a.htm. Accessed 12 July 2013.

104 American Convention on Human Rights, Article 64, "The member states of the Organization may consult the Court regarding the interpretation of this Convention or of other treaties concerning the protection of human rights in the American states." http://www.oas.org/dil/treaties_B-32_American_Convention_on_Human_Rights.htm. Accessed 13 July 2013.

105 IACHR Case 11.142 Avilán v. Colombia [1998] Report No. 26/97, OEA/Ser.L./V/ 11.98, doc. 6 rev., para 132.

106 One commentator, writing in 1998, predicted "at some point in the future, the Court may be in the position to give an opinion on the Commission's decision to apply international humanitarian law directly." Zegveld 1998, p. 511.

107 IACtHR (2000) Las Palmeras Case, Judgment on Preliminary Objections of February 4, 2000, Inter-Am. Ct. H.R. (Ser. C) No. 67. Although it is correct that this was the first case in which the Court addressed the application of IHL, one commentator highlights that the Court had previously considered the challenges inherent in the application of other treaties, notably the Inter-American Convention on Torture, the Inter-American Convention to Prevent and Punish Torture and the Convention on the Rights of the Child; See *also* Buis (2008).

108 "Other Treaties" Subject to the Consultative Jurisdiction of the Court (Article 64 of the American Convention on Human Rights), Advisory Opinion OC-1/82, September 24, 1982, Inter-Am. Ct. H.R. (Ser. A) No. 1 (1982), para 42. http://www1.umn.edu/humanrts/iachr/b_11_4a.htm. Accessed 12 July 2013.

against a state, it demonstrated a more relaxed approach toward the utilization of IHL by the Court than that which it ultimately arrived at. This occurred in a series of cases in which the Court explicitly opined on the status of state violations of IHL.

The Court's decision in *Las Palmeras* demonstrates a decidedly more conservative and legalistic approach to consideration of IHL than that of the Commission. The Court held that the human rights instruments of the Inter-American System lack competence to find violations of any international law other than of its constitutive instrument, the American Convention on Human Rights.[109] The Commission brought *Las Palmeras* to the Court after completing an investigation in Colombia into the deaths of at least six victims who had been killed extra-judicially by members of the National Police Forces, aided by the Colombian armed forces. It specifically requested that the Court find violations not only of the right to life, codified in Article 4 of the ACHR, but also of "Article 3, common to all of the 1949 Geneva Conventions."[110] The Commission's proactive approach reaffirmed its position that both it and the Court were competent to apply IHL directly and to find state violations of the Geneva Conventions.

Ultimately, both the Court and Colombian State disagreed with the Commission's position. Colombia countered with preliminary objections, claiming that both the Commission and the Court lacked competence to find these violations.[111] Importantly, it did not contest that the case arose from facts that qualified as an internal conflict giving rise to Common Article 3; it merely contested the competence of *these instruments* to find such a violation under IHL.[112] The Court admitted these preliminary objections, holding that it could evaluate humanitarian law only in the context of its compatibility with the American Convention.[113] The Court stressed that the ACHR offers competence only to evaluate whether a state's actions are compatible with the convention itself, and not with the Geneva conventions or IHL more broadly.[114]

Many critics viewed the *Las Palmeras* decision as a lost opportunity to build bridges between human rights and IHL.[115] Others argued that the ACHR was

---

[109] IACtHR (2000) Las Palmeras Case, Judgment on Preliminary Objections of February 4, 2000, Inter-Am. Ct. H.R. (Ser. C) No. 67, pp. 60–61.

[110] IACtHR (2000) Las Palmeras Case, Judgment on Preliminary Objections of February 4, 2000, Inter-Am. Ct. H.R. (Ser. C) No. 67, pp. 60–61, para 28.

[111] Ibid.

[112] Ibid at para 29 ("...Colombia had not objected to the Commission's observation that, at the time that the loss of lives set forth in the application occurred, an internal armed conflict was taking place on its territory...").

[113] *Id.* at para 34 "Although the Inter-American Commission has broad faculties as an organ for the promotion and protection of human rights, it can clearly be inferred from the American Convention that the procedure initiated in contentious cases before the Commission, which culminates in an application before the Court, should refer specifically to rights protected by that Convention (cf. Articles 33, 44, 48.1 and 48)."

[114] *Id.* at pp. 60–62.

[115] Martin 2001.

"perfectly clear" on how IHL should be approached by a human rights body, claiming that the two branches of international law interact and complement each other exactly as stated in Article 29(d) of the American Convention.[116] The Court reinforced its holding in later cases addressing internal armed conflict.[117] Its jurisprudence has also reaffirmed the importance of the proper contextualization of human rights within the broader scope of public international law, demonstrating that IHL can be useful to achieve appropriate interpretation of the HRL laws in a context in which IHL applies.[118]

The Court's rebuke of the Commission's activist application of IHL was reinforced in *Bámaca Velásquez*. Here, however, it was less categorical in its analysis, and while confirming its rejection of the direct application of IHL, it simultaneously recognized the role that IHL played as an interpretive reference for cases of armed conflict.[119] In this case, the Commission had requested that the Court find Guatemala in breach of both the ACHR and Common Article 3 of the Geneva Conventions, as a result of the Guatemalan military's torture and murder of a guerilla fighter during the internal armed conflict there.[120] The Court refused, finding state violations only of the ACHR, cementing its lack of competence to find state violations of a treaty that was not explicitly contemplated in the Convention. It did, however, find it proper to make an observation that certain acts violating the ACHR also violate other types of law, such as IHL.[121] The Court found that "the relevant provisions of the Geneva Conventions *may* be taken into account, as elements for interpretation of the American Convention."[122] This holding permits the organs of the IAHRS to employ IHL as an interpretive tool, though they may not determine whether a state has definitively violated IHL.[123] This case, as well as the case of the *Santo Domingo Massacre* v. *Colombia*, reaffirm the Court's capacity to use IHL as *lex specialis* when adjudicating an alleged breach of human rights that has occurred in a context of armed conflict.[124] This finding presumably applies to the Commission as well as the Court.

---

[116] Burgorgue-*Larsen and Ubeda* de Torres 2011, p. 69; Article 29(d) of the American Convention on Human Rights states "..." http://www.oas.org/dil/treaties_B-32_American_Convention_on_Human_Rights.htm. Accessed 13 July 2013.

[117] In the *Serrano-Cruz Sisters* case, for example, the Court recalled the "complementarity of international human rights law and international humanitarian law." IACtHR Preliminary Objections [2004] Serrano-Cruz Sisters v. El Salvador Series C No. 118, para 112.

[118] See *also* IACtHR [2005] Mapiripan Massacre v. Colombia Series C No. 134, para 115.

[119] IACtHR Judgment [2000] Bámaca Velásquez v. Guatemala Series C No. 70.

[120] Ibid at para 2.

[121] Ibid at para 208.

[122] IACtHR Judgment [2000] Bámaca Velásquez v. Guatemala Series C No. 70, para 209 (author's emphasis).

[123] For a more complete discussion of the importance of the Bámaca Velásquez case, see Byron 2006–2007, pp. 861–862.

[124] In the 2012 case of Caso Masacre de Santo Domingo Vs. Colombia. Sentencia de Excepciones Preliminares, Fondo y Reparaciones de 30 de noviembre de 2012. Serie C No. 259 ,

Through this jurisprudence the Court has sought to curtail the direct application of IHL by the instruments of the IAHR System. The Court's strict interpretation of the jurisdictional limits within the ACHR resulted in an abrupt end to the Commission's capacity to find direct violations of IHL by states. Despite this, as the Commission's later jurisprudence reveals, the use of IHL as an interpretive reference within the Inter-American System remains quite viable.

8.4.3 The Commission: A More Tempered Approach?

After this series of IACtHR decisions curtailing the direct application of IHL, the Commission was again presented with accusations of human rights violations within the context of armed conflict, triggering the question of whether and how IHL applied. In *Oscar Romero v. El Salvador*, the Commission issued a report in which it found that El Salvador had violated "the right set forth in Article 4 of the American Convention, *in conjunction* with the principles codified in common Article 3 of the Geneva Conventions."[125] The report in *Romero* was published only two months after *Las Palmeras*, and it appears that the Court's decision may have affected the Commission's analysis. This ambiguous wording does not go so far as to apply IHL, though it does subtly reference IHL in a manner that appears to imply that an Article 3 violation had indeed occurred. It has been suggested that this wording was drafted intentionally, so as not to be read as flouting the Court's mandate on this topic.[126] Since *Las Palmeras* and *Bámaca Velazquez*, the Commission has maintained this approach, noting or discussing violations of IHL as an

(Footnote 124 continued)
the Court in no uncertain terms reiterated its commitment to using IHL as an interpretive reference, but remained unwilling to directly apply it ("Based on the foregoing considerations, the Court reiterates that although the American Convention has only empowered it to determine the compatibility of the States' acts and omissions or laws with this Convention and not with the provisions of other treaties or customary norms, when making this analysis, it can, as it has in other cases… interpret the obligation and the rights contained in the American Convention in light of other treaties. In this case, by using IHL as a supplementary norm of interpretation to the treaty-based provisions, the Court is not making a ranking between normative systems, because the applicability and relevance of IHL in situations of armed conflict is evident. This only means that the Court can observe the regulations of IHL, as the specific law in this area, in order to make a more specific application of the provisions of the Convention when defining the scope of the State's obligations.") It should be noted that at the time of this writing, two cases are pending at the IACtHR which concern the intersections between IHL and HRL, yet there is no indication that the Court will deviate from its previous holdings in either of these cases: Case No. 12.444, Eduardo Nicolás Cruz Sánchez et al. (Operation Chavín de Huántar) v. Peru, and Case No. 12.167 Hugo Oscar Arguelles et al. v. Argentina.

[125] IACHR Case 11.481 Romero y Galdimez v. El Salvador [2000] Report No. 37/00, OEA/Ser.L./V/II.106, doc. 6 rev., p. 66–72.

[126] Moir 2003.

interpretive reference, but declining to base its holdings on direct state violations of IHL.[127]

Although these cases seem to indicate that the Commission has tempered its own inclination to directly find violations by states of IHL, it is not entirely accurate that, as one commentator describes, the Commission in these cases finally and fully adopted the Court's opinion.[128] Instead, the Commission has continued to be more active in its employment of IHL as *lex specialis,* utilizing IHL as an interpretive reference, than has the Court. This position has proven particularly salient in light of its role in claims against the United States regarding treatment of detainees in the Guantanamo Bay Detention Center.

Two major factors distinguish the Commission's cases regarding the United States involving IHL from other Commission cases that consider this law. First, previous cases addressing the intersection of these bodies of law principally concerned internal armed conflict.[129] In contrast, the U.S.'s so-called "war on terrorism" has led to allegations of human rights and humanitarian law violations *outside* the territory of the respondent state, injecting questions of extraterritoriality into the Commission's legal analysis. It is generally understood that a state must respect human rights within its boundaries.[130] Yet, the United State's obligations as an OAS member are complicated due to U.S. control over Guantanamo, thus the U.S. as respondent state exercises control over a detention center outside its territory. In instances such as these, the IACHR has adopted an "effective control" test to determine whether HRL merits application in a particular circumstance.[131] At the IACHR, individuals falling within a state's control, yet outside their territory, are still subject to the requirements of HRL under the ACHR, although those same situations are also governed by IHL.[132] Considerations of extraterritorial violations of IHL within the IAHRS add an additional layer of complexity to these deliberations.

Second, these cases against the U.S. differ from cases against other nations in that only the Commission, not the Court, has competence to hear claims against the United States. The U.S., as a member of the OAS, is obligated by the ADHR

---

[127] See IACHR Case 10.247 Extrajudicial Executions and Forced Disappearances v. Peru, et al. [2001] Report No. 101/01, OEA/Ser.L./V/II.114 doc. 5 rev., p. 208–15; IACHR Case 11.654 Rio Frio Massacre v. Colombia [2001] Report No. 62/01, OEA/Ser.L./V/ 11.111 doc. rev., p. 54–58; IACHR Case 11.710 Bolaio Castro v. Colombia [2001] Report No. 63/01, OEA/Ser.L./V/II.102 doc. rev., p. 32–35; IACHR Case 11.565 Gonzalez Perez v. Mexico [2001] Report No. 53/01, OEA/Ser.L/V/I11.I doc. 20 rev., 45, 54.

[128] Moir 2003, p. 212.

[129] Cerna 2006.

[130] American Convention on Human Rights Article 1(1) http://www.oas.org/dil/treaties_B-32_American_Convention_on_Human_Rights.pdf. Accessed 29 Sept. 2013.

[131] Cleveland 2010, p. 229 ("Regional human rights tribunals, the U.N. treaty bodies, and the International Court of Justice (ICJ) all have recognized that human rights obligations travel with a state when a state or its agents place persons or territories under the state's 'effective control.'"); See pp. 248–270.

[132] Goldman 2013, p. 106.

but did not ratify the ACHR. Therefore, the Commission may hear claims against the U.S. with regard to violations of the Declaration, but not the Convention.[133] Although it is impossible to speculate to what extent this may impact deliberations at the Commission, claims against the U.S. will thus never benefit from an additional level of analysis at the Court, and will never be subjected to its binding jurisdiction.

Starting in 2002, the Commission has served as a principle forum of legal activity for advocates working on behalf of detainees in Guantanamo Bay.[134] Recourse to the Inter-American System became an important alternative forum to U.S. Courts due to U.S. federal courts' lack of a satisfactory response to these allegations of human rights abuse facing detainees in Guantanamo. The leading Supreme Court cases addressing the rights of these detainees demonstrate that despite the demands of the United States Constitution, U.S. courts have proven to be an unsuccessful venue for the realization of US obligations under human rights and IHL toward these detainees.[135] Thus, detainees' advocates presented the Commission with a request for Precautionary Measures against the U.S., filed on behalf of some 300 persons who were transferred to Guantánamo Bay from Afghanistan and elsewhere, and were being held there as 'unlawful

---

[133] American Declaration of Rights of Man, Organization of American States, American Declaration of the Rights and Duties of Man, Articles. XVIII, XXV, XXVI, Apr. 30, 1948, Hein's No. KAV 7225. Charter of the Organization of American States, Apr. 30, 1948, 2 U.S.T. 2394 (entered into force Dec. 13, 1951) (ratified by the United States, June 15, 1951); amended by Protocol of Buenos Aires, 721 U.N.T.S. 324, O.A.S. Treaty Series, No. 1-A (entered into force Feb. 27, 1970); amended by Protocol of Cartagena, O.A.S. Treaty Series, No. 66, 25 I.L.M. 527 (entered into force Nov. 16, 1988); amended by Protocol of Washington, 1-E Rev. OEA Documentos Oficiales OEA/Ser.A/2 Add. 3 (SEPF), 33 I.L.M. 1005 (entered into force Sept. 25, 1997); amended by Protocol of Managua, 1-F Rev. OEA Documentos Oficiales OEA/Ser.A/2 Add.4 (SEPF), 33 I.L.M. 1009 (entered into force Jan. 29, 1996). See *also* IACHR Case 9647 Roach v. United States [1987] Resolution No. 3/87, OEA/Ser.L/V/II.71, doc. 9 rev. 1, para 46; IACHR Petition 8-03 Smith v. United States [2006] Report No. 56/06, OEA/Ser.L/VII.127, doc. 4 rev. 1, paras 32–33.

[134] University of Minnesota Human Rights Library (2002) Detainees in Guantanamo Bay, Cuba; Request for Precautionary Measures, Inter-Am. C.H.R. http://www1.umn.edu/humanrts/cases/guantanamo-2003.html. Accessed 29 Sept. 2013.

[135] Boumediene v. Bush, 553 U.S. 723, 732, 792 (2008) (holding that detained individuals in Guantanamo Bay have the constitutional right to file petitions for habeas corpus proceedings and challenge the legality of their detention and finding that "the constitutional privilege of habeas corpus" extends to aliens detained as enemy combatants at Guantanamo); Al-Bihani v. Obama, No. 09-5051, LEXIS 102, at *871 (D.C. Cir. Jan. 5, 2010) (deciding not to engage in an assessment of international law and laws of war or "quibble over the intricate application of vague treaty provisions and amorphous customary principles"); Final Report: Guantanamo Review Task Force (2010) 2–3 http://www.justice.gov/ag/guantanamo-review-final-report.pdf Accessed 17 Sept. 2013 (demonstrating detainees remained in jurisdictional limbo as 48 detainees "determined to be too dangerous for transfer but not feasible for prosecution," and 30 Yemeni detainees were kept in "conditional" detention "based on the current security environment in that country").

combatants.'[136] Specifically, the request sought to protect the detainees' right to be treated as prisoners of war under the Geneva Conventions, to be free from arbitrary, incommunicado and prolonged detention, and to not be subject to unlawful interrogations and trials by military commissions in which they could be sentenced to death.[137]

In its response to this petition, the Commission found that as a signatory to the American Declaration on the Rights of Man, the U.S. had violated certain articles of the declaration that ensured the right to a fair trial, due process and protection from arbitrary arrest. Further, the Commission evaluated the rights of Guantanamo detainees within the context of IHL as *lex specialis*, given first, that "the respondent in this situation is responsible for relocating an individual to an area of its effective control or occupation, thus implying that IHL may be applied in this instance," and second, that particular rights guaranteed under the American Declaration, such as the right to liberty, may take on distinct meaning in a situation of armed conflict as opposed to a time of peace.[138]

The U.S. response to this request for precautionary measures garnered much attention because it revealed—for the first time—the U.S. legal posture toward detainees in Guantanamo Bay. The U.S. claimed that, in the first place, as a human rights body, the IACHR had no competence to apply humanitarian law even as *lex specialis*.[139] In the alternative, it argued, precautionary measures were unnecessary because the captured individuals, as "unlawful combatants," were disqualified from protection under the Geneva Conventions.[140] As such, the conditions of their detention at Guantanamo could not violate IHL.

The Commission, in its response to the U.S., reiterated that international law "dictates that it may be necessary…to deduce the applicable human rights standard by reference to IHL as the applicable *lex specialis,*" and emphasized that "in *all* circumstances, the minimum regime of non-derogable human rights remain applicable and subject to supervision by the Commission."[141] This approach was reinforced in 2003 with the issuance of the Commission's report on Terrorism and

---

[136] United States (2002) Response of the United States to Request for Precautionary Measures—Detainees in Guantanamo Bay, Cuba, reprinted in 41 I.L.M. 1015, p. 1022.

[137] University of Minnesota Human Rights Library (2002) Detainees in Guantanamo Bay, Cuba; Request for Precautionary Measures, Inter-Am. C.H.R. http://www1.umn.edu/humanrts/cases/guantanamo-2003.html. Accessed 15 July 2013.

[138] Ibid.

[139] United States (2002) Response of the United States to Request for Precautionary Measures—Detainees in Guantanamo Bay, Cuba, reprinted in 41 I.L.M. 1015, p. 1022.

[140] Ibid. p. 3.

[141] University of Minnesota Human Rights Library (2002) Detainees in Guantanamo Bay, Cuba; Request for Precautionary Measures, Inter-Am. C.H.R. http://www1.umn.edu/humanrts/cases/guantanamo-2003.html. Accessed 15 July 2013. 112 Id. (emphasis added). Note that one of the non-derogable rights in the Inter-American system is the judicial remedy of *habeas corpus*. IACtHR (1987) Habeas Corpus in Emergency Situations (Articles 27(2) and 7(6) of the ACHR), Advisory Opinion (ser. A) No. 8.

Human Rights.[142] There, the Commission reiterated that it had the competence to apply IHL as *lex specialis* in instances in which there was a potential breach of Articles 27 or 29.[143]

This recent chapter in the Commission's jurisprudence reveals the on-going role of IHL within the Americas as the Commission continues to utilize one of the two approaches to IHL that it had taken in its initial 1997 analysis of the law. Although the Commission has not, as it did in the era of *Avilán* and *Abella*, considered itself capable of finding violations of IHL in the respondent states, it has continued to use IHL as an interpretive device to assist in evaluating violations of HRL. In contexts such as Guantanamo, IHL provides particularly useful interpretive guidance for how fair trial protections should function, under ACHR Article 8.[144] It also provides important guidance with regard to the ACHR Article 7 prohibition against arbitrary arrest or detention. In its analysis of these protections, the Commission utilized a definition of "arbitrary" informed by IHL, rather than that of HRL. IHL authorizes the detention of combatants during international armed conflicts; therefore, there would be no need to derogate from Article 7 of the ACHR in order to detain an enemy combatant. As explained by Robert Goldman, "[t]he commission in this context looks to IHL as *lex specialis* and finds that, since permissible under the laws of IHL, under Article 7 of the ACHR, these detentions then do not constitute "arbitrary" detentions."[145] With regard to prisoners of war, however, IHL does not provide the same protections for a right to trial as does HRL. The Commission recognizes that POWs are not entitled "to be informed of the reasons for their detention, to challenge the legality of their detention, or, in the absence of disciplinary or criminal proceedings, to be provided with access to legal counsel."[146]

The finding that POWs' right to trial receives less protection under IHL than that of non-POWs under HRL constitutes a carve-out from the rights typically granted under *habeus corpus* law in the ACHR. This is an especially stark contrast when compared to HRL, considering that the Inter-American Court has found that although Article 7 may be derogable, the procedural safeguards of *habeas corpus* and *amparo* cannot be derogated from during emergencies.[147]

---

[142] IACHR Report on Terrorism and Human Rights, paras 29, 78. http://www.cidh.org/Terrorism/Eng/toc.htm. Accessed 31 June 2013.

[143] *Id.* para 62 ("It is therefore appropriate, and indeed imperative, for the Commission to consider all relevant international norms, including those of international humanitarian law, while interpreting the international human rights law instruments for which it is responsible."

[144] Additional Protocol I Article 75(4) ("No sentence may be passed and no penalty may be executed on a person found guilty of a penal offense related to the armed conflict except pursuant to a conviction pronounced by an impartial and regularly constituted court respecting the generally recognized principles of regular judicial procedure").

[145] Goldman 2013, p. 118.

[146] IACHR Report on Terrorism and Human Rights, para 142. http://www.cidh.org/Terrorism/Eng/toc.htm. Accessed 31 June 2013.

[147] *Judicial Guarantees in States of Emergency, Articles 27(2), 25 and 8 of the American Convention on Human Rights,* IACtHR, Advisory Opinion, 6 October 1987.

The Commission tempered its position that POWs' treatment is exclusively governed by IHL, though, by indicating that in situations of uncertain duration, protections of IHL might not suffice, and might prove inadequate to safeguard the personal liberty of detainees:

> Notwithstanding the existence of these specific rules and mechanisms governing the detention of persons in situations of armed conflict, there may be circumstances in which the supervising mechanisms under IHL are not properly engaged or available, or where the detention or internment of civilians or combatants continue [sic] for a prolonged period of time. Where this occurs, the minimum safeguards of IHL may prove inadequate to properly safeguard the minimum standards of detainee treatment.[148]

The Commission's evaluation, therefore, is not based on a strict rule that the existence of armed conflict results in the unambiguous application of IHL norms. Instead, the Commission seeks to balance IHL and HRL, and recognizes the element of uncertainty of length of detention as a key factor in determining when and if protections under IHL are insufficient. This analysis proved central in the issuance of precautionary measures in the case of Guantanamo; the Commission evaluated a number of mitigating factors, such as the length and conditions of detention, yet was so concerned with the conditions that it relied on the stronger protections of HRL rather than IHL.

8.5 Evaluating the Use of IHL Within the IAHR System

In addition to the rationale articulated by the Inter-American Commission in defense of its use of IHL, other large-scale factors emerge, weighing either in support or against the use of IHL by human rights bodies generally. Some of these arguments weigh factors including the lack of enforcement options, concern about jurisdiction, expertise of the adjudicatory bodies, and the nature of IHL itself. Scholars who engage in these conversations do not always distinguish between reference to a direct application of IHL, or to IHL as an interpretive reference.[149] This distinction, however, is a crucial one because it is relevant to concerns regarding jurisdiction and the nature of international treaty obligations under international law.

Perhaps one of the most important factors that may underlie the Commission's rationale for use of IHL is never explicitly expressed: the need for global mechanisms capable of enforcement of IHL. Do the Commission and the Court have an obligation, as the preeminent regional adjudicative bodies in the Americas, to promote the enforcement of IHL in the hemisphere? It is certainly possible to interpret the Commission's reliance on Article 29(d) as articulating this concern. If

---

148 IACHR Report on Terrorism and Human Rights, para 14. http://www.cidh.org/Terrorism/Eng/toc.htm. Accessed 31 June 2013.

149 See for example, Hathaway et al. 2012.

the judicial organs of the IASHR, according to the statute, are precluded from ruling in a manner that would be inconsistent with other legal obligations of states, then perhaps they must ensure that other obligations, including IHL, are not violated.

As discussed earlier, the lack of enforcement mechanisms available for IHL is perceived as one of its key weaknesses. Although one proposed solution to this problem is the creation of an IHL-specific adjudicatory instrument, it is also reasonable to assume that integration of IHL and HRL will lead to better state enforcement of IHL through clarification and interpretation of these norms. This application might be especially relevant in circumstances of internal armed conflict, when a human rights body already has jurisdiction to hear a case against a state and is already engaged with facts that may trigger IHL.[150] One author suggests that reference by human rights bodies to IHL serves to reinforce the observance of IHL, even though these bodies may never determine whether violations have occurred.[151]

Consideration of the relevance of IHL may be important simply as a reminder to states of their humanitarian law obligations. Indeed, awareness of IHL may be more crucial than actual enforcement mechanisms with teeth, if we take literally Harold Koh's claim that "[l]ike most laws, international laws are rarely enforced, but usually obeyed".[152] Also, because there are a limited array of options for enforcement of IHL, the practice of human rights bodies who use IHL, whether directly applying it or using it only as guidance, has the potential to strengthen states' compliance with IHL.[153] This may also reinforce the duty of states to prosecute domestically those who have breached IHL.[154]

Efficiency may also dictate that human rights organs consider IHL in their deliberations. Resources for adjudication of international law are extremely limited, and most regional human rights tribunals suffer from a lack of resources and a tremendous backlog of cases awaiting evaluation.[155] Further, the fragmentation of international law has led to the possibility that the same set of facts could be adjudicated at a variety of tribunals, lessening efficiency and the likelihood of compliance. If a human rights body is already evaluating a set of facts for compliance with HRL, and assuming that adequate and balanced analysis of IHL is possible by the tribunal, it is certainly more efficient for one tribunal to consider the same set of facts than for various bodies to consider it. Indeed, if two tribunals consider the same set of facts, they may arrive at contradictory outcomes, reinforcing one of the principal concerns regarding fragmentation of international law.

---

150 Moir 2003. Moir argues that better state self-regulation may ensue from consideration of IHL by human rights tribunals.

151 O'Donnell 1998, pp. 485–486.

152 Koh 1996 p. 2603.

153 Heintze 2004, p. 797.

154 Byron 2006–2007, p. 877.

155 Dulitzky 2011.

The IAHR System's consideration of IHL may indeed be required under the ACHR. Article 25 of the ACHR dictates that state parties provide a remedy for any breaches of the Convention.[156] It can be argued, as did the Commission in *Abella*, that in enforcing Article 25, the Inter-American system is obligated to uphold IHL, otherwise, individual victims of humanitarian law violations have no recourse through domestic courts. The Court, in *Velazquez Rodriguez*,[157] emphasized the need for the state to investigate and prosecute those responsible for human rights violations, holding that "[t]he State has a legal duty to take reasonable steps to prevent human rights violations and to use the means at its disposal to carry out a serious investigation of violations committed within its jurisdiction, to identify those responsible, to impose the appropriate punishment and to ensure the victim adequate compensation. …"[158] This holding may have positive repercussions for IHL—if the IACHR increases pressure on states to prosecute and investigate members of their armed forces who torture and murder in the context of an armed conflict, they may effectively be forced to increase their own self-compliance with the Geneva Conventions.

One of the Commission's most compelling arguments for the use of IHL as an interpretive reference as opposed to the direct application thereof, is that in order to carry out its mandate of interpreting the ACHR during armed conflict, finders of fact benefit from additional guidance offered by IHL. The Commission has explained that some features of IHL may be crucial to legal interpretation in a conflict situation, such as the capacity to distinguish between non-combatants and other legitimate military targets.[159] It observed that, "the provisions of conventional and customary humanitarian law generally afford victims of armed conflicts greater or more specific protections than do the more generally phrased guarantees in the American Convention and other human rights instruments."[160] Therefore, when IHL is utilized as interpretive reference, ideally all parties involved benefit from a more nuanced understanding of the interplay between the two areas of law. Elucidation of these principles and the distinctions should be permitted to provide context to finders of fact and they should benefit from the insights from this branch of international law, even if the statute does not explicitly grant competence to find violations thereof.

Principles of international treaty interpretation between states do not provide a clear resolution as to whether IHL should be applied by the human rights bodies of the IAHRS. Article 44 of the ACHR provides that only denunciations or complaints of violations to the treaty itself can provide a basis for proceedings. Thus, it

---

156 American Convention on Human Rights *supra* note 114, Article 25.

157 IACtHR Velasquez Rodriguez Case [1988] (ser. C) No. 4, para 155.

158 IACtHR Velasquez Rodriguez Case [1988] (ser. C) No. 4.

159 IACHR, Case 11.137 Abella v. Argentina [1997] Report No. 55/97, 271, OEA/ Ser.L/V/II.98, doc. 6 rev., para 161; see *also* IACHR Case 10.480 Parada Cea v. El Salvador [1999] Report No. 1/99, OEA/Ser.L./V/II.102 doc. 6 rev. 165.

160 IACHR Case 11.137 Abella v. Argentina [1997] Report No. 55/97, 271, OEA/ Ser.L/V/II.98, doc. 6 rev., para 161.

appears that *prima facie*, it is impossible for the Commission to examine any normative behavior outside that described in its constitutive instrument. This would constitute a violation under the VCLT, which promulgates the norm of "express consent," allowing evaluation of states' behavior under a treaty only if the state has consented to be bound by that treaty.[161] Furthermore, the Court in *Las Palmeras* cited Article 62.3 of the ACHR to reinforce states' obligations only to norms to which they have previously committed:

> The American Convention is an international treaty according to which States Parties are obliged to respect the rights and freedoms embodied in it and to guarantee their exercise to all persons subject to their jurisdiction. The Convention provides for the existence of the Inter-American Court to hear "all cases concerning the interpretation and application" of its provisions.[162]

This concern, articulated by the Court, may be all the more relevant today, considering the current crisis within the Inter-American system as more and more states express concerns about its viability and its impartiality.[163] Importantly, however, within the IASHR, it is not that states have not committed to norms under IHL, rather, they have not consented to evaluation of their compliance at a body with binding jurisdiction. This distinction links directly to questions about enforcement, namely, if a state is willing to comply with a treaty, but is not willing to comply with a treaty under binding jurisdiction, the sincerity of its commitment to the intent and purpose of that treaty might be called into question.

Although the VCLT cannot oblige states to comply with treaties to which they are not party, it does require treaty parties interpreting their obligations to take into account "any relevant rules of international law applicable in the relations between the parties."[164] Article 29 of the ACHR contains a similar proscription. These provisions provide rationale that in contexts in which IHL may be relevant, it should be included in the deliberations of the adjudicative body. Alexsander Orakhelashvili claims that

> "the subjects governed by one body of law are frequently also governed by the other body of law, whatever the formal and procedural constraints on the powers of national and international decision-making bodies, in the exercise of their mandate they are expected, at least by implication, to consider the impact of both HRL and humanitarian law, to reach the outcomes permissible at the level of international law."[165]

---

161 Vienna Convention on the Law of Treaties. 1115 UNTS 331. http://untreaty.un.org/ilc/texts/instruments/english/conventions/1_1_1969.pdf. Accessed 13 July 2013.

162 IACtHR (2000) Las Palmeras Case, Judgment on Preliminary Objections of February 4, 2000, Inter-Am. Ct. H.R. (Ser. C) No. 67, pp. 60–61, para 32.

163 During the October 2012 Sessions of the IACHR, states gathered to discuss the crisis in the Inter-American system, changes to the system etc. (CITE to press releases from IACHR).

164 Vienna Convention on the Law of Treaties. 1115 UNTS 331. http://untreaty.un.org/ilc/texts/instruments/english/conventions/1_1_1969.pdf. Accessed 13 July 2013.

165 Orakhelashvili 2008, p. 168.

Further, as Emiliano Buis indicates, any given state is always responsible for respecting both IHL and HRL in accordance with all of its international obligations.[166] A key distinction must be recalled: although a state may be obligated to respect IHL, this does not imply that any monitoring or supervisory instrument has competence to adjudicate possible breaches of IHL without state consent.

Lack of expertise has also been cited as rationale that human rights bodies should not adjudicate IHL claims. Meron, for example, has expressed concern that a lack of expertise may result in "conclusions that humanitarian law experts find problematic."[167] Others have proposed that if the same adjudicative bodies analyze both IHL and HRL with an integrated approach, the result might lead to greater confusion. One potential outcome might be a muddying of the bright lines within IHL that provide crucial guidance to military personnel on the battlefield who require quick and clear answers to life-or-death situations.[168] HRL may set unrealistically high standards that are not feasible to evaluate in this context. Rene Provost also fears that human rights bodies may slant their interpretation of IHL unduly in the direction of HRL, since those bodies are expert in interpretation of HRL.[169] Perhaps in recognition of these valid concerns, the Inter-American system has offered substantive trainings in IHL for its staff and members.[170] Yet, whether adjudicative bodies use IHL as an interpretive device, or are directly applying it and finding violations thereof, lack of expertise in this complex field of law can pose problems. Assuming that the IAHRS ceases to directly apply IHL, even if applied as *lex specialis*, in order to do so adjudicators need to determine when IHL is triggered. The determination of whether an armed conflict or occupation exists is determined by relatively well-established standards of international law, but there are still gray areas that benefit from close attention and expertise.[171] If the

[166] Buis 2008, p. 274.

[167] Meron 2000, p. 247.

[168] Garraway, "To Kill or Not to Kill?" Dilemmas on the Use of Force, referenced in Happold 2010.

[169] Provost 2005, pp. 349–350.

[170] See IACtHR Annual Report (2002), OEA/Ser.L/ V/III.57, doc. 5 *(111)45* (2003), which refers to the "Second Study and Exchange Workshop on International Humanitarian Law (IHL) and Related Issues."

[171] Broad scholarship exists here discussing the establishment of armed conflict or occupation. See *generally,* Anthony Cullen, *Key Developments Affecting the Scope of Internal Armed Conflict in International Humanitarian Law*, 183 Mil Law Rev 66, 69–77 (2005) (distinguishing rebellion and insurgency from belligerency and internal armed conflict which is capable of invoking rights and obligations under IHL); John A Cohan, *Legal War: When Does it Exist, and When does it End?* 27 Hastings Int Comp L Rev 221, 223–224 (2003–2004) (assessing the existence of a war in the legal sense and whether wartime legislation and obligations are triggered); Theodor Meron, *Classification of Armed Conflict in the Former Yugoslavia: Nicaragua's Fallout*, 92 Am J Int Law 236, 241 (criticizing the characterization of armed conflict following the ICJ decision in Nicaragua and argues that "the reality, dimensions, scope and duration of a foreign military intervention, the foreign state's direct involvement in the conflict…the relative involvement of local and foreign forces, and…factual and military considerations" should determine the existence of armed conflict).

Commission or Court were to inadequately determine whether armed conflict or occupation exists in the first place, this might also undermine the efficacy of their subsequent determination of HRL violations.

Another significant concern of a human rights tribunal's application of IHL stems from a central tenant of the field: IHL must be applied between equal parties, with equal rights and equal duties. Indeed, Rene Provost finds this concept of reciprocity to be so central to IHL that he claims IHL is not applicable in non-international armed conflict, only in international armed conflict.[172] Thus, when IHL is considered at a tribunal that only has jurisdiction over states, that tribunal's application of IHL will necessarily be imbalanced. This concern was demonstrated in the *Abella* decision.[173] There, the Commission found itself competent to apply IHL directly, yet it was forced to limit its application of IHL to the conduct of the Argentine state. Therefore, it was incapable of evaluating the actions of the armed opposition group in conflict with the state, although it was clear that the conflict occurred between the state and the armed group of attackers. In its decision, the Commission went so far as to observe that both the state and the opposition group had obligations under IHL, yet the limitations within the Commission's *ratione personae* jurisdiction resulted in an imbalanced application of IHL. In an attempt to recognize this imbalance, the Commission has gone so far as to monitor the conduct of non-state actors under its power to examine the general situation of human rights in a particular state.[174] In a report on the situation in Colombia, for example, the Commission recognized that many actors, including non-state actors, contribute to the situation of violence there.[175] Yet, a purists IHL analysis would still find this analysis problematic, because at a judicial body dedicated to enforcing human rights obligations upon a state, a non-state actor will never have equal standing.

It is not entirely clear what parties benefit when IHL is applied. Orakhelashvili challenges the commonly held notion that HRL necessarily offers greater protection for civilians; indeed, there are several examples in the IACHR's jurisprudence where the opposite is true.[176] In *Abella* for instance, individual combatants were granted less protection under IHL than they would have been if only HRL applied. Through the application of IHL as an interpretive device, the Commission defined the petitioners as combatants, meaning that under IHL the State had a valid right to derogate from the right to life, and thus was not held accountable for their deaths. This demonstrates that petitioners to the Inter-American system should not assume that employment of IHL by the Commission is always in their best interest, or always puts states in a more vulnerable position.

---

[172] Provost 2005, p. 161.

[173] See generally Zegveld 1998.

[174] Martin and Rodríguez-Pinzón 2006, p. 148.

[175] Inter-Am. C.H.R., *Third Report on the Human Rights Situation in Colombia,* OEA/Ser.L/V/II.102 Doc. 9 rev. 1, February 26, 1999, Chap. 1, paras 1–6.

[176] Orakhelashvili 2008.

Although the "express consent" argument defending a state's obligation to be evaluated at the IAHRS only for the laws that it has consented to is valid,[177] *Abella* demonstrates that occasionally, a human rights body's use of IHL may benefit a state's position as respondent, rather than exposing that state to a more legally vulnerable position.

8.6 Conclusion

This chapter has explored the complexities that arise when the Inter-American System of Human Rights is confronted with situations which may give rise not only to the application of international HRL, but also of IHL. As demonstrated, IHL has been incorporated into the jurisprudence of the IASHR in two primary means. When it was initially asked by petitioners to adjudicate on cases involving armed conflict, the Commission saw it fit to directly apply IHL to a set of facts. In those limited instances, the Commission found itself capable of determining that states had violated their obligations under IHL. Second, both the Commission and the Court have applied IHL as an interpretive reference, utilizing it as *lex specialis* to provide added context to the interpretation of HRL during conflict situations. This practice has proven especially useful to the organs of the IASHR in situations such as those discussed above, involving interpretation of legal concepts for which the meaning may be significantly altered during armed conflict. This second approach is decidedly less controversial than the first approach, as it is theoretically in line with direction from the ICJ regarding the interrelationship between IHL and HRL, although no practical guidance was offered as to how this interplay should operate in practice. A review of the cases in which IHL has been considered within the IASHR reveals that the Court's interpretation of jurisdiction *ratione materiae*, as codified in the ACHR, results in the limited scope of IHL's *lex specialis* within the Inter-American System. As a result, direct application of IHL is not considered within the scope of the Court of the Commission. Use of IHL as an interpretive tool is permitted.

In seeking to clarify the System's two approaches to the integration of IHL within a human-rights based system, this chapter emphasizes the important distinction between application of IHL and reference to IHL. It is an oversimplification of the jurisprudence to simply state that the IASHR should, or should not, not employ IHL. The distinction between the two approaches is crucial. This chapter posits that there is no legal rationale preventing the use of IHL as an interpretive reference. As has been articulated by both the Court and the Commission, when these judicial organs consult IHL as an interpretive reference, they do so not to find countries in violation

[177] Infra Sect. 8.3.2, p. 10 (discussing the Vienna Convention on the Law of Treaties prohibiting the enforcement of treaty obligations on States who have not consented to be bound, "Noting that the principles of free consent and of good faith and the *pacta sunt servanda* rule are universally recognized" preamble).

of IHL, but instead, seek to use IHL in order to bring greater precision to their holdings on violations of international HRL within the context of armed conflict or occupation. One caution regarding IACHR and the Court's use of IHL as an interpretive reference is that expertise, as discussed above, may be lacking in the IASHR in this arena. Even if these organs do not seek to find direct violations of IHL, a lack of expertise may lead to misunderstandings in references of IHL. This concern, however, is not so problematic as to imply that IHL should not be utilized in this matter, yet it should serve as a cautious reminder.

Direct application of IHL is without a doubt the more complicated and controversial approach. Due to the lack of other enforcement mechanisms, if it is not directly applied by the IAHRS, it is unlikely that IHL would be directly applied at any other forum to hold countries accountable in the Americas. Thus, it is reasonable that advocates, or Commission members, may have believed that failures to apply IHL constitute missed opportunities for further development of this jurisprudence. Indeed, if the IASHR is already engaged in the examination of a set of facts that give rise to the use of IHL as an interpretive reference, efficiency argues that they should also then consider and have the capacity to find violations of IHL.

Even more provocative is the question of whether the direct application of IHL by a judicial body makes any difference – does it matter? This chapter argues that the use of IHL as an interpretive reference, though it renders a judicial body unable to find a direct violation of IHL, serves a similarly important purpose, and therefore, it may not matter that the Court in *Las Palmeras* prevented the Commission from continuing to find direct violations of IHL. For example, in *Bámaca Velazquez*, the Court held that it lacked competence to find violations of IHL. Yet, it did permit reference to IHL as an interpretive reference, stating, "[t]he relevant provisions of the Geneva Conventions may be taken into considerations as elements for the interpretation of the American Convention."[178] This reference to Geneva Conventions, though it does not explicitly find that IHL has been violated, is enormously powerful by reference alone. Once an adjudicative body refers to IHL in this manner, it has flagged that a situation exists which gives rise to the application of IHL. This reference to IHL serves as an important reminder to state parties that the laws of war are at play and must not be violated. Perhaps reference to IHL, in and of itself, is sufficient as it achieves the goal of shining a light on a state's violations of this law. Thus, direct application by a tribunal is perhaps beneficial, but certainly not crucial.[179] From the perspective of enforcement of IHL, it symbolically appears important for the Court and Commission to have the competence to find direct violations of IHL. Yet, the benefits to considering IHL as an interpretive reference alone are so significant, that this utilization of IHL may be just as influential, if less controversial, than direct application of IHL.

---

[178] IACtHR Judgment [2000] Bámaca Velásquez v. Guatemala Series C No. 70, para 209.

[179] Zegveld 1998, p. 509, makes a similar claim: "it is not obvious that the aim of protection can only be achieved by applying international humanitarian law. Would it not have sufficed for the Commission to apply provisions of the American Convention interpreted in the light of international humanitarian law."

Reference to IHL also ensures that states are made aware in a public forum of their obligations under IHL. This may continue to promote the self-monitoring of IHL by states during conflict. For example, in *Las Palmeras*, when the Commission attempted to evaluate violations of IHL, Colombia never questioned that the situation under examination gave rise to IHL, or that it was obligated to comply with certain obligations under IHL. Further, reference to IHL benefits and reinforces the ACHR, as there are clearly circumstances in which the human rights delineated in the Convention benefit from clarification offered by IHL.

For over a decade, since the Court's rebuke of the Commission's application of IHL in *Las Palmeras*, both the Commission and the Court have limited their use of IHL to interpretation, not application, of the law of war. The Court's evaluation of jurisdiction *ratione materiae* as excluding the application of IHL within the IAHRS has resulted in this strict approach. Thus, in the IAHR system, the institutional and procedural constraints have dominated the conversation regarding IHL more so than a substantive debate about the way in which the two bodies of law intersect.

Might this pattern shift in the future? What circumstances might prompt the Commission to return to its application of IHL? Although the Commission's application of IHL in several early cases was criticized by many scholars, and by the majority of the Court as well, this approach should not be dismissed as a fringe approach. Indeed, not only were the distinguished scholars who comprised the Commission in favor of the direct application of IHL, but so too members of the Court itself. Judge Cançado Trindade, who was at the time President of the Court, approved of the Commission's approach in his separate opinion which he described as a "coextensive interpretation and application of Article 4 of the ACHR and of Article 3 common to the four Geneva Conventions on IHL."[180]

It is possible that situations will arise in which the Court becomes more approving of the application of IHL, but these would require extreme circumstances. For example, were the International Law Commission to take a position on this issue, or were the ICJ to further elaborate upon its recommendations regarding the overlap of the two areas of law, or were the state parties to the OAS to amend the statute reflecting a desire for enforcement of IHL in the Americas, a change in the interpretation of the *rationae materie* might be feasible. It would likely take extreme circumstances such as these for the Court to change its approach to the application of IHL. The Commission's language in recent cases regarding the egregious situation in Guantanamo has already proven so similar to Judge Cançado Trindade's separate opinion that it is not unimaginable that the Commission would decide to revert to its previous position. Despite this, for the time being, in considering cases that arise during armed conflict, the Inter-American System's interpretation of humanitarian law is restricted by the Court's strict reading of its jurisdiction *ratione materiae*. This legalistic approach results in a system that is hamstrung from finding direct state violations of the law of war.

---

[180] Las Palmeras, Cançado Trindade, Separate opinion para 2.

Yet, the outcome is one that is politically viable, as no state can claim that its rights under the Vienna Convention are violated through the use of IHL as an interpretive reference, legally less controversial than direct application of IHL, and ultimately, effective in balancing the complicated interplay between state obligations under IHL and HRL in the face of the violent armed conflict that has plagued the continent for decades.

References

Bowring B (2009) Fragmentation, lex specialis and the tensions in the jurisprudence of the European Court of Human Rights. Univ Nottm J Confl Secur Law 14:485

Buergenthal T (1975) The revised OAS charter and the protection of human rights. AJIL 69:828

Buis E (2008) The implementation of international humanitarian law by human rights courts: the example of the Inter-American Human Rights System. In: Arnold R, Quenivet N (eds.) International humanitarian law and human rights law: towards a new merger in international law, Martinus Nijhoff Publishers, Boston, pp 277–302

Burgorgue-Larsen L, Ubeda de Torres A (2011) The Inter-American Court of Human Rights, case law and commentary. Oxford University Press, USA

Byron C (2006–2007) A blurring of boundaries: the application of international humanitarian law by international human rights bodies. Va J Int Law 47:839, 862

Caceres Brun J (2003) Aspectos destacados de la aplicacion del derecho internacional humanitario y de los derechos humanos. Lecciones y Ensayos 78:49

Cassese A (2001) International law. Oxford University Press, USA

Cerna C (2006) Out of bounds? The approach of the Inter-American system for the Promotion and Protection of Human Rights to the extraterritorial application of human rights law, CHRGJ Working Paper No. 6

Cleveland S (2010) Embedded international law and the constitution abroad. Colum Law Rev 111:225, 229, 248–270

Cryer R (2010) The interplay of human rights and humanitarian law: the approach of the ICTY, referenced in Happold M, introduction: symposium on the relationship between international humanitarian law and international human rights law. J Confl Secur Law 14:441

Darcy S (2003) The evolution of the law of belligerent reprisals. Mil Law Rev 175(184):199–216

Droege C (2008) Elective affinities? Human rights and humanitarian law. Int Rev Red Cross 871:501

Dulitzky A (2011) The Inter-American Human Rights System fifty years later: time for changes. Quebec J Int Law (Special Edition):127

Escorihuela A (2011) Humanitarian law and human rights law the politics of distinction. Mich St U Coll Law J Int Law 19:299

Gardam J (2001) The contribution of the International Court of Justice to international humanitarian law. Leiden J Int Law 14:353

Goldman R (2013) Extraterritorial application of the human right to life and personal liberty, including habeas corpus, during situations of armed conflict. In: Research handbook on human rights and humanitarian law. Edward Elgar, Cheltenham, UK, p 14

Greenwood C (1989) The twilight of the law of belligerent reprisals. Neth Yearb Int Law 20:35–69

Hampson F (2008) The relationship between international humanitarian law and international human rights law. Int Rev Red Cross 871:559

Happold M (2010) Symposium on the relationship between international humanitarian law and international human rights law. J Confl Secur Law 14:441

Hathaway Oona A et al (2012) Which law governs during armed conflict? The relationship between international humanitarian law and human rights law. Minn Law Rev 96:1883

Heintze H (2004) On the relationship between human rights law protection and international humanitarian law. Int Rev Red Cross 856(789):797

Holland E (2011) The qualification framework of international humanitarian law: too rigid to accommodate contemporary conflicts. Suffolk Transnatl Law Rev 34:145

Kleffner J, Zegveld L (2000) Establishing an individual complaints procedure for violations of international humanitarian law. Yearb Int Humanitarian Law 3:384

Koh H (1996–1997) Why do nations obey international law? Yale Law J 106:2602

Koskenniemi M (2006) Fragmentation of international law: difficulties arising from the diversification and expansion of international law. Report of the study group of the International Law Commission. A/CN.4/L.682, pp 13–14; para 5

Le Mon C (2002–2003) Unilateral intervention by invitation in civil wars: the Effective Control Test tested. NYU J Int Law Pol. 35:741

Martin F (2001) Application du droit international humanitaire par la Cour interaméricaine des droits de l'homme. Int Rev Red Cross 844:1037

Martin C, Rodríguez-Pinzón D (2006) The prohibition of torture in the Inter-American System of Human Rights. A handbook for victims and advocates

Meron T (2000) The humanization of humanitarian law. AJIL 94:239

Mitchell A (2001) Does one illegality merit another? the law of belligerent reprisals in international law. Mil Law Rev 170(155):164–170

Moir L (2003) Decommissioned? international humanitarian law and the Inter-American Human Rights System. Hum Rights Q 25:182

O'Donnell D (1998) Trends in the application of international humanitarian law by United Nations human rights mechanisms. Int Rev Red Cross 324(481):485–486

Orakhelashvili A (2008) The interaction between human rights and humanitarian law: fragmentation, conflict, parallelism, or convergence? EJIL 19:161

Pierce G (1980) Humanitarian protection for the victims of war: the system of protecting powers and the role of the ICRC. Mil Law Rev 90:89

Provost R (2005) International human rights and humanitarian law. Cambridge University Press, Cambridge, pp 349–50

Schindler D (1979) The International Committee of the Red Cross and human rights. Int Rev Red Cross 208:3

Scobbie I (2009) Principle or pragmatics? the relationship between human rights law and the law of armed conflict. In: Symposium: The Relationship between International Human Rights Law and International Humanitarian Law. J Confl Secur Law 14:449

Weissbrodt D (2009–2010) The role of the human rights committee in interpreting and developing humanitarian law. U Pa J Int Law 31:1185

Zegveld L (1998) The Inter-American Commission on Human Rights and international humanitarian law: a comment on the Tablada case. Int Rev Red Cross 38:505

Chapter 9
The European Court of Human Right's Engagement with International Humanitarian Law

Samuel Hartridge

Contents

S. Hartridge JD (Hons) is a Research Associate, Faculty of Law, University of New South Wales, Kensington, NSW 2052. The author would like to thank Associate Professor Christopher Michaelsen for his considerable advice and assistance in writing this chapter.

S. Hartridge (✉)
University of New South Wales, Kensington, NSW 2052, Australia
e-mail: sam.hartridge@gmail.com

D. Jinks et al. (eds.), *Applying International Humanitarian Law in Judicial and Quasi-Judicial Bodies*, DOI: 10.1007/978-94-6265-008-4_9,

9.1 Introduction

Since at least the Tehran Conference of 1968[1] there has been a growing recognition that international human rights law ("IHRL") applies in situations of armed conflict. Any doubt about this has largely been removed by the International Court of Justice ("ICJ") *Nuclear Weapons* advisory opinion,[2] but the exact nature of the relationship between IHRL and international humanitarian law ("IHL") is far from certain. This chapter will examine cases brought before the European Court of Human Rights ("ECtHR" or "the Court") that have arisen from situations of armed conflict and assesses the engagement of the Court with IHL. It will consider whether it was either open to or necessary for the Court to apply IHL in order to interpret rights under the European Convention on Human Rights ("ECHR" or "the Convention") and if so, whether the Court did, in fact, consider IHL. A survey of the leading judgments reveals a reluctance of the Court to engage with general principles and rules of IHL in order to give content to rights under the ECHR. This can either be seen as a missed opportunity to develop both legal regimes in a mutually supportive way or, alternatively, as an appropriate outcome of a court exercising a clearly defined jurisdiction.

The chapter begins with a brief exposition of the context in which the Court decides on violations of rights under the ECHR. The Court's jurisdiction is the interpretation of Convention rights and this means that there is no direct jurisdiction to consider IHL. However, the interpretive context in which the Court operates arguably requires at least some advertence to IHL. After a brief discussion of why this is so, the chapter will then proceed to examine particular cases that arise out of situations of armed conflict. The second section will discuss the case law on the general applicability of the Convention in situations of armed conflict, its extraterritorial application as well as its applicability in non-international armed conflicts ("NIACs") within the territory of a State Party. The final section will examine the substantive and procedural content of the right to life and the right to be free from arbitrary detention.

---

[1] Resolution XXIII "Human Rights in Armed Conflicts" adopted by the International Conference on Human Rights, Tehran, 12 May 1968; for a discussion of the relationship between the two disciplines, see Prud'Homme 2007, pp. 359–362.

[2] *Legality of the Threat or Use of Nuclear Weapons, Advisory Opinion*, [1996] ICJ Rep 226, 8th July 1996.

9.2 Interpretive Context: Why Should the European Court of Human Rights Consider IHL?

9.2.1 Conceptual Differences Between IHL and IHRL

At the outset, it is important to consider whether there is any reason for the ECtHR to consider IHL. When evaluating the treatment of IHL by the ECtHR, it is essential to note its lack of direct jurisdiction to apply or interpret this body of law. The Court's jurisdiction is generally limited to interpreting and applying the ECHR[3] and to awarding just satisfaction where a violation is found which has not been awarded appropriate compensation.[4] The Court does not have the power to determine State responsibility for breaches of IHL nor can it attribute individual criminal responsibility for war crimes or grave breaches of the Geneva Conventions. Thus a strict construction of the constituent instrument of the Court suggests that IHL is outside its purview.[5]

In addition to this apparent jurisdictional limit, there are fundamental differences between IHL and IHRL. While both bodies of law have a protective function, regulating the use of military force by states, the origins,[6] object and purpose of the two areas of law are different.[7] IHL was developed in the traditional public international law framework which focused primarily on the state's responsibility to other states. It is designed for application in armed conflict and seeks to balance the pursuit of legitimate military objectives with an obligation to prevent unnecessary suffering; in other words to support the protection of human dignity in armed conflict.[8] This is particularly so in the case of military occupation, wherein IHL gives the occupying state certain powers and rights as well as imposing obligations upon it.[9] Contrast this with IHRL, which speaks of the relationship between the individual and the state. The "fundamental concern" of IHRL is "regulating the essentially unequal relationship between state and individual"[10] and accordingly it circumscribes legitimate use of state power against those under that state's jurisdiction.

---

[3] European Convention on the Protection of Human Rights and Fundamental Freedoms, Nov. 4, 1950, 213 UNTS 221, Article 32.

[4] ECHR Article 41.

[5] Additionally, the textual opening through which IHL is made relevant to other human rights treaties, namely interpreting what constitutes *arbitrariness,* is foreclosed by the wording of relevant provisions; see below Sect. 9.5.

[6] Hampson and Salama 2005 at para 41.

[7] Prud'Homme 2007, p. 360.

[8] Schabas 2007; Doswald-Beck and Vité 1993, pp. 99–128: "The fundamental concepts of the laws of war ... are ... based on the balance between military necessity and humanity".

[9] Hampson 2008, p. 561; Benvenisti 2012

[10] Schabas 2007, p. 607; for a brief outline of the philosophical foundations of IHRL see Doswald-Beck and Vite 1993 at p. 5 of 17.

The conceptual foundation for each area of law is different and, accordingly, the legal frameworks are conceived of in different ways. William Schabas encapsulates the fundamental difference in the approach of the two legal regimes. He notes that "[i]nternational humanitarian law is predicated on an indifference to the origin of the conflict" whereas, for human rights lawyers, the "inquiry into whether killing in wartime amounts to arbitrary deprivation of life involves an assessment of … whether the use of force was compatible with the *jus ad bellum*."[11] Essentially IHL seeks to regulate the behaviour of combatants by divorcing that regulation from any overriding questions of legitimacy of the respective causes of either side. This means that each combatant is expected to comply with the laws of armed conflict. Conversely, IHRL assesses any use of lethal force by reference to certain enumerated aims that are considered normative. This means that human rights law only speaks of the legitimacy or otherwise of the state's actions.

There are also differences in the application and use of the law. IHL is supposed to be applied prospectively and is a framework to guide decision making.[12] It seeks to provide simple and understandable rules that can be applied in combat so as to minimise unnecessary suffering while still allowing military commanders to achieve their objectives. IHL is a "series of duties that combatants have to obey."[13] On the other hand, IHRL concentrates on the intrinsic value of the persons themselves. For that reason individuals can expect the benefit of certain freedoms and forms of protection from the state. As Doswald-Beck and Vite explain, IHL "indicates how a party to a conflict is to behave in relation to people at its mercy, whereas human rights law concentrates on the rights of the recipients of a certain treatment."[14] We can see this difference in the manner in which humanitarian law and human rights treaties are worded. The operative provisions of IHL are manifold and complex, whereas IHRL is framed in terms of general obligations and tends to be directed towards post hoc application.[15] The precise content of rights is usually derived from application of these general specific fact scenarios in order to determine if there has been a violation.[16]

Bearing all this in mind, it may be that striving to harmonise the two regimes is doomed to fail. Schabas notes, for instance, that "because of this conceptual difference between international human rights law and international humanitarian law, it is impossible to entirely reconcile the two systems."[17] So, in light of the Court's jurisdictional limits and the fundamental differences between IHL and IHRL, it is important to consider the question of why the ECtHR should consider IHL at all. Notwithstanding these seemingly intractable differences, there is an

[11] Schabas 2007, p. 593.
[12] Hampson 2008, p. 562.
[13] Doswald-Beck and Vité 1993, p. 7.
[14] Doswald-Beck and Vité 1993, pp. 4–5.
[15] Hampson 2008, p. 561.
[16] Doswald-Beck and Vité 1993, p. 7.
[17] Schabas 2007, p. 610.

unmistakeable interdependency between the two bodies of law. In armed conflict, both bodies of law seek to protect people by regulating the means and methods used by belligerents. In that sense, the application of one should influence the other.

9.2.2 Public International Law Context

There are a number of considerations which flow from the international context in which the Court operates to suggest some consideration of IHL is necessary. The foremost of these are the rules of treaty interpretation and the jurisprudence of the ICJ. As already noted, the Court has jurisdiction to interpret and apply the Convention. It does so using customary rules of treaty interpretation as codified by the Vienna Convention on the Law of Treaties ("VCLT").[18] Article 31(3) of the VCLT, for instance, requires that in interpreting treaty obligations, "[t]here shall be taken into account, together with the context...(c) any relevant rules of international law applicable in the relations between the parties." This rule of interpretation requires that the interpretive approach include some engagement of IHL when applying Convention rights. If nothing more, the rule suggests that the Court should prefer an interpretation of a Convention right that accords with or is not contrary to a right or obligation under IHL. To achieve such an outcome it would arguably be necessary to discuss those IHL obligations of states.

The ICJ has developed the relationship between IHL and IHRL in three influential judgments. The first case to deal with it directly was the *Nuclear Weapons* Advisory Opinion.[19] In dealing with the question of the applicability of the right to life under the International Covenant on Civil and Political Rights[20] ("ICCPR") in war, the Court observed:

> that the protection of the International Covenant on Civil and Political Rights does not cease in times of war ... In principle, the right not arbitrarily to be deprived of one's life applies also in hostilities. The test of what is an arbitrary deprivation of life, however, then falls to be determined by the applicable *lex specialis*, namely, the law applicable in armed conflict which is designed to regulate the conduct of hostilities. Thus whether a particular loss of life, through the use of a certain weapon in warfare, is to be considered an arbitrary deprivation of life contrary to Article 6 of the Covenant, can only be decided by reference to the law applicable in armed conflict and not deduced from the terms of the Covenant itself.[21]

---

[18] Vienna Convention on the Law of Treaties 23 May 1969 (entered into force 27 January 1980). 1155 UNTS 331.

[19] See, note 2.

[20] International Covenant on Civil and Political Rights, GA res 2200A (XXI), 21 UN GAOR Supp (No. 16), UN Doc A/6316 (1966); 999 UNTS 171.

[21] At para 25.

The *Wall* Advisory opinion[22] reiterated the concurrent applicability of the two bodies of law, decisively putting to rest the argument that IHL applies in war and IHRL applies in peace, to their mutual exclusion. The judgment also advanced the proposition of the extraterritorial application of human rights treaties. Ultimately, the ICJ found that Israel was in violations obligations under IHL and IHRL[23] which seems to have made detailed discussion of the interaction between the two superfluous. However, on this question, the ICJ found that:

> As regards the relationship between international humanitarian law and human rights law, there are[24] thus three possible situations: some rights may be exclusively matters of international humanitarian law; others may be exclusively matters of human rights law; yet others may be matters of both these branches of international law. In order to answer the question put to it, the Court will have to take into consideration both these branches of international law, namely human rights law and, as *lex specialis*, international humanitarian law.

The helpfulness of this remark is questionable[25] because it does not give clear guidance on how to resolve conflicting rules or even the precise nature of the *lex specialis* relationship.[26] However, it does slightly develop the position from *Nuclear Weapons*. And importantly for our purposes, it has been suggested that the judgment may be authority for the proposition that "human rights bodies should interpret a human rights norm in the light of [IHL]."[27] In the last of the relevant ICJ cases, *Armed Activities*[28] the ICJ notes that

> Uganda at all times has responsibility for all actions and omissions of its own military forces in the territory of the DRC [Democratic Republic of Congo] in breach of its obligations under the rules of international human rights law and international humanitarian law which are relevant and applicable in the specific situation.[29]

The importance of the *Armed Activities* case is twofold: first it is a contentious judgement, binding on the parties and second, it unambiguously forms part of the *ratio decidendi* of the case and is therefore, *res judicata*.[30]

---

[22] *Legal Consequences of the Construction of a Wall in the Occupied Palestinian Territory, Advisory Opinion,* [2004] ICJ Rep 136, 9th July 2004.

[23] Ibid at para 137.

[24] Ibid at para 106.

[25] Report of the expert meeting on the right to life in armed conflicts and situations of occupation, University Centre for International Humanitarian Law, Geneva, 1–2 September 2005, www.ucihl.org/communication/Right_to_Life_Meeting_Report.pdf cited in Doswald-Beck 2006.

[26] For the fact that this human rights-IHL nexus may in some cases not be subject to reconciliation, ultimately leading to non justiciability claims see Solomon 2009, p. 140.

[27] Hampson and Salama 2005, at para 57.

[28] *Case Concerning Armed Activities on the Territory of the Congo (DRC v. Uganda)* [2005] ICJ rep 116 Judgment of 19 December 2005.

[29] Ibid at para 180.

[30] Alston et al. 2008, p. 194.

In addition to the ICJ case law, there are a number of other important factors in relation to the legal context in which the Court operates. For example, it is relevant to note the position of the Human Rights Committee, which does not use the term *lex specialis*, but does take the view that "both spheres of law are complimentary, not mutually exclusive."[31] Additionally, this dual applicability is also evidenced by the increasing tendency of organisations such as Human Rights Watch applying IHL in their reports on the military actions of states.[32] There remains significant debate as to the precise ambit of the *lex specialis* doctrine, whether it is an appropriate way of conceiving the relationship and, more generally, how the two bodies of law interact.[33] Nonetheless, there are two clear points that can be established. The first is that both IHL and IHLR apply in situations of armed conflict. The second is that there is *some* interpretive relationship between the two, so that where they both operate, consideration of IHL should at least inform consideration of rights under IHRL. This approach has the advantage of lending "some unity and coherence to the otherwise fragmented standards governing armed conflicts."[34]

In many of the cases considered below, the ECtHR cites the three cases from the ICJ. The Court explicitly recognises that there is some kind of interdependence. While there is no express rejection of the *lex specialis* doctrine, neither is there any express application of it. The judgments evince a reluctance to engage with IHL where it would be appropriate or necessary to do so. In the cases that have come before the Court, the IHL dimension has primarily arisen in two ways. The first is NIACs, where an internal armed conflict is clearly occurring within the territorial boundary and jurisdiction of a Convention state. The second situation is violations resulting from foreign military interventions by states. These interventions involve the projection of military power outside the territorial limits of the state and therefore it is necessary to resolve the extent to which convention applies extraterritorially. Thus we now turn to the particular jurisprudence of the Court and the next section will analyse this question of extraterritorial application of the ECHR in situations of armed conflict.

---

[31] UN Human Rights Committee ("HRC"), General comment no. 31 [80], The nature of the general legal obligation imposed on States Parties to the Covenant, 26 May 2004, CCPR/C/21/Rev.1/Add.13, available at: http://www.refworld.org/docid/478b26ae2.html [accessed 18 October 2013]; as to the consensus see Alston et al. 2008, p. 197.

[32] For example Human Rights Watch 2007, Why They Died: Civilian Casualties in Lebanon during the 2006 War.

[33] McCosker 2013; Prud'Homme 2007; Schabas 2007.

[34] Abresch 2005.

9.3 Jurisdiction: Extraterritorial Application of the ECHR in Armed Conflicts

This section will examine the circumstances in which the ECHR is applicable in situations of armed conflict that occur outside the territory of Convention states. Under the ECHR, states are required to "secure to everyone within their *jurisdiction* the rights and freedoms."[35] This means that what constitutes the state's jurisdiction is a preliminary question that the Court is frequently confronted with and, unsurprisingly, this question is usually live when a Convention state intervenes militarily. As will be demonstrated below, not only are the bases for extending jurisdiction in situations of armed conflict unclear, the judgments are unwilling to deal with the overlap between IHL and IHRL. In these cases, the impugned acts were usually committed by the armed forces of the various respondent states operating outside their territorial boundaries and the Court needed to determine whether these actions were susceptible to its oversight.

The legal basis for the applicability of IHL in international armed conflicts is provided for in Common Article 2 of the Geneva Conventions.[36] It states:

> In addition to the provisions which shall be implemented in peacetime, the present Convention shall apply to all cases of declared war or of any other armed conflict which may arise between two or more of the High Contracting Parties, even if the state of war is not recognized by one of them.
>
> The Convention shall also apply to all cases of partial or total occupation of the territory of a High Contracting Party, even if the said occupation meets with no armed resistance.

There are two important points to keep in mind regarding Common Article 2. The first is that the threshold for applying IHL in inter-state conflict is relatively low; essentially any use of force by one state against another will engage IHL.[37] The second point, brought out in the second paragraph of the provision, is that IHL applies in situations of occupation. Where a state occupies territory of another state, IHL provides a comprehensive framework which regulates the rights and responsibilities of the occupying state.[38] These rules will apply once the state has *effective control* over the territory in question.[39] This is generally considered to be

---

[35] ECHR Article 1.

[36] Geneva Convention for the Amelioration of the Condition of the Wounded and Sick in Armed Forces in the Field, Aug. 12, 1949 75 UNTS 31; Geneva Convention for the Amelioration of the Condition of Wounded, Sick and Shipwrecked Members of Armed Forces at Sea, Aug. 12, 1949, 75 UNTS 85; Geneva Convention Relative to the Treatment; of Prisoners of War, Aug. 12, 1949, 75 UNTS 135; Geneva Convention Relative to the Protection of Civilian Persons in Time of War, Aug. 12, 1949, 75 UNTS 287 ("First Geneva Convention", "Second Geneva Convention", "Third Geneva Convention" and "Fourth Geneva Convention" respectively).

[37] See Melzer 2008, pp. 244–252.

[38] Benvenisti 2012.

[39] Benvenisti 2012 at para 1.

a question of fact[40] and the extent of the occupation will be limited to the areas where the occupying power is actually in control.[41] The state has the responsibility to restore and maintain public order and civil life[42] in the occupied territory and this forms the foundation for certain legislative and administrative powers.[43] This can be contrasted with one of the bases for establishing that a state is exercising *jurisdiction* so that the ECHR will apply, which is where that state is exercising *effective control over an area.* It is immediately apparent that the ECtHR has used very similar terminology and indicia to discuss this basis for the extraterritorial application of the Convention. Unfortunately, it does not discuss the relationship between the two tests nor explain why they are or should be different.

The *Loizidou*[44] case was an early leading case establishing the extraterritorial jurisdiction of a Convention state where that state was occupying territory of another Convention state. The case was a claim by a Cypriot citizen against the Turkish regarding its occupation of Northern Cyprus. In addressing the question of the extraterritorial application of the ECHR in this case, the Court made a statement that would have significance for all subsequent cases concerning the application of the ECHR in circumstances of belligerent occupation:

> The responsibility of Contracting States can be involved by acts and omissions of their authorities which produce effects outside their own territory. Of particular significance to the present case the … responsibility of a Contracting Party could also arise when as a consequence of military action — whether lawful or unlawful — it exercises effective control of an area outside its national territory. The obligation to secure, in such an area, the rights and freedoms set out in the Convention, derives from the fact of such control.[45]

It is important to recognise that the obligation derives from the *fact* of such control. Thus we see that, as with the IHL test, the IHRL test also requires a consideration of the factual situation to determine whether there is effective control. This passage could be authority for the proposition that if an (IHL) occupation is established then, *ipso facto*, the occupying state is exercising effective control for the purposes of the Convention. However, subsequent cases have demonstrated that this will not necessarily be the case.

In addition to establishing the framework of application of the extraterritorial application of the Convention, the *Louizidou* case is an early authority for the proposition that the ECHR should be interpreted in conjunction with IHL.

---

[40] Benvenisti 2012 at para 5.

[41] Ibid.

[42] Annex to Convention (IV) respecting the Laws and Customs of War on Land and its annex: Regulations concerning the Laws and Customs of War on Land. The Hague, 18 October 1907 Regulation 43, cf. Fourth Geneva Convention Article 64.

[43] See Sassoli 2004.

[44] App no. 15318/89, Judgment of 18 December 1996.

[45] At para 52, see also preliminary objections at para 62.

The judgments explicitly acknowledges the relevance of VCLT Article 31(3)(c) and noted that "[i]n the Court's view, the principles underlying the Convention cannot be interpreted and applied in a vacuum."[46]

9.3.1 Bankovic

The *Bankovic* case[47] was a claim that arose out of the NATO intervention in the Balkans in the late 1990s as a response to ethnic conflict in Kosovo. NATO initiated a campaign of airstrikes against Serbian forces operating in Kosovo and targets throughout the rest of Serbia such as command and control infrastructure. The application was made by relatives of victims of an attack by NATO aircraft on the Radio Televizije Srbije facilities in Belgrade.[48] In order to establish the claim the applicants needed to show that they came within the jurisdiction of the respondent states.

The applicants argued that the airstrike came within the responsibility of the respondent states because those states were exercising jurisdiction over the victims. This was advanced on a two alternative bases.[49] The first was that the "positive obligation under Article 1 ... to secure Convention rights would be proportionate to the level of control in fact exercised."[50] Thus where a state did not have effective control, it would be required to ensure such rights "within their control in the situation in question."[51] The applicants found support for this proposition in preceding case law, including the cases discussed above, and in Article 15(2) of the ECHR. This provision required derogation from the right to life in situations of armed conflict in order for deaths resulting from military actions to be lawful. This necessarily meant that the Convention was intended to apply to states engaging in such action extraterritorially. The second argument was in essence that the victims were under the jurisdiction of the governments in question because those governments had effective control *of the airspace* over Serbia. Such control was indicated by the impunity with which the NATO air forces operated.[52] The Court considered that this argument was basically a variation of the first.[53]

---

[46] At para 43.

[47] App no. 52207/99 Judgment of 12 December 2001.

[48] And another victim who was injured but survived.

[49] The third argument (at [53]) based on *Soering v. United Kingdom*, App no. 14038/88, proposed that the decision to launch the strike was made on the territory of the respondents and the consequent creation of extraterritorial effects bought the victims within jurisdiction. This was rejected by the court which found that the impugned act was the attack itself which was clearly extraterritorial, see [68].

[50] At para 46.

[51] At para 47.

[52] At para 52.

[53] At para 76.

The Court decided that the act of entering another state's airspace and killing a resident in that state was not sufficient to establish jurisdiction. This was because jurisdiction would only exist where either the state exercised effective control over the area in which the violation occurred[54] or "customary international law and treaty provisions have recognised the extra-territorial exercise of jurisdiction by the relevant State."[55] As for the argument that the obligation to secure Convention rights in proportion to the amount of control exercised, the Court rejected the proposition that rights under the Convention could be "divided and tailored in accordance with the particular circumstances of the extra-territorial act in question."[56]

The decision completely disregards the jurisdictional basis proposed in *Cyprus v. Turkey*.[57] This case stated that jurisdiction could be found where the agents of the state operating extraterritorially exercise authority or control over the victim. An application of such a test would establish jurisdiction in circumstances where the state plans and executes military action. The lawfulness of any deprivation of life resulting from that action would then be determined by reference to the laws of armed conflict. The judgment does not engage directly with IHL in any substantive way, however, it has significant implications for the application of IHL in armed conflict. The rejection of an alternative to effective control of an area as a basis for extraterritorial jurisdiction in armed conflict means that a state will not be subject to the Convention unless it is actually occupying foreign territory. The NATO operation was undoubtedly an armed conflict as defined by Common Article 2. Accordingly the expansive and detailed provisions of IHL regarding targeting would have been applicable. This would have been a paradigm case for applying the *Nuclear Weapons* approach. Accordingly, a finding of jurisdiction in this case would not have resulted in an unacceptable widening of the Courts remit[58] but would have improved the harmonisation of IHL and IHRL in the way envisaged by the ICJ jurisprudence and the rules of treaty interpretation.

There has been widespread criticism of the outcome in *Bankovic*,[59] and, as will be shown below, subsequent case law has changed the position to a certain extent.

---

[54] At para 71.

[55] At para 73.

[56] At para 75.

[57] Milanovic 2012, p. 123; Cyprus v. Turkey App nos. 6780/74 and 6950/75, 26 May 1975 "Authorised agents of a state, including [its] armed forces...bring any other persons "within the jurisdiction" of that that, to the extent that they exercise authority over such persons. Insofar as, by their acts or omissions, they affect such persons or property, the responsibility of the state is engaged" Cyprus v. Turkey App. Nos. 6780/74 and 6950/75, 26 May 1975; quoted in Lawson 2004. See also HRC in Lopez Burgos v. Uruguay, Communication No. R.12/52, UN Doc. Supp. No. 40 (A/36/40) at 176 (1981); General Comment No. 31.

[58] Milanovic, 2012, makes the convincing suggestion that the lack of consideration of a "state agent authority and control" basis for jurisdiction was because the Court was unable to find a non-arbitrary limitation that would achieve its unstated policy objectives, see p. 123.

[59] See Milanovic 2012 footnote 12.

However, *Bankovic* has not been expressly overturned and as such the judgment appears to create a concerning impunity gap for foreign military interventions by Convention states.

9.3.2 Issa, Issak and Pad

The next case that considered this question the extraterritorial application of the Convention in an armed conflict situation was *Issa*.[60] This case was an application by relatives of victims allegedly killed by the Turkish military in northern Iraq in 1995. The applicants alleged that the Turkish military had entered the area and detained the deceased, whose bodies were later found in a cave after the military had withdrawn. The Court held that a temporary occupation of the area by Turkish forces *could* have meant that Turkey was exercising jurisdiction for the purposes of the Convention. However, in contradistinction to *Loizidou* and despite the fact that similar numbers of troops were involved,[61] effective control was found not to have been established.[62] This was because of the limited timeframe of the Turkish incursion and, unlike Northern Cyprus, the area was not "constantly patrolled" and did not have "checkpoints on all main lines of communications."[63] Interestingly, these factors were not relied upon by the *Loizidou* judgment which saw the existence of effective control as being "obvious from the large number of troops engaged in active duties in northern Cyprus."[64] In *Issa,* the facts were largely disputed and the judgment indicates significant evidential deficiencies in the applicants' case.[65] Importantly, the Court was not satisfied to the requisite standard that the Turkish military was even operating in the specific area where the deceased were alleged to have been killed.

Issa reinforces the "effective control of an area" doctrine as an exception to the territorial limits to the concept of "jurisdiction" under Article 1 of the Convention. The distinction made between the facts in this case and those of *Loizidou* support the proposition that the IHL test for occupation and the IHRL test for jurisdiction do not correspond exactly. As a military operation, it would *prima facie* be subject to IHL, although whether Common Article 2 applies is not entirely clear cut.[66] However, it is apparent on the facts that the Turkish military did have the

[60] Issa and others v. Turkey App no. 31821/96, Admissibility Decision of 30 May 2000, Decision of Second Chamber, 16 November 2004.

[61] At para 75.

[62] ibid.

[63] At para 74.

[64] *Loizidou* merits judgement of 18 December 1996 at para 56.

[65] Ibid at paras 76–81.

[66] In light to the Northern Iraq's autonomous status and the nature of the intervention, it may be arguable that a belligerent intent was absent see further Melzer 2008, p. 250.

capacity[67] to control the area in question, arguably enlivening the law of occupation. The Court did not discuss the relationship between the two tests notwithstanding that the facts of the case and the Court's discussion of the effective control test strongly suggest consideration of how the IHRL test interacts with the IHL test for belligerent occupation.

The Court also made certain comments that would become relevant in an armed conflict context outside the territory of a Convention State. The Court found:

> Moreover, a State may also be held accountable for violation of the Convention rights and freedoms of persons who are in the territory of another State but who are found to be *under the former State's authority and control through its agents* operating — whether lawfully or unlawfully — in the latter State … Accountability in such situations stems from the fact that Article 1 of the Convention cannot be interpreted so as to allow a State party to perpetrate violations of the Convention on the territory of another State, which it could not perpetrate on its own territory.[68]

Exercising "authority and control through its agents" would presumably apply where a state conducts extraterritorial military interventions. This comment is probably best understood as *obiter dicta* because the Court was not satisfied to the requisite evidentiary standard that the "Turkish armed forces conducted operations in the area in question."[69] Nonetheless, this statement and the phrase 'authority and control' in particular have been reprised in subsequent cases to the extent that states have been held responsible for violations committed by their agents in territory that was not controlled by the state.

Issak[70]was a case concerning the death of a Cypriot civilian at the hands of Turkish Cypriots, including members of the police force of the Turkish Republic of Northern Cyprus, in a buffer zone established by the UN[71] separating north and south Cyprus. The Turkish government claimed that it was not responsible for any violation of the ECHR because it did not have control over Northern Cyprus, nor the UN buffer zone. The Court[72] reprised its position that jurisdiction, whilst "primarily territorial," would be found where the state in question had effective control, citing *Bankovic* and *Loizidou*. As with the preceding cases, there was no discussion on the relationship between the IHL and the IHRL tests for effective control. Evidently, the situation in Northern Cyprus is one in which the Court considers both tests have been satisfied. But the judgment is more illuminating for its comments regarding the exercise of jurisdiction by the agents of a state. The Court repeated its previous comments in *Issa* that jurisdiction will exist where the

---

[67] It is not entirely settled as to whether the Occupying Power has "actually substituted its own authority… or whether it is sufficient that the foreign army … is in a position" to do so. Although it appears that the weight of international judicial opinion favours the later Benvenisti 2012 at para 5.

[68] At para 71.

[69] At para 81.

[70] App no. 44587/98.

[71] Judgment of 24 June 2008, p. 2.

[72] Preliminary Judgment of 26 September 2006 at p. 19.

agents of a state exercise *authority and control* over the victim.[73] The court rejected the notion that the jurisdiction requirement could "be interpreted so as to allow a State party to perpetrate violations of the Convention on the territory of another State, which it could not perpetrate on its own territory."[74] This is important to keep in mind because it provides a basis for finding jurisdiction where a State's military forces operate outside of their own territory but do not exercise effective control. In such situations, the conduct of the soldiers should be appraised by reference to IHL as a matter of law.

In *Pad*[75] a number of Iranian Nationals were killed by Turkish soldiers firing on them from combat helicopters on the Iranian-Turkish border. It is important to note that for present purposes, it is unlikely, even on the broadest reading of common Article 2 that this was an armed conflict situation. Nonetheless, the judgment is important because it was found that the act of firing upon the victims from the helicopter *was* sufficient to ground jurisdiction. There was a factual dispute as to whether the deceased were in Iranian or Turkish territory.[76] However, the Court did not find it necessary to resolve this, because it held that in either case, the victims were under the jurisdiction of the Turkish military.[77] Although not explicitly stated, this seems to be based on the *authority and control* test which is germane to the exercise of jurisdiction by agents of the state. It provides a further foundation for applying IHRL standards to the conduct of soldiers acting extra-territorially. The judgment seems to be a retreat from problematic[78] and potentially arbitrary[79] position established in *Bankovic.* The authority and control test is

---

[73] "State may also be held accountable for a violation of the Convention rights and freedoms of persons who are in the territory of another State but who are found to be under the former State's authority and control through its agents operating—whether lawfully or unlawfully—in the latter State" preliminary judgment, p. 19.

[74] *Issak* preliminary judgment at p. 20—cf López Burgos v. Uruguay, Comm. No. 52/1979, UN Doc. CCPR/C/13/D/52/1979 (1981).

[75] App no. 60167/00.

[76] At paras 49, 54. One of the interesting features of the case was that the Turkish government argued that the victims *were* on Turkish territory notwithstanding that this would unequivocally establish jurisdiction, albeit on a 'territorial' basis. The Government "vigorously denied … Turkish security forces had carried out a cross-border operation." (at [51]) It is not clear from the judgment whether this was to avoid the political ramifications of conceding to a violation of Iranian sovereignty or whether it was an attempt to avoid strengthening the jurisprudence "authority and control of agents" basis for extraterritorial jurisdiction.

[77] At para 54.

[78] See, note 59.

[79] A number of scholars have highlighted the uncertain and tenuous distinctions that may be required to be drawn as a result of the *Bankovic* judgment. For example if a soldier points a gun at a civilian and thereby detains them, jurisdiction is probably established, whereas if the same soldier simply shoots and kills the civilian there may be no jurisdiction. Hampson suggests another example, where a plane drops two bombs simultaneously, one landing inside a border, thus within jurisdiction, and the other landing outside the territorial limits of the state. The victim of the first bomb will be legally protected by the ECHR whereas the other is not. See Hampson 2008, p. 570; see also Milanovic 2012, p. 123, 129.

evidently the test applied in the *Al Skeini*, the leading case on the extraterritorial applicability of the ECHR in the context of an (international) armed conflict and subsequent belligerent occupation.

9.3.3 Al-Skeini

The *Al-Skeini* case is presently the leading authority of the Court on the extra-territorial applicability of the Convention. The matter was an application by the relatives of six Iraqis who had been killed in Basrah when it was occupied by the UK armed forces in 2003–2004. The Court found that where the complaints were admissible,[80] the UK government was exercising jurisdiction over the victims so as to enliven its procedural obligations under Article 2 of the Convention.[81]

The judgment made extensive reference to IHL, primarily those provisions concerned with the law of belligerent occupation. The case had been argued on the basis that IHL applied and UK government accepted that it was an occupying power in Iraq. This was based on the Security Council resolutions[82] that authorised the presence of the multinational force. The Court reproduced[83] Articles 42 and 43 of the Hague Regulations in full. These provisions are central to the application of the law of belligerent occupation because they set out when an occupation begins and the duties and rights of an occupying force. The Court also discussed[84] Article 64 of the Fourth Geneva Convention[85] which expands on the obligations of occupation forces. It referred to the obligations under IHL to investigate deaths or wilful killings of protected persons as found in the Fourth Geneva Convention.[86] This is immediately followed by an extract from a report from the Special Rapporteur on Extra-Judicial Killings which discusses the obligation to investigate violations of the right to life during armed conflict.[87]

---

[80] The sixth applicant's complaint was found to be inadmissible because he was no longer a "victim of any breach of the procedural obligation under Article 2 at para 176.

[81] See, Sect. 9.5.

[82] UN Security Council resolution 1483, 1511; see para 143–148.

[83] At para 89.

[84] Ibid.

[85] At para 92.

[86] Ibid, Article 121 of the Third Geneva Convention and Article 131 of the Fourth Geneva Convention. the Court also cites the obligation to investigate and prosecute alleged grave breaches of the Conventions, which include "wilful killing of protected persons" in Articles 49 and 50 of the First Geneva Convention, Articles 50–51 of the Second Geneva Convention; Articles 129 and 130 of the Third Geneva Convention and 146 and 147 of the Fourth Geneva Convention.

[87] At para 93.

The Court then turned to the jurisprudence of the ICJ with regard to the relationship between IHL and HRL.[88] This discussion takes place in the context of the extraterritorial applicability of IHRL instruments. The ECtHR quotes, with apparent approval, the passage from the *Wall* judgment (extracted above) that concluded that there will be three possible situations.[89] The first is governed solely by IHL, the second is governed solely by IHRL and the final situation is where both areas of law are applicable. In the last situation, it will necessary consider both "branches" of law, applying IHL as *lex specialis*. The Court also extracts a passage from that case which addresses the Human Rights Committee's conclusion that the ICCPR applies extraterritorially, particularly in the case of the Occupied Palestinian Territories. Finally, reference is made to the *Armed Activities* Case. As mentioned above, this case is notable in that it eschews reference to uncertain concept of *lex specialis* and simply states that IHL and IHRL both apply in situations of occupation, reiterating that IHRL treaties, in that case the ICCPR, have extraterritorial application.

The Court ultimately decided that all the victims were within the jurisdiction of the UK. The judgment seems to merge the two previous foundations for jurisdiction, namely *effective control of an area* and *authority and control* exercised by the agents of the state. However, in light of the preceding case law the judgment does not provide a firm or coherent conceptual foundation for establishing extraterritorial jurisdiction. Furthermore, while the Court was obviously aware of the relevance of IHL, it does not feature in its reasoning for the extraterritorial application of the Convention and the relationship is not clearly discussed. As noted above, the case was conducted on the basis that the UK was an occupying power for the purposes of IHL and this was the starting point for Court's application of the law to the facts.[90] From there it progressed through various diplomatic, political and military circumstances that led to the conclusion that the UK was exercising "public powers normally to be exercised by a sovereign government."[91] This suggests the effective control test in one form or another. But then the Court went on to find that "the UK, *through its soldiers*, engaged in security operations in Basrah during the period in question and exercised *authority and control* over 'the victims' so as to establish a jurisdictional link between the deceased and the United Kingdom."[92]

This reasoning is problematic for a number of reasons. First, the Court starts from the position that the UK was an occupying power, which necessarily means that the government was in effective control of the occupied territory. However, the facts as related in the judgment suggest that effective control *in Basrah* was not established to an IHL standard. The judgment seems to proceed on the assumption

[88] At para 90 and following.

[89] At para 90.

[90] At para 143.

[91] At para 149.

[92] At para 149.

that simply because the US and UK were occupiers of Iraq, writ large, then the law of belligerent occupation must apply. It is important to keep in mind that because belligerent occupation is a question of fact, the absence of a declaration by the occupying power is not determinative.[93] Similarly, the fact that the UK said it *was* an occupying power should not be dispositive of the question. An occupation only exists so far as the occupier exerts control over the territory and this must be considered in light of the facts on the ground.

A second problem with the Court's reasoning is that the considerations it takes into account are very similar to those that would be taken into account in determining whether the UK was actually an occupying power under IHL. These include examining whether the UK was exercising public functions, the amount of troops stationed in the area and, as a question of fact, whether UK forces were in control of an area. It is evident that the law of belligerent occupation should have been a relevant factor in evaluating the lawfulness of the actions of UK troops in Basrah. Droege notes that "in humanitarian law control over a territory is a notion pertaining to the law of occupation and triggers a number of absolute obligations of the occupying power. In international human rights law the notion of 'effective control' has a broader meaning since human rights obligations are more flexible and vary with varying degrees of control."[94] Despite it being entirely appropriate to consider the issue, the Court declined to do so.

While there is no necessary reason why the test for occupation under IHL and that for jurisdiction under IHRL should be the same, the preferable position would have been to explicitly consider the relationship between the two. The failure to do so, coupled with the use of startlingly similar terminology serves only to further obfuscate the relationship between the two areas of law. The potential confusion is problematic for a number of related reasons. The first is that combat situations are not areas that are amenable to systems of rules that lack clarity. This kind of ambiguity clouds decision making. Second, it serves to further fragment an already decentralised and diffuse public international legal system. Finally, it fails to recognise the universal acceptance of IHL norms and the protective role these norm play in armed conflicts.

9.4 IHL in Non-international Armed Conflicts (NIACs)

In cases concerning the extraterritorial application of the ECHR, the Court has acknowledged the existence of IHL as applicable law even if it is reluctant to engage with it. This position stands in stark contrast to applications arising out of NIACs where the Court consistently overlooks IHL. However, humanitarian law applies in these armed conflicts to create different rights and obligations to those

[93] Benvenisti 2012.

[94] Droege 2007, p. 332.

created by the Convention. Admittedly the Court may ultimately decide that these conflict with Convention rights and cannot be reconciled. However, such a conclusion should be reached through a transparent process of reasoning, which is conspicuously absent in the decided cases. This section will discuss the failure to apply IHL in these cases.

IHL in NIACs is less clearly established than its international counterpart. For much of the post-war period the *lex scripta* was essentially common Article 3 of the Geneva Conventions and the second additional protocol thereto.[95] More recently, we have seen a significant expansion in the law applicable to NIACs. As far as treaty law is concerned, the Rome Statute[96] gives the ICC jurisdiction over war crimes committed in NIACs[97] and aspects of the Conventional Weapons Convention have been formulated so as to apply in internal conflicts, too. Furthermore, there is a large and growing consensus that many of the fundamental legal concepts that govern international armed conflicts also apply to NIACs as customary law.[98] However, it is important to keep in mind this position is contentious.[99] The ambiguity of IHL in this context is relevant to appraising the Court's decisions. First the argument that IHL should be applied as *lex specialis*, because law is more fully developed and specialised for the situation, is less persuasive. Similarly, its use as an interpretive prism does not provide the same degree of assistance.

It has also been suggested that IHRL is more specialised and better able to deal with these situations.[100] Certainly this may be the case for some questions such as the use of lethal force against members of rebel groups.[101] Furthermore, it is important to recognise the different international context of an NIAC; that is an insurgency occurring within the territory of the state. IHL is firmly rooted in a traditional public international law context which prioritises the sovereignty of states and which would only regulate the conduct of states internally in limited circumstances. This explains the general reluctance of states to create detailed rules for these armed conflicts and why certain thresholds must be met before it can be said that IHL applies.[102]

The thresholds for IHL to apply relate to the intensity of the violence and the organisation of the groups involved. In this sense, NIACs can be contrasted with "internal disturbances and tensions, such as riots, isolated and sporadic acts of

95 Protocol Additional to the Geneva Conventions of 12 August 1949, and relating to the Protection of Victims of Non-International Armed Conflicts (Protocol II), Geneva 8 June, 1977.

96 Rome Statute entered into force on 1 July 2002 2187 UNTS 90/37 Article 8(2)(c) and (e).

97 Convention on Prohibitions or Restrictions on the Use of Certain Conventional Weapons Which May be Deemed to be Excessively Injurious or to Have Indiscriminate Effects. Geneva, 10 October 1980. Amendment Article 1, 21 December 2001.

98 Henckaerts and Doswald-Beck 2005.

99 Bellinger and Haynes 2007.

100 See for example Lubell 2005, p. 749; Abresch 2005; Doswald-Beck 2006.

101 Sassòli and Olson 2008, p. 621; Abresch 2005, p. 760.

102 See Chap. 2.

violence."[103] From an international law perspective, this threshold delineates situations that are solely governed by IHRL and fall within the "law enforcement" paradigm[104] from situations where an armed conflict is occurring and accordingly subject to regulation under IHL. For humanitarian lawyers, this question is of critical importance and is a prerequisite for legal questions such as individual responsibility for war crimes.[105] Thus if the Court were to consider IHL it would need to consider this threshold question.

It is important to bear in mind that once an NIAC exists, IHL applies as a matter of law.[106] The requirements of the rules of treaty construction and the jurisprudence of the ICJ require at least some consideration of it where relevant. By refusing to apply it the Court potentially creates conflicting obligations. As Hampson correctly points out "if the human rights body fail to take account of IHL, there is a real risk that the state will be found responsible for a killing in breach of human rights law which would not have been unlawful under IHL."[107] Furthermore, IHL has a clear role to play in NIACs; it binds non-state armed groups as well as the government, whereas IHRL only binds the state. In this sense, IHL has an additional protective function that is not present in IHRL. For these reasons "[t]he long-established IHL rules for these situations cannot be easily … discarded,"[108] nor should they be. Nonetheless, the cases that show a distinct reluctance to consider IHL in the contexts of alleged violations of convention rights that have occurred in the context of NIAC. In the three cases discussed below, it is noteworthy that despite the arguments advanced by various parties, the Court did not consider IHL in interpreting and applying rights under the convention.

The *Ozkan*[109] case concerned claims arising from operations by the Turkish security forces in south east Turkey. The court explicitly recognised that there existed an "armed conflict between the security forces and members of the PKK."[110] However, it does not appear that the Court is using the phrase as a term of art and does not discuss the Common Article 3 threshold. Indeed the Court noted that "evidence obtained concerning the PKK activity in [the relevant area] at

---

[103] Protocol II Article 1(2).

[104] This was the approach explicitly taken by the court in the *Isayeva* cases discussed below. See for example *Isayeva v. Russia* at [191]. For a detailed discussion of the law enforcement paradigm in the context of targeted killings see Melzer 2008, pp. 88–90.

[105] see for example ICTY, Prosecutor v. Kunarac, Kovac and Vokovic, Case No. IT-96-23 and IT-96-23/1 (Appeals Chamber), 12 June 2002, para 56 cf "protracted armed violence between governmental authorities and organised armed groups or between such groups within a State" Prosecutor v. Dusko Tadic, ICTY Appeals Chamber, IT-94-1-AR72, at para 70.

[106] Common Article 3 and Protocol II. see the dissenting commission members in *Cyprus v. Turkey;* Hampson 2008 p. 556.

[107] Hampson 2008, p. 563.

[108] Lubell 2005, p. 749.

[109] *Ozkan and others*, App no. 21689/93, Judgment, 6 April 2004.

[110] At para 85.

the material time is contradictory."[111] It is far from clear that the intensity requirement had been met and there was evidence, albeit of dubious quality, that suggested the insurgent activity in the area was low. Consequently, the conclusion that the armed conflict threshold has not been reached is probably sound, albeit unstated in the judgment.

The *Isayeva, Yusupova and Bazayeva*[112] cases concerned applications based on a violation of the right to life of the relatives of three applicants. The deceased were killed in an airstrike by Russian aircraft during the conflict in Chechnya in the late 1990s. In this case the victims had driven to the border between Chechnya and Ingushetia. They had been told that there would be a humanitarian corridor open to allow civilians to leave the area. However, when they arrived at the border they ordered to return to the city. As they were returning to the city, the column of cars was attacked by two Russian aircraft. The missiles killed the relatives of the applicants. The applicants alleged both substantive and procedural violations of the right to life.

It is a fairly strong position to suggest that the intensity and organisational threshold requirements for the applicability of Common Article 3 had been reached in this conflict.[113] This can be ascertained from the judgment itself, which makes reference to nature of the insurgency and the government response to it, which involved sizeable military formations equipped with tanks, combat helicopters and ground attack aircraft. Furthermore, it is arguable that Protocol II, to which the Russian Federation is a party, was also applicable. The Chechen rebels had taken control of significant areas of the region, including the administrative capital Grozny. Indeed, the applicability of IHL was proposed by an NGO that intervened in the case.[114] However, despite this evident applicability and express reference to it by the intervener, the Court evidently did not turn its mind to whether the threshold for an NIAC had been reached. The discussion on the lawfulness of the use of lethal force proceeded from the position that the government forces were carrying out a law enforcement operation. In terms of the broader context the Court did note

> that the situation that existed in Chechnya at the relevant time called for exceptional measures on behalf of the State in order to regain control over the Republic and to

---

[111] At para 87.

[112] App nos. 57947/00, 57948/00, 57949/00. Judgment in this case and *Isayeva v. Russia*, below, was given in conjunction with a third case arising out of Russian military involvement in Chechnya, namely *Khashiyev and Akayeva v. Russia* app nos. 57942/00 and 57945/00. This case involved the extrajudicial execution of five Chechens by Russian servicemen during the assault on Grozny. In that case the Russian government did not argue justification under any of the exceptions in Article 2(2) (at [140]) but simply denied that its soldiers were responsible for the deaths. The comments regarding the characterisation question made regarding the two *Isayeva* cases would also apply.

[113] Kaye 2005, p. 873.

[114] At para 161–167.

> suppress the illegal armed insurgency. These measures could presumably include employment of military aviation equipped with heavy combat weapons.[115]

This is the closest the Court comes to discussing the armed conflict threshold. In everything preceding the substantive discussion of violations of the right to life, the Court looks at the specific circumstances of the incident itself but does not discuss the general situation in Chechnya. For example, the judgment refers to the victims' attempt to use a humanitarian corridor without discussing why such a corridor was necessary or whether the term is being used in a technical IHL sense.[116]

The *Isayeva v. Russia*[117] case arose from an assault on a village in Chechnya in autumn 1999. While there was some dispute of the facts, it emerges in the judgment that there was high intensity fighting in the area, including the use of large calibre weapons, armoured vehicles, "heavy aviation bombs"[118] and multiple rocket launchers. There were at least 1,000 troops on the rebels' side.[119] According to the Government's submissions, 53 government troops, over 180 rebels and 46 civilians were killed during the assault on the village.[120] In discussing the lawfulness of the use of lethal force in the context of what was considered a law enforcement operation the Court reproduced almost verbatim much of what it had said in the first *Isayeva* case. The Court accepted

> that the situation that existed in Chechnya at the relevant time called for exceptional measures by the State in order to regain control over the Republic and to suppress the illegal armed insurgency. Given the context of the **conflict** in Chechnya at the relevant time, those measures could presumably include the **deployment of army units equipped with combat weapons, including military aviation and artillery**. The presence of **a very large group of armed fighters** in Katyr-Yurt, and their **active resistance to the law-enforcement** bodies, which are not disputed by the parties, may have justified use of lethal force by the agents of the State, thus bringing the situation within paragraph 2 of Article 2.[121]

It is clear from the factual situation of both cases that the question as to whether the threshold for an NIAC had been reached was a live one. In these two cases,[122] this question was incorporated into the submissions of at least one of the parties. Notwithstanding this, the Court interpreted and applied the Convention in a way

[115] At para 178.

[116] See Articles 14 and 15 of the Fourth Geneva Convention and Articles 59 and 60 of 1977 Protocol I.

[117] App no. 57950/00 Judgment of 24 February 2005.

[118] At para 19.

[119] At para 23.

[120] At para 27.

[121] At para 180 (emphasis added).

[122] *Isayeva v. Russia* 57950/00 paras 165–67; *Isayeva, Yusupova and Bazayeva* App nos. 57947/00, 57948/00, 57949/00 paras 155–58, 161–67.

that not only ignored IHL, but was potentially contrary to its provisions.[123] The applicability of the ECHR does not turn on the existence of an armed conflict. However, the existence of an armed conflict makes IHL applicable and if it applies it is necessary to examine the relationship between the two. Even if the conclusion of the Court was that the threshold had not been met, the facts of the case necessitated some consideration thereof. Consequentially, the avoidance of IHL suggests that these cases "mark a paradigm shift in the approach of international law to regulating internal armed conflicts."[124]

9.5 Right to Life in Armed Conflicts

The remainder of this chapter will deal with violations of two substantive Convention rights, the right to life and the freedom from arbitrary detention. These have been the basis for the various armed conflict cases considered by the Court. From the outset, it can be noted that the lack of consideration of IHL in the context of threshold or jurisdictional questions is carried through to discussion of substantive rights. Even when considering the situation explicitly envisaged by the ICJ in the *Nuclear Weapons* case, the ECtHR has elected not to apply IHRL viewed through the filter of IHL.

The right to life is the paradigm example of why it is necessary to interpret IHRL in light of IHL. Under these two legal frameworks, the use of lethal force is regulated in profoundly different ways. It is also the situation in which lawyers have the most specific guidance from the ICJ. This section will examine the way in which the ECtHR has interpreted the substantive and procedural aspects of Article 2 of the ECHR in situations of armed conflict. Unsurprisingly, it is the violation of the right which has seen the most attention from the Court when dealing with complaints coming out of war zones. The jurisprudence of the Court surrounding the right to life has established two distinct aspects, namely the substantive protection and the requirement for procedural safeguards, particularly the requirement for effective investigations of potential contraventions.[125] The right that Convention states owe to individuals within their jurisdiction[126] is that a person may not be "intentionally deprived of their life save in the execution of a sentence of a court following his conviction of a crime for which this penalty is provided by law." There are three enumerated exceptions which are when force is used (by the state) "(a) in defence of any person from unlawful violence; (b) in order to effect a lawful arrest or to prevent the escape of a person lawfully detained; (c) in action

[123] See right to life (Sect. 9.5).

[124] Abresch 2005, p. 742.

[125] *McCann and Ors v. UK* App No 18984/91 judgment of 27 September 1995 (investigations must be "practical and effective").

[126] See, Sect. 9.3.

lawfully taken for the purpose of quelling a riot or insurrection." That force must be no more than is absolutely necessary.[127]

It is important to note that the wording of the provision is fundamentally different to that considered by the ICJ in *Nuclear Weapons*. In that case, which considered the operation of the right to life provision in the ICCPR, the prohibition was less precisely worded, namely the prohibition on the *arbitrary* deprivation of life.[128] The question of what constituted arbitrary deprivation was to be answered by IHL as the *lex specialis*. The ECHR provision takes a different approach; the prohibition in general and absolute except in the case of the four enumerated exceptions. In considering armed conflicts situations, two of these exceptions are particularly important, namely where death results from the "defence of any person from unlawful violence" or "action lawfully taken for the purpose of quelling a[n] ... insurrection." The difference in wording is important because there is no elegant argument for the applicability of IHL to Article 2 of the ECHR in the context of armed conflicts. The clear wording of the section does not admit IHL unless it has something to say about either of the two relevant exceptions.

The exception in Article 2(2)(c) raises the question of the lawfulness of action taken to quell an insurrection. Assuming the NIAC threshold has been reached, logically this would be governed at least in part by IHL. Clearly, the force used would remain subject to the proviso that it be no more that absolutely necessary. But it would not be impossible to gauge necessity in this sense, in the context of an armed conflict, as being necessity as understood by IHL and reflected in its various rules, especially the principle of proportionality in attacks.[129] Such an interpretation would accord with the broader legal context and the existence of an armed conflict would provide an appropriate basis for distinguishing the peace time rules regarding the use of force as established in cases as *McCann*. However, the Court has not taken this approach and the ambit of this exception is unsettled because the cases have generally not been conducted on the basis of Article 2(2)(c). Even when considering large-scale insurrection, governments have tended to argue their cases based on the exception in Article 2(2)(a), namely defending someone from unlawful violence.

The role of IHL is less clear in the case of the exception for defending someone from unlawful violence. The unlawfulness of the violence being defended against is undoubtedly to be assessed by reference to human rights law on the use of lethal force. In NIAC, this inevitably brings us back to the original question of the

[127] ECHR Article 2.

[128] ICCPR Article 6(1) "Every human being has the inherent right to life. This right shall be protected by law. No one shall be arbitrarily deprived of his life."

[129] In this sense it is noted that in IHL, military necessity is generally a concept which underlies the formal rules. These rules are a balance between military necessity and the "competing" concept of humanity. This means that except where the specific rule makes explicit allowance for military necessity (see for example Hague Regulation 23(g)) a participant to an armed conflict cannot justify a violation of a rule by reference to military necessity. On this point see further Dinstein 2010, pp. 4–8.

relationship between the two regimes. However, domestic law will also be relevant in assessing the lawfulness of the violence. Even if rebel groups complied scrupulously with IHL and IHRL, they would invariably be outlawed domestically. This would mean that their belligerent acts would therefore be unlawful. Thus any government could always claim that the acts of their military fell under the exemption in Article 2(2)(a). This was the situation in both *Isayeva* cases. The Russian government proposed a very expansive understanding to this exception, namely that the extensive military operations undertaken in those cases were done in defence of people from unlawful violence. While the Court found that the rights of the applicants had been violated, it nonetheless accepted that in principle such significant military operations could be justified on those grounds.[130]

Thus we see that wholesale military intervention could be said to be taken in "defence of any person from unlawful violence." Nevertheless, as with Article 2(2)(c), there is no immediately apparent reason why the necessity requirement in Article 2 could not be openly interpreted so as to correspond with IHL. In terms of the relationship between the right to life and lawful targeting under IHL, both gauge lawfulness by reference to necessity, be it "absolute" or "military," and the proportionality of the use of force. Thus, the problem is compounded by the use of similar terminology to describe legal tests and concepts. This can lead to confusion and obfuscation. For example, until the Chechen cases, it had been suggested that the court was in fact applying IHL without explicitly saying so.[131] As Lubell succinctly puts it "it would be wise to clarify which language is being spoken, and not jump between them using terms from the different bodies of law within the same sentence, or perhaps not even in too close proximity to each other."[132]

A related area that is ripe for confusion is the proportionality tests of each body of law, which are fundamentally different. In IHRL, the test requires that the minimum force be used to achieve one of a number of lawful aims. Thus use of lethal force is only permitted when "absolutely necessary."[133] The Court is of the opinion that "the primary aim of [any] operation should be to protect lives from unlawful violence."[134] Under IHL, it is lawful to kill an enemy combatant[135] or civilian[136] who is directly participating in hostilities, provided that the anticipated

---

[130] *Isayeva v. Russia* 57950/00 at para 181.

[131] Abresch 2005, p. 742.

[132] Lubell 2005, p. 746

[133] ECHR Article 2 see also *McCann and Ors v. UK* App No 18984/91 judgment of 27 September 1995.

[134] *Isayeva v. Russia* at para 191 "Even when faced with a situation where, as the Government submit, the population of the village had been held hostage by a large group of well-equipped and well-trained fighters, the primary aim of the operation should be to protect lives from unlawful violence. The massive use of indiscriminate weapons stands in flagrant contrast with this aim and cannot be considered compatible with the standard of care prerequisite to an operation of this kind involving the use of lethal force by State agents."

[135] As defined in the Third Geneva Convention, Article 4.

[136] Additional Protocol I Article 50(3).

military advantage in doing so is not disproportionate to any expected incidental civilian casualties.[137] Lubell[138] suggests the first question in the *Isayeva* cases should have been whether there was a lawful military objective. If that was answered in the affirmative, then the anticipated military advantage would need to be assessed against the expected incidental civilian casualties.[139] The IHL rules would have been relevant in assessing the lawfulness of the attack but were not considered.

Ultimately, in the two *Isayeva* cases, the use of lethal force probably falls afoul of IHL rules, as well as those of IHRL. As Kaye notes, it may be that "the hard case is yet to come, where a close call in IHL—or an obviously permitted use of force under IHL—is pitted against the rules of the European Convention"[140] In the cases that discussed the lawfulness of the use of force in what could be considered an NIAC, the Court has applied the jurisprudence on the use of lethal force in the context of a law enforcement operation without considering the law relating to lawful targeting under IHL. This is understandable considering the jurisdictional framework and political context in which the court is operating. But it is problematic from a jurisprudential perspective. Even putting aside the guidance of the ICJ, if it is accepted that IHL applies as a matter of law giving rise to obligations for the State, then these obligations should be considered by the Court. While it may be that the Court cannot resolve any conflict, it is inappropriate for the Court to simply refuse to address these questions. That is not to say that the Court cannot conclude that it is not possible to resolve that conflict.

9.5.1 Derogations From the Right to Life

As with the difference in the wording of the right to life clause, there is also a fundamental difference in the derogation regime of the ECHR regarding the right to life. Whereas the ICCPR and the American Convention on Human Rights[141] both make the right to life[142] non-derogable,[143] Article 15 of the ECHR permits derogations from Article 2 in the case of deaths that result from lawful acts of war.

---

137 Additional Protocol I Article 51(5)(b).

138 Lubell 2005, p. 744.

139 Additional Protocol I Article 51(5).

140 Kaye 2005, p. 881.

141 Organization of American States (OAS), American Convention on Human Rights, "Pact of San Jose," Costa Rica, 22 November 1969, available at: http://www.refworld.org/docid/3ae6b36510.html [accessed 14 October 2013].

142 that is to say prohibition on the *arbitrary* deprivation of life is non-derogable; Article 6 ICCPR; Article 4 ACHR.

143 ICCPR Article 4, ACHR Article 27(2) the African (Banjul) Charter On Human And Peoples' Rights , 27 June 1981, CAB/LEG/67/3 rev. 5, 21 I.L.M. 58 (1982) does not provide for derogations.

The precise ambit of this provision[144] has not been raised in the Court because, to date no state has derogated from Article 2 in accordance with Article 15.[145]

As far as international armed conflicts are concerned it is unsettled whether it is necessary for a state to enter a derogation when engaging in a foreign intervention. The position of the Court after *Bankovic* would suggest that derogation would only be necessary where the state is in effective control of foreign territory. However, this test for jurisdiction has been somewhat complicated by subsequent judgements.[146] In light of this, it may now be the better position that a derogation be entered by a state participating in such interventions. However, it is also a live question as to whether such a derogation would be legitimate and the Court is able to determine whether it will accept the derogation.[147] The derogations clause requires an emergency threatening the life of the nation.[148] This makes it questionable whether it would be possible to derogate where a state is participating an external military intervention, such as the interventions in Kosovo or Iraq. Nevertheless, it is important to note that the Court has been very permissive as far as emergency situations were concerned and has accepted their existence is most cases employing a margin of appreciation that shows deference to the determinations of governments.[149]

The ability to derogate is also open to a State where it is dealing with an NIAC. However, it is interesting to note that no state has taken advantage of this provision as regards the right to life.[150] Turkey has entered derogations in regards to the situation in the south east of the country, but has not derogated from Article 2. Similarly, at various times the UK entered a derogation in relation to Northern Ireland, although whether this amounted to an NIAC is unclear. Finally, it is noteworthy that the Russian government did not derogate in regard to its military action in Chechnya.[151] The judgments in the *Isayeva* cases clearly indicate that absent a derogation the Court will apply a standard "law-enforcement" context

---

[144] Prud'Homme 2007 makes an interesting argument that the requirement in Article 15(1) that "provided that such measures are not inconsistent with its other obligations under international law" requites the ECtHR to "consider international humanitarian law and examine *proprio motu* whether derogation is consistent with this legal framework" (at p. 365). The lack of derogations to Article 2 means that the issue has not been raised and it does not appear that this argument has been run in regards derogations from other provisions of the convention which have been lodged in relation to armed conflict.

[145] Doswald-Beck 2006, p. 883.

[146] See, Sects. 9.3.2 and 9.3.3.

[147] ECommnHR, *Greek Colonels' Case*, 12 Ybk, 1970; p. 71; *A v. United Kingdom* app no. 3455/05 at para 177; *Aksoy v. Turkey*, app no. 21987/93, Judgment of 18 December 1996 see also HRC general comment 29 at para 3.

[148] ECHR Article 15.

[149] See for example *Brannigan* and *McBride* no 14553/89, and, most recently *A and Others*. See r Michaelsen 2012, pp. 287–314.

[150] Abresch 2005, p. 745.

[151] At paras 133 and 191.

with the associated rules on the use of lethal force.[152] In *Isayeva v. Russia* the Court held

> No martial law and no state of emergency has been declared in Chechnya, and no derogation has been made under Article 15 of the Convention. The operation in question therefore has to **be judged against a normal legal background**.[153]

Here, the Court implicitly disavows IHL. It may be that the proper construction of Article 15(2) is that absent a derogation, IHL does not apply. But in light of the broader legal context and the role of IHL in regulating the conduct of hostilities, such a result should be achieved through careful legal reasoning. It is suggested that the existence of a derogation from obligations under the ECHR cannot be dispositive of the question of whether IHL applies. Likewise it is inappropriate to rely on the derogations regime to avoid discussion of the relationship between the two regimes.

9.6 Freedom From Arbitrary Detention

The power to detain is a central concern to both IHL and IHRL. Article 5 of the ECHR specifies the circumstances in which a person's liberty can be deprived. As with Article 2, the provision is circumscribed and the text does not directly admit a role for IHL in its interpretation. The six grounds for detention enumerated in this provision do not extend to the power to detain enemy combatants or civilians under the Geneva Conventions. While the question may not be entirely foreclosed, the weight of authority form the Court suggests that power to detain under IHL cannot operate as an additional ground of detention, separate to those found in Article 5. It may be that detention in armed conflict is only lawful where Article 5 has been derogated from. The case law is clear that such derogation would be effective.[154]

An early case to consider the question of detention in armed conflict was *Cyprus v. Turkey*.[155] In this case, the European Commission found that because there was no derogation by Turkey, its detention of POWs was a violation of Article 5 of the ECHR. It was in this case that the dissenting commission members suggested that IHL should be applied as a matter of law. As has been noted elsewhere,[156] the comprehensive and exhaustive detention provisions under the Geneva Conventions have a long history in international law and have received the

---

[152] See for example *McCann*; 1990 U.N. Basic Principles on the Use of Force and Firearms by Law Enforcement Officials, 9, U.N. Doc. A/CONF.144/28/Rev.

[153] At para 191, emphasis added.

[154] *Brannigan and McBride v. UK*, app no 14553/89.

[155] App nos. 6780/74 and 6950/75, Report of the Commission, adopted on 10 July 1976.

[156] Hampson 2008, p. 565.

explicit assent of 194 state parties. As such, they should not be disregarded out of hand.

The *Ozkan*[157]case raised allegations of violations of Article 5 in the context of a potential NIAC. Unlike the expansive provisions of the third and fourth Geneva Conventions, the humanitarian law regulating detention in NIACs is far less developed. Nevertheless, Common Article 3 and Protocol II[158] do provide a degree of guidance and there is evidence and a weight of academic opinion to support the proposition that many of the provisions established in the Geneva Conventions apply to NIACs as customary law.[159] As seems to be its approach with all cases involving internal conflicts, the Court did not consider IHL at all. Importantly, on the question of detention, there are fundamental differences between NIACs and IACs. First, the distinction between combatants and civilians is absent. The second and associated point is that there is no immunity from prosecution for those who directly participate in hostilities against the government. Accordingly domestic law plays a central part in the treatment of people detained. In light of this, the reluctance to apply IHL norms is entirely understandable. However, the precise ambit of customary humanitarian law applying to detention in NIAC is ripe for judicial consideration. Furthermore, the fundamental point remains that there are relevant legal norms that directly apply to the situation and that these norms should be considered in assessing the legality of the actions of the state.

The *Al-Jedda*[160] case arose from the detention of a UK/Iraqi dual national by the British military in Iraq during its occupation of Basrah. The applicant argued that the detention was a violation of Article 5 of the ECHR. The UK submitted that the acts in question were attributable to the UN, not the UK and alternatively that UN Security Council resolutions authorised the detention and accordingly overrode the UK obligations under Article 5 of the ECHR by virtue of Article 103 of the UN Charter.[161] The main thrust of the Court's judgment focused on the resolution of the attribution and the application of Article 103 of the UN Charter. On these points, the Court found that the detention was attributable to the UK[162] and Article 103 did not create obligations that conflicted with the ECHR.[163]

[157] *Ozkan and others*, app no. 21689/93, Judgment, 6 April 2004.

[158] Although it is debatable whether Protocol II would have applied in this situation in South Eastern Turkey.

[159] See Henckaerts and Doswald-Beck 2005; Abresch 2005, p. 749.

[160] App no. 27021/08 judgment of 7 July 2011.

[161] "In the event of a conflict between the obligations of the Members of the United Nations under the present Charter and their obligations under any other international agreement, their obligations under the present Charter shall prevail." Charter of the United Nations, 24 October 1945, 1 UNTS XVI entered into force 31 August 1965.

[162] At para 80.

[163] At para 109.

The Court then turned to examine whether there was another legal ground for the detention of the applicant. The court decided that the detention provisions under international humanitarian law could not "disapply" the provisions of Article 5.[164] This was because those provisions did not create an *obligation* to detain.[165] This is clearly correct and to interpret the provision in question as creating an obligation to detain would be impractical.[166] Thus, it is implicit in the judgment's discussion of IHL that if there was an *obligation* to detain, it is possible that this may affect Article 5. However, these provisions clearly do *authorise,* i.e. provide a "legal basis"[167] for detention. The Court did not elaborate on why only an *obligation* to detain under IHL could displace the provisions of Article 5[168] nor did the Court say whether obligations under IHL treaties *could* disapply the Convention, although this may be implicit in the reasons. Similarly, the Court did not advert in this context to the general obligation of occupiers to restore public order. An alternative approach may be one that recognises this obligation and the concomitant power to detain as a tool in achieving this end. It would not place the interpretive relationship under undue strain to hold that the IHL provisions relating to detention as an additional ground operating alongside, the provisions of the ECHR. Here, the Third and Fourth Geneva Conventions are more to the point of the particular situation. As noted above, there is authority for the proposition that IHL should be applied as a matter of law in situations of armed conflict. If this approach were to be taken then detention provisions would operate along side of those under the ECHR and IHRL would fill any gaps. Such an approach would also take into account the (near) universal ratification of the Geneva Conventions.[169]

The cases that consider the right to life and the freedom from arbitrary detention demonstrate the difficulty that the Court is faced with when dealing with situations of armed conflict. On one hand it has a body of jurisprudence giving content to enumerated rights that apply at all times, not just in war. Furthermore, the Court is expressly constituted to interpret those rights. On the other hand, it operates within a broader legal and institutional context which includes a well-defined body of law that applies to the unique situation of armed conflicts. The use of lethal force and the deprivation of liberty are fundamental concerns of both bodies of law. While it was often open to the Court to engage IHL, and arguably necessary to do so in some circumstances, the cases where these rights have been violated in armed conflicts unambiguously demonstrate the reluctance of the Court to play a role in the development of the relationship between the IHL and IHRL.

[164] At para 107.

[165] ibid.

[166] Pejic 2011, p. 847.

[167] cf *Al-Jedda* at para 174.

[168] See Pejic 2011; Milanovic 2012.

[169] Pejic 2011.

9.7 Conclusion

This chapter has reviewed the key case law of the ECtHR that deals with situations of armed conflict and underscored the reluctant engagement of the Court with IHL norms. In her thorough discussion of *lex specialis*, Nancie Prud'Homme cites Kammerhofer who states:

> Any doctrine of international law is automatically based on a theory, even if the writer does not consciously realise it. He who does not explicitly argue for one theoretical basis simply implies a theory and since that implied theory is not expressed and discussed, it is much more likely to be incoherent, inconsistent or simply false.[170]

It may be that the jurisprudence of the ECtHR implies a theory, the outcome of which is that there is no relationship between IHL and IHRL to which the Court should have regard. The implication may be that the Court will only apply legal rules which it has jurisdiction to apply, namely the Convention. Perhaps, as Milanovic suggests, the Court "would not find itself the ultimate arbiter of all European overseas adventures."[171] However, there is broad consensus among international institutions and lawyers that both legal regimes apply in situations of armed conflict. Furthermore there is general acceptance that this relationship is one of interdependence at some level. Interpreting and applying one set of rules without reference to the other has the potential to further fragment public international law and create conflicting obligations.

If this chapter is also based on a theory, then it is probably this; that the process of judicial reasoning should properly engage with all relevant considerations. Even if they are ultimately dispensed with, rules of law binding on states should be considered in decision, not cited and then ignored, as in *Al Skeini*, nor overlooked altogether, as in the *Isayeva* cases. IHL has a clear and necessary role within the constellation of international law. In armed conflict decisions to use lethal force are made in high-pressure situations and IHL seeks to provide the clear, unambiguous rules to guide those decisions. The goal of this is to avoid unnecessary suffering in the interests of humanity, a goal which is not so separate from the goal of human rights law.

References

Abresch W (2005) A human rights law of internal armed conflict: the European Court of Human Rights in Chechnya. EJIL 16:741

Alston P, Morgan-Foster J, Abresch W (2008) The competence of the UN Human Rights Council and its special procedures in relation to armed conflicts: extrajudicial executions in the 'War on Terror'. EJIL 19:183

---

170 Jörg Kammerhofer, Unearthing Structural Uncertainty through Neo-Kelsenian Consistency: Conflicts of Norms in International Law, 7 (2005) cited in Prud'Homme 2007, p. 393.

171 Milanovic 2012.

Bellinger J, Haynes W (2007) A US government response to the International Committee of the Red Cross study customary international humanitarian law. Int Rev Red Cross 89:866–443
Benvenisti E (2012) Belligerent occupation. In: Wolfrum R (ed) The Max Planck Encyclopaedia of public international law, 2008 [www.mpepil.com]. Accessed 2 Nov 2012
Dinstein Y (2010) The conduct of hostilities under the law of international armed conflict, 2nd edn. Cambridge University Press, Cambridge
Doswald-Beck L (2006) The right to life in armed conflict: does international humanitarian law provide all the answers? Int Rev Red Cross 88:864
Doswald-Beck L, Vité S (1993) Le droit international humanitaire et le droit des droits de l'homme. Rev Int de la Croix-Rouge 800:99
Droege C (2007) Interplay between international humanitarian law and international human rights law in situations of armed conflict. Isr Law Rev 40:310
Hampson F (2008) The relationship between international humanitarian law and human rights law from the perspective of a human rights treaty body. Int Rev Red Cross 90(871):549
Hampson F, Salama I (2005) UN Sub-commission on the Promotion and Protection of Human Rights, Administration of Justice, Rule of Law and Democracy: Working paper on the relationship between human rights law and international humanitarian law, 21 June 2005, E/CN.4/Sub.2/2005/14
Henckaerts J, Doswald-Beck L (2005) Customary international humanitarian law. Cambridge University Press, Cambridge
Kaye D (2005) Khashiyev and Akayeva v. Russia. App. nos. 57942/00 & 57945/00; Isayeva, Yusupova and Bazayeva v. Russia. App. nos. 57947/00, 57948/00, & 57949/00; Isayeva v. Russia. App. no. 57950/00; European Court of Human Rights, February 24, 2005. Am J Int Law 99(4):873
Lawson R (2004) Life after Bankovic: on the extra territorial application of the European Convention on Human Rights. In: Coomans F, Kamminga, M (eds) Extraterritorial application of human rights treaties, vol. 2. Intersentia, Antwerp, pp 83–123
Lubell N (2005) Challenges in applying human rights law to armed conflict. Int Rev Red Cross 87(860):737
McCosker S (2013) The 'interoperability' of international humanitarian law and human rights law: evaluating the legal tools available to negotiate their relationship. In: Byrnes A, Hayashi M, Michaelsen C (eds) International law in the new age of globalization. Martinus Nijhoff Publishers, Leiden, pp 145–178
Melzer N (2008) Targeted killing in international law. Oxford University Press, Oxford
Michaelsen C (2012) Permanent legal emergencies and the derogation clauses in international human rights treaties: a contradiction? In: Masferrer Aniceto (ed) Post 9/11 and the state of permanent legal emergency. Springer, New York, pp 287–314
Milanovic M (2012) Al-Skeini and Al-Jedda in Strasbourg. EJIL 23:121
Pejic J (2011) The European Court of Human Rights' Al-Jedda judgment: the oversight of international humanitarian law. Int Rev Red Cross 93(883):837
Prud'Homme N (2007) Lex specialis: oversimplifying a more complex and multifaceted relationship? Isr Law Rev 40:355
Sassoli M (2004) Article 43 of the Hague Regulations and peace operations in the twenty-first century. Background paper prepared for informal high-level expert meeting on current challenges to international humanitarian law. Cambridge
Sassòli M, Olson M (2008) The relationship between international humanitarian and human rights law where it matters: admissible killing and internment of fighters in non-international armed conflicts. Int Rev Red Cross 90(871):599
Schabas W (2007) Lex specialis—belt and suspenders—the parallel operation of human rights law and the law of armed conflict, and the conundrum of jus ad bellum. Isr Law Rev 40:592
Solomon S (2009) The justiciability of international disputes: the advisory opinion on Israel's security fence as a case study. Wolf Legal Publishers, The Netherlands

Chapter 10
The Interaction Between Domestic Law and International Humanitarian Law at the Extraordinary Chambers in the Courts of Cambodia

Patricia Hobbs

Contents

10.1 Introduction

The aim of this chapter is to evaluate how the Extraordinary Chambers in the Courts of Cambodia (ECCC) apply norms of international humanitarian law and domestic law in order to provide justice for the atrocities committed by the Khmer Rouge regime between 17 April 1975 and 6 January 1979.[1] The discussion reflects

Patricia Hobbs is Lecturer at Brunel University Law School, Uxbridge, UK.

[1] See infra Sect. 10.2.

P. Hobbs (✉)
Brunel Law School, Brunel University, London, UB8 3PH, UK
e-mail: Patricia.Hobbs@Brunel.ac.uk

D. Jinks et al. (eds.), *Applying International Humanitarian Law in Judicial and Quasi-Judicial Bodies*, DOI: 10.1007/978-94-6265-008-4_10,

modern developments in international criminal justice, as the ECCC represent a relatively new judicial model that attempts to bring standards of international criminal justice closer to home. The hybrid model allows the judiciary to interact with both domestic and international sets of laws applicable to the particular crimes committed during the relevant period within the jurisdiction of the Chambers. In this way, there is a closer collaboration between the international community—under the auspices of the United Nations—and the domestic judicial institutions. They are 'hybrid' tribunals precisely

> ...because they involve the combined effort of the international community and the national institutions of the country where the crimes were committed. The hybrid tribunals typically employ both national and international judicial actors and incorporate both domestic and international law in their statutes.[2]

This is in contrast to the *ad hoc* tribunals of the Former Yugoslavia and Rwanda, set up through Security Council Resolutions and therefore representing the will of the international community, rather than the country itself.[3] The grave breaches of the Geneva Conventions perpetrated by the Khmer Regime[4] are a reminder that, in times of conflict, where human suffering is a guaranteed outcome of a conflict situation, certain categories of people must be protected in order to minimise such suffering. The discussion that follows will evaluate the way the ECCC have applied those rules in conjunction with existing rules from the Cambodia Penal Code.[5] This will ensure that criminal responsibility will be applicable in situations where a particular conduct does not fall within the ambit of the Geneva Conventions.

In order to evaluate the application and interaction of domestic laws and international humanitarian law, the discussion that follows will analyse contemporary judicial decisions to demonstrate the Chambers' reasoning when faced with situations or conduct that may not easily fit within Cambodia domestic laws. After this introduction, Sect. 10.2 will provide a historical background to the conflict itself, setting the scene for the need to fight impunity for the crimes and violations committed during the relevant period. Section 10.3 will present a discussion on the establishment of the ECCC, reflecting aspirations and concerns both from a domestic perspective and an international one. Section 10.4 will then provide the background for the rules applicable by the Chambers, although this is focussed specifically on the Geneva Conventions and domestic law. Section 10.5 will use some specific examples to demonstrate the interaction between the laws applied by the Chambers, namely the doctrine of Joint Criminal Enterprise and the *Duch* case. Section 10.6 will then focus on another aspect of judicial creativity and analysis,

---

[2] Cohen 2007, p. 2.

[3] The *ad hoc* criminal tribunals of Rwanda and the Former Yugoslavia were established by the Security Council, acting under Chapter VII UN Charter; SC Resolution 955 of 8 November 1994 and SC Resolution 827 of 25 May 1993 respectively.

[4] See infra Sect. 10.2.

[5] Code Penal et Lois Penales, Ministry of Justice of the Kingdom of Cambodia 1956.

namely the relevancy of amnesties in the context of international humanitarian law, and the conclusion will follow in Sect. 10.7, reflecting on the work of the ECCC to combat impunity and achieve justice.

10.2 Historical Background

Between 1975 and 1979 Cambodia experienced some of the worse human rights atrocities in modern history. Under the rule of the Khmer Rouge regime, led by Pol Pot, two-thirds of Cambodian people lost their lives.[6] The much criticised idealism that led to such widespread atrocities had not much in common with mainstream conceptions of communism or socialism[7] as it amounted to a clear attempt to create a '*pure Khmer nation, one completely sovereign and self-reliant, free of subjugation by foreign and class enemies*'.[8] This extremist Maoist-inspired ideology practically entailed the notion that any ideas from outside the pure Khmer ideology, and specifically from Western liberal democracies, had to be completely eradicated from the new Khmer society that was going to be developed under the new regime.[9] The natural result of this ideology led to the persecution and killing of millions of people for the sake of a purification process through genocidal means. Whatever grudge was held by the new regime leaders, the way it was dealt with was so much more severe and horrendous than the original offence, that all connection to it became a vanishing memory, leading to the taking of disproportionate measures[10]:

> To outsiders, and often to ourselves, Cambodia looked peaceful enough. The farmers bound to their planting cycles. Fisherman living on their boats...The wide boulevards and the flowering trees of our national capital, Phnom Penh. All that beauty and serenity was visible to the eye. But inside, hidden from sight the entire time, was *kum*. Kum is a Cambodian word for a particularly Cambodian mentality of revenge – to be precise a long standing grudge leading to revenge much more damaging than the original injury. If I hit you with my fist and you wait five years and then shoot me in the back one dark night, that is kum...Cambodians know all about kum. It is the infection that grows on our national soul.[11]

The result of this culture of revenge led to a period of heinous human rights violations, evidenced by massive scale executions, torture, imprisonments without trials, religious and ethnic persecutions and forced labour.[12] The general aim was to

---

[6] Although the actual number of deaths that occurred during the Pol Pot regime has been subject to different estimates, one of the latest studies proposed a range between 1.2 millions and 3.4 million deaths; see De Walque 2005.

[7] Jackson 1989.

[8] Ratner et al. 2009.

[9] See Hinton 2005.

[10] Ibid.

[11] Ngor and Warner 1987.

[12] Ciorciari 2006, p. 11.

eliminate any of the existing traditional and foreign influences and return Cambodia to the "Year Zero",[13] a reference to a new beginning or a new birth for Cambodia and for its inhabitants, with the ultimate goal of creating an 'agrarian communist utopia'.[14] An exclusive agrarian community, capable to support itself, would remove the need for any outside dependency, signalling the repudiation for any need of modernity, a customary by-product of any level of interaction with other States and societies.[15] This revengeful purification project was therefore achieved through acts of utmost brutality that swept the country in just over three years, separating communities, families and friends, and established a reign of terror.[16]

The horrors of the Democratic Kampuchea[17] regime came to an end in 1979. Despite the amount of evidence concerning the perpetration of some of the worst crimes ever committed, there was a general failure at the domestic level to bring any perpetrators to justice. Pol Pot and Ieng Seri were tried *in absentia* in 1979; they both were found guilty of genocide and sentenced to death. Depending on domestic or international rules,[18] trials *in absentia* may indeed attract a sufficient level of legitimacy,[19] and they can serve the purpose of sending out a strong message that justice will be done, even in the absence of the perpetrators. However, it does not follow that trials *in absentia* represent the State's genuine willingness to deal with atrocities.

10.3 The Establishment of the Extraordinary Chambers of the Courts of Cambodia (ECCC)

The 1990s witnessed a major development of international criminal law, with the establishment of the *ad hoc* international criminal tribunals of the Former Yugoslavia (ICTY) and Rwanda (ICTR) through Security Council Resolutions taken

---

[13] Ibid.

[14] Montesano 2009, p. 72.

[15] Klein 2006, p. 553.

[16] Chandler 1999.

[17] Democratic Kampuchea refers to the period of Khmer Rouge regime from 17 April 1975 to 6 January 1979, when the Pol Pot regime was overthrown by Vietnam. However, the regime established by Vietnam in Cambodia was not recognised internationally and the Khmer Rouge continued to represent Cambodia at the UN until 1993; see McCargo 2005.

[18] Generally speaking, trials in absentia may be allowed in civil jurisdictions (e.g. Italy, France and Germany) but even in this case strict rules apply in order to ensure compliance with minimum human rights protection (see, for example *Colozza* vs. *Italy* (1985) 7 E.H.R.R. 516, paras 27 and 29). However, among international and hybrid tribunals, the Statute of the Special Tribunal for Lebanon (SC Res. 1757 (2007)) is the only one that allows such trials (Article 22).

[19] It must be stated, however, that the notion of trials *in absentia* is controversial as it appears to conflict with the defendant's right to be tried in his presence, in accordance with Article 14(3)(d) of the International Covenant on Civil and Political Rights (UN Doc. A/6316, 1966).

under Chapter VII of the UN Charter.[20] The founding of these two tribunals represented the first instance that the issue of impunity was dealt with for the perpetration of international crimes since the establishment of the Nuremberg and Tokyo Tribunals.[21] The message sent was the international community's resolve to deal with impunity after a long period throughout the Cold War during which the international community had been practically paralysed.[22] In other words, the achievement of justice for the victims of international crimes became an issue that went beyond the interests of States, as the international human rights phenomenon inherently promotes a paradigm shift in international law, namely from a State-centric approach to a person-centred approach.[23]

However, the *ad hoc* tribunals' contribution to the fight against impunity, although commended, was also accompanied by much criticism.[24] This was partly due to questions surrounding the innovative use of the Security Council powers,[25] and partly because of the difficult relationship between the domestic courts and the international ones,[26] impacting on cooperation, effectiveness and ultimately on the success of the courts and the fight against impunity. The regime of the two *ad hoc* tribunals was based on their primary role to investigate and prosecute,[27] a jurisdictional practice that was reversed with the establishment of the International Criminal Court (ICC) through the principle of complementarity.[28]

Notwithstanding the above, the fight against impunity concerning the crimes committed in Cambodia by the Khmer Rouge regime was going to take a different course from the models set up by previous international criminal tribunals. Given the multiple problems that arose in the context of the *ad hoc* tribunals and

---

[20] The ICTY and ICTR were established through SC Resolutions 827 of 25 May 1993 and SC Resolution 955 of 8 November 1994 respectively.

[21] The International Military Tribunal at Nuremberg was established in pursuance of the Agreement for the Prosecution and Punishment of the Major War Criminals of the European Axis (82 U.N.T.S 279, 8th August 1945); The International Military Tribunal for the Far East was established in Tokyo on 16th January 1946 in pursuance of the Cairo Declaration (1st December 1943), the Declaration of Potsdam (26th July 1945), the Instrument of Surrender (2nd September 1945) and the Moscow Conference (26th December 1945), 4 Bevans 20.

[22] Notably, the International Law Commission was unable to establish an international judicial body to try individuals charged with genocide after the adoption of the Convention on Prevention and Punishment of the Crime of Genocide in 1948; see Bassiouni 1999.

[23] See Teitel 2008.

[24] See Barria and Roper 2005.

[25] The Security Council can take action under Chapter VII of the UN Charter where there is a threat to international peace; the link between the establishment of a tribunal and the Security Council's objective has not always been clear; see Tavernier 1997.

[26] See Brown 1998.

[27] See Article 9 ICTY Statute and Article 8 ICTR Statute.

[28] The Rome Statute of the International Criminal Court was adopted in 1998 and entered into force on 1 July 2002, UN Treaty Series, vol. 2187, No. 38544; see the Preamble (para 6) and Article 1 concerning the role of the State as the entity with primary responsibility to investigate and prosecute international crimes.

even the issues associated with the situations currently before the ICC,[29] it could be argued that, in an ideal world, it would be more effective for domestic courts to exercise their jurisdictions over international crimes. As Cassese points out, '...whenever we are faced with widespread, large-scale atrocities, the best response should be resort to *national* criminal courts...because all the evidence normally is there, witnesses are there, and so on'.[30] This is a logical and common-sense supposition. The other side of the coin is that international crimes are normally committed by State organs or organs under the control or direction of the State. This fact feeds into the well-known discourse of impunity[31] and the use of sovereignty as a shield[32] to avoid effective investigations and prosecutions of international crimes.

Given the above accounts, the situation in Cambodia represented a turning point and a new development for international criminal justice. On the one hand, the Security Council was reluctant to establish another *ad hoc* tribunal for Cambodia; on the other hand, Cambodia was equally unenthusiastic about potential prosecutions conducted outside its territory.[33] However, it was definitely clear that there was national Cambodian and international support for the investigation and prosecution of the crimes committed in Cambodia.[34] It is also fair to assert that, because of the strong US involvement and encouragement to move towards investigations and prosecutions of these particular crimes, the willingness and momentum to make this happen was essentially there. For example, in 1994 Yale University set up the Cambodian Genocide Program (CGP) and received funding of $499,000 from the US Department of State in order to research and document the killings that took place during the Democratic Kampuchea regime.[35] This led to the establishment of the Documentation Center of Cambodia and the enactment of the Cambodian Justice Genocide Act in 1994,[36] giving full support to the pursuit of justice for the crimes committed by the Khmer Rouge regime between April 17, 1975 and January 7, 1979.[37]

Despite the Cambodian and US clear commitment to deal with these crimes, the nature of the tribunal to carry out these investigations and prosecutions kept the

[29] Current concerns include the possibility of bias, especially as some situations are not referred to the ICC prosecutor (Dugard 2013); there has also been too much emphasis on African States, leading to a high degree of dissatisfaction within the African Union (Schabas 2013); lastly, there are difficulties in relation to State cooperation (Delmas-Marty 2013).

[30] Cassese in Romano et al. 2004, p. 4.

[31] See Akhavan 2001.

[32] See Cassese 1998; interestingly, Cassese points to the fact that, even though the shield of sovereignty loses power in the context of international criminal tribunals, the shield appears to gain power again in the context of the much needed cooperation with international tribunals.

[33] Ratner et al. 2009, pp. 341–351.

[34] For U.S. support see Cerone 2007; for the support at domestic level see Sperfeldt 2012.

[35] See http://www.yale.edu/cgp/cgpintro.html (last accessed on 22 May 2013).

[36] 22 U.S.C. 2656, Part D, ss. 571–574.

[37] S. 572 (a).

relevant interested parties and UN agencies busy for a number of years due to the inability to agree on a model that would satisfy the interests of justice, that is, a model considered to be sufficiently impartial and effective to deal with the alleged perpetrators of these crimes.[38] After several attempts, an agreement between Cambodia and the UN was finally achieved in March 2003, approved by the General Assembly in May 2003[39] and implemented by the Cambodian Government in October 2004.[40] The UN-Cambodia agreement set out to regulate the cooperation between the United Nations and the Royal Government of Cambodia in the pursuit of justice for the crimes perpetrated during the Khmer Rouge regime, namely 'crimes and serious violations of Cambodian penal law, international humanitarian law and custom, and international conventions recognized by Cambodia'.[41] The new hybrid international criminal tribunal model represents a clear departure from the previous *ad hoc* tribunals and it is also a model of international criminal justice that attempts to ensure impartiality, independence and fairness, despite an initial UN Expert Group investigation that Cambodian courts were not equipped to deal fairly with these crimes.[42]

In fact, it can be argued that the establishment of the ECCC reflects an attempt to deal with several issues concerning the pursuit of justice for international crimes and breaches of the Geneva Conventions. Notwithstanding the fact that the punishing of individuals is still seen as one of the main objectives of criminal investigations and prosecutions, there are broader goals that look into the long-term benefits of such prosecutions in order to rebuild the social fabric of the country.[43] Justice, truth-telling, deterrence and social reconstruction, after a period of physical and psychological trauma, are amongst those objectives. In the case of Cambodia, there is the added benefit that the ECCC can provide a model of justice for Cambodia's future legal system.[44] As a hybrid tribunal, the ECCC can accomplish objectives possibly beyond the reach of the previous *ad hoc* tribunals, which is to bring international criminal justice standards home.

---

[38] See Ratner et al. 2009, pp. 350–353. Some of the proposals put forward by the UN and Cambodia form the foundation of this long dispute; see, *inter alia*, A/53/850-S/1999/231 and Annex, A/57/769, GA Res. 55/95.

[39] GA Res. 57/228 (2003).

[40] Law on the Establishment of Extraordinary Chambers in the Courts of Cambodia for the Prosecution of Crimes Committed During the Period Of Democratic Kampuchea, adopted on 27 October 2004 (NS/RKM/1004/006) [henceforth ECCC Law].

[41] Article 1 UN-Cambodia Agreement; Article 9 also clearly defines the jurisdiction of the new hybrid tribunal.

[42] Report of the Group of Experts for Cambodia, established pursuant to GA Resolution 52/135, 16th March 1999, UN Doc. A/53/850-5/1999/321, paras 123–130.

[43] See Fletcher and Weinstein 2002; Filatova et al. 2008.

[44] Chansok and Theara 2008.

This is reflected in the laws applicable by the ECCC. A mixture of international norms and domestic criminal laws are applied, reflecting the distinctive nature of the Cambodian conflict and cultural identity.[45] Unlike the Special Court for Sierra Leone (SCSL), the ECCC is considered by some academics as part of the Cambodian judicial system,[46] even if the ECCC Pre-Trial Chamber[47] stated in the Duch case that the ECCC is distinct from other Cambodian courts, based on three specific arguments: first of all, the specific expertise of international law, international criminal law and international humanitarian law, is a necessary requirement for appointment, and domestic judges would lack this particular skill; secondly, the ECCC is an independent entity as other judicial bodies cannot review its decisions and the Chambers have no right to review the actions of other Cambodian judicial bodies; thirdly, using the SCSL as an example, it reiterated the fact that the establishment of the ECCC represented an expression of the will of the international community to deal with international crimes.

It must be borne in mind, however, that in this particular case the scope of the appeal before the Pre-Trial Chamber was very narrow, as it concerned the possibility that the Military Court—which originally carried out the arrest—infringed the rights of the accused, as protected under Article 9 of the International Covenant of the Civil and Political Rights (ICCPR).[48] If a wider interpretation is adopted, then one can construct the ECCC as a highly specialised Cambodian judicial body, providing a jurisdictional narrative aimed at instructing and guiding other domestic courts.[49] Moreover, it would not be an unusual occurrence if, in the future, the ECCC was to widen its scope and rule on issues that were once deemed to be beyond its jurisdiction.[50]

---

[45] It is a well-documented fact that the Cambodian Buddhist ideology was targeted by the Khmer Rouge regime, resulting in the persecution of monks and destruction of temples (see Kiernan 2008). For example, Article 3 of the ECCC Statute makes a clear reference to religious persecutions (as contained in Articles 209 and 210 of the 1956 Penal Code) and Article 7 is aimed at the prosecutions of individuals for the destruction of cultural property, as contained in the Convention for the Protection of Cultural Property in the Event of Armed Conflict (14th May 1954).

[46] See Romano et al. 2004; Cryer et al. 2007.

[47] *Prosecutor v. Kaing Guek Eav* ('Duch'), ECCC Pre-Trial Chamber, Decision on Appeal Against Provisional Detention Order, 3 December 2007, paras 17–20.

[48] International Covenant on Civil and Political Rights, U.N. Doc. A/6316 (1966), 999 U.N.T.S. 171, entered into force on 23rd March 1976.

[49] Jeudy et al. 2013.

[50] For example, see the European Court of Justice review of the legality of a Security Council Resolution taken under Chapter VII of the UN Charter, which potentially infringed fundamental human rights; see *Kadi and Al Barakaat International Foundation* v. *Council and Commission* [2008] ECR I–6351, Case C–402/05 P and C–415/05. The decision attracted much criticism; see Kokott and Sobotta 2012.

10.4 The ECCC Jurisdiction: IHL and Domestic Law

International Humanitarian Law (IHL) comprises the body of rules that normally apply in times of conflict and aim to regulate the parties' conduct in order to minimise the human suffering that typically ensues in such situations.[51] IHL is also traditionally referred to as *jus in bello* (the law that applies in time of war) as opposed to *jus ad bellum* (the law that regulates the State's right to enter into conflict).[52] The Hague Conventions[53] and the 1949 Geneva Conventions[54] make up a substantial part of IHL, though these instruments have been supplemented by the Additional Protocols[55] and a variety of other instruments, which provide for more extensive protection in specific areas.[56] Generally speaking, IHL regulates States' conduct in the context of international armed conflicts, namely conflicts between two or more States.[57] To ensure a minimum level of protection in a non-international conflict, Article 3, common to all four Conventions, stipulates that State parties to the Geneva Conventions, involved in an *internal* conflict, must treat

[51] See International Committee for the Red Cross (ICRC) Manual, p. 13.

[52] Article 2(4) of the UN Charter sets out a clear prohibition on the use of force; there are, however, two exceptions: first, through a Security Council Resolution taken under Chapter VII of the UN Charter (Articles 42–46) in order to restore peace and security; secondly, Article 51 of the UN Charter allows States to use force in the case of individual or collective self-defence.

[53] The Hague Conventions of 1899 and 1907 aimed to regulate the pacific settlement of disputes, respect for the laws and customs of war on land and maritime provisions for the regulation and respect of conflicts at sea; many provisions contained in the Hague Conventions reflected a refinement of the First Geneva Convention for the Amelioration of the Condition of the Wounded in Armies in the Field, adopted in 1864.

[54] Convention (I) for the Amelioration of the Condition of the Wounded and Sick in Armed Forces in the Field; Convention (II) for the Amelioration of the Condition of Wounded, Sick and Shipwrecked Members of Armed Forces at Sea. Geneva; Convention (III) Relative to the Treatment of Prisoners of War and Convention (IV) Relative to the Protection of Civilian Persons in Time of War; all four Geneva Conventions were adopted on 12 August 1949.

[55] Protocol I Additional to the 1949 Geneva Conventions and Relating to the Protection of Victims of International Armed Conflict (8th June 1977); Protocol II Additional to the 1949 Geneva Conventions and Relating to the Protection of Victims of Non-International Armed Conflict (8th June 1977) and Protocol III Additional to the 1949 Geneva Conventions Relating to the Adoption of an Additional Distinctive Emblem (8th December 2005).

[56] 1925 Protocol for the Prohibition of the Use of Asphyxiating, Poisonous or Other Gases, and of Bacteriological Methods of Warfare; 1954 Hague Convention for the Protection of Cultural Property in the Event of Armed Conflict, plus its two Protocols of 1954 and 1999; 1972 Biological Weapons Convention; 1976 Convention on the Prohibition of Military or any Hostile Use of Environmental Modification Techniques; 1980 Convention on Certain Conventional Weapons and its five Protocols; 1993 Chemical Weapons Convention; 1997 Mine Ban Convention; 1998 Statute of the International Criminal Court; 2000 Optional Protocol to the Convention on the Rights of the Child on the involvement of children in armed conflict; and the 2008 Convention on Cluster Munitions.

[57] ICRC Manual, supra n. 51, p. 14.

> persons taking no active part in the hostilities, including members of armed forces who have laid down their arms and those placed 'hors de combat' by sickness, wounds, detention, or any other cause, shall in all circumstances be treated humanely, without any adverse distinction founded on race, colour, religion or faith, sex, birth or wealth, or any other similar criteria.[58]

In the case of the IHL violations that took place in the realm of Cambodia during the DK regime, these stemmed largely from the Vietnam intervention in the country and the international conflict that erupted. As the Trial Chamber clarified in the first case tried by the ECCC, the Cambodian and Vietnamese armed forces engaged in hostilities from 17 April 1975 (the entry of Kampuchean forces into Phnom Penh) until 7 January 1979 (the day the Vietnamese forces invaded Cambodia and captured Phnom Penh).[59] The reality, therefore, about the application of IHL in the context of the crimes perpetrated by the Khmer Rouge, is that the requirement of the existence of an international conflict becomes an essential element of the proceedings. In addition, to incur liability for grave breaches of IHL, a nexus must be established between the conduct or act of the accused and the conflict itself.[60]

According to Article 3 of the ECCC Statute,[61] the Extraordinary Chambers have jurisdiction over selected domestic crimes set out in the 1956 Penal Code, and which were committed during the relevant period, from 17 April 1975 to 6 January 1979. The specific offences listed are Homicide (Articles 501, 503, 504, 505, 506, 507 and 508), Torture (Article 500) and Religious Persecution (Articles 209 and 210) and all offences are subject to a maximum life imprisonment, in accordance with Article 32 of the Cambodian Constitution, and as further specified in Articles 38 and 39 of the ECCC Statute. The 1956 Penal Code was the applicable domestic criminal law during the relevant period within the ECCC jurisdiction, as it remained in force following the promulgation of both the Khmer Republic Constitution on 10 May 1972 and the Democratic Kampuchea Constitution on 5 January 1976.[62]

It must be acknowledged that the jurisdiction over domestic crimes by international and hybrid tribunals is a novel development in international law, but it is one that can bolster the legitimacy of such tribunals and, in the case of Cambodia, may also help towards the creation of an effective and credible judicial model. Issues of legitimacy can arise in the context of the 'source', especially given the

---

[58] Geneva Conventions, Common Article 3(1). Also, the 1977 Optional Protocol II extends the protection offered by common Article 3, thus ensuring the IHL effectiveness in the context of international and non-international conflicts.

[59] Case 001/18-07-2007/ECCC/TC, Judgment of 26 July 2010, paras 59–81 (henceforth Duch Case).

[60] Ciorciari 2006, p. 65.

[61] Law on the Establishment of Extraordinary Chambers in the Courts of Cambodia for the Prosecution of Crimes Committed during the Period of Democratic Kampuchea, promulgated on 27th October 2004 (NS/RKM/1004/006).

[62] Duch Case, supra n. 59, para 29.

criticism concerning the establishment of the *ad hoc* international criminal tribunals[63]; the 'process', as procedural standards differ depending on different cultural traditions,[64] and the 'outcome', as courts have an inherent inclination to interpret rules in a creative manner, and this could interfere with established principles of international criminal law.[65]

In fact, the ECCC jurisdictional competencies could determine the effectiveness and success of the prosecutions. Although the substantive scope of the ECCC jurisdiction has never attracted much criticism, the ability to link the actions of the accused to grave breaches of IHL may prove to be very difficult.[66] This is because the ongoing border disputes with Vietnam, which eventually led to a 'traditional' international conflict between Vietnam and Cambodia, cannot account for the ideological initiative to re-shape Cambodia and its people. Therefore, although some actions can be directly attributed to an international conflict, the discussion that follows points to a co-existence of a variety of laws (IHL, domestic and crimes against humanity) with a clear aim to fill jurisdictional gaps and ensure effective prosecutions.

10.5 ECCC Law and Its Application

Reiterating the Chambers' temporal jurisdiction over the crimes committed during the Khmer Rouge regime, Article 6 of the ECCC Law stipulates that the Extraordinary Chambers

> ...shall have the power to bring to trial all Suspects who committed or ordered the commission of grave breaches of the Geneva Conventions of 12 August 1949, such as the following acts against persons or property protected under provisions of these Conventions...

The acts listed in Article 6 include willful killing; torture or inhumane treatment; willfully causing great suffering or serious injury to body or health; destruction and serious damage to property, not justified by military necessity and carried out unlawfully and wantonly; compelling a prisoner of war or a civilian to serve in the forces of a hostile power; willfully depriving a prisoner of war or civilian the rights of a fair and regular trial; unlawful deportation or transfer or unlawful confinement of a civilian and taking civilians as hostages.

At the time of the conflict, both Cambodia and Vietnam were party to the Geneva Conventions,[67] the 1948 Convention on the Prevention and Punishment of

---

[63] See Shany 2013, p. 8.

[64] Ibid at pp. 8–9.

[65] Ibid.

[66] Ciorciari 2006, p. 48.

[67] Cambodia ratified the Geneva Conventions on 8 December 1958, whereas Vietnam ratified them on 28th June 1957.

Genocide,[68] and the 1954 Hague Convention and Protocol for the Protection of Cultural Property.[69] The investigations and prosecutions of crimes that fitted the above categories have been encapsulated within Articles 6, 4 and 7 respectively. It must also be noted that the 1899 and 1907 Hague Conventions, the first treaties that set out to regulate the laws on warfare, are widely considered to be the embodiment of existing customary international law, and will therefore bind all States, irrespective of whether a State engaged in a conflict has signed and ratified a specific convention.[70]

Given the potential difficulty in proving the nexus between the act and the conflict, the prosecution of individuals accused of crimes against humanity must also be considered. Crimes against humanity are included in the ECCC Statute[71] and require that acts are committed as part of widespread and systematic attacks. There is no added element that the crimes should be committed in times of peace or conflict, and may therefore offer an easier alternative to prosecutions for IHL breaches. The text of the ECCC Statute does not go as far as Article 8 of the 1998 Rome Statute, where war crimes are defined, *inter alia*, as 'other serious violations of the laws and customs applicable in armed conflicts not of an international character, within the established framework of international law…'[72] This is not to say that both types of crimes are the same, as the context will normally dictate whether a certain conduct should be classified as a war crime or as a crime against humanity. Additionally, a war crime can be committed following just one specific act, whereas for crimes against humanity to apply, the prohibited acts must be carried out in a systematic and extensive manner. Also, the sentencing for both types of crimes is different, thus potentially rendering crimes against humanity more serious than war crimes.[73]

10.5.1 Joint Criminal Enterprise

Whenever widespread violations of human rights and IHL occur, it is often difficult to identify the individual perpetrators because of the sheer number of individuals who have taken part in the hostilities.[74] Moreover, the context of these serious violations is such that, whilst orders are given by senior State officials, the

---

[68] Ratified on 14 October 1950.

[69] Both the Convention and the Protocol were ratified on 4 June 1962.

[70] This was confirmed by the Nuremberg Judgment in relation to an assertion that some States were not bound by the Conventions because they had not ratified them; see Nuremberg Judgment 1947, pp. 248–249.

[71] Article 5 ECCC Statute.

[72] Article 8(2)(e) Rome Statute.

[73] See Frulli 2004.

[74] See Drumbl 2005.

crimes are usually perpetrated by a large number of individuals intending to carry out those orders. The aim of the Joint Criminal Enterprise (JCE) doctrine is therefore to ensure that, once a link is made between the crimes committed and the orders given, then even those officials can be investigated and prosecuted.[75] A JCE model was initially incorporated into the Nuremberg Trials by the 1945 London Charter, where in Article 6 it was stated that 'Leaders, organizers, instigators and accomplices participating in the formulation or execution of a common plan or conspiracy to commit any of the foregoing crimes are responsible for all acts performed by any persons in execution of such plan'.[76] It was however the *Tadić*[77] case that reformulated a new, and much criticised, JCE model, whereby three different stages of responsibility were established: according to JCE I, responsibility will arise for acts committed in pursuit of a common design; in JCE II, responsibility will arise for acts committed by individuals enforcing a repression regime. It is, however, JCE III that extends liability beyond what was initially envisaged by the Nuremberg Tribunal, as acts committed outside the common design framework can be considered as a natural and foreseeable consequence.

At the time of the Cambodian conflict, JCE was recognised as being part of international customary law[78] as well as being part of Cambodian law recognised under the Cambodia Penal Code and French Law, the latter providing the foundation for the development of Cambodia's criminal law.[79] In 2011, the ECCC Pre-Trial Chamber (PTC) had the opportunity to consider the application of the JCE doctrine to four defendants—Nuon Chea, Ieng Sary, Ieng Thirith,[80] and Khieu Samphan—indicted for a series of crimes ranging from genocide, crimes against humanity, war crimes and other violations of Cambodia's criminal code.[81] The seniority of the four defendants meant that the application of the JCE doctrine was a necessity, especially in the context of such serious and widespread violations that can only be explained through a central or higher command, and this particular doctrine represents an effective method to prosecute the individuals involved.[82] However, the ECCC was keen to ensure that the scope of application of the JCE doctrine was not expanded too far to the detriment of the principle of legality. The issue rested with the *mens rea* to be applicable to the different forms of JCE, being a shared intent to commit the crime, in the context of JCE I, and the knowledge of ill-treatment and the intent to further it, in the context of JCE II. The *mens rea*

[75] See Danner and Martinez 2005.

[76] Article 6 of the Charter of the International Military Tribunal 1945.

[77] ICTY Judgment, *Tadić* (IT-94-1-A), Appeals Chamber, 15 July 1999, paras 185–229.

[78] See Cassese 2009.

[79] Ibid.

[80] Proceedings against Ieng Thirith were terminated on 13 September 2012, following the Trial Chamber Decision that she was unfit to stand trial; Case 002/19-09-2007/ECCC/TC.

[81] *Decision on the Appeals against the Co-Investigative Judges Order on Joint Criminal Enterprise (JCE)*, ECCC Pre-Trial Chamber, 20 May 2010, Case No. 002/19-09-2007-ECCC/OCIJ (ECCC JCE Appeals Decision).

[82] See Marsh and Ramsden 2011.

applicable to JCE III is a little more problematic because it imports elements of foreseeability and willingness to take a risk; this would, in turn lead to criminal liability.[83] Reviewing its first application during the Nuremberg Trials and the humanitarian law violations committed by the Nazi regime, the Chamber agreed that the doctrine is necessary, but the consensus goes as far as JCE I and II, the basic and systemic forms, especially as their substance resembles similar Cambodian Laws.[84] As for the extended version, JCE III, the PTC did not consider this form of liability to be part of customary international law at the time of the Cambodian conflict, or at least it was not foreseen as such by the individuals indicted:

> JCE III purports to attach liability for crimes falling outside the common criminal purpose but which were natural consequences of the realization of that purpose and foreseeable to the accused. The Pre-Trial Chamber has not been able to identify in the Cambodian law, applicable at the relevant time, any provision that could have given notice to the Charged Persons that such extended form of responsibility was punishable as well. In such circumstances, the principle of legality requires the ECCC to refrain from relying on the extended form of JCE.[85]

Therefore, by ensuring compliance with the principle of legality, *nullum crimen sine lege*, the ECCC demonstrated the willingness to investigate and prosecute, *inter alia*, violations of international humanitarian law, but within the parameters of the legality principle.[86]

10.5.2 The Duch Case

Kaing Guek Eav, also known as Duch, was the commandant of S-21, an institution created by the Khmer Rouge regime in order to further and protect the aims of the regime itself. S-21 has been described as an example of a 'total institution',[87] cut off from the rest of the world, and kept busy by killing prisoners and amending their biographies to suit the requirements of the Party.[88] It was, for all intents and purposes, a torture and interrogation facility, set up in the style of the Soviet secret police 'to uncover and combat all tendencies and developments inimical to the State…',[89] where the only escape was death.[90]

---

[83] ECCC JCE Appeals Decision, para 39.

[84] ECCC JCE Appeals Decision, para 41.

[85] ECCC JCE Appeals Decision, para 87.

[86] See Marsh and Ramsden 2011; Shany 2013. For a contrasting opinion see Karnavas 2010.

[87] Goffman 1961, p. 11.

[88] Chandler 1999, pp. 14–15.

[89] Ibid at p. 15.

[90] It is estimated that between 12,000 and 14,000 men, women and children were executed in S-21; see Dunlop 2005.

As the commander of such facility, Duch was charged with planning, instigating, ordering, committing, or aiding and abetting crimes against humanity, grave breaches of the Geneva Conventions of 1949, and national crimes of premeditated murder and torture.[91] Given that the Duch case represented a significant step forward in terms of justice for the crimes committed by the DK regime,[92] the court examined the crimes meticulously, ensuring consistency with modern developments of international humanitarian law, with the practice of other tribunals and with international customary law. With regard to violations of the 1949 Geneva Conventions, Duch was charged with (i) willful killing; (ii) torture or inhumane treatment; (iii) willfully causing great suffering or serious injury to body or health; (iv) willfully depriving a prisoner of war or civilian of the rights of fair and regular trial; and (v) unlawful confinement of a civilian.[93]

After establishing that the grave breaches of the Geneva Conventions were binding on Cambodia at the relevant time, the Trial Chamber adopted the five-part test devised by the ICTY[94] to ensure compliance with the jurisdictional requirements for the application of the Geneva Conventions law: existence of an armed conflict; international character of the armed conflict; nexus between the acts of the accused and the armed conflict; status of the 'protected persons' under the Geneva Conventions and knowledge of the accused. Given the high number of Vietnamese detainees present at S-21, and given their unambiguous status as soldiers or civilians, the Chamber found it relatively easy to establish that they fell within the 'protected groups' in the context of IHL.[95] The Chamber also concluded that an international armed conflict existed at that particular time, though it carefully added 'at all times relevant to the Amended Closing Order'.[96]

The Trial Chamber then turned its attention to the issue of criminal responsibility of the accused.[97] According to Article 29 of the ECCC Law, 'any Suspect who planned, instigated, ordered, aided and abetted, or committed the crimes referred to in Articles 3 new, 4, 5, 6, 7 and 8 of this law shall be individually responsible for the crime' and '...acts...committed by a subordinate does not relieve the superior of personal criminal responsibility if the superior had effective command and control or authority...'. The Chamber pointed out that two of these elements, planning and superior responsibility, did not form part of the 1956 Cambodian Penal Code.[98] However, the Chamber circumvented the 'planning' element of the offence by looking at other provisions of the Penal Code and introducing an element of foreseeability in order to ensure that such conduct would

---

91 *Duch* Case.

92 See Wilson 2011.

93 *Duch* Case, para 401.

94 *Prosecutor* v. *Natelitić* et al., Judgment, ICTY Appeals Chamber (IT-98-34-A), 3 May 2006.

95 Duch Case, para 425.

96 Duch Case, para 423.

97 *Duch* Case, para 470 *et seq.*

98 Code Penal et Lois Penales, Ministry of Justice of the Kingdom of Cambodia, 1956.

be criminalised.[99] With regard to superior responsibility, the Chamber restated the Nuremberg Tribunals practice of extending responsibility to individuals other than the ones who physically perpetrated the crimes, something specifically applicable to IHL violations.[100] Moreover, it also considered the superior responsibility attached to the failure to carry out duties properly, especially when witnessing criminal conduct by subordinates.[101] Although this type of responsibility was later codified within Additional Protocol I, the Chamber found that at the time of the conflict it already formed part of international customary law, and was therefore applicable.[102]

10.5.3 Ieng Sari, Amnesty and Cambodian Law

Case 002 concerned Ieng Sari, an official of the Khmer Rouge regime who served as Deputy Prime Minister for Foreign Affairs during the relevant period under the jurisdiction of the ECCC.[103] According to the Closing Order, Ieng Sari was charged with crimes against humanity (namely murder, extermination, enslavement, deportation imprisonment, torture, persecution on political, racial and religious grounds and other inhumane acts), grave breaches of the 1949 Geneva Conventions (wilful killing, torture or inhumane treatment, wilfully causing great suffering or serious injury to body or health, wilfully depriving a prisoner of war or civilian the rights of fair and regular trial, unlawful deportation or unlawful confinement of a civilian), genocide and crimes under the 1956 Penal Code of Cambodia.[104]

As Pol Pots' brother-in-law, Ieng Sari was responsible for persuading many educated Cambodians to leave the cities for the countryside, which eventually led to their torture and deaths.[105] As a high-ranking Government official, Ieng Sari shared power with Pol Pot and he himself gave the order for the recall of students and intellectuals from abroad and was ultimately responsible for their execution.[106] Given that IHL aims to protect certain categories of people from the harm caused by an armed conflict, Ieng Sari's actions represented unequivocal IHL

---

[99] Articles 223, 239 and 290 of the Cambodia Penal Code.

[100] *Duch* Case, para 475.

[101] *Duch* Case, para 476.

[102] *Duch* Case, para 477.

[103] It must be noted that criminal proceedings against Ieng Sari terminated on 14 March 2013, following his death on the same day.

[104] Closing Order 002/19-09-2007-ECCC-OCIJ, 15th September 2010.

[105] ECCC Pre-Trial Chamber Decision on Appeal against Provisional Detention Order of Ieng Sary, Case No. 002/19-09-2007-ECCC/OCIJ, 17 October 2008 (ECCC Detention Order Appeal).

[106] ECCC Detention Order Appeal, para 25.

breaches, which led to starvation, inhumane suffering and the death of thousands of civilians.[107]

When Vietnam invaded, Ieng Sari fled the country and, together with Pol Pot, was convicted of genocide *in absentia* by the People's Revolutionary Tribunal and sentenced to death. However, in 1996 King Norodom Sihanouk granted him a royal pardon for the sentence of death and confiscation of his property. Moreover, under the same Royal Decree dated 14 August 1996,[108] he also received an amnesty from prosecution with reference to the 1994 Cambodian law outlawing the Khmer Rouge regime.[109]

States are in fact able to pardon individuals for crimes committed within that State's territory, using a special mechanism called amnesty.[110] It is a tool that reflects the sovereign power to bestow immunity from criminal prosecution for past offences, and it is sometimes used in conjunction with the truth and reconciliation mechanism to grant amnesty in exchange for truth, as in South Africa.[111] Amnesties have often been applied to transitional societies in order to bring about stability and peace,[112] but they can also be construed as tools to shield perpetrators.[113] Moreover, even if the amnesty can bring about a quick solution to a conflict, victims often undergo a 'secondary victimisation' process due to the fact that their voices and experiences were never heard after the perpetration of the crimes.[114]

The granting of amnesties in relation to serious human rights violations, which would include violations of the Geneva Conventions, is however generally not allowed nor tolerated by the international community. In fact, the acceptability of an amnesty depends on the existence of an obligation to prosecute certain crimes; treaty law or customary international laws generally dictate the existence of such obligation. For example, the Geneva Conventions (GC), the Genocide Convention and the Convention Against Torture all include specific provisions, which obligate the State parties to enact domestic laws to ensure that these acts are effectively dealt with.[115]

---

107 Closing Order 002, paras 268–269, 285.

108 Royal Decree NS/RKT/0996/72, Article 1 (Unofficial Translation).

109 Law to Outlaw the Democratic Kampuchea Group, promulgated by Reach Kram No. 1, NS 94 of 14th July 1994 [henceforth the 1994 Law]; Article 7 of the 1994 Law allows the King to grant amnesties, either partial or complete, a power further supported by Article 27 of the Cambodian Constitution, adopted by the Constitutional Assembly on 21st September 1993.

110 The word *amnesty* derives from the Greek *amnestia*, which translates as *forgetfulness* or *oblivion*; see Weisman 1972, p. 529.

111 Moon 2008, p. 15.

112 Bassiouni 1996.

113 Roht-Arriaza 1996.

114 Condry 2010.

115 See Article 49 GC I, Article 50 GC II, Article 129 GC III and Article 146 GC IV; Article 5 of the 1948 Convention on the Prevention and Punishment of the Crime of Genocide and Article 2 of the 1984 Convention Against Torture.

The crimes committed in Cambodia, which represent clear violations of the Geneva Conventions, are no exceptions. This is notwithstanding the fact that some academics may argue that the establishment of a special tribunal to investigate and prosecute the crimes committed during the DK regime run counter to Article 52 of the Cambodian Constitution,[116] according to which Cambodia must '...adopt the policy of national reconciliation to insure national unity, and preserve the good national traditions of the country'. This policy is embedded within the long-established Buddhist tradition embraced by Cambodia and reaffirmed in the Cambodian Constitution itself.[117] As part of the Theravada Buddhist concept, individuals have 'no-self', which means that neither the victims nor the perpetrators of the crimes have any individual rights,[118] making the concept of crime practically redundant.

As mentioned above,[119] Ieng Sari was granted an amnesty for the part he played in the violations of IHL during the Khmer Rouge regime. However, given the seriousness of these crimes it would be unthinkable that perpetrators could so easily become immune to prosecutions. To illustrate the point, in the *Furundzija* case it was stated—in the context of torture only—that the granting of an amnesty is no bar to prosecution by an international court, another State or a subsequent regime.[120] This is in line with the serious violations of international humanitarian and international criminal laws, as well as the new culture against impunity that provided the original impetus for the establishment of international tribunals. Article 40 of the ECCC Law reiterates the current development, as it is stated that:

> The Royal Government of Cambodia shall not request an amnesty or pardon for any persons who may be investigated for or convicted of crimes referred to in Articles 3, 4, 5, 6, 7 and 8 of this law. The scope of any amnesty or pardon that may have been granted prior to the enactment of this Law is a matter to be decided by the Extraordinary Chambers.

This is in line with the ECCC Agreement, according to which the Government of Cambodia is precluded from requesting 'an amnesty or pardon for any persons who may be investigated or convicted of crimes referred to in the present agreement'.[121] The Pre-Trial Chamber (PTC) had the opportunity to rule on the validity of Ieng Sary's amnesty in an appeal against an order of provisional detention.[122] On examination of the Royal Decree granting amnesty to Ieng Sari, the PTC concluded that the Khmer word for 'amnesty' is used inconsistently, leading to a

[116] See Capeloto 2008.

[117] See Articles 43 and 68.

[118] Hancock 2008–2009, p. 88.

[119] See supra n. 105.

[120] *The Prosecutor* v. *Anto Furundzija*, ICTY IT-95-17/1-T, Judgement (Trial Chamber, 10 December 1998), para 155.

[121] Article 11(1) ECCC Agreement.

[122] Decision on Appeal Against Provisional Detention Order of Ieng Sary, 17 October 2008 (Ieng Sary Appeal).

dual interpretation to be applied: 'amnesty from a sentence' and 'amnesty from prosecution', but both of them were inconsistent with the amnesty provision in the new Cambodian Constitution.[123] It concluded that the first type of amnesty was uncertain, and certainly would not apply to acts of genocide;[124] whereas the second one pertained to acts involving the Law to Outlaw the Democratic Kampuchea Regime, and was not therefore under the subject-matter jurisdiction of the ECCC Law.[125]

The Chamber also had the opportunity to discuss the principle of *ne bis in idem* in order to evaluate whether Ieng Sari's conviction for genocide in 1979 would prevent the ECCC to investigate and prosecute him, for the IHL breaches again.[126] The Chamber proceeded to consider Articles 7 and 12 of the 1956 Cambodia Penal Code,[127] and Article 14 ICCPR.[128] Given that the initial investigations only put forward general charges concerning violations of crimes against humanity and grave breaches of the 1949 Geneva Conventions,[129] the Chamber concluded that it was not manifest or evident that the 1979 conviction would prevent a conviction by the ECCC, or indeed violate the *ne bis in idem* principle.[130]

10.5.4 Case 002 and the Severance Procedure

Case 002 currently deals with the criminal responsibility of two defendants who, at the time of the DK regime, were prominent members of the governing body: Nuon

[123] Ieng Sary Appeal, para 57.

[124] Ieng Sary Appeal, para 59.

[125] Ieng Sary Appeal, para 61. The Chamber did not widen the scope of the amnesty issue and therefore the validity of the Royal/Decree was not examined.

[126] According to the principle of *ne bis in idem*, a court may not institute proceedings against an individual for a crime that has already been the object of previous criminal proceedings and for which the accused has been found guilty or acquitted. In other words, the accused 'shall not be tried twice for the same crime'. As the principle is not mentioned within the ECCC law, the Chamber examined its interpretation under both Cambodian Law and International Law (specifically the ICCPR), where 'same crime' is interpreted as 'same act' and 'same offence' respectively. Although semantically similar, 'act' is not necessarily synonymous with 'offence', and this classification can lead to a weakening of the *ne bis in idem* principle, though it also leaves it open to the judges' discretion to determine whether the legislature intended to impose just one conviction.

[127] Article 7 clarified the extinction of criminal action, namely (1) the death of the offender; (2) the expiration of the Statute of limitations; (3) a grant of general amnesty; (4) abrogation of the criminal law and (5) the *res judicata* principle. Article 12 defined the *res judicata* principle, where the 'same act' phrase is adopted.

[128] Article 14(7) ICCPR incorporates the *ne bis in idem* principle, 'no one shall be liable to be tried or punished again for *an offence* for which he has already been convicted or acquitted in accordance with the law…'.

[129] Ieng Sary Appeal, para 52.

[130] Ieng Sary Appeal, para 53.

Chea, former Chairman of the Democratic Kampuchea National Assembly, Deputy Secretary of the Communist Party of Kampuchea, and Khieu Samphan, former Head of State of Democratic Kampuchea. Both of them are charged with crimes against humanity, grave breaches of the 1949 Geneva Conventions, and genocide against the Muslim Cham and the Vietnamese.[131]

In January 2011 the Trial Chamber completed the Closing Order for Case 002, compiling a 739-page document, which included grave breaches of the Geneva Conventions, genocide, crimes against humanity and offences under Cambodian law.[132] Between January and April 2011, the parties to this case had to deal with over 1,000 witnesses and gathered over 7,000 documents in relation to the offences committed by the four accused.[133] Faced with elderly accused, and defence lawyers about to submit motions of unfitness to stand trial in reference to three accused, the Trial Chamber decided to sever the Case into more manageable parts and to ensure a more timely justice for all parties concerned.[134] Although the defence teams objected to the severance order and appealed for the inclusion of all the offences set out in the original Closing Order, the Chamber stated that:

> These offences include killings and other deprivations of fundamental rights and international humanitarian law allegedly committed at 11 security centres, six worksites, three execution sites, as well as two allegations of genocide and two of religious persecution, spanning the entire territory of the Kingdom of Cambodia over approximately a four-year period. It was apparent to the Trial Chamber from the outset that a case containing even a single example of each category of crime or serious violation of humanitarian law would be one of such breadth and scope as to be unable to conclude within the Accused's natural life-span or whilst they remained fit to be tried.[135]

The ECCC Internal Rule 89*ter* stipulates that:

> When the interest of justice so requires, the Trial Chamber may at any stage order the separation of proceedings in relation to one or several accused and concerning part or the entirety of the charges contained in an Indictment. The cases as separated shall be tried and adjudicated in such order as the Trial Chamber deems appropriate.[136]

Case 002/01 will deal specifically with the forced movement of the population,[137] though the killings carried out at Toul Pot Chrey were added as they were

---

[131] Case 002 originally also included Ieng Sari (see supra 10.5.3) and Ieng Tirith, who was found unfit to stand trial in November 2011 due to dementia (Decision on Ieng Tirith's Fitness to Stand Trial, Case 002/19-09-2007IECCCITC, 17th November 2011.

[132] Decision on Severance of Case 002 Following Supreme Court Chamber Decision of 8th February 2013, 002/19-09-2007/ECCC, 26th April 2013, para 5 (henceforth SCC Severance Order).

[133] SCC Severance Order, para 5.

[134] SCC Severance Order, para 6.

[135] SCC Severance Order, para 109.

[136] ECCC Internal Rules (Rev. 8), as revised on 3rd August 2011.

[137] Severance Order para 2, Trial Chamber Case 002/19-09-2007-ECCC/TC, 22nd September 2011 (henceforth TC Severance Order).

deemed to be consistent with the overall theme of the trial[138] and was going to widen the number of victims affected by these specific offences.[139] The new indictments for Case 002/01 now include offences only in relation to crimes against humanity (enslavement, imprisonment, torture and other inhumane acts). Although grave breaches of the Geneva Conventions[140] were originally part of the Closing Order for Case 002, the Supreme Court of Cambodia concluded that the scope of grave breaches of the Geneva Conventions were too narrow because of the requirement for an international armed conflict.[141] The Chamber also indicated that Case 001, in relation to IHL breaches perpetrated at S-21, was much simpler and straightforward, described as a 'single-Accused trial of a co-operative, healthy defendant who in large part admitted his role and responsibility in relation to the crimes at issue'.[142]

Moreover, the focus of the Severance Order - the forced movement of population - represented a theme that involved the entire Cambodian population. The use of this method, therefore, allowed a large variety of groups to be represented within this stage of the trial process, despite the fact that, for example, the killings in the infamous S-21 camp were not going to feature at this particular trial for these defendants.[143]

10.6 The Destruction of Cultural Property

One of the main features of the Cambodian conflict was the ultimate intent to eliminate all kinds of foreign and intellectual influences from Cambodian society, including religious ones.[144] The religious persecution of Buddhist monks became part of the regime's efforts to cleanse Cambodian society.[145] Moreover, this cleansing was accompanied by the destruction of thousands of temples to ensure that these religious symbols scattered over the land would cease to exist.[146] The Khmer Rouge destroyed the majority of the existing pagodas, inflicting extensive damage to statues, monuments and other religious items.[147] The destruction was not

[138] SCC Severance Order, para 9.

[139] SCC Severance Order, para 56.

[140] Namely, wilfully causing great suffering, wilfully depriving a prisoner of war to a fair trial, unlawful deportation of civilians and unlawful confinement of civilians.

[141] SCC severance Order, para 113. According to the TC Severance Order, grave breaches of the Geneva Conventions were going to be deferred to the late stages of Case 002 (para 7).

[142] SCC severance Order, para 138.

[143] SCC severance Order, paras 112–122.

[144] See supra Sect. 10.2.

[145] Ratner et al. 2009, p. 311.

[146] Hawk 1986.

[147] See Becker 1998.

limited to Buddhist temples but extended to Christian places of worship, including the Catholic cathedral of Phnom Penh, which was destroyed stone by stone.[148]

As stated above, IHL's main objective is to protect certain categories of vulnerable people during times of conflict. Quite significantly, IHL also protects cultural property. Whilst it may be considered rather peculiar that property should feature in the context of HIL, cultural property is deemed to be part of the 'common human culture, whatever [its] origin or its present location, independent of property rights or current jurisdiction'.[149] The Hague Convention for the Protection of Cultural Property[150] is the most significant piece of international law concerning this specific issue. The Preamble clearly indicates the importance of cultural property for all peoples as it represents the cultural heritage of all mankind.[151] Cultural property is defined as

> movable or immovable property of great importance to the cultural heritage of every people, such as monuments of architecture, art or history, whether religious or secular; archaeological sites; groups of buildings which, as a whole, are of historical or artistic interest; works of art; manuscripts, books and other objects of artistic, historical or archaeological interest; as well as scientific collections and important collections of books or archives or of reproductions of the property defined above.[152]

The State parties are under positive duties to safeguard[153] and respect[154] cultural property, and only a state of military necessity may provide the necessary exception for such duties.[155] Moreover, the provision of the 1954 Convention apply in respect of an international conflict between two or more State parties,[156] whereas the minimum level of respect for cultural properties provided in Article 4 will apply in the context of non-international conflicts;[157] the State party is also under a duty to enact domestic laws to ensure that appropriate sanctions will apply in case these provisions are breached, including the prosecution of individuals.[158]

The evidence of the intentional destruction of cultural property in Cambodia during the Khmer Rouge regime is indeed overwhelming.[159] The question now turns to the ECCC effectiveness to deal with this particular IHL violation. The

---

148 Ratner et al. 2009, p. 329.

149 Merryman 1986, p. 831.

150 Convention for the Protection of Cultural Property in the Event of Conflict, The Hague, 14th May 1954 (henceforth 1954 Hague Convention). Cambodia ratified the Convention on 4th April 1962.

151 1954 Hague Convention, Preamble.

152 Article 1(a) 1954 Hague Convention.

153 Article 3 1954 Hague Convention.

154 Article 4(1) 1954 Hague Convention.

155 Article 4(2) 1954 Hague Convention.

156 Article 18 1954 Hague Convention.

157 Article 19 1954 Hague Convention.

158 Article 28 1954 Hague Convention.

159 Ang 1990.

ECCC has the power to bring to trial individuals responsible for the destruction of cultural property during an armed conflict in conformity to the 1954 Hague Convention and in relation to the period under the control of the Khmer Rouge regime.[160] The main drawback with this provision is that its source is a treaty, where there is no reference to the concept of individual criminal responsibility for the destruction of cultural property or to a crime.[161] As a treaty provision it is binding on contracting parties only, giving rise to international responsibility according to established rules of international law.[162] Therefore, in accordance with the principle of *nullum crimen sine lege*, an individual cannot be prosecuted for a crime if, at the time of the specific conduct, such conduct was not criminalised.[163]

On the other hand, the ECCC Co-Prosecutors could try and use the 1949 Geneva Conventions[164] as the basis for possible prosecutions for the destruction of cultural property; this is incorporated within Article 6, even though there is no specific reference to cultural property but it refers instead to the 'destruction and serious damage to property, not justified by military necessity and carried out unlawfully and wantonly'.[165] As Article 6 lists grave breaches of IHL,[166] the breach will give rise to individual criminal responsibility and the State is under a duty to prosecute.[167] Still, the ability to use Article 6 as the basis for prosecutions for the destruction of cultural property is curtailed by the fact that it can only be used in the context of an international conflict. Common Article 3 of the 1949 Geneva Conventions will apply in the context of a non-international conflict, but there is doubt that a prosecution can proceed on this basis given the conduct that falls within Common Article 3 is not widely recognised as a grave breach of IHL.[168] Alternatively, customary international law could be invoked as a basis for prosecution,[169] though the finding of an armed conflict, international or non-international, will dictate the success of this

---

[160] Article 7 ECCC Statute.

[161] Ciorciari 2006, p. 69.

[162] Responsibility of States for Internationally Wrongful Acts, adopted by the Commission in its 53rd Session in 2001.

[163] See Mokhtar 2005.

[164] Specifically, Article 53 Geneva Convention IV Relative to the Protection of Civilian Persons in Time of War, 1949 (henceforth Geneva Convention IV).

[165] Article 6 ECCC Statute.

[166] Namely wilful killing; torture or inhumane treatment; wilfully causing great suffering or serious injury to body or health; destruction and serious damage to property, not justified by military necessity and carried out unlawfully and wantonly; compelling a prisoner of war or a civilian to serve in the forces of a hostile power; wilfully depriving a prisoner of war or civilian the rights of fair and regular trial; unlawful deportation or transfer or unlawful confinement of a civilian; taking civilians as hostages.

[167] See Article 147 Geneva Convention IV.

[168] See, for example, Tadić (Decision on Defence Motion for Interlocutory Appeal on Jurisdiction), ICTY Appeals Chamber, paras 79–84, Case No. IT-94-1-AR/72, 2nd October 1995; see also Prosecutor v. Naletilić and Martinović, ICTY Trial Chamber, Case No. IT-38-34-T, 31st March 2003.

[169] Article 2 ECCC Statute.

action.[170] Given the potential problems mentioned above, prosecutions for crimes against humanity as the basis for prosecutions for the destruction of cultural property may provide an easier and less problematic course of action, given that crimes against humanity can occur in times of peace or conflict.[171] Article 5 ECCC Statute refers to 'acts committed as part of a widespread or systematic attack directed against any civilian population, on national, political, ethnical, racial or religious grounds'. Even though the provision lacks a clear reference to the destruction of property, cultural or otherwise, attacks motivated by religious persecutions could facilitate prosecutions for the destruction of cultural property.[172]

10.7 Conclusion: Final Reflections on the Application of IHL in the ECCC

It is overwhelmingly clear that the successful application of IHL norms rests on the nature of the conflict. The Cambodian conflict was a very complex one and was characterised by international and non-international elements, and by an ideology that led to utter destruction and atrocities. As IHL applies mainly in the context of international conflicts, the nature of the conflict must be determined and decided with utmost clarity. The discussion above points to the fact that IHL has been applied in very selected situations so far. More specifically, the S-21 prison camp and the killing of Vietnamese people have provided the ideal scenario for the straightforward application of IHL in the forms of grave breaches of the Geneva Conventions.

In addition, the Severance Order in Case 002 and the focus on offences that amount to crimes against humanity is evidence to the fact that the ECCC is increasingly more interested in timely and effective justice. The nature of crimes against humanity has changed in recent years, leading to a wider scope for their application; that is not the same for IHL. It could also be said that time is running out for the ageing defendants, and finding culpability on the basis of crimes against humanity may be a more effective use of ECCC resources. As for the destruction of cultural property, the academic speculation points towards the use of crimes against humanity rather than IHL, again because of the extra requirement to prove the existence of an international conflict and the problems that may be encountered by the ECCC with regard to the principle of legality.

---

170 See O'Keefe 2010.

171 See Prosecutor v. Kunarac et al., ICTY Appeals Chamber, Case No. IT-26-93, 12th June 2002, paras 85–92.

172 See Prosecutor v. Kupreŝkić, ICTY Trial Chamber, IT-95-16-T, 14th January 2000, paras 616–627.

References

Ang S (1990) Preserving a cultural tradition: ten years after the Khmer Rouge. Cult Surviv Q 14:3

Akhavan P (2001) Beyond impunity: can international criminal justice prevent future atrocities? AJIL 95:7

Barria L, Roper S (2005) How effective are international criminal tribunals? An analysis of the ICTY and the ICTR. Int J Hum Rights 9:349

Bassiouni M (1999) A draft international criminal code and draft statute for an international criminal tribunal. Martinus Nijhoff, Dordrecht

Becker E (1998) When the war was over. PublicAffairs

Brown B (1998) Primacy or complementarity: reconciling the jurisdiction of national courts and international criminal tribunals. Yale J Int Law 23:383

Capeloto T (2008) Reconciliation in the wake of tragedy: Cambodia's Extraordinary Chambers undermines the Cambodian constitution. Pac Rim Law Policy J Assoc 17:103

Cassese A (1998) On the current trends towards criminal prosecution and punishment of breaches of international humanitarian law. EJIL 9:2

Cassese A (2009) Amicus curiae brief on joint criminal enterprise doctrine. Crim Law Forum 20:289

Cerone J (2007) Dynamic equilibrium: the evolution of US attitudes toward international criminal courts and tribunals. EJIL 18:277

Chandler D (1999) Voices from S-21—terror and history. University of California Press, Berkley

Chansok L, Theara K (2008) In pursuit of transitional justice in Cambodia: from theoretical to pragmatic applications CICP working paper 47

Ciorciari JD (ed) (2006) The Khmer Rouge Tribunal. Documentation Center for Cambodia, Phnom Penh

Cohen J (2007) Hybrid justice in East Timor, Sierra Leone, and Cambodia: lessons learned and prospects for the future. Stanf J Int Law 43:1–38

Condry R (2010) Secondary victims and secondary victimization. International handbook of victimology. CRC Press, Boca Raton

Cryer R et al (2007) An introduction to international criminal law and procedure. Cambridge University Press, Cambridge

Danner A, Martinez J (2005) Guilty associations: joint criminal enterprise, command responsibility, and the development of international criminal law. Calif Law Rev 93:75

Delmas-Marty M (2013) Ambiguities and lacunaes—the International Criminal Court ten years on. J Int Crim Justice 11:553

De Walque D (2005) Selective mortality during the Khmer Rouge period in Cambodia. Popul Dev Rev 31:351

Drumbl M (2005) Collective violence and individual punishment: the criminality of mass atrocity. Northwest Univ Law Rev 99:539

Dugard J (2013) Palestine and the International Criminal Court—institutional failure or bias? J Int Crim Justice 11:563

Dunlop N (2005) The last executioner. Bloomsbury, London

Ehlert C (2013) Prosecuting the destruction of cultural property in international criminal law, Martinus Nijhoff, Leiden

Evans C (2005) The double-edged sword: religious influences on international humanitarian law. Melb J Int Law 6:1

Filatova E et al (2008) Transitional justice and human rights in Cambodia. European Institute for Asian Studies

Fletcher L, Weinstein H (2002) In pursuit of transitional justice in Cambodia: from theoretical to pragmatic applications. Hum Rights Q 24:573

Frulli M (2004) Are crimes against humanity more serious than war crimes? EJIL 12:329

Goffman E (1961) Asylums: essays on the social situations of mental patients and other inmates. New York, Garden City

Hancock V (2008-2009) No-self at trial: how to reconcile punishing the Khmer Rouge for crimes against humanity with Cambodian buddhist principles. Wis Int Law J 26:87
Hawk D (1986) International human rights law and Democratic Kampuchea. Int J Polit 16:3
Henckaerts J, Doswald-Beck (eds) (2005) Customary international humanitarian law, vol 1, Rules. Cambridge University Press, Cambridge
Hilaire M (2005) United nations law and the security council. Ashgate, Aldershot
Hinton AL (2005) Why did they kill? Cambodia in the shadow of genocide. University of California Press, Berkeley
Jackson K (ed) (1989) Cambodia 1975–1978: rendezvous with death. Princeton University Press, Princeton
Jeudy O et al (2013) Workshop report on the implementation of the ECCC legacies for domestic legal and judicial reform (Cambodian Human Rights Action Committee). http://www.chrac.org/eng/CHRAC%20Statement%20in%202013/03_12_2013_Report%20on%20Legacy%20Workshop_English_FINAL.pdf
Karnavas MG (2010) Joint criminal enterprise at the ECCC: a critical analysis of the pre-trial chamber's decision against the application of JCC iii and two divergent commentaries on the same. Crim Law Forum 21:445
Kiernan B (2008) The Pol Pot regime: race, power and genocide in Cambodia under the Khmer Rouge. Yale University, New Haven
Klein KM (2006) Bringing the Khmer Rouge to justice: the challenges and risks facing the joint tribunal in Cambodia. Northwest J Int Hum Rights 4:549
Kokott J, Sobotta C (2012) The Kadi case—constitutional core values and international law—finding the balance? EJIL 23:1015
Marsh L, Ramsden M (2011) Joint criminal enterprise: Cambodia's reply to Tadic. Int Crim Law Rev 11:137
McCargo D (2005) Cambodia: getting away with authoritarianism. J Democr 16:98
Merryman J (1986) Two ways of thinking about cultural property. Am J Int Law 80:831
Mokhtar A (2005) Nullum Crimen, Nulla Poena Sine Lege: aspects and prospects. Statute Law Rev 26:41
Montesano M (2009) Current international efforts in Cambodia: developing a court system to protect human rights. J Law Soc Chall 11:71
Moon C (2008) Narrating political reconciliation: South Africa's Truth and Reconciliation Commission. Lexington Books, Lanham
Ngor H, Warner R (1987) A Cambodian Odyssey. Macmillan, New York
O'Keefe (2010) Protection of cultural property under international criminal law. Melb J Int Law 11:1
Ratner S et al (2009) Accountability For human rights atrocities in international law: beyond the Nuremberg legacy. OUP, Oxford
Romano C et al (eds) (2004) Internationalized criminal courts: Sierra Leone, East Timor, Kosovo, and Cambodia. Oxford University Press, Oxford
Schabas W (2013) The banality of international justice. J Int Crim Justice 11:545
Shany Y (2013) Seeking domestic help. International criminal tribunals. J Int Crim Justice 11:5
Sperfeldt C (2012) Cambodian Civil Society and the Khmer Rouge Tribunal. Int J Transit Justice 6:149
Tavernier P (1997) The experience of the International Criminal Tribunals for the Former Yugoslavia and for Rwanda. Int Rev Red Cross, No 321
Teitel R (2008) Humanity law: a new interpretive lens on the international sphere. Fordham Law Rev 77:667
Thomas G (1995) A blameworthy act approach to the double jeopardy same offence problem. Cal Law Rev 83:1027
Weisman N (1972) A history and discussion of amnesty. Colum Hum Rights Law Rev 4:529
Wilson P (2011) Observations of the Cambodian trial of 'Duch'. Curr Issues Crim Justice 22:473

Part III
The Institutional Expansion: Applying International Humanitarian Law In Domestic Jurisdictions and Quasi Judicial Bodies

Chapter 11
Applying the Laws of Armed Conflict in Swiss Courts

Roberta Arnold

Contents

11.1 Introduction

Switzerland, the depositary state of the Geneva Conventions of 1949 and their Additional Protocols of 1977 and 2005, has a long tradition in the dissemination of the Laws of Armed Conflict (LOAC).[1] Paradoxically, however, its judicial history in this field is pretty recent and can only record two proceedings that were brought to trial: the *G. case* and the *Niyonteze case.*[2] Both were judged by the Swiss

Roberta Arnold, PhD (Bern, hons), LLM (Nottingham), is attorney. Researcher at the Military Academy at ETH Zurich, Switzerland and investigating military magistrate within the Swiss Military Justice (specialist officer). The views expressed here are the author's only and do not necessarily represent those of her employer.

[1] Arnold 2011, p. 1 et seq.
[2] Niyonteze Case, MAT Judgment, p. 45; MCC Judgment, p. 30; G case, Judgement of the Divisional Military Tribunal I, 14–18 April 1997; Arnold 2005, p. 764.

R. Arnold (✉)
Military Academy, ETH Zurich, Zürich, Switzerland
e-mail: rarnold74@hotmail.com

D. Jinks et al. (eds.), *Applying International Humanitarian Law in Judicial and Quasi-Judicial Bodies*, DOI: 10.1007/978-94-6265-008-4_11,

Military Justice (MJ), which had the exclusive competence to prosecute and adjudicate war crimes until 1st January 2011.[3] This date coincides with the entry into force of major revisions of the existing legislation, that were undertaken following to the ratification of the Rome Statute for an International Criminal Court (ICC Statute).[4] Its aim was to equip the Swiss prosecutorial and judicial authorities with the adequate tools and teeth to fight against impunity in the field of international criminal law.

The first step was the redefinition of jurisdiction over international crimes. With the entry into force of the new federal Criminal Procedure Code (CrimPC), which now applies uniformly at both cantonal and federal level, the primary competence to prosecute violations of the LOAC was delegated to the Office of the Federal Attorney General (OAG).[5] The MJ retained jurisdiction over cases in which these offences have been committed (a) by or against members of the Swiss armed forces; or (b) in the framework of an armed conflict to which Switzerland is/has been a Party.[6] At the same time, in order to fully comply with the ICC Statute, the Parliament amended also the Military Criminal Code (MCC)[7] and the Criminal Code (CC).[8] The main concern regarding the existing legislation, in particular the general clause on violations of the LOAC contained in Article 109 of the old MCC (oMCC), was its compatibility with the principle of legality,[9] reason for which detailed war crimes[10] and, for the first time, crimes against humanity catalogues were introduced in the MCC and CC.[11] These amendments entered into force on

[3] The basis was Article 109 oMCC.

[4] The ICC Statute was ratified on 12th October 2001 and entered into force in Switzerland on 1st July 2002.

[5] Articles 23(1)(g) and 25 CrimPC. Pursuant to the CrimPC, all cases, including those pending on 1st January 2011, must be prosecuted by the OAG. The first competent judicial instance is the Federal Criminal Court, whose judgments may be appealed to the Swiss Federal Supreme Court.

[6] Article 2 et seq MCC; Appendix to the Message on the modification of federal laws for the implementation of the Rome Statute of the International Criminal Court, 23rd April 2008, BBl 2008 3863, at 3971.

[7] Swiss Military Criminal Code of 13th June 1927 (MCC), with the amendments introduced on 1st January 2011.

[8] Swiss Criminal Code of 21st December 1937 (CC).

[9] Van Wijnkoop 2009, p. 8 et seq; Federal law on the modification of the Military Criminal Code, BBl 1967 I 587.

[10] Articles 264b–264j CC; Articles 111–112d and Article 114 MCC.

[11] Articles 264a CC and 109 MCC. Crimes against humanity were introduced for the first time into Swiss legislation, with these provisions.

1st January 2011.[12] At the same time, the crime of genocide, which was first introduced in the CC on 15th December 2000, was extended to "social" and "political" groups, too,[13] and a mirror provision was integrated in the MCC.[14]

11.2 The Legal Landscape

11.2.1 The Criminal Code (CC)

International crimes are now defined in the Special Part of the CC.[15] Genocide and crimes against humanity are addressed in Articles 264 and 264a CC (Chapter 12bis), whereas war crimes are enlisted in Articles 264b–264j CC (Chapter 12ter). Aggression has not been included, yet, but on 26th June 2013 the Federal Council launched the consultation procedure on the ratification of the amendments made to the ICC Statute on 10th and 11th June 2010, which would allow the ICC to exercise jurisdiction over this crime, too. The Message of the Federal Council of 19.02.2014 is yet to be discussed by the Parliament.[16]

Major legal issues arise from the inclusion of the provision on command responsibility also in the same chapter together with war crimes. Ultimately, it will be the task of the Federal Criminal Court to clarify whether it is to be considered as a *sui generis* crime—consisting in the failure of a commander to discharge his duties—or a special form of participation to the underlying crimes (*sui generis accomplice liability/complicity*).[17] The qualification has important effects on aspects such as causality, cumulative conviction, punishment, non-retroactivity and *mens rea* requirements.[18]

---

[12] Federal Law of 18th June 2010 on the modification of federal laws for the implementation of the Rome Statute of the International Criminal Court (BBl 2010 4277); Message on the modification of the federal laws for the implementation of the Rome Statute of the International Criminal Court of 23rd April 2008 (BBl 2008 3863). For the legislative history see Arnold 2011, p. 6.

[13] Jurius, 'Guerres et genocides: le Conseil des Etats prône un arsenal pénal encore plus sevère', Jusletter (22 March 2010); Trial Watch, Genocide, Crimes against Humanity and War Crimes: Switzerland to Have a New Law—But with Limited Application (19 March 2010).

[14] Article 264 CC; Article 108 MCC.

[15] Article 111 et seq CC.

[16] Federal Department of Foreign Affairs, Amendments to the Rome Statute of the International Criminal Court: consultation procedure launched, 26th June 2013; Message of the Federal Council of 19.02.2014 (FF 2014 1973).

[17] Méttraux 2009, p. 18 et seq; 37, 54–56, 58, 69; Arnold 2013, FN 16; Triffterer 2008, Commentary to Article 28, N 81; Prosecutor v. Oric, TJ, §§ 293, 724.

[18] Arnold and Wehrenberg 2014 (forthcoming).

Universal jurisdiction applies to the offences contained in Chapters 12bis and 12ter CC, as well as Article 264k CC. The requirement is the suspect's presence in Switzerland and the impossibility to extradite or surrender him/her to an international tribunal recognised by Switzerland. Extradition shall not be granted when it is obvious that the requesting State only did it in order to hinder prosecution. In order to avoid cases the outcome of which would probably be unsuccessful, Article 264m (2)(b) CC states that if "*the suspected perpetrator is no longer in Switzerland and is not expected to return there*", the prosecutor may suspend or abandon the investigation, provided that he has taken the necessary conservatory measures. This provision is to be read jointly with Article 7(2)(b) CC,[19] according to which if neither the offender nor the victim are Swiss nationals and other traditional forms of jurisdiction do not come under consideration, the CC may apply only if the offender committed a particularly serious crime that is "*proscribed by the international community*".[20] Article 264m CC is *lex specialis* with regard to the crimes enlisted under Chapters 12bis and 12ter CC.

11.2.1.1 War Crimes

The war crimes enlisted in the CC and MCC reflect those established by international law. An important requirement is the existence of an armed conflict and of a nexus between the crime and the conflict.[21] The underlying idea of the war crimes defined in Articles 264b–264j CC is that their gravity shall not depend on the qualification of the armed conflict during which they were committed (international or non-international).[22] Article 264b CC, however, specifies that:

> Articles 264d–264j apply in connection with international armed conflicts including occupations as well as, unless the nature the offences requires otherwise, in connection with non-international armed conflicts.

This reference to the nature of the offences is made to recall that war crimes qualifying as 'grave breaches' of the GCs only apply in the context of international armed conflicts (IAC), whereas all the others, may apply to non-international armed conflicts, too. This is relevant, for instance, with regard to crimes committed against prisoners of war (POW), such as delay in their repatriation under Article 264i CC, or to the transfer of the population by the occupation power (Article 264 g(1)(h) CC).[23] This distinction is made in Article 264c CC (*'serious violations of the Geneva Conventions'* and Article 264d CC (*'other war crimes'*).

---

[19] BBl 2008, 3895, p. 3954; Fiolka 2013b, p. 2274 et seq.

[20] BBl 2008, 3895 et seq.

[21] Fiolka and Zehnder 2013, p. 2158, N 33 et seq.

[22] Fiolka and Zehnder 2013, N 12, p. 2142.

[23] Fiolka and Zehnder 2013, p. 2157, N 29.

The language used by the legislator, however, is somewhat misleading, in that Article 264c CC actually refers to the grave breaches of the GCs.[24] Another consideration guiding the legislator was that some LOAC treaties providing the basis for some international crimes may be exclusively applicable to IAC. For example the extension to non-international armed conflicts (NIAC) of the ban on the use of poison or poisoned weapons, gas and similar substances and devices as well as "dum-dum bullets", was only proposed on 10th and 11th June 2010, as an amendment of the ICC Statute.[25] In general, however, the war crimes provisions of the CC may apply to both types of armed conflicts.

11.2.1.2 Crimes Against Humanity

The crimes against humanity enlisted under Article 264a CC correspond to those foreseen by Article 7 ICC Statute.[26] They do not require a nexus with an armed conflict. The underlying offences—wilful killing, extermination, enslavement, unlawful deprivation of freedom, enforced disappearance, torture, violation of sexual rights, deportation or forcible transfer, persecution and apartheid, other inhumane acts—must have been committed as part of a widespread or systematic attack directed against any civilian population. Due to the lack of jurisprudence, it will be the Federal Criminal Court's task to interpret this provision. The crime may be committed by everyone, against any national.[27] Protected persons are also members of the armed forces who have surrendered their weapons or who are 'hors de combat'. A widespread or systematic attack may be committed also via omission, for instance when a State or an organisation intentionally fails to prevent the underlying offences, thereby tolerating them.[28] The offences must have a link to the attack, which may be either widespread or systematic (alternative condition). Thus, they are characterised by either their dimension, such as a high number of victims, or their high degree of organisation. The protected good is humanity, so that it covers a collectivity, rather than a single victim.[29] However, it is sufficient that the perpetrator committed a single offence against a single victim, as long as

---

[24] Even though the unofficial English version of the provision is entitled as 'serious violations'. Article 2 ICTY Statute clearly refers to grave breaches, whereas Article 3 ICTY Statute refers to serious violations. The wording of the Swiss CC, thus, is somewhat misleading. Article 264c CC on serious violations actually means the grave breaches, whereas Article 264d CC on 'serious violations' actually means other serious violations of the laws of armed conflict.

[25] On 26th June 2013 the Federal Council launched a consultation procedure on its ratification. See 'Amendments to the Rome Statute of the International Criminal Court: consultation procedure launched', Bern, 26.6.2013, at http://www.news.admin.ch/message/index.html?lang=en&msg-id=49423.

[26] Wehrenberg and Ehlert 2013, p. 2116, N 2.

[27] BBl 2008, 3895 et seq, p. 3920, with reference to the ICTR and ICTY jurisprudence.

[28] BBl 2008, 3895 et seq, p. 3921.

[29] Wehrenberg and Ehlert 2013, p. 2118, N 10.

the contextual element was given. The perpetrator, however, must have been aware of the attack, even though it is not necessary that he knew all the details. The *mens rea* may be determined on the basis of circumstantial evidence.[30]

Most of the underlying offences need to be read in light of the corresponding provisions under Article 7 ICC Statute. For instance, wilful killing may be read in conjunction with Article 111 CC; enslavement, *inter alia*, with human trafficking (Article 182 CC); torture with Articles 183–184 CC on false imprisonment; violation of sexual rights with Articles 189–191 CC (offences against sexual liberty and honour; rape and sexual acts with persons incapable of judgement or resistance); other inhumane acts with Article 122 CC (assault).[31]

11.2.1.3 Genocide

Genocide was introduced in the CC on 15th December 2000 (Article 264 CC), following to the conclusion of the Military Court of Appeal in the *Niyonteze Case*,[32] that the Genocide Convention of 1948,[33] did not provide a sufficient basis for a charge for genocide, under the perspective of the principle of legality. Only in 2010, a mirror provision was introduced in the Military Criminal Code (Article 108 MCC), following to the adoption of the Law on the changes of Federal Laws for the implementation of the Rome Statute of 18th June 2010.[34] Genocide may be committed by everyone; the envisaged protected groups are those which are characterised by their nationality, race, religion or ethnic, social or political affiliation. The list is exhaustive.[35] The real novelty is the extension of the protection to social or political groups, which include groups of persons defined by cultural and economic criteria, as well as 'medical' criteria (e.g. paraplegics). The underlying idea was the necessity to encompass also those groups of people that had been explicitly targeted by the Nazi regime during WWII and the fact that the alternative possibility to prosecute their extermination as a crime against humanity, did not attach the appropriate stigma. A social group is a group of persons that feels permanently united by constitutive identifying criteria and that is perceived as such by the external world. A political group is a group of persons that has a nexus to general, public interests and that organises itself in a manner

---

30 BBl 2008, 3895 et seq, p. 3922.

31 BBl 2008, 3895 et seq, pp. 3923–3932.

32 Judgment of the Military Appeal Court 1A, 26th May 2000, pp. 28–29.

33 Convention on the Prevention and Punishment of the Crime of Genocide of 9th December 1948.

34 Bundesgesetz über die Änderung von Bundesgesetzen zur Umsetzung des Römer Statuts des Internationalen Strafgerichtshofs vom 18. Juni 2010, BBl 2010 4277. Wehrenberg/BS/Vor Articles 264–264m, p. 2086 et seq, N 6 et seq.

35 Wehrenberg/BS/Article 264, p. 2095, N 29.

allowing it to pursue these interests. It is not necessary to have a program or a high degree of organisation. Also spontaneously constituted groups for individual political issues may qualify. The idea was to encompass the suicidal genocide of groups like the Khmer Rouge in Cambodia during 1975–1979.[36]

Instigation to commit genocide, as seen, constitutes a separate offence (CC, Article 259 (1bis)) that aims at protecting public freedom.[37] This provision covers only genocides that are planned to take place, in part or in whole, in Switzerland. Since it was not included in either Chapter 12 bis, ter or quater, a question that may arise is whether the 'general principle' of command responsibility, along with the other general principles under Chapter 12quater, may apply in relation thereto. Another controversy is its extraterritorial applicability. Since Article 264m CC cannot apply, also in this case reliance must be made on Articles 6–7 CC.[38]

11.2.2 The Military Criminal Code (MCC)

The revised MCC contains a detailed war crimes (Chapter 6bis, Articles 110–114) and crimes against humanity catalogue (Chapter 6, Article 109), along with genocide (Chapter 6, Article 108). Incitement to genocide is outlawed by Article 171a (1bis) MCC, whereas preparatory acts to international crimes are proscribed by Article 171b(1) MCC.[39] These mirror the CC provisions. The following paragraphs, thus, will focus on the differences. Important novelties concern the personal and territorial[40] scope of application of the MCC and the jurisdiction of the Military Justice.[41] Of particular interest is further Chapter 6ter containing the general principles applicable to international crimes.

11.2.2.1 War Crimes

War crimes are enlisted under Chapter 6bis (Articles 110–114) MCC and are divided into grave breaches (Article 111 MCC), war crimes (Articles 112–113 MCC) and other violations of the LOAC (Article 114 MCC). As discussed, Article 109 oMCC already provided a basis for their prosecution. It is noteworthy that plundering has not been included in the list. Nevertheless, it is banned as an ordinary crime under Article 139 MCC. The other new provisions of the MCC mirror Articles 264b–264j CC; reference, thus, is made to the comments made to the CC.

---

[36] Wehrenberg/BS/Article 264, pp. 2096–2097, N 34–35.

[37] Fiolka 2013a, p. 1926, N 5.

[38] Fiolka 2013a, p. 1931, N 27.

[39] BBl 2008, 3895 et seq, p. 3958.

[40] Article 10 (1bis, 1ter and 1quater MCC).

[41] Articles 3, 5, 7, 220 and 221a MCC.

11.2.2.2 Crimes Against Humanity

Article 109 MCC on crimes against humanity mirrors Article 264a CC. Reference is thus made to the comments on that provision of the criminal code.

11.2.2.3 Genocide

Article 108 MCC on genocide mirrors Article 264 CC. It is worth noting, however, that members of the Swiss armed forces remain subject to the military jurisdiction regardless of whether they committed the crime in Switzerland or abroad.[42] Incitement to genocide, instead, is specifically banned under Article 171a MCC as long as the genocide was intended to occur in Switzerland.

11.3 Applying the LOAC in the Swiss Domestic Jurisprudential Sphere

The Swiss judicial mechanism has been occupied by questions of LOAC application in a number of cases. Quite interestingly and pursuant to the legal regime described above, Swiss courts have dealt also with indictments based on the correlation of genocide with war crimes, as demonstrated in the Niyonteze case. As such, the cardinal cases of LOAC application will be analysed below.

11.3.1 The G Case

The *G* case[43] dealt with Mr. G, a Serbian asylum seeker accused of being Goran Karlica, a guard responsible for the mistreatment of several inmates at the Omarska and Keraterm prison camps in Bosnia. In February 1997, the military prosecutor of the Military Divisional Tribunal 1 indicted G.G. for violations of the laws and customs of war under the Swiss Military Criminal Code.[44] It was the first Swiss case dealing with war crimes and determining the Swiss military courts' jurisdiction over foreign nationals accused of serious violations of the laws and customs of war, based on 109 oMCC.[45] It is, thus, an important precedent confirming the compatibility of Article 109 oMCC with the principle of legality.

---

[42] BBl 2008 3863, p. 3961.

[43] G case. In: Ziegler 1998, p. 431; Arnold 2005, p. 764.

[44] Ziegler 1998.

[45] In particular breaches of the III and IV GC of 1949 and of the Additional Protocols of 1977. The main charge was for the beating up, in July 1992, of at least six detainees of the Omarska prison camp and the causing of several wounds to two of them. G was also charged with the

Due to the numerous contradictions in the evidence and the fact that during the period of the indicted fact, the accused was apparently working in Austria and Germany,[46] the Tribunal eventually acquitted him,[47] concluding that G had been probably confused with someone else. The tribunal examined further (a) the issue of damage compensation for the endured years of preventive detention (two)[48] and (b) whether an indictment for *war crimes* may constitute a grave prejudice. The Tribunal concluded that in G's case the indictment for war crimes had not constituted a grave prejudice, since such an eventuality, for citizens coming from the former Yugoslavia in that period, was not exceptional. It could, thus, be presumed that G's reputation within the Serbian community of Bosnia had not been discredited. The highest military judicial authority, the Military Court of Cassation (MCCa), eventually granted him 50,000 Swiss Francs as moral compensation.[49]

11.3.2 The Niyonteze Case

The *Niyonteze Case* dealt with a Rwandan asylum seeker (F.N.) suspected of participation to the 1994 genocide.[50] F.N. was indicted for serious violations of the laws of war, as well as for the ordinary offences of murder, attempted murder and incitement to murder. In 1999, the Military Divisional Tribunal 2 found him guilty under all three counts and sentenced him to life imprisonment and expulsion from Switzerland for 15 years. In 2000 the Military Appeal Tribunal (MAT) confirmed the judgment for serious violations of the laws and customs of war, but reversed the convictions for the other counts. The sentence was reduced to 14 years imprisonment and 15 years expulsion. Both parties appealed to the Military Court of Cassation.[51] (MCCa)

Noteworthy is the MCCa's dismissal of the appeal against the applicability of Article 109 oMCC. The MCCa concluded that this provision may provide a basis for the prosecution of violations of the laws and customs of war also in times of non-international armed conflicts (NIAC), particularly in relation to common

(Footnote 45 continued)
alleged participation, jointly with two uniformed individuals, in the beating up of prisoners, and the alleged attempt to the dignity of several inmates of Keraterm prison camp, in particular by forcing one of them to lick the shoes of one of the guards. G Case, supra, at 3.

46 G case. In: Ziegler 1998, p. 438 ("en droit").

47 G case. In: Ziegler 1998, p. 439 ("en droit"): "Le doute doit profiter à l'accusé et il sera dont acquitté de tous les chefs d'accusation".

48 G Case, p. 4 ("Dommages intérêts et tort moral") (in the original version).

49 G Case, Decision of the Military Court of Cassation, 5.9.1997, p. 2.

50 Niyonteze Case, Jugement du Tribunal militaire d'appel 1A, 26.5.2000, p. 45; Arrêt du Tribunal militaire de cassation, 27.4.2001, p. 30; Arnold 2005, JICJ, p. 764 ; Roth and Henzelin 1998, p. 84 et seq ; Reydams 2002, p. 231 et seq; Ziegler 1997, Revue p. 576 et seq ; Sassoli and Bouvier 1999, pp. 1255–1263 ; Sassoli 2002, p. 151 ; Roth and Henzelin 1998, p. 223.

51 For a commentary see Ziegler 2002, p. 215.

Article 3 to the Geneva Conventions of 1949 and Additional Protocol II of 1977 (APl).[52] Another significant aspect is that no one contested the applicability of Article 109 oMCC in relation to international customary law.[53] In this regard, however, the MAT highlighted a significant restriction. Pursuant to it, Article 109 of MCC must be read in conjunction with Article 108 of MCC. The latter defines the scope of application of issues relating to the violation of the laws and customs of war. The MAT specified that Article 109 of MCC, as indicated by Article 108 (1) oMCC,[54] applies without reservations in the event of an *international* armed conflict (IAC). In the event of a *non-international* armed conflict (NIAC) instead, Article 108 (2) oMCC provides that breaches of the laws of warfare may be pursued only on the basis of an international *treaty* which provides for a larger scope of application than mere IAC. In the MAT's view, this means that in order to apply to NIAC, Articles 109 and 108(2) of MCC require the existence of an international convention ratified by Switzerland, that may be applicable to NIAC, too. *International customary law* per se instead, is an insufficient legal basis to establish the jurisdiction of the Swiss military courts over LOAC breaches committed during a NIAC. Therefore, the MAT restricted its exam to violations of common Article 3 to the GCs and of AP II, on the basis of Article 109 oMCC.[55] For the same reason, since the 1948 Convention on the Prevention on Genocide had not been ratified by Switzerland and since the situation in Rwanda qualified as a NIAC, the latter could not be invoked.

Another interesting aspect was the implicit reference in the judgement to the principle of superior responsibility. In Chapter 5 ("Violation of the duties of a *bourgmestre*"), the MAT highlights the Military Divisional Tribunal's conclusion that the accused, in his role of *bourgmestre* (mayor) had not done everything in his

[52] Judgment of the Military Court of Cassation of 27th April 2001, p. 5 et seq of the original document.

[53] Judgment of the MAT, original version, p. 28: "Le Tribunal d'appel considère que l'art 109 CPM énonce une clause générale réprimant non seulement les violations des conventions internationales signées et ratifiées par la Suisse, mais aussi les violations des normes coutumières reconnues par la communauté internationale (cf. Message du Conseil fédéral concernant une révision partielle du code pénal militaire du 6 mars 1967, publié à la Feuille fédérale 1967 I 605 et seq, 610 et 612). (unofficial) English translation: The Appeals Tribunal considers that Article 109 MCC states a general clause repressing not only violations of international conventions signed and ratified by Switzerland, but also violations of customary norms recognised by the international community."

[54] Article 108 oMCC: 1 Les dispositions de ce chapitre sont applicables en cas de guerres déclarées et d'autres conflits armés entre deux ou plusieurs Etats; à ces conflits sont assimilés les atteintes à la neutralité, ainsi que le recours à la force pour repousser de telles atteintes. 2 La violation d'accords internationaux est aussi punissable si les accords prévoient un champ d'application plus étendu. (unofficial) English translation: 1 The provisions of this chapter are applicable in the event of a declared war and other armed conflicts between two or more States; attacks against neutrality, as well as the use of force in order to counteract such attacks, are associated to these conflicts. 2 The violation of international conventions is also punishable, if such conventions provide for a wider scope of application.

[55] Judgment of the MAT, original version, p. 29.

power to prevent or limit the massacres. It further adds, however, that these omissions on his part did not constitute an additional and complementary crime to those perpetrated actively by him.[56] Therefore, the MAT seems to consider command responsibility as a complementary charge to active participation, rather than as a *sui generis* and independent crime. The concurrent or alternative application of war crimes provisions and the principle of command responsibility has been a long disputed issue.[57] It will be interesting to see how the Federal Criminal Tribunal will assess the question.

A consequent application of the principle as a *sui generis* offence, corresponding to a dereliction of a commander's duties, would require a concurrent application of the two forms of liability (e.g. active perpetration and command responsibility out of omission). This position was held, for instance, in the *Oric Case*, where the Trial Chamber of the ICTY sentenced the accused to two years of imprisonment for failure to prevent the crimes committed by his soldiers,[58] considering his guilt the dereliction of his duties as commander, rather than his participation in the crimes.

The view held here is that the protected goods differ. The war crimes provisions protect the physical or mental integrity of a person (e.g. the war crime of murder). The provisions on command responsibility, instead, protect the rule of law (i.e. in particular the observance of the LOAC and discipline within the armed forces/ groups). This approach, thus, justifies a concurrent application of the two forms of liability. On the other hand, one may argue that it would be illogical to condemn a superior for having ordered the commission of crimes and, at the same time, for having failed to prevent their occurrence. In this case, an alternative would be to consider the two modes of liability concurrently. In this case, however, the perpetrator's rank should be an aggravating circumstance. This aspect, however, should be considered during the phase of sentencing, rather than of the indictment. The Military Divisional Tribunal 2 added that these omissions by a superior were not sanctioned by any applicable legal provision.[59] This is astonishing, since the principle of command responsibility, as discussed, finds a basis both in the Swiss military legislation and in Articles 86–87 AP I.

---

[56] Judgment of the MAT, original version, p. 25.

[57] Bonafé 2007, p. 612 et seq; Meloni 2007, pp. 620–621.

[58] Prosecutor v. Oric, TJ, §§ 293, 724. On the issue of cumulative convictions for individual and superior responsibility, see § 339 et seq.

[59] Decision of the Military Divisional Tribunal 2 of 26th August 1999, Chapter 4, C. Violation des devoirs du bourgmestre, reprinted in Ziegler et al., p. 328: "En effet, d'une part, les manquements sont absorbés par le comportement actif retenu à la charge de l'accusé en rapport avec la réunion du Mont Mushubati et le camp de Kabgayi et, d'autre part, ils ne sont sanctionnés par aucune norme légale applicable." (unofficial) English translation: "in fact, on the one hand, the omissions are absorbed by the active behaviour charged against the accused in relation to the meeting held at Mount Mushubati and at camp Kabgayi and, on the other hand, they are not sanctioned by any applicable legal provision."

Since the Military Prosecutor did not appeal against the Divisional Tribunal's conclusions on the failures of the *bourgmestre* to prevent the crimes, the MAT did not consider the matter any further. This was a lost opportunity to obtain a jurisprudential basis clearly qualifying the nature of breaches of the principle of command responsibility and determining its application to civilian superiors (such as mayors) and to NIAC.

With regard to the appeal grounds raised by the Military Prosecutor, the MCCa concluded that the MAT had not made an arbitrary consideration of the facts.[60] It concluded that the MAT had been sufficiently severe.

In sum, the MCCa rejected all the grounds of appeal, confirmed the sentence and revoked the expulsion, asking the MAT to reconsider this aspect.[61] On 29th December 2005, Niyonteze was given release on parole. The immigration authorities having decided to expel him from Switzerland after his release from prison, the Swiss Supreme Court, by decree dated 11 September 2006, validated the decision to deport him from Switzerland.[62]

11.4 Conclusion

With the revision of the MCC and the CC Switzerland fully implemented the ICC Statute and proved its humanitarian tradition, by introducing some legislative novelties such as the extension of the crime of genocide to social and political groups, or by generally extending the war crimes catalogue to all armed conflicts, regardless of them being international or non-international. This humanitarian approach, on the one hand, is to be appreciated, but on the other hand, from a systematic point of view, it raises several legal issues, especially when these provisions must be applied to foreign nationals, whose countries of origin have implemented differently the LOAC and other international treaties proscribing international crimes.

On the other hand, in other instances, the legislator's approach has been much stricter. For instance, its narrow interpretation of the principles of non-retroactivity and legality with regard to the new provisions on crimes against humanity and genocide will pose major obstacles to the prosecution of these crimes, notwithstanding their long-established recognition as customary law by the international community.

---

[60] Decision of the MCC, p. 51.

[61] Arnold 2005, JICJ, p. 764.

[62] A.X. contre Service de la population et des migrants du canton de Fribourg, et Tribunal administratif du canton de Fribourg (A.X. Against the immigration service of Canton Fribourg, cantonal administrative tribunal of Fribourg), judgment of 11th September 2006, 2nd Court of Public Law of the Swiss Federal Tribunal, case no. 2A.328/2006, available online at http://competenceuniverselle.files.wordpress.com/2011/08/niyonteze-tribunal-fc3a9dc3a9ral-11-septembre-2006.pdf (in French).

The author's impression, moreover, is that in adopting the new provisions of the CC and MCC, the legislator was too "ICC Statute" oriented. This focus may have led the legislator to overlook the fact that the ICC Statute was the result of a *compromise* and that its provisions were derived from well-rooted LOAC principles. This should be kept in mind, however, by the judicial authorities. When applying principles such as command responsibility, these should not be interpreted exclusively from a criminal law perspective, but also in the light of their aim and objective under the LOAC and military law.

In the final line, the Swiss legislator and its judicial authorities have proven their commitment to fight against impunity. The question of LOAC application, thus, is not one of "if" but of "when" and "how". And on this, the Swiss judicial system has demonstrated prudence and a strict adherence to the fundamental principles of criminal law.

Appendix: Documentation

Military Legislation (Service Regulations)

- Regulations nr. 51.007.04 "Legal bases for conduct during an engagement" of 1st July 2005 (Rechtliche Grundlagen für das Verhalten im Einsatz) (cited as RVE)
- Regulations nr. 51.7/II d on the Laws and Customs of War (Regl. Nr. 51.7/II d Gesetze und Gebräuche des Krieges)
- Booklet nr. 51.7/III on the Laws and Customs of War (Lehrschrift 51.7/III d f i "Gesetze und Gebräuche des Krieges"
- Pocket card nr. 51.7/IV d on the principles of the laws of armed conflict for the commander (Merkblatt 51.7/IV d "Kriegsvölkerrechtliche Grundsätze für den Kommandanten")
- Regulations nr. 52.11 on the interrogation of prisoners of war (Regl. 52.11 d "Kriegsgefangenenbefragung").

Online Document

Papers

- Amendments to the Rome Statute of the International Criminal Court: consultation procedure launched', Bern, 26.6.2013, at http://www.news.admin.ch/message/index.html?lang=en&msg-id=49423
- Federal Department of Foreign Affairs (2013) Amendments to the Rome Statute of the International Criminal Court: consultation procedure launched, 26th

June 2013 http://www.eda.admin.ch/eda/en/home/recent/media/single.html?id=49423
- Jurius (2010) Guerres et genocides: le Conseil des Etats prône un arsenal pénal encore plus severe. *Jusletter* 22nd March 2010. In: Trial Watch (19.3.2010) *Genocide, Crimes against Humanity and War Crimes: Switzerland to Have a New Law—But with Limited Application* (19 March 2010) www.trialch.org/en/activities/details/article/genocide-crimes-against-humanity-and-war-crimes-switzerland-to-have-anew-law-but-with-limited-a.html?tx_ttnews[backPid]=50&cHash=dc1d25f5d5.

Legislation

International

- Rome Statute for an International Criminal Court of 17.7.1998, in force in Switzerland since 1st July 2002 http://www.admin.ch/opc/de/classified-compilation/20002381/index.html
- Convention against Torture and Other Cruel, Inhuman or Degrading Treatment or Punishment, New York, 10 December 1984, at http://legal.un.org/avl/ha/catcidtp/catcidtp.html. Accessed 26 May 2014
- Convention on the Prevention and Punishment of the Crime of Genocide of 9th December 1948. http://untreaty.un.org/cod/avl/ha/cppcg/cppcg.html.

Domestic

- Federal Constitution of the Swiss Confederation of 18 April 1999, RS 101. http://www.admin.ch/ch/e/rs/c101.html.
- Swiss Military Criminal Code (MCC) of 13th June 1927, RS 321, in French, Italian and German on the website of the Swiss Military Attorney General (cited as oMCC) http://www.vbs.admin.ch/internet/vbs/fr/home/documentation/oa010.html.
- Swiss Criminal Code (CC) of 21st December 1937, SR 311.0 http://www.admin.ch/opc/de/classified-compilation/19370083/index.html.
- Federal law of 5th October 1967 on the modification of the Military Criminal Code (Bundesgesetz betreffend die Änderung des Militärstrafgesetzes vom 5. Oktober 1967) BBl 1967 I 587 (cited as BBl 1967 I 587) http://www.amtsdruckschriften.bar.admin.ch/viewOrigDoc.do?id=10043764.
- Service Regulations of 22nd June 1994 (Dienstreglement der Schweizerischen Armee), SR 510.107.0 (cited as DR 04) http://www.admin.ch/opc/de/classified-compilation/19950175/index.html.

- Federal Law of 22nd June 2001 on the cooperation with the ICC (*Loi fédérale du 22 juin 2001 sur la coopération avec la Cour pénale internationale (LCPI)*), SR 351.6 www.admin.ch/ch/f/rs/c351_6.html.
- Swiss Criminal Procedure Code (CrimPC), RS 312.0, in English at http://www.admin.ch/opc/en/classified-compilation/20052319/index.html.
- Federal Law of 18th June 2010 on the modification of federal laws for the implementation of the Rome Statute of the International Criminal Court (Bundesgesetz vom 18. Juni 2010 über die Änderung von Bundesgesetzen zur Umsetzung des Römer Statuts des Internationalen Strafgerichtshofs), BBl 2010 4277 (cited as BBl 2010 4277) http://www.admin.ch/opc/de/federal-gazette/2010/4277.pdf.

Jurisprudence

Swiss

- Niyonteze Case:

- Judgment of the Military Divisional Tribunal 2 of 26th August 1999 (in French), reprinted in Ziegler/Wehrenberg/Weber (Eds), *Procès de criminels de guerre en Suisse* (Zürich : Schulthess Verlag)(2009), at 298
- Judgment of the Military Appeal Tribunal 1A of 26th May 2000 (in French), reprinted in Ziegler/Wehrenberg/Weber (Eds), *Procès de criminels de guerre en Suisse* (Zürich : Schulthess Verlag)(2009), at 334; original version available online at http://www.vbs.admin.ch/internet/vbs/de/home/documentation/oa009.parsys.0025.downloadList.00251.DownloadFile.tmp/urteiln2instanz.pdf (Decision of the MAT)
- Judgment of the Military Court of Cassation of 27th April 2001 (in French), reprinted in Ziegler/Wehrenberg/Weber (Eds), *Procès de criminels de guerre en Suisse* (Zürich : Schulthess Verlag)(2009),at 359. Original version in: Armee Suisse, Arrêts du TMC, 12ème Volume, pp 1–30 (Decision of the MCC), online at http://www.vbs.admin.ch/internet/vbs/de/home/documentation/oa009.parsys.0026.downloadList.00261.DownloadFile.tmp/entscheid021.pdf
- A.X. contre Service de la population et des migrants du canton de Fribourg, et Tribunal administratif du canton de Fribourg (A.X. Against the immigration service of Canton Fribourg, cantonal administrative tribunal of Fribourg), judgment of 11th September 2006, 2nd Court of Public Law of the Swiss Federal Tribunal, case no. 2A.328/2006, available online at http://competenceuniverselle.files.wordpress.com/2011/08/niyonteze-tribunal-fc3a9dc3a9ral-11-septembre-2006.pdf (in French).

- *G* case:

– Judgement of the Divisional Military Tribunal I, 14–18 April 1997, Lausanne, reprinted in A. Ziegler, S. Wehrenberg, R. Weber, *Procès de criminels de guerre en Suisse* (Zurich : Schulthess Verlag)(2009), at 431.
– Decision of the Military Court of Cassation, 5.9.1997, available in the Swiss Military Justice's Collection of Decisions of the Military Court of Cassation, Volume 12 (5), at 2.

- *Prosecutor v. Brima, Kamara and Kanu* SCSL-04-16-T, TJ, 20.6.2007 (*Brima TJ*)
- *Prosecutor v. Halilovic,* Case No. IT-01-48-T, Judgment, 16 November 2005 (*Halilovic TJ*);
- *Prosecutor v. Hadžihasanović* et al., Case No. IT-01-47-T, Judgment, 15 March 2006 (*Hadžihasanović TJ*)
- *Prosecutor v. Enver Hadzihasanovic* et al., Decision on interlocutory appeal challenging jurisdiction in relation to command responsibility, Case No. IT-01-47-AR72, 16.7.2003 (*Hadžihasanović Interlocutory Appeal*)
- *Prosecutor v. Delalić* et al., *TJ*, Case no. IT-96-21, Judgment of 16th November 1998 (*Delalić TJ*)
- *Prosecutor v. Oric*, TJ, Case no. IT—03-68-T, Judgment of 30th June 2006 (Oric TJ)
- Arrest Warrant Case (Democratic Republic of Congo vs. Belgium) ICJ Rep. 2002.

Other

- Amsterdam Court of Appeal, Bouterse case (Gerechtshof Amsterdam, 20 November 2000).

References

Arnold R (2005) Military criminal procedures and judicial guarantees: the example of Switzerland. J Int Crim Justice 3(3):749 (cited as Arnold JICJ)
Arnold R (2011) Correspondent's report for Switzerland. Yearb Int Humanit Law 14:1
Arnold R (2013) Book Review of Maria Nybondas' 'Command responsibility and its applicability to civilian superiors'. J Int Crim Justice 11(4):943 (cited as Arnold–Nybondas)
Arnold R, Wehrenberg S (2014: forthcoming) Die Strafbarkeit des Vorgesetzten nach Art. 264k StGB, [The criminal responsibility of the superior under Art. 264K of the Swiss criminal code]. The Military Law and Law of War Review
Bonafé B (2007) Finding a proper role for command responsibility. J Int Crim Justice 5:599
Fiolka G (2013a) Kommentar zu Article 259. In: Niggli MA, Wiprächtiger H (eds) Basler Kommentar zum StGB, Vol. II, 3rd edn. Helbing & Lichtenhahn, Basel, pp 1923–1932

Fiolka G (2013b) Kommentar zu Article 264 k. In: Niggli MA, Wiprächtiger H (eds) Basler Kommentar zum StGB, Vol. II, 3rd ed. Helbing & Lichtenhahn, Basel, pp 2245–2264

Fiolka G, Zehnder B (2013) Kommentar zu Article 264b-j. In: Niggli MA, Wiprächtiger H (eds) Basler Kommentar zum StGB, Vol. II, 3rd edn. Helbing & Lichtenhahn, Basel, pp 2139–2160

Meloni C (2007) Mode of liability for the crimes of subordinates or separate offence of the superior? J Int Crim Justice 5:619

Méttraux G (2009) The law of command responsibility. Oxford University Press, Oxford

Reydams L (2002) International decisions, Nyionteze v Public prosecutor. AJIL 96:231

Roth R, Henzelin M (1998) La répression des violations du droit international humanitaire en Suisse. In: Pellandini C (ed) Répression nationale des violations du droit international humanitaire (systèmes romano-germaniques): rapport de la réunion d'experts, 23–25 September 1997. ICRC, Geneva, pp 84–201

Sassoli M, Bouvier A (1999) How does law protect in war?. Int Comm Red Cross, Geneva

Sassoli M (2002) Le génocide rwandais, la justice militaire suisse et le droit international. Rev Suisse de Droit Int et Eur 2:151

Triffterer O. (2008) Commentary to Article 28 ICC Statute. In: Triffterer O (ed) Commentary on the Rome Statute of the International Criminal Court, 2nd edn. Oxford University Press, Oxford

Van Wijnkoop J (2009) Das Engagement der Schweiz—Grundlagen und erste Schritte. In: Ziegler A et al (ed) Procès de criminels de guerre en Suisse. Schulthess, Zurich, pp 3–16

Wehrenberg S, Ehlert C (2013) Kommentar zu Article 264a StGB, In: Niggli MA, Wiprächtiger H (eds) Basler Kommentar zum StGB, Vol. II, 3rd edn. Helbing & Lichtenhahn, Basel, pp 2112–2137

Ziegler A (1997) Domestic prosecution and international cooperation with regard to violations of international humanitarian law: the case of Switzerland. Rev Suisse de Droit Int et Eur 5:561

Ziegler A (1998) International Decision in Re G. Military Tribunal, Division 1, Lausanne, Switzerland, April 18, 1997. AJIL 92:78

Ziegler A (2002) Militärkassationsgericht, Entscheid vom 27.4.2001. Aktuelle Juristische Praxis 215

Chapter 12
International Humanitarian Law in the Courts of Australia

Emily Crawford

Contents

12.1 Introduction

Australia was involved in nearly every major international war in the twentieth century. Starting with the formation of the fabled ANZAC—Australian and New Zealand Army Corps—in World War I, who fought during the Battle of Gallipoli in 1915,[1] and reformed to fight during the Second World War,[2] Australian troops

E. Crawford, Postdoctoral Fellow, Sydney Law School, New Law Building F10, Eastern Avenue, University of Sydney, New South Wales, 2006, Australia. The author wishes to thank Ms. Melissa Martin for her excellent research assistance on this article, and to Professor Mary Crock at the University of Sydney for her advice and guidance.

[1] *Oxford Companion to Australian Military History* 2008.
[2] See generally Laffin 1965.

E. Crawford (✉)
Sydney Law School, Camperdown, NSW 2006, Australia
e-mail: emily.crawford@sydney.edu.au

D. Jinks et al. (eds.), *Applying International Humanitarian Law in Judicial and Quasi-Judicial Bodies*, DOI: 10.1007/978-94-6265-008-4_12,

have fought in the wars in Korea, Vietnam, the Gulf, and Afghanistan,[3] as well as been part of international peace-keeping missions in places such as Timor-Leste and the Solomon Islands.[4] Australia also has the 'lucky honour'—if you will—of being spared the ravages of civil war.[5] While Australia was subject to attack on its territory during the Second World War,[6] it has not been beset by widespread internal violence, nor has it been invaded in since its initial colonization in 1788.

Australia is party to the major international humanitarian law treaties, including the Geneva Conventions of 1949,[7] the Additional Protocols to the Geneva Conventions,[8] the Rome Statute of the International Criminal Court,[9] as well as a number of the weapons treaties.[10] These treaties have been given domestic

---

[3] See the Australian Defence Force website regarding current Australian deployments, specifically http://www.defence.gov.au/media/download/2004/aug/250804/Defence_Winning%20Peace_War.pdf; and the Australian War Memorial website for information regarding past deployments, at http://www.awm.gov.au/atwar/.

[4] Ibid.

[5] Australia ranks 22nd 'most peaceful country in the world', according to the Global Peace Index survey conducted in 2012 by the Institute for Economics and Peace. Peace is correlated to indicators such as income, schooling and the level of regional integration, as well as transparency of government and lack of institutional corruption. See further http://www.visionofhumanity.org/globalpeaceindex/2012-gpi-findings/.

[6] Lockwood 2005.

[7] The Geneva Conventions, as they are collectively known (and as they will be referred to in this book) are Geneva Convention for the Amelioration of the Condition of the Wounded and Sick in Armed Forces in the Field of August 12 1949, 75 *UNTS* 31 (hereinafter Geneva Convention I or GCI); Geneva Convention for the Amelioration of the Condition of Wounded, Sick and Shipwrecked Members of Armed Forces at Sea of August 12 1949, 75 *UNTS* 85 (hereinafter Geneva Convention II or GCII); Geneva Convention Relative to the Treatment of Prisoners of War of August 12 1949, 75 *UNTS* 135 (hereinafter Geneva Convention III, the POW Convention, or GCIII); and Geneva Convention Relative to the Protection of Civilian Persons in Time of War of August 12 1949, 75 *UNTS* 287 (hereinafter Geneva Convention IV, the Civilians Convention, or GCIV).

[8] The Additional Protocols comprise Protocol Additional to the Geneva Conventions of 12 August 1949, and relating to the Protection of Victims of International Armed Conflicts of 8 June 1977, 1125 *UNTS* 3, and Protocol Additional to the Geneva Conventions of 12 August 1949, and relating to the Protection of Victims of Non-International Armed Conflicts of 8 June 1977, 1125 *UNTS* 609.

[9] Rome Statute of the International Criminal Court, 2187 *UNTS* 90.

[10] Including the 1972 Convention on the Prohibition of the Development, Production and Stockpiling of Bacteriological (Biological) and Toxin Weapons and on their Destruction, 1015 *UNTS* 163; the 1993 Convention on the Prohibition of the Development, Production, Stockpiling and Use of Chemical Weapons and on their Destruction, 1974 *UNTS* 45; the 1997 Ottawa Convention on the Prohibition of the Use, Stockpiling, Production and Transfer of Anti-Personnel Mines and on their Destruction, 2056 *UNTS* 211; the 2008 Cluster Munitions Convention, Depositary notification C.N.776.2008.TREATIES-2 of 10 Nov 2008; and the 1980 Convention on the Prohibition or Restriction on the Use of Certain Conventional Weapons which may be deemed to be Excessively Injurious or Have Indiscriminate Effects, 1342 UNTS 137, and its protocols: weapons that injure by fragments which are not detectable in human body by X-rays (Protocol I; adopted 1980 1342 *UNTS* 168; non-detectable anti-personnel mines (Protocol II; adopted 1980, 1342 *UNTS* 168; anti-personnel incendiary weapons (Protocol III, adopted 1980);

legislative effect.[11] As such, Australian courts have had recourse to examine them and to assess and apply the obligations they embalm. The bulk of these cases has tended to deal with refugee matters and extradition orders, though some cases have raised issues of extraterritorial application of Australian law. This chapter will examine some of those cases to develop an overview of how international humanitarian law (IHL) in particular has been received and implemented in Australia.

12.2 Australia and International Law: A Prefatory Note

Before analysing the instances of IHL in Australian case law, it is useful to note, if briefly, the reception of international law in the courts of Australia. Australia takes an essentially dualist approach to international law[12]—treaties are only given direct effect in the Australian legal system if there is legislation that expressly implements the treaty obligations.[13] In keeping with this dualist approach, Australian courts will follow the intent of the legislation even if the legislation clearly and unambiguously intends to operate contrary to international law. Put another way, "the provisions of a Commonwealth or state statute, validly made, must be applied even though they are in contravention of accepted rules of international law."[14] However, as a general rule, Courts will attempt to interpret legislation in line with Australian obligations under international law.[15] The *Acts Interpretation Act 1901* (Cth), as amended in 1984, allows for courts to refer to extrinsic materials—such as treaties—in the interpretation of federal statutes if provisions within the statutes are ambiguous or obscure, or if treaties are specifically referred to in the statute.[16]

Regarding customary international law, Australian courts have not accepted the English position, enunciated in *Trendtex Trading Corp v. Central Bank of Nigeria,*[17] that customary international law is automatically part of Australia law.[18] However, case law has demonstrated that Australian courts have not clearly adopted the

(Footnote 10 continued)
laser weapons that cause permanent blindness (Protocol IV; adopted 1996), 1380 *UNTS* 370; explosive remnants of war (Protocol V; adopted 2005) 2399 *UNTS* 100.

[11] *Criminal Code Act 1995* (Cth), *Geneva Conventions Act 1957* (Cth) amended to include the Additional Protocols, *International Criminal Court Act 2002* (Cth), *International Criminal Court (Consequential Amendments Act) 2002* (Cth); Chemical Weapons (Prohibition) Act 1994 (Cth); Weapons of Mass Destruction (Prevention of Proliferation) Act 1995 (Cth); Crimes (Biological Weapons) Act 1976 (Cth).

[12] Balkin 2005, p. 119.

[13] Ibid, 127.

[14] Allars 1997, p. 239.

[15] Balkin 2005, pp. 132–135.

[16] Sections 15AB(1)(i)(ii), and (2)(d)–(f) and (h).

[17] [1977] QB 529 (CA) per Denning MR.

[18] 'It is apparent that Australian judges, while not entirely consistent in their approaches, have not accepted the proposition, enunciated by English courts in the eighteenth century and

transformation approach either. Australian Courts have evidenced a cautious acceptance of international law in their decisions; while not accepting outright automatic incorporation of customary international law into Australian law, the Courts have nonetheless demonstrated a willingness to accept customary international law as a persuasive factor in interpretation, even in the absence of implementing legislation.[19]

In these realms, questions of international humanitarian law most often come in for judicial consideration in the context of legislation relating to refugee law and extradition; however, Australia does have some limited experience with war crimes prosecutions—these will be explored in this next section.

12.3 IHL in the Courts of Australia

12.3.1 World War II War Crimes Prosecutions

The laws of armed conflict were first dealt with in the courts of Australia in the post-World War II trials of Japanese war criminals. From 1943 onwards, as information came to light regarding Japanese conduct towards captured prisoners of war (POWs), civilian internees, and the civilian population at large, the Australian government began to put into place measures to investigate and prosecute the perpetrators of such acts at the cessation of hostilities.[20] The Australian government appointed Sir William Webb, then Chief Justice of Queensland, Commissioner under National Security (Inquiries) Regulations; with the objective to investigate whether the Japanese armed forces had violated the laws of armed conflict.[21] Between 1943 and 1945, Webb undertook three commissions of inquiry into Japanese conduct,[22] culminating in the adoption of the *War Crimes Act 1945* (Cth). Under that Act, Australian military courts had jurisdiction to prosecute a variety of criminal acts committed against any person who was at any time an Australian resident or a citizen of any power allied or associated with Australia during World War II.[23] The criminal acts included ill-treatment of prisoners of war in labour camps, the massacre or execution of captured allied servicemen, local inhabitants or civilian internees, and widespread acts of assault, torture and

(Footnote 18 continued)
reaffirmed by the English Court of Appeal…that international law *in its fullest extent* is automatically incorporated as part of the law of the land.' Balkin 2005, p. 115, 117.

[19] This cautious approach has been seen in key Australian cases, such as *Nulyarimma v. Thompson* (1999) 165 ALR 621.

[20] Anderson 1996, pp. 138–139.

[21] Evatt 1945, pp. 1–3.

[22] The Third Commission was jointly run by Webb, Justice Mansfield of the Queensland Supreme Court and Judge Kirby of the New South Wales District Court.

[23] *War Crimes Act 1945* (Cth), s5.

murder.[24] Following the cessation of hostilities, between 30 November 1945 and 9 April 1951, 924 enemy nationals were tried for war crimes in 296 trials conducted by Australian military courts. Of those found guilty by these trials, 148 were sentenced to death and executed. An additional 496 were given prison sentences.[25]

Australia became signatory to the Geneva Conventions of 1949 in 1950, giving the Conventions domestic legislative effect in the *Geneva Conventions Act 1957* (Cth). Under the Act, grave breaches of the Geneva Conventions of 1949 are crimes under Federal law, over which Australian courts have jurisdiction. Under s7(1) of the Act:

> a person who, in Australia or elsewhere, commits, or aids, abets of procures the commission by another person, of a grave breach of any of the Conventions in guilty of an indictable offence.

However, by the end of the 1950s, there was apparent groundswell within Australia to wind-up such prosecutions.[26] Perceived public fatigue at the duration of the war crimes trials,[27] along with the fact that Australia did not invoke the *War Crimes Act* after 1951, led Acting Minister for External Affairs and Attorney-General Sir Garfield Barwick to remark in the House of Representatives that "the time has come to close the chapter",[28] to allow the nation to rebuild and move forward.[29]

By the 1980s, renewed interest was shown regarding the prosecution of Axis war criminals. Media reports in April of 1986[30] raised the possibility that UK, US and Australian governments in power during the 1950s had knowingly allowed "substantial numbers of Nazi war criminals"[31] to enter Australia, facilitated in part "by American and UK intelligence agencies deceiving or withholding information from Australian officers and even by the involvement of these Australian officers in the deception."[32] Around this same time, commissions of inquiry in the United Kingdom[33] and Canada[34] had uncovered compelling evidence that both countries were home to hundreds of suspected war criminals. A similar inquiry in Australia[35] was launched; known as the *Menzies Report*, it uncovered evidence that

---

[24] *War Crimes Act 1945* (Cth), s6.

[25] http://www.naa.gov.au/collection/fact-sheets/fs61.aspx. See generally Dickinson 1952.

[26] Triggs 1988, p. 382; Menzies 1987, p. 9.

[27] Triggs 1997, p. 126.

[28] Commonwealth of Australia, *Parliamentary Debates*, House of Representatives, 22 March 1961, 449, 451.

[29] Boas 2010, p. 316.

[30] ABC Radio National, *Background Briefing*, "Nazis in Australia", first broadcast 13 April 1986; see also ABC TV, *Don't Mention the War*, first broadcast 22 April 1986.

[31] Menzies 1987, p. 7.

[32] Ibid.

[33] *The Hetherington-Chalmers Report* 1989.

[34] Deschênes 1986.

[35] Menzies 1987.

Australia was "more likely than not"[36] home to a significant number of persons alleged to have committed war crimes during the Second World War, leading to the perception that Australia was a "welcoming sanctuary"[37] for war criminals.

In response to the investigations undertaken by the *Menzies Report* into war criminals living in Australia, Attorney-General Lionel Bowen went on record to rebut his predecessor Sir Garfield Barwick's comments,[38] stating that the Australian government "does not regard the chapter as closed... justice must be done, no matter how much time has passed since the events in question."[39] The Government established a Special Investigations Unit to examine whether any of the persons named in the *Menzies Report* could potentially be prosecuted in Australian courts. However, in order for such prosecutions to proceed, amendment of the *War Crimes Act 1945* (Cth) was necessary; the *Menzies Report* had made it clear that it was "unthinkable"[40] to prosecute Australian residents and citizens under the military court schema provided for in the *War Crimes Act*. The Australian government thus passed the War Crimes Amendment Act 1988 (Cth), which enabled the regular court system to handle these cases.[41] The amended Act varied from the 1945 Act, in that it dealt with war crimes committed in Europe between 1 September 1939 and 8 May 1945—thus excluding any war crimes committed in the Pacific theatre of war.[42]

Under the amended Act, prosecutions were brought against three Ukrainians who were living in South Australia—Ivan Polyukhovich,[43] Michael Berezowsky,[44] and Heinrich Wagner.[45] An initial challenge to the constitutional validity of the Act was resolved by the High Court of Australia,[46] and the trials were able to proceed. However, none of the cases were heard to completion. The trial of Ivan Polyukhovich was terminated in the Supreme Court of South Australia, due to eyewitness evidence being deemed inherently unreliable;[47] the Magistrate hearing the preliminary proceedings against Michael Berezowsky refused to allow the case to proceed to trial, refusing an application to allow evidence against Berezowsky

---

36 Ibid 177.

37 Aarons 2001, p. 2.

38 See infra.

39 Commonwealth of Australia, *Parliamentary Debates*, House of Representatives, 24 February 1987, 594–595.

40 Menzies 1987, p. 163.

41 For more on the *War Crimes Amendment Act* see Triggs 1988, 1997; Boas 2010.

42 Triggs 1997, p. 129.

43 Ivan Timofeyevich Polyukhovich, No. S3782, Supreme Court of South Australia, 22 December 1992 (unreported).

44 Mikolay Berezowsky, File NO. 91/25241, Adelaide Magistrates Court, 16 July 1992.

45 Peter Hughes, "Man Committed for Trial on War Crimes Charges", *The Age*, 21 November 1992.

46 *Polyukhovich v. Commonwealth*, 172 CLR 501 (1991).

47 *Polyukhovich*, Supreme Court of South Australia, 19; see also Boas 2010, p. 319; Triggs 1997, pp. 130–132.

to be taken from two elderly Ukrainian witnesses located overseas. The Magistrate held that Berezowsky could not receive a fair trial if he was not able to confront the eyewitnesses in person.[48] The third accused, Heinrich Wagner, suffered a heart attack during the preliminary proceedings of his trial; the prosecution decided to drop the case, believing that Wagner would not survive a criminal trial.[49]

Following the failure of all three cases, the Attorney-General, Michael Duffy, announced the closure of the War Crimes Special Investigation Unit.[50] On-going investigations were, ostensibly, to continue, but no new investigations were to be opened; by September 1992, a proposed fourth prosecution was abandoned by the Australian government.[51] Australia's history of war crimes prosecutions was thus, as Triggs puts it, "spasmodic, selective and short."[52] Indeed, in the years that followed the closure of the War Crimes Special Investigation Unit, concerns regarding the harbouring of war criminals continued to emerge—Konrad Kalejs, believed to have been a member of the Arajs Kommando in World War II,[53] was investigated by Australian Federal Police, who eventually abandoned their investigation, citing insufficient evidence.[54] Kalejs died in 2001, fighting attempts to extradite him to Latvia to face war crimes charges.[55] Since then, the issue of World War II Axis criminals has essentially disappeared from view.

Since the abortive attempts at war crimes prosecutions towards the end of the twentieth century, Australian courts have had little cause to examine the issue of IHL. Visits to Australia by then-US President George W Bush brought on calls for a 'citizen's arrest' of Bush for war crimes in Iraq and Afghanistan;[56] unsurprisingly, such an 'arrest' did not take place.

However, attempts to bring charges against another sitting head of state did come to the Australian courts in 2011, when an attempt was made to bring charges against the President of Sri Lanka, Mahinda Rajapaksa, for the commission of alleged war crimes in the Sri Lankan civil war.[57] Arunachalam Jegatheeswaran, a Sri Lankan-born Australian citizen, filed the indictment, with the charges laid in the Melbourne Magistrates' Court, preparatory to Rajapaksa's arrival in Australia

---

48 *Berezowsky*, per DC Gurry SM.

49 Maryann Stenberg, "End to War Crimes Trials", *The Age*, 11 December 1993.

50 Triggs 1997, p. 134.

51 Ibid.

52 Triggs 1997, p. 123.

53 The Arajs Kommando was a unit of the Nazi-sponsored Latvian Auxiliary Police, named for Victor Arajs, who headed the unit. The Kommando who gained a reputation for their brutality and savagery—see generally Angrick, Klein 2012.

54 Boas 2010, p. 322.

55 Alan Gold, "We Must Pursue All War Criminals", *The Canberra Times*, 11 November 2001.

56 Dan Harrison, "Students Stirke Over Bush", The Age, 5 September 2007;

57 See Michael Gordon, "Sri Lankan President Accused of War Crimes in Australian Court", *The Sydney Morning Herald*, 25 October 2011, available at http://www.smh.com.au/national/sri-lankan-president-accused-of-war-crimes-by-australian-citizen-20111024-1mgd2.html.

for the Commonwealth Heads of Government Meeting (CHOGM).[58] Jegatheeswaran alleged that he witnessed the deliberate targeting of civilians and civilian infrastructure, such as schools and hospitals, during 2007–2008, and that the commission of such acts by the Sri Lankan government were war crimes.[59] The instigation of the case by Jegatheeswaran was done under the *International Criminal Court (Consequential Amendments) Act 2002* (Cth), which amended the *Criminal Code Act 1995 (Cth)* in order to incorporate the international crimes recognised under the Rome Statute of the International Criminal Court within Australian domestic criminal law. Less than a day after the indictment was filed, the Attorney-General, Robert McLelland, moved to quash the charges,[60] citing s268.121(1) of the Criminal Code, which states that any proceedings concerning genocide, war crimes, crimes against humanity, and crimes against the administration of justice of the International Criminal Court, "must not be commenced without the Attorney-General's written consent"—which was absent in this instance. At the time, the Attorney-General did not give any written reasons behind the decision to quash; however, a spokesperson stated that Rajapaksa was entitled to head of state immunity, and thus any case brought against him in an Australian domestic court would put Australian in violation of its international obligations.[61] This approach, though undoubtedly disappointing for Jegatheeswaran, nonetheless was an accurate and appropriate response in line with current international law approaches to head of state immunity.[62]

A war crimes investigation which was still open in 2013 has originated from an inquiry into the deaths of five journalists killed in Timor-Leste in October 1975.[63] Known as the 'Balibó Five',[64] the journalists—two Australians, two

---

[58] Ibid.

[59] http://jurist.org/paperchase/2011/10/australia-citizen-files-war-crimes-charges-against-sri-lanka-president.php

[60] http://www.abc.net.au/news/2011-10-25/mcclelland-sri-lanka-decision/3600104

[61] http://www.watoday.com.au/wa-news/sri-lankan-pm-will-not-answer-war-crimes-claims-20111025-1mi4c.html. See also Hood and Cormier 2012.

[62] The current situation regarding head of state immunity is highly contested. As a general principle, incumbent heads of state enjoy both personal and functional immunity from prosecution, in domestic criminal and civil courts. However, at the international level, a number of treaties have eroded this absolute immunity for sitting heads of state (such as the Rome Statute of the International Criminal Court in Article 27)—it can no longer be said that heads of state have absolute immunity from prosecution for international criminal acts. As such, the precise contours of head of state immunity remain in flux; the International Law Commission of the UN is currently examining the issue, and its conclusions will be a valuable addition to the current discourse—see further http://untreaty.un.org/ilc/guide/4_2.htm.

[63] http://www.abc.net.au/news/2009-09-09/afp-launches-balibo-war-crimes-probe/1422816

[64] *Inquest into the Death of Brian Raymond Peters* (Unreported, Coroner's Court of New South Wales, Magistrate Pinch, 16 November 2007) 3.

Britons and one New Zealander[65]—were in the Timorese town of Balibó, preparing a report on the rumoured impending Indonesian invasion. The five men were killed during the invasion. Indonesian authorities reported at the time, and two Australian government inquiries confirmed, that the journalists had been killed in cross-fire 'in the heat of battle'.[66] However, the families of the journalists were adamant that they had been deliberately targeted by Indonesian authorities.[67] The sister of one of the journalists was able to ask for a coronial inquest into the death of her brother, Brian Peters, based on his residency in New South Wales.[68] The Coroner found that the journalists had surrendered to Indonesian forces at the time of invasion, and were claiming their status as journalists and thus civilians, when the Captain of the Indonesian Special Forces in Balibó ordered that they be killed.[69] Once the journalists had been killed, Special Forces troops dressed the journalists in old Portuguese army uniforms, and photographed them to indicate that they had been taking direct part in the hostilities and thus liable to be targeted under the international law of war. The bodies were burnt to conceal the fact that they had been shot with AK-47 rifles—which were not in use by local forces.[70] The Coroner's findings opened the possibility for the prosecution of those involved in the murder of the journalists; in September 2009, the AFP thus launched a war crimes investigation into the killings. However, as of May 2013, the investigation seems to have stalled[71]; key witnesses have died, and relevant evidentiary materials have been difficult to locate. Whether the case is ever brought to trial remains to be seen.[72]

12.3.2 IHL in Refugee and Extradition Cases

International humanitarian law is now mostly raised in Australian courts in the context of refugee and asylum cases, with some cases looking at extradition.

---

65 Greg Shackleton and Tony Stewart were Australian; Brian Peters and Malcolm Rennie were Britons and Gary Cunningham from New Zealand.

66 Tom Sherman, 'Report of the Deaths of Australian-Based Journalists in East-Timor in 1975' June 1996; 'Second Report on the Deaths of Australian-Based Journalists in East Timor in 1975' January 1999.

67 http://www.abc.net.au/worldtoday/content/2007/s1840561.htm

68 Ibid.

69 *Coroners Findings* 111–113.

70 Ibid.

71 http://www.smh.com.au/national/fears-balibo-five-killing-investigation-is-stalling-20130505-2j1h1.html

72 See generally Saul 2009.

12.3.2.1 Australian Case Law on IHL and Refugee Status

Australia is party to the Refugee Convention,[73] and has given the Convention domestic effect in the *Migration Act 1958* (Cth). Of relevance to the current discussion, the Refugee Convention contains the following exclusion clause, outlining a category of persons who do not qualify for refugee status:

> The provisions of this Convention shall not apply to any person with respect to whom there are serious reasons for considering that: (a) he has committed a crime against peace, a war crime, or a crime against humanity, as defined in the international instruments drawn up to make provision in respect of such crimes.[74]

The *Migration Act* incorporates the Article 1F exclusion in Article 36(2C)(a)(i), regarding the ineligibility for the grant of a protection visa, stating that a "non-citizen is taken not to satisfy the criteria" for admission to Australia as a refugee if the Government has serious reasons for considering that the person in question has "committed a crime against peace, a war crime or a crime against humanity, as defined by international instruments prescribed by the regulations." The Regulations[75] list the relevant international instruments, including the Geneva Conventions and Additional Protocols, the Rome Statute of the International Criminal Court, the Statutes of the International Criminal Tribunal for the Former Yugoslavia[76] and the International Criminal Tribunal for Rwanda,[77] and the Genocide Convention.[78]

The Australian courts have interpreted this section, on 'serious reasons', to mean that the government, through the Minister for Immigration and Citizenship, need only have "'serious reasons for considering' that one of the three exclusion provisions in Art 1F applies"[79]; that is to say, it is not necessary for conclusive proof to be provided, nor for evidence of an arrest[80]: "it is enough to adduce strong evidence that a crime has been committed".[81] Australian courts and review tribunals[82] have had a number of occasions to consider the Article 1F exclusion

---

73 Convention relating to the Status of Refugees, 189 *UNTS* 150.

74 Article 1F, Refugee Convention.

75 Migration Regulations 1994, Reg 2.03B.

76 Statute of the International Tribunal for the Prosecution of Persons Responsible for Serious Violations of International Humanitarian Law Committed in the Territory of the Former Yugoslavia since 1991, UN Doc. S/25704 at 36, annex (1993) and S/25704/Add. 1 (1993), adopted by Security Council Resolution 827, UN Doc. S/RES/827 (1993).

77 Statute of the International Tribunal for Rwanda, UN Doc. S/RES/955 (1994), adopted by Security Council Resolution 955 (1994).

78 Convention on the Prevention and Punishment of the Crime of Genocide, 78 *UNTS* 277.

79 Crock and Berg 2011, p. 424.

80 Rikhof 2009, p. 470.

81 Ibid.

82 These include, for the purposes of refugee and asylum decisions, the Federal Court of Australia, the Refugee Review Tribunal and the Administrative Appeals Tribunal—for a list of the numerous cases dealing with the 1F exclusion, see further Rikhof 2009.

regarding war crimes, including cases which have touched on the conflicts in Afghanistan, Nepal, Sri Lanka, Lebanon, Liberia, Sierra Leone and Kosovo. While these courts have had reference to the statutes of the ICTR and ICTY, as well as the Statute of the International Military Tribunal at Nuremburg,[83] the Rome Statute of the International Criminal Court "has been held to be the most authoritative in the context of international crimes."[84]

One of the most significant recent cases in Australia dealing with IHL was the case of *SRYYY*.[85] In that instance, the Full Court of the Federal Court[86] had cause to look at the issue of how to define war crimes, crimes against humanity, and the defence of superior orders. One of the issues raised was whether the Administrative Appeals Tribunal (AAT) had erred in applying the definitions of crimes against humanity and war crimes as outlined in the Rome Statute, as the crimes at issue in *SRYYY* had been committed between 1997 and 2000—before the Rome Statute had been adopted.[87] The applicant also argued that the AAT had not adequately addressed the questions required when making an assessment of the commission of crimes against humanity or war crimes; specifically, that the AAT did not consider whether the appellant's acts were committed as part of a widespread or systematic attack directed against the civilian population pursuant to or in furtherance of a State or organisational policy to commit such an attack.[88]

In considering these issues, the Full Federal Court held that "it is permissible to seek guidance on the elements of relevant crimes from any such instrument, whether or not the instrument was in force at the time the alleged crime was committed."[89] The Court affirmed that Article 1F(a) was designed to recognise that:

> the rules of international law are dynamic and their content inevitably turns on the future evolution of international law… the drafters of [Article 1F(a) allow]… the decision-maker to draw upon the definitions of such crimes by reference to unspecified international instruments drawn up to provide for the crimes in question.[90]

Thus, the AAT had *not* erred in making reference to the Rome Statute, even though it had been adopted after the criminal acts at issue had been committed.

---

[83] United Nations, Charter of the International Military Tribunal—Annex to the Agreement for the Prosecution and Punishment of the Major War Criminals of the European Axis, 8 August 1945, available at: http://www.refworld.org/docid/3ae6b39614.html.

[84] Rikhof 2009, p. 471.

[85] *SRYYY v. Minister for Immigration and Multicultural and Indigenous Affairs* [2005] FCAFC 42.

[86] *The Federal Court of Australia Act 1976* (Cth) requires that certain matters must be heard and determined by a Full Court (comprising three or more judges) sitting in the Court's original jurisdiction; see ss 20 and 25 of the *Federal Court of Australia Act* regarding when a Full Court is considered necessary, either in original or appellate jurisdiction.

[87] *SRYYY* [13].

[88] Ibid.

[89] Ibid at paras 63–67.

[90] [31].

However, the court did find that the AAT had failed to determine whether all the requisite elements of the alleged criminal acts in *SRYYY* could be made out. Specifically, the AAT appears to have mixed the elements of crimes against humanity with those of war crimes, by finding that the Sri Lankan army was involved in systematic persecution of a civilian group—as required for a finding of crimes against humanity—and thus concluding that there were serious reasons for considering that a war crime had been committed by the applicant. As noted by the Court:

> the definition of a war crime in Article 8 contains no requirement that there be evidence of a 'widespread or systematic attack', whether directed against a civilian population, or otherwise. Manifestly, this is a critical and distinguishing feature of 'crimes against humanity'.[91]

Thus, the Federal Court rejected the AAT finding in regards to that specific issue, and urged that Courts needed to take a cautious approach stating that all elements of the crimes at issue should be addressed.[92]

SRYYY also looked at the question of 'defence of superior orders'. The Court examined the question of whether the AAT should have considered whether the applicant was entitled to claim the benefit of the Article 33 defence of superior orders. The Court affirmed the necessity of determining whether relevant defences may be applicable when considering if a refugee applicant falls within the Article 1F(a) ambit. The Court stated that:

> Article 1F(a) refers to serious reasons for considering that the relevant person 'has committed a crime'. We are unable to accept the proposition that a person may be said to have committed a crime when that person has a defence which, if upheld, will absolve or relieve that person from criminal responsibility.[93]

SRYYY was one of a number of Australian cases during the first decade of the twenty-first century that had cause to examine the interplay between Australia's obligations under the Refugee Convention, and its obligations under international humanitarian law. In *SZCWP v. Minister for Immigration and Multicultural and Indigenous Affairs*,[94] the Federal Court examined whether the term 'civilian population', under international humanitarian law, could include members of the police force. In *SZCWP*, the applicant argued that the police force of Nepal could not be considered part of the civilian population, and therefore systematic and widespread acts of violence against the police could not amount to a crime against humanity. In that instance, the Federal Court found that the police force is not part of the armed forces, and are not deprived of their civilian status if they were involved in attempting to repel attacks by the Maoist insurgents.[95] That same year, the Federal

---

91 [107].

92 [109].

93 [127].

94 *SZCWP v. Minister for Immigration and Multicultural and Indigenous Affairs* [2006] FCAFC 9 (20 February 2006).

95 [119].

Court in *SZITR v. Minister for Immigration and Multicultural Affairs*[96] examined the elements of the crime of torture as a crime against humanity. The case was an appeal against a decision by the Administrative Appeals Tribunal, which had rejected a visa application on the basis that the applicant had been involved in acts of torture during his tenure as a member of the Sri Lankan Army. The applicant argued that he did not have the requisite legal custody or control of the detainees being tortured, and thus, he had not personally fulfilled the requisite elements of torture as defined in the ICC Statute's Elements of Crime[97]—severe pain, victim under custody or control, unlawful sanction, part of a widespread attack against the civilian population with knowledge of the conduct as part of the attack.[98] The Court rejected this argument, stating that it was not necessary for the applicant to have strict legal control over detainees—all that was necessary was that the victim was "at the mercy"[99] of the accused.[100] These few cases, dealt on a Federal Court level, are just a sample of the many cases in Australia dealing with Article 1F(a), the majority of which are ultimately tried on a lower, Tribunal level.[101]

12.3.2.2 Australian Case Law on IHL and Extradition

Australian courts have also had cause to examine IHL issues in relation to extradition requests. In 2006, the High Court of Australia had cause to consider the constitutionality of the *Extradition Act 1988* (Cth) and the Extradition (Croatia) Regulations 2004 (Cth).[102] The facts in that case relate to attempts to extradite Dragan Vasiljkovic to Croatia to face charges of war crimes in relation to conduct during the Balkans conflict in the early 1990s. Vasiljkovic, a naturalised Australian citizen and citizen of Serbia and Montenegro, had been arrested in Sydney in January of 2006 pursuant to an arrest warrant that had been issued in Croatia.[103] Vasiljkovic challenged the legality of his detention in the High Court. Under the 2004 Regulations, no evidence need be provided by the country seeking extradition in order to commence the extradition process.[104] Vasiljkovic argued that this

---

96 [2006] FCA 1759 (15 December 2006).

97 [30].

98 http://www.icc-cpi.int/NR/rdonlyres/336923D8-A6AD-40EC-AD7B-45BF9DE73D56/0/ElementsOfCrimesEng.pdf

99 Rikhof 2009, p. 473.

100 *SZITR* [46].

101 See Rikhof 2009 for a more detailed exploration of Article 1F(a) in the courts of Australia.

102 *Dragan Vasiljkovic v. Minister for Justice and Customs* [2006] HCA 40 (3 August 2006).

103 Vasiljkovic, also known as Daniel Snedden, had been investigated by the County Court of Sibenik in Croatia, who then issued Warrant KIO-86/05, charging that Vasiljkovic had committed offences under the Basic Criminal Code of the Republic of Croatia—see *Dragan Vasiljkovic v. Minister for Justice and Customs and Ors* [2006] FCA 1346, [5].

104 Extradition (Croatia) Regulations 2004 (Cth), reg. 4; see s 19(3) of the *Extradition Act 1988* (Cth).

was constitutionally invalid, as it authorised his detention without requiring that a *prima facie* case against him be made out.[105] The High Court dismissed the application, finding his detention to be a valid exercise of Commonwealth authority pursuant to the legislation, which it also held to be a valid exercise of the Commonwealth's constitutional powers.[106] Vasiljkovic then made a new application to the Federal Court of Australia, seeking to stop his extradition, on the basis that, among other claims, he would not receive a fair trial in Croatia. After a long progress through the Australian courts, Vasiljkovic, now going by Daniel Snedden, was successful in the Federal Court,[107] who found that there was a "substantial or real chance of prejudice"[108] against Snedden if tried in Croatia, and thus he should not be extradited.[109] The Australian government successfully appealed against the decision in the High Court,[110] and the Federal Court upheld the appeal.[111] In November 2012, the Australian government ordered the extradition of Snedden.[112]

Another recent attempt to extradite an alleged war criminal has been equally as protracted as the Snedden case. Since 2007, attempts had been made to extradite Charles Zentai, formerly Károly Steiner, to Hungary to stand trial for war crimes committed during the Second World War. Zentai had long been listed in the Simon Weisenthal Centre's *Annual Status Report on the Worldwide Investigation and Prosecution of Nazi War Criminals*,[113] which included a 'top ten most wanted list'. Numerous appeals were made to the Federal Court[114] and High Court[115] regarding the extradition, culminating in a decision by the High Court in 2012,[116] who found that the Minister for Home Affairs, who had originally approved the extradition of

---

105 *Dragan Vasiljkovic v. Minister for Justice and Customs* [2006] HCA 40 (3 August 2006), [72].

106 Ibid, [85]–[88] per Gummow and Hayne JJ.

107 *Snedden v. Republic of Croatia* [2009] FCAFC 111 (2 September 2009).

108 Ibid, [54].

109 Ibid, [44–47], [54–55].

110 *Republic of Croatia v. Snedden* [2010] HCA 14 (19 May 2010).

111 *Vasiljkovic v. Honourable Brendan O'Connor* [2010] FCA 1246 (19 November 2010).

112 http://www.theaustralian.com.au/national-affairs/croatia-bid-for-dragan-vasiljkovic-extradition-approved/story-fn59niix-1226518481625

113 http://www.wiesenthal.com/atf/cf/%7B54d385e6-f1b9-4e9f-8e94-890c3e6dd277%7D/ANNUAL%20STATUS%20REPORT%20ON%20THE%20WORLDWIDE%20INVESTIGATION%20AND%20PROSECUTION%20OF%20NAZI%20WAR%20CRIMINALS.PDF

114 Including *Zentai v. Republic of Hungary* [2006] FCA 1226 (12 September 2006); *Zentai v. Republic of Hungary* [2007] FCAFC 48 (16 April 2007); *Zentai v. Republic of Hungary* [2007] FCA 842 (29 May 2007); *Zentai v. Republic of Hungary* [2008] FCA 1335; *Zentai v. Republic of Hungary* [2009] FCA 511; *Zentai v. Honourable Brendan O'Connor* [2009] FCA 1597; *Zentai v. Honourable Brendan O'Connor* (No 3) [2010] FCA 691; *O'Connor v. Zentai* [2011] FCAFC 102.

115 Including *Zentai v. Republic of Hungary & Ors; O'Donoghue v. Ireland & Anor* [2007] HCATrans 491 (3 September 2007); *O'Donoghue v. Ireland; Zentai v. Republic of Hungary; Williams v. United States of America* [2008] HCA 14 (23 April 2008).

116 *Minister for Home Affairs of the Commonwealth v. Zentai* [2012] HCA 28 (15 August 2012).

Zentai to Hungary, was unable to prove that the offence of 'war crime was an offence against the law of Hungary on 8 November 1944'.[117] As such, Zentai could not be extradited to Hungary.

12.3.3 Cases from the 'War on Terror'

Australia's involvement in the conflicts in Iraq and Afghanistan has also opened up possibilities for IHL to be raised in Australian courts. Some of the first people captured during the invasion of Afghanistan in 2002 were Australian citizens—David Hicks[118] and Mamdouh Habib.[119] Both men were eventually released from the Guantánamo Bay detention facilities, and returned to Australia. Both men then brought cases against the Australian government in relation to their detention by the US. In *Hicks v. Ruddock*,[120] Hicks alleged that the Australian government had failed to afford his application for diplomatic protection proper consideration, having taking into consideration irrelevant issues, namely whether Hicks could be prosecuted under Australian law if he returned to Australia on release from Guantánamo. In determining whether Hick's could have his argument tested on the merits, the Court made reference to Geneva Convention III, and that Hicks had been denied the protections of the Convention by the detaining authority—the United States.[121] However, this was the extent of IHL discussion in that case.

International humanitarian law was also raised in *Habib v. Commonwealth*.[122] In that case, Habib alleged that, following his October 2001 arrest in Pakistan, he was subject to various acts of torture while he was being detained in various locations including Pakistan, Egypt, and Guantánamo Bay.[123] Habib claimed that these acts of torture were undertaken by local authorities with the knowledge and/or assistance of US officials in Pakistan, Egypt and Guantánamo Bay[124]; Habib further claimed that Australian officials from the Australian Security and Intelligence Organisation (ASIO), the Australian Federal Police, and/or the Department

[117] Ibid, [74].

[118] Hicks—Detainee 002 as he was known—was one of the first people charged by the US after capture—see http://www.defense.gov/news/d20070301hicks.pdf.

[119] Habib was detained in Guantánamo Bay for three years before being released without charge. See the US Department of Defence, List of Individuals Detained by the Department of Defense at Guantanamo Bay, Cuba from January 2002 through May 15, 2006, http://www.dod.mil/news/May2006/d20060515%20List.pdf.

[120] *David Matthew Hicks v. The Honourable Philip Ruddock MP, Attorney-General for the Commonwealth of Australia, The Honourable Alexander Downer MP, Minister for Foreign Affairs and Commonwealth of Australia* (2007) FCA 299 (8 March 2007).

[121] Ibid, [8].

[122] *Mamdouh Habib v. The Commonwealth of Australia* [2010] FCAFC 12 (25 February 2010).

[123] Ibid, [2], per Black CJ.

[124] [16], per Perram J.

of Foreign Affairs and Trade, were complicit in the acts of torture, in that they had provided information to Egyptian authorities that was employed during his interrogation.[125] Habib also claimed that, based on his appearance, it would have been evident to the Australian governmental officials when they visited him that he had been subject to acts of torture.[126] Habib argued that these acts constitute offences under Australian law, specifically s6 of the *Crimes (Torture) Act 1988* (Cth), which gives effect to the Convention Against Torture and Other Cruel, Inhuman or Degrading Treatment or Punishment[127] as well as ss 268.26 and 268.74 of the *Criminal Code Act 1995* (Cth), which relate to torture.[128] The Commonwealth argued that the matter was non-justiciable, as any finding against Australia would necessitate a finding that foreign agents had acted illegally on their own territory—which would amount to a breach of the act of state doctrine.[129]

While the Court in that case did not analyse the substantive issues regarding torture and IHL, the Court did hold that the act of state doctrine did not bar Habib from bringing the case in the first instance, as "the act of state doctrine—whatever it might be—has no application where it is alleged that Commonwealth officials have acted beyond the bounds of their authority under Commonwealth law."[130] Moreover, "where fundamental human rights are in play, the courts of this country will not abstain from reviewing the legitimacy of the actions of a foreign sovereign state."[131] As noted by Jagot J:

> international humanitarian law has been codified through the Geneva Conventions of 1949 and Additional Protocols of 1977, the Torture Convention has been rapidly and almost universally acceded to, and certain violations of international law (including torture) are recognised to involve contraventions of peremptory norms, or *jus cogens*, being norms about which all nations agree or are taken to agree and from which no derogation is permitted.[132]

Habib settled with the Australian government out of court; later press reports claimed that the settlement was authorised after the Australian government received intelligence from Egyptian authorities that implicated Australian officials in Habib's torture.[133]

---

125 Ibid, [17].

126 Ibid, [18].

127 1465 *UNTS* 85.

128 Originally contained in s 7(1) of the *Geneva Conventions Act 1957* (Cth), ss 268.26 and 268.74 of the *Criminal Code Act 1995* (Cth) make it an offence of extraterritorial operation to torture a person protected by Geneva Convention III or Geneva Convention IV.

129 *Habib*, [5], per Black CJ.

130 *Habib*, [24], per Perram J.

131 *Habib*, [105], per Jagot J.

132 *Habib*, [108], per Jagot J.

133 See Natalie O'Brien, "Australians saw Habib Tortured, Says Officer", *The Sydney Morning Herald*, 13 February 2011, http://www.smh.com.au/national/australians-saw-habib-tortured-says-officer-20110212-1aran.html#ixzz2J1vuk5wZ.

Finally, an example of international humanitarian law being dealt with in a potentially *inappropriate* manner in the courts of Australia was seen in 2011, when two Australian commandos found themselves subject to charges as a result of activities in Afghanistan. In February of 2009, Australian commandos conducted a raid in Oruzgan province, in which six Afghan civilians were killed—five of the deceased were children. Following the raid, two of the commandos—a sergeant and a lance corporal—were charged with manslaughter and, in the alternative, two counts of dangerous conduct with negligence as to consequence. It was alleged that the two commandos had thrown a grenade into a room (which contained women and children) without being under direct threat of continued small arms fire. As such, it was alleged that the throwing of the grenade was negligent, possibly amounting to manslaughter.[134] Of concern to many—and to IHL lawyers specifically—was the notion that Australian defence force personnel were now unable to rely upon compliance with IHL as a guarantee of lawful conduct in armed conflict. As noted by Tim McCormack:

> Australian Defence Force legal officers have been taught for years that the law governing combat operations is international humanitarian law (or the law of armed conflict) implemented into Australian domestic law through Commonwealth legislation. Rules of engagement are drafted in strict compliance with that body of law, ensuring troop confidence in the legality of combat operations... [the court martial charges] challenged that orthodoxy by laying charges without reference to an alleged violation of international humanitarian law.[135]

The prosecution in the court martial did not allege that a war crime had been committed, but rather an act of manslaughter and/or negligence. In doing so, the grounds were laid for a situation whereby Australian criminal law 'imposed a higher standard on ADF members, who could no longer assume that compliance with international humanitarian law would guarantee lawful conduct'.[136] The potential for problems was evident—Australian military courts would be imposing a set of criteria for conduct for defence force personnel that was not mirrored in IHL or international criminal law, criteria that could lead to ADF members returning home from operations believing themselves to have complied with IHL, only to face charges upon their return to Australia. As McCormack rightly noted, 'negligence has never been an acceptable fault element for the perpetration of a war crime'.[137] In the end, the accepted, correct, orthodoxy prevailed—the charges were dismissed in a pre-trial hearing.

---

[134] See Sophie MacNeil and Rafael Epstein, 'Diggers' Court-Martial Twist', *The Age*, 30 March 2011 http://www.theage.com.au/national/diggers-courtmartial-twist-20110329-1ceu3.html.

[135] Tim McCormack, Commandos finally get justice. The Sydney Morning Herald, 25 May 2011, http://www.smh.com.au/federal-politics/society-and-culture/commandos-finally-get-justice-20110524-1f2dl.html.

[136] Ibid.

[137] Ibid.

12.4 Conclusions

This chapter has examined some of the major cases in Australia's legal history whereby Australia has attempted to give domestic effect to its obligations under international humanitarian law and international criminal law. In some cases, other considerations—international and domestic, legal and policy-based—have overridden attempts to bring alleged war criminals to justice. As such, Australia seems to have "returned to the position of Sir Garfield Barwick in 1961"[138]—to want to close the chapter on domestic prosecution of war criminals. This is understandable in some respects. The Australian judicial system is, like many judicial systems, under significant financial and time constraints. For example, a study conducted in 2007 by the Victorian Department of Justice found that the costs associated with an aborted criminal trial are on average AUD$7419, with the average costs of a retrial conducted over a week in the Supreme Court of Victoria estimated at $47,572.[139] The increasing number of self-represented litigants in the Australian court system has also greatly stressed courts in terms of time management and costs.[140] As such, one can understand the reluctance of the Australian government to expend funds on war crimes cases that are unlikely to result in convictions due to the factors such as unavailable or unreliable witnesses, lack of evidence, and the passage of time on memory. Political exigencies and international diplomatic pressures may also account for a failure to act in cases such as the Balibó Five. It would be tempting to confirm the prevailing perception of Australia as it was in the 1980s—as a welcoming haven for war criminals. However, this would arguably be too harsh an assessment, when one looks at the robust jurisprudence in the realms of refugee law and extradition in Australian courts. Despite failures and abortive attempts to prosecute war crimes outright, the courts of Australia nonetheless remain a lively forum for the discussion and application of IHL principles, and a continuing arena for ensuring that, even if only in small ways, persons who commit violations of IHL must account for their conduct.

References

Aarons M (2001) War criminals welcome: Australia, a sanctuary for fugitive war criminals since 1945. Black Inc, Melbourne

Allars M (1997) International law and administrative discretion. In: Opeskin B, Rothwell D (eds) International law and Australian federalism. Melbourne University Press, Melbourne, pp 232–279

Anderson R (1996) War crimes and Australia. Pub Law Rev 7:138

---

[138] Triggs 1997, p. 149.

[139] Victorian Bar, *Review of Fees Paid by Victoria Legal Aid to Barristers in Criminal Cases April 2008*, cited in Law Council of Australia 2009, p. 6.

[140] Ibid.

Angrick A, Klein P (2012) The 'Final Solution' in Riga: exploitation and annihilation, 1941–1944. Berghahn Books, Oxford

Balkin R (2005) International law and domestic law. In: Blay S, Piotrowicz R, Tsamenyi M (eds) Public international law: an Australian perspective, 2nd edn. OUP, Melbourne, pp 119–145

Boas G (2010) War crimes prosecutions in Australia and other common law countries: some observations. Crim Law Forum 21:313

Crock M, Berg L (2011) Immigration, refugees and forced migration: law, policy and practice in Australia. Federation Press, Annandale

Deschênes J (1986) Report of the commission of inquiry on war criminals: part 1 (public). Minister of Supply and Services, Ottawa

Dickinson G (1952) Japanese war trials. Aust Quart 24:69

Evatt HE (1945) Current notes on international affairs, vol 16. Department of External Affairs, Canberra

Hetherington T, Chalmers W (1989) Report of the war crimes enquiry. CM 744, Great Britain Home Office

Hood A, Cormier M (2012) Prosecuting international crimes in Australia: the case of the Sri Lankan president. Melbourne J Int Law 13:1

Law Council of Australia (2009) Inquiry into access to justice. Senate Legal and Constitutional Affairs Committee, Canberra

Laffin J (1965) Anzacs at war: the story of Australian and New Zealand battles. Abelard-Schuman, New York

Lockwood D (2005) Australia under attack: the bombing of Darwin 1942. New Holland Press, Frenchs Forest

Menzies ACC (1987) Review of material relating to the entry of suspected war criminals into Australia. Aust Gov Publ Serv, Canberra

Rikhof J (2009) War criminals not welcome: how common law countries approach the phenomenon of international crimes in the immigration and refugee context. Int J Refugee Law 21:435

Saul B (2009) Prosecuting war crimes at Balibo under Australian law: the killing of five journalists in East Timor by Indonesia. Sydney Law Rev 31:83

Triggs G (1988) Australia's war crimes trials: a moral necessity of legal minefield? Melbourne Univ Law Rev 16:382

Triggs G (1997) Australia's war crimes trials: all pity choked. In: McCormack T, Simpson G (eds) The law of war crimes: national and international approaches. Kluwer, The Hague, pp 123–150

Chapter 13
Aut Deportare Aut Judicare: Current Topics in International Humanitarian Law in Canada

James Yap

Contents

James Yap, B.Sc. (McGill), J.D. (York), LL.M. (Yale). The author is indebted to Matt Eisenbrandt, Marjan Firouzgar, Elise Groulx, Sue Guan, Tasha Manoranjan, William J. Moon, Stavroula Papadopoulos, Allison Rhoades, Craig Scott, François Tanguay-Renaud, and the editors for their invaluable guidance and support.

J. Yap (✉)
Siskinds LLP, Toronto, Canada
e-mail: james.yap@gmail.com

D. Jinks et al. (eds.), *Applying International Humanitarian Law in Judicial and Quasi-Judicial Bodies*, DOI: 10.1007/978-94-6265-008-4_13,

13.1 Introduction

Canada's legal system is one that is infused with dualities. Canada is a federal state, with federal and provincial levels of government legislating and governing concurrently with respect to separate—but often overlapping—fields of jurisdiction.[1] There are also parallel federally- and provincially administered court systems.[2] The federal legislature is itself a bicameral apparatus, emulating the British Parliamentary tradition with an elected House of Commons and an appointed "upper house," called the Senate.[3] Even the world's two major legal traditions co-exist side by side: while most of the country follows a common law legal system, the province of Québec—Canada's second most populous—follows the civilian tradition, a reflection of its historical French roots.[4]

In characteristic fashion, therefore, there also exist two parallel legal avenues that are customarily used to bring proceedings against people suspected of committing war crimes. The first is a conventional criminal prosecution, accompanied by the typical punishment of a custodial sentence. However, immigration proceedings, featuring removal from the country as the prospective sanction, are also widely used as a means to pursue suspected war criminals. Both are key components of an integrated strategy to ensure that individuals who come to Canada having committed international crimes in their countries of origin do not escape some measure of accountability.

Many other countries also rely on a combination of criminal and immigration remedies in order to ensure that war criminals residing inside their borders do not escape punishment. As such, the discussion in this chapter has practical relevance for countries outside Canada as well. At the same time, Canada has been particularly aggressive among its peers in developing a sophisticated and integrated system that incorporates immigration proceedings as a key component, to the near exclusion of criminal proceedings.

Section 13.2 will examine the historical and legal background that led to this dynamic, while Sect. 13.3 will conduct a comparative examination of the two different types of proceeding. While this last part will account for the vast majority of proceedings in Canada that raise questions of international humanitarian law, Sect. 13.4 will explore some other cases where international humanitarian law has come into play—most notably in recent civil litigation claims against Canadian corporations for complicity in war crimes committed abroad—before Sect. 13.5 closes the chapter with some concluding remarks.

---

[1] Hogg 2007, pp. 5-1–5-47.

[2] Ibid at pp. 7-1–7-57.

[3] Ibid at pp. 2–11.

[4] Ibid at pp. 2–8.

13.2 Historical and Legal Background

If a Canadian tribunal is considering a question of international humanitarian law, the probability is very high that it is doing so because it has been tasked with determining whether a foreign-born individual has committed a war crime in his or her country of origin. This feature is by no means unique to Canada, and in fact is probably common to a large number of western countries. However, the fact is that owing to Canada's relatively low rate of getting involved in military conflict, Canadian tribunals are rarely in a position to apply international humanitarian law to acts committed by or against Canada's own military personnel.[5] At the same time, Canada does accept immigrants from many parts of the world that have been ravaged by war. Among those who arrive in Canada to establish new lives for themselves, there are occasionally individuals who have been implicated in grave breaches of international humanitarian law, or other international crimes, in their countries of origin.

Such individuals are relatively few in number, but are sufficiently numerous that cases assessing their culpability constitute the overwhelming majority of occasions that Canadian tribunals have had to consider and apply international humanitarian law. This can happen two ways.

13.2.1 Criminal Proceedings

In Canada, criminal law falls within the exclusive jurisdiction of the federal government.[6] For over four decades after the end of World War II, the only criminal provisions with respect to war crimes were contained in the *War Crimes Act*,[7] providing summary procedures for war crimes trials designed for a military tribunal

[5] Often, Canadian military personnel are simply deployed overseas in circumstances where international humanitarian law, or the rules concerning war crimes which are the most likely context in which individual military personnel might find themselves in court, do not apply. Perhaps the most notorious example is the case of Shidane Arone, a Somali teenage civilian who was brutally tortured and murdered by Canadian military personnel in 1993. The military operation in question was a UN-led peacekeeping mission and not an international armed conflict (see e.g. Graditzky 1998). However, the direct perpetrators and various other personnel were charged with conventional offenses ranging from second-degree murder, to torture, to negligent performance of a military duty. See *R. v. Brown*, Court Martial Appeal Court Case No. CMAC-372, 6 January 1995; *R. v. Brocklebank* (1995), 106 (3d) C.C.C. 234 (Court Martial Appeal Court); *R. v. Boland*, Court Martial Appeal Court Case No. CMAC-374, 16 May 1995; *R. v. Seward*, Court Martial Appeal Court Case No. CMAC-376, 27 May 1995. Prosecution for conventional offenses was also used in a more recent case involving a Canadian infantry officer alleged to have shot and killed a fatally-wounded insurgent in Afghanistan in 2008. He was charged with second degree murder, but the military jury found him not guilty on this charge, and convicted him instead on the lesser charge of disgraceful conduct. See *R. v. Semrau*, 2010 CM 4010.

[6] *Constitution Act, 1867*, s. 91(27).

[7] (1946) 10 George VI, c. 73.

in times of war, and, after 1965, the *Geneva Conventions Act*,[8] which specified that any act constituting a "grave breach" of the *Geneva Conventions of 1949*[9] was a criminal offense. The latter had far greater practical significance, not only in that it contemplated conventional civilian criminal proceedings, but in that it also explicitly circumvented the territoriality principle by applying to any offense committed "whether within or outside Canada."[10] It did not, however, circumvent the *nullum crimen sine lege praevia* principle,[11] having no retroactive effect.

In the late 1970s and 1980s, the concern that fugitive Nazi-era war criminals were hiding in Canada began to grow in the country's public consciousness.[12] In the earlier years of the Cold War era, the government had accepted many refugees from eastern European countries.[13] Keen not to admit Communist agitators, it freely embraced those who had fought for the Nazis against the Soviets, which it saw as a sure indicator of political reliability.[14] Many years later, the wisdom of this practice came to be called into question, as aversion to the idea of harboring perpetrators of war crimes and other atrocities began to outpace anti-Red hysteria. The media and prominent public figures fanned the flames[15]; famed Nazi hunter Simon Wiesenthal during this time speculated that Nazi-era war criminals hiding in the country may number as many as 6,000,[16] and it was even suggested that the notorious "Angel of Death" Josef Mengele may be among them.[17]

In 1985, in response to the growing public consternation, the government appointed Jules Deschênes, a judge on Québec's Court of Appeal, to lead an independent Commission of Inquiry to investigate the alleged presence of Nazi war criminals in Canada, and how they had obtained entry into the country.[18] In its

---

[8] R.S.C. 1985, c. G-3.

[9] *Convention for the Amelioration of the Condition of the Wounded and Sick in Armed Forces in the Field*, 12 August 1949, 75 U.N.T.S. 31 [*First Geneva Convention*]; *Convention for the Amelioration of the Condition of the Wounded, Sick, and Shipwrecked Members of Armed Forces at Sea*, 12 August 1949, 75 U.N.T.S. 85 [*Second Geneva Convention*]; *Convention Relative to the Treatment of Prisoners of War*, 12 August 1949, 75 U.N.T.S. 135 [*Third Geneva Convention*]; *Convention Relative to the Protection of Civilian Persons in Time of War*, 12 August 1949, 75 U.N.T.S. 287 [*Fourth Geneva Convention*].

[10] Ibid., s. 3(1).

[11] The principle, well recognized in both international and domestic legal systems, that a law cannot criminalize prior conduct. See e.g. Cassese 2008, pp. 37–38. In Canada, see *Constitution Act, 1982*, s. 11(g).

[12] Deschênes 1986, pp. 245–249.

[13] Abella and Troper 1982.

[14] Abella and Troper 1982; Purves 1998, p. 3.

[15] Deschênes 1986, pp. 245–249.

[16] Deschênes 1986, pp. 247–249.

[17] Deschênes 1986, pp. 67–68.

[18] Deschênes 1986.

report released the following year, the Deschênes Commission found that reports of Nazi war criminals hiding in Canada were "grossly exaggerated."[19] Of a master list of 774 suspects drawn to its attention, the Commission found *prima facie* evidence of war crimes warranting official action in just 20 cases, while recommending the outright closure of another 606—341 of these for the reason that the suspects in question were not and never had been in Canada.[20] Similarly, it also found no evidence that Dr. Mengele had ever entered Canada or attempted to enter Canada.[21] Nevertheless, noting that there was no viable way to prosecute any individuals who there were reasonable grounds to believe had committed international crimes during World War II,[22] it recommended that Canada's *Criminal Code* be amended to give Canadian criminal courts jurisdiction over war crimes and crimes against humanity committed outside Canada and before the entry into force of the amendment.[23]

These recommendations were accepted, and in 1987 Canadian criminal courts for the first time were given extraterritorial and retrospective jurisdiction over the criminal prosecution of war crimes and crimes against humanity. A constitutional challenge to the legislation's retrospectivity was rejected by a decision of the Supreme Court of Canada in 1994, removing another potential obstacle.[24]

With the adoption of the *Rome Statute of the International Criminal Court*[25] in 1998, however, the need to update the legislation became clear. Accordingly, in 2000, the *Crimes Against Humanity and War Crimes Act*[26] (hereafter referred to as the "*War Crimes Act*"—but not to be confused with the obscure 1940s statute of the same name mentioned above) harmonized the Canadian law with the definitions of war crimes, crimes against humanity, and genocide set out in the *Rome Statute*, making Canada the first country to incorporate the *Rome Statute* into domestic law. The *War Crimes Act* also implements the laws pertaining to command responsibility set out in Article 28 of the *Rome Statute*.[27]

In terms of jurisdiction, it is like its predecessor provisions both retrospective and extraterritorial in scope. The Act explicitly applies to any offense committed "either before or after [its] coming into force."[28] Further, anyone who commits a

---

[19] Ibid., at p. 249. Of a master list of 774 suspects drawn to its attention, the Commission found prima facie evidence of war crimes warranting official action in just 20 cases, while recommending the outright closure of another 606—341 of these for the reason that the suspects in question were not and never had been in Canada. Ibid., at pp. 262–270. Similarly, it found no evidence that Dr. Mengele had ever entered or attempted to enter Canada. Ibid at pp. 67–82.

[20] Ibid., at pp. 262–270.

[21] Ibid., at pp. 67–82.

[22] Ibid., at pp. 111–126.

[23] Ibid., at 157–158.

[24] *R. v. Finta*, [1994] 1 S.C.R. 701.

[25] 17 July 1998 2187 U.N.T.S. 90.

[26] S.C. 2000, c. 24.

[27] Ibid., ss. 5, 7.

[28] Ibid., s. 6.

war crime, a crime against humanity or genocide outside Canada may be prosecuted for that crime if, at any time after the offense is committed, he or she is present in Canada.[29]

The *War Crimes Act* remains in force and to date has resulted in the successful prosecution of one individual,[30] and the acquittal of another.[31]

13.2.2 The Munyaneza and Mungwarere Cases

The first prosecution attempted under the new legislation was that of Désiré Munyaneza, a Rwandan national and former militia commander, who in 2009 was found guilty by a Québec court of war crimes, crimes against humanity, and genocide charges arising from incidents that took place in 1994 in the Butare prefecture of Rwanda.[32] The decision is presently under appeal.

The trial decision in *R. c. Munyaneza* is not particularly noteworthy from a strictly legal perspective. In a very efficient and mechanistic manner, the judge states the law, resolving any legal questions simply by adopting the positions of the international tribunals, summarizes the witnesses' testimony, makes findings of fact, and reaches a verdict.[33] As has already been observed elsewhere, meanwhile, the judge offers only the most cursory discussion concerning the application of the law to the facts.[34]

There is also no discussion of modes of participation, as the judge appears to have considered the accused liable as a principal. This has led to observations that some of the factual conclusions as to the accused's conduct—such as his contribution of vehicles and weapons to facilitate the commission of atrocities—do not support a finding of principal liability.[35] At the same time, there are clearly some that do,[36] and those that do not could just as easily have been used as evidence of the specific intent required for the offence of genocide.[37]

Moreover, while the judge relies on the jurisprudence of international tribunals to settle questions of international law, there are some questions he does not address. For instance, Munyaneza was found guilty on charges of war crimes, even though it is not clear that customary international law at the time recognized acts

---

29 Ibid., s. 8.

30 *R. c. Munyaneza*, 2009 QCCS 2201.

31 *R. c. Mungwarere*, 2013 ONCS 4594.

32 *Munyaneza*, supra n. 30.

33 Lafontaine 2010b, pp. 271–272. See also Currie and Stancu 2010.

34 Lafontaine 2010b, pp. 271–272.

35 Ibid., p. 272.

36 See *Munyaneza*, supra n. 30 at paras 2061–2075.

37 Specifically, the "intent to destroy, in whole or in part, a national, ethnical, racial or religious group." See *Convention on the Prevention and Punishment of the Crime of Genocide*, Article 2.

committed in non-international armed conflicts as war crimes[38]; in fact one other Canadian court has explicitly ruled that this was not the case.[39] Accordingly, at the hearing of Munyaneza's appeal, this question became a major preoccupation of the appeal panel.[40]

However, while perhaps not noteworthy as a paragon of IHL jurisprudence, *Munyaneza* is nevertheless a significant milestone, in that it shows that Canada has finally developed a regime that is capable of bringing to justice those responsible for war crimes and other international crimes committed overseas.

On the heels of *Munyaneza* came *R. c. Mungwarere*, another case from Rwanda. There, Rwandan national Jacques Mungwarere was charged with genocide and crimes against humanity, this time in the Kibuye prefecture. He was acquitted of these charges, the judge finding insufficient credible evidence to affirmatively establish his guilt (although he allowed that there may be enough evidence to establish a probability of guilt).[41] The prosecution declined to appeal the decision.

Unlike Munyaneza, Mungwarere was not charged with war crimes, and so much of the legal analysis in the decision is not relevant to the present discussion. However, also unlike *Munyaneza*, the judge in *Mungwarere* did discuss the rules on modes of participation applicable in Canadian courts to international crimes, holding that the rules on modes of participation under Canadian criminal law applied to all offenses under the *War Crimes Act*. Nevertheless, he also hastened to add that "[TRANSLATION] in a criminal prosecution of an international nature, it is necessary to draw as much as possible on the jurisprudence of international criminal tribunals."[42] True to his word, he drew heavily from ICTY case law in his discussion on modes of participation, and reconciled it with the corresponding domestic rules as much as possible.

Despite the fact that the prosecution resulted in an acquittal, and so in that narrow sense was not strictly successful, it is important not to frame *Mungwarere* as a failure. In fact, nothing could be further from the truth. The result was not due to any systemic limitations or shortcomings in the legislation. Rather, it was due to the fact that the prosecution's case simply was not strong enough—more specifically, the evidence of the prosecution's key witnesses did not withstand rigorous cross-examination and judicial scrutiny at trial. In other words, the system functioned exactly as it was supposed to. The accused received a fair trial—which, fittingly, may have been the very concern that motivated the initial decision to prosecute these individuals domestically rather than remove them from the country in the first place.

---

38 See Graditzky 1998.

39 *Bermudez v. Canada (Minister of Citizenship and Immigration)* (2000), 24 Admin LR (3d) 65 (Fed. Ct.).

40 See Correspondence with Matt Eisenbrandt, Legal Counsel for the Canadian Centre for International Justice (August 26, 2013).

41 *Mungwarere*, supra n. 31 at para 1260–1261.

42 Ibid at para 62.

13.2.3 Immigration Proceedings

As we have seen, the fear of becoming a haven for fugitive war criminals is primarily responsible for spurring the development of Canada's modern regime of criminally prosecuting war crimes and other international crimes. However, during its early years, the nascent system struggled to successfully discharge its function. After all, the barriers to prosecuting crimes committed decades earlier halfway around the world were not just legal in nature. The first few prosecutions initiated under the new laws all failed to result in convictions, often due to procedural and logistical complications. These included:

- The case of Imre Finta, a former Hungarian police captain, accused of kidnapping and manslaughter of 8,617 Jews in 1944. Finta was acquitted by a jury in 1990 after an eight-month trial. His acquittal was upheld by the Supreme Court in 1994.
- The case of Michael Pawlowski, accused of participating in the 1942 murder of 410 Jews and 80 Poles by Nazi-supported local police in Minsk. Charges against Pawlowski were dropped in 1992 due to problems gathering evidence in the Soviet Union.
- The case of Stephen Reistetter, charged with kidnapping 3,000 Jews and sending them to death camps in Slovakia in 1942. Charges against Reistetter were dropped in 1991 due to a lack of evidence.
- The case of Radislav Grujicic, a former Yugoslav police officer, accused of murder. The Crown stayed proceedings against him in September 1994 on account of his ill health.[43]

As these failures mounted, the pressure to find an expedient solution rose. Half a century after World War II, suspects and victims alike were dying, witnesses' memories were fading, and windows of opportunity were, accordingly, closing. Therefore, the focus began to shift to the use of immigration proceedings as a means of visiting a less complete but more pragmatic form of justice upon World War II-era war criminals.

Under Canadian law, a foreign-born individual who immigrates to Canada and acquires Canadian citizenship can have their citizenship revoked, and consequently be deported, if it is shown that their citizenship was obtained as a result of a material misrepresentation. Because the criteria for evaluating a candidate's suitability for citizenship at the most relevant time included a requirement of "good character,"[44] involvement in war crimes was a material circumstance, the concealment of which would provide grounds to revoke a naturalized person's citizenship. The Deschênes Commission report had urged the government

---

[43] The history of Canada's experience pursuing war criminals on its territory is crucial to understanding how the system in place today has developed into what it is. For a more detailed discussion, see Purves 1998; Lafontaine 2012.

[44] See *Canadian Citizenship Act*, 1946, 10 G. VI, c. 15, s. 10(d).

to strengthen enforcement of this rule against Nazi-era war criminals,[45] a recommendation the government implemented with somewhat more success[46] (and continues to use against post-World War II war criminals today[47]).

However, aside from urging steps to remove Nazi-era war criminals who had obtained Canadian citizenship, the Deschênes Commission report also suggested measures to prevent the admission of such individuals into the country in the first place. At the time, Canada's refugee laws did not implement Article 1F(a) of the 1951 *Refugee Convention*, which excludes an asylum seeker from refugee status if "there are serious reasons for considering that he has committed a crime against peace, a war crime, or a crime against humanity."[48] The Deschênes Commission report recommended that the government incorporate a similar exclusionary clause into Canada's immigration laws.[49]

This advice, too, the Canadian government heeded. Currently, Article 1F(a) of the *Refugee Convention* is implemented referentially through Section 98 of the *Immigration and Refugee Protection Act* (*IRPA*),[50] which reads simply: 'A person referred to in section E or F of Article 1 of the Refugee Convention is not a Convention refugee or a person in need of protection.'

This provides a mechanism to adjudicate whether a refugee claimant who is suspected of committing war crimes has actually done so, and to deny that person's claim if there are serious reasons for so considering. Moreover, because not every person who seeks to immigrate to Canada does so as a refugee claimant, section 35(1) of the *IRPA* further provides that any permanent resident or foreign national may be found inadmissible to Canada for:

> (a) committing an act outside Canada that constitutes an offence referred to in sections 4 to 7 of the *Crimes Against Humanity and War Crimes Act*;
> (b) being a prescribed senior official in the service of a government that, in the opinion of the Minister, engages or has engaged in terrorism, systematic or gross human rights violations, or genocide, a war crime or a crime against humanity.

Thus, any non-citizen is liable to removal from the country if found not only to have committed an international crime, but also merely to have been a "prescribed senior official" in a government that has committed such crimes. Further, the procedure is highly judicialized and sophisticated. Both refugee and admissibility decisions are made by appointed members of a federal administrative tribunal

---

45 Deschênes 1986, pp. 7–8.

46 See e.g. *Canada (Secretary of State) v. Luitjens* [1992], 142 N.R. 173 (Fed. Ct. App.); *Canada (Minister of Citizenship and Immigration) v. Bogutin* (1998), 144 F.T.R. 1 (Fed. Ct. Trial Div.); *Canada (Minister of Citizenship and Immigration) v. Baumgartner* (2001); 211 F.T.R. 197 (Fed. Ct. Trial Div.), *Canada v. Obodzinsky*, 2003 FC 1080 (Fed. Ct.).

47 See *Canada (Citizenship and Immigration) v. Rogan*, 2011 FC 1119.

48 *Convention relating to the Status of Refugees*, 189 U.N.T.S. 150, entered into force April 22, 1954.

49 Deschênes 1986, pp. 230–232.

50 S.C. 2001, c. 27.

called the Immigration and Refugee Board (IRB). The IRB holds quasi-judicial hearings where the individuals whose interests are concerned have basic procedural rights, such as the right to legal representation, the right to know the case against them, and the right to make oral submissions at the hearing.[51] Further, as with any federal administrative actor, decisions of IRB members are also subject to judicial review by the Federal Court. Decisions of the Federal Court, in turn, may be appealed all the way up to the Supreme Court. At all levels, written reasons for decision are given, and once proceedings reach the level of the Federal Court reasons are usually made available publicly online. The system is sophisticated and mature enough that an extensive body of case law has developed around it.

In this way, suspected foreign war criminals who have sought refuge in Canada may be subject either to criminal prosecution or removal from the country. The substantial functional overlap between these two mechanisms is self-evident: a great number of cases that are candidates for one type of proceeding will be candidates for the other. Indeed, as noted above, the widespread use of one was the result of a deliberate strategic choice made by federal government officials in response to the perceived practical limitations of the other.[52] In these circumstances, therefore, the most intriguing theme that emerges in the narrative of international humanitarian law in Canadian courts involves examining the characteristics of these two types of proceedings, as well as what their comparative features and differences have meant in terms of practical ramifications.

13.3 How They Operate in Practice

The second question is the easiest to answer: the mechanisms to deal with suspected war criminals through immigration proceedings—notably refugee or admissibility hearings—are far more heavily used than the available criminal procedures.

In Canada, the government has implemented a coordinated approach to managing the various mechanisms available to pursue persons in Canada suspected of being war criminals. Since 1998, the operational units and personnel responsible for administering the different mechanisms have been integrated through a single unit known as the Crimes Against Humanity and War Crimes Program ("War Crimes Program").

As of 2011, the War Crimes Program had an annual budget of CAD $15.6 million,[53] and issues reports on its activities on a periodic basis. Statistics drawn from these reports demonstrate a strong preference for the pursuit of immigration remedies against suspected war criminals. On the immigration side, the figures are

---

[51] At least in the case of refugee hearings, these rights are constitutionally protected. *Singh v. Minister of Employment and Immigration*, [1985] 1 S.C.R. 177.

[52] "Federal Government Announces WWII War Crimes Strategy," Government of Canada news release, January 31 1995.

[53] Canada, Canada Border Services Agency et al. 2011, p. 3.

impressive. In the 2010–2011 fiscal year alone, for instance, 31 refugee claimants were excluded from refugee protection on the grounds of suspected involvement in war crimes, crimes against humanity, or genocide, while 22 others withdrew or abandoned their claims after the government filed exclusion arguments against them.[54] A further seven individuals were found inadmissible to Canada under s. 35(1) of the *IRPA*.

Meanwhile, as discussed above, in all the time since the enactment of the *War Crimes Act* in 2000 implemented the *Rome Statute* into Canadian law, there have been only two prosecutions undertaken under the *War Crimes Act*. The discrepancy in figures between the immigration and criminal mechanisms is thus staggering. For reference, in the same period of time, the War Crimes Program has secured the 1F exclusion of 500 refugee claimants and counting.[55] While the immigration aspect of the War Crimes Program's activities has clearly been a success, the dramatic imbalance in frequency of use between the immigration and criminal options is not the statistic one would intuitively expect to see in a healthy and properly functioning system. Can it really be that such a startlingly skewed ratio truly represents the optimal balance? What accounts for this discrepancy?

13.3.1 Accounting for the Predominance of Immigration Proceedings

At least part of the answer must lie in the fact that it is simply easier to remove a suspected war criminal from the country than to prove that they actually are a war criminal. There are a number of reasons why this is the case.

The most important reason is the standard of proof. In criminal proceedings, as is well known, the prosecution must prove its case beyond a reasonable doubt.[56] Further, Canada being a predominantly common law jurisdiction, the accused also has a right to elect a trial by jury, in which case the prosecution must persuade so thoroughly as to extinguish all reasonable doubt in the minds of twelve individuals.[57]

In IRB hearings, on the other hand, the standard of proof is far lower. The typical standard of proof in non-penal proceedings is the civil standard of balance of probabilities.[58] However, the standard of proof for 1F exclusion is lower even than this. Under Article 1F, all that is required to exclude an asylum seeker from refugee protection are "serious reasons for considering" that they have committed

---

[54] Ibid., at p. 7.

[55] Canada, Canada Border Services Agency et al. 2011, p. 17.

[56] See e.g. Whitman 2008. See also Langbein et al. 2009, pp. 696–698.

[57] *Constitution Act, 1982*, s. 11(f).

[58] See e.g. *Mutual Life Assurance Co. of Canada v. Aubin*, [1979] 2 S.C.R. 298 at p. 301.

a war crime or crime against humanity.[59] In Canada, this has been interpreted as equivalent to "reasonable grounds to believe," meaning something more than suspicion or conjecture, but something less than proof on a balance of probabilities.[60]

For instance, Canadian courts have consistently held that if there is an organization with a "limited, brutal purpose," mere membership in that organization is sufficient to give rise to reasonable grounds to believe the claimant has been complicit in war crimes or crimes against humanity.[61] This means that in theory, government attorneys could secure the exclusion of a refugee claimant simply by showing membership in a limited, brutal purpose organization and nothing else. The presumption can of course be rebutted,[62] and a claimant occasionally succeeds in doing so.[63] Further, the Supreme Court has cautioned that decision makers must carefully consider whether it can be inferred that the individual's contribution to the group was voluntary and had a significant enough impact on the group's crime or criminal activity.[64] Nevertheless, this still falls far short of what would be required to secure a criminal conviction, and it is easy to see why immigration proceedings present such an alluring alternative to criminal prosecutions.

In admissibility proceedings where the person concerned is alleged to have committed an international crime, the same standard of "reasonable grounds to believe" is also applied.[65] Moreover, another mechanism handicaps the process in the government's favor in a similar way. As set out above, subsection (b) of *IRPA* s. 35(1) provides that a foreign national is inadmissible to Canada if he or she is a "prescribed senior official in the service of a government that, in the opinion of the Minister, engages or has engaged [among other things] genocide, a war crime or a crime against humanity." Under this provision, certain senior officials of regimes designated by the government are automatically considered inadmissible to Canada. For example, currently designated regimes include 1990–1994 Rwanda and the 1992–1995 Bosnian Serb Republic.

However, pointing to specific differences such as these scarcely begins to convey the breadth of the tactical advantage the government enjoys in immigration proceedings as opposed to criminal proceedings. The simple fact is that the immigration system and the criminal justice system are fundamentally different in character. The common law criminal justice system has evolved over centuries to adapt to the numerous challenges that have confronted it. To address the danger of

---

59 Supra, n. 48.

60 *Ramirez v. Canada (Minister of Employment and Immigration)*, [1992] 2 F.C. 306 (C.A.) at pp. 311–312.

61 Ibid at 317–318.

62 *Saridag v. Canada (Minister of Employment and Immigration)*, [1994] F.C.J. No. 1516 at para 10.

63 See e.g. *Canada (Minister of Citizenship and Immigration) v. Mohsen*, [2000] F.C.J. No. 1285.

64 *Ezokola v. Canada (Citizenship and Immigration)*, 2013 SCC 40.

65 *IRPA* s. 33.

abuses by the state, as embodied in popular lore by the excesses of the Star Chamber,[66] the system developed procedural safeguards to ensure trial fairness and judicial impartiality. To counteract the impressionability of lay juries too readily swayed by the dramatic flair and showmanship of skilled oral advocates, the system developed evidentiary rules to deny such advocates the use of certain highly prejudicial classes of evidence whose value is judged to be more rhetorical than real.[67]

In short, the criminal process is designed from the ground up with the protection of the rights of the accused as a central pillar.[68] The IRB, in contrast, has a statutory mandate to "deal with all proceedings before it as informally and quickly as the circumstances and the considerations of fairness and natural justice permit,"[69] and its procedure accordingly lacks many of the core prophylactic features of a criminal trial. The criminal accused, for instance, has a privilege against self-incrimination, and cannot be compelled to testify at his or her own trial.[70] Not so, however, for the person whose rights are concerned at an admissibility hearing, who is a fully compellable witness at the hearing.[71] Moreover, at a refugee hearing, it would make no sense for the refugee claimant to have a right to silence, as it is his or her own onus to establish the claim.[72] Further, IRB members presiding over refugee or admissibility hearings are not bound by the strict rules of evidence that apply in criminal proceedings, and are authorized to consider any evidence they deem credible or trustworthy in the circumstances.[73] It is, in general, a process that is conducted with far less formality and rigor than a criminal proceeding. Often, the person concerned is represented not by a lawyer but an immigration consultant—a profession that is not regulated nearly as rigorously as the legal profession, and that has been plagued by reports of rampant fraud and unscrupulous exploitation of vulnerable clients.[74] So widespread and notorious is the problem that the government addressed it by enacting legislation which was colorfully introduced as the *Cracking Down on Crooked Consultants Act*.[75]

---

66 It does not escape the author that the Star Chamber was technically a court of equity.

67 See e.g. Langbein 1996, pp. 1194–1195.

68 See e.g. Langbein et al. 2009, pp. 647–728.

69 *IRPA* s. 162(2).

70 See e.g. *R. v. Henry*, 2005 SCC 76.

71 See *Bowen v. Canada*, [1984] 2 F.C. 507 (C.A.).

72 *Canada (Attorney General) v. Ward*, [1993] 2 S.C.R. 689.

73 *IRPA* ss. 170–175; *Thamotharem v. Canada (Minister of Citizenship and Immigration)*, 2007 FCA 198, [2008] 1 F.C.R. 385, at para 41; *Kumar v. Canada (Minister of Citizenship and Immigration)*, 2009 FC 643 (CanLII), at paras 28–29.

74 Nicholas Keung, Surya Bhattacharya, and Jim Rankin, "How to stay in Canada by cooking up a story." The Toronto Star, June 17 2007.

75 Citizenship and Immigration Canada, "News Release—Legislation targeting crooked immigration consultants receives Royal Assent," March 23, 2011.

In the author's opinion, the "reasonable grounds to believe" standard is problematic because it is ambiguous and therefore difficult to apply with certainty. To an extent, this is understandable given that it is tethered to the equally imprecise wording of the *Refugee Convention*. However, it is essential that judges remain diligent in maintaining a suitable degree of rigor in applying this standard. This is because a finding of inadmissibility on the grounds of war crimes or other international crimes potentially has very serious consequences for the person concerned. They are liable to removal from Canada to face whatever dangers and risks they may have left behind in their country of origin—with the added component that their names are now affirmatively associated with very serious criminal acts.

The implications of 1F exclusions and findings of inadmissibility under *IRPA* s. 35(1) are made all the more serious by the way the government makes use of them. Since 2011, the government has published on the CBSA website a "wanted" list of individuals who have been the subject of 1F exclusions or findings of inadmissibility under s. 35(1) of the *IRPA*, asking for the public's help in locating them and facilitating their removal from the country.[76] Each name is accompanied by a high resolution photo and vital information, and where the reason for an individual's inclusion in the list relates to suspicions of war crimes or other international crimes, the caption affirmatively states that "It has been determined that he violated human or international rights under the *Crimes Against Humanity and War Crimes Act* or under international law"[77]—prompting The Economist in its coverage of the issue to wryly note, "Canada is making little pretence of presuming the suspects' innocence of these vague allegations."[78]

The author's view is that given the serious consequences of this determination, the standard of "reasonable grounds to believe" should not fall very much lower than the civil standard of balance of probabilities. After all, if someone "believes" something, it is presumably because one thinks it more likely than not to be true. Of course people may "believe" all kinds of fantastical things, but a reasonable belief is one that has an objectively adequate evidentiary basis for being held. Thus, the "reasonable grounds to believe" standard should not be considered met unless it is at least possible for a reasonable person to conclude, on the basis of the evidence, that the case has been met on a balance of probabilities.

---

[76] Canada Border Services Agency, "News Release Government of Canada Enlists Help of Canadians to Enforce Canada's Immigration Laws," July 21, 2011.

[77] http://www.cbsa.gc.ca/wc-cg/wanted-recherchees-eng.html

[78] "Canada and international justice: Be off with you", The Economist, August 4, 2011. http://www.economist.com/blogs/americasview/2011/08/canada-and-international-justice. The Economist also made note of the case of Francisco Manuel Hernández Hernández, a former soldier in the Salvadoran army who filed a failed refugee claim in Canada in the early 1990s. Hernández, now a US citizen and evangelical pastor, had been living in New York since 1993, but his name found its way onto the list anyway, prompting him to come forward in order to clear his name. His name was subsequently removed from the list.

13.3.2 Criticism

The War Crimes Program has been perfectly candid in acknowledging its preference for immigration procedures, citing cost as the primary factor.[79] In this way, after some early struggles in Canada's efforts to avoid being a safe haven for war criminals, the War Crimes Program has managed to find a formula for success by targeting suspected war criminals primarily through immigration proceedings. At the same time, this success—and particularly the way in which it has been achieved—has caused some controversy and drawn criticism from academic[80] and NGO[81] sources alike. The two principal concerns articulated are complementary: concern for the accountability of those who are actually guilty of the acts alleged against them, and concern for the procedural rights of those who may not be.

First, critics argue that Canada is merely perpetuating impunity by simply deporting suspected war criminals without ensuring that they will be tried for their alleged crimes. After all, Canada has a statute with sweeping temporal and extraterritorial jurisdiction over such crimes, which was enacted after a laborious 15-year process for this very purpose. Critics further point to Canada's international obligations, citing the principle of *aut dedere aut judicare*. While the existence of an international legal obligation "to extradite or prosecute" is not settled with respect to all core crimes as defined under the *Rome Statute* as a matter of customary international law,[82] it is established as a matter of treaty law with respect to grave breaches of the *Geneva Conventions*.[83] Moreover, the preamble to

---

[79] See e.g. Canada, Canada Border Services Agency et al. 2011, p. 4 ("The War Crimes Program emphasizes immigration remedies, … [which] have been found to be effective and cost-efficient. The most expensive and resource-intensive remedies are the criminal investigation and prosecution of war criminals—these methods are therefore pursued infrequently. Nonetheless, the ability to conduct criminal investigations and to prosecute is an important element of the War Crimes Program. In some cases, a criminal justice response is the most appropriate action and sends a strong message to Canadians and the international community that the Government of Canada does not tolerate impunity for war criminals or for persons who have committed crimes against humanity, or genocide."); Canada, Canada Border Services Agency et al. 2008, p. 2 ("Remedies are restricted by available funding. Criminal investigations and prosecution, widely seen as essential to international justice, are the most expensive options and only pursued in a fraction of the cases. Therefore partners diligently seek the more cost-effective remedies…").

[80] See e.g. Lafontaine 2010a; Weiss 2012.

[81] See e.g. Amnesty International Canada, "Open Letter to Ministers Toews and Kenney about "Wanted by the CBSA"," August 2, 2011; Letter of September 20, 2011 to Jason Kenney and Vic Toews from 16 organizations including Canadian Council for Refugees, Canadian Centre for International Justice, and Canadian Civil Liberties Association. http://www.criminallawyers.ca/pdf/Most_wanted-Letter_Kenney_Toews.pdf.

[82] For views in favor see e.g. Bassiouni and Wise 1995; International Law Commission, *Fourth Report on the obligation to extradite or prosecute (*aut dedere aut judicare*) by Zdzislaw Galicki, Special Rapporteur*, UN GAOR, 63rd Sess., UN Doc. A/CN.4/648 (2011); cf Cryer et al. 2010. See also Bassiouni 2003, pp. 337–346.

[83] *First Geneva Convention* Article 49; *Second Geneva Convention* Article 50; *Third Geneva Convention* Article 129; *Fourth Geneva Convention* Article 146.

the *Rome Statute* states that "it is the duty of every State to exercise its criminal jurisdiction over those responsible for international crimes,"[84] a passage which is seen by some as evidence of the *aut dedere aut judicare* obligation.[85]

The second criticism echoes the concern articulated earlier in the course of the discussion on the "reasonable grounds to believe" standard—the concern that abuse of the low standard of proof and less stringent procedural and evidentiary safeguards in immigration proceedings could end up casting too wide a net, and unfairly place the stigma of very serious crimes on innocent individuals—with all its attendant repercussions, both in Canada and abroad, both for the individual and the individual's relatives.

It blunts this second concern somewhat that there is a safeguard in place to ensure that no individual is removed from Canada to a country where he or she faces a risk of death, torture, or cruel and unusual punishment. Any person who feels they face such a risk upon return to their country of origin may apply for a pre-removal risk assessment (PRRA).[86] A successful PRRA application stays any existing removal order against the applicant.[87]

Nevertheless, what both these criticisms demonstrate is that immigration proceedings are not a complete standalone remedy to deal with perpetrators of war crimes and other international crimes. According to the *travaux préparatoires*, Article 1F(a) of the Refugee Convention was conceived to serve two purposes: to ensure that the benefits of refugee protection are not enjoyed by those who by virtue of their actions do not deserve them, and to ensure that perpetrators of war crimes and similar heinous acts do not use the institution of asylum to escape facing justice for their crimes.[88] It is thus an inherently incomplete remedy: it was not designed to itself be the mechanism by which war criminals are brought to justice, and, arguably, even implicitly anticipates that another mechanism will intervene to accomplish this function. Thus, it performs entirely inadequately when conscripted to fill this role. It sweeps up the innocent, and does not fully bring the guilty to justice.

This is not to suggest that criminal proceedings ought always to be used instead. Clearly, first of all, not every case is suitable for prosecution. Much depends on the strength and nature of the case and evidence, and the investigative steps required to compile it.[89]

---

[84] *Rome Statute*, Preamble, sixth recital.

[85] See e.g. *Qadafi case*, Cour d'appel de Paris, 20 October 2000, Revue Générale de Droit International Public (2001), 475.

[86] *IRPA*, ss. 112–114.

[87] Ibid., s. 114(1)(b).

[88] Conference of Plenipotentiaries on the Status of Refugees and Stateless Persons, Summary Record of the 24th Meeting, UN doc. A/CONF.2/SR.24, 27 Nov. 1 951, statements of Herment (Belgium) and Hoare (UK); Gilbert 2003, pp. 427–428.

[89] The War Crimes Program suggests that in order for a case to be considered for prosecution, "the allegations must disclose personal involvement or command responsibility, and the evidence pertaining to the allegation must be corroborated and obtainable in a reasonable and rapid fashion, among other considerations." Canada, Canada Border Services Agency et al. 2011, p. 10.

Further, practical constraints of trying an offense alleged to have occurred on another continent in another era abound. In the *Munyaneza* trial, for instance, the trial judge described the logistical challenges as a “colossal undertaking.”[90] The trial itself lasted 19 months.[91] From the time the investigation opened in 1999, to Munyaneza’s arrest 5 years later, to his conviction in 2009, the process up to the completion of trial lasted 10 years—and is still mired at the appeal stage.

Financially, meanwhile, it is estimated that prosecution costs alone totalled $4 million,[92] a number that is in line with the experience of other countries.[93] The average prosecution costs in immigration proceedings, in comparison, come in at under $50,000.[94] It is highly questionable whether such a monstrous investment in both time and money is justifiable for each of the dozens of suspected perpetrators of international crimes who are pursued through immigration proceedings by government officials each year. These are, after all, hardly the Bashirs and Milosevics of the world. They are typically very low-level, relatively unknown actors and the atrocities alleged against them tend to be smaller in scale and more localized.

Where criminal prosecution is not a feasible proposition, however, it is important that other remedies be fully explored instead of, or in conjunction with, immigration proceedings. Extradition and surrender to an international criminal tribunal are two other options that the War Crimes Program actively considers, for instance,[95] and both are more suited to the objective of bringing perpetrators to justice than immigration remedies. Some scholars have also suggested that new, alternative remedies could perhaps be fashioned to supplement all these options.[96]

However, there are some instances where no alternative option to criminal prosecution is available. International criminal tribunals generally concern themselves with the most serious cases,[97] while many countries will not have the political will to seek the extradition of and prosecute their own citizens. For instance, in *Kuruparan v. Canada (Citizenship and Immigration)*,[98] the government secured the exclusion of a former commodore in the Sri Lankan Navy who had applied for refugee status in Canada. In a decision that was upheld by the Federal Court, the IRB found that the Sri Lankan Navy was an organization that had committed war crimes and crimes against humanity during the course of that

---

[90] Ibid., at para 23. For instance, the court traveled to take witness evidence in Paris, Dar Es Salaam, and Kigali (twice), and most of the witnesses testified in Kinyarwanda, requiring extensive translation and interpretation. All told, the court heard 66 witnesses generating 16,000 pages of stenographic notes, and the parties filed briefs of 600 pages with tens of thousands of pages of additional authorities.

[91] Ibid., at paras 25–29.

[92] Canada, Department of Justice 2008.

[93] See e.g. Helsingin Sanomat, Bazaramba plans to appeal genocide conviction (June 14, 2010).

[94] Ibid.

[95] Canada Border Services Agency et al. 2011, p. 4.

[96] Lafontaine 2010a, pp. 43–44.

[97] See e.g. Rome Statute Article 5(1).

[98] 2012 FC 74.

country's brutal 26-year civil war between government forces and the separatist Liberation Tigers of Tamil Eelam (LTTE). Given the applicant's long and illustrious service in the navy and his admitted long-time knowledge of that organization's atrocities, it was found that there were reasonable grounds to believe he had been complicit in war crimes or crimes against humanity.[99]

It is unknown whether the evidence against Nadarajah Kuruparan was strong enough to support a criminal prosecution, and indeed no evidence appears to have been adduced linking him to specific atrocities,[100] suggesting that this may not have been the case. It is thus unclear how suitable this particular case was for criminal prosecution. Nevertheless, the background context of the case provides a perfect illustration of circumstances where a domestic criminal prosecution may be the only viable option to bring perpetrators of war crimes and other international crimes to justice. There is no international criminal tribunal currently prosecuting cases from Sri Lanka. Further, there is absolutely no prospect of the Sri Lankan government seeking extradition of a member of its own security forces for prosecution for war crimes or crimes against humanity. The government of Sri Lanka has persistently and vehemently rejected allegations that its forces have been complicit in war crimes or crimes against humanity,[101] despite clear evidence to the contrary.[102]

---

[99] Ibid., at paras 21–32, 88–90.

[100] Ibid., at paras 91–116.

[101] See e.g. Amnesty International, *Sri Lanka: Report exposes the government's violent repression of dissent*, 30 April 2013, available at: http://www.amnesty.org/en/news/sri-lanka-report-exposes-government-s-violent-repression-dissent-2013-04-30 ("It is abundantly clear that Colombo is unwilling and unable to investigate the credible allegations of crimes under international law, including war crimes, during the conflict."); United States Department of State, *2012 Country Reports on Human Rights Practices—Sri Lanka*, 19 April 2013 at p. 34 ("Many international and national observers stated that the LLRC did not adequately address accountability for alleged war crimes committed by the government and the LTTE during the final months of the conflict and that the LLRC report exonerated the government of any wrongdoing."); United Kingdom: Foreign and Commonwealth Office, *Human Rights and Democracy: The 2011 Foreign & Commonwealth Office Report*, April 2012 at p. 318 ("No concrete progress was made in holding accountable those alleged to be responsible for violations of international human rights and humanitarian law during the final stages of the war."); Freedom House, *Freedom in the World 2013—Sri Lanka*, 10 June 2013, available at: http://www.freedomhouse.org/report/freedom-world/2013/sri-lanka ("The government continued to reject credible allegations of war crimes committed in the final phase of its military campaign against the Tamil Tiger rebel group in 2009, even as the UN Human Rights Council passed a critical resolution calling for an investigation into these issues."); Human Rights Watch, World Report 2013—Sri Lanka, 31 January 2013, available at: http://www.hrw.org/world-report/2013/country-chapters/sri-lanka ("The Sri Lankan government in 2012 continued its assault on democratic space and failed to take any meaningful steps towards providing accountability for war crimes committed by either side during the internal armed conflict that ended in 2009," "There has been no information regarding actions of the special army courts of inquiry, supposedly established in 2012 to look into allegations of war crimes.").

[102] Ibid.; see also UN Secretary-General (UNSG), *Report of the Secretary General's Panel of Experts on Accountability in Sri Lanka*, 31 March 2011 ("the Panel found credible allegations, which if proven, indicate that a wide range of serious violations of international humanitarian law

In such instances, where alternative means of justice are unavailable, the War Crimes Program ought to pursue criminal prosecutions wherever a reasonable prospect of conviction exists. Although there were good reasons historically for the initial shift in strategic focus from criminal prosecutions to immigration proceedings, those reasons do not apply with the same force today. The temporal difficulties associated with aging evidence and witnesses are diminished now that the body of cases arising out of World War II-era atrocities figures less prominently in the War Crimes Program's work. The enactment of the *War Crimes Act* in 2000 eliminated many of the practical difficulties that led to the failures of the earliest prosecutions.[103] The successful prosecution of Désiré Munyaneza has definitively demonstrated that the legislation works and convictions are attainable. Meanwhile, the trial of Jacques Mungwarere, despite failing to produce a conviction, offered indications that some of the logistical extravagances of the *Munyaneza* trial may in fact be avoidable. Due to the accused's initial election for a trial by jury, witnesses located overseas had to be heard by videoconference rather than on location, a process the trial judge wrote had "worked very well" and was suitable for use in any kind of trial.[104] Subject to relief from budgetary constraints imposed by government, therefore, the time is right for the War Crimes Program to slowly begin reviving the long-neglected criminal prosecution component of its holistic war crimes strategy.

None of this, of course, is meant to discount the tremendous value that successful immigration proceedings can have, particularly where the evidence is not sufficiently strong to obtain a conviction. In *Kuruparan* and similar cases from Sri Lanka,[105] for instance, the mere judicial finding that there was a "widespread and systematic attack" against the Tamil population in Sri Lanka[106] provides a powerful and compelling indictment of the Sri Lankan government, and amplifies the mounting international pressure to ensure accountability for wartime atrocities committed on all sides during the civil war. There is no doubt that such a decision is a positive and welcome development in the global struggle for justice for war crimes and crimes against humanity. Nevertheless, the fact remains that immigration proceedings are an imperfect remedy, and many of the practical reasons that once existed in Canada for relying disproportionately on them no longer apply.

(Footnote 102 continued)
and international human rights law was committed both by the Government of Sri Lanka and the LTTE, some of which would amount to war crimes and crimes against humanity."); International Crisis Group, *War Crimes in Sri Lanka*, Asia Report N°191, 17 May 2010, available at: http://www.crisisgroup.org/en/regions/asia/south-asia/sri-lanka/191-war-crimes-in-sri-lanka.aspx ("This evidence also provides reasonable grounds to believe the Sri Lankan security forces committed war crimes with top government and military leaders potentially responsible.").

[103] See e.g. Currie and Stancu 2010.

[104] *Mungwarere*, supra n. 31 at para 17.

[105] See e.g. *Loordu v. Canada (Minister of Citizenship & Immigration)* [2001] F.C.J. No. 141.

[106] *Kuruparan* at paras 106–109.

13.3.3 General Principles of Individual Liability

Instruments of international humanitarian law define the broader, fundamental elements of what acts constitute an offense or breach, but tend to be silent on the principles of individual criminal liability to be applied, such as modes of participation and defenses. These lacunae must be filled independently.

To do this, Canadian tribunals rely heavily on international criminal law and the jurisprudence of international tribunals. In the leading case of *Mugesera v. Canada (Minister of Citizenship and Immigration)*,[107] the Supreme Court emphasized that international law plays "a crucial role as an aid in interpreting domestic law"[108] governing crimes of international concern. The Supreme Court also remarked that decisions of international criminal tribunals are also highly persuasive authority, noting that:

> These tribunals have generated a unique body of authority which cogently reviews the sources, evolution and application of customary international law. Though the decisions of the ICTY and the ICTR are not binding upon this Court, the expertise of these tribunals and the authority in respect of customary international law with which they are vested suggest that their findings should not be disregarded lightly by Canadian courts applying domestic legislative provisions…[109]

As such, many Canadian decisions applying international humanitarian law cite liberally from international legal authorities.

That said, there is not always complete convergence between international humanitarian/criminal law as applied by Canadian courts and international humanitarian/criminal law as applied by international tribunals. One interesting illustration of this is the law relating to the defense of duress. In *Prosecutor v. Erdemović*, the accused, a former member of the Bosnian Serb army, admitted that he personally participated in a massacre of several hundred Bosnian Muslim civilians in July 1995.[110] His evidence was that he initially refused to participate, but was told "If you are sorry for them, stand up, line up with them and we will kill you too."[111] The Appeals Chamber of the ICTY ruled in a narrow 3-2 decision that duress could not afford a complete defense to a charge of war crimes or crimes against humanity involving the killing of innocent human beings.[112]

In Canada, however, a long line of immigration decisions dating to before *Erdemović* establishes that the defense of duress is available in such circumstances.[113] This is ironic, given that in *Erdemović*, both the leading majority (on

---

[107] 2005 SCC 40.

[108] Ibid., at para 82.

[109] Ibid., at para 126.

[110] *Prosecutor v. Erdemović*, Judgement. Case No. IT-96-22-A, at para 3.

[111] Ibid., at para 4.

[112] Ibid, at para 19.

[113] See *Ramirez*, supra n. 60; *Oberlander v. Canada (Attorney General)*, 2009 FCA 330; *Ezokola*, supra n. 64 at para 86.

the question of duress) opinion of Judges McDonald and Vohrah[114] and the separate concurring opinion of Judge Li[115] drew heavily from the laws and decisions of common law countries, including Canada. This created the rather unusual result of an international tribunal drawing upon Canadian law, and a Canadian tribunal drawing upon international law, with each coming to different decisions.

Compounding the irony, a number of the major developed common law countries on which the majority in *Erdemović* relied have now aligned themselves with the Canadian position on the defense of duress,[116] while the United States Supreme Court has left the possibility open as well.[117] Further, any tension is now substantially diminished given that the *Rome Statute* has expressly adopted the defense of duress.[118] Nevertheless, this is a cogent illustration of the occasional discrepancies that inevitably arise between ostensibly harmonized bodies of law. It also makes a strong case for why international criminal tribunals might be well advised to consider paying closer attention to Article 1F exclusion decisions in national courts, particularly when examining state practice.

As an example, in his minority opinion in *Erdemović*, Judge Cassese noted the difficulty in assessing the requirement for duress that the harm inflicted not be disproportionate to the threat against the accused, given the seriousness of crimes involving the taking of innocent lives.[119] International tribunals pondering this question in future might very well find that the cases where Canadian tribunals have grappled with the same issue prove instructive.

For instance, in *Canada (Minister of Citizenship and Immigration) v. Asghedom*, the refugee claimant had been forcibly recruited into the Ethiopian military in 1986 at the age of 18, and spent most of the next 2 years at a military camp in Eritrea, where rebels were at the time still fighting for independence from Ethiopia.[120] The claimant's duties included going into villages to conduct house-to-house searches for weapons. Those with weapons he forced into trucks and brought back to the camp, where they were tortured and killed. The claimant and others then buried the bodies.[121] Despite these circumstances, the Federal Court

---

[114] *Prosecutor v. Erdemović*, Joint Separate Opinion of Judge McDonald and Judge Vohrah. Case No. IT-96-22-A, at paras 42, 49, 60.

[115] *Prosecutor v. Erdemović*, Separate and Dissenting Opinion of Judge Li. Case No. IT-96-22-A, at para 7.

[116] *Refugee Appeal No. 1655/93 Re MSI*, New Zealand Refugee Status Appeals Authority (23 November 1995); *Gurung v. Secretary of State for the Home Department*, [2002] UKIAT 04870, United Kingdom Asylum and Immigration Tribunal (14 October 2002); *Sryyy v. Minister for Immigration and Multicultural and Indigenous Affairs* (2005) 220 A.L.R. 394 (Federal Court of Australia).

[117] *Negusie v. Holder* (2009), 555 U.S. 511.

[118] *Rome Statute* Article 31(1)(d).

[119] *Prosecutor v. Erdemović*, Separate and Dissenting Opinion of Judge Cassese. Case No. IT-96-22-A, at para 49.

[120] 2001 FCT 972 at paras 3–6.

[121] Ibid at paras 7, 12.

accepted the IRB's finding that the claimant was entitled to invoke the defense of duress, because the evidence showed that he would have faced death by execution if he deserted.[122] The judge added that, "The law does not function at the level of heroism and it does not require that a person tries to desert or disobey an order at the risk of his life."[123]

However, in *Valle v. Canada (Citizenship and Immigration)*, the applicant was a Honduran military intelligence operative in Battalion 3–16, a CIA-trained military death squad that abducted, tortured, and murdered civilians with suspected communist or leftist sympathies.[124] Despite the finding that he would have been killed had he left the unit without permission, the IRB ruled that this did not justify the defense of duress, given the greater harm inflicted on a greater number of people.[125]

There appears to be very little to distinguish *Valle* from *Asghedom*. Perhaps the key difference was Valle's more active and higher-level involvement in the atrocities committed. Whatever the case, decisions such as these illustrate that Canadian courts applying international humanitarian law in the context of immigration proceedings may have some useful experience with questions that may be the subject of some difficulty or debate under international law.

The principles of individual criminal liability at international law have also required some adaptation to the lower standard of proof under Article 1F(a) of the *Refugee Convention*. For instance, it was mentioned above that proof of membership in a "limited, brutal purpose organization" gives rise to a presumption of complicity in the context of an immigration proceeding. This is because mere membership in such an organization is thought to supply reasonable grounds to infer that the constituent elements of the offense alleged are present.

Thus, circumstances that may not be sufficient to prove complicity under international criminal law may still provide reasonable grounds to infer complicity under the Article 1F(a) standard. At the same time, however, there is also a danger of straying too far from what constitutes complicity under the criminal standard.

For instance, where the organization in question is not one with a "limited, brutal purpose," Canadian courts have struggled with the question of what level of participation in an organization's activities is sufficient to give rise to an inference of complicity. Initially, they adopted a test of whether the person in question's involvement with the organization constitutes "personal and knowing participation,"[126] with reference to a list of relevant factors: the nature of the organization; the method of recruitment; position/rank in the organization; knowledge of the organization's atrocities; the length of time in the organization; and the opportunity

---

[122] Ibid at paras 29–35.

[123] Ibid at para 38.

[124] 2010 FC 403.

[125] Ibid at para 40.

[126] *Ramirez*, supra n. 60.

to leave the organization.[127] Canadian courts have suggested that this test—which has also been adopted to varying extents in the United Kingdom,[128] New Zealand,[129] and Australia[130]—harmoniously transposes[131] into the 1F exclusion context the "joint criminal enterprise" theory of liability at international law[132] as expounded by the ICTY[133] and in related provisions of the *Rome Statute*.[134]

However, in *Ezokola v. Canada (Citizenship and Immigration)*, the Supreme Court noted that in practice the standard of "personal and knowing participation" had become susceptible to overextension, and elected to replace it with a "significant contribution" test, requiring the decision maker to determine whether an individual "has voluntarily made a significant and knowing contribution to a group's crime or criminal purpose."[135] This was part of what appeared to be a concerted effort to caution against an overly liberal application of the exclusion clause—as mentioned earlier, the court also placed constraints on the "limited, brutal purpose organization" test.

The Supreme Court was correct in recognizing a need to inject additional rigor into the test, as there were signs that it was being too broadly applied. For instance, in *Ezokola*, the IRB had excluded the applicant from refugee protection purely on account of his having been a high-ranking diplomat in the service of a government known to have committed crimes against humanity (the Democratic Republic of the Congo).[136] However, it remains to be seen whether the Supreme Court's recalibration will have any appreciable impact.

---

[127] *Fabela v. Canada (Minister of Citizenship and Immigration)*, 2005 FC 1028 at para 24; *Ali v. Canada (Solicitor General)*, 2005 FC 1306 at para 10. The Supreme Court in *Ezokola*, supra n. 64, later revised these factors slightly to include: (i) the size and nature of the organization; (ii) the part of the organization with which the refugee claimant was most directly concerned; (iii) the refugee claimant's duties and activities within the organization; (iv) the refugee claimant's position or rank in the organization; (v) the length of time the refugee claimant was in the organization, particularly after acquiring knowledge of the group's crime or criminal purpose; and (vi) the method by which the refugee claimant was recruited and the refugee claimant's opportunity to leave the organization. See *Ezokola*, supra n. 64, at para 91.

[128] *R (on the application of* JS*)* (Sri Lanka*) (Respondent) v Secretary of State for the Home Department (Appellant)*, [2010] UKSC 15 at para 30.

[129] *Refugee Appeal No. 1248/93, Re TP*, No. 1248/93, New Zealand Refugee Status Appeals Authority, 31 July 1995.

[130] *W97/164 and MIMA* [1998] AATA 618, para 7.

[131] Although not in the strict sense, as the "personal and knowing participation" test predates the modern articulation and formulation of the joint criminal enterprise theory.

[132] *Canada (Citizenship and Immigration) v. Ekanza Ezokola*, 2011 FCA 22 at para 68.

[133] *Prosecutor v. Tadić*, Judgment. Case No. IT-94-1-A, 15 July 1999; *Prosecutor v. Delalić et alia*, Judgment. Case No. IT-96-21-A, 20 February 2001; *Prosecutor v. Kvočka et alia*, Judgment. Case No. IT-98-30/1-A, 28 February 2005.

[134] *Rome Statute* Article 25(3).

[135] *Ezokola* (Supreme Court), supra at para 84.

[136] Ibid at para 19.

As for the "limited, brutal purpose organization" presumption, meanwhile, it might be sensible for Canadian tribunals to follow the more restrained approach adopted in *Pourjamaliaghdam v. Canada (Citizenship and Immigration).*[137] There, the applicant was a telephone receptionist at a military hospital in Iran who recorded telephone conversations at the request of the Shah's secret police, SAVAK, from 1976 until the revolution.[138] The IRB had found that SAVAK was an organization with a limited, brutal purpose, and excluded the applicant from refugee protection by virtue of her association with it.[139]

On application for judicial review to the Federal Court, this ruling was overturned. In particular, the judge cautioned against overzealous application of the "limited, brutal purpose organization" presumption, noting that it was no more than an extension of the common-sense proposition that "in some cases, it will simply be self-evident that the person, being an active member of such a group, was a knowing participant in its crimes."[140] However, cases where this was all government attorneys had to prove would be the exception, and even in such cases tribunals would still have to consider all the remaining evidence in deciding whether there are, in fact, serious reasons for considering that the applicant had committed an international crime.[141] Further, if a decision against the applicant were to be made solely on the basis of the applicant's membership in an organization, the characterization of that organization as having a limited, brutal purpose must be "free from doubt."[142] Meanwhile, in those cases where it is not "fairly clear" that the presumption applies, it is preferable to perform the conventional multi-factor analysis.[143]

In the context of criminal proceedings, meanwhile, there is an additional gloss on the question of what general principles of individual liability to apply. Immigration tribunals seek to mirror international law as closely as possible in this regard.[144] After all, s. 98 of the *IRPA* incorporate Article 1F(a) of the *Refugee Convention* by reference, and as pointed out in *Ramirez v. Canada (Minister of Employment and Immigration)*, "An international convention cannot be read in the light of only one of the world's legal systems."[145]

However, the situation in criminal proceedings is subtly different. There, the question of what general principles of criminal liability are to be applied is

---

[137] 2011 FC 666.

[138] Ibid at para 6.

[139] Ibid at paras 7–21.

[140] Ibid at para 51.

[141] Ibid at para 52.

[142] Ibid at para 54. See also *Canada (Minister of Citizenship and Immigration) v. Hajialikhani*, [1999] 1 FC 181 (T.D.), at para 24.

[143] Ibid at para 53.

[144] See *Zazai v. Canada (Minister of Citizenship and Immigration)*, 2004 FC 1356 at paras 49–50.

[145] *Ramirez*, supra n. 60.

primarily governed by s. 34(2) of the *Interpretation Act*,[146] which reads "All the provisions of the *Criminal Code* relating to indictable[147] offences apply to indictable offences created by an enactment, and all the provisions of that Code relating to summary conviction offences apply to all other offences created by an enactment, except to the extent that the enactment otherwise provides."

Although many substantive criminal offenses in Canada are defined in special legislation such as the *War Crimes Act*, the central repository of criminal law in Canada is a voluminous statute known as the *Criminal Code*.[148] The *Criminal Code* does not just define substantive offenses, it also sets out many of the auxiliary rules of criminal law, such as procedural rules, sentencing rules, and, indeed, general principles of criminal liability. This means that s. 34(2) of the *Interpretation Act* prescribes the application of all the general principles of criminal liability contained in the *Criminal Code* to offenses defined in the *War Crimes Act*.[149] This includes provisions regarding modes of participation such as aiding and abetting,[150] counselling,[151] and common purpose,[152] as well as defenses such as mental disorder[153] and intoxication,[154] to list a few examples. Meanwhile, the *War Crimes Act* is silent on what should happen in cases of conflict or inconsistency between the Canadian and international law principles, and, as noted above, the Supreme Court has remarked that Canadian provisions on international crimes ought to be interpreted harmoniously with international law. As such, Canadian courts considering criminal liability under the *War Crimes Act* have sought to reconcile the two bodies of law as much as possible.[155] However, there can be little question that, Canada being a dualistic state,[156] the Canadian law prevails in event of an unresolvable conflict.[157]

One notable implication of this arrangement is the criminal liability of corporations. This is a topic that is the subject of considerable controversy as a matter of

---

[146] R.S.C. 1985, c. I-21.

[147] The terms "indictable" and "summary conviction" merely refer to the two main classifications of crimes in the Canadian criminal law system, with the former category generally being the more serious. All that need be known for the present purposes is that all the core crimes defined in the *War Crimes Act* are indictable offenses.

[148] R.S.C. 1985, c. C-46.

[149] This has recently been confirmed judicially in *Mungwarere*, supra n. 31, at paras 50–51.

[150] Ibid., s. 21(1).

[151] Ibid., s. 22.

[152] Ibid., s. 21(2).

[153] Ibid., s. 16.

[154] Ibid., s. 33.1.

[155] *Mungwarere*, supra n. 31 at para 62.

[156] See *Baker v. Canada (Minister of Citizenship and Immigration)*, [1999] 2 S.C.R. 817 at para 69.

[157] For a thorough discussion on the differences between the general principles of criminal liability applicable under Canadian and international criminal law, see Lafontaine 2012, Part III.

international law.[158] In Canada, however, the *Criminal Code* contains a regime of corporate criminal liability that, by virtue of s. 34(1) of the *Interpretation Act*, is applicable to the offenses defined in the *War Crimes Act* as well. The criminal liability of a corporation is tied principally to the acts or omissions of its "senior officers."[159] For a corporation to be found criminally liable of an offense,[160] one of its senior officers must be a party to the offense, direct a representative of the corporation to commit the offense, or, knowing that a representative of the corporation is about be a party to the offense, neglect to take reasonable measures to stop them.[161] In so doing, the senior officer must be acting within the scope of their authority, and with the intent at least in part to benefit the corporation.[162] If all these conditions are met, a corporation could in theory be convicted of war crimes, crimes against humanity, or genocide in a Canadian court[163]—making Canada one of a number of jurisdictions in the world where this appears to be possible.[164]

13.4 Other Current International Humanitarian Law Topics in Canadian Courts

While IHL has typically come before Canadian courts in the manners discussed above, modern challenges of IHL, such as cases of prolonged occupations or the dilemmas posed by the war on terror, have also found their way into the Canadian jurisprudence. The following sections examine some of these cases.

13.4.1 Civil Claims Against Canadian Corporations for Complicity in War Crimes Overseas

A pair of distant military conflicts—Israel's prolonged occupation of the West Bank on the one hand, and the most recent civil conflict in the Democratic Republic of the Congo (DRC) on the other—have managed to find their way to

---

158 See e.g. *Kiobel Lafontaine Royal Dutch Petroleum Co.*, 621 F.3d 111 (2d Cir. 2010).

159 Meaning "a representative who plays an important role in the establishment of an organization's policies or is responsible for managing an important aspect of the organization's activities and, in the case of a body corporate, includes a director, its chief executive officer and its chief financial officer." *Criminal Code* s. 2, "senior officer."

160 Other than offenses requiring the prosecution to prove negligence, to which different rules of corporate liability apply. See *Criminal Code* s. 22.1.

161 *Criminal Code* s. 22.2.

162 Ibid.

163 See also Dragatsi 2011; Wanless 2009.

164 See e.g. Kyriakakis 2007.

Canadian courts, in the form of civil claims filed against Canadian corporations alleging complicity in war crimes overseas.

In *Yassin c. Green Park International Inc.*,[165] inhabitants of the Palestinian village of Bil'in in the West Bank filed suit in Montréal against a Québec-registered construction company that had been contracted to build Israeli settlements on village land.[166] They alleged that this made the defendant complicit in an occupying power's unlawful transfer of population onto occupied land, constituting a grave breach of the *Fourth Geneva Convention* and a war crime.[167] In response, the defendant sought to invoke *forum non conveniens*—the doctrine, imported from the common law, that gives the court discretion to decline jurisdiction if there is a clearly more appropriate forum elsewhere.[168] They argued that Israel was the proper forum for the dispute.

The motion judge recognized, for the first time in Canada, that involvement in a war crime could form the basis for civil liability.[169] He also acknowledged that the plaintiff's cause of action, as framed, was not justiciable in Israel because Article 49 of the *Fourth Geneva Convention*, which prohibits the transfer of an occupying power's population onto occupied land, was not considered customary international law (and therefore automatically incorporated into Israeli domestic law[170]) by Israeli courts,[171] as it was in Canada.[172] However, in a decision that was upheld on appeal,[173] he granted the defendant's *forum non conveniens* motion, suggesting that the plaintiff should argue to an Israeli court that Article 49 of the *Fourth Geneva Convention* had in fact become part of customary international law in the 30 years since the question was last decided there.[174]

In another Québec case, *Anvil Mining Ltd. c. Association canadienne contre l'impunité*,[175] the plaintiff filed a claim against a copper mining company with an office in Québec and a mining operation in the DRC, alleging complicity in war crimes and crimes against humanity for furnishing trucks and other supplies to government soldiers, which they used to brutally quell a small uprising in a town near the site of the mine.[176] As in the *Yassin* case, the defendant sought to have the claim dismissed on jurisdictional bases.

---

[165] 2010 QCCA 1455 [*Bil'in* Appeal Judgment].

[166] Ibid at paras 9–15.

[167] *Fourth Geneva Convention*, Article 49, para 6; *Rome Statute* Article 8(2)(b)(viii).

[168] *Code Civil du Québec*, L.R.Q., c. C-1991, Article 3135.

[169] 2009 QCCS 4151 at para 175 [*Bil'in* Motion Judgment].

[170] Lapidoth 1992 at p. 452.

[171] *Bil'in* Motion Judgment at paras 280–288.

[172] *War Crimes Act*, s. 6(4).

[173] *Bil'in* Appeal Judgment at para 99.

[174] *Bil'in* Motion Judgment at paras 324–326.

[175] 2012 QCCA 117 [*Anvil Mining* Appeal Judgment].

[176] *Association canadienne contre l'impunité (ACCI) c. Anvil Mining Ltd.*, 2011 QCCS 1966 at para 26 [*Anvil Mining* Judgment Decision].

The plaintiff was successful at first instance, with the motion judge ruling that the Québec court had jurisdiction, and that this jurisdiction should not be declined on the basis of *forum non conveniens*.[177] However, this ruling was overturned on appeal. The Québec Court of Appeal held that the claim did not have a sufficient connection to the defendant's particular activities in Québec to form the basis of jurisdiction there.[178]

The results in both cases are disappointing. In *Yassin*, the motion judge engaged in improper speculation when he suggested that the plaintiff could petition an Israeli court to simply change its interpretation of Israeli domestic law.[179] In *Anvil Mining*, meanwhile, the Court of Appeal could easily have asserted jurisdiction using Québec's forum of necessity doctrine,[180] which allows a Québec court to assert jurisdiction where the plaintiff cannot reasonably be required to institute proceedings elsewhere.[181] At first instance, the motion judge himself had found that the plaintiff had no recourse to justice elsewhere.[182]

13.4.2 International Humanitarian Law and Canadian Constitutional Law

In *R. v. Hape*, the Supreme Court of Canada was confronted with the question of whether the prosecution should be entitled to evidence collected overseas by Canadian police in a manner that would have violated the Canadian constitutional rights of the accused if collected domestically.[183] In a remarkable display of legal contortionism, a narrow majority found a way to rule that the *Canadian Charter of Rights and Freedoms*—a constitutional document that guarantees a wide range of basic individual rights—does not apply to government action overseas,[184] unless the state on whose territory the conduct occurred gives its consent.[185] In order to soften the impact of such a sweeping pronouncement, the majority also suggested

---

[177] Ibid at paras 13–39.

[178] *Anvil Mining* Appeal Judgment at paras 52–94.

[179] For a detailed analysis of this decision, see Yap 2010.

[180] *Code civil du Québec*, Article 3136.

[181] The doctrine is Swiss in origin. See *Loi fédérale sur le droit international privé*, R.O. 1988 1776, Article 3. The provision reads, "Lorsque la présente loi ne prévoit aucun for en Suisse et qu'une procédure à l'étranger se révèle impossible ou qu'on ne peut raisonnablement exiger qu'elle y soit introduite, les autorités judiciaires ou administratives suisses du lieu avec lequel la cause présente un lien suffisant sont compétentes."

[182] *Anvil Mining* Motion Judgment at para 39.

[183] 2007 SCC 26.

[184] Ibid at para 69.

[185] Ibid at para 68.

that this rule may yield in circumstances where the government action would violate Canada's international human rights obligations.[186]

Neither aspect of this decision has any basis whatsoever in either text or jurisprudence. It has been sharply criticized both in the concurring opinions[187] and in subsequent academic commentary,[188] and lower courts have expressed regret in being bound to apply it.[189] However, it also created another opening for the application of international humanitarian law in Canada, in the context of constitutional law. In *Canada (Justice) v. Khadr*, the question arose whether Canadian security service officials violated the *Charter* when they shared with US authorities the product of interviews conducted with a Canadian citizen who had been taken prisoner by US forces in Afghanistan in 2002 and was being held at the US detention facilities in Guantanamo Bay.[190] Applying *Hape*, the Supreme Court acknowledged that Canadian participation in a process that violated Canada's international human rights obligations would violate the *Charter* in these circumstances,[191] but expressed concerns over the appropriateness of ruling on the legality of a foreign state's actions with respect to international law.[192] Fortunately, however, the Supreme Court of Canada was relieved of the necessity to resolve this issue in this case, because the United States Supreme Court had already declared that the process being conducted at the time was in violation of international humanitarian law.[193] Thus, the court could simply rely on the US ruling,[194] and the claimant's *Charter* rights were subsequently upheld.

However, no such outlet was available in *Amnesty International Canada v. Canada (Chief of the Defence Staff)*, leading to a different result.[195] That case arose in the context of widespread public concern over suggestions that had emerged that Canadian forces in Afghanistan had been transferring detainees to Afghan authorities in spite of a known and substantial risk of torture.[196] In *Amnesty International Canada*, the Federal Court of Appeal considered whether the *Charter* protected the rights of these detainees, given that the circumstances involved alleged violations of international humanitarian law. Desjardins J.A., writing for a unanimous three-judge panel, distinguished *Khadr* on the basis that that case involved the rights of a Canadian citizen – a distinction whose legal

---

186 Ibid at para 101.

187 See e.g. Ibid., Reasons of Binnie J., paras 181–192.

188 See e.g. Currie J H 2007; Currie R J 2010 at 530–37.

189 *Amnesty International Canada v. Canada (Chief of the Defence Staff)*, 2008 FC 336 [*Amnesty International Canada* Motion Judgment] at para 340.

190 2008 SCC 28.

191 Ibid. at para 19.

192 Ibid. at para 21.

193 *Hamdan v. Rumsfeld*, 126 S. Ct. 2749 (2006).

194 *Hape* at para 23.

195 2008 FCA 401 [*Amnesty International* Appeal Judgment].

196 See e.g. *Amnesty International Canada v. Canada* Motion Judgment at para 76.

significance is unclear given that the section of the *Charter* invoked clearly protects non-Canadians as well,[197] as she herself recognized.[198]

This result, once again, is disappointing. The meager reasoning offered by the Federal Court of Appeal as to why the *Charter* does not apply in this case is unsatisfying, and once again, a Canadian court is relieved of potentially having to rule on a controversial question of international humanitarian law in a case brought by a private litigant.

This evasiveness, meanwhile, stands in stark contrast to the situation in the UK, where the Administrative Court has assertively made itself available as a forum to adjudicate whether Afghan detainees in the hands of British forces should be transferred to Afghan authorities amid fears of torture.[199]

Thus, three Canadian courts have offered questionable (to varying degrees) reasons for dismissing a claim that raised a question of international humanitarian law without having to adjudicate it, and a fourth avoided the issue altogether simply by deferring to the findings of a foreign court. This pattern discloses an admittedly emerging but discernible trend: when petitioned by a private litigant to adjudicate the acts of a foreign state with respect to international humanitarian law, Canadian courts have consistently chosen to punt the ball instead of run with it. This may not be surprising to some, as studiously avoiding controversy could perhaps be considered something of a Canadian pastime. Sadly, in this situation, it comes at the expense of some very fundamental international human rights.

13.5 Concluding Remarks

This chapter is entitled "*Aut Deportare Aut Judicare*"—a Latin phrase meaning roughly, "to deport or to prosecute." The phrase—a play on the words *aut dedere aut judicare*—was chosen because it succinctly encapsulates the principal tension in the Canadian international humanitarian law experience—the question of whether to pursue suspected war criminals found on Canadian soil through criminal prosecution to properly bring them to justice, or through immigration proceedings with the less ambitious but more pragmatic aim of simply removing them from the country.

The title is also apt *precisely* because it is a play on words, and the real choice is not actually supposed to be "to deport or to prosecute." Reliance on the immigration remedy began as a secondary alternative to criminal proceedings, only resorted to due to the logistical difficulties of prosecuting World War II-era crimes. Today, however, there is no doubt that immigration proceedings have come to be

---

197 See e.g. *Suresh v. Canada (Minister of Citizenship and Immigration)*, 2002 SCC 1.

198 *Amnesty International* Appeal Judgment at para 20.

199 See e.g. *Mohammed, R (On the Application Of) v. The Secretary of State for Defence* [2012] EWHC 3454 (Admin).

considered the primary option to deal with suspected war criminals found inside Canada. One Minister in a statement at a press conference recently outlined what seems to be the new conception of Canada's role in bringing war criminals to justice: that it was the responsibility of the countries where the crimes are committed to prosecute them, and that Canada's role was limited to simply removing them from the country.[200]

Hopefully, this strikingly insular view does not prevail everywhere in government, because the fact remains that immigration proceedings are a highly incomplete remedy. There is no doubt that they have a valuable role to play, and that the achievements of Canada's War Crimes Program have delivered this value. However, they cannot support the heavy load they bear under the current system, where they occupy an almost exclusive role in Canada's strategy on suspected war criminals found in the country. They are only a rough indicator of actual guilt at best, and are not designed to properly bring perpetrators of war crimes to justice. It is thus hoped that with the early promising results of prosecutions under the *War Crimes Act*, criminal proceedings will eventually be restored to some measure of prominence, with occasional resort to extradition and other alternative options where domestic prosecutions are not feasible.

It was stated at the outset that Canada's legal system is rife with dualities, and several of these have been exposed throughout the course of this chapter. However, a broader, holistic appraisal of the totality of the Canadian experience with international humanitarian law reveals the most puzzling duality of all.

One author has described Canadian courts' experience with respect to international humanitarian law as "both extensive and limited" at the same time.[201] This characterization, though a contradiction in terms, is nevertheless uncannily accurate. When it comes to applying international humanitarian law through 1F exclusion cases, Canadian courts are bold, pioneering trailblazers, issuing decisions whose influence reverberates globally in refugee law spheres. However, their character transforms dramatically when a claim brought by a private litigant raises a question of international humanitarian law. Then, they suddenly become flustered and timid, preferring to defer to foreign courts, or, better yet, evade the issue entirely by any legally acrobatic means necessary, and awkwardly fumbling what they do venture to take on (the motion judge in *Yassin*, for instance, embarrassingly betrayed a complete ignorance of the fact that there is a difference between international humanitarian law and international human rights law[202]).

It is difficult to explain the root cause of this Jekyll-and-Hyde act. It could be that Canadian judges as an institution see a limited political role for the judiciary,

---

[200] Embassy, "War criminal campaign derided as 'misleading': Government accused of muddying the waters between immigration, criminal law," Kristen Shane, 3 August 2011.

[201] Lafontaine 2012 at p. 282.

[202] *Bil'in* Motion Judgment at para 248. Cullen J. specifically makes note of an expert witness' use of the term "international humanitarian law," and goes on to cite one author's opinion that the term "international human rights law" is "a convenient but perhaps confusing category of reference devoid of intrinsic substance."

and shy away from making decisions that could cause a political stir unless called on to do so by government actors. Or, it could merely be a symptom of inexperience—the tentative, uncertain skepticism that is perhaps only natural when encountering something new has not yet given way to a confident belief that such claims brought by private litigants do, in fact, belong in court. Only one thing is certain: private litigants will not stop bringing these claims just because Canadian courts would prefer not to have to decide them. As such, it is hoped that Canadian courts will find a way to overcome this inexplicable reticence whatever its cause may be, before many more private litigants are denied their day in court.

In stark contrast, the refugee and immigration decisions of Canada's Federal Court system contain a trove of jurisprudential consideration of war crimes and crimes against humanity. International criminal tribunals do make occasional scant use of this resource,[203] but it still remains largely untapped. This is a call to such tribunals to make better use of the accumulated insights of courts in Canada (as well as other countries) that have considered very similar issues—in some instances exceedingly thoroughly—in the context of refugee and immigration decisions. Of course, certain care needs to be taken, given the lower standard of proof set out by Article 1F(a) of the *Refugee Convention*, as well as the different objectives of refugee protection generally. For instance, the jurisprudence on complicity by membership in the Canadian refugee and immigration jurisprudence may be useful for its philosophical discussions of the principles governing individual criminal liability, but the ultimate legal conclusions on membership in an organization as a basis for liability are probably too rooted in the "serious reasons for considering" standard of Article 1F(a) to provide any useful guidance in the criminal context. Nevertheless, Canadian case law considering the commission of war crimes and crimes against humanity is in many areas more developed than in the international jurisprudence, and presents a potentially valuable resource for international tribunals to draw upon.[204]

References

Abella I, Troper H (1982) None is too many: Canada and the Jews of Europe, 1933–1948. University of Toronto Press, Toronto

Bassiouni MC (2003) Introduction to international criminal law. Transnational Publishers, Ardsley

Bassiouni MC, Wise EM (1995) *Aut Dedere Aut Judicare*: The Duty to Extradite or Prosecute in International Law. Martinus Nijhoff, Dordrecht

Canada, Canada Border Services Agency, Citizenship and Immigration Canada, Department of Justice, Royal Canadian Mounted Police (2008) Canada's Program on Crimes Against Humanity and War Crimes: Eleventh annual report, 2007–2008

[203] See e.g. ICTY: *Prosecutor v. Kunarac*, Judgement. Case No. IT-96-23/1-A & IT-96-23/1-A, fn. 114; ICTR: *Nahimana v. Prosecutor*, Judgement. Case No. ICTR-99-52-A, para 699.

[204] See also Rikhof 2006, pp. 719–22.

Canada, Canada Border Services Agency, Citizenship and Immigration Canada, Department of Justice, Royal Canadian Mounted Police (2011) Canada's Program on Crimes Against Humanity and War Crimes: Twelfth annual report, 2008–2011
Canada, Department of Justice (2008) Crimes Against Humanity and War Crimes Program—Summative Evaluation: Final Report. Evaluation Division, Office of Strategic Planning and Performance Management, Ottawa
Cassese A (2008) International criminal law, 2nd edn. Oxford University Press, Oxford
Cryer R, Friman H, Robinson D, Wilmshurst E (2010) An introduction to international criminal law and procedure, 2nd edn. Cambridge University Press, Cambridge
Currie JH (2007) Weaving a tangled Web: *Hape* and the obfuscation of Canadian reception law. Can Yearb Int Law 45:55
Currie RJ (2010) International and transnational criminal law. Irwin Law, Toronto
Currie RJ, Stancu I (2010) *R. v. Munyaneza*: pondering Canada's first core crimes conviction. Int Crim Law Rev 10(5):829–853
Deschênes J (1986) Commission of Inquiry on War Criminals Report, Part 1: Public. Canadian Government Publishing Centre, Ottawa
Dragatsi H (2011) Criminal liability of Canadian corporations for international crimes. Carswell, Toronto
Gilbert G (2003) Current issues in the application of the exclusion clauses. In: Feller E, Turk V, Nicholson F (eds) Refugee protection in international law. Cambridge University Press, Cambridge, pp 425–478
Graditzky T (1998) Individual criminal responsibility for violations of international humanitarian law committed in non-international armed conflicts. Int Rev Red Cross 322:29
Hogg PW (2007) Constitutional Law of Canada, 5th edn. Carswell, Toronto
Kyriakakis J (2007) Australian prosecution of corporations for international crimes: the potential of the Commonwealth Criminal Code. J Int Crim Justice 5:809
Lafontaine F (2010a) The unbearable lightness of international obligations: when and how to exercise jurisdiction under Canada's *Crimes Against Humanity and War Crimes Act*. Revue québécoise de droit international 23(2):1
Lafontaine F (2010b) Canada's Crimes against Humanity and War Crimes Act on Trial: An Analysis of the *Munyaneza* Case. J Int Crim Justice 8:269
Lafontaine F (2012) Prosecuting genocide, crimes against humanity and war crimes in Canadian Courts. Carswell, Toronto
Langbein JH (1996) Historical foundations of the law of evidence: a view from the Ryder Sources. Columbia Law Rev 96:1168
Langbein JH, Lerner RL, Smith BP (2009) History of the common law: the development of the Anglo-American legal institutions. Wolters Kluwer Law & Business, New York
Lapidoth R (1992) International law within the Israel legal system. Israel Law Rev 24:451
Purves G (1998) War Criminals: The Deschênes Commission. Parliamentary Research Branch, Library of Parliament, Ottawa
Rikhof J (2006) Complicity in international criminal law and Canadian refugee law: a comparison. J Int Crim Justice 4:702
Wanless WC (2009) Corporate liability for international crimes under Canada's *Crimes Against Humanity and War Crimes Act*. J Int Crim Justice 7:201
Weiss N (2012) Somebody else's problem: how the United States and Canada violate international law and fail to ensure the prosecution of war criminals. Case West Reserve J Int Law 45:579
Whitman JQ (2008) The origins of reasonable doubt: theological roots of the criminal trial. Yale University Press, New Haven
Yap J (2010) Corporate civil liability for war crimes in Canadian courts lessons from *Bil'in (Village Council) v. Green Park International Ltd.* J Int Crim Justice 8:631

Chapter 14
International Humanitarian Law in Indian Courts: Application, Misapplication and Non-application

Chintan Chandrachud

Contents

14.1 Introduction

India is no stranger to warfare and the rules that govern its conduct. Some of the oldest laws and customs of war can be traced back to the Vedic period, dating from about 1500 BC to 500 BC.[1] Ancient texts such as the *Ramayana*, the

The author is a PhD Candidate at the University of Cambridge. Chritarth Palli from the Government Law College, Mumbai provided excellent research assistance. All errors remain those of the author.

[1] Mani 2001, p. 61.

C. Chandrachud (✉)
University of Cambridge, Cambridge, UK
e-mail: chintan.dc@gmail.com

D. Jinks et al. (eds.), *Applying International Humanitarian Law in Judicial and Quasi-Judicial Bodies*, DOI: 10.1007/978-94-6265-008-4_14,

Mahabharata, the *Agni Purana* and the *Manusmriti* include prescriptions on the legitimate conduct of war.[2] They distinguished between *dharma yuddha* (just war) *and adharma yuddha* (unjust war).[3] Using poisoned or disproportionately harmful weapons, attacking disarmed soldiers and inflicting harm upon non-combatants was proscribed.[4] Rulers were duty bound to inform their rivals of their intention to go to war.[5]

In contemporary times, post-independence India has fought four wars with Pakistan,[6] one with China[7] and has militarily intervened in the Sri Lankan civil war.[8] Governments have also persistently faced situations of internal armed conflict against Maoists in the 'red corridor'[9] and insurgents in Kashmir[10] and the Northeast.[11] But counterintuitively, international humanitarian law (IHL) finds less reference than expected in the judgments of Indian courts.

This chapter has three primary objectives. First, it seeks to thematically analyse Indian courts' consideration and application of norms of IHL. Greatest emphasis has been placed on this objective. Second, it seeks to expound upon the cases in which Indian courts have misunderstood basic principles of IHL on some occasions when they have chosen to cite it. Third, it seeks to critically analyse a few cases in which IHL was not invoked, even though its application would have been apposite.

With this context in mind, the chapter proceeds as follows. Section 14.2 briefly examines the legal status of international law (including IHL) in India. Section 14.3 thematically analyses the Indian case law concerning the application of IHL norms. Section 14.4 takes a step back by looking at the overall picture of application, misapplication and non-application of IHL norms in India. Concluding comments are given in Sect. 14.5.

---

2 Ibid. See also Penna 1980, p. 181.

3 Sinha 2005, p. 287; Subedi 2003, p. 356.

4 Sinha 2005, pp. 291–292.

5 Subedi 2003, p. 353.

6 Ganguly 2002, p. 1.

7 Krishna 1998, p. 23.

8 Rao 1988.

9 See Poprzeczny 2010.

10 Patankar 2009.

11 Bhaumik 2007.

14.2 The Status of International Law in India

Several provisions of the Indian Constitution make direct or indirect references to international law.[12] How a judicial system views international law in general is an important factor in understanding its approach to principles of IHL.[13] With regard to the relationship between international law and the municipal law, Indian courts have steadily moved from a transformationalist approach, requiring international law to be transformed into the municipal law through constitutional machinery before it has any effect, to an incorporationalist approach that recognises international law as having become part of the municipal law without the intervention of domestic constitutional processes. The Supreme Court and High Courts have increasingly relied upon international treaties and custom, particularly in the sphere of human rights and environmental law.[14] In what remains one of the most authoritative cases on this subject, the Supreme Court said:

> The comity of nations requires that rules of international law may be accommodated in the municipal law even without express legislative sanction provided they do not run into conflict with Acts of Parliament. But when they do run into such conflict, the sovereignty and the integrity of the Republic and the supremacy of the constituted legislatures in making the laws may not be subjected to external rules except to the extent legitimately accepted by the constituted legislatures themselves. National courts cannot say yes if Parliament has said no to a principle of international law. National courts will endorse international law but not if it conflicts with national law.[15]

---

[12] See, for e.g., Article 51(c) (requiring the state to 'foster respect for international law and treaty obligations'), Article 73 (stating that the executive power of the Union extends to the exercise of such rights, authority and jurisdiction as are exercisable by the Government of India by virtue of any treaty), Article 246 read with entries 10–19 of List I of the Seventh Schedule (granting the Union Parliament the exclusive power to legislate on matters relating to international law in India), Article 253 (enabling the Union Parliament to make any law for the whole or any part of India for implementing any treaty or decision made at an international conference) and Article 372(1) (stipulating that the laws in force in India prior to the commencement of the Constitution, including British common law rules governing the incorporation of international law into municipal law, shall continue in force until altered, repealed or amended).

[13] Blank 2012, pp. 18–19.

[14] Hegde 2010, p. 55. The judicial structure of India is unitary, with the Supreme Court as the highest appellate and constitutional court, followed by the twenty-four state High Courts. Each state has a High Court, which is the highest appellate court within the state (in some cases, two or more states share a High Court). The High Courts are linked to the Supreme Court within the federal system, which is the apex appellate and constitutional court in India. The Supreme Court and High Courts have far-reaching constitutional powers, including the power to 'strike-down' primary and secondary legislation. The common law doctrine of precedent holds sway, with the result that courts bind those that are below them in the judicial hierarchy. Rules of standing were liberalised considerably in the 1980s, thereby allowing public-spirited (not necessarily personally injured) citizens to move the Supreme Court and High Courts through 'public interest litigation' petitions.

[15] *Gramophone Company of India v. Birendra Pandey* (1984) 2 SCC 534 [5].

In *Vellore Citizens' Welfare Forum v. Union of India*,[16] in the context of sustainable development in environmental law, the Supreme Court reiterated that the rules of customary international law are deemed to be incorporated into the domestic law, so long as they are not inconsistent. In a case concerning the sexual harassment of women in workplaces, the Supreme Court observed that in the absence of domestic legislation in the field, international conventions and norms can be read into fundamental rights under the Constitution.[17] Therefore, international conventions and custom can supplement existing legislation or relevant constitutional provisions.[18]

India has ratified the four Geneva Conventions of 1949[19] but has neither signed nor ratified the three additional protocols.[20] The Geneva Conventions Act 1960 (GCA) incorporates the Geneva Conventions into domestic law.[21] Other statutes also incorporate aspects of IHL into Indian domestic law. The Chemical Weapons Convention Act 2000 gives effect to the Chemical Weapons Convention,[22] which was ratified by India in 1996. It establishes a national authority for implementing the provisions of the Chemical Weapons Convention, prohibits the use of chemical weapons, sets up an inspection regime and contains provisions relating to offences and penalties. The Weapons of Mass Destruction and their Delivery Systems

[16] (1996) 5 SCC 647 [15]. See also *People's Union for Civil Liberties v. Union of India* (1997) 1 SCC 301 [22].

[17] *Vishaka v. State of Rajasthan* (1997) 6 SCC 241.

[18] However, the extent to which international law (whether treaties or customary law) can be relied upon in domestic courts without transformation into municipal law has its limits. It is questionable whether courts will permit a litigant to rely upon international law as a self-standing source of law, rather than as a tool to supplement existing constitutional or statutory provisions (*Jolly George Varghese v. Bank of Cochin* (1980) 2 SCC 360 [6, 7]). It is also unlikely that courts will rely on international law to justify restrictions on the rights of citizens (See *Maganbhai Ishwarbhai v. Union of India* (1970) 3 SCC 400 [80]; Basu 2011, p. 9014). Therefore, Indian courts do not subscribe to the doctrine of incorporation in its purest form (See *State of West Bengal v. Kesoram Industries* (2004) 10 SCC 201 [490–492]).

[19] Convention for the Amelioration of the Condition of the Wounded and Sick in Armed Forces in the Field; Convention for the Amelioration of the Condition of Wounded, Sick and Shipwrecked Members of Armed Forces at Sea; Convention relative to the Treatment of Prisoners of War; Convention relative to the Protection of Civilian Persons in Time of War. The conventions were ratified by India on 9 November 1950.

[20] Protocol relating to the Protection of Victims of International Armed Conflicts (1977); Protocol relating to the Protection of Victims of Non-International Armed Conflicts (1977); Protocol relating to the Adoption of an Additional Distinctive Emblem (2005).

[21] Section 20 of the GCA repealed two statutes: the Geneva Convention Act 1911, passed by the Imperial Legislature (which sought to give effect to certain provisions of the Second Geneva Convention for the Amelioration of the Condition of Wounded, Sick and Shipwrecked Members of Armed Forces at Sea) and the Geneva Convention Implementing Act 1936, passed by the Indian Legislature pre-independence (which sought to discharge the obligations imposed by Article 28 of the Geneva Convention for the Amelioration of the Conditions of the Wounded and Sick in Armies in the Field 1929 insofar as this had not been done by the 1911 statute).

[22] Convention on the Prohibition of the Development, Production, Stockpiling and Use of Chemical Weapons and on their Destruction 1993.

(Prohibition of Unlawful Activities) Act 2005[23] provides for 'integrated legal measures' to exercise controls over the export of materials, equipment, and technologies and prohibits unlawful activities in relation to weapons of mass destruction and their means of delivery. It was enacted in pursuance of Resolution 1540 of the UN Security Council.[24]

These statutes provide a framework for IHL discourse in India's judicial system. The next section will analyse judgments that have applied norms of IHL.

14.3 Thematic Analysis of IHL in Indian Domestic Courts

This section analyses the judgments that apply norms of IHL under four broad themes: occupation and annexation of territory, prisoners of war, terrorism and the war on terror and the meaning of aggression.[25] These themes are employed with the objective of demonstrating the range of matters which have given rise to a discussion of IHL in Indian courts, rather than constructing distinctive jurisprudential approaches to different kinds of subject matter. Therefore, the themes should not be understood as being mutually exclusive either in the kinds of IHL issues that arise for consideration or in courts' treatment of them.

14.3.1 Occupation and Annexation of Territory

Rev Monterio v State of Goa[26] arose in the backdrop of post-independence India's annexation of Goa. Goa, a territory that is part of the Indian sub-continent, was a Portuguese colony for over four centuries.[27] In December 1961, Indian armed forces launched a short military operation that led to the surrender of the Portuguese.[28] In March 1962, the Parliament of India passed a constitutional amendment[29] to recognise Goa as a union territory[30] of India from 20 December 1961 onwards. The petitioner, a resident of Goa, had the option under the law of

---

[23] Long Title, The Weapons of Mass Destruction and their Delivery Systems (Prohibition of Unlawful Activities) Act 2005.

[24] Kanodia and Bhalla 2012, p. 1.

[25] I have considered cases in which IHL has played some meaningful role (but not necessarily the predominant or a significant role) in the judgment of the court. This naturally means that judgments which have made cursory references to IHL either in the description of parties' arguments or in the substantive portion of the decision have been excluded from consideration in this section.

[26] AIR 1970 SC 329.

[27] Sakshena 2003, p. 19.

[28] Prabhakar 2003, p. 41.

[29] Constitution (Twelfth Amendment) Act 1962.

[30] Unlike states, union territories are under the direct administration of the central government. Goa was converted into a state in 1987.

retaining his Portuguese nationality instead of becoming an Indian national. He chose to exercise this option, was registered as a foreigner and obtained a temporary residential permit to stay in India until November 1964.[31] He did not seek an extension or renewal of the permit on the expiry of his term of residence. As a result, he was ordered to leave India by the Lieutenant Governor General of Goa. He was prosecuted and sentenced to thirty days' imprisonment and a fine for disobeying the order.[32] After appealing unsuccessfully, he filed a special leave petition[33] to the Supreme Court of India.

The petitioner contended that his deportation was contrary to the GCA, which incorporated the four Geneva conventions into domestic law. His argument relied upon Articles 1, 2, 4, 6, 8, 47 and 49 of the Fourth Geneva Convention. Central to the discussion were Articles 47[34] and 49[35] of the Fourth Geneva Convention.[36] Since the benefits that arise from these provisions for the civilian population are contingent on the territory in question being 'occupied', the most important question for the Court was whether Goa could still be described as an occupied territory. A further question arose under Article 49—could the order of the Lieutenant Governor General be considered as an order of deportation of a protected person?

The petitioner chose not to question the legality of the annexation itself.[37] Instead, he contended that Goa was 'occupied territory' and that the occupation had not come to an end.[38] His argument sought to interpret the provisions of the Fourth Geneva Convention in the light of developments in international law, under which acquisition of territory by the use of force did not end occupation and confer title.[39] Moreover, the constitutional amendment passed by Parliament did not legitimize the unilateral military annexation in the eyes of international law.[40] The

---

[31] *Rev Monterio v. State of Goa* AIR 1970 SC 329 [1].

[32] Ibid.

[33] Article 136 of the Indian Constitution enables the Supreme Court, in its discretion, to grant 'special leave to appeal from any judgment, decree, determination, sentence or order in any cause or matter passed or made by any court or tribunal' in India (except under any law relating to the armed forces).

[34] This provision stipulates that protected persons who are in occupied territory shall not be deprived of the benefits of the Convention as a result of the occupation or annexation of the territory (see Fourth Geneva Convention, Article 47).

[35] This provision prohibits the deportation of protected persons from occupied territory to the territory of the Occupying Power or to that of any other country (see Fourth Geneva Convention, Article 49).

[36] For commentary on the implications of Articles 47 and 49 of the Fourth Geneva Convention, see Korman 1996, p. 219; Arai-Takahashi 2009, p. 273.

[37] *Rev Monterio v. State of Goa* AIR 1970 SC 329 [5].

[38] Ibid.

[39] Ibid [10].

[40] Ibid [10].

occupation would not come to an end until the territory was formally ceded by the original power (in this case, Portugal) or until the occupying power (India) withdrew from the territory.[41] Thus, Goa should be considered occupied territory for the purposes of Articles 47 and 49. Further, according to the petitioner, the order made by the Lieutenant Governor General was a deportation order.[42] The state contended that one of the legitimate ways in which occupation comes to an end is through conquest followed by subjugation.[43] Therefore, Goa was a part of India and could not be described as 'occupied territory'.

The judgment of the Court is interesting, both in terms of the result it arrived at as well as with reference to the observations made in the course of the decision. At the outset, the Court observed that the GCA did not give a specific right to anyone to approach the court. This on account of the fact that the GCA was passed in pursuance of Article 253 of the Constitution and only provided 'for certain matters based on Geneva Conventions'.[44] The Court remarked:

> ...the Act by itself does not give any special remedy. It does give indirect protection by providing for penalties for breaches of Convention. The Conventions are not made enforceable by Government against itself nor does the Act give a cause of action to any party for the enforcement of Conventions. Thus there is only an obligation undertaken by the Government of India to respect the Conventions regarding the treatment of civilian population but there is no right created in favour of protected persons which the Court has been asked to enforce. If there is no provision of law which the courts can enforce the court may be powerless and the court may have to leave the matter to what Westlake aptly described as indignation of mankind.[45]

Thus, the Court was unsure about the method that an aggrieved party needed to adopt in order to invoke the jurisdiction of a municipal court, but it chose not to consider the issue since on the merits, it agreed with the contentions of the state.

Since the Geneva Conventions do not define the notion of occupation, the Court relied upon Article 42 of the Hague Regulations concerning the laws and customs of war on land of 1907, according to which a territory is considered occupied when it is actually placed under the authority of the hostile army.[46] From this definition, the Court inferred that occupation under Articles 47 and 49 referred to military occupation, a temporary situation that does not deprive the occupying power of its sovereignty or statehood. Annexation, however, takes place when possession is supplemented by 'uncontested sovereignty' over territory and gives rise to a

[41] Ibid [10].

[42] Ibid [10].

[43] Ibid [11].

[44] Ibid [13].

[45] Ibid [15].

[46] Article 42 of the Hague Regulations concerning the laws and customs of war on land of 1907 states that '[t]erritory is considered occupied when it is actually placed under the authority of the hostile army'.

de jure right to administer the territory.[47] The Court then distinguished between 'premature annexation' and 'true annexation'.[48] Whereas the former takes place in situations where hostilities are continuing, the latter is said to occur when the territory is conquered and subjugated.

The Court recognized that Article 47 of the Geneva Convention specified that annexation had no impact on protection. However, the nature of annexation spoken of in this provision was premature annexation and not true annexation. True annexation confers title and destroys the source of authority of the existing government.[49] Following true annexation, the inhabitants would be bound to follow the laws of the annexing state.[50] The military operation conducted by India lasted for only a few hours and was not resisted.[51] Thus, in this case, the occupation ended and gave way to true annexation when the hostilities ceased. The date of true annexation was 20 December 1961, when the government was taken over and there was neither an army in occupation, nor an army in opposition.[52] The Court also asserted that the annexation had given rise to a transfer of title: '[i]f cession after defeat can create title, occupation combined with absence of opposition must lead to the same kind of title'.[53] It arrived at the conclusion that the petitioner could not claim the benefit of the relevant provisions of the Geneva Conventions. He was bound by the order of the Lieutenant Governor General, since sovereign states had the prerogative to distinguish between citizens and non-citizens. The Supreme Court therefore held in favour of the state.

To date, this remains the case that engaged most with concepts of IHL. Some of the issues that arose in the court's decision are now worth analyzing. To begin with, the petitioner decided not to question the legality of the annexation itself. At one level, this was a strategic and ingenious move, although it did not yield dividends. If the petitioner had chosen to question the legality of the annexation itself, it would have left him with a big mountain to climb. How comfortable would a group of five Supreme Court judges have been declaring that India's annexation of Goa was illegal in the eyes of international law? The petitioner sought to separate the question of the legality of the military operation from the question of acquisition of sovereignty. But the Court did not accept this argument. On the contrary, it noted that:

> It must be remembered that Mr. Gardiner [counsel for the petitioner] concedes that the annexation was lawful. Therefore, since occupation in the sense used in Article 47 [of the fourth Geneva Convention] had ceased, the protection must cease also.[54]

---

47 *Rev Monterio v. State of Goa* AIR 1970 SC 329 [21].

48 Ibid [22].

49 Ibid [23].

50 Ibid [23].

51 The Court's judgment seems to indicate that India's military opposition went completely unopposed (Ibid [26]). But a few commentators suggest that there was some resistance (Anderson 2000, p. 153; Rakove 2013, p. 105).

52 *Rev Monterio v. State of Goa* AIR 1970 SC 329 [26].

53 Ibid [25].

54 Ibid [26].

It is problematic to draw the bridge between the legality of the military operation and the transfer of title over territory as the Court did. It is plausible to argue that the unilateral use of force against the territory of another state may be lawful in some situations and not in others. What the petitioner contended was that *regardless* of whether the use of force was lawful or not, acquisition of sovereignty or title over the territory could never follow under international law.

At the outset, the Court should have decided the question about whether the petitioner had the standing to challenge the order of the Lieutenant Governor General under the GCA in the first place, rather than have said that his challenge failed in any event. The Supreme Court flipped the logical order of analysis by answering the substantive question and sidestepping the equally important threshold question. Further, the court's remark that the GCA did not seem to provide any specific remedies against the government[55] is peculiar. This argument implies that a statute that does not specifically provide for remedies is meaningless and unenforceable in the eyes of the law. But this is a mistaken conclusion. For instance, any delegated legislation or executive action that is inconsistent with the provisions of such a statute can be struck down by the courts in exercise of their powers of judicial review. Thus, a statute in the nature of the GCA imposes an injunction on the executive not to act contrary to principles of IHL. If a representative of the state does act contrary to the GCA, that would trigger the remedy of judicial review under the common law.

Finally, the Court's conclusion that 'true annexation' brought the occupation to an end seems to contradict fundamental notions of modern IHL.[56] However, although the Court's analysis that the annexation led to a transfer of title may seem flawed when examined exclusively through the funnel of IHL, it finds greater justification when viewed in the context of the broader political and legal issues of de-colonisation, self-determination and acceptance by the international community of states, all of which were precipitated by the annexation of Goa.[57]

14.3.2 Prisoners of War

Another issue that has been brought before Indian courts concerns the treatment and repatriation of prisoners of war. Both cases that will be discussed arose in the context of the 1971 Indo-Pakistan war. In December 1971, a war broke out between India and Pakistan.[58] The war lasted for only about two weeks and led to

---

[55] Ibid [15].

[56] Gasser 2004, p. 242; UK Ministry of Defence 2004, p. 278.

[57] Mastorodimos 2009, p. 145; Wright 1962; Korman 1996, pp. 273–274; Bains 1962, pp. 195–208.

[58] Roy-Chaudhury 2010, p. 544.

the secession of East Pakistan as the independent state of Bangladesh.[59] The three countries agreed to release and repatriate prisoners of war thereafter.[60] On the Indian side, there were concerns that some prisoners of war remained in Pakistani jails despite assertions to the contrary by the government of Pakistan.[61]

A remarkable set of circumstances provide the backdrop for the Supreme Court's judgment in *Angrej Kaur v. Union of India*.[62] The wife of a constable on the Border Security Force, who was declared to have died during the war, petitioned the Supreme Court under Article 32 of the Constitution.[63] Based on news reports and verbal testimonies of prisoners of war who had been repatriated, she believed that her husband was alive and languishing in Pakistani jails for over three decades. Accordingly, she prayed for a writ of habeas corpus seeking the repatriation of her husband.[64]

The Court recognised that issuing a writ of habeas corpus to Pakistani authorities was beyond the boundaries of its jurisdiction.[65] But it sought to pass appropriate directions, since in its view, human emotions made it difficult to accept the 'legal landline' between the two nations.[66] The Court was satisfied that the Indian authorities had taken a number of steps, including engaging in bilateral discussions with Pakistan, to trace the whereabouts of the petitioner's husband. It disposed of the petition by issuing a direction asking the authorities to continue their efforts. Clarifying that its directions related to Indian officials alone, the court said:

> If a soldier, while fighting for the country's security, is captured and taken to other [sic] country's prison contrary to the official belief that he was dead, it would be in the interest of not only petitioner and her family members but also for the armed forces of this country to see that he is brought back to our country.[67]

Although the Court did not categorically cite principles of IHL in its judgment, its judgment was in furtherance of accepted norms concerning the release and repatriation of prisoners of war after the close of hostilities, specifically laid down in Article 118 of the Third Geneva Convention.[68]

---

[59] Ibid.

[60] The Indian Government initially refused to repatriate over 90,000 Pakistani prisoners of war on the basis that a renewal of hostilities could not be excluded (UK Ministry of Defence (2004), p. 205).

[61] Singh 2009, p. 533.

[62] (2005) 4 SCC 446.

[63] Article 32 provides for the right to petition the Supreme Court at first instance for the enforcement of fundamental rights under Part III of the Constitution. It also states that the Supreme Court has the power to issue directions, orders or writs for the enforcement of fundamental rights.

[64] *Angrej Kaur v. Union of India* (2005) 4 SCC 446.

[65] Ibid [2].

[66] Ibid [2].

[67] Ibid [4].

[68] Article 118 of the Third Geneva Convention relative to the treatment of prisoners of war.

Under IHL, the obligation to release prisoners of war is triggered as soon as active hostilities cease.[69] Hence, the mere fact that hostilities may resume at some point in the future is not a sufficient basis to be absolved of this obligation.[70] The duty of release and repatriation after the termination of hostilities is absolute and is not contingent on the behaviour of the home state.[71] Given that the Supreme Court is a national court, it was of course not open to it to seek the direct enforcement of IHL by issuing directions to Pakistani authorities. Its directions, however, did seek the proxy-enforcement of IHL by requiring Indian authorities to continue to engage with their Pakistani counterparts on the issue of the release of the petitioner's husband.

The second case under this theme arose in similar circumstances, but on a larger scale. In *Jagjit Singh Arrora v. Union of India*,[72] former members of the Indian armed forces petitioned the Gujarat High Court in relation to fifty-four prisoners of war who were allegedly languishing in Pakistani jails for over three decades after the 1971 war, and were presumed dead by the Government of India. The petitioners had two principal contentions. First, that since the prisoners of war were still alive, they should be treated as having been alive for the purposes of the payment of salary, pension and benefits to their next of kin.[73] In other words, rather than being treated as dead since the 1971 war, members of the armed forces should be treated as though they had served their full tenure until retirement. The second argument was more contentious. The court was asked to direct the government to petition the International Court of Justice (ICJ) requesting Pakistan to honour its agreements on the repatriation of prisoners of war.[74]

The second contention of the petitioners was based on the fact that the Indian and Pakistani governments had entered into the Simla Agreement in July 1972, under which it was agreed that the modalities for the repatriation of prisoners of war would be discussed.[75] Pursuant to this agreement, it was subsequently decided that the governments would release and repatriate the prisoners of war.[76] The petitioners claimed that India acted in accordance with the Geneva Conventions by treating prisoners with respect and repatriating them in accordance with the agreement with Pakistan. The government of Pakistan, on the other hand, was in breach of IHL and their treaty obligations by failing to repatriate a large number of Indian prisoners of war.[77]

---

[69] Fischer 2004, p. 364.

[70] Ibid, p. 365.

[71] UK Ministry of Defence (2004), p. 205.

[72] 2012 GLH (1) 362.

[73] Ibid [3].

[74] Ibid [3].

[75] Agreement Between the Government of India and the Government of the Islamic Republic of Pakistan on Bilateral Relations (Simla Agreement) (2 July 1972), Clause VI.

[76] *Jagjit Singh Arrora v. Union of India* 2012 GLH (1) 362 [3].

[77] Ibid [1].

As in the *Agrej Kaur* case, the government of India argued that it had made sustained diplomatic efforts in seeking to discover the whereabouts of these prisoners of war.[78] It also staunchly opposed the contention that it should be directed to take the issue to the ICJ for two reasons. First, the government was not in a position to take the case to the ICJ unilaterally. The ICJ would have jurisdiction only if a reference was made by both India and Pakistan.[79] Second, invoking the International Court's jurisdiction would contradict India's consistent approach that its disputes with Pakistan should be resolved bilaterally without any third-party intervention.[80]

The Gujarat High Court held that since the prisoners of war were still alive, the state could not presume them dead. Hence, their next of kin would be entitled to service and retirement benefits as though they were in service until the age of retirement.[81] Controversially, the Court also directed the government to refer the matter to the ICJ, since Pakistan was in breach of an international treaty.[82] It correctly recognised that apart from a special agreement referring a dispute to the court, the ICJ's jurisdiction can also be invoked through compromissory clauses[83] in treaties.

The evidence relied upon by the Court in arriving at this conclusion was tenuous. It cited the first clause of the Simla Agreement which states that 'the principles and purposes of the Charter of the United Nations shall govern the relations' between the parties.[84] According to the Court, since the Statute of the ICJ is included as an annex to the Charter of the United Nations, the parties, both signatory to the U.N. Charter, could be deemed as having consented also to the referral of disputes to the ICJ. Further, since the repatriation was in pursuance of the Simla Agreement, Pakistan's failure to repatriate the prisoners of war could be taken to the ICJ.

The Court also stated that referring the matter to the ICJ would not affect India's policy of dealing with Pakistan-related issues on a bilateral basis, since all that was sought here was the enforcement of an agreement that was entered into between the two countries, which the state was obliged to pursue in the light of the right to life of the prisoners of war under the Indian Constitution.[85] Thus, the Court attempted to secure the fulfilment of Pakistan's obligations under IHL through the unprecedented route of directing the Union of India to approach the ICJ within two months' time.

---

[78] Ibid [2].

[79] Ibid [9].

[80] Ibid [9].

[81] Ibid [24].

[82] Ibid [25].

[83] Compromissory clauses refer to clauses in international treaties and conventions that provide for the resolution of disputes through the ICJ or other international bodies. See Shaw 2008, p. 1079; Charney 1987.

[84] Agreement Between the Government of India and the Government of the Islamic Republic of Pakistan on Bilateral Relations (Simla Agreement) (2 July 1972), Clause I (i).

[85] Article 21 of the Indian Constitution states as follows: 'No person shall be deprived of his life or personal liberty except according to procedure established by law'.

This is problematic for a number of reasons. First, it raises the question about whether a municipal court can direct a government to approach the ICJ, something which seems to fall squarely within the prerogative of the executive.[86] The Court seemed to justify its conclusion on the basis that it was only mandating the government to enforce the provisions of the treaty that it had entered into. But this argument erroneously assumes that petitioning the ICJ is the only way of securing the enforcement of IHL in general, and of treaty obligations in particular. Judicial redress is neither the only, nor necessarily the most optimal, method of securing compliance with treaties embodying IHL norms. Pursuing bilateral diplomatic channels, mounting international pressure or reconfiguring trade relations could all be effective methods of securing the same objective.[87]

The Court's decision is also questionable on grounds of institutional competence—how appropriate is it for the judiciary to decide that a sovereign state should petition the ICJ against another? This is a decision which should be left to the government, since it has polycentric implications[88] going far beyond the release of prisoners of war. Even if the Court's decision is framed in rights-based terms, on the argument that the fundamental rights of the prisoners of war are at stake, it could have far reaching rights-based implications on many others who are caught in the political crossfire between the two nations.

Finally, the court's understanding of international law, which had a bearing on its interpretation of the Simla Agreement, was questionable. Article 36(1) of the Statute of the ICJ provides that the International Court has jurisdiction in all matters where this is *specially provided for* in the Charter of the United Nations or in treaties and conventions. Thus, compromissory treaty clauses must provide for the referral of disputes to the ICJ with at least some degree of specificity. For instance, in the *Nicaragua* case,[89] the clause that led to the invocation of the court's jurisdiction was as follows: '[a]ny dispute between the Parties as to the interpretation or application of the present Treaty, not satisfactorily adjusted by diplomacy, shall be submitted to the International Court of Justice, unless the Parties agree to settlement by some other pacific means'.[90] Similarly, in *Bosnia*

---

[86] Article 73(b) of the Indian Constitution, which was referred to earlier, states that the executive power of the Union extends to the exercise of rights, authority and jurisdiction as are exercisable by the government of India by virtue of any treaty or agreement.

[87] See Damsrosch 1997, p. 19.

[88] Fuller 1978.

[89] *Military and Paramilitary Activities in and against Nicaragua (Nicaragua v. US)* (1984) ICJ Rep 392 (Jurisdiction and Admissibility).

[90] Treaty of Friendship, Commerce and Navigation between the United States and Nicaragua (21 January 1956), Article XXIV, para 2. Another example is Article 1 of the Optional Protocol to the Vienna Convention on Consular Relations, concerning the compulsory settlement of disputes. This compromissory clause reads as follows: '[d]isputes arising out of the interpretation or application of the Convention shall lie within the compulsory jurisdiction of the International Court of Justice and may accordingly be brought before the Court by an application made by any party to the dispute being a Party to the present Protocol'.

and Herzegovina v Yugoslavia,[91] the compromissory clause that founded the Court's jurisdiction stated that '[d]isputes between the Contracting Parties relating to the interpretation, application or fulfillment of the present Convention... shall be submitted to the International Court of Justice at the request of any of the parties to the dispute'.[92] The opening clause of the Simla Agreement, which simply states that the 'principles and purposes' (and not even the methods and means) of the UN Charter will govern the relations between the parties,[93] is not sufficiently specific to establish the jurisdiction of the ICJ. The second clause in the Simla Agreement addresses the methods of dispute resolution more directly and only states that the two countries will settle disputes through 'bilateral negotiations or by any other peaceful means mutually agreed upon between them'.[94]

The government has filed an appeal to the Supreme Court against the High Court's direction to petition the ICJ.[95] The appeal is still pending, although the Supreme Court has temporarily suspended the effect of the Gujarat High Court's judgment.[96] It has to be seen whether the Supreme Court takes a more nuanced approach to the IHL issues at stake.

14.3.3 Terrorism and the War on Terror

This section examines the application of IHL norms in cases relating to terrorism. Terrorism has a long and complex history in independent India and remains one of the biggest challenges to national security.[97] Terrorist operations have not only affected the lives of those in the middle classes, but have also found their way into the corridors of influence. The terrorist attack on Parliament, which provides the context of the cases that are discussed in this part, is a good example.

On 13 December 2001, a group of five terrorists infiltrated the Parliament of India in New Delhi while it was in session.[98] Their objective was to take members of Parliament and government officials hostage and blow up the parliamentary premises.[99] The attempt failed. The terrorists were killed following an exchange

---

91 *Application of the Convention on the Prevention and Punishment of the Crime of Genocide* (*Bosnia and Herzegovina v. Yugoslavia*)(1996) ICJ Rep 595 (Preliminary Objections).

92 Convention on the Prevention and Punishment of the Crime of Genocide 78 UNTS 277 (9 December 1948), Article IX.

93 Agreement Between the Government of India and the Government of the Islamic Republic of Pakistan on Bilateral Relations (Simla Agreement) (2 July 1972), Clause I (i).

94 Ibid, Clause I (ii).

95 D Mahapatra (2012) SC stays Gujarat HC fiat to Centre to move ICJ on 1971 POWs in Pakistan, 3 May 2012, The Times of India.

96 Ibid.

97 Mohan and Sahni 2012, p. 6.

98 Goswami 2012, p. 127.

99 *State v. Mohammed Afzal* (2003) 107 DLT 385 [1, 12].

of fire with security personnel.[100] Four people were tried for engaging in a conspiracy along with the terrorists to perpetrate the attack. Three of them were convicted by a special court,[101] while the fourth was convicted for a lesser offence. *State v Mohammed Afzal*[102] concerned the appeals from the judgment of the special court.

Although the accused were charged with committing a range of criminal offences, the offence that is of interest for this chapter is provided for in Section 121 of the Indian Penal Code 1860, which penalises the waging of war against the government of India.[103] Before Indian independence, this capital offence was invoked by the British colonial government to prosecute and punish those who attacked state institutions and sometimes, even those who instigated violence against the government.[104] Post-independence, it has frequently been employed against those accused of committing terrorist acts.[105]

In *Mohammed Afzal*, the state and the defendant parted ways on the interpretation of the notion of 'war' under Section 121 of the Indian Penal Code. The defendant argued that 'war' should be interpreted as seeking to overthrow the government by conquest or rebellion and attacking combatants as opposed to civilians.[106] War was fought between nations according to the rules of international conventions. Since the terrorists did not seek to overthrow the government of the day, they could not be prosecuted under Section 121.[107] Further, unlike war, which signified an ongoing state of hostilities, terrorist acts were intermittent, and hence fundamentally different.[108]

In response, the state contended that there was a difference between inter-state war and intra-state war.[109] The illustration accompanying Section 121 provided a glimpse into the minds of the enacting legislature. Since joining an insurrection against the government constitutes 'waging war' against the government of India,

---

[100] *State v. Najot Sandhu* AIR 2005 SC 3820 [3].

[101] The special court was constituted under Section 23 of the Prevention of Terrorists Activities Act 2002.

[102] (2003) 107 DLT 385.

[103] Section 121 of the Indian Penal Code 1860 reads as follows: 'Waging, or attempting to wage war, or abetting waging of war, against the Government of India—Whoever wages war against the Government of India, or attempts to wage such war, or abets the waging of such war, shall be punished with death, or imprisonment for life and shall also be liable to fine. *Illustration*. A joins an insurrection against the Government of India. A has committed the offence defined in this section.'

[104] Chandrachud (2011).

[105] *State v. Mohammed Afzal* (2003) 107 DLT 385; *State v. Najot Sandhu* AIR 2005 SC 3820; *State of West Bengal* v. *Mohammed Jamiluddin Nasser* MANU/WB/0007/2010; *Ajmal Kasab v. State of Maharashtra* AIR 2012 SC 3565.

[106] *State v. Mohammed Afzal* (2003) 107 DLT 385 [181].

[107] Ibid [182].

[108] Ibid [182].

[109] Ibid [183].

the legislative intent was not meant to restrict the meaning of 'war' to cases where rival states were engaged in an armed conflict of a certain magnitude.[110]

Speaking for the Court, Justice Nandrajog rejected the interpretation of Section 121 put forth by the counsel for the defendant. The Court held that 'war' was a flexible expression that had different connotations in international law and municipal law.[111] Insurgency, as a legal concept, fell within the auspices of 'waging war' as understood in Indian domestic law.[112] Even international law drew a distinction between inter-state wars and intra-state wars. Although the volume of international law applying to internal armed conflict has been expanding progressively, the rules governing intra-state war are still fundamentally different from those governing inter-state war. Further, wars as understood in the international sense did not imply continuous conflict, and could be interspersed with periods of cease-fire. Responding to the defendant's contention that war would necessarily implicate an objective to overthrow the government, the Court clarified that wars can conceivably have more limited or modest objectives, for instance the partial conquest of a territory or the coercion of a rival government.[113] Terrorist tactics may be adopted in war.[114]

Thus, the Court concluded that wars could occur even where the belligerents were not states. Individuals who had a different allegiance could use arms to engage against the state. The scale of aggression would be determinative in order to ascertain whether an act constituted war against the government under Section 121.[115] The number of combatants would only be a relevant factor in deciding whether an act of violence could be described as an act of war. The Court provided an example to drive home the point:

> ... a single person may have infiltrated into India with a nuclear bomb, a missile and a navigation system to guide a missile. He uses it to bomb the parliament when it is in Session and particularly when the President of India is to address it. The entire executive and the legislature is present...He intends by his attack to wipe out the entire legislative and executive body. This solitary act by one man would be more devastating then a 1,000 armed men attacking the Parliament. Indeed, it would be an act of war.[116]

The Court found that where a group of five terrorists attacked Parliament, the seat of Indian sovereignty, while it was in session, this would constitute an act of war for the purposes of Section 121 considering the cache of arms and fire-power that was at their disposal. Thus, Justice Nandrajog relied upon the difference between

---

[110] Ibid [183].
[111] Ibid [185].
[112] Ibid [190].
[113] Ibid [186–187].
[114] Ibid [188].
[115] Ibid [189].
[116] Ibid [190].

international armed conflict and non-international armed conflict in order to expound upon the meaning of war under Section 121 of the Indian Penal Code.[117] Two of the defendants were sentenced to death under this provision.

The matter went in appeal to the Supreme Court.[118] The Supreme Court agreed with the Delhi High Court's interpretation of the term 'war' under Section 121 of the Indian Penal Code.[119] According to it, there was a difference between the understanding of war in municipal law and international law.[120] In international law, war referred to military operations between two or more hostile states. Given the illustration to Section 121,[121] it was clear that war was ascribed a different meaning under the Indian Penal Code. It was intended to include acts of insurrection or insurgency (as opposed to belligerency) against the government. As a result, the court stated that although every terrorist act did not amount to waging war under Section 121,[122] some terrorist acts could attain the threshold of waging war.

Writing the Court's judgment, Justice Venkatarama Reddi did not acknowledge the distinction between international armed conflict and non-international armed conflict that was expounded upon by the High Court.[123] Instead, the Supreme Court chose to highlight that there was divergence of opinion about how war was defined in the international sphere as well.[124]

In failing to identify that IHL draws a distinction between international armed conflict and non-international armed conflict, the court misunderstood the law in two ways. To begin with, its judgment conveys the impression that the concept of war in international law is always understood as involving belligerency between states (although the court did accept that precise definitions of war within this framework varied). Second, it implies that rules of international law govern only war between sovereign states. Both of these propositions are mistaken, since IHL not only takes cognizance of intra-state wars, but also prescribes rules for the conduct of such wars.[125] In fact, Additional Protocol II to the Geneva Conventions relates exclusively to the protection of victims of non-international armed conflicts.

---

117 Ibid [190].

118 *State v. Najot Sandhu* AIR 2005 SC 3820.

119 Ibid [(xi)].

120 This conclusion has been cited in several subsequent cases. See, for example, *Mohammed Afzal Kumhar v. State* (2009) 158 DLT 549; *State of Maharashtra v. Ajmal Kasab* AIR 2011 Bom 648.

121 The illustration accompanying Section 121 of the Indian Penal Code 1860 is as follows: '*Illustration*. A joins an insurrection against the Government of India. A has committed the offence defined in this section.'

122 *State v. Najot Sandhu* AIR 2005 SC 3820 [(xi)].

123 Ibid.

124 Ibid.

125 See, generally, Sivakumaran (2012).

14.3.4 The Meaning of Aggression

Under the final theme, I will briefly examine a case in which the Supreme Court relied upon understandings of war in IHL to distinguish it from the notion of 'aggression'. In *Sarbananda Sonowal v Union of India*,[126] a public interest litigation petition challenging the constitutional validity of the Illegal Migrants (Determination by Tribunals) Act 1983 (IMDT Act) was filed. The objective of the IMDT Act was to detect and deport primarily Bangladeshi illegal immigrants from the state of Assam.[127] This law was special legislation that applied only to Assam and was meant to override the provisions of the Foreigners Act 1946,[128] which was applicable to illegal immigrants in the rest of India.[129]

The petitioner contended that the IMDT Act failed to achieve its objective and stood in breach of provisions of the Constitution.[130] One of the grounds of challenge was based on Article 355 of the Constitution, which reads as follows.

> Duty of the Union to protect States against external aggression and internal disturbance- It shall be the duty of the Union to protect every State against external aggression and internal disturbance and to ensure that the government of every State is carried on in accordance with the provisions of this Constitution.

The petitioner contended that the influx of a large number of illegal immigrants from Bangladesh into Assam constituted 'external aggression and internal disturbance' for the purposes of Article 355.[131] Thus, by virtue of being an ineffective law passed for Assam to replace the more effective law applicable to the rest of the country, the IMDT Act should be struck down for violating this constitutional mandate.

The moot question was whether the entry of illegal immigrants could fall within the purview of the word 'aggression' in Article 355. Addressing this issue, the Court held that the term was of a very wide import and should not be confused with 'war'.[132] Though war would be included within the scope of aggression, the converse would not necessarily be true. The Court cited three different definitions of the notion of war[133] in IHL to substantiate its opinion. It asserted that war is a contest between two or more belligerent states and can sometimes involve the general population as well.[134] According to the Court, the framers of the Constitution

---

126 AIR 2005 SC 2920.

127 See Long Title, Illegal Migrants (Determination by Tribunals) Act 1983.

128 Illegal Migrants (Determination by Tribunals) Act 1983, Section 4.

129 Section 1(2), The Foreigners Act 1946.

130 *Sarbananda Sonowal v. Union of India* AIR 2005 SC 2920 [2].

131 Ibid.

132 Ibid [32].

133 Ibid [32].

134 Ibid [32].

consciously used the word 'aggression' rather than 'war' to avoid these connotations.[135] In its view, the influx of illegal immigrants fell within the purview of the notion of aggression.[136] The IMDT Act was struck down as unconstitutional.[137]

14.4 Norms of IHL in Indian Courts: The Overall Picture

14.4.1 Infrequent References to IHL

The first thing that is discernible when sifting through Indian case law is that references to IHL and the Geneva Conventions have been scant, especially when compared to international human rights conventions such as the International Covenant on Civil and Political Rights[138] and the Convention on the Elimination of All Forms of Discrimination Against Women.[139] The reasons for this could be manifold and go beyond the consideration of this chapter. But they could include the nature and profile of litigation in the Supreme Court and High Courts, the greater appeal and superior accessibility of international human rights law compared to IHL and the lack of emphasis on IHL in the curricula of university law courses.[140]

---

135 Ibid [32].

136 Ibid [38].

137 Ibid [42].

138 See, for e.g., *Madha v. Hoskot v. State of Maharashtra* AIR 1978 SC 1548 [20]; *Prem Shankar Shukla v. Delhi Administration* AIR 1980 SC 1535 [4]; *Bachan Singh v. State of Punjab* (1982) 3 SCC 24 [141–143, 231]; *Indian Express Newspapers v. Union of India* AIR 1986 SC 515 [26]; *Nilabati Behera v. State of Orissa* AIR 1993 SC 1960 [23]; *D C Saxena v. Union of India* AIR 1996 SC 2481 [31]; *TMA Pai Foundation v. State of Karnataka* AIR 2003 SC 355 [228]; *Swamy Shraddananda v. State of Karnataka* (2007) 12 SCC 288; *Selvi v. State of Karnataka* AIR 2010 SC 1974 [81].

139 See, for e.g., *Madhu Kishwar v. State of Bihar* AIR 1996 SC 1864 [9–11, 13]; *Vishaka v. State of Rajasthan* AIR 1997 SC 3011 [12, 13]; *Githa Hariharan v. Reserve Bank of India* AIR 1999 SC 1149 [14, 22]; *Municipal Corporation of Delhi v. Female Workers (Muster Roll)* AIR 2000 SC 1274 [34]; *Seema v. Ashwani Kumar* AIR 2006 SC 1158 [2]; *National Insurance Co v. Deepika* (2009) 6 MLJ 1005 [8]; *All India Lawyers Union (Delhi Unit) v. Government of Delhi* (2009) 172 DLT 319 [33].

140 The Bar Council of India does not include IHL in the list of compulsory subjects for university LLB courses (see http://www.barcouncilofindia.org/wp-content/uploads/2010/05/BCI RulesPartIV.pdf accessed 24 August 2013). See also the syllabi of the LLB Programmes at the following universities, which do not contain an IHL component: University of Calcutta (available at: http://www.caluniv.ac.in/academic/law.htm accessed 24 August 2013), University of Mumbai (available at: http://www.glcmumbai.com/uploads/notices/124_file.pdf accessed 24 August 2013), University of Allahabad (available at: http://www.allduniv.ac.in/images/course/syllabus/law/syb-law-llb3years.pdf accessed 24 August 2013), University of Karnataka (available at: http://lawschool.cmr.ac.in/application/362-Syllabus%203 %20Years.pdf accessed 24 August 2013).

14.4.2 The Importance and Nature of the Role of IHL in Case Law

The relative importance of the IHL question in the overall context of the court's judgment has varied. In the *Rev Monterio* case[141] the whole matter hinged on the IHL issue of whether and when India's occupation of Goa had ceased. Similarly, in the prisoners of war cases, the IHL norms requiring the repatriation of prisoners of war after the close of hostilities provided the substratum for the courts' judgments. In the terrorism cases, the definition of war under IHL was relevant to one aspect of the courts' judgments—the interpretation of 'waging war' against the government under Section 121 of the Indian Penal Code. In *Sarbananda Sonowal*,[142] the application of IHL played a peripheral role, as the Court attempted to define the concept of war vis-à-vis that of aggression.

In practice, where it has been cited, IHL has played two different roles in Indian case law. First, it has been applied directly in order to justify or form the basis of the Court's judgment. This will be referred to as the 'applicatory role' of IHL. The cases examined under the first two themes discussed in the previous section demonstrate IHL's applicatory role. In the case concerning the annexation of Goa, the Supreme Court directly relied upon the notions of occupation and annexation as understood in the Geneva Conventions and Hague Regulations in order to determine whether India's belligerent occupation had ceased. In the cases relating to prisoners of war, the principle of repatriation of prisoners of war after the close of hostilities and the agreements between India and Pakistan in pursuance of this principle formed the basis for the courts' decisions.

The second role IHL plays in Indian jurisprudence encompasses situations where a principle or concept of IHL has been cited to distinguish it from a concept in domestic law. This will be referred to as IHL's 'distinguishing role'. The cases analyzed under the third and fourth themes of the previous part bring out the distinguishing role of IHL. In the terrorism cases, the definition of 'war', as understood in IHL, was used as a point of contrast with the meaning of 'war' under the Indian Penal Code. In the case under the final theme on aggression, the concept of aggression under Article 355 of the Indian Constitution was distinguished from the understanding of war in IHL.

---

141 *Rev Monterio v. State of Goa* AIR 1970 SC 329.

142 *Sarbananda Sonowal v Union of India* AIR 2005 SC 2920.

14.4.3 Misapplication and Mislabelling

The *Jagjit Singh Arrora*[143] and *Navjot Sandhu*[144] cases reflect a failure to appreciate and take account of the nuances of IHL, even though it was referred to. In *Jagjit Singh Arrora*, the infirmity lies in failing to understand the specificity required for clauses to be considered as 'compromissory' under Article 36(1) of the ICJ Statute. The Supreme Court's error in *Navjot Sandhu* was more subtle: it was a failure to appreciate the qualitatively different kinds of armed conflict that IHL may be applicable to.

Further, on at least one occasion, what has been labelled as IHL actually fell within the domain of international refugee law. In *Ktaer Abbas Habib v Union of India*,[145] the petitioners were Iraqi refugees who had left their home country to avoid having to serve in the army. They had a fear of persecution in their home country and requested that they be handed over to the United Nations High Commissioner for Refugees instead of being deported to Iraq. Treating the problem as one of international humanitarian law, the Gujarat High Court said:

> There is no law in India which contain [sic] any specific provision obliging the State to enforce or implement the international treaties and conventions including the implementation of International Humanitarian Law (IHL). Amongst the domestic legislation, the only law that directly deals with the principle of IHL is the Geneva Convention Act, 1960.[146]

It then cited the *Rev Monterio* case,[147] which has been discussed above, for the proposition that the GCA did not provide any special remedies. The court laid down a group of principles applicable to IHL norms (which, in its view, included the concept of non-refoulment). Admittedly, the lines of distinction between IHL, international criminal law, international human rights law and international refugee law have been increasingly blurring.[148] But to treat non-refoulement as a principle which squarely falls within IHL reflects a failure to recognize the broad jurisdictional domains of different aspects of international law.

14.4.4 The Non-application of IHL

Sometimes, courts have not applied IHL norms in cases where they would have been particularly apposite or relevant. *Nandini Sundar v State of Chattisgarh*[149] was a high profile and politically charged case that was adjudicated upon by the

---

143 *Jagjit Singh Arrora v. Union of India* 2012 GLH (1) 362.

144 *State v. Najot Sandhu* AIR 2005 SC 3820.

145 1999 Cri LJ 919.

146 *Ktaer Abbas Habib v. Union of India* 1999 Cri LJ 919 [9].

147 *Rev Monterio v. State of Goa* AIR 1970 SC 329.

148 See Quénivet 2008; Dugard 1998.

149 AIR 2011 SC 2839.

Supreme Court in 2011. Throughout the last few decades, the state of Chhattisgarh has been critically affected by insurgent militant groups with a Maoist ideology.[150] With the objective of combating this insurgency, the state established an armed civilian vigilante group which went by the name of 'Salwa Judum'.[151] Untrained and poorly paid tribal youth were appointed as special police officers, participating in anti-insurgency operations.[152] It is widely believed that the Salwa Judum itself was involved in widespread human rights violations and atrocities.[153] As a result, a petition was filed in the Supreme Court seeking that this force be declared unconstitutional.

The Court held that the mobilisation of the Salwa Judum violated Article 14 of the Constitution, the right to equality before the law.[154] According to the Court, subjecting untrained, poorly educated members of the tribal communities to the same dangers as the regular state police force was discriminatory.[155] Moreover, the right to life[156] was breached on account of the fact that, as experience had shown, employing such persons in counter-insurgency operations endangered the lives of others in society.[157] The Court therefore disbanded the Salwa Judum and directed the state to recall the firearms provided to its members.[158]

The Court did not cite principles of IHL in its judgment. This case would have been a paradigm scenario for the application of Additional Protocol II to the Geneva Convention, which concerns the protection of victims of non-international armed conflicts. As renowned journalist Siddharth Varadarajan has noted in the context of the insurgency in Chhattisgarh and the Salwa Judum, 'if ever there was a textbook case of the kind of conflict envisaged by Protocol II, the tragedy that is playing out in Chhattisgarh is surely it'.[159]

Various provisions of the Protocol would have been relevant to the facts of the case. For instance, Article 4 provides for the humane treatment of those who do not or have ceased to take part in hostilities. Article 13 provides that '[t]he civilian population and individual civilians shall enjoy general protection against the dangers arising from military operations'. Article 17 prohibits the displacement of

---

150 For a brief background and context of the naxalite insurgency, see Gupta 2007; Vora and Buxy 2011.

151 Sundar 2006.

152 *Nandini Sundar v. State of Chattisgarh* AIR 2011 SC 2839 [42].

153 Ibid [59].

154 Ibid [61].

155 Ibid [61].

156 The right to life is embodied in Article 21 of the Indian Constitution, which provides that '[n]o person shall be deprived of his life or personal liberty except according to procedure established by law'.

157 *Nandini Sundar v. State of Chattisgarh* AIR 2011 SC 2839 [64].

158 Ibid [75].

159 Varadarajan 2007.

civilian populations on account of the conflict. Even if one were to attribute the Court's omission to cite the Additional Protocol to the fact that India is not a party to it, the court could have referred to common Article 3 of the Geneva Conventions, which applies to non-international armed conflicts and requires the humane treatment of persons not taking active part in the hostilities.

Another case[160] was set in the backdrop of insurgency movements in the state of Assam. A group of petitions in the Gauhati High Court challenged the Presidential proclamation of emergency[161] in the state, as well as the characterisation of the state as a 'disturbed area' under two statutes.[162] The 'disturbed area' status granted the army sweeping powers in conducting counter-insurgency operations.[163] One of the petitioners sought the enforcement of Additional Protocol II of the Geneva Convention. The petitioner described the army as a combatant force and the people of Assam as non-combatant civilian population.[164] He claimed that the army action had forced villagers to flee their villages. Army personnel kidnapped civilians and raped women. Farmers were prevented from working.[165] Although the court broadly agreed with the petitioners and imposed some safeguards in the form of directions to the government,[166] it neither expressed an opinion on, nor engaged with, the IHL norms invoked in the argument of one of the petitioners. Like in the *Nandini Sundar* case, this would have been a fit case for the invocation of Additional Protocol II or common Article 3.

It is difficult to attribute the judicial reticence on IHL norms to a single factor. A number of factors might bear partial responsibility. For instance, in *Nandini Sundar*, the parties did not seem to invoke IHL norms, and so it is possible that the application of IHL norms simply did not cross the Court's mind. Another explanation could be that the courts had homegrown legal tools, such as constitutional provisions, at their disposal in order to achieve the same result that would have been achieved by resorting to norms of IHL. A third explanation could be that, at least vis-à-vis Additional Protocol II, India is not a party to the international convention. Nevertheless, in other spheres of international law, such as international criminal law or international human rights law, Indian courts have not been as reluctant to refer to agreements to which India is not a party.[167]

---

[160] *People's Union for Human Rights v. State of Assam* AIR 1992 Gau 23.

[161] The proclamation was made under Article 356 of the Indian Constitution.

[162] Armed Forces (Special Powers) Act 1958 and the Assam Disturbed Areas Act 1955.

[163] *People's Union for Human Rights v. State of Assam* AIR 1992 Gau 23 [13].

[164] Ibid [20].

[165] Ibid [20].

[166] Ibid [64].

[167] See, for example, the Supreme Court's invocation of the Rome Statute in *Imtiyaz Ahmed v. State of Uttar Pradesh* (2012) 2 SCC 688 and the Second Optional Protocol to the International Covenant on Civil and Political Rights in *Swamy Shraddananda v. State of Karnataka* (2007) 12 SCC 288.

14.5 Conclusion

As the title suggests, this article has made an attempt to expound upon the application, misapplication and non-application of IHL in Indian courts. Norms of IHL have been applied on some occasions by the Supreme Court and High Courts. In cases where they have been cited, they have either performed an applicatory role, enabling courts to support their judgments on the basis of IHL norms, or a distinguishing role, providing a useful point of contrast from an allied concept in domestic law. The importance of IHL norms in the context of the cases has varied, being the substratum of the judgment in cases on one end of the spectrum, and peripherally relevant in cases on the other end. Judgments have also misapplied IHL norms, on account of a failure to appreciate the nuances of the law. Some cases provided good opportunities for courts to cite IHL norms. Yet, for a variety of reasons, these opportunities were missed and provide notable examples of the non-application of IHL. The challenge of the application of IHL norms still lies ahead.

References

Anderson J (2000) The history of Portugal. Greenwood Press, Westport

Arai-Takahashi Y (2009) The law of occupation. Martinus Nijhoff, Leiden

Bains JS (1962) India's international disputes: a legal study. Asia Publishing House, London

Basu DD (2011) Commentary on the Constitution of India, 8th edn. LexisNexis Butterworths Wadhwa, Nagpur

Bhaumik S (2007) Insurgencies in India's Northeast: conflict, co-option & change. East-West Center Washington Working Paper No. 10 (July)

Blank L (2012) Understanding when and how domestic courts apply IHL. Emory University School of Law, Legal Studies Research Paper Series 12–200

Chandrachud C (2011) The evolution of section 121 of the Indian Penal Code: from the revolutionary to the terrorist. Madras Law J (Crim) 1:9

Charney J (1987) Compromissory clauses and the jurisdiction of the International Court of Justice. AJIL 81:855

Damsrosch LF (1997) Enforcing international law through non-forcible measures. Recueil des Cours 269, Martinus Nijhoff, Leiden

Dugard J (1998) Bridging the gap between human rights and humanitarian law: the punishment of offenders. Int Rev Red Cross 38(324):445

Fischer H (2004) Protection of prisoners of war. In: Fleck D (ed) The handbook of humanitarian law in armed conflicts. Oxford University Press, Oxford, pp 321–367

Fuller L (1978) The forms and limits of adjudication. Harv Law Rev 92:353

Ganguly S (2002) Conflict unending: India–Pakistan tensions since 1947. Oxford University Press, New Delhi

Gasser H (2004) Protection of the civilian population. In: Fleck D (ed) The handbook of humanitarian law in armed conflicts. Oxford University Press, Oxford, pp 209–292

Goswami A (2012) 3D: deceit, duplicity and dissimulation of U.S. foreign policy towards India, Pakistan and Afghanistan. AuthorHouse, Bloomington

Gupta D (2007) The Naxalites and the Maoist movement in India: birth, demise, and reincarnation. Democr Secur 3:157

Hegde KS (2010) Indian courts and international law. Leiden J Int Law 23:53
Kanodia R, Bhalla A (2012) Transit and transhipment of dual-use items: India. WorldECR 1–4
Korman S (1996) The right of conquest: the acquisition of territory by force in international law and practice. Oxford University Press, Oxford
Krishna A (1998) India's armed forces: fifty years of war and peace. Lancer, New Delhi
Mani V (2001) International humanitarian law: an Indo-Asian perspective. Int Rev Red Cross 83(841):59–75
Mastorodimos K (2009) How and when do military occupations end? Sri Lanka J Int Law 21(1):109–152
Mohan CR, Sahni A (2012) India's security challenges at home and abroad. Natl Bur Asian Res, Report 39
Patankar VG (2009) Insurgency, proxy-war and terrorism in Kashmir. In: Ganguly S, Fidler D (eds) India and counterinsurgency. Routledge, Abingdon, pp 65–78
Penna LR (1980) Traditional Asian approaches: an Indian view. Aust Yearb Int Law 9:168
Poprzeczny J (2010) India's 'Red Corridor' and the Naxalite threat, 29 May 2010 News Weekly (Australia)
Prabhakar PW (2003) Wars, proxy-wars and terrorism: post independent India. Mittal, New Delhi
Quénivet N (2008) Introduction—the history of the relationship between international humanitarian law and international human rights law. In: Arnold R, Quénivet N (eds) International humanitarian law and human rights law: towards a new merger in international law. Martinus Nijhoff, Leiden, pp 1–14
Rakove R (2013) Kennedy, Johnson and the nonaligned world. Cambridge University Press, Cambridge
Rao PV (1988) Ethnic conflict in Sri Lanka: India's role and perception. Asian Surv 28(4):419
Roy-Chaudhury R (2010) The Security Council and the India–Pakistan wars. In: Lowe V, Roberts A, Welsh J, Zaum D (eds) The United Nations Security Council and war: the evolution of thought and practice since 1945. Oxford University Press, Oxford, pp 522–555
Sakshena RN (2003) Goa: into the mainstream. Abhinav Publications, New Delhi
Shaw M (2008) International law, 6th edn. Cambridge University Press, Cambridge
Singh S (2009) India's wars since independence. Lancer International, Frankfort
Sinha MK (2005) Hinduism and international humanitarian law. Int Rev Red Cross 87(858):285
Sivakumaran S (2012) The law of non-international armed conflict. Oxford University Press, Oxford
Subedi S (2003) The concept in Hinduism of 'Just War'. J Confl Secur Law 8:339
Sundar N (2006) Bastar, Maoism and Salwa Judum. Econ Polit Wkly XLI 29:3187
UK Ministry of Defence (2004) The manual of the law of armed conflict. Oxford University Press, Oxford
Varadarajan S (2007) Salwa Judum and international humanitarian law. 8 September 2007 The Hindu
Vora P, Buxy S (2011) Marginalization and violence: the story of Naxalism in India. Int J Crim Justice Sci 6:358
Wright Q (1962) The Goa incident. AJIL 56:617–632

Chapter 15
Interpretations of IHL in Tribunals of the United States

Michael W. Lewis and Peter Margulies

Contents

Portions of this chapter are adapted from Margulies 2013.

M. W. Lewis
Ohio Northern University School of Law, 525 S. Main Street, Ada, OH 45810, USA
e-mail: m-lewis@onu.edu

P. Margulies (✉)
Roger Williams University School of Law, 10 Metacom Avenue, Bristol, RI 02908, USA
e-mail: pmargulies@rwu.edu

D. Jinks et al. (eds.), *Applying International Humanitarian Law in Judicial and Quasi-Judicial Bodies*, DOI: 10.1007/978-94-6265-008-4_15,

15.1 Introduction

On the whole, US tribunals applying international law have followed what we call a membership conception, in which the US has valued its place as a member of the community of nations and has acted accordingly. This conception was adopted by the Framers of the US Constitution, and has been the predominant view ever since. Like most nations, of course, the US has on occasion deviated from the membership view.[1]

This approach to international law writ large can also be seen in the way US tribunals have interpreted the more specialized field of IHL. Some post-9/11 initiatives within the executive branch of the US government, including efforts to expand the scope of military commission jurisdiction and the criteria it applied to the scope of detention and interrogation authority, have clashed with the membership conception. However, US courts have pushed back, realigning the US with that conception. This chapter will examine some of the more important decisions of the past 150 years and how these decisions and their interpretations of IHL have influenced that body of law.

While a great deal of attention has been paid to the jurisprudence of American courts and military commissions since 9/11 on a variety of issues shaping how modern conflicts between states and non-state actors are regarded, there were a number of pre-9/11 cases whose impact on IHL continues to be felt today. Although it is impossible to discuss all such cases in a single chapter, this chapter will begin with a discussion of significant pre-9/11 cases before turning to the some of the most familiar modern cases.

15.2 The Founding Era

The framers of the U.S. Constitution had learned through practice and experience the importance of compliance with international law. The case of *Rutgers v. Waddington*,[2] which Alexander Hamilton argued in a New York State court in the chaotic era before the Constitution's enactment provides one example. Hamilton represented a British subject who, during the American Revolution, had obeyed an order from the British commander in New York to seize property belonging to an American citizen. New York's Trespass Act allowed citizens to seek damages against British nationals who had seized their property during the war. Hamilton contended that international law protected his client's reliance on military orders.

---

[1] See e.g. U.S. v. Alvarez-Machain (Justice Rehnquist's opinion that the abduction of Alvarez-Machain from Mexico was not a violation of the extradition treaty between the US and Mexico was roundly criticized by international law scholars and undermined cooperation between the two nations in combating drug trafficking).

[2] See Rutgers v. Waddington, reprinted in Goebel 1964, pp. 393–419.

According to Hamilton, international law governed the scope of the New York statute. While Hamilton's opponents jeered that international law could not change a statute that seemed clear on its face, Hamilton argued that New York could not rid itself of the law of nations.[3] The court read the law of nations into the New York law, fearful of the chaos that would result if each nation could defy the laws of the "civilized world."[4]

Hamilton's *tour de force* of advocacy in *Rutgers v. Waddington* was one of a number of indications that curbing defiance of international law in the new republic was central to the Framers' goals. Violations of the core customary principle of diplomatic immunity, including an assault in Philadelphia on the French Consul General and another such attack in New York, had ignited confrontations with European powers.[5] Edmund Randolph, who was to become the first Attorney General of the United States, opened the Constitutional Convention in Philadelphia with a warning about these incidents. A strong federal government, Randolph insisted, was necessary to deter such lawlessness.[6] To give the federal government more power to combat such abuses and signal the new republic's membership in the world community, the Framers included in the Constitution the Define and Punish Clause, which gave Congress authority to "Define and Punish... Offenses against the Law of Nations."[7]

15.3 The Civil War

The United States' interpretation of international law during the Civil War followed the membership conception. Attorney General James Speed, in an opinion justifying the use of military commissions to try individuals accused of conspiring with John Wilkes Booth to assassinate President Lincoln, acknowledged the Framers' view that the law of nations was "part of the law of the land."[8] Speed reiterated Edmund Randolph's warning that "every change [in the law of nations] is at the peril of the nation which makes it."[9] This commitment to the law of

---

[3] Ibid.

[4] Ibid at pp. 405–406.

[5] See Sosa v. Alvarez-Machain at pp. 716–717 (2004) (noting that concern over "inadequate vindication of the law of nations persisted through the time of the Constitutional Convention"); but see Bradley 2002, pp. 640–641and Kent 2007, pp. 874–888.

[6] 1 Records of the Federal Convention of 1787, at 24–25 (Max Farrand ed., rev. edn. 1966) (warning that, under the Articles of Confederation, "\[]i]f a State act against a foreign power contrary to the laws of nations or violates a treaty, [the federal government] cannot punish that State, or compel its obedience to the treaty. It can only leave the offending State to the operations of the offended power.... [i]t therefore cannot prevent a war"); but see Kent 2007, pp. 897–899.

[7] U.S. Const.. Article I, § 8, cl. 10.

[8] Speed 1865 at p. *4, citing Randolph, p. *1.

[9] Randolph, p. *1.

nations was reflected both in the ordinary convening of military commissions to quell the Southern rebellion and try charges of violations of IHL associated with the conflict, and in the reasoning of the best-known case involving military commissions, *Ex parte Milligan*.[10]

15.3.1 Commissions in General

Military commissions served a hybrid role, adjudicating law of war offenses like sabotage and offenses such as aiding the enemy related to violations of martial law. In the former category were "bushwhackers"[11] who assaulted and robbed civilians. Since attacks on civilians were considered war crimes, bushwhackers who were part of an organized armed group participating in the conflict had committed offenses triable in law of war commissions. Military commissions were also used to try bushwhackers who were no longer affiliated with an organized armed group if they committed offenses in areas where the institutions of civil society had broken down.

US officials defined the war crime of sabotage as including individuals who feigned civilian status in order to destroy military objectives. Hundreds of military commissions were convened in the violence-torn state of Missouri, where they tried individuals for acts of sabotage, including bridge burning.[12] Commissions also tried individuals on charges of espionage: General Henry Halleck, a senior commander of the U.S. government forces, was also a noted international law expert, who wrote in a well-regarded treatise that some forms of espionage involving "*disguise*, or *false pretence*... constitutes... perfidy" punishable by death.[13] The highest-profile military commission—that convened for the Lincoln conspirators, involved the age-old war crime of perfidy: feigning civilian status to facilitate the use of lethal force. Attorney General Speed's opinion authorizing military commissions to try the Lincoln conspirators called them "secret active enemies"[14] who had willingly aided John Wilkes Booth's plan to use civilian disguise to kill Lincoln.

Commissions functioned, as noted US law of war expert William Winthrop had explained, as tribunals to enforce the law of occupation in areas held by forces of

[10] See infra note 21.

[11] See General Order (G.O.) No. 13 at p. 403; see also Lieber 1862, pp. 16–17 (noting nature and scope of prohibition); but see Neely 1991, pp. 36–39 (noting Halleck's repeated requests for this authority, which first met with inertia from the ever-cautious General George McClellan, but were ultimately approved by Lincoln).

[12] See, e.g., G.O. No. 20, HQ, Dep't of the Missouri (Jan. 14, 1862), 1 OR ser. II at 403 (noting charges against one James R.J. Jones).

[13] Halleck 1893, p. 572 (emphasis in original).

[14] Ibid at p. 34.

the U.S. government.[15] In Washington, D.C., for example, an area that was near the front lines of the Civil War for much of the conflict, commissions regularly tried residents for offenses like trading with the enemy. Commission jurisdiction in such cases did not stem from the Define and Punish Clause's authority to adjudicate violations of the law of war. Instead, jurisdiction emerged from a corollary of war itself—the need to preserve order in areas under military control. Because civil institutions such as the courts had broken down in certain areas, such as the state of Missouri, military commissions also preserved order by trying violations of ordinary criminal law.[16]

Procedural safeguards were also part of the plan for military commissions. Review by generals like Halleck or by President Lincoln himself cured procedural irregularities and introduced mercy into decisions that might otherwise have been unduly harsh.[17] Demonstrating the integrity of the commissions, acquittals occurred in a significant number of cases. The proof is in the pudding: Missouri was the site of almost half of the over 4,000 military commissions during the Civil War.[18] In a representative sample of the Missouri proceedings, acquittals occurred in 15 percent of the contested cases and administrative review of the sentence produced commutations in another 40 percent of the proceedings.[19] No mere drum-head tribunal could have produced such disparate results.

15.3.2 Ex Parte Milligan (1866)

The Civil War era military commissions case that has proven to be the most influential on IHL was *Ex parte Milligan*, decided just as the codification of IHL was beginning. Three years after the Lieber Code was promulgated to Union troops during the Civil War in 1863,[20] the United States Supreme Court heard the case. The rationale underlying its holding shaped subsequent understandings of limitations on the scope of internal armed conflicts.

Lamdin Milligan, a US citizen and resident of the state of Indiana was arrested on the order of the military commandant for the District of Indiana in 1864.

---

[15] Winthrop 1886, p. 69.

[16] Hamdan, infra n. 59, at 608.

[17] See Chomsky 1990, pp. 86–90 (analyzing Lincoln's review of military commission verdicts regarding members of the Dakota nation who had allegedly killed captives and targeted civilians for killing and sexual violence). The Lincoln administration was careful to comply with international law in other respects, including the treatment of blockade-runners. See Golove 2006, pp. 364–370.

[18] See Neely 1991, p. 168.

[19] Ibid at p. 43.

[20] See e.g. Witt 2012, pp. 229–237; Paust 2001, p. 114; Baxter 1963, p. 171. The Lieber Code, which was transmitted as General Order No. 100 to Union troops in the field at President Lincoln's direction, is widely viewed as the first attempt at codifying the laws of armed conflict.

Lamdin was charged with conspiracy against the government of the United States, affording aid and comfort to rebels against the authority of the United States, inciting insurrection, disloyal practices, and violations of the laws of war.[21] He was tried before a military commission which heard evidence that Lamdin had communicated with the enemy and had conspired to seize munitions stored in arsenals, free Confederate prisoners of war and resist the draft that the United States government instituted to strengthen the Union army. He was convicted by the military commission and sentenced to death.[22] He filed a petition for a writ of habeas corpus challenging the jurisdiction of the military commission to adjudicate his case.[23] Manifest throughout the Court's judgment was the tension, all too familiar to modern audiences, between due process rights and the need for executive branch discretion on security measures in times of trouble. On the one hand, the Court recognized that "[i]t is essential to the safety of every government that, in a great crisis, like the one we have just passed through, there should be a power somewhere of suspending the writ of habeas corpus."[24] The Court did not hesitate in finding that such power lay with the executive when such a crisis threatened. "Unquestionably, there is then an exigency which demands that the government, if it should see fit in the exercise of a proper discretion to make arrests, should not be required to produce the persons arrested in answer to a writ of habeas corpus."[25] However, the Court also made clear that the suspension of habeas corpus did not necessarily mean that the establishment of military commissions was in all cases justified. In siding with Milligan and finding his trial by military commission to be an illegal exercise of executive power, the Court placed geographic as well as temporal limits on the scope of the exigency and therefore upon the scope of the extraordinary powers justified by such an exigency. Just as the temporal end of an armed conflict would signal the end of the extraordinary executive powers relating to prosecuting an armed conflict, so too the geographical boundaries of an armed conflict limited the areas in which such powers could be exercised.

In determining how the boundaries of this exigency should be drawn the Court looked to the institutions of civil society, specifically the courts, to decide where such extraordinary powers could appropriately be wielded.

> Martial rule can never exist where the courts are open, and in the proper and unobstructed exercise of their jurisdiction. It is also confined to the locality of actual war. Because, during the late Rebellion it could have been enforced in Virginia, where the national authority was overturned and the courts driven out, it does not follow that it should obtain in Indiana, where that authority was never disputed, and justice was always administered.[26]

---

[21] Ex parte Milligan, 71 U.S. 2, 6–7 (1866).

[22] Ibid at p. 7.

[23] Ibid.

[24] Ibid at p. 125.

[25] Ibid at pp. 125–126.

[26] Ibid at p. 127.

By imposing geographical as well as temporal limits on the scope of the laws of armed conflict the Court recognized that the extraordinary measures taken during war time pose a real threat to constitutionally protected due process interests. The Court ameliorated this threat by defining the scope of the laws of armed conflict as narrowly as possible, thereby taking a rights-maximizing view of internal armed conflicts. This view, that the scope of the laws of armed conflict-or at least the laws of armed conflict that infringe upon human rights- should be viewed narrowly because their application inevitably infringes on fundamental human rights interests that are inviolable in peacetime, has been echoed by modern international interpretations of IHL.

Over 125 years later, the International Criminal Tribunal for the Former Yugoslavia (ICTY) was created by the UN Security Council to "prosecute persons responsible for serious violations of international humanitarian law committed in the territory of the former Yugoslavia".[27] Among those prosecuted before the ICTY was Dusko Tadić. Tadić was charged with beating, stabbing and sexually mutilating prisoners in a camp near Prijedor, a district in northwestern Bosnia that was occupied by Bosnian Serb forces in 1992.[28] The ICTY's jurisdiction to try Tadić for these acts (which could also have been prosecuted as violations of domestic criminal law by domestic criminal courts) was based upon their characterization as "serious violations of international humanitarian law."[29]

During the course of the proceedings against him, Tadić challenged the jurisdiction of the ICTY to hear his case and when that challenge was denied by the trial chamber he filed an interlocutory appeal with the appeals chamber.[30]

Because the ICTY's jurisdiction was tied to IHL violations, one of the bases for Tadić's interlocutory appeal was a claim "that there was no armed conflict at all in the region where the crimes were allegedly committed."[31] There were no active combat operations occurring in the vicinity of Prijedor at the time the alleged beatings, stabbings, and mutilations occurred, therefore Tadić claimed that these actions did not occur in the context of an armed conflict. This was based upon the notion that without an armed conflict, IHL could not apply. While the appeals chamber agreed that the existence of an armed conflict was a precondition to the application of IHL, it refused to limit the geographic scope of all of IHL's provisions to just "the vicinity of actual hostilities."[32] At the same time, it did not find that all of IHL's provisions applied throughout the entire territory of the parties involved in the conflict. Instead it took a more nuanced view about the scope of

---

27 ICTY Statute, Article 1.

28 Prosecutor v. Tadic, Case No. IT-94-1-T, Trial Chamber Judgment, at para 9.

29 See ICTY Statute, Article 1.

30 Prosecutor v. Tadic, Decision on the Defence Motion for Interlocutory Appeal of Jurisdiction, at paras 1–2, 8.

31 At para 65.

32 Ibid at para 68.

internal armed conflicts that draws on the distinctions made over a century earlier in the *Milligan* case.

In considering the geographic scope of IHL in internal armed conflicts, the appeals chamber conceded that "some of [IHL's] provisions are clearly bound up with the hostilities and the geographical scope of those provisions should be so limited. Others, particularly those relating to the protection of prisoners of war and civilians, are not so limited."[33] This seems to echo the rights-maximizing provisions that *Milligan* applied to the internal armed conflict that was the backdrop for that case. Only where there are actual hostilities taking place, or as the *Milligan* court said "where the national authority was overturned," will normal peace time rules yield to the exigencies of wartime. But this narrow geographic view will only apply to provisions such as the use of lethal force as a first resort or targeting rules that recognize the inevitability of collateral damage. For provisions like the proper treatment of prisoners, the appeals chamber found that IHL should apply broadly, throughout the entire territory of parties to the conflict.[34]

As this chapter will develop in the following sections, this rights-maximizing view for internal armed conflicts became more controversial after 9/11 when a US tribunal applied it to something other than a purely internal armed conflict.

15.4 World War II

The American role in the interpretation of IHL during and after World War II followed the membership pattern, as well. Of course, in some ways America's influence was most notable in the prosecution and adjudication of war crimes at Nuremberg. However, U.S. domestic courts also had a role. That role was not free of controversy. Some of these major cases will be analyzed in the following section.

15.4.1 Ex parte Quirin

Quirin addressed Congress's power to define and punish espionage and sabotage in a case involving individuals who disembarked from German submarines on the eastern coast of the United States and then donned civilian attire.[35] The defendants largely conceded that the German high command had tasked them with destroying military objectives within the U.S. The Supreme Court suggested that Congress could authorize military commissions to try individuals charged with espionage or

[33] Ibid.

[34] Ibid at paras 67–69.

[35] Ex parte Quirin at pp. 20–23.

sabotage, even though the former has an ambiguous status under international law and the defendants had not consummated the acts normally required for the latter.[36] The Court also adopted a definition of unprivileged belligerency that encompassed the use of feigned civilian status to advance a plot to destroy military objectives behind an enemy's lines.

The Court's discussion of sabotage extends international law in a fashion that is true to IHL's spirit. Sabotage, defined as the use of civilian disguise to destroy a military objective, is still considered a war crime.[37] The wrinkle in *Quirin* was that the defendants made little concrete progress in destroying military objectives within U.S. territory: although the defendants conceded that the German high command had tasked them with orders to destroy military objectives, they did not get beyond disembarking on U.S. territory, donning civilian clothes to conceal their mission and identities, and dispersing to conduct reconnaissance. However, the Supreme Court declined to hold that this failure to destroy or even attempt the destruction of a particular military objective undermined the sabotage charges against the defendants.[38] At first blush, this failure to strictly limit the scope of sabotage charges might be viewed as clashing with international law. However, a more careful look supplies a convincing justification for the Court's view.

In essence, the Supreme Court viewed even preliminary acts undertaken to further wartime espionage and sabotage as requiring the robust deterrence that trial in military commissions provided. Allowing a defendant to assert that his plot had not progressed further than the assumption of civilian disguise would encourage such plots, with the possibility of bloodshed and chaos that such plans entailed. This implied concern with impunity foreshadowed the focus on eliminating impunity that typifies the Rome Statute of the International Criminal Court[39] and much modern international criminal law. One could accomplish this goal, as the noted international law publicist Lassa Oppenheim explained, by designating as a war crime, the mere acts of combatants who "exchange their uniforms for plain clothes and thereby appear as members of the peaceful private population" in

---

[36] See Fisher 2003, p. 175. All members of the group were convicted. Two defendants, who after their entry into the United States informed the Federal Bureau of Investigation of the group's plans, ultimately had their sentences commuted. The rest were executed. Among those executed was Herbert Haupt who held both German and American citizenship. The Court found that his citizenship changed neither the process he was entitled to nor the punishment that he faced. Adding to the controversy around the decision, the executions occurred *before* the Court's decision. For different views of the case, compare Bryant and Tobias 2003, p. 309 (contending that *Quirin*, along with changes in law of habeas corpus, provides significant protection for defendants in military tribunals), with Turley 2002, pp. 735–739 (criticizing *Quirin*).

[37] See Oppenheim p. 225.

[38] Quirin, supra n. 35, at p. 38.

[39] See Preamble, Rome Statute of the International Criminal Court.

order to facilitate the destruction of a military objective.[40] The Court took this approach, citing Oppenheim for the proposition that even these minimal preparations constituted sufficient action to support culpability.[41]

To justify the added deterrent provided by military commissions, the Court distinguished between lawful belligerency, which involved combatants wearing insignia identifying themselves as participants in hostilities, with this form of unlawful belligerency, which consisted of donning civilian garb for the purpose of committing acts of sabotage.[42] This reading of unlawful belligerency effectively extended the temporal scope of sabotage and was viewed as a "completed" offense once a defendant moved behind U.S. lines "in civilian dress and with hostile purpose."[43] The Court relied in part on considerations of institutional memory and competence, asserting that "a long course of practical administrative construction by... military authorities... here and abroad" had developed an appreciation for the evils of such conduct and expertise in identifying its commission—a skill-set that civilian fact finders in ordinary courts might not possess.[44] Military commissions were thus the appropriate venue for trial of such violations of the laws of war.

The Court's viewing the conduct at issue in *Quirin* as "complete" prior to either completion of the harm or even a concrete attempt may have pushed the envelope of international law, but did not clash with international law's precepts. Publicists like Oppenheim have recognized the conduct in question as transgression of the laws of war, distinguishing between such conduct and "legitimate warfare".[45] If any daylight remained between the Court's holding and international law, the complementary relation between international and domestic law, as expressed in the margin of appreciation doctrine, closes the gap.

In assessing state compliance with international law, publicists and tribunals have always accorded state interpretations a measure of deference.[46] That deference is integral to a membership conception. In the realms of international criminal law, the ICC has noted that complementarity "strikes a balance" that

---

[40] Oppenheim p. 315 (providing example of Japanese officers during Russo-Japanese War who disguised themselves as Chinese civilians for the purpose of attempting to destroy a railway bridge behind Russian lines in Manchuria).

[41] Quirin, supra n. 35, at p. 35 n. 12, see also pp. 36–37.

[42] Ibid at pp. 36–37.

[43] Ibid at p. 38.

[44] Ibid at p. 35.

[45] Oppenheim p. 315.

[46] Handyside at p. 47 (in interpreting protection of free expression under European Convention on Human Rights, granting a "margin of appreciation" or deference to state decision banning a book on sexuality that was marketed to teenagers).

harmonizes state interests and international law.[47] Preserving a measure of discretion for state decisions promotes a healthy partnership with other states and with international institutions. Collaboration is necessary for the drafting, ratification, and execution of international agreements, and for the development of customary international law.

Abandoning complementarity would endanger that collaboration, because it would decrease each state's stake in collective action. As the International Criminal Court (ICC) conceded in a recent case involving alleged election-related killings in Kenya, "[w]ithout [complementarity]... there would have been no agreement" possible among states parties to the Rome Statute that established the ICC.[48] Complementarity does not allow wholesale defiance of international law, but it does counsel the wisdom of some deference to state interpretation. The *Quirin* Court seemed to invoke this concept, as it rejected any effort to hamstring Congress with an unduly "meticulous" demarcation of the law of nations' "ultimate boundaries."[49]

15.4.2 In re Yamashita

In re Yamashita is another World War II case that illustrates the evolution of the membership conception. In *Yamashita*, the Supreme Court articulated an innovative view of the doctrine of command responsibility. That doctrine has been a vital building block in accountability for war crimes, even as procedural problems in the case have spurred enhanced safeguards.

General Tomoyuki Yamashita[50] was the commander of the 14th Area Army in the Philippines in 1944 when American forces began landing to recapture the island. Although he withdrew most of his forces from the major cities some elements remained behind in Manila. During the ensuing battle for the city a large number of civilians and Allied POW's were massacred by Japanese forces before

---

[47] See Prosecutor v. Muthara, at ¶19; but see Newton 2011, p. 332 (warning of "presumption of supranational superiority" in which transnational tribunals like International Criminal Court override domestic decisions, thereby sending wrong message about development of domestic capabilities).

[48] Ibid.

[49] Quirin, supra n. 35, at pp. 45–46.

[50] See Yamashita Tomoyuki's Last Message to the Japanese People available at http://japanfocus.org/-Yuki-TANAKA/1753. Nicknamed the "Tiger of Malaya" after his much smaller force captured over 130,000 British and Commonwealth troops in his successful campaign to take Malaya and Singapore, Yamashita was one of the most successful Japanese generals of the war. Reassigned to Manchukuo for 18 months after falling out of favor with Tojo he was put in charge of Japanese forces in the Philippines after the Tojo government fell. As American force closed in he declined to commit suicide to save the lives of his soldiers who otherwise would have followed suit. [].

they withdrew.[51] After he was captured, General Yamashita was tried by a military commission that lasted a little over a month and heard from two hundred eighty-six witnesses.[52] The commission sentenced him to death and he filed a writ of habeas corpus challenging the jurisdiction of the tribunal because, *inter alia*, the charge against him was not a violation of the laws of war.[53]

The charge against Yamashita was that:

> while commander of armed forces of Japan at war with the United States of America and its allies, unlawfully disregarded and failed to discharge his duty as commander to control the operations of the members of his command, permitting them to commit brutal atrocities and other high crimes against people of the United States and of its allies and dependencies, particularly the Philippines; and he … thereby violated the laws of war.[54]

Justice Stone writing for a sharply divided Court, found support for the doctrine of command responsibility in the nature and purpose of IHL. Stone cited portions of the Fourth and Tenth Hague Conventions and the Geneva Red Cross Convention of 1929 that prohibited the targeting of civilians and the abusive treatment of prisoners of war.[55] Without the restraint exercised by a diligent commander, Stone observed, military personnel would engage in "excesses… result[ing] in violations which it is the purpose of the law of war to prevent."[56] Imposing a responsibility on commanders for their subordinates' abuses would promote diligence and deter IHL violations. Yamashita's conviction, Stone concluded, was a fitting response to the general's "affirmative duty" as the overall commander of Japanese forces in the Philippines "to take such measures as were within his power and appropriate in the circumstances to protect prisoners of war and the civilian population."[57]

Justices Rutledge and Murphy in dissents that have perhaps become more famous than the majority opinion argued that this standard required proof that Yamashita had actual knowledge of the atrocities committed by his subordinates.[58] Absent proof that he committed, ordered, or condoned the atrocities the dissenters argued that personal criminal liability should not attach. The dissenters felt that Yamashita's conviction was particularly unfair because the same US forces that

---

[51] In re Yamashita, at p. 14 (the opinion describes the massacre of 25,000 men, women and children at the hands of Japanese soldiers; other sources place the total number of civilian casualties in Manila at close to 100,000).

[52] Ibid at p. 5.

[53] Ibid at p. 6.

[54] Ibid at pp. 13–14.

[55] Ibid at p. 14.

[56] Ibid at p. 15.

[57] Ibid at p. 16.

[58] Ibid at pp. 32–35.

actively and successfully destroyed Yamashita's ability to control his forces were now holding him accountable for failing to exercise proper control.[59]

Sixty years later this case, along with several of the decisions handed down by the Nuremburg and International Military Tribunal for the Far East courts and Article 86 and 87 of Additional Protocol I, were used by the ICTY to establish the modern understanding of "command responsibility".[60] The ICTY drew on the dissenters' call for some showing of actual knowledge (although it also allowed for a showing of constructive knowledge) in eschewing strict liability and establishing the elements required to support a charge of command responsibility. The Halilović trial court, quoting the standard established in the Čelibići trial court and reiterated in a half dozen other intervening ICTY cases, described the elements as being:

i. The existence of a superior-subordinate relationship;
ii. the superior knew or had reason to know that the criminal act was about to be or had been committed; and
iii. the superior failed to take the necessary and reasonable measures to prevent the criminal act or punish the perpetrator thereof.[61]

The ICTY also heeded the dissenters' objection about Yamashita's inability to prevent the actions complained of by making it clear that the "necessary and reasonable measures" required of the commander must be materially possible for him to accomplish.[62]

15.5 Post 9/11 Developments

In the wake of 9/11, some US officials deviated from the membership conception of IHL, but this divergence was generally short-lived. Responses from Congress, the courts, and US military lawyers curbed the scope and duration of these departures. However, the dialectic between deviation and response left IHL less clear in one vital case, *Hamdan v. Rumsfeld.* Starting with *Hamdan*, this section will examine a range of post-9/11 IHL issues, including the classification of armed conflicts, interrogation, detention, and military commission jurisdiction.

---

[59] Ibid. In his opinion for the Supreme Court in Boumediene v. Bush, 553 U.S. 723 (2008), Justice Kennedy noted that the procedural lapses in Yamashita had been "sharply criticized by Members of this Court." Id at 786, citing Hamdan v. Rumsfeld, 548 U.S. 557, 617 (2006).

[60] See e.g. Prosecutor v. Delalić, et al., at paras 330–343, see also Prosecutor v. Halilović, at paras 44–48.

[61] Halilović, supra n. 60, at paras 56 and 65.

[62] Ibid at para 73 quoting Delalić at para 395.

15.5.1 Hamdan v. Rumsfeld

Salim Hamdan, a Yemeni national, was Osama bin Laden's driver and one of his bodyguards in Afghanistan.[63] In November 2001 during hostilities between the Taliban and US forces, he was captured by militia forces allied with the US. In June 2002 he was transported to the detention facility in Guantanamo Bay, Cuba where he was eventually charged with violations of the laws of war by a military commission.[64] Hamdan filed a writ of habeas corpus challenging the jurisdiction of the military commission to try him and claiming that its procedures violated international law.[65]

The Bush Administration argued against the applicability of the Geneva Conventions to Hamdan's case. The government claimed that the conflict between the United States and al Qaeda was neither an international armed conflict, governed by Common Article 2 of the Geneva Conventions, nor a conflict "not of an international character" governed by Common Article 3.[66] These claims were based upon both the plain language of these two articles of the Conventions which establish their applicability to a given conflict and the broadly accepted scope of IHL that existed at that time. The government argued that al Qaeda was not a "High Contracting Party"[67] (i.e. a signatory) to the Conventions and therefore the conflict could not be considered an international armed conflict. Likewise it took the position that Common Article 3 only applied to internal armed conflicts based upon its statement that its provisions applied to an "armed conflict not of an international character occurring in the territory of one of the High Contracting Parties."[68] This understanding that Common Article 3 applied exclusively to internal armed conflicts was black-letter IHL prior to the Supreme Court's opinion in this case.[69]

Justice Stevens, writing for a majority of five, found that at a minimum the provisions of Common Article 3 applied to Hamdan's trial by a military commission.[70] In an opinion that eschewed the typically thorough reading of

---

63 See Hamdan v. Rumsfeld, p. 570.

64 Ibid, p. 566.

65 Ibid., p. 567.

66 A conflict under Common Article 2 would mean that the full panoply of the Geneva Conventions applied to the conflict, while a Common Article 3 conflict would only invoke the protections provided by that article.

67 Geneva Conventions I–IV, Article 2 state that "the Convention shall apply to all cases of declared war or of any other armed conflict which may arise between two or more of the High Contracting Parties".

68 Geneva Conventions I–IV, Article 3.

69 See e.g. Fleck 1995, p. 47 stating in bold type that: "A non-international armed conflict is a confrontation between the existing governmental authority and groups of persons subordinate to this authority, which is carried out by force of arms within national territory and reaches the magnitude of an armed riot or a civil war."

70 See Hamdan v. Rumsfeld, pp. 629–631.

international law sources, commentaries, negotiating histories and preparatory documents that characterized most Supreme Court cases analyzing international law issues[71] Stevens found that the term "conflict not of an international character" [NIAC] is used as a term of "contradistinction to a conflict between nations" and that it bears no more than its literal meaning of not being a conflict between nations.[72]

This simplistic classification of the conflict as a NIAC was to have profound effects on IHL in the coming years. To understand why Stevens reached for an international law hook on which to hang his opinion it is necessary to recall the context in which the *Hamdan* case arose. The Bush Administration had taken an extraordinarily aggressive approach to interrogation particularly in 2002 and 2003.[73] Vice President Cheney had initiated this policy, receiving legal support from a law professor turned Justice Department attorney, John Yoo.[74] Secretary of Defense Donald Rumsfeld had triggered a similar process.[75] Each official had relied on the legal conclusion discussed above, which classified the conflict with al Qaeda as entirely outside IHL's coverage because it was neither an international armed conflict nor a conflict not of an international character. Additionally, both Cheney and Rumsfeld had consciously stifled the dissenting voices of military lawyers that questioned the validity of this approach.[76] Because the detainees were not protected by any provisions of the Geneva Conventions, administration officials asserted that the prohibition on "cruel, inhuman, and degrading treatment" in Common Article 3 of the Geneva Conventions did not constitute a bar to practices such as waterboarding or intensive sleep deprivation. To clear the path for use of such techniques, Yoo had narrowly interpreted a US statute implementing the United Nations Convention Against Torture.[77]

---

[71] See Lewis 2008, pp. 689–695, 705–706 (describing the exhaustive thoroughness that the Court displayed in determining the legal meaning of numerous phrases in international law opinions and contrasting that with Stevens' brevity in answering several important questions about the scope of IHL).

[72] See Hamdan, supra n. 59, pp. 630–631.

[73] Margulies 2010, pp. 56–57.

[74] See Memorandum from Jay S. Bybee 2002.

[75] Margulies 2010, p. 61.

[76] Ibid.; compare Kramer and Schmitt 2008, p. 1407 (arguing for vigorous dialogue between military lawyers and civilian officials), and McNeal 2009, pp. 126–34 (praising resistance to political influence within the military), with Sulmasy and Yoo 2007, pp. 1820–1823 (depicting military lawyers who opposed Bush Administration policies on detention and interrogation as entrenched bureaucrats).

[77] See United Nations Convention Against Torture and Other Cruel, Inhuman or Degrading Treatment or Punishment, Article 2; Memorandum from Jay S. Bybee 2002 at pp. 3–8 (construing US anti-torture statute, which like CAT defined torture as intentional infliction of "severe pain," as requiring proof that interrogator wished to inflict pain for its own sake (not just to gain information) and that pain inflicted was equivalent to pain associated with organ failure). A Justice Department review conducted during the Obama administration found that while Yoo's opinions were unwise and unduly aggressive, they did not constitute unethical professional

The pushback against aggressive interrogation policies started to gain momentum by the end of 2003. At the Justice Department, new Assistant Attorney General Jack Goldsmith withdrew the most sweeping of Yoo's memos.[78] In the second term of the Bush administration, new Secretary of State Condoleezza Rice and deputies like John Bellinger, Matthew Waxman, and Philip Zelikow began to put the US back on a Geneva footing.[79] While Congress responded to the *Hamdan* opinion by passing the Military Commissions Act,[80] effectively remedying the domestic law infirmities Stevens found and attempting to address the international law ones as well, it also pushed back on the aggressive interrogation policy by passing the McCain Amendment that placed tighter limits on interrogations.[81]

The Supreme Court also pushed back. *Hamdan* was not the first case in which the Supreme Court had opined on the conduct of the conflict with al Qaeda. Decisions like *Hamdi v. Rumsfeld*[82] and *Rasul v. Bush*,[83] which required judicial review of detention decisions, emerged against the backdrop of the revelations of detainee abuse at Abu Ghraib. The Justices who formed the majority in each of these cases were surely aware that the Abu Ghraib story broke on the same day that an administration lawyer declared in an oral argument that the US did not engage in torture.[84] In *Hamdan*, Stevens alluded in an oblique but unmistakable fashion to the aggressive post-9/11 interrogations regime, mentioning that the convicted war criminal, Dr. Henry Wirz, the commandant of the Confederacy's notorious Andersonville prison during the Civil War, had personally engaged in torture and the use of dogs to mistreat prisoners.[85] As Stevens almost surely knew, a Defense Department investigation had found that interrogators at Guantanamo had used dogs in questioning detainees.[86] Stevens' classification of the struggle

(Footnote 77 continued)
conduct. See Margolis (2010), Assoc. Deputy Att'y Gen., Memorandum for the Attorney General (Jan. 5, 2010) available at http://judiciary.house.gov/hearings/pdf/DAGMargolisMemo100105.pdf, p. 67; see also Padilla v. Yoo, (holding that Yoo was entitled to qualified immunity in lawsuit brought by US citizen detainee Jose Padilla because Yoo's conduct in Padilla's case did not violate clearly established law). For debate on Yoo's ethics, see Finkelstein and Lewis 2010 at p. 214 compare Luban 2007 at pp. 176–180, 200–202 and Clark K 2005 with Margulies P 2012 pp. 825–829 (agreeing that Yoo's legal reasoning was strained and shortsighted, but also observing that imposition of professional discipline such as suspension or disbarment would be inappropriate because underlying legal rules were not wholly settled when Yoo drafted his opinions).

78 Goldsmith 2007, pp. 153–155.

79 Margulies 2010, p. 159.

80 Military Commissions Act of 2006.

81 Interrogation of Detainees, pp. 1–6.

82 Hamdi v. Rumsfeld at p. 507.

83 Rasul v. Bush at p. 466.

84 Margulies 2010, p. 56.

85 Hamdan, at p. 609.

86 See Army Regulation 15-6. The Defense Department banned the practice after the issuance of the investigative report. See White 2005 (barring use of dogs in interrogations).

against al Qaeda as a NIAC added an international law barrier to a return to an aggressive interrogation program.

Nevertheless, although undoubtedly well-intentioned, the effects on IHL of Justice Stevens' opinion were not always positive. The categorization of the conflict as NIAC crowded out other meritorious suggestions on how IHL should be applied to conflicts between non-state actors and states that cross international boundaries. The approach advanced by Geoffrey Corn and Eric Jensen to regulate such conflicts suggested that a third category of "transnational armed conflict"[87] should be considered. Had *Hamdan* made it plain that the current legal architecture was insufficient to deal with such conflicts, the urgency to define a third category would have been significant. Instead, those who applauded the result in *Hamdan* regarded the classification question as settled. This has led to some odd interpretations of IHL.

One example of *Hamdan*'s sometimes muddled legacy is the debate over the boundaries of the battlefield in such conflicts. Supporters of the idea that the *Tadic* factors should determine where the law of armed conflict applies in transnational armed conflicts point to the designation of this conflict as a NIAC.[88] While such a test is appropriate for internal armed conflicts in which the state actor controls uncontested territory and has the unquestioned right to recapture contested territory, this is not the case in transnational armed conflicts. Applying *Tadic* to transnational armed conflicts results in non-state actors effectively being granted sanctuaries in ungoverned spaces such as Somalia, parts of Yemen, the FATA-region of Pakistan, etc. if the level of violence requirement of *Tadic* is not present in that locality.[89] This reading of the law effectively denies states the ability to pursue non-state actors across borders, thereby granting terror groups like al Qaeda an important first-mover advantage.

Another negative effect of the *Hamdan* opinion on IHL was that it blurred the lines between the legal regimes applicable to IACs and NIACs in ways that undermine how those very different types of conflict are regarded. Although the opinion designated the conflict as a NIAC, it turned to the provisions of Additional Protocol I [AP I] to determine whether the military commissions complied with the

[87] Corn and Jensen 2009.

[88] See e.g. O'Connell 2009, pp. 860–864; Heller 2011, "No, the UN Has Not Said the U.S. Is Engaged in an 'Armed Conflict' with Al Qaeda", Opinio Juris blog, May 21, 2011 available at http://opiniojuris.org/2011/05/21/no-the-un-has-not-affirmed-that-the-us-is-engaged-in-an-armed-conflict-with-al-qaeda/; Dehn and Heller 2011; Report of the Special Rapporteur on Extrajudicial, Summary or Arbitrary Executions 2010 at para 86.

[89] As a remedy for this problem, scholars and state representatives have drawn analogies to the law of neutrality, which permits a state victimized by a party to an armed conflict to use force on the territory of an ostensibly neutral state if that state is "unwilling or unable" to stop the harm directed against the victim state. See Deeks 2012, pp. 499–503 (exploring "unwilling or unable" test based on law of neutrality).

"indispensable judicial guarantees" requirement of Common Article 3.[90] Stevens, now writing for a plurality of four, looked to the requirements of Article 75 of AP I to determine which "indispensable judicial guarantees" Hamdan was entitled to under Common Article 3.

This was problematic because, by its terms AP I applies to international armed conflicts[91] while Additional Protocol II [AP II] explicitly applies to NIACs.[92] Referencing AP I to determine the scope of rights applicable in a NIAC might be justifiable if AP II was silent as to the issue at hand, but that was not the case here. Article 6 of AP II was practically identical to Article 75 of AP I, except that it was shorter and did not include a right to cross examine witnesses which Stevens included as a defect of the proposed commissions. To reach his desired result Stevens ignored the treaty law which explicitly applied to Common Article 3 (AP II) in favor of the law applicable to international armed conflicts. In doing so he erased the line between the two types of conflicts which has led to unfortunate interpretations of IHL in both directions.

To the dismay of human rights advocates, states have imported the targeting and collateral damage standards from IAC's into their conduct of transnational (and in some cases internal) NIAC's. This has undermined the rights-maximizing nature of the law applicable to NIAC's that had developed from *Milligan* to *Tadic*. Meanwhile, humanitarians have argued that rights-maximizing features of NIAC's ought to apply to all armed conflicts, going so far as to claim that a duty to capture exists in all armed conflicts.[93] These are some examples of the turmoil created by the *Hamdan* opinion.

In sum, Justice Stevens' opinion in *Hamdan* worked best as a signal that the Supreme Court would not countenance gaps in IHL. That signal was salutary as a response to unduly narrow readings of IHL ventured by senior US officials immediately after September 11. However, *Hamdan* has spawned unintended consequences that continue to challenge IHL scholars and practitioners.

---

[90] Geneva Conventions I–IV, Article 3(1)(d) forbids "the passing of sentences and the carrying out of executions without previous judgment pronounced by a regularly constituted court, affording all the judicial guarantees which are recognized as indispensable by civilized peoples."

[91] See Additional Protocol I, Article 1 para 3 "[t]his Protocol, which supplements the Geneva Conventions of 12 August 1949 for the protection of war victims, shall apply in the situations referred to in Article 2 common to those Conventions."

[92] See Additional Protocol II, Article 1 [Protocol II] "develops and supplements Article 3 common to the Geneva Conventions of 12 August 1949 without modifying its existing conditions of application, shall apply to all armed conflicts which are not covered by Article 1 of the Protocol Additional to the Geneva Conventions of 12 August 1949, and relating to the Protection of Victims of International Armed Conflicts (Protocol I)".

[93] Goodman 2013; but see Corn et al. 2013, pp. 562–563 (arguing that IHL does not require priority for least harmful means of incapacitating adversary in armed conflict).

15.5.2 Detention

Post-9/11 practice on detention of individuals who are part of Al Qaeda fits the membership conception snugly, without the question marks raised in *Hamdan v. Rumsfeld*. In implementing the US Supreme Court's groundbreaking decision in *Boumediene v. Bush*, which granted Guantanamo detainees access to the Great Writ of habeas corpus,[94] federal courts have employed a test that harmonizes with IHL to determine an individual's initial detainability. Moreover, after some delay, the US has indicated that it will implement procedures consistent with Article 78 of the Fourth Geneva Convention[95] for administrative review of detainees' present dangerousness.

The Supreme Court's post-9/11 affirmation that detention authority stemmed from IHL actually started before *Boumediene*, in *Hamdi v. Rumsfeld*.[96] In *Hamdi*, the Court observed that the "capture and detention" of combatants is an "important incident[]" of armed conflict.[97] In refining this insight after *Boumediene*, the case law of the US Court of Appeals for the District of Columbia Circuit (D.C. Circuit), which by statute has jurisdiction over Guantanamo habeas cases, has adopted IHL's linking between detainability and membership in an organized armed group (OAG).[98] Under IHL, a state engaged in a NIAC with a non-state actor can detain members of the OAG and civilians participating directly in hostilities (DPH). Commanders of a group possessing basic indicia of organization,[99] as well as other fighters further down the chain of command, qualify as members of an OAG. By requiring *judicial* review of detention at the US naval base at Guantanamo Bay, Cuba, US courts have in fact gone further than IHL requires.[100]

---

[94] Compare Cole 2008 (praising judicial review); and Corn 2008 (arguing that judicial review of detention by US courts tempers arbitrariness in executive branch decisionmaking and vindicates IHL values), with Kent 2011 (arguing that *Boumediene* was based on faulty reading of US precedents).

[95] See Geneva Convention IV Article 78.

[96] Hamdi v. Rumsfeld at p. 507.

[97] Ibid at p. 518.

[98] See Uthman v. Obama at pp. 403–408; but see Prosecutor v. Tadic, Decision on Defence Motion for Interlocutory Appeal on Jurisdiction, at para 70 (setting out the IHL test).

[99] See Prosecutor v. Limaj, at paras 113–117 but see Pejic 2011, pp. 191–192

[100] In traditional conflicts between states, IHL only requires administrative review of combatant status. See Geneva Convention III, Article 5 Under the Fourth Geneva Convention, a state also may detain civilians who are dangerous to security. See Geneva Convention IV, Article 78. In that case, however, the state must not only rely on a competent body's determination of an individual's *initial* status, but must also provide periodic administrative review of the individual's ongoing dangerousness. For more discussion of detention, see Wittes 2010; Chesney 2011; Goodman 2009, pp. 53–55; Graham and Tomatz 2013; but see Waxman 2009, pp. 17–23 (discussing administrative detention); Bellinger III J, Padmanabhan 2011 (analyzing continued legal debates concerning detention in NIACs).

D.C. Circuit case law since *Boumediene* has adopted a pragmatic test for membership in an OAG. In finding evidence of membership, the court has relied on convergence of several factors, including participation in an Al Qaeda training camp, a stay at an Al Qaeda guest-house, and living with Al Qaeda or Taliban fighters near battle lines while in possession of a military-grade firearm.[101] The court has viewed mere coincidence as an unlikely explanation for the confluence of such factors.[102] With coincidence ruled out, membership in Al Qaeda is the most plausible explanation for the convergence.

One D.C. Circuit decision, *Latif v. Obama*,[103] strayed from this common sense approach, taking deference to the government too far. In *Latif*, the D.C. Circuit accorded a "presumption of regularity" to intelligence reports that classified the detainee as a member of Al Qaeda.[104] As Judge David Tatel pointed out in his dissent, the intelligence report at issue in *Latif*, which linked the detainee to Al Qaeda and a known Qaeda recruiter, was assembled hastily in the field, featured "multiple layers of hearsay, depend[ed] on translators of unknown quality, and include[d] cautionary disclaimers" that alerted a reasonable reader that the entire composition process was "prone to significant errors."[105] Moreover, the majority, in an opinion by Justice Janice Rogers Brown, failed to credit the narrative of the petitioner, which had been viewed as "plausible" by the district judge. The petitioner submitted ample documentation of a long-standing medical condition that would have hindered his participation in combat and explained his extended hospital stay prior to his capture.[106] The trial court had evaluated all of the evidence and found for the detainee, but the *Latif* majority took an unduly narrow view of the trial court's findings. The D.C. Circuit's decision to remand the case for further fact-finding was made even more troubling by the detainee's subsequent suicide.[107] Fortunately, *Latif* is an outlier. Most D.C. Circuit opinions have adhered to a common sense view, with measured but not excessive deference to the government's position.

---

[101] See Hussain v. Obama at p. 968.

[102] See ibid. (employing the "duck-test" to identify members of an OAG—if an observed entity "looks like a duck... walks like a duck, and... quacks like a duck," it seems reasonable to conclude that it is in fact a duck). This view of probabilistic inferences and evidence is consistent with mainstream legal thought. See Park and Saks 2006, at p. 992 (discussing Bayes' Theorem and assessments of probability).

[103] Latif v. Obama at pp. 1178–1183.

[104] But see ibid at pp. 1180–1181 (asserting that presumption merely shifts burden to detainee to show that US official writing report misinterpreted or mistranscribed claims related by others, but does not presume that such claims are accurate); ibid at 1188–1189 (buttressing applicability of presumption of regularity in Latif's case by citing details in Latif's subsequent statements which were consistent with material in intelligence report).

[105] Ibid at p. 1210 (Tatel, J., dissenting).

[106] Ibid at p. 1188.

[107] See Savage 2012.

The US has been more deliberate in establishing and implementing procedures to review the ongoing dangerousness of detainees. Although IHL is ambiguous on this score, many scholars and practitioners view Article 78 of the Fourth Geneva Convention, with its requirement of periodic administrative review of detention, as either a state duty or a sound prudential step.[108] In 2011, President Obama issued an Executive Order outlining a periodic review mechanism.[109] In 2012, with the review mechanism not yet operational, Congress asked the US Secretary of Defense to report regularly on review procedures at Guantanamo.[110] In July of 2013, the Department of Defense announced that it would initiate administrative review proceedings for 71 Guantanamo detainees.[111]

15.5.3 Military Commission Jurisdiction

The Military Commission act (MCA) Congress passed as a reaction to Hamdan, broadened the definition of material support of terrorism and rendered conspiracy a stand-alone offense involving mere agreement, which also exceeded the internationally recognized boundaries of IHL.[112] This section discusses the use of material support and conspiracy in two cases. The first is *Hamdan v. United States (Hamdan II)*, in which the D.C. Circuit vacated the defendant's conviction, and the second is that of *al Bahlul v. United States*, still pending in the same appellate court. We take a stance against the U.S. government's theory of liability in these cases, but also would like to argue that a narrower form of material support tied to conspiracy and aiding and abetting as modes of liability for completed war crimes would support al Bahlul's conviction.

15.5.4 The U.S. Government's Theory of a "U.S. Common Law of War"

Because both inchoate conspiracy and the broad form of material support found in federal criminal law are not recognized by IHL, the government decided to claim that culpability for acts prior to enactment of the MCA was not governed solely by

[108] See Waxman 2010, p. 350.

[109] Exec. Order No. 13,567, Periodic Review of Individuals Detained at Guantanamo Bay Naval Station Pursuant to the Authorization for Use of Military Force.

[110] See National Defense Authorization Act for Fiscal Year 2012, Section 1023(a), (b); Graham and Tomatz 2013 at p. 10 (discussing provisions of legislation).

[111] See Rosenberg 2013.

[112] See 18 U.S.C. Sect.s 2339A & B (2013).

international law, as the Define and Punish Clause would appear to require,[113] but was instead controlled by a "U.S. common law of war."[114] The "U.S. common law of war" argument relies on Congress's power under Article I, Sect. 8 to "make rules" for the army and navy, as well as other textual anchors of Congress's authority over making war. Arguing that the "U.S. common law of war" before 9/11 permitted trial of both material support and inchoate conspiracy in military commissions, adoption of this theory would mean that convictions for pre-MCA conduct did not violate the Constitution's Ex Post Facto Clause,[115] which incorporates the international law principle of legality, barring prosecutions based on conduct that did not violate a binding norm in place at the time of the defendant's acts. Unfortunately, the U.S. common law of war argument does not fit the Framers' constitutional design or most American practice, which reflects the membership view.

The Framers, with their deep understanding of publicists like Vattel, would have deplored assertions of a "U.S. common law of war."[116] Hamilton had argued in *Rutgers v. Waddington* that the law of nations had to inform state law.[117] He and Madison, with their memories of attacks on ambassadors and states' failure to observe treaties during the Articles of Confederation period, had pressed for a Constitution to signal the United States' allegiance to international law.[118] They and their fellow Framers would have found the notion of a "U.S. common law of war" distressingly familiar; that same notion, when articulated by the states during the Articles of Confederation period, had crystallized the case for a new Constitution. Indeed, for the Framers, positing a "U.S. common law of war" would have been the legal equivalent of announcing a "U.S. law of gravity."

As evidence from the Founding Era and beyond suggests, both the text and purpose of the Define and Punish Clause show that it was supposed to be the *exclusive* source for Congress's power to authorize military commission trials of individuals without a duty of loyalty to the United States. The government's argument in *Hamdan* II and *Bahlul* that Congress can invoke its war powers to do an end run around the Define and Punish Clause undermines that framework. Randolph, in his capacity as Attorney General, noted that when dealing with foreign nationals, "every change [in the law of nations] is at the peril of the nation which makes it."[119] Invoking Congress's war powers to achieve a result that was materially different from the one permitted under the Define and Punish Clause

---

[113] See Margulies 2013, pp. 63–65.

[114] See Brief for the United States, Hamdan v. United States, No. 11–1257.

[115] U.S. Constitution Article I §9 (a clause prohibited the passing of any "ex post facto Law").

[116] But see Margulies 2013 at pp. 63–66, Alexander 2013 at p. 615 (warning against threat to constitutional framework posed by allowing Congress to 'define anything it pleases as a war crime').

[117] Rutgers v. Waddington, supra note 2.

[118] The Federalist No. 42, 262 (James Madison) (Clinton Rossiter ed., 1961).

[119] Randolph, Who Privileged From Arrestat p.1.

would clearly have been viewed by Randolph as a substantial "modification"[120] which the Constitution barred. Attorney General Speed's opinion in 1865 grounds similar sentiments in the text of the Clause. Speed, as we have seen, made much of the distinction between the term "define," which gives the Clause its name, and the Framers' use of the term "make" in establishing Congress's power to regulate the armed forces.[121] While Randolph and Speed conceded that Congress had some latitude in its work when it invoked the Define and Punish Clause, they both viewed such latitude as circumscribed compared with Congress's expansive war powers. Permitting war powers to expand Congress's discretion under the Define and Punish Clause would make these linguistic differences superfluous, and risk the confrontations with foreign powers that the Framers wished to avoid.[122]

A "US common law of war" approach also conflicts with IHL. While the complementary relation between international and domestic law offers states some leeway in interpreting IHL, it does not give them also "carte blanche" to remake it. Any theory that gives states such sweeping discretion would undermine IHL's clarity as a guide to combatants in the fog of war.

15.5.4.1 Material Support

Judge Kavanaugh's opinion for the court in *Hamdan II* rejected the U.S. common law of war theory regarding material support, noting correctly that the U.S. could inform, but not displace the law of nations, at least if it wished to permit the MCA 2006 to apply retroactively. In assessing whether material support was a crime under the law of nations, Judge Kavanaugh looked to treaties, case law, and commentary. He observed that no treaty listed material support as a crime punishable by a transnational tribunal.[123] Furthermore, no tribunal had convicted anyone of the offence, or even entertained such charges. Commentators, the judge continued, also typically declared that material support was not a recognized war crime prior to the MCA's passage.[124] However, Judge Kavanaugh did not consider whether a more tailored form of material support would pass muster.

A narrower version of material support charges would look much like aiding and abetting. The tailored definition would still preclude the broadest uses of the

---

[120] Ibid.

[121] Speed Military Comm'ns 1865 11 Op. Att'y Gen. 297, at p. 4.

[122] Padmanabhan 2009, pp. 471–490 (arguing that military commissions that are perceived as illegitimate impair global counterterrorism efforts); Vladeck 2010, p. 295 (arguing for narrow view of military commission jurisdiction).

[123] See Hamdan v. US at p. 1251. Responding to the Hamdan II decision, Brig. Gen. Mark Martins, chief prosecutor of the military commissions system, recently dropped stand-alone conspiracy charges pending against Khalid Shaikh Mohammed and four others accused of complicity in the 9/11 attacks. See Savage 2013. This was a sound tactical decision, given Gen. Martins' assessment of the strength of the remaining charges.

[124] See Hamdan v. US at p. 1251.

federal criminal prohibition. The touchstone for aiding and abetting liability would be the codification effort by the International Law Commission (ILC). The ILC noted that collective attributions of guilt were generally inappropriate, and that conviction of crimes against humanity such as the murder of civilians rested on "individual responsibility."[125] The ILC recognized that individual responsibility could include the actions of one who "[k]nowingly aids, abets or otherwise assists, directly and substantially, in the commission of… a crime."[126] The commentary to this section noted that the accomplice must "knowingly provide… assistance which facilitates the commission of a crime in some significant way."[127]

Aiding and abetting liability includes assistance after the crime's commission, as long as the perpetrator and accomplice agreed on this assistance before the fact.[128] Assistance that a perpetrator knows will be forthcoming upon commission of a crime facilitates commission of the crime just as surely as direct assistance before the fact.[129] Aiding after the fact is an in-kind insurance policy, guaranteeing that the perpetrator will not face obstacles that may well have dampened the perpetrator's ardor for the entire operation.

Aiding and abetting liability covers many of the offenses supposedly included in the "U.S. common law of war." The Civil War bridge burning cases clearly fall under this rubric, with most defendants convicted of conduct that entailed concrete assistance to acts of violence against government targets.[130] The bushwhacker cases often involved similar proof of violence against civilian persons and/or property, in the context of units so small that an individual who slacked off in engaging in such conduct would receive substantial and immediate peer pressure from his colleagues in crime.[131]

The Nuremberg prosecutors' refinement of the London Charter's "membership offenses" is also analogous to aiding and abetting liability, albeit with somewhat greater play at the joints. The bushwhacker scenario explains the conviction of the noncommissioned officer Graf, who was part of the murderous *einsatzgruppen* that engaged in face-to-face killing of hundreds of thousands of civilians in Central and Eastern Europe.[132] Although Graf was reluctant to continue in the unit—a fact that reduced his sentence—it would be difficult for a noncommissioned officer in such

---

125 See Report Of The International Law Commission on the Work of its Forty-eighth Session, Article 2.

126 Ibid. Article 2 para 3(d).

127 Ibid. Article 2 Commentary, para 11.

128 Ibid. Article 2 Commentary, para 12.

129 See Dawson and Boynton 2008, p. 271 (noting importance of perpetrator's knowledge prior to crime's commission that he would receive help afterward).

130 See General Order (G.O.) No. 20 at pp. 403–404 and pp. 478–479 (describing how bridge-burners were often complicit in acts against the government).

131 See Winthrop 1886, pp. 10–11(outlining the establishment of commissions to prosecute bushwhackers).

132 See Trials of War Criminals Before the Nuernberg Military Tribunals Under Control Council Law No. 10 at p. 587 (finding Graf guilty of membership in the SD).

a unit to avoid conduct such as assisting in transportation or logistics that facilitated the *einsatzgruppen*'s activities.

A later case arising out of the activities of the *einsatzgruppen* is *Public Prosecutor v. Menten*,[133] in which a Dutch court convicted a translator of crimes against humanity in connection with the killing of Jews, Polish nationalists, and suspected communists. Although the trial occurred decades after the events in question and evidence of the defendant's participation in actual killing was slim,[134] the court found that Menten had assisted forces engaged in killing through his services as a translator[135] and his "accurate knowledge of persons and places" in the area.[136] Aiding and abetting also covers the conduct of the German financiers and industrialists like Flick and Steinbrinck who banded together as "Friends of Himmler" to assist the SS's murderous mission.[137] An efficient war crimes machine requires care and feeding, and Flick and Steinbrinck provided the resources that made that possible. The tribunal also found that they contributed eagerly with full knowledge of the SS's lethal activities.[138]

The recent case law on aiding and abetting is mixed. In 2012, the trial chamber of the Special Court for Sierra Leone convicted the Liberian leader Charles Taylor of aiding and abetting murder, mutilation, and sexual abuse in Sierra Leone by providing arms and logistical support to groups that engaged in such activity.[139] The court defined aiding and abetting broadly as lending "practical assistance, encouragement, or moral support to the perpetration of a crime or underlying offence."[140] The ICTY has taken a more restrictive tack, holding that the *actus reus* of aiding and abetting requires that the defendant's conduct was "specifically… directed towards relevant crimes."[141] However, even the ICTY's formulation is broader than it seems upon initial examination.

In *Perisić*, the tribunal ruled that the "specifically directed" test precluded culpability for a senior commander in the Yugoslav Army for genocidal acts committed by a paramilitary group without stronger evidence of the commander's own ties to the group. The decision has markedly less relevance for individuals

---

133 Public Prosecutor v. Menten.

134 Ibid at p. 345 (noting that defendant's joint responsibility was proven, although his "exact part [in the killings] could not be precisely established after such a long time").

135 Ibid at p. 347.

136 See ibid at pp. 351, 360, 365 (discussing defendant's use of his skills to aid the police and render "incidental services" to unit).

137 See Trials of War Criminals Before the Nuernberg Military Tribunals Under Control Council Law No. 10 at p. 1221(finding that the donation of money to Himmler, which in turn went to fund illegal activities, was sufficient for conviction).

138 Ibid at 1216, 1222–1223 (noting that Flick and Steinbrinck were convicted of having "knowledge of the criminal activities of the SS [and still] contribut[ing] funds and influence to its support."

139 Prosecutor v. Taylor, at paras 6910–6912.

140 Ibid para 482 (defining "aiding and abetting").

141 See Prosecutor v. Perisić, Case No. IT-04-81-A, Appeals Chamber Judgment, ¶ 27.

within the *same* group, such as al Qaeda. Moreover, the ICTY has emphasized that the "specifically directed" requirement goes to *actus reus*, not *mens rea*. To be guilty of aiding and abetting, a defendant need not have knowledge of the particular crime that his conduct has facilitated. He need only know that crimes of a certain type, such as the murder of civilians, will "probably" be committed, due in part to his aid.[142] The case law also would yield different results in Hamdan's and al Bahlul's cases. As Judge Kavanaugh said in his opinion for the court in *Hamdan II*, Salim Hamdan's acts were limited to generic activities such as driving Osama bin Laden to "various planning meetings."[143] That sort of generic conduct clearly did not meet the "specifically directed" standard of the ICTY. Al Bahlul's case is different. Because al Bahlul administered the *bayat* to two of the key September 11 hijackers and helped "keep them on task,"[144] his conduct met the ICTY's requirements for aiding and abetting liability. Even if fitting his conduct under the ICTY's definition pushes the IHL envelope in a modest fashion, that interpretive move fits well within the measure of discretion that the principle of complementarity provides.

15.5.4.2 Conspiracy

Even if one agrees with the *Hamdan II* panel that material support isn't a violation of the law of nations, the future of conspiracy charges in military commissions may be brighter. Conspiracy is a plausible mode of liability in military commission cases, including *al Bahlul*. Applying the *Hamdan II* analysis, conspiracy's main advantage over material support is its pedigree in international treaties, case law, and commentary. The lack of this pedigree was fatal to material support in Judge Kavanaugh's *Hamdan II* opinion.[145] The lineage of conspiracy as a mode of liability for a completed war crime is more substantial.

Analysis begins with the 1996 ILC Draft Code of Crimes Against Peace and Security of Mankind.[146] Article 2(e) of the Draft Code prohibits "planning or conspiring" to engage in war crimes, such as targeting civilians that "in fact occur." The ILC Draft Code's standing provides some evidence of conspiracy's acceptance, of the kind that the *Hamdan II* panel found lacking in the case of material support. Conspiracy as mode of liability, however, encounters problems

---

142 See Prosecutor v. Stanisic & Simatovic, Case No. IT-03-69-T, Trial Chamber Judgment, ¶ 1264 (noting that a defendant, "does not…need to know either the precise crime that was intended or the one that was actually committed; it is sufficient that he or she be aware that one of a number of crimes will probably be committed, if one of those crimes is in fact committed").

143 See Hamdan v. US at p. 1242.

144 See Transcript of Military Commission Hearing, United States v. Al Bahlul (Tr.) 555–556 (testimony of Federal Bureau of Investigation agent regarding Al Qaeda tradecraft).

145 See Hamdan v. US.

146 See Report Of The International Law Commission on the Work of its Forty-eighth Session Article 2.

elsewhere in the indicia of legitimacy that Judge Kavanaugh outlined in his opinion for the court. The London Charter governing the Nuremberg tribunals expressly provided for conspiracy, and the Nuremberg tribunals permitted such charges, albeit in a limited manner.[147] The statutes of more recent tribunals, such as the International Criminal Tribunal for the former Yugoslavia (ICTY), are more restrictive. They do not include conspiracy as a mode of liability, although they do allow charging conspiracy to commit genocide (and genocide only) as a separate offense.[148] Whether this is an insurmountable obstacle depends on how one reads Judge Kavanaugh's opinion.

If one reads the indicia of authority in the opinion as conjunctive, conspiracy as mode of liability is problematic. On this view, the failure to include conspiracy as a mode of liability in the statutes of the ICTY and other recent tribunals would be fatal. However, one can also read Judge Kavanaugh's discussion as a more flexible guide to the range of authority that could support military commission jurisdiction. On this more flexible view, the ILC's endorsement of conspiracy would still be meaningful, along with conspiracy's inclusion in the London Charter of the Nuremberg tribunals. This pedigree also creates room for the analogical reasoning that Judge Kavanaugh rejected in the case of material support. As Cornell's Jens David Ohlin mentions in an important recent article,[149] conspiracy as a mode of liability shares many attributes with another mode of liability involving concerted activity, Joint Criminal Enterprise (JCE), which *is* included in the statutes of recent tribunals and figures heavily in the case law.[150] Under international law, an individual is guilty of participation in a JCE if he intentionally aids a common plan that results in a completed war crime.[151] Participation in a JCE encompasses serving as a "cog in the wheel of events leading up to the result which in fact occurred."[152] This pairing of joint intention with action is very close to conspiracy as a mode of liability—close enough that no individual charged with the latter as a mode of liability can claim lack of notice.

In light of the birfurcation above, once again the case law leads to disparate views of the respective cases of Hamdan and al Bahlul. Although Judge Kavanaugh's opinion in *Hamdan II* did not mention conspiracy, Hamdan's conduct was too generic even under the ICTY's broad JCE standard. A different conclusion is in order for al Bahlul. The members of the commission specifically found that the defendant had committed overt acts corresponding to a role in the 9/11 plot, including his administration of Mohammed Atta's and Ziad al Jarrah's *bayat* or

[147] See London Agreement of 8 August 1945, Charter of the International Military Tribunal, and the Nuremberg Tribunal's Rules of Procedure; Ohlin 2011, p. 702.

[148] See Statute of the International Criminal Tribunal for the Former Yugoslavia Article 4(3)(b).

[149] See Ohlin 2011, p. 702.

[150] *Prosecutor v. Tadic*, Case No. IT-94-1-A, Appeals Chamber Judgment, para 196.

[151] Ibid.

[152] Ibid at para 199 (quoting from World War II-era precedent).

loyalty oath to Osama bin Laden.[153] The *bayat* to Atta, the 9/11 plot's ringleader in the United States, and al Jarrah, the pilot on Flight 93, set the 9/11 machinery in motion. The *bayat* bound Atta and al Jarrah to "obey [bin Laden] at all times,",[154] and "die for the sake of Jihad... against the American[s] and the Jews."[155] Moreover, the defendant groomed Atta and al Jarrah for a mission of particular "sensitivity," living with them to "keep them on task."[156] Al Bahlul embraced his role with the intention of aiding in the targeting of civilians—indeed he asserted that Americans were not civilians because they supported the policies of the United States government.[157] Al Bahlul's lack of advance knowledge of the specifics of the 9/11 plot is irrelevant, given his intent to participate in a plan to murder civilians.[158] Al Bahlul's intent and conduct thus meet the requirements for JCE liability.

This argument about al Bahlul's culpability under IHL has one procedural flaw: al Bahlul's charge sheet mentioned only an *agreement* to murder civilians, and al Bahlul was charged with conspiracy, not with the actual murder of civilians, as would be the case where the prosecution relied on conspiracy or JCE as a mode of liability for a completed war crime. As we have discussed, mere agreement is an inchoate offense not generally recognized in IHL. However, this omission in the charge sheet does not undermine the validity of al Bahlul's conviction.

While the charge sheet in al Bahlul's case did not allege that he had committed murder, the list of overt acts included in the charging document mentioned conduct related to the 9/11 attacks, including the administration of the *bayat* to Atta and al Jarrah. A letter that al Bahlul wrote to Ramzi bin al Shibh, a senior Al Qaeda figure, had acknowledged that al Bahlul played a "simple... indirect role"[159] in the attacks by virtue of his administration of the *bayat* and role regarding the martyr wills of Atta and al Jarrah, which supplied both the rationale for the two men's participation in the attacks and a propaganda benefit intended by bin Laden as a consequence of the attacks' consummation. Al Bahlul's comments to the commission while acting as his own counsel demonstrated ample awareness that he was being charged with a role in the 9/11 plot.[160] Moreover, when the prosecution in its opening statement mentioned al Bahlul's involvement in the 9/11 attacks and

---

153 Al Bahlul v. United States, Findings Work Sheet at pp. 3–4.

154 See note 71 supra at 509.

155 Ibid at p. 510.

156 Ibid at pp. 555–556.

157 Transcript of Military Commission Hearing at p. 503.

158 See Prosecutor v. Brdanin, Case No. IT-99-36-A, Appeals Chamber Judgment at para 418 (noting that JCE liability does not require, beyond a finding of a common purpose, "an additional... agreement to commit... [a] *particular* crime between the accused and the principal perpetrator of a crime") (emphasis added).

159 United States v. Al Bahlul, Prosecution Exhibit 15.

160 See Transcript of Military Commission Hearing at pp. 193–194.

followed up with testimony from an FBI agent discussing his role, the defense did not object or pose a single question by way of cross-examination. Under the circumstances viewing the omission in the charge sheet as harmless error does not clash with IHL.

15.6 Conclusion

Even before the enactment of the US Constitution, pivotal figures, like Alexander Hamilton, believed that membership in the community of nations was a fundamental aim of the new republic. In the more than two centuries since the Constitution's enactment, US policy and practice have typically remained within the membership conception. This chapter has described this pattern, as well as occasional departures in times of crisis that have driven the creation or recalibration of existing standards.

From the US Civil War through the aftermath of the September 11 attacks, US departures from IHL have usually involved measures taken by the executive branch. Other players, including courts, Congress, and military lawyers, have responded, sometimes accepting these initiatives, but often rejecting them or tailoring measures to IHL principles. This pattern emerged after the Civil War, when the US Supreme Court held in *Ex parte Milligan* that a military commission could not try a non-belligerent for acts committed outside the theater of war. In *In re Yamashita*, the Supreme Court upheld a military commission conviction based on a then-novel theory of command responsibility. The doctrine of command responsibility became a key building block for international tribunals, which provided more robust procedural safeguards, learning from the flaws in Yamashita's prosecution.

The September 11 attacks provide the latest illustration of the membership argument. The executive branch responded to the attacks with efforts to change IHL rules on interrogation, detention, and the jurisdiction of military commissions. Courts and other players pushed back. These responses were often effective, although the Supreme Court's decision in *Hamdan v. Rumsfeld* classifying the struggle with al Qaeda as a NIAC may have raised more questions than it answered. On interrogation policy, the US has returned to the IHL fold. With regard to detention courts have applied IHL principles to determine membership in an OAG and the US has begun to implement administrative review of present dangerousness based on the Fourth Geneva Convention. As of August, 2013, issues regarding military commission jurisdiction are still working their way through US courts. However, the D.C. Circuit's decision in *Hamdan v. United States* vacating a conviction for material support of terrorism in the absence of evidence that the defendant had committed an established war crime reaffirmed the US Constitution's commitment to international law.

Documentation

Cases

US Supreme Court

Boumediene v. Bush, 553 U.S. 723 (2008).
Ex parte Milligan, 71 U.S. 2 (1866).
Ex parte Quirin, 317 U.S. 1 (1942).
Hamdan v. Rumsfeld, 548 U.S. 557 (2006).
Hamdi v. Rumsfeld, 542 U.S. 507 (2004).
Rasul v. Bush, 542 U.S. 466 (2004).
Sosa v. Alvarez-Machain, 542 U.S. 692 (2004).
U.S. v. Alvarez-Machain, 504 U.S. 655 (2007).

Federal Circuits

Hamdan v. U.S., 696 F.3d 1238 (D.C. Cir. 2012).
Hussain v. Obama, 718 F.3d 964 (D.C. Cir. 2013).
Latif v. Obama, 677 F.3d 1175 (D.C. Cir. 2012) (reissued); cert. denied, 132 S. Ct. 2741 (2012).
Padilla v. Yoo, 678 F.3d 748 (9th Cir. 2012).
Uthman v. Obama, 637 F.3d 400, 403–408 (D.C. Cir. 2011).

European Court of Human Rights

Handyside v. United Kingdom, 24 Eur. Ct. H.R. (ser. A) (1976).

International Crime Tribunal for the Former Yugoslavia

Prosecutor v. Brdanin, Case No. IT-99-36-A, Appeals Chamber Judgment (Int'l Crim. Trib. for the Former Yugoslavia Apr. 3, 2007).
Prosecutor v. Delalić, et al. (also known as the Čelibići case), Case No. IT-96-21-T, Trial Chamber Judgment (Int'l Crim. Trib. for the Former Yugoslavia, Nov. 16, 1998).
Prosecutor v. Halilović, Case No. IT-01-48-T, Trial Chamber Judgment (ICTY, Nov. 16, 2005).
Prosecutor v. Muthara, No. ICC-01/09-02/11-342.
Prosecutor v. Perisić, Case No. IT-04-81-A, Appeals Chamber Judgment (Int'l Crim. Trib. for the Former Yugoslavia Feb. 28, 2013).
Prosecutor v. Stanisic & Simatovic, Case No. IT-03-69-T, Trial Chamber Judgment (Int'l Crim. Trib. for the Former Yugoslavia May 30, 2013).
Prosecutor v. Tadic, Case No. IT-94-1-T, Trial Chamber Judgment (Int'l Crim. Trib. for the Former Yugoslavia May 7, 1997).
Prosecutor v. Tadic, Case No. IT-94-1-A, Appeals Chamber Judgment (Int'l Crim. Trib. for the Former Yugoslavia July 15, 1999).
Prosecutor v. Tadic, Decision on the Defence Motion for Interlocutory Appeal of Jurisdiction, 2 Oct. 1995.

Special Court for Sierra Leone

Prosecutor v. Taylor, Case No. SCSL-03-01-T, Judgment (Special Court for Sierra Leone, May 18, 2012).

Supreme Court of the Netherlands

Public Prosecutor v. Menten, 75 I.L.R. 331 (Neth. Sup. Ct. 1981).

New York Mayor's Court

Rutgers v. Waddington, Opinion of the New York Mayor's Court, Aug. 27, 1784 *reprinted in* 1 The Law Practice Of Hamilton: Documents And Commentary 393–419 (Julius Goebel, Jr. ed., 1964)

Case Materials

Al Bahlul v. United States, Findings Work Sheet (Completed by Members) (dated Oct. 31, 2008) at 3-4, available at http://www.mc.mil/CASES/MilitaryCommissions.aspx ("Docket" tab) (last visited Aug. 15, 2013).

Brief for the United States, Hamdan v. United States, No. 11-1257 (D.C. Circuit), filed Jan. 17, 2012, at 24–46, available at http://www.lawfareblog.com/wp-content/uploads/2012/01/Hamdan-Brief-for-US-As-Filed.pdf.

Trials of War Criminals Before the Nuernberg Military Tribunals Under Control Council Law No. 10 available at http://www.loc.gov///_Law//NT_war-criminals_Vol-IV.pdf and http://www.loc.gov///_Law//NT_war-criminals_Vol-VI.pdf.

Transcript of Military Commission Hearing, United States v. Al Bahlul, available at http://www.mc.mil/CASES/MilitaryCommissions.aspx (last visited Aug. 15, 2013).

United States v. Al Bahlul, Prosecution Exhibit 15, Al Bahlul Letter to Ramzi bin al Shibh at 4 (Sept. 20, 2005), available at http://www.mc.mil/CASES/MilitaryCommissions.aspx (last visited Aug. 15, 2013).

Attorney General Opinions/Memorandums

Memorandum from Jay S. Bybee, Assistant Attorney Gen., to Alberto R. Gonzales, Counsel to President, Standards of Conduct for Interrogation Under 18 U.S.C. §§ 2340–2340A (Aug. 1, 2002), *in* The Torture Papers: The Road to Abu Ghraib 172 (Karen J. Greenberg & Joshua L. Dratel eds., 2005).

Memorandum from Jay S. Bybee, Assistant Attorney Gen., to John Rizzo, Acting Gen. Counsel of the Cent. Intelligence Agency, Interrogation of al Qaeda Operative, at 4 (Aug. 1, 2002), *available at* http://www.fas.org/irp/agency/doj/olc/zubaydah.pdf.

Randolph, Who Privileged From Arrest, 1 Op. Att'y Gen. 26, at *1.

Speed, Military Comm'ns, 11 Op. Att'y Gen. 297 (1865), at *4.

Constitutions/Statutes/Regulations/Conventions/Agreements

Army Regulation 15-6: Final Report: Investigation into FBI Allegations of Detainee Abuse at Guantanamo Bay, Cuba Detention Facility 14 (June 9, 2005), available at http://www.defense.gov/news/jul2005/d20050714report.pdf.

Exec. Order No. 13,567, Periodic Review of Individuals Detained at Guantanamo Bay Naval Station Pursuant to the Authorization for Use of Military Force (March 7, 2011), available at https://www.fas.org/irp/offdocs/eo/eo-13567.htm.

General Order (G.O.) No. 13, Headquarters, Dep't of the Missouri (Dec. 4, 1861), 1 OR ser. II.

General Order (G.O.) No. 20, Headquarters, Dep't of the Missouri (Jan. 14, 1862), 1 War of the Rebellion: A Compilation of the Official Records of the Union and Confederate Armies, ser. II.

Geneva Convention for the Amelioration of the Condition of the Wounded and Sick in Armed Forces in the Field, opened for signature Aug. 12, 1949, 6 U.S.T. 3114, 75 U.N.T.S. 31 [Geneva I]; Geneva Convention for the Amelioration of the Condition of Wounded, Sick and Shipwrecked Members of Armed Forces at Sea, opened for signature Aug. 12, 1949, 6 U.S.T. 3217, 75 U.N.T.S. 85 [Geneva II]; Geneva Convention Relative to the Treatment of Prisoners of War, opened for signature Aug. 12, 1949, 6 U.S.T. 3316, 75 U.N.T.S. 135 [Geneva III]; Geneva Convention Relative to the Protection of Civilian Persons in Time of War, opened for signature Aug. 12, 1949, 6 U.S.T. 3516, 75 U.N.T.S. 287 [Geneva IV].

Interrogation of Detainees: Overview of the McCain Amendment, CRS Report for Congress, Oct. 23, 2006, available at http://fpc.state.gov/documents/organization/76919.pdf.

London Agreement of 8 August 1945, Charter of the International Military Tribunal, and the Nuremberg Tribunal's Rules of Procedure, reprinted in 2 Virginia Morris & Michael P. Scharf, An Insider's Guide to the International Criminal Tribunal for the Former Yugoslavia (1995).

Military Commissions Act of 2006, Pub. L. No. 109–366 (2006), available at http://www.gpo.gov/fdsys/pkg/BILLS-109s3930es/pdf/BILLS-109s3930es.pdf

National Defense Authorization Act for Fiscal Year 2012, Pub. L. No. 112–181 (2012), available at http://www.gpo.gov/fdsys/pkg/PLAW-112publ81/pdf/PLAW-112publ81.pdf

Protocol Additional to the Geneva Conventions of 12 August 1949, and Relating to the Protection of Victims of International Armed Conflicts (Additional Protocol I), June 8, 1977, 1125 U.N.T.S. 3

Protocol Additional to the Geneva Conventions of 12 August 1949, and Relating to the Protection of Victims of Non-International Armed Conflicts (Additional Protocol II), June 8, 1977, 1125 U.N.T.S. 609; 26 I.L.M. 568 (1987); S. Treaty Doc. No. 100–102 (1987).

Report of the International Law Commission on the Work of its Forty-eighth Session, Draft Code of Crimes against the Peace and Security of Mankind with commentaries, U.N. Doc. A/51/10 (May 6–July 26, 1996).

Report of the Special Rapporteur on Extrajudicial, Summary or Arbitrary Executions, Philip Alston, Addendum, Study on Targeted Killings, U.N. Doc. A/HRC/14/24/Add. 6 (May 28, 2010).

Rome Statute of the International Criminal Court, July 17, 1998, 2189 U.N.T.S. 90.

Statute of the International Criminal Tribunal for the Former Yugoslavia S.C. Res. 827, U.N. Doc. S/RES/827 (May 25, 1993).

United Nations Convention Against Torture and Other Cruel, Inhuman or Degrading Treatment or Punishment, G.A. Res. 39/46, U.N. Doc. A/RES/39/708 (Dec. 10, 1984).

18 U.S.C. Sect.s 2339A & B (2013).

U.S. Constitution. Article I, § 8, cl. 10.

References

Alexander JC (2013) The Law-Free Zone and Back Again. U Ill L Rev 2013:551

Baxter RR (1963) The first modern codification of the law of armed conflict—Francis Lieber and General Order No. 100. IRRC 25:171

Bellinger J III, Padmanabhan V (2011) Detention operations in contemporary conflicts: four challenges for the Geneva Conventions and other existing law. AJIL 105:201

Bradley C (2002) The Alien Tort Statute and Article III. Va J Int'l L 42:587

Bryant AC, Tobias C (2003) Quirin revisited. Wis L Rev 2003:309

Chesney R (2011) Who may be held? Military detention through the Habeas Lens. B C L Rev 52:769

Chomsky C (1990) The United States-Dakota War Trials: a study in military injustice. Stan L Rev 43(13):86–90

Clark K (2005) Ethical issues raised by the OLC Torture Memorandum. J. Nat'l Security L. & Pol'y 1:455

Cole D (2008) Rights over borders: transnational constitutionalism and Guantanamo Bay, 2007–2008 Cato Sup. Ct Rev 47

Corn G (2008) The role of the courts in the war on terror: the intersection of hyperbole, military necessity, and iudicial review. N Eng L Rev 43:17

Corn G, Jensen ET (2009) Transnational armed conflict: a 'Principled' approach to the regulation of counter-terror combat operations. Isr L Rev 42:46

Corn G, Blank L, Jenks C, Jensen ET (2013) Belligerent targeting and the invalidity of a least harmful means rule. Int'l L Stud 89:536

Dawson G, Boynton R (2008) Reconciling complicity in Genocide and Aiding and Abetting Genocide in the jurisprudence of the United Nations Ad Hoc Tribunals. Harv Hum Rts J 21:241

Deeks A (2012) Unwilling or unable: toward a normative framework for extraterritorial self-defense. Va J Int'l L 52:483

Dehn JC, Heller KJ (2011) Targeted killing: the case of Anwar al-Aulaqi. U Pa L Rev PENNumbra 159:175

Finkelstein C, Lewis MW (2010) Should Bush administration lawyers be prosecuted for authorizing torture? U Pa L Rev PENNumbra 158(195):205

Fisher L (2003) Nazi saboteurs on trial: a, military tribunal and American law. Kansas University Press

Fleck D, ed (1995) Handbook of humanitarian law in armed conflicts. Oxford University Press, Oxford

Goebel J (ed) (1964) The law practice of Hamilton: documents and commentary, 1st edn. Columbia Univ Press, New York

Goldsmith J (2007), The terror presidency: law and judgment inside the Bush administration. W W Norton & Company

Golove D (2006) Leaving customary international law where it is: Goldsmith and Posner's the limits of international law. Ga J Int'l Comp L 34:333
Goodman R (2009) The detention of civilians in armed conflict. AJIL 103:48
Goodman R (2013) The power to kill or capture enemy combatants. EJIL 24:819
Graham L, Tomatz M (2013) Congress and Consensus on Enemy Detention. Air Force L Rev. 69:1
Halleck HW (1893) Halleck's international law or rules regulating the intercourse of states in peace and war. Sherston Baker, 3rd edn
Heller KJ (2011) "No, the UN Has Not Said the U.S. Is Engaged in an 'Armed Conflict' with Al Qaeda", Opinio Juris blog, May 21, 2011 available at http://opiniojuris.org/2011/05/21/no-the-un-has-not-affirmed-that-the-us-is-engaged-in-an-armed-conflict-with-al-qaeda/
Kent JA (2007) Congress's under-appreciated power to define and punish offenses against the law of nations. Tex L Rev 85:843
Kent JA (2011) Boumediene, Munaf, and the Supreme Court's misreading of the Insular cases. Iowa L Rev 97:101
Kramer ML, Schmitt MN (2008) Lawyers on Horseback? Thoughts on judge advocates and civil-military relations. UCLA L Rev 55:1407
Lewis MW (2008) International Myopia: Hamdan's shortcut to "Victory". U Rich L Rev 42:687
Lieber F (1862) Guerrilla parties considered with reference to the laws and usages of war. D van Nostrand, New York
Luban D (2007) Legal ethics and human dignity. Cambridge University Press, Cambridge
Margulies P (2010), Law's Detour: justice displaced in the Bush administration
Margulies P (2012) Reforming lawyers into irrelevance?: reconciling crisis and constraint at the office of legal counsel. Pepperdine L Rev 39:809
Margulies P (2013) Defining, punishing, and membership in the community of nations: material support and conspiracy charges in military commissions. Fordham Int'l L J 36:1
McNeal G (2009) Organizational culture, professional Ethics and Guantánamo case W. Res J Int'l L 42:125
Neely M (1991) The fate of liberty: Abraham Lincoln and Civil Liberties
O'Connell ME (2009) Combatants and the combat zone. U Rich L Rev 845:43
Ohlin JD (2011) Joint intentions to commit international crimes. Chi J Int'l L 11:693
Oppenheim LF 2 International Law: A Treatise: War and Neutrality International Law page 315 section 255 (2d ed.), available at http://www.gutenberg.org/files/41047/41047-h/41047-h.htm#Page_313
Padmanabhan V (2009) Norm internalization through trials for violations of international law: four conditions for success and their application to trials of detainees at Guantanamo Bay. U Pa J Int'l L 31:427
Park R, Saks M (2006) Evidence scholarship reconsidered: results of the interdisciplinary turn. BC L Rev 46:949
Paust JJ (2001) Dr Francis Lieber and the Lieber Code. ASIL Proc 95:112
Pejic J (2011) The protective scope of common Article 3: more than meets the eye. Intl Rev Red Cross 93(881):189–225
Records of the Federal Convention of 1787, at 24–25 (Max Farrand, ed, rev edn 1966)
Rosenberg C (2013) At Guantanamo, 71 detainees will get parole-style hearings. Wash Post July 22, 2013, A4
Savage C (2012) Investigators said to question how detainee died of overdose. NY Times 29(2012):A18
Savage C (2013) U.S. to press fight of Detainee's Appeal, N.Y. Times, Jan 10, 2013, at A14
Sulmasy G, Yoo J (2007) Challenges to civilian control of the military: a rational choice approach to the war on terror. UCLA L Rev 54:1815
Turley J (2002) Trials and tribulations: the antithetical elements of military governance in a Madisonian democracy. Geo Wash L Rev 70:649
Vladeck S (2010) The laws of war as a constitutional limit on military commission jurisdiction. J Nat'l Security L Pol'y 4:295

Waxman M (2009) Administrative detention of terrorists: why detain, and detain whom? J Nat'l Sec L Pol'y 3:1
Waxman M (2010) The law of Armed conflict and detention operations in Afghanistan. Int'l L Stud 85:343
White J (2005) Defense document bans detainee torture. Wash Post 9(2005):A25
Winthrop W (1886) Military law and precedents. Morrison Publisher, W.H
Witt JF (2012) Lincoln's code: the laws of war in American History. Free Press, New York
Wittes B (2010) Detention and denial: the case for Candor. Brookings Institution, Washington DC

Chapter 16
The International Commission of Inquiry on Darfur and the Application of International Humanitarian Norms

Makane Moïse Mbengue and Brian McGarry

Contents

Makane Moïse Mbengue is Associate Professor, University of Geneva, Faculty of Law, Department of Public International Law and International Organization; Visiting Professor, Sciences Po Paris (School of Law). Brian McGarry is Ph.D. Candidate, University of Geneva, Faculty of Law, Department of Public International Law and International Organization.

M. M. Mbengue (✉) · B. McGarry
University of Geneva, Geneva, Switzerland
e-mail: makane.mbengue@unige.ch

B. McGarry
e-mail: brian.mcgarry@unige.ch

D. Jinks et al. (eds.), *Applying International Humanitarian Law in Judicial and Quasi-Judicial Bodies*, DOI: 10.1007/978-94-6265-008-4_16,

16.1 Introduction

The region of Darfur, a sovereign territory for centuries under a sultanate, has spent its last century marginalized under British colonial and Sudanese policies that have concentrated resources eastward in Khartoum.[1] The relationship between nomadic herdsmen and sedentary farmers in the region was dramatically destabilized in the 1970s and 1980s by a perfect storm of factors, including the abolition of customary land rights, the ravages of drought and famine, a sharp rise in access to automatic firearms, and the efforts of State media in the Sudan and Darfur-neighboring Libya to politically exploit an "historically bogus, but disturbingly powerful"[2] dichotomy between sedentary 'Arabs' and nomadic 'Africans'.[3]

The flashpoint for the current phase of the conflict was in 2003, when burgeoning rebel groups known as the Sudanese Liberation Army/Movement (SLA/M) and the Justice and Equality Movement (JEM) drew attention to their political and human rights grievances by staging large attacks on Sudanese military garrisons and supply convoys.[4] The government of President Omar al-Bashir sought to quickly stamp out the insurrection, but was impeded by both its focus on resolving civil war in the nation's southern region (present-day South Sudan) and its army's unpreparedness to meet the challenges of guerilla attacks.[5] The government's solution—fortifying its military response by arming, training, and bankrolling an extant militia known to the group's targets as the *Janjaweed* (a traditional Darfurian term denoting any armed bandit on a horse)[6]—quickly led to a humanitarian crisis endangering and displacing communities across Darfur.

Following allegations that the government of the Sudan (in collaboration with these paramilitaries) had committed internationally criminal acts during the escalating attacks and counterattacks, the UN Security Council authorized[7] Secretary-General Kofi Annan in September 2004 to establish the International Commission of Inquiry on Darfur (hereinafter, the 'Darfur Commission').[8] The Commission's mandate required it to "investigate reports of violations of international humanitarian law and human rights law in Darfur by all parties," to "determine also whether or not acts of genocide have occurred," and to "identify the perpetrators of such violations [...] with a view to ensuring that those

---

1 Prunier 2005, p. 33.

2 De Waal 2005, pp. 181, 197.

3 For a brief but comprehensive overview of these factors, see Elliesie 2010, pp. 193, 196–205.

4 For a factual framing of the conflict escalation that is more concise than the survey undertaken by the Commission, see Kastner 2012, pp. 30–35.

5 Ibid., p. 30.

6 Report of the International Commission of Inquiry on Darfur to the United Nations Secretary-General pursuant to Security Council Resolution 1564 of 18 September 2004 (Geneva, 25 January 2005), para 69.

7 Charter of the United Nations (San Francisco, 26 June 1945), Chap. 7.

8 UN Security Council Resolution 1564 (18 September 2004).

responsible are held accountable."[9] The Commission also presented detailed recommendations concerning the establishment and implementation of accountability mechanisms to address the existing situation in Darfur and avoid its reoccurrence.[10] These parameters establish the Commission as a quasi-judicial body and it is in this framework that this chapter will examine the Commission's findings on individual and State accountability in the course of a non-international armed conflict, such as that in Darfur.[11]

Moreover, the chapter will focus on the Commission's assertion that genocide did not occur, analyzing genocidal component elements such as the specificity of the targeted group, the specificity of intent to kill, the question of State responsibility for such acts and the distinctions that the Commission drew between genocide and other internationally criminal acts. Finally, this contribution will compare the Commission's normative methodology in this regard to those of the International Court of Justice (ICJ) and major criminal courts and tribunals, before offering conclusions based on the resulting contrasts.

16.2 The View from Above: Contextualizing the Commission's Report

16.2.1 A Unique Methodological Approach

The Darfur Commission, composed of the Secretary-General's appointees and chaired by Professor Antonio Cassese, began its work in Geneva in October 2004 with a three-month deadline and an investigative team assembled by the UN High Commissioner for Human Rights.[12] The Commission's fact-finding involved field trips and extensive interviews with representatives of the government of the Sudan, senior officials at both the state and local levels in the Darfur region, members of the military and police force, rebel force leaders, tribal leaders, internally displaced persons, other victims and their witnesses, as well as representatives of the UN and external NGOs.[13]

This fact-finding methodology can be contextualized by contrast with the ICJ's approach to another instance of regional African conflict. Like the Darfur Commission, the ICJ in *Democratic Republic of the Congo v. Uganda* was faced with fact-intensive issues concerning the identity of actors and the scope of paramilitary

[9] Ibid., para 12.

[10] Report of the International Commission of Inquiry on Darfur, supra n. 6, paras 565–625.

[11] For the Commission's analysis of modes of criminal liability for violations of humanitarian law, see ibid., paras 533–564.

[12] Ibid., para 1.

[13] Ibid., paras 3, 20–39.

activities.[14] However, the ICJ's Rules of Court prevent it from soliciting information from NGOs engaged on the ground level during the conflict.[15] The Court circumvented this by declaring that the NGO reports referred to in the parties' pleadings were in the public domain, and thus consultable without direct solicitation by the Court for a 'submission'.[16]

Nevertheless, some judicial bodies specifically empowered to address humanitarian claims have been endowed with expansive fact-finding abilities akin to those of the Darfur Commission. For example, the Rome Statute of the International Criminal Court (ICC) indicates that the Court's Prosecutor may request information from any "reliable sources that he or she deems appropriate", while the Statute of the International Criminal Tribunal for the Former Yugoslavia (ICTY) lacks even this qualified limit.[17] Both texts explicitly include "non-governmental organizations" as fact-finding sources.[18]

Despite this strong similarity to the investigative powers of such adjudicative fora, however, the Darfur Commission declared that it was "not a judicial body."[19] This was a highly consequential statement that freed the Commission of any obligation to apply standard criminal law thresholds concerning evidentiary burdens. The Commission instead determined that the requirement of "a reliable body of material consistent with other verified circumstances, which tends to show that a person may reasonably be suspected of being involved in the commission of a crime" was the most appropriate standard for its task.[20] This 'reasonable suspicion' threshold differs from evidentiary standards commonly found in domestic and international criminal proceedings—such as *prima facie* burdens for indictment,[21] and 'reasonable doubt' burdens for incrimination[22]—and perhaps finds its

[14] *Armed Activities on the Territory of the Congo (Democratic Republic of the Congo v. Uganda)*, Judgment, I.C.J. Reports 2005, p. 168.

[15] Rules of Court of the International Court of Justice, Articles 69(1)(4). The Court faces no such procedural hurdle in soliciting information from intergovernmental organizations, and indeed has been criticized for relying too heavily in its fact-gathering on secondary sources provided by the UN. See, generally, Halink 2008, p. 13. For an analysis of issues unique to the role of the International Committee of the Red Cross in fact-finding inquiries, see Wiebalck 2003, pp. 198–216.

[16] *Democratic Republic of the Congo v. Uganda*, Judgment, supra n. 14, paras 129, 135. Former ICJ Judge Abdul Koroma has outlined a number of pragmatic reasons to limit the use of evidence gathered by NGOs. See Koroma 2011, pp. 199–204, at 203. For a detailed discussion of evidentiary concerns particular to investigations of human rights law and humanitarian law violations, see Ratner and Abrams 2001, p. 253 ('Developing the Case: Comments on Evidence and Judicial Assistance').

[17] Rome Statute of the International Criminal Court (17 July 1998), Article 15(2); Statute of the International Criminal Tribunal for the Former Yugoslavia (25 May 1993), Article 18(1).

[18] Ibid.

[19] Report of the International Commission of Inquiry on Darfur, supra n. 6, para 14.

[20] Ibid., para 15.

[21] Eg, Statute of the ICTY, supra n. 17, Article 18(4).

[22] Eg, Rome Statute, supra n. 17, Article 66(3).

closest cousin at international law in the customary rules of seizure under prize law.[23]

In January 2005, the Commission submitted its findings in its Report to the Secretary-General (hereinafter, the 'Report').[24]

16.2.2 Conclusions Under Review

16.2.2.1 Copious Violations of Human Rights Law and Humanitarian Law

After culling reports and witness accounts, the Darfur Commission found that it had established that the government of the Sudan and the *Janjaweed* had committed serious violations of international human rights and humanitarian law.[25] While the Commission found credible evidence that rebel forces may be responsible for some of the same violations, it also held that the role of the Government of the Sudan and the *Janjaweed* was widespread in the perpetration of these acts.[26] The specific conduct of government forces and militias, according to the Commission, included the murder of civilians, torture, rape and sexual violence, enforced disappearances and forced displacement, and destruction and pillaging of villages.[27] The Commission considered that the widespread and systematic nature of these acts approached the threshold for crimes against humanity.[28] The overwhelming majority of the victims involved in these incidents had been from tribes labeled as 'African', primarily the Fur, Zaghawa, Massalit, Jebel, and Aranga.[29]

The Commission considered that it had clearly established that the attacks of the government forces had been deliberately waged in an indiscriminate manner against civilians in Darfur, many of whom lost their livelihood and means of survival in the process.[30] As such, the Commission did not accept the government's argument that military attacks in Darfur had been waged for counter-insurgency purposes.[31] The Commission instead found that rebels were often not present at the scene of these attacks, that civilians had not been afforded an

---

[23] Colombos 1926, pp. 361–362. See *Sudden & Christenson v. United States (The Edna)*, 22 December 1934 (John C. Knox, Arbitrator), available in Morgenstern and Lauterpacht 1942, pp. 578–579.

[24] Report of the International Commission of Inquiry on Darfur, supra n. 6.

[25] Ibid., paras 273–418.

[26] Ibid.

[27] Ibid.

[28] Ibid., paras 291–296.

[29] Ibid., para 271.

[30] Ibid., paras 277, 283, 331.

[31] Ibid., paras 628, 638.

opportunity to flee or be shielded from attack, and that military force had been grossly disproportionate to any exigent threat of rebel aggression.[32]

16.2.2.2 ...in the Absence of Genocide

Genocide is central to the current chapter's analysis in part because it is a broad concept that can occur both in times of war and peace, and which may create both individual and State criminal liability.[33] In the context of the non-international armed conflict in Darfur, the Commission found plausible evidence that government forces and militias within their control had killed and committed acts likely to destroy multitudes of people.[34] Moreover, in addition to this element of *actus reus*, the Commission found that these entities had targeted protected groups for their criminal acts.[35]

However, the Commission did not find the presence of genocidal intent on the part of central government authorities.[36] Rather, it found that established policies of attacking and displacing members of particular tribes did not sufficiently demonstrate a *dolus specialis* to exterminate a protected group.[37] Interestingly, and as opposed to its evaluation of crimes against humanity and war crimes, the Commission found some application for the government's counter-insurgency argument when considering the allegation of genocide, concluding that the State's goal of driving victims from their villages implied that there had been no specific intent to annihilate them.[38]

Despite its finding of an absence of genocidal policy on the part of the government of the Sudan, the Commission left open the possibility that individuals—including officials within the State government—might have committed atrocities with genocidal intent.[39] The Commission pointedly left this possibility to the ad hoc analysis of courts and tribunals competent to evaluate questions of individual criminal responsibility, such as the ICC.[40]

---

[32] Ibid., para 267.

[33] On this point, the Darfur Commission noted the assertion by the Appeals Chamber of the International Criminal Tribunal for Rwanda that "genocide is not a crime that can only be committed by certain categories of persons. As evidenced by history, it is a crime which has been committed by the low-level executioner and the high-level planner or instigator alike." *Kayishema and Ruzindana*, ICTR Appeals Chamber, ICTR-95-1-A (1 June 2001), at para 170.

[34] Report of the International Commission of Inquiry on Darfur, supra n. 6, paras 507–522.

[35] Ibid.

[36] Ibid., paras 513–517.

[37] Ibid.

[38] Ibid., para 518.

[39] Ibid., paras 520–521. For an overview of this general issue, see Dupuy 2002.

[40] Report of the International Commission of Inquiry on Darfur, supra n. 6, paras 520–521. For scholarship that matches the Commission's State-centric perspective, see Pellet 1999, pp. 425, 428.

While the present chapter critiques the effects of the Darfur Commission's refusal to more fully embrace a judicial function, the fact that it lacked authority to summon and adjudge individual defendants in criminal trials may reflect a broader issue for UN responses to allegations of genocide. Passing the question of individual criminal responsibility to bodies such as the ICC may suggest an inherent structural weakness in quasi-judicial bodies vis-à-vis their conventional judicial counterparts. Therefore, despite the Commission's stated mandate "to identify the perpetrators of such violations,"[41] one may fairly wonder whether the UN Security Council's establishment of a commission of inquiry or other quasi-judicial body is, in fact, an appropriate response to an escalating humanitarian crisis. Given the comparable investigative powers of the ICC and a number of ad hoc criminal tribunals, it may be worth considering whether a more direct path to publicizing and processing individual accountability would better serve to halt atrocities in progress. The effectiveness of such international prosecutorial bodies is especially vital in the absence of any clearly established legal justification for authorizing military intervention into the territory of another State in order to stop violations of humanitarian law.[42]

16.3 Method of Modern Hate: Appraising the Genocide Conclusion *in Vacuo*

16.3.1 Sizing Up the Target

A primary concern in analyzing the Darfur Commission's conclusions on genocide is its characterization of the absence of genocidal intent. Neither Article II of the 1948 Genocide Convention, nor its *travaux preparatoires*, are particularly helpful in clarifying the meaning of such intent[43]—a perhaps unsurprising revelation, given that the Convention was drafted in the postwar shadow of the Nazi Holocaust, a paradigm of clarity in terms of genocidal intent. Article II of the Convention states:

> In the present Convention, genocide means any of the following acts committed with intent to destroy, in whole or in part, a national, ethnical, racial or religious group, as such:

---

[41] Report of the International Commission of Inquiry on Darfur, supra n. 6, para 2.

[42] See Murphy 2009, p. 23 ("[T]here exists considerable confusion and disagreement about the contemporary parameters of the *jus ad bellum*; if you were to ask a random group of legal advisors to foreign ministries their views on whether, for example, humanitarian intervention [...is] permissible under the *jus ad bellum*, you are likely to receive varied answers: some saying yes; some saying no; some insisting that it depends on the circumstances; and some refusing to respond to the question.").

[43] *Travaux preparatoires* available as U.N. GAOR C.6, 75th meeting, A/633, pp. 115–116 (1948). See discussion in Leblanc 1988.

(a) Killing members of the group;
(b) Causing serious bodily or mental harm to members of the group;
(c) Deliberately inflicting on the group conditions of life calculated to bring about its physical destruction in whole or in part;
(d) Imposing measures intended to prevent births within the group;
(e) Forcibly transferring children of the group to another group.[44]

The International Law Commission (ILC), in the Commentary to its 1996 Draft Code of Crimes against the Peace and Security of Mankind (hereinafter, the 'Draft Code of Crimes'), articulated "members of a tribal group" to be an objectively sufficient target of intent to destroy under this legal instrument.[45] Yet when dealing with the Convention's more rigid quartet of 'group' characteristics listed above, the Darfur Commission progressed to a subjective view of the protected group criterion,[46] citing International Criminal Tribunal for Rwanda (ICTR) and ICTY case law and States' conduct to conclude that an expansive interpretation of the protected group element—one which permits the inclusion of tribal peoples based on their self-perception and the perception of their attackers—had seeped into the body of international customary law.[47] This was particularly useful in supplementing the Commission's analysis of the victims in Darfur, who spoke the same Arabic as their assailants, shared the same Muslim faith as their assailants, and frequently intermarried with members of their assailants' lineage.[48]

Given this purported lack of objective distinctions between the attackers and their victims, the Commission found sufficient 'otherness' between these persons by relying upon: popular epithets hurled by the attackers as they invaded communities;[49] the common connotation that the umbrella term *Janjaweed* held for interviewed victims[50]; and a media-fueled perception of the Sudan's Arab–African divide as analogous to divergent sympathies for the government and rebels, causing those at the heart of the conflict in Darfur to self-identify as belonging to either one group or the other.[51] Notably, after the Commission's Report was used as the fact-finding basis for the ICC Prosecutor's charges against incumbent Sudanese President Omar Al-Bashir,[52] the President publicly derided the charges as follows: "Whoever has visited Darfur, met officials and discovered their

---

[44] Convention on the Prevention and Punishment of the Crime of Genocide (Paris, 9 December 1948), Article II.

[45] International Law Commission Draft Code of Crimes against the Peace and Security of Mankind with Commentaries (1996), Article 17, Comment (9).

[46] Report of the International Commission of Inquiry on Darfur, supra n. 6, paras 509–512.

[47] Ibid., paras 498–501.

[48] Ibid., para 508.

[49] Ibid., para 511.

[50] Ibid.

[51] Ibid., para 510.

[52] The Court's first warrant of arrest against President Al-Bashir was issued in March 2009. *Prosecutor v. Omar Hassan Ahmad Al Bashir*, ICC Pre-Trial Chamber I, Warrant of Arrest for Omar Hassan Ahmad Al Bashir, ICC-02/05-01/09-1 (4 March 2009).

ethnicities and tribes [...] will know that all of these things are lies."[53] This statement can be readily interpreted as an objectivist theory of the 'protected group' element, since in the absence of any fundamental difference between assailants and victims under the objective criteria of Article II of the Genocide Convention, there can be no finding of genocide. However, if this statement had been intended to dissuade further ICC actions by pleading in the court of public opinion, it did not entirely succeed: the following year, the ICC amended its indictment of President Al-Bashir to include charges of genocide,[54] a significant departure from the conclusion reached by the Commission in its Report.

Beyond the notion of a 'protected group', however, the Commission has attracted perhaps its greatest share of attention for its interpretation of Article II's more cryptic phrase, "in whole or in part".[55] The ILC's Commentary to its Draft Code of Crimes states that it is "not necessary to intend to achieve the complete annihilation of a group from every corner of the globe."[56] In a similar sense, the Darfur Commission noted approvingly a geographical interpretation of "in part" advanced by Professor William Schabas, who stated that the Turkish government, the Nazis and the Rwandan extremists all committed genocide despite, of course, limiting their respective destruction of Armenians, Jews and Tutsi to the territory that their forces controlled.[57] However, in its analysis of protected groups "in whole", the Darfur Commission rejected the same scholar's classification of tribes as distinct protected groups within the meaning of Article II of the Genocide Convention.[58]

In this light, the pertinent question is whether the Commission properly identified the relevant 'part' and 'whole' in its analysis of genocide in Darfur. The Commission recounted one telling example of its reasoning in this respect, stating:

> [A]fter occupying the villages the Government Commissioner and the leader of the Arab militias that had participated in the attack and burning, gathered all those who had not managed to escape into a large area. Using a microphone they selected 15 persons (whose name they read from a written list), as well as 7 *omdas*, and executed them on the spot. They then sent all elderly men, all boys, many men and all women to a nearby village, where they held them for some time, whereas they executed 205 young villagers, who they

[53] E. Thomasson, 'ICC prosecutor seeks arrest of Sudan's Bashir', Reuters, 14 July 2008. Electronic version available at: http://www.reuters.com/article/2008/07/14/us-warcrimes-sudan-idUSL1417202620080714.

[54] The Court's second warrant of arrest was issued in July 2010. *Al Bashir*, supra n. 52, Second Warrant of Arrest for Omar Hassan Ahmad Al Bashir, ICC-02/05-01/09-95 (12 July 2010).

[55] Genocide Convention, supra n. 44., Article II.

[56] ILC Draft Code of Crimes, supra n. 45, Article 17, Comment (8). See also *Prosecutor v. Jelisić*, ICTY Trial Chamber, Judgment (14 December 1999), para 80; *Prosecutor v. Krstić*, ICTY Trial Chamber, Judgment (2 August 2001), para 584.

[57] Report of the International Commission of Inquiry on Darfur, supra n. 6, para 492.

[58] Ibid., para 496. According to Prof. Schabas, "[i]t is not difficult to understand why tribal groups fit within the four corners of the domain, whereas political and gender groups do not". The Darfur Commission dismissed this proposition as legally baseless. Schabas 2000, p. 112.

> asserted were rebels (*Torabora*). According to male witnesses interviewed by the Commission and who were among the survivors, about 800 persons were not killed….[59]

On these grounds, the Commission concluded that the perpetrators lacked the intent to commit genocide, as the systematic murders were limited to men considered as rebels, while the displacement of local populations had been intended to prevent rebels from hiding in the villages.[60] In other words, the Commission interpreted the 'whole' protected group as all 'African' Darfurians, while it discerned the relevant 'part' to be those military-aged male 'African' Darfurians who had been deliberately killed during village raids.

16.3.2 Gauging Intent

In addition to illustrating the above said point that the proportional scope of 'part/whole' analysis can lead to a finding of insufficient "intent to destroy" under Article II of the Genocide Convention,[61] the Commission highlighted a more direct issue at stake: the logically porous relationship between 'intent' and 'motive' in this context. As noted earlier, the Commission found that the State conducted itself with the purpose of driving victims from their villages.[62] In the eyes of the Commission, this precluded any finding of a *dolus specialis* to annihilate 'African' Darfurians.

The Commission was careful to distinguish this analysis of 'intent' from any consideration of 'motive', stating that "special intent must not be confused with motive, namely the particular reason that may induce a person to engage in criminal conduct […]. From the viewpoint of criminal law, what matters is not the motive, but rather whether or not there exists the requisite special intent to destroy a group."[63] The coherence of this distinction will be further discussed, infra, via comparison to the fact-finding work of courts and tribunals.

16.3.3 Whose Hand on the Trigger?

Although its mandate from the Secretary-General instructed it to determine culpability for crimes against humanitarian law and human rights law, it is doubly striking that the Darfur Commission took the step of exculpating State responsibility on the part of the Sudan for the crime of genocide. First, the Commission did

[59] Report of the International Commission of Inquiry on Darfur, supra n. 6, para 513.

[60] Ibid., para 514.

[61] Genocide Convention, op. cit., Article II.

[62] Report of the International Commission of Inquiry on Darfur, supra n. 6, para 514.

[63] Ibid., para 493.

so after concluding that no genocide had, in fact, occurred.[64] Second—and more germane to this commentary—the Commission exonerated the State while acknowledging that government officials in the Darfur saga may have possessed genocidal intent.[65] This point is notable for not only its implication that an international court or tribunal might subsequently find sufficient evidence of genocide, as has indeed been the case,[66] but also its implication that high-ranking government officials may possess and implement genocidal intent without incurring or evidencing the international criminal responsibility of the State. This latter aspect of the Commission's analysis merits further exposition.[67]

The major issue of attribution for genocide in the Sudan was the nature of the relationship between the State and the various actors attacking villages in Darfur, meaning not simply the Sudanese armed forces, but also the *Janjaweed* and other non-State entities such as the Popular Defence Forces (PDF) and various regional militias.[68] On the basis of its investigation, the Commission clarified that "[t]he 'Janjaweed' to whom most victims refer in the current conflict are Arab militias that raid the villages of those victims [and] frequently operate with, or are supported by, the Government, as [demonstrated by, *inter alia*,] the recruitment, arming and training of militias by the Government."[69]

In light of this, the Commission determined that the *Janjaweed* served as a *de facto* organ of the State, since "[w]hen militias attack jointly with the armed forces [...] they act under the effective control of the Government, consistently with the notion of control set out in 1999 in *Tadić (Appeal)* [...]."[70] The Commission's reference to 'effective control' is perhaps misleading, as it suggests a very high threshold for State attribution under the eponymous test advanced by the ICJ in *Nicaragua v. United States*[71] and subsequently affirmed by the Court in its more substantively pertinent 2007 judgment in *Bosnia and Herzegovina v. Serbia and*

---

[64] Ibid., para 518.

[65] Ibid., paras 529–521.

[66] For an updated list of indictments, see 'Situation in Darfur, Sudan', ICC website, available at: http://www.icc-cpi.int/EN_Menus/ICC/Situations%20and%20Cases/Situations/Situation%20ICC%200205/Pages/situation%20icc-0205.aspx.

[67] The very notion of customarily applying international legal norms to purely internal State acts may itself prove a point of contention for scholars, some of whom characterize the approach of courts and tribunals in this area as "somewhat creative [...] and not easy to justify." Greenwood 2006, p. 808. For further exploration of this general issue, see Yihdego 2009, pp. 37, 39–45. In terms of the Darfur crisis and the Genocide Convention, the question of customary law is removed, as the Sudan acceded to the Convention in October 2003.

[68] The Sudanese government diverted State budgetary funds to tribal leaders with the understanding that this money would pay PDF members' salaries. Report of the International Commission of Inquiry on Darfur, supra n. 6, para 68.

[69] Ibid., para 121.

[70] Ibid., para 123, citing *Prosecutor v. ICTY* Appeals Chamber, Judgment (15 July 1999), paras 98–145.

[71] *Military and Paramilitary Activities in and against Nicaragua (Nicaragua v. United States of America)*, Merits, Judgment, I.C.J. Reports 1986, p. 14, para 115.

Montenegro.[72] Instead, the Commission's clear analogy to the methodology of the ICTY in the *Tadić* case indicates that the Commission is, in fact, embracing the lower threshold for State attribution known under the 'overall control' test promulgated by that Tribunal.[73]

In contrast to its finding as to the status of the *Janjaweed*, the Commission found that the PDF existed as a *de jure* organ of the State, as it had an official "legislative basis under Sudanese law" for fighting alongside the regular armed forces during the conflict in Darfur.[74] By this logic, the Commission also surmised that any militias integrated into and uniformed by the PDF would necessarily absorb the status of *de jure* organs of the State as well.[75]

In this light, the Commission made a superfluous determination when it stated that certain militia attacks had been undertaken with the acquiescence of State officials.[76] Such proof by omission should be unnecessary because these mercenaries had already been outfitted and inculcated by the PDF and had performed joint operations in Darfur with the formal Sudanese military. By the Commission's own reasoning, these arrangements actively promoted those militia units to *de jure* organs of the State. There is thus no need to assess mere acquiescence.

Of course, the Commission also had recourse to public statements made by cabinet Ministers of the Sudan (some of whom have since been indicted for war crimes by the ICC) and President al-Bashir (who, as discussed earlier, has additionally been indicted for genocide).[77] These statements varied over time from appearing to affirm coordination in Darfur between the government and non-State actors to relative ambiguity on the subject.[78] In this context, the Commission's 'uniform' criterion for evaluating *de jure* organs of the State appears to be quite straightforward.[79]

---

[72] *Application of the Convention on the Prevention and Punishment of the Crime of Genocide (Bosnia and Herzegovina v. Serbia and Montenegro)*, Judgment, I.C.J. Reports 2007, p. 43.

[73] *Tadić*, op. cit., paras 116–145.

[74] Report of the International Commission of Inquiry on Darfur, supra n. 6, para 108.

[75] Ibid., para 124.

[76] Ibid., para 364.

[77] See 'The Prosecutor v. Omar Hassan Ahmad Al Bashir', ICC website, available at: http://www.icc-cpi.int/en_menus/icc/situations%20and%20cases/situations/situation%20icc%200205/related%20cases/icc02050109/Pages/icc02050109.aspx.

[78] For example, while the Minister of Defense stated during a January 2004 press conference that that the *Janjaweed* were "gangs of armed bandits" (and the PDF a contingent of volunteers), President al-Bashir during the prior month had publicly stated "[w]e will use the army, the police, the mujahedeen, the horsemen to get rid of the rebellion." Report of the International Commission of Inquiry on Darfur, supra n. 6, paras 118–119.

[79] The Commission's streamlining of the *de jure* question is also apparent in light of issues of State attribution arising in recent world events (see N. Shachtman, 'Intercepted Calls Prove Syrian Army Used Nerve Gas, U.S. Spies Say', Foreign Policy, 27 August 2013, available at: http://thecable.foreignpolicy.com/posts/2013/08/27/exclusive_us_spies_say_intercepted_calls_prove_syrias_army_used_nerve_gas (urgently attempting to determine government responsibility for the use of chemical weapons, and tentatively concluding that "[i]t's unclear where control

16.3.4 Tracing the Lines Between Crimes

The Commission took pains to both preface and conclude its findings on genocide with a refutation of the ICTR's hierarchical notion of genocide, described in both *Kambanda* and *Serushago* as "the crime of crimes".[80] Rather, the Darfur Commission stated categorically that other offenses falling under the label 'crimes against humanity' and requiring elements of proof distinct from genocide may be nonetheless similar to it in gravity and stigma.[81]

How, then, has the Commission distinguished between genocide and crimes against humanity? The latter term has been in use since the extermination of Armenians in 1915, and was subsequently a commonplace label for the conduct of authorities in the Nazi regime.[82] The fact that both of these events have since been labeled genocides, however, is revealing. Following codification in the Genocide Convention, the crime of genocide stood in contrast to the fluid status of crimes against humanity at customary law, a dynamic that would not change until 50 years later, when the ICC's Rome Statute (and the crimes against humanity incorporated therein) entered into force.[83] Further diminishing their prominence, scholars have considered crimes against humanity to be limited exclusively to wartime, whereas genocide may occur at any time.[84]

The Darfur Commission, however, rejected this particular categorization. The Report distinguished crimes against humanity from the tertiary category of 'war crimes' on this basis, stating that crimes against humanity may occur "either in time of peace or of armed conflict."[85] Interestingly, the Commission also discriminated between these two categories based on the level of coordination each requires. According to the Commission, war crimes cannot rise to the level of crimes against humanity unless they are systematic or "widespread", which—unlike its findings concerning genocide—does not require "the existence of a policy or plan".[86]

Often discussed in separate terms from the aforementioned crimes is 'ethnic cleansing.' In his Separate Opinion in the case of *Bosnia and Herzegovina v.*

(Footnote 79 continued)
lies")), as well as issues of individual attribution arising in recent jurisprudence (see K. Roth, 'A Tribunal's Legal Stumble', New York Times, 9 July 2013, available at: http://www.nytimes.com/2013/07/10/opinion/global/a-tribunals-legal-stumble.html (critiquing the ICTY under Prof. Theodor Meron for developing a 'specific direction' element for aiding-and-abetting liability in the 2013 Appeals Chamber acquittal of Momčilo Perišić)).

[80] *Prosecutor v. Kambanda*, ICTR Judgment, ICTR 97-23-S (4 September 1998), para 16; *Prosecutor v. Serushago*, ICTR Sentence, ICTR-98-39 (5 February 1999), para 15.

[81] Report of the International Commission of Inquiry on Darfur, supra n. 6, para 506.

[82] UN War Crimes Commission 1948, p. 35.

[83] Rome Statute, supra n. 17, Article VII.

[84] See, eg, Schabas 2006, pp. 1703, 1719–1720.

[85] Report of the International Commission of Inquiry on Darfur, supra n. 6, para 178.

[86] Report of the International Commission of Inquiry on Darfur, supra n. 6, para 179.

Serbia and Montenegro,[87] Judge ad hoc Elihu Lauterpacht succinctly described this particular crime as "the forced migration of civilians,"[88] and posited that the Genocide Convention empowered the Court to address it through provisional measures.[89] The Darfur Commission, however, adopted a different interpretation of ethnic cleansing. The Commission did not find any grounds in the Genocide Convention for addressing this practice, citing instead a legal opinion by the Canadian Department of Foreign Affairs concerning the plight of Kosovar Albanians.[90] The Commission agreed with the Canadian ministry that the drafters of the Genocide Convention had expressly excluded ethnic cleansing from its purview because forcible expulsion was fundamentally different from the "intent to destroy" in Article II of the Convention.[91] Moreover, the Commission did not classify ethnic cleansing as a categorically separate crime from genocide and crimes against humanity. Rather, its Report explicitly filed "deportation or forcible transfer of population" under the umbrella term 'crimes against humanity',[92] in a manner similar to provisions of the Rome Statute.[93]

Regarding the variable divisions between the aforementioned crimes, it should be noted that the UN General Assembly's adoption in September 2005 of the World Summit Outcome Document endorsed a less semantic, non-treaty-based standard of protection that attempts to assimilate the various criminal labels associated with humanitarian crises.[94] The text advances a broad obligation of each State "to protect its populations from genocide, war crimes, ethnic cleansing and crimes against humanity,"[95] which—presuming a criminal court or tribunal were to consider such an obligation customarily binding—would also promote a new judicial tool for securing the livelihood and continued existence of threatened peoples. This is because it transforms third-party analysis from 'did the State perpetrate the crime' to 'did the State fail to take adequate steps to prevent the perpetration of the crime'.

This latter approach appears to be critically distinct from the Commission's existing findings concerning 'command responsibility', as it does not establish any formal State connection with the perpetrators of these crimes[96] Nor does it establish any State superiority over them. Rather, the important element is whether

[87] *Bosnia and Herzegovina v. Serbia and Montenegro*, Provisional Measures, Order of 13 September 1993, I.C.J. Reports 1993, p. 325, Separate Opinion of Judge ad hoc Lauterpacht.

[88] Ibid., para 69.

[89] Ibid., para 123(A)(ii).

[90] Report of the International Commission of Inquiry on Darfur, supra n. 6, para 504.

[91] Ibid.

[92] Ibid., para 178.

[93] Rome Statute, supra n. 17, Article 7. For an analysis of the gap between genocide and ethnic cleansing in the wake of the Commission's Report, see Schabas 2005, pp. 871, 874–877.

[94] 2005 World Summit Outcome Document, UNGA 60th session, A/RES/60/1 (24 October 2005).

[95] Ibid., para 138.

[96] Report of the International Commission of Inquiry on Darfur, supra n. 6, paras 558–564.

the State, as an act of omission, failed to protect the life and dignity of its "populations," namely the distinct peoples within its borders, from the assailants. This may also be viewed as an improvement upon the ambiguity of the Genocide Convention's prohibition against "complicity in genocide," both in terms of clarification and scope of application beyond genocide.[97] Furthermore, if a third-party body concludes that the obligation to protect has been breached, this approach would well-serve the humanitarian legal order by eschewing the kind of complex attribution issues with which the Darfur Commission wrestled in its analysis of State responsibility for genocide.[98]

16.4 Discerning the Judicial Function: Analogies to Courts and Tribunals

16.4.1 Sizing Up the Target

To assess the Commission's treatment of the protected group element of genocide, comparison should be drawn to instances such as *Krstić*, wherein the Trial Chamber of the ICTY noted that "while '[t]he [Bosnian Serb Army, or 'VRS'] may have initially considered only targeting military men for execution'", a decision was taken "to capture and kill all the Bosnian Muslim men indiscriminately. No effort was made to distinguish the soldiers from the civilians."[99] One may infer from this that if the VRS had just killed Bosnian Muslim men of military age—rather than Bosnian Muslims indiscriminately—the Tribunal may have found a lack of specific genocidal intent. Subsequently, the Appeals Chamber in the same case raised a basic but important point about these gender classifications, stating that the annihilation of so many males would "inevitably result in the physical disappearance of the Bosnian Muslim population at Srebrenica."[100]

In its judgment in *Bosnia and Herzegovina v. Serbia and Montenegro*, the ICJ staked out a geographical approach, stating that a crime "may be found to have been committed where the intent is to destroy the group within a geographically limited area."[101] Yet the Court's clearest statement on the issue in this case was proportional in nature, noting that "since the object and purpose of the Convention

---

97 Genocide Convention, supra n. 46, Article III(e).

98 Report of the International Commission of Inquiry on Darfur, supra n. 6, paras 77–141.

99 *Krstić*, ICTY Trial Chamber, supra n. 56, para 547. See discussion in *Bosnia and Herzegovina v. Serbia and Montenegro*, Judgment, supra n. 72, para 292.

100 *Prosecutor v. Krstić*, ICTY Appeals Chamber, Judgment, IT-98-33-A, para 28 (citing *Krstić*, ICTY Trial Chamber, supra n. 56, para 595).

101 Genocide Convention, supra n. 46, para 199. See also ILC Draft Code of Crimes, supra n. 45, Article 17, Comment (9).

as a whole is to prevent the intentional destruction of groups, *the part targeted must be significant enough to have an impact on the group as a whole.*"[102]

Without the ratio aspect, little benefit may be derived from numeric quantifiers, such as the standard drawn by the ICTR in *Kayishema and Ruzindana*, stating that there must be "a considerable number" of victims to meet the threshold for genocide.[103] While the ICTY in *Jelisić* offered proportional criteria in the form of "a substantial part", it is also ambiguously qualified as *not* a "very important part."[104] This sort of complication could be seen as risking what the ICTY Trial Chamber in *Stakić* characterized as a narrow interpretative approach that could deflate the practical legal effect of humanitarian norms.[105]

With respect to the case at hand, it is certainly arguable—as some commentators believe[106]—that the 'in whole or in part' criterion was misapplied. Some have raised the issue that the relevant 'whole' is the portion of 'African' Darfurians trapped by assailants (generally speaking, military-aged males).[107] This would certainly make it easier to prove that a significant part of that whole had been intentionally killed.

Yet this criticism of the Commission's approach to the question of 'in whole or in part' is perhaps misplaced. The purpose of the Genocide Convention is to protect defined groups of peoples. They have been objectively defined by the drafters, and have been subjectively defined by some of the judges and scholars who have studied the Convention in practice, including the Darfur Commission.[108] But while the notion of 'whole' must be limited to only those members of a group that live within a State's territorial boundaries,[109] the notion that a 'whole' should be further limited to those areas within the State's territory that the assailants choose to or are able to attack threatens to effectively rob Article II of its original aims.

---

[102] *Krstić*, ICTY Appeals Chamber, supra n. 100, para 8 [emphasis added].

[103] *Prosecutor v. Kayishema and Ruzindana*, ICTR Trial Chamber II, Judgment, ICTR-95-1-T (21 May 1999), para 97.

[104] *Prosecutor v. Jelisić*, ICTY Trial Chamber, Judgment, IT-95-10-T (19 October 1999). See also *Prosecutor v. Bagilishema*, ICTR Trial Chamber I, ICTR-95-1A-T (7 June 2001), paras 56–59.

[105] *Prosecutor v. Stakić*, ICTY Trial Chamber II, Judgment, IT-97-24-T (31 July 2003).

[106] For a discussion that praises the Commission's analysis of protected group status as "sterling" while asserting that objective criteria were sufficient to achieve that status, see Abass 2008, pp. 871, 882.

[107] See UN Economic & Social Council, Sub-Committee on Prevention of Discrimination & Protection of Minorities (B. Whitaker, rapporteur), *Review of Further Developments in the Fields with which the Sub-Commission has been Concerned: Revised and Updated Report on the Question of the Prevention and Punishment of the Crime of Genocide*, E/CN.4/Sub.2/1985/6 (2 July 1985), para 29. The Whitaker Report herein espouses the proportionality criterion in conjunction with a consideration of sheer volume.

[108] Report of the International Commission of Inquiry on Darfur, supra n. 6, paras 509–512.

[109] See Schabas 2000, p. 235.

A related issue concerning the Commission's approach to the part/whole criterion is the aforementioned 'subjective' approach, based on self-identification among victims, and a common, reciprocal identification of 'otherness' between the victims and their attackers. In *Akayesu*, the Trial Chamber of the ICTR stated that the attackers and victims were so similar that it was impracticable to discern between them.[110] Yet the Tribunal held that the tribes were in fact sufficiently distinct because their common colonial overlords from Belgium had created an identification card system to distinguish between them.[111]

From a methodological perspective, the question arises as to whether the judge reviewing this material considers it a subjective analysis, or else utilizes the self-identification of witnesses as evidence of an objective distinction. The Chamber in *Akayesu* appears to fall into the latter camp, stating that any group qualifying for protection under the Genocide Convention must be not only "stable", but also "constituted in a permanent membership of which is determined by birth."[112] This interpretation is commendable for utilizing subjective methodology *only* to the minimum extent necessary to satisfy the principle of *res magis valeat quam pereat* at international law, which the Darfur Commission explicitly embraced in its Report.[113]

Indeed, the Chamber in *Akayesu* formulated that a group should be evaluated by congenital commonalities—perhaps requiring an expansive contemporary interpretation of Article II of the Genocide Convention, but not deviating from the objective character of its example—and only supplemented with subjective self-identification if there do not exist any objective factors more compelling than stability and permanence.[114] This approach aligns fairly well with the treaty interpretation rules proscribed in the Vienna Convention on the Law of Treaties, which insists upon utilizing the objective meaning of the Genocide Convention unless it would lead to a manifestly unreasonable outcome, at which point more novel interpretative tools may be introduced.[115] While not spelled out as clearly in this respect, the methodology of the Report of the Darfur Commission can be analogously interpreted: Just as Rwandan witnesses' self-identification as Hutu or Tutsi allowed the ICTR to overcome Article II's inchoate application to complex but objective tribal distinctions,[116] the ethnic self-identification as 'African' or

---

110 *Prosecutor v. Akayesu*, ICTR Trial Chamber I, Judgment, ICTR-96-4-T (2 September 1998).

111 Electronic images of these identity cards are available at: http://trim.unictr.org/webdrawer/rec/2116/view/Akayesu%20-%20Identity%20Card.PDF.

112 *Akayesu*, supra n. 110, para 511.

113 Report of the International Commission of Inquiry on Darfur, supra n. 6, para 494.

114 *Akayesu*, supra n. 110, paras 702, 712.

115 Vienna Convention on the Law of Treaties (Vienna, 23 May 1969), Article 32(b).

116 The Tribunal noted that "a common criterion in the four types of groups protected by the Genocide Convention is that membership in such groups would seem to be normally not challengeable by its members," and that "it is particularly important to respect the intention of the drafters of the Genocide Convention, which according to the *travaux preparatoires*, was patently to ensure the protection of any stable and permanent group." *Akayesu*, supra n. 110,

'Arab' by witnesses interviewed by the Darfur Commission supplemented existing objective distinctions in both lineage and sedentariness between these groups.[117]

From a narrow methodological point of view, the principle of *res magis valeat quam pereat* may seem to be well served by embracing a subjective test for "in whole or in part" without any of the restraints advanced by the Chamber in *Akayesu*.[118] It is, after all, true that employing a subjective analysis is likely to increase the number of 'groups' recognized as protected. However, introducing a subjective analysis may result in greater difficulty when trying to determine what constitutes a sufficient 'part' of that group under Article II of the Genocide Convention. In tribal instances, where the objective analysis is arguably sufficient to qualify a group as protected under Article II, it may be doing victims a disservice to unnecessarily rely upon identification-based subjective criteria. The twofold—and somewhat paradoxical—issue with superfluously applying the subjective test is illustrated by the Darfur Commission's equation between identification as 'Arab' and 'African' and identification as 'pro-government' and 'pro-rebel'.[119]

On the one hand, these are fluid concepts that may easily evolve as a violent conflict escalates, resulting in a group that self-identifies as a domestic resistance front in a civil war, but which has no other discernible characteristic to unite them as an internationally protected people. On the other hand, and for the same reason, it may become more difficult to state definitively that government forces intend to destroy a significant 'part' of this expanding 'whole'.

In summation, the subjective test does not limit itself to the establishment of a protected group, and the criticisms which it may invite are not limited to the conceptual—it bears concrete, methodological consequences both for evaluating parts of that group and for proving intent to destroy.

Before transitioning from our comparative analysis of 'in whole or in part' to a discussion of genocidal intent, it is worth recalling at this juncture the ICJ's proportionality requirement in its judgment in *Bosnia and Herzegovina v. Serbia and Montenegro*, finding that the targeted 'part' "be significant enough to have an impact on the group as a whole."[120] Inarguably, the significance to a group of destroying a set number of its people is far greater when those killings are highly gender-imbalanced. This is because a very skewed gender balance will dramatically decrease the diversity of the gene pool for future procreation within the tribe, as implied by the above said statements of the ICTY Appeals Chamber in

(Footnote 116 continued)
paras 511, 516. On the notion of a "national group" in particular, the Tribunal defined this as a "collection of people who are perceived to share a legal bond based on common citizenship." Ibid., para 512, citing *Nottebohm Case (second phase)*, Judgment of April 6th, 1955, p. 4.

117 Report of the International Commission of Inquiry on Darfur, supra n. 6, para 508.

118 *Akayesu*, supra n. 110.

119 Report of the International Commission of Inquiry on Darfur, supra n. 6, para 510.

120 *Bosnia and Herzegovina v. Serbia and Montenegro*, Judgment, supra n. 72, para 198.

Krstić.[121] In Darfur, when assailants systematically executed men of military age, they were at the same time destroying men of prime procreative age. Notably, the relatively low life expectancy for black Darfurians further consolidates the overlap between these two Venn diagram sets, closer to the point of eclipse.[122]

16.4.2 Gauging Intent

In terms of evidencing intent to destroy through aggregate acts, the ICTY Trial Chamber in the *Blagojević* case found *dolus specialis* even though video footage demonstrated that assailants in Srebrenica had not annihilated entire villages. This is because the Chamber found that all of the assailants' acts "constituted a single operation" that had been intended, in the aggregate, to annihilate the group as a whole: "Bosnian Serb forces not only knew that the combination of the killings of men with the forcible transfer of women, children and elderly, would inevitably result in the physical disappearances of the Bosnian Muslim population of Srebrenica, but clearly intended through these acts to physically destroy this group."[123]

In addition to aggregated acts, courts and tribunals may take into account circumstantial evidence to conclude that assailants possessed genocidal intent. In *Jelisić*, the ICTY Appeals Chamber stated: "As to proof of specific intent, it may, in the absence of direct explicit evidence, be inferred from [...] general context, the perpetration of other culpable acts systematically directed against the same group, the scale of atrocities committed, the systematic targeting of victims on account of their membership of a particular group, or the repetition of destructive and discriminatory acts."[124]

In its Report, the Darfur Commission characterized repeatedly that many attacks by government forces and the *Janjaweed* were carried out in an "indiscriminate" fashion.[125] This label is difficult to reconcile with what the Commission considered to be exculpatory evidence that the State had pursued counter-insurgency measures,

---

[121] *Krstić*, ICTY Appeals Chamber, supra n. 100, para 28 (citing *Krstić*, ICTY Trial Chamber, supra n. 56, para 595).

[122] Life expectancy in Sudan currently ranks 185th among countries, and is undoubtedly worse within Darfur as its humanitarian crisis continues. Notably, the lowest average life expectancy currently exists in Chad, which has absorbed the greatest share of Darfurian refugees as a result of the crisis. US Central Intelligence Agency, *The World Factbook* (2013). Electronic version available at: https://www.cia.gov/library/publications/the-world-factbook/rankorder/2102rank.html?countryName=Sudan&countryCode=su&regionCode=afr&rank=185#su.

[123] *Prosecutor v. Blagojević*, ICTY Trial Chamber, Judgment, IT-02-60-T (17 January 2005), para 677.

[124] *Prosecutor v. Jelisić*, ICTY Appeals Chamber, Judgment, IT-95-10-A (5 July 2001), para 47.

[125] Report of the International Commission of Inquiry on Darfur, supra n. 6, paras 238–268.

not an intentional plan of genocide.[126] It also conflicts with evidence that the assailants conducted executions after reading names from a predetermined list,[127] as well as evidence that assailants left alone those villages with mixed Arab and African populations. Moreover, the notion of 'indiscriminate' attacks is perhaps just as problematic for the central issue of *specific* intent to destroy a protected group. Truly 'indiscriminate' killings would not suffice for specific genocidal intent, because there would need to first be an act of perception and discrimination between 'Arab' and 'African' villages and peoples before acting upon any specific intent to destroy a protected group. This distinction might not have been so easily drawn because, as the Commission noted, differences between tribal groups may not be readily apparent.[128]

The scope of destruction ancillary to the Sudan's stated goal of stamping out the insurrection is further suggested by the context of *Bosnia and Herzegovina v. Serbia and Montenegro*, in which the ICJ noted that "an essential motive of much of the Bosnian Serb leadership—to create a larger Serb State, by a war of conquest if necessary—did not necessarily require the destruction of the Bosnian Muslims and other communities, but their expulsion."[129] The Darfur Commission would have done well to develop similar reasoning, as it properly suggests that counter-insurgency motives do not foreclose the possibility of genocidal intent. This distinction between specific intent and motive surfaced as well before the ICTY, which in *Tadić* stated that there is no motive-based element in international criminal law.[130] While the Appeals Chamber did not grant any legal weight to the Prosecutor's argument that proving a subjective negative such as this would be evidentiarily "onerous,"[131] it did capture the senselessness of such a requirement through a *reductio ad absurdum* concerning a high-ranking Nazi officer who pleads for acquittal by claiming either that his participation in genocide was based on purely personal hatred, or else that it was based on his purely personal motivation to stay employed.[132]

However, this remains an issue wherein neither the Commission nor the other bodies under discussion have succeeded in quelling voices advocating for a different approach to the question of motive.[133] In contrast to the Commission's approach, some scholars have argued that an analysis of specific intent not only

[126] Ibid., para 518.

[127] Ibid., para 513.

[128] Ibid., para 498.

[129] *Bosnia and Herzegovina v. Serbia and Montenegro*, Judgment, supra n. 72. para 372.

[130] *Tadić*, op. cit., para 248.

[131] Ibid., para 254.

[132] Ibid., para 269.

[133] For an analysis concluding that both the Commission and the ICJ adopted a 'purpose-based' approach to intent that, in fact, does evaluate motives, see Loewenstein and Kostas 2007, 839, 844–845 (notably citing, in support of this approach, Cassese 2002, p. 338.

benefits from but "*must* be coupled with" an analysis of motive when examining allegations of genocide.[134]

16.4.3 Whose Hand on the Trigger?

As emphasized in the *Nuclear Tests* case, the interpretation of government authorities' acts from which state responsibility allegedly derives must be considered in the context of those prospective obligations, not *in vacuo*.[135] Thus the Court in *Bosnia and Herzegovina v. Serbia and Montenegro* refused to treat as an admission a Serbian Minister's televised statement that appeared to acknowledge the mass murders at Srebrenica.[136] Under the circumstances, the Court found it to be a political statement to which no legal weight could be applied, let alone the incurrence of State responsibility for genocide.[137]

Bosnia and Herzegovina v. Serbia and Montenegro is particularly relevant to the Darfur Commission's discussion of State responsibility because it embodies the ICJ's most recent thinking on the subject of genocide in the context of paramilitary implementation. In its Judgment, the Court created the language of whether a State has used paramilitaries as "in fact the instruments of its action,"[138] in order to qualify as a State organ *de jure* under the ILC Articles on State Responsibility.[139] Failing that, the Court reasoned that a State could still accrue responsibility for the acts of an entity that is under the established and "complete dependence" of the State in all of its actions.[140] While the Court appears to have considered these constructs as simply new phrasings of uncodified customary international law, they have not been universally hailed as beacons clarifying the ILC Articles.

It is difficult to see how the Darfur Commission could have reached a different conclusion concerning genocide by simply applying the ICJ's subsequent approach. Both the *Janjaweed* and the paramilitaries in *Bosnia and Herzegovina v. Serbia and Montenegro* were compensated and trained by the State. Yet, the Genocide Convention case involved a single massacre concentrated into a very brief period in Srebrenica, a prominent general at the helm of State military forces during the attacks, and a participating paramilitary group that evidence suggested

---

[134] Shaw 1989, p. 806 [emphasis added]. For further exposition on this divide, see van Haren 2006, pp. 205, 237–243.

[135] *Nuclear Tests (New Zealand v. France)*, Judgment, I.C.J. Reports 1974, p. 457.

[136] *Bosnia and Herzegovina v. Serbia and Montenegro*, Judgment, supra n. 72.

[137] Ibid.

[138] Ibid., para 384.

[139] International Law Commission Articles on Responsibility of States for Internationally Wrongful Acts (UN General Assembly Resolution 56/83 of 12 December 2001), Article 4.

[140] *Bosnia and Herzegovina v Serbia and Montenegro*, Judgment, supra n. 72, para 393.

had grown from within a State ministry.[141] Given the comparatively fragmented nature of the killings at issue before the Darfur Commission, it is unlikely that its application of the "instruments of its action" or "complete dependence" tests for *de jure* organs would have yielded any different results. For the same factual reasons, the fluid dynamics of the killings in Darfur would not likely permit the ICJ to find that they rise to the level of "effective control," in other words to the instruction, direction or control of every ad hoc act at issue, as explained by the Court's discussion in *Nicaragua v. United States*[142] and codified as Article 8 of the ILC Articles on State Responsibility.[143]

Interestingly, while the Commission ultimately took its own path to reject State responsibility for genocide in Darfur, Chairman Antonio Cassese subsequently published on the subject with a substantially different conclusion than that reached by the Commission. Professor Cassese stated:

> [If] the militias act under the overall control of that government [...] the violations of international human rights law and humanitarian law perpetrated by those militias must be attributed to that government—without any need to prove that in each specific instance of violation instructions or directives were issued by Khartoum authorities.[144]

Given that the Commission, as earlier discussed, had declared the Janjaweed as a *de facto* organ under the overall control test employed in *Tadić*,[145] this was a very striking statement from Professor Cassese. Under his logic, the Commission's search for a 'central plan' was moot, because the State automatically incurred liability for the crimes committed by the *Janjaweed* in their capacity as a *de facto* organ of the State. Nor would any additional analysis be needed concerning whether the *Janjaweed*—whom the Commission noted to have committed early morning mass murders side-by-side with the Sudanese army[146]—perhaps qualified as a *de jure* body, trained and administered by the State.

The Commission stated in its Report that militias absorbed into and given uniforms by the PDF are necessarily *de jure* organs of the State.[147] It is interesting to note the link between this principle and the Commission's studious analysis of subjective criteria in ascertaining distinctions between protected groups and their

---

[141] See *Bosnia and Herzegovina v Serbia and Montenegro*, Judgment, supra n. 72, para 389 ("In two of the intercepted documents presented by the Applicant (the authenticity of which was queried [...]), there is reference to the 'Scorpions' as '[Ministry of the Interior] of Serbia' and 'a unit of Ministry of Interiors of Serbia'. The Respondent identified the senders of these communications [...] as being 'officials of the police forces of Republika Srpska.'"). For further analysis, see Milanović 2007, pp. 669–694.

[142] *Nicaragua v. United States of America*, Merits, Judgment, supra n. 71.

[143] ILC Articles on State Responsibility, supra n. 139, Article 8. See also Article 5 concerning the conduct of persons or entities exercising elements of governmental authority.

[144] Cassese 2007, pp. 649–668.

[145] Report of the International Commission of Inquiry on Darfur, supra n. 6, para 121, citing *Tadić*, op. cit., paras 98–145.

[146] Report of the International Commission of Inquiry on Darfur, supra n. 6, para 241.

[147] Ibid., para 124.

assailants. A military uniform is the sole concrete element discussed by the Commission that instantly turns militias into *de jure* organs in accordance with the ILC Articles on State Responsibility.[148] This is logical in the sense that a military uniform essentially—and often literally—places a State flag on a man's attire. Yet, in the cavalcade of criteria by which a relationship to the State can be deduced (for example, through the arming, training or financial support of the militants), the color of one's attire is easily the least consequential to his capacity to violate human rights and humanitarian norms.

Nevertheless, the identification value of the uniform serves to formalize what the Commission had already heard victims surmise when interviewed: that their attackers, regardless of how they were dressed, were all "one and the same" in their efforts.[149]

Interestingly, this 'otherness' was reciprocated by *Janjaweed* assailants, who many reported had told their victims, "we are here to eradicate blacks (nuba)."[150]

16.4.4 Tracing the Lines between Crimes

As concerns crimes against humanity, the Darfur Commission's 'widespread or systematic' requirement draws from *Kunarac, Kovac, and Vokovic*, wherein the ICTY Appeals Chamber stated that "the possible participation of officials or authorities or any identifiable patterns of crimes, could be taken into account to determine whether the attack satisfies either or both requirements of a 'widespread' or 'systematic' attack."[151] Differently framed, the ICTY Trial Chamber in *Kordić and Čerkez* declared the sufficiency of a "cumulative effect of a series of inhumane acts or the singular effect of an inhumane act of extraordinary magnitude."[152]

Since the Commission stated in its Report that the possibility of criminal involvement by government officials is germane to a finding of crimes against humanity,[153] it may seem odd that the apparent certainty of involvement in Darfur by government officials did not register a similar effect on its analysis of genocide, instead placing the conduct of those government actors within the purview of a

---

[148] ILC Articles on State Responsibility, supra n. 139, Article 4.

[149] Report of the International Commission of Inquiry on Darfur, supra n. 6, para 246.

[150] Report of the International Commission of Inquiry on Darfur, supra n. 6, para 245.

[151] *Prosecutor v. Kunarac, Kovac and Vokovic*, ICTY Appeals Chamber, Judgment, IT-96-23&IT-96-23/1-A (12 June 2002), para 95.

[152] *Kordić and Čerkez*, ICTY Trial Chamber, Judgment, IT-95-14/2-T (26 February 2001), para 179 (citing *Prosecutor v. Blaškić*, ICTY Trial Chamber, Judgment, IT-95-14-T (3 March 2000), para 206).

[153] Report of the International Commission of Inquiry on Darfur, supra n. 6, para 293.

future court or tribunal's analysis of individual criminal responsibility.[154] The difference, for the Commission, seems to be a canyon between what it considered the essentiality of a central policy or government plan for a finding of genocide, and the purely supplementary role such evidence plays in the analysis of crimes against humanity. In this respect, the Commission cited with approval the ICTR Appeals Chamber in *Kayishema and Ruzindana*.[155] The practical effect of adopting these distinctions advanced in the case law is that it supports the Commission's conclusion that there is no 'crime of crimes';[156] therefore, crimes against humanity should be more esteemed in the court of public opinion and more frequently applied in cases involving allegations of genocide.

On this point, the public statements by Security Council members in the lead-up to the establishment of the Darfur Commission may indeed suggest a perception that to assign such a travesty with a charge other than genocide is to forsake justice.[157] Yet not only might that view be groundless at this point, it may also be more productive in practice to obtain an indictment for crimes against humanity. This is not solely for evidentiary expedience. Since the ICC Prosecutor amended his indictments to include genocide, President Al-Bashir has expelled international aid organizations caring for internally displaced Darfurians.[158] Moreover, he has found several other heads of State to welcome his visits, setting up legal clashes between, on the one hand, their Rome Statute obligations *lex specialis* to arrest and submit President Al-Bashir to ICC custody and, on the other, their customary obligations to respect the immunity of heads of State.[159] Formal indictments for genocide have thus far resulted only in the African Union reinforcing this

[154] Ibid., paras 520–521. It may be particularly difficult to parse this issue in light of doctrine positing that the evidence of internationally criminal intent will nearly always exist at the individual level. See Fletcher and Ohlin 2005, pp. 539, 539–561. On this particular point, see also Udombana 2006, pp. 167, 178–182.

[155] *Prosecutor v. Kayishema and Ruzindana*, ICTR Appeals Chamber, supra n. 103, para 170.

[156] See, eg, *Prosecutor v. Semanza*, ICTR Trial Chamber, Judgment, ICTR-97-20 (15 May 2003), para 555.

[157] See, eg, conclusory statements made in an address by then-U.S. Secretary of State Colin Powell before the UN Security Council sprang into action: "Sudan [...] is obliged under the Convention to prevent and to punish acts of genocide. To us, at this time, it appears that Sudan has failed to do so." *The Crisis in Darfur: Hearing before the Senate Foreign Relations Committee*, 108th Congress (2004). Electronic version available at: http://2001-2009.state.gov/secretary/former/powell/remarks/36042.htm.

[158] Admittedly, however, President al-Bashir had already exerted this form of retaliation following the initial arrest warrant. J. Lauria, 'Darfur aid agencies leave after expulsion by Sudan', Wall Street Journal, 9 March 2009. Electronic version available at: http://online.wsj.com/article/SB123655809808566323.html.

[159] On this critical issue, see Gaeta 2009, pp. 315, 323–324.

customary obligation with resolutions.[160] Such animosity toward international criminal procedure within the Rome Statute framework poses dangers for the ICC in terms of both its global standing and regional effectiveness in Africa.

16.5 Conclusion

While specific elements of the Report have troubled commentators, it is the systemic aspects of the Darfur Commission's approach that are most problematic. In particular, the extraneous application of a subjective test when discerning 'part' and 'whole' under Article II of the Genocide Convention poses dangers to the ultimate effectiveness of that provision. Importantly, such aspects of the Report cannot be divorced from the Commission's disavowal of any primary judicial function.[161] As a result, while the 'reasonable suspicion' evidentiary standard may seem less burdensome than the threshold for indictment employed by international tribunals, this deviation may have ultimately deprived the Commission's work of some degree of guidance from and contribution to the international criminal law system.[162]

More fundamentally, this refusal to acknowledge its judicial capacities is at odds with the rhetoric of other ad hoc bodies, some of which are also closely tied to insurrection in the Sudan. In the *Abyei* arbitration between the government of the Sudan and the Sudan People's Liberation Movement, the Tribunal noted that fact-finding bodies may be required "to reach a decision on the basis of these

[160] After President al-Bashir's initial arrest warrant, the African Union formally pledged to "not cooperate pursuant to the provisions of Article 98 of the Rome Statute of the ICC relating to immunities"; following his State visits to Djibouti, Chad and Kenya in the aftermath of the warrant's amendment to include genocide, the African Union resolved that such States "were implementing various AU Assembly Decisions on non-cooperation with the ICC on the arrest and surrender [...]." Assembly of the African Union, 13th ordinary session, Assembly/AU/Dec.245(XIII) Rev.1 ('Decision on the Meeting of African States Parties to the Rome Statute of the International Criminal Court (ICC)') (Sirte, 3 July 2009), Item 10; Assembly of the African Union, 18th ordinary session, Assembly/AU/Dec.397 (XVIII) ('Decision on the Progress Report of the Commission on the Implementation of the Assembly Decisions in the International Criminal Court (ICC)') (Addis Ababa, 30 January 2012), Item 7.

[161] See, generally, Abi-Saab 2012.

[162] It is interesting to note the evidentiary standards subsequently applied by the ICC in issuing its arrest warrants in the Darfur case. The Appeals Chamber, in agreement with a dissenting Trial Chamber Judge, found that the issuance of an arrest warrant depended only upon a reasonable inference of genocidal intent (i.e., no conclusion as to that inference need be drawn before issuing a warrant). As this appears to align closely with the 'reasonable suspicion' standard that the Commission had adopted ad hoc, a logical outgrowth of the UN's response to Darfur may be greater and more expedient synergy between the ICC and commissions of inquiry in future crises. See *Al Bashir*, ICC Pre-Trial Chamber I, Warrant of Arrest for Omar Hassan Ahmad Al Bashir, ICC-02/05-01/09-3 (4 March 2009), Dissenting Opinion of Judge Anita Ušacka.

facts",[163] an aspect of the Darfur Commission's mandate which is clearly indicated by its duty to not simply 'investigate' human rights and humanitarian law violations, but "to *determine* also whether or not acts of genocide have occurred," and to identify those responsible.[164] The decisive nature of 'determine'—in contrast to 'investigate'—clearly endowed the Commission with a judicial or at least accusatory function, in addition to its fact-finding function.

From this essential point, all subsequent questions confronted by the Commission—such as the evidentiary standards it would apply—could have been resolved in a more assertive fashion on the basis of the *compétence de la compétence* which is a "fundamental pre-requisite of the autonomy of the international judicial function."[165] This traditional ability of adjudicative bodies to determine the scope of their own powers is robust because there is a "paucity of authority on what 'excess of mandate' concretely represents in law."[166] Moreover, just because a commission is "not an adjudicative body *strictu* sensu does not mean that it lack[s] *Kompetenz-Kompetenz*."[167]

Strangely, the denial of judicial function—which led the Darfur Commission to eschew the standards of established criminal tribunals—led to the adoption of ad hoc standards that, in practice, proved "stifling and surrealistically high."[168]

Moreover, any opportunity for ad hoc commissions established in response to separate ongoing crises to transcend these disparate roots and contribute to the normalization of international humanitarian law should be encouraged. The fears of fragmentation in international law expressed in the ILC's 2006 report on the subject accrue the highest stakes in the area of humanitarian law and human rights.[169] The ICJ's distinguishing itself in *Bosnia and Herzegovina v. Serbia and Montenegro* from the ICTY—on the basis of the former's role at the vanguard of general international law, and the latter's context as a specialized forum for criminal prosecution[170]—can be seen as having created a normative gap that the ILC would encourage bodies such as the Darfur Commission to fill to the greatest extent possible.

Therefore, to disavow all judicial function in the face of a mandate to "determine" the occurrence of genocide is not simply to distinguish the fact of the crime from its legal weight. It is moreover to sidestep a systemically important

---

163 *Arbitration before a Tribunal constituted in accordance with Article 5 of the Arbitration Agreement between the Government of Sudan and the Sudan People's Liberation Movement/ Army on Delimiting Abyei Area*, Final Award (22 July 2009), para 482.

164 UN Security Council Resolution 1564, supra n. 8, para 12.

165 Boisson de Chazournes 2011, p. 1028.

166 *Abyei Arbitration*, supra n. 163, para 401.

167 Ibid., para 502.

168 Abass 2008, p. 886.

169 International Law Commission, 'Fragmentation of International Law: Difficulties arising from the Diversification and Expansion of International Law', A/CN.4/L.682 (Geneva, 13 April 2006).

170 *Bosnia and Herzegovina v. Serbia and Montenegro*, Judgment, supra n. 72, paras 402–403.

opportunity for cross-fertilization between a variety of bodies that share, at base, an enjoined purpose in the international community. This shared purpose calls for judicial dialogue and legal certainty based on a gradually crystallizing methodological approach to the question of genocide. The development and practice of international humanitarian law depends upon a greater degree of normative harmonization than the Darfur Commission saw fit to contribute.

References

Abass A (2008) Proving state responsibility for genocide: the ICJ in *Bosnia v. Serbia* and the International Commission of Inquiry for Darfur. Fordham Int Law J 31(871):882

Abi-Saab G (2012) 'The metamorphosis of the international judicial function' (lecture), UN Office of Legal Affairs, Codification Division. Lecture available at UN Audiovisual Library of International Law: http://untreaty.un.org/cod/avl/ls/Abi-Saab_CT.html

Boisson de Chazournes L (2011) The principle of *Compétence de la Compétence* in international adjudication and its role in an era of multiplication of courts and tribunals. In: Arsanjani MH et al (eds) Looking to the future: essays of international law in honor of W. Michael Reisman. Martinus Nijhoff, Leiden, p 1028

Cassese A (2002) Genocide. In: Cassese A, Gaeta P, Jones JRWD (eds) The Rome Statute of the International Criminal Court: a commentary, vol II. Oxford University Press, Oxford, p 338

Cassese A (2007) The Nicaragua and Tadić tests revisited in light of the ICJ judgment on genocide in Bosnia. EJIL 18:649

Colombos CJ (1926) A Treatise on the law of prize. Sweet & Maxwell, London, pp 361–362

de Waal A (2005) Who are the Darfurians? Arab and African identities, violence and external engagement. Afr Aff 104(181):197

Dupuy P-M (2002) International criminal responsibility of the individual and international responsibility of the state. In: Cassese A, Gaeta P, Jones JRWD (eds), The Rome Statute of the International Criminal Court: a commentary, Vol. II, Oxford University Press, Oxford

Elliesie H (2010) Sudan under the constraints of (International) human rights law and humanitarian law: the case of Darfur. Beiträge zum Islamischen Recht, vol. VII, pp 193, 196–205

Fletcher GP, Ohlin JD (2005) Reclaiming fundamental principles of criminal law in the Darfur case. J Int Crim Justice 3(3):539–561

Gaeta P (2009) Does president Al Bashir enjoy immunity from arrest. J Int Crim Justice 7(315):323–324

Greenwood C (2006) The law of war. In: Evans M (ed) International law, 2nd edn. Oxford University Press, Oxford, p 808

Halink S (2008) All things considered: how the International Court of Justice delegated its fact-assessment to the United Nations in the *Armed Activities* Case. NYU J Int Law Polit 40:13

Kastner P (2012) International criminal justice in Bello? The ICC between law and politics in Darfur and Northern Uganda. Martinus Nijhoff, Leiden, pp 30–35

Koroma AG (2011) Challenges of evidence gathering. In: Odello M, Beruto GL (eds.), Global violence: consequences and responses, International Institute of Humanitarian Law, FrancoAngeli, Milan, pp 199–204

Leblanc LJ (1988) The United Nations Genocide Convention and Political Groups: should the United States propose an amendment? Yale J Int'l L. 13(268):271

Loewenstein AB, Kostas SA (2007) Divergent approaches to determining responsibility for genocide. The Darfur Commission of Inquiry and the ICJ's judgment in the *Genocide* Case. J Int Crim Justice 5(839):844–845

Milanović M (2007) State responsibility for genocide: a follow-up'. EJIL 18:669
Morgenstern F, Lauterpacht H (1942) Annual digest and reports of public international law cases, 1938–1940 (International Law Reports, Vol. 9), Case No. 221, pp 578–579
Murphy SD (2009) Protean Jus Ad Bellum. Berkeley J Int Law 27:23
Pellet A (1999) Can a state commit a crime? definitely, yes! EJIL 10(425):428
Prunier G (2005) Darfur: the ambiguous genocide. Cornell University Press, Ithaca, p 33
Ratner SR, Abrams JS (2001) Accountability for human rights atrocities in international law. Beyond the Nuremberg legacy. Oxford University Press, Oxford
Schabas WA (2000) Genocide in international law. Cambridge University Press, Cambridge, p 112
Schabas WA (2005) Darfur and the 'odious scourge: the commission of inquiry's findings on genocide. Leiden J Int Law 18(871):874–877
Schabas WA (2006) Genocide, crimes against humanity, and Darfur: the commission of inquiry's findings on genocide. Cardozo Law Rev 27(1703):1719–1720
Shaw MN (1989) Genocide and international law. In: Dinstein Y (ed) International law at a time of perplexity: essays in honour of Shabtai Rosenne. Martinus Nijhoff, Dordrecht, p 806
Udombana NJ (2006) An escape from reason: genocide and the International Commission of Inquiry on Darfur. Sri Lanka J Int Law 18(167):178–182
UN War Crimes Commission (1948) The history of the UN war crimes commission and the development of the laws of war. HMSO, London, p 35
Van Haren MK (2006) The report of the international commission of inquiry on Darfur & genocidal intent—a critical analysis. Netherlands Int Law Rev 53:205
Wiebalck A (2003) International humanitarian law and the ICRC in the Republic of the Sudan. Comp Int Law J Southern Africa 36:198
Yihdego Z (2009) Darfur and humanitarian law: the protection of civilians and civilian objects. J Confl Secur Law 14(37):39–45

Chapter 17
The *Mavi Marmara* Incident and the Application of International Humanitarian Law by Quasi-Judicial Bodies

Russell Buchan

Contents

17.1 Introduction

From June 1967 until May 1994, Israel occupied the Gaza Strip and the West Bank without any self administering rights to be awarded to the Palestinian population.[1] In 1994, Israel and the Palestinian Liberation Organization (PLO) concluded a peace agreement known as the Oslo Accords,[2] which divided the Gaza Strip and the West Bank in areas A, B and C, largely granting autonomy over the major

Russell Buchan is a Lecturer in International Law at the University of Sheffield. He has published widely in the field of international peace and security and his book *International Law and the Construction of the Liberal Peace* (2013) is published by Hart.

[1] See generally Kimmerling and Migdal 1994.
[2] For a critical overview of the Oslo Accords see Miller 1998.

R. Buchan (✉)
University of Sheffield, Yorkshire, UK
e-mail: r.j.buchan@sheffield.ac.uk

D. Jinks et al. (eds.), *Applying International Humanitarian Law in Judicial and Quasi-Judicial Bodies*, DOI: 10.1007/978-94-6265-008-4_17,

Palestinian population centres and thereby paving the way for the negotiation of a permanent status agreement that would establish a sovereign Palestinian state existing alongside the state of Israel. However, the two-state solution suffered a serious setback in 2006 when Hamas secured enough seats in the Palestinian Legislative Council (PLC) to become the elected government.[3] This resulted in a period of prolonged fighting between Hamas and Fatah.[4] In June 2007, Hamas took control of Gaza and Fatah retained control of the West Bank.[5] Given that Hamas adopted an extremely belligerent stance towards Israel, on 19 September 2007 Israel declared Hamas a 'terrorist organisation' and Gaza 'hostile territory'.[6]

In order to prevent war material being delivered to Hamas fighters, Israel imposed a land blockade against Gaza on 14 November 2001.[7] To reinforce this land blockade, Israel imposed a naval blockade against the Gazan coast on 3 January 2009.[8] Concerned that a humanitarian crisis was occurring in Gaza, in May 2010 the Free Gaza Movement dispatched a flotilla of ships—referred to by those organising the movement as the Peace Flotilla—with the express intention of violating the naval blockade and delivering humanitarian aid to Gaza.[9] On 31 May 2010, the flotilla approached the naval blockade and was advised by Israeli forces to either turn back or to dock at a nearby Israeli port in order for their cargo to be inspected.[10] With the flotilla rejecting the offer, Israel sought to enforce its naval blockade. In general, this occurred relatively peacefully. However, one boat, the *Mavi Marmara*, resisted the interception and violence erupted between the crew members and Israeli forces. Nine crew members were killed and several Israeli

---

[3] BBC News, 'Hamas Sweeps to Election Victory', 26 January 2006, available at http://news.bbc.co.uk/1/hi/4650788.stm. Accessed 24 September 2013.

[4] New York Times, 'Hamas Seize Broad Control in Gaza Strip', 13 June 2007, available at http://www.nytimes.com/2007/06/14/world/middleeast/14mideast.html. Accessed 24 September 2013.

[5] Ibid.

[6] Statement of Israel's Foreign Minister Regarding Israel's Policy towards Hamas and its Terrorism, 1 October 2007, available at http://www.mfa.gov.il/MFA/About+the+Ministry/Foreign+Minister+Livni/Speeches+interviews/Statements+by+Israeli+FM+Livni+regarding+Israeli+policy+toward+the+Hamas+and+its+terrorism+11-Sep-20.htm. Accessed 24 September 2013.

[7] These land crossings were implemented in response to the Second Intifada, which began in September 2000. See generally Pressman 2003.

[8] Number 1/2009 Blockade of the Gaza Strip 3 January 2009, publicised by the Israeli government at http://en.mot.gov.il/index.php?option=com_content&view=article&id=124:no12009&catid=17:noticetomariners&Itemid=12. Accessed 24 September 2013.

[9] For an overview of the activities of the Free Gaza Movement see their webpage at http://www.freegaza.org/.

[10] The Public Commission to Examine the Maritime Incident of 31 May 2010, 23 January 2011, para 3 available at http://www.turkel-committee.gov.il/files/wordocs/8808report-eng.pdf. Accessed 24 September 2013 (herein referred to as the Turkel Report).

military personnel were injured. Israel eventually assumed control of the situation and confiscated the boat and detained the crew members.[11]

Israel's interception of the *Mavi Marmara* attracted considerable media attention. Although much of the media reported that Israel's actions were in violation of international law, and in particular that the interception was in contravention to well-established international legal principles applicable to the high seas,[12] Israel claimed that the interception was justified on the basis of the laws of war; specifically, international humanitarian law.[13]

Significantly no court, either international or domestic, has had the opportunity to authoritatively examine the interception and thus pronounce upon the legality of Israel's conduct. This being said, four quasi-judicial bodies[14] produced detailed reports examining the legality of the *Mavi Marmara* interdiction. Two of these reports are domestic and two are international. On the domestic level, both Israel and Turkey produced their reports into the incident. The Turkish Report was

[11] These facts have been determined and outlined by a fact-finding mission established by the UN Human Rights Council; United Nations Human Rights Council, Report of the International Fact-Finding Mission to Investigate Violations of International Law, Including International Humanitarian and Human Rights Law, Resulting from the Israeli Attacks on the Flotilla of Ships Carrying Humanitarian Assistance, A/HRC/15/21, 27 September 2010 (herein the UN Human Rights Council Report).

[12] The Washington Post, 'Israel's Flotilla Raid revives Questions of International Law', 1 June 2010, available at http://www.washingtonpost.com/wp-dyn/content/article/2010/06/01/AR2010060102934.html?hpid=topnews. Accessed 24 September 2013.

[13] 'We were acting totally without our legal rights. The international law is very clear on this issue ... if you have a declared blockade, publicly declared, legally declared, publicised as international law requires, and someone is trying to break that blockade and though you have warned them ... you are entitled to intercept even on the high seas'; M Regev, Spokesman for Israeli Prime Minister Binyamin Netanyahu, quoted in The Washington Post, 1 June 2010, available at http://www.washingtonpost.com/wp-dyn/content/article/2010/06/01/AR2010060102934.html. Accessed 24 September 2013.

[14] I refer to these bodies as quasi-judicial on the basis that they satisfy the definition outlined by Alvarez in his seminal work on this topic. For Alvarez, a quasi-judicial body is a body that can be 'characterized by some serious attempt, primarily through rules for the type of expertise required of the dispute settlers, their method of selection, or their tenure in office (or all three), to recognize the "independent" status of the third party decision-maker from the governments involved in their creation'; Alvarez 2005, p. 459. The four bodies under consideration in this chapter can be regarded as quasi-judicial because their members were selected on the basis of their professional standing; namely, their expertise in international law and/or experience and knowledge of international relations. Consequently, there was a serious attempt by their creators to establish bodies that were capable of independently adjudicating the dispute. The reports compiled by the bodies established by the Turkish government and the Israeli government are perhaps most susceptible to being criticised for lacking independence. However, it should be noted that both these reports were formulated in response to a Presidential Statement of the Security Council requiring that both governments conduct a 'prompt, *impartial*, credible and transparent investigation conforming to international standards' (emphasis added); Presidential Statement of the Security Council, UN Doc SC/9940 (31 May 2010). Both reports confirmed that they adhered to this requirement of impartiality.

produced at the request of the Turkish government.[15] In Israel, the Turkel Report was published after the request of the Israeli government.[16] On the international plain, a UN Fact-Finding Report was published on 22 September 2010, compiled by the UN Human Rights Council (herein referred to as the Human Rights Council Report),[17] while the Palmer Report was published in September 2011, at the behest of the UN Secretary-General.[18]

The purpose of this chapter is not to engage in an in-depth analysis of whether Israel's interception of the *Mavi Marmara* was in conformity with international humanitarian law. I have discussed the legality of the interception in detail elsewhere.[19] Rather, my intention is to compare and contrast the four reports of these quasi-judicial bodies, identifying significant discrepancies between them as to the interpretation and application of international humanitarian law. This is achieved in Sects. 17.2 and 17.3 of this chapter. In Sect. 17.4, my focus dilates, locating the role of quasi-judicial bodies within the broader context of international adjudication. In particular, I flag up some of the potential problems that this new type of adjudication may yield for international law generally and international dispute resolution in particular.

17.2 The International Law of Naval Blockade

A fundamental principle of the law of the high seas is that ships are subject to the exclusive sovereignty of the state of the flag under which the vessel sails.[20] This principle is however subject to a number of recognised exceptions. A well-recognised exception is that, as a principle of *lex specialis*,[21] during times of armed conflict international humanitarian law permits states to interdict ships on the high seas where they violate or intend to violate a lawfully established blockade.[22]

---

[15] Report of Turkish National Commission of Inquiry, 11 February 2011, available at http://www.mfa.gov.tr/data/Turkish%20Report%20Final%20-%20UN%20Copy.pdf. Accessed 24 September 2013.

[16] Turkel Report 2011, supra n. 10.

[17] UN Human Rights Council Report 2010, supra n. 11.

[18] Report of the Secretary-General's Panel of Inquiry on the 31 May 2010 Flotilla Incident, July 2011, available at http://www.un.org/News/dh/infocus/middle_east/Gaza_Flotilla_Panel_Report.pdf. (Accessed 24 September 2013).

[19] Buchan 2011, 2012.

[20] Article 92 of the Law of the Sea Convention 1982. Although note that many argue that there must be a 'genuine link' between the vessel and the state under which the vessel sails; see generally Solomon and Maogoto 2013.

[21] *Lex specialis* is a principle of legal interpretation that provides that where two laws govern the same factual situation the law governing a specific subject matter (*lex specialis*) overrides a law which only governs general matters (*lex generalis*).

[22] Jones 1983, p. 760 (arguing that the law of blockade has created an exception to the principle of exclusive jurisdiction).

The important question, then, is whether Israel's naval blockade was lawfully deployed. The law of naval blockade is located in customary international humanitarian law.[23] However, although not a binding document, the San Remo Manual is often considered to represent a codification of customary international law that is applicable during times of armed conflict at sea.[24] In this sense, the Manual is considered authoritative.[25] The Manual explains that in order for a naval blockade to be lawfully deployed it must be publically announced, enforced and effective. It must also apply impartially and cannot be imposed against the ports or coasts of neutral states. Furthermore, the blockade must be in response to an international armed conflict and in all cases it must be proportionate.[26]

Although the culmative nature of the San Remo Manual makes it clear that all six requirements have to be satisfied in order for a blockade to be lawful, it is in relation to the interpretation and application of the final two requirements where the four quasi-judicial bodies examining the interception of the *Mavi Marmara* exhibit greatest divergence. For this reason, this is where my attention will be focused.

17.2.1 International Armed Conflict

Historically, public international law has always been an inter-state system; a system of law created by sovereign states, for sovereign states.[27] As a branch of public international law international humanitarian law has followed this premise. Traditionally its focus has been on international armed conflicts, namely conflicts between states[28] rather than armed conflict within states or between states and non-state actors.[29] What was therefore required in order to apply international humanitarian law was to first determine that, factually, and armed conflict of sufficient intensity was persisting and, second, that it was between two or more states and could therefore be classified as international in character. This said, as non-state actors became increasingly powerful in the world order, and in particular their ability to organise themselves into armed groups that can perpetrate large-scale violence, many rules applicable during times of international armed conflict

---

23 Green 2008, p. 204.

24 See the Introduction to the San Remo Manual on International Law Applicable to Armed Conflicts at Sea, 12 June 1994.

25 Doswald-Beck 1995.

26 Section II, San Remo Manual on International Law Applicable to Armed Conflicts at Sea, 12 June 1994.

27 Buchan 2011, pp. 217–218.

28 An international armed conflict is defined as 'recourse to armed force between States'; *Prosecutor* v. *Tadić*, Case No. IT-94-I-I, Judgement, 15 July 1999, para 70.

29 Although this is a position that would of course change over time, not least with the introduction of Common Article 3 of the Four Geneva Conventions of 1949.

gradually became applicable to non-international armed conflicts alike, namely to 'protracted armed violence between governmental authorities and organised groups or between such groups.'[30]

In determining the legality of Israel's naval blockade of Gaza two questions need to be addressed. First, on 31 May 2010 was Israel engaged in an armed conflict with Hamas? If so, what was its classification; was it an international or non-international armed conflict? Second, if it was a non-international armed conflict, is there sufficient evidence of state practice accompanied by *opinio juris* to substantiate the claim that international humanitarian law has evolved to the extent that it now recognises the right to impose a naval blockade during times of non-international armed conflict? As we shall see, when the San Remo Manual was drafted in 1994 its drafters were clearly of the opinion that the right to naval blockade is only available in times of international armed conflict. The four quasi-judicial bodies examining the legality of Israel's interception of the *Mavi Marmara* arrive at very different conclusions when addressing these important questions, and it is interesting to compare and contrast their approaches and findings.

Surprisingly, the Turkish Report does not consider whether Israel and Hamas were, factually, engaged in an armed conflict on 31 May 2010. Rather, this is assumed. Moreover, the Turkish Report does not address the issue of whether the armed conflict was of an international or non-international character. The Turkish Report thus determines that Israel possessed the right to impose a naval blockade under international humanitarian law on the basis that an armed conflict was occurring.[31]

In contrast, the Turkel Report concludes that the violence between Israel and Hamas was of sufficient intensity to amount to an armed conflict on 31 May 2010 and that this armed conflict was international in character.[32] The armed conflict was classified as international on the basis of the *Targeted Killings* case.[33] In this case, Israel's Supreme Court held that although Hamas is not the governing authority of a state, Israel and Hamas were nevertheless engaged in an international armed conflict because the violence crossed Israeli borders.[34] Interestingly, the Turkel Report goes on to explain that even if this is not grounds for interna-

[30] supra n. 28.

[31] Turkish Report 2011, supra n. 15, p. 33 ff.

[32] Turkel Report 2011, supra n. 10, para 38.

[33] HCJ 769/02 *Public Committee Against Torture v. Government* [2006] (2) IsrLR 459. In actual fact, the Turkel Report identifies two grounds for internationalising an armed conflict between a state and an organised armed group; the *Targeted Killings* scenario and where the state occupies the territory within which the armed group is located. However, the report clearly states that Gaza was not occupied by Israel on 31 May 2010, and therefore the only conclusion is that the Turkel Report sought to internationalise the armed conflict on the basis of the *Targeted Killings* judgement.

[34] Ibid., para 18.

tionalising the armed conflict, a naval blockade can still be imposed in the realms of a non-international armed conflict.[35]

This interpretation is justified on the basis that there is sufficient state practice to substantiate the claim that customary international humanitarian law now recognises the right to impose naval blockades in non-international armed conflicts. As the Turkel Report notes

> '[n]aval blockades have, nevertheless, been imposed in non-international armed conflict...In certain situations, States have imposed a military or economic blockade against an enemy that is not a *de jure* government'.[36]

The Turkel Report provides three examples; first, the naval blockade imposed by the Union against the Southern ports controlled by the Confederates during the American Civil War; second, the Nationalist Chinese government's (purported) blockade of ports under control of the Community forces in 1949; and third, Israel's blockade of Lebanon in its armed conflict with Hezbollah in 2006.[37]

Although the UN Human Rights Council Report determines that Israel and Hamas were engaged in an armed conflict on 31 May 2010, it does not classify the conflict as international or non-international in character.[38] Similar to the Turkish Report, the UN Human Rights Council Report appears to suggest that because an armed conflict was occurring Israel possessed the right to blockade and that it is not necessary to classify the legal status of this armed conflict.

The Palmer Report considers that Israel and Hamas were engaged in hostilities of sufficient intensity and violence on 31 May 2010 in order to qualify as an armed conflict for the purposes of international humanitarian law.[39] In relation to the classification of the character of this armed conflict the Palmer Report concludes that it has 'all the trappings of an international armed conflict', justifying this determination on the basis that Hamas is in control of territory and possesses state-like features.[40] In essence, the Palmer Report is implying that Hamas amounts to a belligerent power under international humanitarian law[41] and thus the conflict between Israel and Hamas should be viewed as an international one.

Moreover, like the Turkel Report, the Palmer Report also finds it necessary to consider whether naval blockades can be imposed also in the realms of non-international armed conflicts. As such, it concludes that customary international

[35] Turkel Report 2011, supra n. 10, para 44.

[36] Ibid., para 39.

[37] Ibid., para 43 and footnote 131.

[38] See for example UN Human Rights Council Report 2010, supra n. 11, para 51 ff.

[39] Report of the Secretary-General's Panel of Inquiry on the 31 May 2010 Flotilla Incident (Palmer Report 2011), paras 73–74.

[40] Ibid., para 73.

[41] M Milanovic (2 September 2011) Palmer Committee Report on the Mavi Marmara Incident, EJIL: Talk! available at http://www.ejiltalk.org/palmer-committee-report-on-the-mavi-marmara-incident/ (Accessed 24 September 2013).

law now recognises such a right.[42] Thus, even if Israel and Hamas were engaged in a non-international armed conflict on 31 May 2010, Israel still possessed the right to impose a naval blockade. The report justifies this approach on two grounds; first, on the basis that the San Remo Manual provides that the right to naval blockade is available in times of non-international armed conflict; and secondly, that there are 'a few examples'[43] of state practice where naval blockades have been imposed in non-international armed conflicts. As it happens, the report only provides one example: the Union's naval blockade of Southern ports during the American Civil War.[44]

Incontrovertibly, the violence between Israel and Hamas on 31 May 2010 was of sufficient intensity to amount to an armed conflict.[45] The question of whether this armed conflict was of an international or non-international character also has to be answered, since this distinction is required under contemporary international humanitarian law.[46] Thus, the Turkish Report and the Human Rights Council Report's failure to specify the classification of the armed conflict stem from a misunderstanding of international humanitarian law.

I argue that the Israel-Hamas armed conflict should be deemed as non-international and as a protracted armed conflict between a state and an organised armed group.[47] True, non-international armed conflicts can be internationalised, as the Turkel Report and Palmer Report make clear. However, the Turkel Report claims that the armed conflict is internationalised because the violence 'crosses the border of a state,' namely the borders of Israel. This approach has been heavily criticised, not least because it is inconsistent with the history of state practice which reveals that 'the single defining feature of international armed conflicts has not been their cross-border, but their interstate, nature'.[48]

The Palmer Report internationalises the armed conflict on the basis of the doctrine of belligerency. However, this approach is also problematic. This is because it is well established in international law that where a non-state actor is engaged in an armed conflict with a state but the non-state actor is recognised as a 'belligerent' under international law then this otherwise non-international armed conflict will be transformed into an international armed conflict. The reason for this is because, as Falk explains, '[i]nternational law treats an internal war with the

[42] Palmer Report 2011, supra n. 39, para 23 of Appendix I.

[43] Ibid., para 21 of Appendix I.

[44] Ibid.

[45] I have discussed this elsewhere; Buchan 2011, pp. 221–223. Cf Guilfoyle 2011, p. 18.

[46] See generally International Law Association 2010.

[47] Applying similar reasoning to the US Supreme Court's determination that the US (a state) is engaged in a non-international armed conflict with Al Qaeda (an organised armed group); *Hamdan* v. *Rumsfeld*, 548 US 557 (2006).

[48] Milanovic 2007, p. 384.

status of belligerency as essentially identical to a war between sovereign states'.[49] This notwithstanding, it is unlikely that Hamas exhibits the necessary features in order to be regarded as a belligerent. Lauterpacht identifies four characteristics that an organised armed group must possess in order to be classified as a belligerent power under international humanitarian law

> [F]irst, there must exist within the State an armed conflict of a general (as distinguished from purely local) character; secondly, the insurgents must occupy and administer a substantial portion of national territory; thirdly, they must conduct hostilities in accordance with the rules of war and through organized armed forces acting under a reasonable authority; fourthly, there must exist circumstances which make it necessary, for outside states to define their attitude by means of recognition of belligerency.[50]

According to this definition, Hamas cannot be regarded as an occupying power. First, belligerency status is intended to apply to organised armed groups that are participating in a particularly fierce and entrenched civil war against the government (note the requirement that 'there must exist within a state'). Demonstrably, Hamas is not 'within' Israel. Second, Hamas does not comply with the third requirement that it conducts hostilities in accordance with the rules of war. As is well known and documented,[51] Hamas frequently engages in the indiscriminate firing of mortar shells into Israel, with wanton disregard for civilian damage. Such conduct is manifestly inconsistent with the basic tenets of international humanitarian law; in particular, the requirement to distinguish between civilians and combatants and between civilian objects and military objects.[52]

Assuming, then, that Israel is engaged in a non-international armed conflict with Hamas, the next question is whether customary international humanitarian law recognises the right to impose a naval blockade in times of non-international armed conflict. In essence, this boils down to whether there is sufficient state practice, accompanied by *opinio juris*, of naval blockades being deployed in non-international armed conflicts. In this respect, the Turkel Report cites three examples.

The first example refers to the Union's blockade of southern ports controlled by the Confederates during the American Civil War.[53] As noted, the Palmer Report also refers to this blockade as being an example of state practice during times of non-international armed conflict.[54] However, to read the American Civil War as a non-international armed conflict is to fundamentally misconceive the nature the

---

[49] Falk 1964, p. 203. Although interestingly note that the Turkel Report concludes that the doctrine of belligerency is 'almost irrelevant' under contemporary international humanitarian law; Turkel Report 2011, supra n. 10, para 39.

[50] Lauterpacht 1947, p. 176.

[51] See for example EU Council Commons Position 2001/931/CFDSP, 27 December 2001.

[52] The use of weapons in an indiscriminate manner constitutes a clear violation of international humanitarian law; see Henckaerts and Doswald-Beck 2005, Rule 11.

[53] Turkel Report 2011, supra n. 10, footnote 131.

[54] Palmer Report 2011, supra n. 39, para 21 of Appendix I.

hostilities. The Confederates were regarded as a belligerent power by many foreign governments and so the armed conflict between the Union and the Confederates is in fact a well-known example of an *international* armed conflict.[55]

The second example given by the Turkel Report is the Chinese government's blockade of ports under control of the Communist forces in 1949.[56] However, careful inspection of the correspondence between the Chinese government and Communist forces reveals that the government was not in fact imposing a naval blockade of the ports.[57] The third example offered by the Turkel Report is Israel's blockade of Lebanon in 2006.[58] The Turkel Report suggests that this was a blockade by a state, namely Israel, in the realms of its armed conflict with Hezbollah, a non-state actor. However, before the Security Council the Israeli representative unambiguously stated that because of the close relationship between the Lebanese government and Hezbollah, Israel was actually in an armed conflict with Lebanon.[59] In other words, the conflict was between two states and thus an international armed conflict. In conclusion, then, the Turkel Report and the Palmer Report identify little state practice to substantiate the claim that customary international humanitarian law now recognises the right to impose a naval blockade in times of non-international armed conflict.

As I have noted, the Palmer Report also refers to the San Remo Manual in order to justify its position that naval blockades can be imposed in times of a non-international conflict. However, the Explanation that accompanies the Manual seems to indicate the opposite. The explanation provides that

> it should be noted that although the provisions of the Manual are primarily meant to apply to international armed conflicts at sea, this has intentionally not been expressly indicated in para 1 in order to dissuade the implementation of these rules in non-international armed conflicts involving naval operations.[60]

From the aforementioned excerpt it is therefore evident that the Manual applies in times of international armed conflict and that, *as a matter of good practice but not of law*, these requirements should be adhered to in the eventuality that a naval blockade is imposed in a non-international armed conflict.

It is interesting to note here that by applying the Manual also to non-international conflicts, the Palmer Report may be deemed as trying to bridge the de lege lata-de

---

[55] US Department of State: Office of the Historian, *The Blockade of Confederate Ports, 1861–1865*, available at http://history.state.gov/milestones/1861-1865/Blockade. Accessed 24 September 2013.

[56] Turkel Report 2011, supra n. 10, footnote 131.

[57] Woosley 1950, p. 350.

[58] Turkel Report 2011, supra n. 10, para 43.

[59] 'Responsibility for this belligerent act of war lies with the Government of Lebanon, from whose territory these acts have been launched into Israel'; Permanent Representative of Israel to the United Nations, *Identical Letters Dated July 12 2006 from the Permanent Representative of Israel to the United Nations Addressed to the Secretary-General and the President of the Security Council*, UN Doc. A/60/937, S/2006/515, 12 July 2006.

[60] Doswald-Beck 1995, p. 73.

lege ferenda nexus in naval warfare.[61] While this opens a new perspective in the application of international humanitarian law to sea operations, it also speaks volumes of the potential impact that quasi-judicial bodies have on shaping international humanitarian law.

17.2.2 Proportionality

Paragraph 102 of the San Remo Manual provides that a blockade is unlawful where its sole purpose is the starving of the civilian population, the denial of objects essential for its survival or in cases where the damage to the civilian population is, or is expected to be, excessive in relation to the concrete and direct anticipated military advantage. In context of the current discussion, it is important to note that Israel has imposed both a land and naval blockade against Gaza. As such, before any assessment of the legality of the Israeli blockade, it is necessary to determine whether it is the naval blockade alone that must be subjected to the proportionality test or, rather, the naval blockade in conjunction with the land blockade.

The Turkish Report, the Turkel Report and the UN Human Rights Council Report all proceed on the basis that the naval blockade and the land blockade constitute one single unified policy (which I will refer to as the closure regime) and thus it is the overall impact of both that needs to be tested against the proportionality requirement.[62]

The Turkish Report concludes that the closure regime amounts to a collective punishment against the people of Gaza. In short, Israel imposed the closure regime in retribution for the Gazan population electing Hamas to power in 2006. In this sense, the sole purpose of the closure regime is to deny objects essential for the survival of the Gazan population and is thus unlawful.[63]

Even if the closure regime is not implemented with the sole purpose of denying the civilian population objects essential to its survival, the Turkish Report argues that the closure regime nevertheless causes excessive damage to the civilian population and is therefore unlawful.[64] In particular, the Turkish Report explains

---

[61] For this nexus see S Solomon , J Maogoto (22 July 2013) Jurisdictional Aspects of the Article 12(2) Rome Statute Vessel Provision: Some Thoughts on the Provision's Dogma and Implementation in Light of the Comoros Referral, *Opinio Juris*, available at http://opiniojuris.org/2013/07/21/jurisdictional-aspects-of-the-article-122-rome-statute-vessel-provision-some-thoughts-on-the-provisions-dogma-and-implementation-in-light-of-the-comoros-referral/. (Accessed 24 September 2013).

[62] Turkish Report 2011, supra n. 15, p. 70; Turkel Report 2011 supra n. 10, para 63; UN Human Rights Council Report 2010, supra n. 11, para 59.

[63] Turkish Report 2011, supra n. 15, p. 38.

[64] Ibid., p. 6 ['The Israeli blockade was excessive in relation to any advantage to Israel's military objective and has a disproportionate impact on the civilian population as documented by numerous UN agencies and the international community at large'].

that the extensiveness and severity of the restrictions render the blockade excessive, and cites claims by various human rights organisations that a 'serious humanitarian crisis' is occurring in Gaza in order to demonstrate its excessiveness.[65]

In juxtaposition, the Turkel Report submits that the closure regime is motivated by legitimate military objectives; that the items prevented from entering Gaza are of dual use, meaning that even materials that are ostensibly for civilian purposes, such as fuel and building materials, can be used by Hamas in its armed conflict with Israel. Thus, the closure regime seeks to prevent the delivery of such material to Gaza. To this end, the *sole* purpose of the closure regime cannot be regarded as an attempt to deny essential objects from reaching the Gazan population.[66]

In determining whether the closure regime caused damage that has been excessive in relation to the anticipated military advantage, the Turkel Report notes that the more significant the military objective, the greater the damage that can be justified.[67] The Turkel Report therefore considers it crucial that the closure regime is pursuant to a significant military objective, namely to protect the Israeli civilian population from the indiscriminate firing of rockets by Hamas from Gaza into Israel.[68] Moreover, the Turkel Report explains that the humanitarian situation in Gaza is not as bad as has been reported, and that it certainly cannot be described as a humanitarian crisis. As an example, the report notes that although the resource of food is scarce, the Gazan population is not starving but instead subject to 'food insecurity'.[69] For these reasons, the Turkel Report does not consider that the naval blockade inflicts disproportionate damage upon the civilian population.[70]

The UN Human Rights Council Report does not address whether the sole purpose of the blockade is to deny essential objects reaching the civilian population.[71] However, the report reaches the conclusion that the blockade is inflicting disproportionate damage upon the civilian population in the Gaza strip and that as such the flotilla interception could not be justified and therefore has to be considered illegal.[72]

Interestingly, and surprisingly given that it was released after the Turkish, Turkel and UN Human Rights Council Reports, the Palmer Report determines that the naval blockade must be distinguished from the land blockade when applying the test of proportionality. The Palmer Report explains that the naval blockade and

---

[65] Ibid., p. 68.

[66] Turkel Report 2011, supra n 10, para 61 ff.

[67] Ibid., para 87.

[68] Ibid., para 89.

[69] Ibid., para 76.

[70] Ibid., para 97.

[71] Nevertheless, the UN Human Rights Council does conclude that the blockade constitutes a collective punishment under Article 33 of the Fourth Geneva Convention; UN Human Rights Council Report 2010, supra n. 11, para 54.

[72] Ibid., para 13.

the land blockade are pursuing different objectives and *cannot* be considered one unified closure policy. To this end, the impact of the naval blockade must be considered in isolation from the impact of the land crossings.[73]

Working on this premise, the Palmer Report concludes that the naval blockade is imposed in order to realise legitimate military objectives such as the prevention of arms delivery to Hamas, and so cannot be regarded as a blockade imposed with the sole purpose of denying the civilian population objects essential to its survival.[74] In relation to whether the naval blockade caused excessive damage, the Palmer Report agrees that a humanitarian crisis was occurring in Gaza. However, and crucially, the Palmer Report determines that this crisis was attributable to the land blockade, and not to the naval blockade, not least because Gaza does not possess a commercial port that could be used to receive humanitarian goods.[75] In short, the naval blockade does not have any significant impact upon the humanitarian situation in Gaza and thus any damage occurring cannot be considered excessive when weighed against the significant military advantage of preventing war material from reaching Gaza.[76]

In line with the Turkish, Turkel and UN Human Rights Council Reports I argue that the land and naval blockade must be considered one unified closure policy. In fact, this is the approach that has been consistently adopted by the Israeli government.[77] Israel imposed the naval blockade subsequent to the land blockade when it realised that Hamas fighters would seek to circumvent the land blockade by receiving war material by sea.[78] Thus, the Palmer Report's conclusion that the two blockades have to be assessed in isolation does not stand up to scrutiny. Indeed, it is interesting to note that whilst the Palmer Report explains that the objective of the naval blockade is motivated by security concerns, and that the objective of the naval blockade and land crossings are different, it does not go on to articulate what the objective of the land crossings is.

Approaching the land and naval blockade as one general closure policy, the question is whether it can be argued that its sole purpose is the intention to deny the Gazan population objects essential to its survival, as the Turkish Report determines. Given the sophistication of modern warfare and how many objects such as spices, milk and plastic can now be used to perpetrate violence and promote the war effort (dual use items), it is difficult to maintain that Israel prevents essential objects from reaching Gaza on the *sole* basis that it intends to deny the civilian population objects essential to its survival.

---

[73] Palmer Report 2011, supra n. 39, para 70.

[74] Ibid., para 47(e).

[75] Ibid., para 78.

[76] Ibid., para 79.

[77] See the discussion in Finkelstein 2011, p. 14 ff.

[78] Number 1/2009 Blockade of the Gaza Strip 3 January 2009, publicised by the Israeli government at http://en.mot.gov.il/index.php?option=com_content&view=article&id=124:no12009&catid=17:noticetomariners&Itemid=12. Accessed 24 September 2013.

In relation to whether the closure regime can be regarded as excessive, the Turkel Report's claim is correct when it explains that the more significant the military objective being pursued, the greater the damage that can be inflicted upon the civilian population. On this, two things have to be noted. First, the Turkel Report correctly states that protecting its civilian population is one of the most important tasks incumbent upon a government.[79] At the same time, the question is how serious the threat is in order to justify a particular state reaction. In the case of Hamas rocket attacks towards southern Israel, it is true that many of the missiles are inaccurate and so fail to cause any damage to property or people. Moreover, Israel possesses sophisticated defence systems that are highly successful in destroying Hamas missiles before they reach land.[80] In this sense, the military objective is perhaps not as considerable as the Turkel Report portrays.

This is important because, as Para 102 of the San Remo Manual requires, the significance of the military advantage must be weighed alongside the extent of the damage being inflicted upon the civilian population. In this context, the Turkel Report's determination that a severe humanitarian crisis is not occurring in Gaza is probably erroneous. Numerous reports from the UN and from human rights organisations have consistently concluded that a 'devastating' human retain crisis is occurring in Gaza.[81] In the light of this, and in light of the fact that many rockets fired into Israel do not successfully strike civilian areas,[82] the Gaza closure regime at the time of the flotilla incident should be perceived as causing excessive damage to the civilian population and therefore be considered unlawful.

17.3 Enforcement

All four reports, including the Turkish Report and the UN Human Rights Council Report which considered the imposition of the blockade to be unlawful, go on to consider whether the enforcement of the naval blockade was lawfully executed. A blockade that is lawfully deployed under international law can be enforced against

---

[79] Turkel Report 2011, supra n. 10, para 89.

[80] See 'Iron Dome: Missile Defense System a Game Change, Israelis Say', *CNN* (20 November 2012), available at http://edition.cnn.com/2012/11/17/world/meast/iron-dome-israel-gaza-conflict. Accessed 24 September 2013.

[81] See ICRC News Release No. 10/103, 14 June 2010.

[82] As the Palmer Report rightly notes, the psychological damage that the constant threat of rocket attacks causes Israeli citizens is considerable; Palmer Report 2011, supra n. 39, para 71. On this see further Eliav Lieblich's chapter in this volume. However, my view is that in terms of justifying a blockade that is having a devastating impact on a civilian population, there is a clear division between damage to property and/or death or injury to people on one hand and psychological damage on the other.

a vessel that violates or expresses an intention to violate it.[83] In this sense, capturing the vessel becomes a legitimate military objective. Indeed, all necessary force can be used in order to capture a vessel that seeks to violate a blockade.[84] However, the degree of the necessary force employed depends very much upon how the individuals on board the vessel are to be classified. In short, if they are regarded as civilians directly participating in hostilities then according to international humanitarian law they can be targeted as if they were combatants.[85] What this means is that the Israeli forces would be subject to very few restrictions in the manner in which they used force against the crew members that resisted capture.[86] In contrast, if the crew members are to be regarded as civilians engaging in political protest, Israeli forces would be limited to only using force that was necessary to defend themselves or to secure capture of the vessel. Moreover, any use of force must have been proportionate in the circumstances.[87] It is therefore of crucial importance to determine the status of the crew members.

Interestingly, the Turkish Report never addresses the question of whether the crew members' decision to violently resist capture of the vessel meant that they were directly participating in hostilities. Instead, the report automatically assumes that the crew members were civilians. As civilians, the Israeli forces could only use force that was necessary and proportionate in the circumstances.[88] Although the report concedes that the crew members did violently resist capture, in the light of the widespread use of lethal force by the Israeli forces the report nevertheless concludes that the force used was 'disproportionate' and therefore unlawful.[89]

The Turkel Report considers in detail whether the crew members that violently resisted capture were directly participating in hostilities.[90] Citing the *Targeted Killings* case of Israel's Supreme Court,[91] the report concludes that the decisive factor is whether the individual is performing the functions of a combatant.[92] If so, the individual can be regarded as directly participating in hostilities and thus be directly targeted. In this context, the report considers it significant that the crew members had brought aboard the *Mavi Marmara* weapons that could be used to

[83] San Remo Manual on International Law Applicable to Armed Conflicts at Sea, 12 June 1994, para 98.

[84] See Bothe 2008, p. 596.

[85] See generally International Committee of the Red Cross 2009.

[86] As Blum notes, '[t]he striking feature of the mainstream literature is its general acceptance (albeit at times, with some moral discomfort) of the near-absolute license to kill combatants and of the law's view of combatants as nothing more than instruments of war'; Blum 2010, p. 118.

[87] *M/V 'Saiga' (No. 2) (Saint Vincent and the Grenadines v. Guinea)*, 38 ILM (1999) 1323, para 156.

[88] Turkish Report 2011, supra n. 15, 53.

[89] Ibid., p. 56.

[90] 'The salient issue is whether the passengers were civilians taking a direct part in hostilities or uninvolved civilians'; Turkel Report 2011, supra n. 10, para 188.

[91] supra n 33.

[92] Ibid., para 195.

repel Israeli forces and had prepared the vessel in such a way as to make boarding and capture particularly difficult. Moreover, the report notes that when faced with capture the crew members committed 'severe violence' against Israeli forces.[93] Indeed, the report explains that the force employed was analogous to that 'associated with combat'.[94] Consequently, the report determines that the violence used by the resisting crew members 'cannot be categorized as civil disobedience'[95] and, on that basis, they could be regarded as directly participating in hostilities.[96] As a result, the use of force used by Israeli forces was governed by international humanitarian law and so there was no requirement that it comply with the principles of necessity and proportionality. For this reason, the report determines that the level of force used by the Israeli forces was lawful.[97]

In contrast to the Turkel Report, the UN Human Rights Council Report explains that '[i]n a situation of armed conflict, military force can only be used against a combatant or against civilians participating actively and directly in combat activities, which cannot be said of the civilians on the *Mavi Marmara*'.[98] The UN Human Rights Council Report therefore clearly regards the crew members to be civilians. In light of this determination, the report goes on to note that

> The Mission is satisfied that much of the force used by the Israeli soldiers on board the Mavi Marmara and from the helicopters was unnecessary, disproportionate, excessive and inappropriate and resulted in the wholly avoidable killing and maiming of a large number of civilian passengers.[99]

On this basis, the UN Human Rights Council Report determines that the level of force used by the Israeli soldiers was unlawful.[100]

In Appendix I, the Palmer Report recognises that when civilians directly participate in hostilities this has significant implications for the level of force that can be permissibly used against them.[101] This being said, the report never expressly states whether the crew members that violently resisted capture were directly participating in hostilities. The implication, however, is that the crew members were not considered to be directly participating in hostilities; instead, they were civilians. This is because the report explains that 'there has been no adequate explanation provided [from Israel] for the nine deaths or why force was used to the extent that it produced such high levels of injury'.[102] If the crew members were to be regarded as directly participating in hostilities questions relating to the level or

---

[93] Ibid., para 213.
[94] Ibid., para 197.
[95] Ibid.
[96] Ibid., para 201.
[97] Ibid., para 239.
[98] UN Human Rights Council Report 2010, supra n. 10, para 66.
[99] Ibid., para 172.
[100] Ibid., para 264.
[101] Palmer Report 2011, supra n. 39, para 47 of Appendix I.
[102] Ibid., para 131.

extent of force would not come into question. All in all, the report concludes that the level of force used by Israeli forces was disproportionate and therefore 'unacceptable,' presumably meaning unlawful, although the report never uses this term.[103]

Apparently, there are striking differences in the way these four reports assess the legality of the use of force during Israel's interception of the *Mavi Marmara*. Ultimately, it seems that the view according to which the crew members that violently resisted capture of the vessel cannot be regarded as directly participating in hostilities, should be adopted. As stated above, the Turkel Report considers the civilians to be directly participating in hostilities on the basis of the *Targeted Killings* case. However, the test for whether a civilian is directly participating in hostilities is usually located in the International Committee of the Red Cross's (ICRC) interpretative guidance on this topic, which is generally regarded as reflective of customary international law.[104] This guidance provides a three stage test to determining whether an individual can be regarded as directly participating in hostilities.[105] In particular, the third stage explicitly stipulates that the act must be specifically designed to directly cause the required threshold of harm in support of a party to the conflict and to the detriment of another. In the context of the current discussion the important question is whether the *Mavi Marmara's* attempt to breach Gaza's naval blockade can be deemed in support of Hamas in its armed conflict with Israel.

As I have noted, the Turkel Report explicitly concludes that the passengers on board the *Mavi* that used violence against Israeli forces did so in support of a party to the armed conflict: namely Hamas.[106] This being said, I argue that the crew on board the *Mavi Marmara* that used violence did so in self-defence, in the sense that they were trying to protect the vessel and the cargo it was carrying. Or to put the matter differently, the violence cannot be regarded as analogous to that of a combatant that is acting in support of Hamas in its armed conflict with Israel. To this end, the persons on board the *Mavi Marmara* were not directly participating in hostilities. Instead, they were civilians and Israeli forces could only use force that was necessary and proportionate in the circumstances in order to defend themselves or enable them to capture the vessel. Given the use of lethal weapons by

---

[103] Ibid., para 134.

[104] It is interesting to note that the Turkel Report explains that the determination that the crew members were directly participating in hostilities would have been reached even if the ICRC's guidance on direct participation in hostilities had been used. On this see Turkel Report 2011, supra n. 10, para 201. For a good discussion of the ICRC's guidance on this topic see Goodman and Jinks 2010.

[105] International Committee of the Red Cross 2009, p. 46.

[106] Indeed, Israel suggests that there is video footage to substantiate this claim; see the website of Israel's Ministry of Foreign Affairs, available at http://mfa.gov.il/MFA/MFA-Archive/2010/Pages/Gaza_flotilla_videos.aspx. Accessed 24 September 2013.

Israeli forces and the large number of deaths and injuries that resulted, the use of force should be deemed disproportionate and consequently Israel's enforcement of the blockade considered unlawful.

17.4 Quasi-Judicial Bodies and International Adjudication

The objective of this chapter has been to reveal the considerable involvement of quasi-judicial bodies in the interpretation and application of international humanitarian law to the interdiction of the *Mavi Marmara*. However, it is important to note that the use of quasi-judicial bodies to interpret and apply international law and international humanitarian law in particular is not an isolated occurrence. In fact, in recent years, there has been a proliferation of quasi-judicial bodies that have been established by states, regional organisations and organs of the UN in order interpret and apply principles of international law to crises that have occurred or are occurring in the world order.[107]

Although these bodies are not fully judicial and therefore the contents of the reports that they produce are not legally binding, this certainly does not mean that they are without significance. On the contrary, often their findings are of immense significance, in both political and legal terms. For example, it has been argued that the International Court of Justice (ICJ) is inclined to accept the facts of a particular scenario as true when they are contained in UN reports.[108] More generally, Akande and Tonkin contend that

> The reports of these commissions and the decisions reached, though not formally binding, may end up being just as authoritative, in the public eye and in relevant political and legal bodies, as proper judicial processes. Often, these reports establish facts that then become difficult to dispute, they are used by the political bodies in taking action against States, they may be used by international tribunals, and they usually have an important effect in public discourse (think of the effect of the Goldstone and Darfur Reports). In addition, commissions of inquiry usually make a series of recommendations, which may include the revision of government practices and institutions, the imposition of sanctions (such as demotion or dismissal of government employees), the initiation of criminal prosecutions and the provision of compensation to victims. In many cases, the factual record of a

---

[107] See for example the International Commission of Inquiry for Darfur (2004) which was established by the UN Security Council in 2004 to determine whether violations of the Genocide Convention had been committed; the Fact-Finding mission established by the UN Human Rights Council in 2009 to investigate whether Israel had committed violations of international law in the Palestinian territories; the Fact-Finding mission created by the Council of the European Union in 2009 to investigate the origins and causes of the conflict in Georgia; the International Commission of Inquiry on Syria was established in 2012 by the UN Human Rights Council to determine whether violations of international humanitarian law and international criminal law had been committed in the conflict in Syria; and the International Commission of Inquiry on Libya created in 2012 by the UN Human Rights Council in order to assess whether international crimes had been committed by Colonel Gaddafi's forces during the recent armed conflict in Libya.

[108] Halink 2008, p. 16.

commission of inquiry serves as the basis for subsequent legal proceedings, including criminal prosecutions of individuals.[109]

Indeed, the significance of these reports can be gleaned from the Palmer Report that was discussed above in relation to the interception of the *Mavi Marmara*. Although the report explains that the Panel is not a court and has no mandate to interpret and apply international law or adjudicate on liability,[110] it is clear that the Panel engaged in exactly these tasks. In fact, the report itself states that 'the Panel hopes that its report may resolve the issues surrounding the incident and *bring the matter to an end*'.[111] This statement is startling, especially given that Turkey had publically declared its intention to lobby the General Assembly to request an Advisory Opinion from the ICJ as to the legality of the *Mavi Marmara* operation.[112] Thus, as Akande and Tonkin note, it seems that the effects of reports of quasi-judicial bodies are comparable to those of international courts and tribunals; or in the words of Alvarez, 'it is apparent that *quasi-judicial* and judicial dispute settlers' contribution to the law is considerable'.[113]

In the light of this, it becomes necessary to question the role that quasi-judicial bodies are now playing in the adjudication of disputes that require the interpretation and application of international law. The rationale for the proliferation of quasi-judicial bodies is clear; they compensate for inadequacies in the current international legal framework. The argument runs that, at least historically, the ICJ was the only adjudicatory body that was capable of hearing international disputes.[114] However, international law has always been an *inter-state* system and is therefore built upon the principle of the sovereignty equality of states.[115] In short, what this means is that a state cannot be compelled to submit to the jurisdiction of the ICJ; the jurisdiction of the ICJ is dependent upon the consent of the concerned states.[116]

The requirement of consent clearly restricts the possibility of bringing disputes before the ICJ. In order to mitigate this restriction, states have sought alternative ways to expose international disputes to adjudication, most notably through the creation of treaty tribunals. This is when a treaty establishes a specific tribunal that is competent to hear disputes arising under that treaty. Thus for example, the United Nations Convention on the Law of the Sea created the Law of the Sea Tribunal in order to adjudicate disputes arising under that treaty.[117] But the issue is

---

109 Akande and Tonkin 2012.

110 'This Panel is not a court. It was not asked to make determinations of the legal issues or to adjudicate on liability'; Palmer Report 2011, supra n. 39, para 1.

111 Ibid., p. 3 (emphasis added).

112 Press Meeting of H E Mr Ahmet Davutoglu, Minister of Foreign Affairs of the Republic of Turkey, on Turkish-Israeli Relations, 2 September 2011.

113 Alvarez 2005, p. 516 (emphasis added).

114 See generally Thirlway 2010.

115 Buchan 2013, pp. 19–29.

116 Article 36 of the Statute of the International Court of Justice 1945.

117 Section 5 of the United Nations Convention on the Law of the Sea 1982.

that many treaties relating to international humanitarian law, such as the Geneva Conventions and their Protocols, do not create these types of tribunals. In the light of this, and in the light of the fact that a state cannot be compelled to appear before the ICJ, the reality of the situation is that there is little possibility of a state that is accused of committing egregious violations of international humanitarian law being brought before a competent tribunal. Consequently, the use of quasi-judicial bodies represents the only way in which determinations of fact and the application of international humanitarian law can be achieved. As Akande and Tonkin explain

> In the absence of universal compulsory jurisdiction by international judicial bodies, these commissions of inquiry are a way in which the international community can obtain an authoritative determination of whether these violations have taken place and who is responsible.[118]

I do express a degree of sympathy with this approach. International law and international humanitarian law in particular must have a forum for application and enforcement in order to maintain their integrity and authority. If there are no avenues available to ensure that those who commit violations of international humanitarian are held to account, international humanitarian law will become increasingly delegitimised and risk fading into irrelevance. This notwithstanding, it does seem necessary to identify some of the potential problems that are associated with 'this new form of adjudication'.[119]

First, emphasis should be placed on the issue of sovereignty. The principle of state sovereignty has long been regarded as the backbone of the international legal order. Indeed, it is often cast as a constitutional norm.[120] In the context of international adjudication what this principle means is that no state can be subject to the jurisdiction of a tribunal without first providing its consent. In this way, state sovereignty is protected and respected. If this is so, the question then is to what extent the use of quasi-judicial bodies depart from, if not flagrantly violate, the principle of state sovereignty. Some bodies, such as the Commission of Inquiry that was established to investigate whether violations of the Genocide Convention occurred in Darfur, have been established by the Security Council under its mandatory Chapter VII powers.[121] In these instances, state consent can be assumed because all states are signatories to the UN and thus knowingly and voluntarily signed up to its legal framework, thus permitting the Security Council to adopt

---

[118] D Akande and H Tonkin 6 April 2012.

[119] Ibid ['[t]hese commissions do seem to be an additional form of resolving, and obtaining authoritative pronouncements on, contested facts and issues of international law'].

[120] 'The sovereignty and equality of states represent the basic constitutional doctrine of [international law], which governs a community consisting primarily of states having a uniform legal personality': Brownlie 2008, p. 289.

[121] The Commission of Inquiry on Darfur was created by SC Res 1564 (18 September 2004).

binding decisions where a threat to international peace and security has been determined.[122]

However, there are other instances where the notion of assumed consent is far more difficult to sustain. As such, the Panel of Experts on Accountability in Sri Lanka was established by the UN Secretary-General in order to determine the nature and scope of any alleged violations of international law in relation to Sri Lanka's non-international armed conflict with the Tamil Tigers.[123] The Panel concluded that a number of violations of international human rights law and international humanitarian law were committed on behalf of both the government and the Tamil Tigers, and indeed suggested international crimes may have been committed and that the situation should be therefore referred to the International Criminal Court.[124]

In such instances, the issue of sovereignty intrusion by the institution of quasi-judicial bodies remains and becomes intense. This is particularly so given that Sri Lanka vehemently opposed the creation and operation of this Panel.[125] This being said, one of the members of the Panel of Experts has argued, albeit writing under his personal academic capacity, that Sri Lanka's consent was in fact respected because the Secretary-General had created the Panel on the basis of his 'inherent powers'.[126] According to the inherent powers doctrine, an international organisation will possess a power provided that the conferral of this power is not specifically precluded by the constituent treaty of the organisation.[127] The doctrine of inherent powers is reconciled with the principle of state consent on the basis that member states voluntarily joined the international organisation and, by doing so, subscribed to the normative framework outlined in its constituent treaty. A state is therefore assumed to have consented to the exercise of an inherent power on the basis that when it joined that organisation it was aware of the possibility of the exercise of such a power because it was not specifically precluded by the treaty.[128]

This approach however gives rise to two problems. The first problem is that the contention that international organisations possess inherent powers is far from accepted in international institutional law, precisely because it stretches the notion of state consent to breaking point. In fact, most recent judicial pronouncements[129] on the topic of powers and the accompanying international legal literature[130]

---

[122] Article 25 of the United Nations Charter 1945.

[123] Press Release, Secretary-General, Secretary-General Names Panel of Experts to Advise on Accountability for Possible Rights Violations During Sri Lanka Conflict, UN Doc SG/SM/12967 (22 June 2010).

[124] Ibid., p. ii.

[125] Ratner 2012, p. 799.

[126] 'As for the legality of the panel, the secretary-general is clearly entitled under his inherent powers to seek advice from outside experts'; ibid., p. 798.

[127] White 2005, pp. 87–89.

[128] Ibid., p. 87 ff.

[129] *Legality of the Threat or Use of Nuclear Weapons* (1996) ICJ Report 226.

[130] See Klabbers 2002, p. 75 ff. Cf Seyersted 1963.

indicate that organisations *do not* possess inherent powers, but only those powers that are expressly conferred by the constituent treaty and those that can be implied from its objects and purposes. If in the case of Sri Lanka, the creation of the Panel is justified on the basis of inherent powers, yet international institutional law does not recognise the legality of inherent powers, then surely a state cannot be regarded as having consented to the unlawful exercise of a power.

The second problem is that even if we do accept that international organisations can lawfully exercise inherent powers, in the context of the Sri Lankan example, it would seem that the Secretary-General did not have an inherent power to establish a Panel of Inquiry to adjudicate a dispute and determine state liability. The UN Charter makes it quite clear that although there is an obligation upon states to settle disputes peacefully, there is no obligation to submit a dispute to an international court or tribunal. On the contrary, and as Alvarez explains, '[t]he Charter's drafters, after all, had *carefully protected the discretion of states* with respect to how they were to resolve their disputes and where the Charter did not include a clause on the compulsory settlement of disputes'.[131] When cast in this light it seems that the UN Charter precludes the possibility that the Secretary-General possesses the power to create a body that is in essence imbued with the authority to make legal determinations relating to the liability of states. Instead, the power to authoritatively determine disputes is invested in the ICJ, whose jurisdiction is dependent upon the expression of state consent.[132]

Second, the proliferation of quasi-judicial bodies raises important issues concerning due process and procedural fairness. The Sri Lankan Report is again of interest here. As a result of the Sri Lankan government's fierce resistance to the mandate conferred on the Panel, the Panel was prevented from visiting the country and conducting investigations on the ground.[133] The Panel did not therefore have a formal fact-finding power, and could not be regarded as a typical Commission of Inquiry like the ones established in relation to Libya and Syria. However, as Ratner notes, '[t]he panel determined early on that its mandate – and in particular, the phrase "taking into account the nature and scope of any alleged violations" - required it to gather information about the conduct of the war, based on the view of any allegations, if credible, would create certain obligations and other responsibilities for the Sri Lankan government with respect to the alleged conduct'.[134] The Panel explained that it considered a fact to be credible where 'there [was] a reasonable basis to believe that the underlying act or event occurred'.[135] As such,

---

[131] Alvarez 2005, p. 420 (emphasis added).

[132] In justifying the creation of the Panel of Inquiry for Sri Lanka Ratner explains that UN Secretaries-General have exercised the power to establish Panel of Inquiries many times in the past; Ratner 2012, p. 798. Yet, frequency of an activity does not in itself make it lawful.

[133] Report of the Secretary-General's Panel of Experts on Accountability in Sri Lanka, available at http://www.un.org/News/dh/infocus/Sri_Lanka/POE_Report_Full.pdf. Accessed 24 September 2013, para 21 (herein referred to as Sri Lanka Report).

[134] Ratner 2012, p. 799.

[135] Sri Lanka Report 2011, supra n. 133 para 51.

by definition, in order to discharge its mandate and determine whether violations of international law had occurred, the Panel was required to make determinations of fact.

As Ratner himself recognises, the problem here lies in the fact that this 'reasonable basis' standard of proof is lower than that stipulated by other Commissions of Inquiry.[136] For example, in relation to the Commission of Inquiry in Syria in 2011 the standard of proof was one of 'reasonable suspicion' which was met when the commission obtained a reliable body of evidence, consistent with other information, indicating the occurrence of a particular incident or event.[137] This disparity in the standard of proof level is potentially problematic because is raises concerns relating to the consistency of international adjudication and, more broadly, could perhaps undermine the international rule of law which in turn requires adherence to uniform standards when the international legal rights and responsibilities of states are being adjudicated.

Third, with this proliferation of quasi-judicial bodies there is of course the problem of conflicting adjudicative opinions relating to the same legal issues, thereby threatening the overall unity and coherence of public international law. This point is particularly salient in relation to the *Mavi Marmara* incident, where as we saw four quasi-judicial bodies produced very conflicting reports in relation to the interpretation and application of international humanitarian law. Consider, for example, the application of the proportionality test by the two reports published under the auspices of the UN: the UN Human Rights Council Report determined that the land and naval blockade taken together had to be assessed against the proportionality test, whereas the Palmer Report considered that only the naval blockade needed to be subjected to the requirement of proportionality. On this basis, the UN Human Rights Council Report determined the blockade unlawful and the Palmer Report determined the blockade lawful. Very different and conflicting interpretations of the law of blockade were therefore projected by these two UN-endorsed reports.

Moreover, there is not just the problem of conflicting interpretations and application of international law between quasi-judicial bodies, but also the fact that these reports themselves often have what Alvarez calls 'normative legs'.[138] This means that the impact of decisions of quasi-judicial bodies are not just restricted to the incident under examination, but can be absorbed more generally into international law. This therefore has the potential to profoundly affect the character, content and trajectory of international law. This seems especially so in relation to UN Reports, which are generally accorded particular weight, significance and authority.[139] This is particularly distressing in the light of the fact that

---

[136] Ratner 2012, pp. 799–800.

[137] Report of the Independent International Commission of Inquiry on the Syrian Arab Republic (23 November 2011) UN Doc A/HRC/S-17/2/Add 1, para 5.

[138] Alvarez 2005, p. 463.

[139] See Halink 2008.

quasi-judicial bodies, which do not necessarily have the legal expertise international courts and tribunals have, may inaccurately interpret and apply international law. For example, in the case of the flotilla incident, the pronouncements of the Palmer Report regarding the legality of blockades in non-international conflicts as well as the international nature of the Israel-Hamas conflict, can lead future judicial and quasi-judicial bodies down erroneous paths regarding the application of international humanitarian law.

17.5 Conclusion

This chapter has pursued three interrelated objectives. First, to demonstrate that quasi-judicial bodies are now actively engaged in the interpretation and application of international law in general and international humanitarian law in particular. Second, to use Israel's interception of the *Mavi Marmara* as a lens to reveal not just the involvement of quasi-judicial bodies in international dispute settlement, but also to demonstrate how drastically quasi-judicial bodies can differ in their interpretation and application of international law. Third, there has been a trend in international legal literature to assume that the use of quasi-judicial bodies inherently yield considerable benefits for the adjudication of international disputes. This is based upon the fact that since the ICJ is the only tribunal that can address disputes relating to international humanitarian law but at the same time is dependent upon state consent in order for it to exercise its jurisdiction, many disputes involving the application of international humanitarian law remain immune from judicial scrutiny. As such, quasi-judicial bodies therefore provide the only avenue for these disputes to receive independent adjudication. Notwithstanding the clear utility of such bodies, this chapter has nevertheless sought to flag up several problems that need to be considered and addressed given that resort to quasi-judicial bodies is likely to take place with similar frequency in the future.

References

Akande D, Tonkin H (2012) International commissions of inquiry: a new form of adjudication? EJIL: *Talk!* Available at http://ejiltalk.org/international-commissions-of-inquiry-a-new-form-of-adjudication/. Accessed 24 Sept 2013

Alvarez J (2005) International Organizations as Law-Makers. Oxford University Press, Oxford

Blum G (2010) The dispensable lives of soldiers. J Leg Anal 2:115

Bothe M (2008) The law of neutrality. In: Fleck D (ed) The handbook on international humanitarian law. Oxford University Press, New York, pp 501–604

Brownlie I (2008) Principles of public international law. Oxford University Press, Oxford

Buchan R (2011) The international law of naval blockade and Israel's interception of the *Mavi Marmara*. Neth Int Law Rev 58:209–241

Buchan R (2012) The Palmer report and the legality of Israel's naval blockade of Gaza. Int Comp Law Q 61:264–273

Buchan R (2013) International law and the construction of the liberal peace. Hart, Oxford
Doswald-Beck L (1995) San Remo manual on international law applicable to armed conflicts at sea. Cambridge University Press, Cambridge
Falk R (1964) Janus Tormented: the international law of internal war. In: Rosenau J (ed) International aspects of civil strife. Princeton University Press, Princeton
Finkelstein N (2011) Torpedoing the law: how the Palmer report justified Israel's naval blockade of Gaza. Insight Turk 13:11–29
Goodman R, Jinks D (2010) The ICRC interpretive guidance on the notion of direct participation in hostilities under international humanitarian law. NYU J Int Law Polit 42:637–640
Green L (2008) The contemporary law of armed conflict. Manchester University Press, Manchester
Halink H (2008) All things considered: how the International Court of Justice delegated its fact-assessment to the United Nations in the *Armed Activities* case. NYU J Int Law Polit 40:13
Henckaerts J-M, Doswald-Beck L (2005) Customary international humanitarian law. Cambridge University Press, Cambridge
International Law Association (2010) The Hague Conference: Use of Force—Final Report on the Meaning of Armed Conflict in International Law
International Committee of the Red Cross (2009) Interpretative Guidance on the Direct Participation in Hostilities under International Humanitarian Law. http://www.icrc.org/eng/assets/files/other/icrc-002-0990.pdf. Accessed 24 Sept 2013
Jones TD (1983) The international law of maritime blockade—a measure of naval economic interdiction. Howard Law J 26:759
Kimmerling B, Migdal J (1994) Palestinians: the making of people. Harvard University Press, Cambridge
Klabbers J (2002) An introduction to international institutional law. Cambridge University Press, Cambridge
Lauterpacht H (1947) Recognition in international law. Cambridge University Press, Cambridge
Milanovic M (2007) Lessons for human rights and humanitarian law in the war on terror: comparing Hamdan and the Israeli targeted Killings case. Int Rev Red Cross 89:373
Miller EB (1998) Implementing the Oslo Accords. Cardozo J Int Comp Law 6:363
Pressman J (2003) The second intifada: Background and causes of the Israeli-Palestinian conflict. J Confl Stud 23:114
Ratner R (2012) Accountability and the Sri Lankan civil war. AJIL 106:795
Seyersted F (1963) Objective personality of intergovernmental organizations: Do their capacities really depend upon the Conventions establishing them? Copenhagen
Solomon S, Maogoto J (2013) Jurisdictional Aspects of the Article 12(2) Rome Statute Vessel Provision: Some thoughts on the provision's dogma and implementation in light of the Comoros Referral, Opinio Juris, available at: http://opiniojuris.org/2013/07/21/jurisdictional-aspects-of-the-article-122-rome-statute–vessel-provision-some-thoughts-on-the-provisions-dogma-and-implementation-in-light-of-the-comoros-referral/. Accessed 24 Sept 2013
Thirlway H (2010) The International Court of Justice 1989–2009: At the heart of the dispute settlement system? Neth Int Law Rev 57:347
White ND (2005) The law of international organisations. Manchester University Press, Manchester
Woosley LH (1950) Closure of ports by the Chinese National Government. AJIL 44:350–356

Index

D. Jinks et al. (eds.), *Applying International Humanitarian Law in Judicial and Quasi-Judicial Bodies*, DOI: 10.1007/978-94-6265-008-4,